CONTENTS

CONTENTS

SECOND EDITION

SELECTIONS FROM

— THE OLD—
TESTAMENT
MADE EASIER

PART THREE:
1 KINGS THROUGH MALACHI

SECOND EDITION

SELECTIONS FROM

— THE OLD —
TESTAMENT
MADE EASIER

PART THREE:
1 KINGS THROUGH MALACHI

DAVID J. RIDGES

CFI
An Imprint of Cedar Fort, Inc.
Springville, Utah

ISBN: 978-1-4621-1494-8

Published by CFI, an imprint of Cedar Fort, Inc., 2373 W. 700 S., Springville, UT 84663
Distributed by Cedar Fort, Inc., www.cedarfort.com

The Library of Congress has cataloged the first volume of this set as follows:

Ridges, David J., author.
Your study of the Old Testament made easier / David J. Ridges. -- Second edition.
    pages cm
Includes bibliographical references.
Summary: Study guide for the King James Version of the Old Testament.
ISBN 978-1-4621-1492-4
1. Bible. Old Testament--Commentaries. I. Title.

BS1151.52.R53 2014
221.071--dc23

2014007358

Cover design by Shawnda T. Craig
Cover design © 2014 Lyle Mortimer
Edited and typeset by Emily S. Chambers

Printed in the United States of America

10 9 8 7 6 5 4 3 2 1

Printed on acid-free paper

BOOKS BY DAVID J. RIDGES

The Gospel Study Series:

- *Your Study of The Book of Isaiah Made Easier, Second Edition*

- *The New Testament Made Easier, Part 1 (Second Edition)*

- *The New Testament Made Easier, Part 2 (Second Edition)*

- *Your Study of The Book of Mormon Made Easier, Part 1*

- *Your Study of The Book of Mormon Made Easier, Part 2*

- *Your Study of The Book of Mormon Made Easier, Part 3*

- *Book of Mormon Made Easier, Family Deluxe Edition, Vols. 1 and 2*

- *Your Study of The Doctrine and Covenants Made Easier, Part 1*

- *Your Study of The Doctrine and Covenants Made Easier, Part 2*

- *Your Study of The Doctrine and Covenants Made Easier, Part 3*

- *The Old Testament Made Easier, Part 1*

- *The Old Testament Made Easier, Part 2—Selections from the Old Testament*

- *The Old Testament Made Easier, Part 3—Selections from the Old Testament*

- *Your Study of the Pearl of Great Price Made Easier*

- *Your Study of Jeremiah Made Easier*

- *Your Study of The Book of Revelation Made Easier, Second Edition*

Our Savior, Jesus Christ: His Life and Mission to Cleanse and Heal

Mormon Beliefs and Doctrines Made Easier

The Proclamation on the Family: The Word of the Lord on More Than 30 Current Issues

Using the Signs of the Times to Strengthen Your Testimony

Doctrinal Details of the Plan of Salvation: From Premortality to Exaltation

FOREWORD

IN THE SECOND edition of volumes 1–3 of this Old Testament study guide, I have added many additional verses, along with notes and explanations not found in the original edition.

By the way, the bolded words and phrases are for teaching emphasis and allow the reader to glean the main ideas and concepts at a glance.

In over 40 years of teaching in the Church and for the Church Educational System, I have found that members of the Church encounter some common problems when it comes to understanding the scriptures. One problem is understanding the language of the scriptures themselves. Another is understanding symbolism. Another common concern is how best to mark their own scriptures and perhaps make brief notes in them. Yet another concern is how to understand what the scriptures are actually teaching. In other words, what are the major messages being taught by the Lord through His prophets?

This book is designed to address each of the concerns mentioned above. One of my objectives in these "Teacher in Your Hand" Gospel Studies Series books is to teach the language of the scriptures. Many Latter-day Saints struggle with the beautiful language of the scriptures. There is a special Spirit that attends it. The Brethren use it often to bring us the word of God, matched to our exact needs by the Holy Ghost. Therefore, I add brackets on occasion within the verses, for the purpose of defining difficult scriptural terms. I hope that as you read and study this work, you will get to the point that you do not need these definitions in brackets anymore. When that happens, please be patient because others may still need them.

The format is intentionally simple, with some license taken with respect to capitalization and punctuation in order to minimize interruption of the flow. It is intended to help readers to

- Quickly gain a basic understanding of these scriptures as they read, through the use of brief explanatory notes in brackets within the verses as well as occasional notes between verses. This paves the way for even deeper testimony and understanding later.

- Better understand the beautiful language of the scriptures. This is accomplished in this book with in-the-verse notes that define difficult terms.

- Mark their scriptures and put brief notes in the margins that will help them understand now and remember later what particular passages of scripture teach.

- Better understand symbolism.

Over the years, one of the most common expressions of gratitude from my students has been "Thanks for the notes you had us put in our scriptures." This book is dedicated to that purpose. Sources for the notes given in this work are as follows:

- The standard works of The Church of Jesus Christ of Latter-day Saints.

- Footnotes in the Latter-day Saint version of the King James Bible.

- The Joseph Smith Translation of the Bible.

- The Bible Dictionary in the back of our Bible.

- Various dictionaries.

- Various student manuals provided for our institutes of religion.

- Other sources as noted in the text and in the "Sources" section.

I hope that this study guide will serve effectively for members of the Church, as well as others, as they seek to increase their understanding of the writings and teachings contained in these portions of the Old Testament. Above all, if this work serves to bring increased understanding and testimony of the Atonement of Christ, all the efforts to put it together will have been far more than worth it. A special thanks goes to my wife, Janette, and to my daughters and sons, who have encouraged me every step of the way.

DAVID J. RIDGES

THE JST
(THE JOSEPH SMITH TRANSLATION OF THE BIBLE)

REFERENCES USED IN STUDY GUIDES BY DAVID J. RIDGES

BE AWARE THAT some of the JST references I use in my study guides are not found in the footnotes nor in the JST section at the back of our LDS version of the King James Bible (the one we use in the English-speaking part of the Church). The reason for this, as explained to me some years ago while writing curriculum materials for the Church, is simply that there is not enough room, for practical purposes, to include all of the JST additions and changes. As you can imagine, as was likewise explained to me, there were difficult decisions that had to be made by the Scriptures Committee and Church leaders as to which JST contributions were included and which were not.

The Joseph Smith Translation of the Bible in its entirety can generally be found in LDS bookstores or ordered through them. It was originally published under the auspices of the Reorganized Church of Jesus Christ of Latter Day Saints in Independence, Missouri. The version of the JST that I prefer to use is a parallel column version, entitled, *Joseph Smith's "New Translation" of the Bible*, published by Herald Publishing House,

Independence, Missouri, in 1970. This parallel column version compares the King James Bible with the JST side by side and includes only the verses that have changes, additions, or deletions made by the Prophet Joseph Smith.

By the way, some members of the Church have wondered whether we can trust the JST since it was published by a breakaway faction from our church who retained the original manuscripts after the martyrdom of the Prophet Joseph Smith. They worry that some changes to the Prophet's original manuscript might have been made to support doctrinal differences between the RLDS Church (the Reorganized Church of Jesus Christ of Latter Day Saints) and us. This is not the case. Many years ago, Robert J. Matthews of the Brigham Young University Religion Department was teaching a summer school class I attended. He told us that he was given permission by leaders of the RLDS Church to come to their Independence, Missouri, headquarters to see their publication of the JST. Brother Matthews was thus able to verify that they had been meticulously true to the Prophet's original work.

1 KINGS

1 KINGS 2

Selection: verses 5–9

I**T IS A sad commentary** on the way David's life ended that his last recorded words consisted of counsel and advice to his son Solomon to get revenge for him. Solomon had been anointed to become the next king (1 Kings 1:39). On his deathbed, David gave wise counsel and then, in a strange twist of events, since he, himself, had promised not to execute Joab, he asked Solomon to do the deed.

5 Moreover thou knowest also what Joab the son of Zeruiah did to me, *and* what he did to the two captains of the hosts of Israel, unto Abner the son of Ner, and unto Amasa the son of Jether, whom he slew, and shed the blood of war in peace, and put the blood of war upon his girdle that *was* about his loins, and in his shoes that *were* on his feet.

6 Do therefore according to thy wisdom, and **let not his hoar head** [*his gray head*] **go down to the grave in peace.**

7 But shew kindness unto the sons of Barzillai the Gileadite, and let them be of those that eat at thy table: for so they came to me when I fled because of Absalom thy brother.

8 **And, behold,** *thou hast* with thee **Shimei** the son of Gera, a Benjamite of Bahurim, which cursed me with a grievous curse in the day when I went to Mahanaim: but he came down to meet me at Jordan, and I **sware to him by the LORD, saying, I will not put thee to death with the sword.**

9 **Now therefore** hold him not guiltless: for thou *art* a wise man, and knowest what thou oughtest to do unto him; but **his hoar head bring thou down to the grave with blood.**

1 KINGS 11

Selection: verses 1–3, 6–8

A**LL WE HAVE** space to do in this study guide, as far as Solomon is concerned, is lament the fact that he, too, ultimately squandered the splendid gifts and blessings the Lord had given him.

It seems that one of the major messages in this portion of the Old Testament is reinforced over and over. It is that we all have tremendous God-given potential for good. But we must be constantly on guard and strictly obey the commandments on a daily basis, or we too can fall.

Solomon did much good. He built the temple in Jerusalem. He solved difficult problems with the wisdom that the Lord gave him. But he eroded away his spiritual strength by beginning to make his own rules, apparently feeling that he was above the laws of God.

Solomon defied the Lord's commandment in one way in particular. As you know, the Israelites were commanded not to marry outside the covenant. Solomon, over the course of his life, married many foreign wives who brought with them idolatry and false doctrines. Ultimately, he apostatized because of them.

1 But **king Solomon loved many strange** [*foreign*] **women**, together with the daughter of Pharaoh, women of the Moabites, Ammonites, Edomites, Zidonians, *and* Hittites;

2 Of the nations *concerning* **which the LORD said unto the children of Israel, Ye shall not go in to them**, neither shall they come in unto you: *for* surely they will turn away your heart after their gods: Solomon clave unto these in love.

3 And **he had seven hundred wives**, princesses, **and three hundred concubines** [*legally married servant wives*]: **and his wives turned away his heart.**

> In verses 6–8, next, we see that Solomon ended his mortal life a wicked man. The JST makes an important change to verse 6, next.

6 And **Solomon** did evil in the sight of the LORD, and **went not fully**

after the LORD, as did David his father.

JST 1 Kings 11:6

6 And Solomon did evil in the sight of the Lord, as David his father, and went not fully after the Lord.

7 Then did Solomon build an high place for Chemosh, the abomination of Moab, in the hill that *is* before Jerusalem, and for Molech [*the fire god, to whom children were sacrificed—see Bible Dictionary, under "Molech"*], the abomination of the children of Ammon.

8 And likewise did he for all his strange wives, which burnt incense and sacrificed unto their gods.

A DIVIDED KINGDOM: REHOBOAM AND JEROBOAM

As you can imagine, Solomon's lifestyle was expensive. Thus, the tax burden on the citizens of Israel was very heavy. After the death of Solomon, the people approached his son, Rehoboam, the next king, and petitioned him to lighten the tax burden. However, his young friends told him to increase taxes in order to show the people who was boss. He listened to his peers and caused a rebellion and split in the kingdom (1 Kings 12:4–11).

ISRAEL AND JUDAH

A man by the name of Jeroboam led the opposition, and Israel split into the northern ten tribes, hereafter referred to as Israel, and the southern two tribes—Judah and part of Benjamin—hereafter known as Judah. Both Rehoboam and Jeroboam led their people into wickedness and idolatry.

Kings and Chronicles both cover much of the same basic historical material.

As you read in your Old Testament, you will notice that Kings and Chronicles often overlap in their coverage of material. For the most part, we tend to use Kings in our gospel discussions.

THE VICIOUS CYCLE OF APOSTASY CONTINUES

As you read Kings and Chronicles in your Bible, you will no doubt become sadly aware that the cycle of apostasy continues. It is much the same in the Old Testament as in the Book of Mormon. In fact, it becomes all too predictable.

Again, the way to personally prevent the cycle of apostasy in one's own life is to remain humble and to comply strictly with God's commandments in daily living. A wonderful safeguard is found in following the living prophet.

ELIJAH

Elijah is one of the best-known Old Testament prophets. He comes on the scene in 1 Kings 17:1. It is a time of great apostasy, led by Ahab, wicked king of the northern kingdom (Israel) and Jezebel, his equally wicked wife. These two firmly established Baal worship in their kingdom.

JEZEBEL, ELIJAH, AND THE EIGHT HUNDRED AND FIFTY PRIESTS OF BAAL

Remember that Baal worship involved sexual immorality as part of the ceremonies used in worshipping Baal. Things got so bad that Elijah challenged the priests of Baal to a contest. You will see it in 1 Kings 18. As you read about Jezebel's reaction in 1 Kings 19, you will see that she makes a vow to see that Elijah is killed within twenty-four hours. She does not succeed.

As you read these chapters, you will sense Elijah's loneliness. But his reward for faithful service to the Lord was to be translated and taken up to heaven without dying.

2 KINGS

FOR THE PURPOSES of this study guide, we will just mention Elijah's being taken up into heaven in a whirlwind, and the jeering and mocking of his successor, Elisha.

2 KINGS 2

Selection: verses 11, 23–24

AT THE END of his earthly mission, Elijah was translated. He was with the Savior on the Mount of Transfiguration (Matthew 17:1-3) and was resurrected with Jesus Christ (Doctrine & Covenants 133:54-55). He appeared to Joseph Smith and Oliver Cowdery in the Kirtland Temple and restored the keys of the sealing power (Doctrine & Covenants 110).

11 And it came to pass, as they still went on, and talked, that, behold, *there appeared* a chariot of fire, and horses of fire, and parted them both asunder; and **Elijah went up by a whirlwind into heaven.**

Again, for purposes of this study guide, we will only mention one thing about Elisha, which may be helpful to you in your reading of this portion of the Old Testament.

After Elijah had been taken up in the whirlwind into heaven, Elisha became the next prophet in Israel. One day as he was out walking, the Bible tells us that several "little children" mocked him, calling him, in effect, "baldy, baldy, baldy" and taunting him for not being translated like Elijah was (verse 23, next). His response was to curse them. As a result, two female bears attacked them and injured forty-two of them.

23 ¶ And he went up from thence unto Beth-el: and as he was going up by the way, **there came forth little children out of the city, and mocked him**, and said unto him, Go up, thou bald head; go up, thou bald head [*a challenge for him to be translated as Elijah was*].

24 And **he turned back, and looked on them, and cursed them** in the name of the LORD. And there came forth **two she bears** out of the wood, and **tare forty and two children of them.**

The main concern most students of the Bible express is that such a punishment upon little children, who are not even accountable, is unthinkable. The fact is, they were not little children. They were youths, which in that culture could include anyone from late teenage up to thirty years of age, when men officially became adults (footnote 23a in your Bible). Thus they were indeed accountable and were intentionally blaspheming the Lord's prophet.

CHRONICLES

THE BOOKS OF First and Second Chronicles summarize from the creation down to the return of the Jews to Jerusalem after the proclamation of Cyrus giving permission for their return, in 538 BC. Many genealogies are included. The two books of Chronicles repeat much of what is recorded in the books of Samuel as well as the books of Kings.

As you have no doubt noticed, righteous kings cause much good and wicked kings cause much damage and evil as their people follow their example. We will take time to look at King Hezekiah, of Judah, who is an example of a good king. Before his reign, the temple in Jerusalem had come into terrible neglect. He cleaned it up and restored its proper use.

2 CHRONICLES 29

Selection: verses 1–11

HEZEKIAH'S FATHER, AHAZ, left a legacy of wickedness, but Hezekiah determined to serve the Lord and not follow the evil example of his father. As you know, this is very rare.

1 HEZEKIAH **began to reign when he was five and twenty years old**, and he reigned nine and twenty years in Jerusalem. And his mother's name was Abijah, the daughter of Zechariah.

2 And **he did that which was right in the sight of the LORD**, according to all that David his father had done.

We suspect that the last phrase of verse 2, above, refers to the first part of David's life, where he lived righteously.

3 ¶ **He** in the first year of his reign, in the first month, **opened the doors of the house of the LORD** [*the temple*], **and repaired them.**

4 And **he brought in the priests and the Levites, and gathered them together** into the east street,

5 And said unto them, Hear me, ye Levites, **sanctify now yourselves, and sanctify the house of the LORD God of your fathers, and carry forth the filthiness out of the holy place.**

6 **For our fathers have trespassed, and done that which was evil in the eyes of the LORD** our God, and have forsaken him, and have turned away their faces from the habitation of the LORD, and turned their backs.

7 Also they have shut up the doors of the porch, and put out the lamps, and have not burned incense nor offered burnt offerings in the holy place unto the God of Israel.

8 Wherefore the wrath of the LORD

was upon Judah and Jerusalem, and he hath delivered them to trouble, to astonishment, and to hissing, as ye see with your eyes.

9 For, lo, our fathers have fallen by the sword, and our sons and our daughters and our wives are in captivity for this.

10 Now it is in mine heart to make a covenant with the LORD God of Israel, that his fierce wrath may turn away from us.

11 My sons, be not now negligent: for the LORD hath chosen you to stand before him, to serve him, and that ye should minister unto him, and burn incense [start up proper worship again].

2 CHRONICLES 30

Selection: verses 26–27

THE RETURN OF righteousness and respect to the temple during King Hezekiah's reign brought happiness to the people.

26 So there was great joy in Jerusalem: for since the time of Solomon the son of David king of Israel there was not the like in Jerusalem.

27 ¶ Then the priests the Levites arose and blessed the people: and their voice was heard, and

their prayer came up to his holy dwelling place, even unto heaven.

NOTE: Isaiah was the prophet during Hezekiah's reign. At one point, righteous King Hezekiah was sick and was on his deathbed. We will quote from Isaiah to see what happened.

Isaiah 38:1–22
1 In those days [about 705–703 BC] was Hezekiah sick unto death. And Isaiah the prophet the son of Amoz came unto him, and said unto him, Thus saith the LORD, Set thine house in order [get ready]: for thou shalt die, and not live.
2 Then Hezekiah turned his face toward the wall, and prayed unto the LORD,
3 And said, Remember now, O LORD, I beseech thee, how I have walked before thee in truth and with a perfect heart, and have done that which is good in thy sight [in other words, I have lived a good life]. And Hezekiah wept sore [bitterly].
4 Then came the word of the LORD to Isaiah, saying,
5 Go, and say to Hezekiah, Thus saith the LORD, the God of David thy father [ancestor], I have heard thy prayer, I have seen thy tears: behold, I will add unto thy days fifteen years [I will add fifteen years to your life].

Major Message

When they are in harmony with the will of the Lord, the

mighty prayers of the faithful can change the Lord's plan temporarily.

6 And **I will deliver thee and this city out of the hand of the king of Assyria**: and I will defend this city [*this would seem to place Hezekiah's illness sometime during the Assyrian threats to Jerusalem as described in chapters 36 and 37*].

7 And this **shall be a sign unto thee** from the LORD, that the LORD will do this thing that he hath spoken;

8 Behold, **I will bring again the shadow of the degrees** [*the shadow on the sundial*], which is gone down in the sun dial of Ahaz, **ten degrees backward.** So the sun returned ten degrees, by which degrees it was gone down [*the sun came back up ten degrees; in other words, time was turned backward*].

9 [*Hezekiah is healed and gives thanks and praise to the Lord for his miraculous recovery.*] **The writing** [*psalm*] **of Hezekiah** king of Judah, **when he had been sick, and was recovered** of his sickness [*after he had been sick and had recovered*]:

Righteous King Hezekiah now tells us what he said, expressing the thoughts of his heart when he was blessed with another fifteen years of life by the Lord.

First, he tells us what was going through his mind when he knew he was going to die.

10 I [*Hezekiah*] **said** in the cutting off of my days [*when I was on my deathbed*], I shall go to the gates of the grave [*I am doomed*]: I am deprived of the residue [*remainder*] of my years [*I am too young to die*].

11 I said, I shall not see the LORD, even the LORD, in the land of the living [*I am about to leave this mortal life*]: I shall behold man no more with the inhabitants of the world [*I won't be around anymore to associate with my fellow men*].

12 Mine age is departed [*German Bible: my time is up*], and is removed from me as a shepherd's tent [*they are taking down my tent*]: I have [*Thou hast*] cut off like a weaver my life [*Thou hast "clipped my threads" as a weaver does when the rug is finished*]: he will cut me off with pining sickness [*fatal illness is how the Lord is sending me out of this life*]: from day even to night wilt thou make an end of me [*I will die very shortly*].

13 I reckoned till morning [*German Bible: I thought, "If I could just live until morning!"*], that, as a lion, so will he break all my bones [*I can't stop the Lord if he wants me to die anymore than I could stop a lion*]: from day even to night wilt thou make an end of me [*my time is short*].

14 Like a crane or a swallow, so did I chatter [*German Bible: whimper*]: I did mourn as a dove: mine eyes fail with looking upward [*falter as I*

look *up to heaven*]: O LORD, I am oppressed [*German Bible: suffering*]; undertake [*German: sooth, moderate my condition*] for me [*be Thou my help, security*].

Next, Hezekiah tells us how he felt when he found out he was not going to die.

15 What shall I say [*how can I express my gratitude*]? he hath both spoken unto me, and himself hath done it [*JST: "healed me"*]: I shall go softly [*German Bible: in humility*] all my years [*JST: "that I may not walk"*] in the bitterness of my soul.

16 O Lord, by these things men live, and in all these things is the life of my spirit [*JST: "thou who art the life of my spirit, in whom I live"*]: so wilt thou recover [*heal*] me, and make me to live [*JST: "and in all these things I will praise thee"*].

17 Behold, for peace I had great bitterness [*JST: "Behold, I had great bitterness instead of peace"*]: but thou hast in love to my soul delivered it [*JST: "saved me"*] from the pit of corruption [*from rotting in the grave*]: for thou hast cast all my sins behind thy back [*the effect of the Atonement*].

18 For the grave cannot praise [*German Bible: Hell does not praise*] thee, death can not celebrate thee: they [*people in spirit prison*] that go down into the pit [*hell; see Isaiah 14:15*]

cannot hope for thy truth [*see Alma 34:32–34*].

19 The living, the living, he shall praise thee, as I do this day [*I am very happy to still be alive*]: the father to the children shall make known thy truth [*I will testify to my family and others of Thy kindness to me*].

20 The LORD was ready to save me: therefore we [*I and my family*] will sing my songs to the stringed instruments [*we will put my words of praise to music*] all the days of our life in the house of the LORD.

Next, Hezekiah refers to something Isaiah instructed him to do in order to be healed.

21 **For Isaiah had said, Let them take a lump of figs, and lay it for a plaister** [*plaster*] **upon the boil, and he shall recover** [*perhaps the lump of figs served the same purpose as the lump of clay to heal the blind man in John 9:6–7, i.e., faith obedience*].

22 Hezekiah also had said, What is the sign that I shall go up to the house of the LORD? [*This verse fits after verse 6— see 2 Kings 20:8.*]

NOTE: In order to address the goal of this study guide to include notes and commentary on most chapters of Ecclesiastes and every verse of Isaiah and Jeremiah, we will only provide brief mention of the next several books in the Old Testament. More on them will have to be done in a future edition of this Old Testament study guide.

EZRA AND NEHEMIAH

THESE TWO BOOKS fit into the Old Testament chronology after the Jews who were taken captive to Babylon (600–588 BC) were released to return to Jerusalem (about 538 BC). They tell the story of Israel from the time of their return, when they began to rebuild Jerusalem, to the end of Nehemiah's second term as governor of Judah, about 400 BC

IN THESE BOOKS you will find a remarkable effort to return to the laws of Moses and a strong reformation in the people's lives. Pay special attention to Nehemiah 8:5–18, where Ezra reads the book containing the laws of God, and the people listen to it day after day for many days.

ESTHER

THE BEAUTIFUL STORY of the courage and faith of Esther fits chronologically with Ezra 7:1.

JOB

JOB CONTAINS SEVERAL major messages. One is that bad things happen to good people. Another is that the only sure strength during times of trial and adversity is personal righteousness and integrity, combined with deep faith in God. Yet another is the value of patience when things keep going wrong.

ONE DEFINITE MESSAGE provided at the end of the book is that ultimately, personal righteousness pays off in ways beyond our ability to comprehend. The ending of the account of Job (Job 42:10–17) can be considered to be a "type" of exaltation.

PSALMS

THE PSALMS ARE songs of praise to God and were usually set to music. They were written by many different authors, David being one of the main ones. We will include a list of the 150 Psalms that appear in our Bible by their author, where known. The quote below and the list come from the *Old Testament Student Manual*, page 310.

"THERE IS A great debate among biblical scholars about the authorship of the Psalms. Superscriptions on many of the Psalms themselves attribute them to various ancient authors:

Psalms with no superscription	18
Psalms attributed to David	70
Psalms attributed to Solomon	2
Psalms attributed to Asaph (a musician in David's court)	12
Psalms attributed to the sons of Korah (Levites)	10
Psalms attributed to Heman (a leader of the temple music)	1
Psalms attributed to Ethan (a leader of the temple music)	1

WE WILL MENTION that Psalm 51 was written by David after he had committed adultery with Bathsheba. You can feel his anguish as you read it. One concern with it is that his thinking is not exactly straight on some issues. For example:

Psalm 51:4

4 Against thee [*the Lord—see verse 1*], thee only, have I sinned, and done this evil in thy sight: that thou mightest be justified when thou speakest, and be clear when thou judgest.

THAT IS NOT correct doctrine. David sinned against Bathsheba, against her husband, against his other wives and children, against the citizens of his kingdom, and so forth. It is often the claim of the sinner that he has done damage only to himself.

PROVERBS

PROVERBS IS SOME-TIMES referred to as "wisdom literature." We will quote from the Bible Dictionary to provide a general background for this book of the Bible.

BIBLE DICTIONARY: PROVERBS

The Heb. word rendered proverb is mashal, a similitude or parable, but the book contains many maxims and sayings not properly so called, and also connected poems of considerable length. There is much in it that does not rise above the plane of worldly wisdom, but throughout it is taken for granted that "the fear of the Lord is the beginning of wisdom" (1:7; 9:10). The least spiritual of the Proverbs are valuable as reminding us that the voice of Divine Inspiration does not disdain to utter homely truths. The first section, Chs. 1–9, is the most poetic and contains an exposition of true wisdom. Chapters 10–24 contain a collection of proverbs and sentences about the right and wrong ways of living. Chapters 25–29 contain the proverbs of Solomon that the men of Hezekiah, king of Judah, copied out. Chapters 30 and 31 contain the "burden" of Agur and Lemuel, the latter including a picture of the ideal wife, arranged in acrostic form. The book is frequently quoted in the New Testament, the use of chapter 3 being especially noteworthy.

ECCLESIASTES

THE WORD "ECCLESI-ASTES," is a Greek translation of a Hebrew word that means "one who convenes a congregation" (see Bible Dictionary, under "Ecclesiastes"). As you can see in your Bible, at the beginning of this book, Ecclesiastes has also come to be known as "The Preacher." In effect, the book gathers us together as a congregation of readers and preaches to us about life.

We do not know for sure who wrote Ecclesiastes; however, many Bible scholars suggest that it was probably written by Solomon because of considerable evidence within the book that leads to this conclusion. Solomon was the son of King David and Bathsheba. The evidence, for example, in Ecclesiastes 1:1, 12, 16; 2:4–10; and 12:9, seems to point to Solomon as the author.

Perhaps the most well known verses of Ecclesiastes are 3:1–8, which begin with "To every thing there is a season, and a time to every purpose under the heaven."

An important key to understanding Ecclesiastes is the word "vanity," as used in one form or another five times in chapter 1, verse 2, and at least thirty-two times elsewhere within the book. If you define the word as "pride," or "self-aggrandizement," you will not understand Ecclesiastes. However, if you correctly understand that in Ecclesiastes "vanity" means a state or situation that is "temporary," "transitory," or "fleeting," (see Bible Dictionary, under "Ecclesiastes"), and thus means "the temporary or transitory nature of mortality," then you will get much more out of it. In fact, look at verse 2 of chapter 1 right now. What it is saying, in effect, is that everything associated with mortal life is fleeting and temporary.

Many students become a bit confused as they study Ecclesiastes because it seems that at one moment, the author is being pessimistic, cynical, bitter, and depicting the philosophies of the world. And then in the next sentence or verse, he seems to be preaching true gospel concepts.

For example, in 9:5, we read, "the dead know not any thing," and 9:10, "there is no work, nor device, nor knowledge, nor wisdom, in the grave." These statements would lead most readers to conclude that there is no life after death. But, in 12:7, we read, "the spirit shall return unto God who gave it." And in 12:14, we see, "God shall bring every work into judgment, with every secret thing, whether it be good, or whether it be evil," which certainly indicates that there is life beyond the grave!

So, what is going on here? Answer: The author of Ecclesiastes (most likely Solomon) appears on the one hand to be presenting the pessimistic, cynical outlook or philosophy of the "natural man"—in other words, the ideas of people of the world who do not believe in God. They do not believe in life beyond the grave and consequently see life as being essentially meaningless. In fact, they look at people who do believe in God and in life beyond the grave as

15

being foolish, perhaps weak, needing religion as a crutch because they can't handle the reality of the futility of life.

On the other hand, the author reminds everyone, including those who believe in God, that life is brief and that it is vital to keep God in mind, separating the important from the relatively unimportant. Chapters 11 and 12, as a whole, are the most spiritual of the book, and teach that obedience to God and His commandments provides lasting value and permanence to mortal souls.

In summary, much of what we are seeing in Ecclesiastes is how people who do not believe in God see life. Their outlook, although not reflecting the truth, is what the author is depicting. If you keep this in mind as you read, it will make much more sense. Putting it another way, the book can be seen as a study in comparison and contrast between the unbelieving "natural man" and those who do believe in God. Life is often dismal and pessimistic for those who do not believe in God nor in life after death, and thus view life only from a worldly point of view (see more on this in Bible Dictionary, under "Ecclesiastes"). Also, mortality is brief and fleeting for all, including the believers.

One approach to understanding Ecclesiastes is to read chapter 1, verses 3–11, which present the outlook or view of the natural man, and then read chapter 12, verses 13–14, which present the view of those who believe in God, and conclude that all people are accountable to Him and will face Him on the day of final judgment. In effect, these two sets of verses form "bookends" to Ecclesiastes, the one bookend being the pessimism and cynicism of the natural man and the other bookend representing the truth that there is a God and that life has meaning and will continue beyond the grave. Between the "bookends," we see the comparison and contrast between the thinking of the natural man and the thoughts of the believers, with most of the emphasis being placed on the natural man.

One of the major messages of the book is that all people—believers and unbelievers—are subject to the trials and tribulations of mortality.

Another message is the obvious warning to avoid relying too much on the things of the world for satisfaction and fulfillment.

Yet another major message is that, by design, mortality is intended to provide many opportunities to enjoy the good things provided by a pleasant, merciful Creator. In other words, the blessings of the earth are provided for all to enjoy. For example, in 2:24 we read (**bold** added for emphasis): "*There is* **nothing better for a man,** *than* **that he should eat** and **drink,** and *that* he should make his soul **enjoy good** in his labour. This also I **saw, that** it *was* **from the hand of God.**"

In other words, there is indeed much to be enjoyed in life (compare with 2 Nephi 2:25). This message is repeated again in 3:12–13.

By the way, Ecclesiastes is read by Jews at their annual Feast of Tabernacles (see Bible Dictionary, under "Feasts") as a sobering reminder of the fleeting nature of mortality.

We will now proceed with our study of Ecclesiastes. Keep in mind that there are many ways to study and interpret this book. We will present some possibilities. You will no doubt see others also, both positive and negative.

Bold will be used for teaching emphasis, suggesting things you may wish to underline or otherwise mark in your own scriptures.

ECCLESIASTES 1

Selection: all verses

1 The words of the Preacher [*possibly Solomon*], the son of David, king in Jerusalem.

2 **Vanity of vanities** [*fleeting and temporary*], saith the Preacher, **vanity of vanities** [*temporary and fleeting*]; **all** *is* **vanity** [*everything in mortality is temporary*].

> One way to look at verses 3–11, next, is to consider them to be the viewpoint of the natural man, the one who neither believes in God or in life after death. You will see that for such people, there is no ultimate purpose or meaning to mortal life. It is a rather pessimistic and dismal view of things. Life, to them, is essentially meaningless.

3 **What profit hath a man of all his labour** [*what good does all the work do*] which he taketh **under the sun** [*which mankind does upon the earth*]?

4 *One* generation passeth away, and *another* generation cometh [*people come and go; we all end up dying*]: but the earth abideth for ever.

5 The sun also ariseth, and the sun goeth down, and hasteth to his place where he arose.

6 The wind goeth toward the south, and turneth about unto the north; it whirleth about continually, and the wind returneth again according to his circuits [*everything remains the same; there is no ultimate purpose nor goal*].

7 All the rivers run into the sea; yet the sea *is* not full; unto the place from whence the rivers come, thither [*there*] they return again.

8 **All things** *are* **full of labour** [*everything requires tiresome work*]; man cannot utter *it* [*more than words can express*]: the eye is not satisfied with seeing, nor the ear filled with hearing [*nothing really satisfies*].

9 The thing that hath been, it *is* that which shall be [*the past will be repeated*]; and that which is done *is* that which shall be done [*everything is mere repetition*]: and **there** *is* no **new** *thing* under the sun [*nothing is new*].

10 Is there *any* thing whereof it may be said, See, this *is* new? it hath been

already of old time, which was before us [*answer: nothing is new*].

11 *There is* **no remembrance of former** *things* [*nobody remembers the past*]; neither shall there be *any* remembrance of *things* that are to come with *those* that shall come after [*neither will the future be remembered by those who come after it; in other words, nothing changes*].

> By the way, you can probably see that verses 9–11, above, could also be interpreted as saying, in effect, that nobody ever seems to learn from the past, which in many ways would be true of worldly societies and people.

12 ¶ I the Preacher was king over Israel in Jerusalem [*probably Solomon referring to himself*].

> In verses 13–18, the author of Ecclesiastes sadly seems to take a pessimistic view of the benefits of wisdom. This outlook could also reflect the viewpoint of the natural man and those who do not believe in God nor in an afterlife.

13 And **I gave my heart to seek and search out by wisdom** concerning **all** *things* that are done **under heaven** [*I dedicated myself to applying my wisdom to the study of all things*]: this sore travail [*heavy burden*] hath God given to the sons of man to be exercised therewith [*in other words, wisdom becomes a heavy burden upon those who possess it*].

14 I have seen all the works that are done under the sun [*in the world*]; and, behold, all *is* vanity and vexation of spirit [*everything in the world is fleeting, meaningless, and frustrating*].

15 *That which is* crooked cannot be made straight [*nothing can be fixed*]: and that which is wanting [*lacking*] cannot be numbered [*counted*].

> Another interpretation of verse 15, above, might depict pessimism in dealing with people. It could be saying that people never learn their lessons, and that their foolishness seems to be infinite.

> Verses 16–18, next, appear to be Solomon speaking about himself.

16 I communed with mine own heart, saying [*I said to myself*], Lo, **I am come to great estate** [*I have become great—see footnote 16a in your Bible*], **and have gotten more wisdom than all** *they* **that have been before me in Jerusalem** [*Solomon was given great wisdom as a gift from God—see 1 Kings 3:12*]: yea, my heart had great experience of wisdom and knowledge.

17 And **I gave my heart** [*I dedicated myself*] **to know wisdom,** and to know [*recognize*] madness and folly: I perceived that **this also is vexation of spirit** [*this was also frustrating*].

18 For [*because*] **in much wisdom** *is* **much grief**: and he that increaseth knowledge increaseth sorrow.

ECCLESIASTES 2

Selection: all verses

AS MENTIONED AT the end of the introductory notes to Ecclesiastes, in this study guide, there are many different ways to approach this particular book of the Bible. One of the major messages of Ecclesiastes can be the warning not to trust too much in the things of the world for satisfaction. For chapter 2, however, the author seems to be pointing out that the Lord has indeed provided many things in this world that are designed to provide appropriate pleasure and enjoyment to mankind. Solomon (assuming he is the author) seems to come to this conclusion at the end of the chapter.

As the chapter progresses, we see a series of things that Solomon samples in order to evaluate their worth. Having investigated them, he draws conclusions about them. We will **bold** several of them as we go along.

1 I said in mine heart, Go to now, I will prove thee with **mirth** [*laughter and merriment*], therefore enjoy **pleasure**: and, behold, this also *is* vanity [*conclusion: this is temporary, fleeting; it doesn't last*].

2 I said of **laughter**, It *is* mad [*crazy*]:

and of **mirth**, What doeth it [*what does it accomplish*]?

In verses 3–10, next, Solomon discusses his experiences with several things in this world to which people turn for satisfaction. He will give his conclusion about them in verse 11.

3 I sought in mine heart to give myself unto **wine**, yet acquainting mine heart with wisdom; and to lay hold on **folly**, till I might see what *was* that good for the sons of men, which they should do under the heaven all the days of their life.

4 I made me **great works**; I builded me **houses**; I planted me **vineyards**:

5 I made me **gardens** and **orchards**, and I planted trees in them of all *kind of* fruits:

6 I made me **pools of water**, to water therewith the wood that bringeth forth trees:

7 I got *me* **servants and maidens**, and had servants born in my house; also I had **great possessions** of great and small cattle above all that were in Jerusalem before me:

8 I gathered me also **silver and gold**, and the peculiar **treasure** of kings and of the provinces: I gat me **men singers and women singers**, and the delights of the sons of men, *as* **musical instruments**, and that **of all sorts**.

9 **So I was great**, and increased more than all that were before me in Jerusalem: **also my wisdom remained with me.**

10 And **whatsoever mine eyes desired I kept not from them, I withheld not my heart from any joy;** for my heart rejoiced in all my labour: and this was my portion of all my labour.

11 **Then I looked on all the works that my hands had wrought** [*accomplished, built, made*], and on the labour that I had laboured to do: **and, behold, all** *was* **vanity and vexation of spirit** [*it was all ultimately of no lasting value, and brought more frustration than it was worth*], and there was no profit under the sun [*I found that there is no lasting value in worldly things*].

12 ¶ And I turned myself to behold wisdom, and madness, and folly: for what *can* the man *do* that cometh after the king [*what can my successor do*]? *even* that which hath been already done.

> In the next verses, we see more of Solomon's conclusions.

13 Then **I saw that wisdom excelleth folly**, as far **as light excelleth darkness.**

14 **The wise man's eyes** *are* **in his head; but the fool walketh in darkness**: and I myself perceived also that **one event happeneth to them all** [*life is essentially the same for all people*].

15 Then said I in my heart, As it happeneth to the fool, so it happeneth even to me; and why was I then more wise? Then I said in my heart, that this also *is* vanity.

16 For *there is* no remembrance of the wise more than of the fool for ever; seeing that which now *is* in the days to come shall all be forgotten. And how dieth the wise *man*? as the fool [*ultimately, the wise man dies just the same as the fool dies*].

> Solomon had concluded, at this point, that he had no basic advantage over any other person in life. He would eventually die and leave all his wealth and possessions behind (see verse 18). This was frustrating to him (verse 17) but reminded him of the temporary nature of worldly possessions.

17 **Therefore I hated life;** because the work that is wrought **under the sun** [*"from a worldly point of view"—see Bible Dictionary, under "Ecclesiastes"*] is grievous unto me: for all *is* vanity [*fleeting, temporary*] and vexation of spirit [*frustration*].

18 ¶ Yea, **I hated all my labour** which I had taken under the sun [*I despised all my worldly accomplishments*]: **because I should leave it unto the man that shall be after me.**

19 And who knoweth whether he shall be a wise *man* or a fool? yet shall he have rule over all my labour wherein I have laboured, and wherein I have shewed myself wise under the sun. This *is* also vanity.

> Next, we see that Solomon despaired because of what he had observed (verses 20–23). However, he will come to a valuable conclusion for all of us in verse 24.

20 Therefore I went about to cause my heart to despair of all the labour which I took under the sun.

21 For there is a man whose labour *is* in wisdom, and in knowledge, and in equity; yet to a man that hath not laboured therein shall he leave it *for* his portion [*I will leave all my worldly possessions and accomplishments to someone who has not worked for it as I did*]. This also *is* vanity and a great evil.

22 For what hath man of all his labour, and of the vexation of his heart, wherein he hath laboured under the sun [*what is the ultimate value of worldly pursuits*]?

23 For all his days *are* sorrows, and his travail [*labor, work*] grief; yea, his heart taketh not rest in the night. This is also vanity [*temporary, fleeting*].

> There are some philosophies and many religious creeds that teach that mankind should avoid physical pleasures because they are inherently evil. In verse 24, next, Solomon concludes that the Lord has provided many things to be enjoyed in life by His children here on earth, and that it is proper to enjoy them. Obviously, he is not endorsing sin and wickedness but rather the proper enjoyment of the good things of the earth created to "please the eye and gladden the heart" (Doctrine & Covenants 59:18).

24 ¶ *There is* nothing better for a man, ***than* that he should eat and drink, and *that* he should make his soul enjoy good in his labour** [*derive satisfaction from his work*]. This also **I saw, that it *was* from the hand of God.**

> The same conclusion is drawn elsewhere.
>
> <u>Ecclesiastes 3:13</u>
> **13** And also that every man should **eat** and **drink,** and **enjoy the good of all his labour,** it *is* **the gift of God.**

25 For who can eat, or who else can hasten *hereunto,* more than I [*can't I enjoy these things just as much as anyone else*]?

> In verse 26, next, Solomon teaches that God gives righteous people wisdom, knowledge, and also joy.
>
> The last phrase of the verse seems to apply to the "sinner" who will ultimately lose any benefit from that which he has "gathered and heaped up."

26 For **God giveth** to a man that *is* good in his sight [*a man who is righteous*] **wisdom**, and **knowledge**, and **joy:** but to the sinner [*the wicked*] he giveth travail, to gather and to heap up, that he may give to *him that is* good before God. This also *is* vanity and vexation of spirit.

ECCLESIASTES 3

Selection: all verses

A S WE MENTIONED in the introductory notes to Ecclesiastes, in this study guide, verses 1–8 are probably the most-quoted verses in Ecclesiastes. They remind us that timing plays a major role in our mortal lives. The ability to wisely discern between these "seasons" (verse 1) and act accordingly, is one of the signs of spiritual maturity and wisdom. We will go ahead with these eight verses now. Notice that they focus primarily upon everything that takes place "under the heaven" (verse 1), in other words, during mortality.

1 To every *thing there is* a season, and a time to every purpose under the heaven:

2 A time to be born, and a time to die; a time to plant, and a time to pluck up *that which is* planted;

3 A time to kill, and a time to heal; a time to break down, and a time to build up;

4 A time to weep, and a time to laugh; a time to mourn, and a time to dance;

5 A time to cast away stones, and a time to gather stones together; a time to embrace, and a time to refrain from embracing;

6 A time to get, and a time to lose; a time to keep, and a time to cast away;

7 A time to rend [*tear*], and a time to sew; a time to keep silence, and a time to speak;

8 A time to love, and a time to hate; a time of war, and a time of peace.

The word "hate" in verse 8 above does not reflect proper gospel living in terms of forgiving others. Remember, though, that much of Ecclesiastes reflects the thinking of the natural man, who is "an enemy to God" (Mosiah 3:19). People who are living in the natural man "mode" are often given to hating others deeply, much to the detriment of their own souls as well as of society in general.

As you have no doubt noticed, the author of Ecclesiastes keeps asking hard questions. For the unbeliever, few if any of the questions have answers. For the believer, many of the questions have answers but some still do not because we do not comprehend the mind and will of God in all things.

Continuing with chapter 3, we

see that the preacher asks a question in verse 9, makes an observation in verse 10, and then states in verse 11 that it is only through an eternal perspective that we can make sense out of mortality.

9 What profit hath he that worketh in that wherein he laboureth [*what benefit does a worker gain from his labor*]?

10 I have seen the travail [*work*], which God hath given to the sons of men to be exercised in it [*to be kept busy by it*].

11 He [*the Lord*] hath made every *thing* beautiful in his [*its*] time [*all things in nature have their time to be beautiful*]: also he [*the Lord*] hath set the world in their heart [*Hebrew: "hath set the eternal in their heart without which man cannot find out the work that God hath done"—see footnote 11b in your Bible*], so that no man can find out the work that God maketh from the beginning to the end.

12 I know that *there is* no good in them, but for *a* man to rejoice, and to do good in his life [*the thing that makes life good is being happy and doing good*].

Next, in verse 13, the preacher concludes that the Lord has given us much that is designed by Him for us to enjoy during our mortal years. In other words, it is okay to be happy and enjoy the good things of life appropriately.

Major Message

By design, mortality is intended to provide many opportunities to enjoy the good things provided by a pleasant, merciful Creator.

13 And also that every man should eat and drink, and enjoy the good of all his labour, it *is* **the gift of God.**

Next, in verse 14, we are taught that God's work is eternal and unchanging. In other words, He is completely dependable and we can always rely on Him and His gospel.

14 I know that, **whatsoever God doeth, it shall be for ever: nothing can be put to it, nor any thing taken from it:** and God doeth *it,* that *men* should fear before him.

15 That which hath been is now; and that which is to be hath already been; and God requireth that which is past.

Verse 17 seems to suggest that an appropriate interpretation of verse 16, next, is that it contains the doctrine of final judgment. All who are accountable will ultimately answer to God for their mortal choices.

16 ¶ And moreover I saw under the sun **the place of judgment,** *that* wickedness *was* there [*the wicked were there*]; and the place of righteousness [*the righteous were there*], *that* iniquity *was* there ["*the filthy were filthy still*"— *see 2 Nephi 9:16*].

17 I said in mine heart, **God shall judge the righteous and the wicked**: for *there is* a time there for every purpose and for every work.

One way to look at verses 18–21 next, is that they represent the incorrect thinking of those who do not believe in God, many of whom conclude that people are simply animals of a higher order and that we are no more important than animals. The Savior provided true doctrine about this. He taught:

Matthew 6:26
26 Behold the fowls of the air: for they sow not, neither do they reap, nor gather into barns; yet your heavenly Father feedeth them. **Are ye not much better than they?**

18 I said in mine heart **concerning the estate of the sons of men**, that God might manifest them, and that they might see that **they themselves are beasts.**

19 For **that which befalleth** [*happens to*] **the sons of men befalleth beasts**; even one thing befalleth them: as the one dieth, so dieth the other; yea, they have all one breath; so that **a man hath no preeminence above a beast**: for all *is* vanity.

20 All go unto one place; all are of the dust, and all turn to dust again.

Verse 21, next, poses a rather interesting question. We do have an answer, which we will give after the verse.

21 Who knoweth the spirit of man that **goeth upward, and the spirit of the beast** that **goeth downward to the earth** [*who knows if there is a heaven and the spirits of men go up to it and the spirits of animals do not*]?

The answer to one question that arises from verse 21 (do animals resurrect?) is given in the Doctrine and Covenants. The answer is yes.

Doctrine & Covenants 29:23–25
23 And the end shall come, and the heaven and the earth shall be consumed and pass away, and there shall be a new heaven and a new earth.
24 For all old things shall pass away, and **all things shall become new** [*will be resurrected*], even the heaven and the earth, and all the fulness thereof [*everything that is in it*], both **men** and **beasts**, the **fowls** of the air, and the **fishes** of the sea;
25 And not one hair, neither mote, shall be lost, for it is the workmanship of mine hand.

Among other things, verse 22, next, can be looked at from the viewpoint of the natural man and also from the perspective of the believers. If viewed as the thinking of the natural man, we might conclude that it means that, since life is basically meaningless, we might as well at least enjoy what we are able to accomplish.

If viewed from the standpoint of those who believe in God,

we might say that it misses the mark. There is much more to life than just what we can accomplish as mortals. We ought to rejoice in the marvelous works of God and in the availability of eternal life.

22 Wherefore I perceive that *there is* nothing better, than that a man should rejoice in his own works; for that *is* his portion: for who shall bring him to see what shall be after him?

ECCLESIASTES 4

Selection: all verses

ONE OF OUR purposes as we study Ecclesiastes is to help you see that there are actually many ways to approach understanding it. One way is to simply read through Ecclesiastes and, on the one hand, mark the verses that seem to be the viewpoint of those who do not believe in God, who do not believe that life has any ultimate purpose, and whose views often reflect pessimism. On the other hand, while reading through it you could also mark the verses that represent the viewpoint of the believer, those that point out the good in mortal life and give an eternal perspective to it.

We will use this approach in chapter 4, realizing that many verses could go either way. Thus, you could go through it using the same approach as we do and come up with quite different results. We will use two headings for this approach:

Pessimist: representing the natural man and those who do not believe in God.

The Positive Approach: representing the viewpoint of those who see things in an eternal perspective, through their belief in God. They are often optimists.

Pessimist (verses 1–5)

1 So I returned, and considered **all the oppressions** that are done under the sun [*in mortality*]: and behold the **tears** of *such as were* oppressed, and they had **no comforter; and on the side of their oppressors *there was* power** [*life is not fair; the power in daily life lies with those who oppress others*]; but they had **no comforter.**

2 Wherefore [*as a result*] **I praised the dead** which are already dead **more than the living which are yet alive** [*people who are dead are the lucky ones*].

3 Yea, **better *is* he than** both **they,** which hath not yet been, **who hath not seen the evil work that is done under the sun** [*the unborn are better off than both the dead and the living, because they have seen none of the evils of mortality*].

4 ¶ Again, **I considered all travail, and every right work, that for this a man is envied of his neighbour** [*everything that is supposedly good has its downside; all achievement comes as a result of people envying their neighbors*]. **This *is* also vanity** [*meaningless,* transitory] **and vexation of spirit** [*frustrating*].

5 The fool foldeth his hands together, and **eateth his own flesh** [*makes decisions leading to his own destruction*].

The Positive Approach (verse 6)

6 Better *is* an handful *with* **quietness, than both the hands full** *with* **travail and vexation of spirit** [*better to be satisfied with what you have than to be constantly striving for more and getting frustrated*].

Pessimist (verses 7–8)

7 ¶ Then I returned, and **I saw vanity under the sun** [*everything in mortal life is fleeting, meaningless*].

8 There is one *alone,* **and** *there is* **not a second** [*we are all basically alone in life*]; yea, he hath neither child nor brother: yet *is* **there no end of all his labour** [*life is basically one big struggle to survive*]; **neither is his eye satisfied with riches;** neither *saith he,* For whom do I labour, and bereave my soul of good? This *is* also vanity, yea, it *is* a sore travail [*it is a miserable life*].

The Positive Approach (verses 9–12)

9 ¶ **Two** *are* **better than one;** because they have a good reward for their labour.

10 For if they fall, the one will lift up his fellow: but woe to him *that* *is* alone when he falleth; for *he hath* not another to help him up.

11 Again, **if two lie together, then they have heat: but how can one be warm** *alone?*

12 And **if one prevail against him, two shall withstand him; and a threefold cord is not quickly broken.**

> Verse 13, next, is a wise saying, and doesn't really fit under the pessimist heading nor the positive heading.

13 ¶ **Better** *is* **a poor and a wise child than an old and foolish king, who will no more be admonished** [*who will not take counsel*].

Pessimist (verses 14–16)

14 For out of prison he cometh to reign; whereas also *he that is* born in his kingdom becometh poor.

15 I considered [*I thought about*] all the living which walk under the sun [*who live on the earth*], with the second child that shall stand up in his stead [*I looked at the successor to the current ruler*].

16 *There is* no end of all the people, *even* of all that have been before them: **they** also that come after shall **not rejoice in him** [*basically, all are oppressed by their rulers, including the successors to the rulers*]. Surely **this also** *is* **vanity and vexation of spirit.**

ECCLESIASTES 5

Selection: all verses

WE WILL CONTIN-
UE the approach we used
in chapter 4 as we consider
chapter 5. You will see that there are
many more positives than negatives in
this chapter. As usual, we will use **bold**
to point things out.

Perspective and Wisdom from the Viewpoint of the Believer (verses 1–10)

1 Keep thy foot **when thou goest to the house of God, and be more ready to hear, than to give the sacrifice of fools:** for they consider not that they do evil.

2 **Be not rash with thy mouth, and let not thine heart be hasty to utter** *any* **thing before God: for God** *is* **in heaven, and thou upon earth: therefore let thy words be few.**

3 For a dream cometh through the multitude of business; and **a fool's voice** *is* *known* **by multitude of words.**

4 **When thou vowest a vow unto God, defer not to pay it;** for *he hath* no pleasure in fools: **pay that which thou hast vowed.**

5 **Better** *is* *it* **that thou shouldest not vow, than that thou shouldest vow and not pay** [*it is better not to make a covenant with God than to make and then break it*].

6 **Suffer not thy mouth to cause thy flesh to sin;** neither say thou before the angel [*the officiator in the temple; see New International Version*], that it *was* an error [*that you made a mistake in making a vow*]: wherefore should God be angry at thy voice, and destroy the work of thine hands?

7 For in the multitude of dreams and many words [*much dreaming and many empty words*] there are also *divers* vanities [*amount to nothing*]: but **fear thou God** [*live in respect and awe of God*].

8 ¶ If thou seest the oppression of the poor, and violent perverting of judgment and justice in a province [*in the government of a particular region*], marvel not at the matter [*don't be surprised that such things take place*]: for **he** *that* *is* **higher than the highest regardeth** [*God is watching everything*]; and *there be* higher than they [*God is indeed higher than mortal government officials*].

9 ¶ Moreover **the profit of the earth is for all** [*God intends the bounties of the earth to bless all people*]: the king himself is served by the field [*is benefited by the crops of the field*].

10 **He that loveth silver shall not be satisfied with silver;** nor he that loveth abundance with increase [*one whose heart is set on wealth is never satisfied with his income*]: this *is* also

vanity [*meaningless, temporary*].

Verse 11, next, probably fits best in the "pessimist" category.

Pessimist (verse 11)

11 When goods increase, they are increased that eat them [*if your income increases, there will just be more mouths to feed*]: **and what good is** there **to the owners thereof, saving the beholding** *of them* **with their eyes?**

Perspective and Wisdom from the Viewpoint of the Believer (verses 12-13)

12 The sleep of a labouring man is sweet, whether he eat little or much: but **the abundance** [*wealth*] **of the rich will not suffer** [*allow*] **him to sleep.**

13 There is a sore [*grievous, serious*] evil *which* I have seen **under the sun** [*among people who view things "from a worldly point of view"—see Bible Dictionary, under "Ecclesiastes"*] namely, **riches kept for** [*hoarded by*] **the owners thereof to their hurt** [*in other words, wealth often ruins worldly people*].

Pessimist (verses 14-17)

14 But those riches perish by evil travail: and he begetteth a son, and *there is* **nothing in his hand.**

15 As he came forth of his mother's womb, naked shall he return to go as he came, and shall take nothing of his labour, which he may carry away in his hand [*this life is meaningless*].

16 And this also *is* **a sore evil,** *that* **in all points as he came, so shall he go:** and what profit hath he that hath laboured for the wind? [*One interpretation of verses 15–16 is that life on earth has basically no real value.*]

Depending on how you look at it, verse 16, above could also be saying that people who spend all their lives only pursuing material things (last half of the verse) have labored for nothing of real value.

17 All his days also he eateth in darkness [*his whole life is spent not knowing what life is about*], **and** *he hath* **much sorrow and wrath with his sickness.**

Perspective and Wisdom from the Viewpoint of the Believer (verses 18-20)

18 ¶ Behold *that* **which I have seen** [*here is what I have concluded*]: **it** *is* **good and comely** [*appropriate*] *for one* **to eat and to drink, and to enjoy the good of all his labour** that he taketh under the sun [*during mortality*] **all the days of his life, which God giveth him:** for it *is* his portion [*it is God's gift to him*].

19 Every man also to whom God hath given riches and wealth, and hath given him power to eat thereof, and to take his portion, and to

rejoice in his labour; **this** *is* **the gift of God.**

20 For he shall not much remember the days of his life; because God answereth *him* **in the joy of his heart** [*in other words, with an eternal perspective, mortal life passes quickly and one has much joy because of the goodness of God*].

> By now you have seen that there are many different ways to look at Ecclesiastes—and even at individual verses within the book. So far, we have given some possible approaches and perspectives for your consideration. We hope this will be helpful to you as you read the rest of Ecclesiastes. We will examine a few more verses and then finish with considerable detail on the last two chapters.
>
> First, we will skip to chapter 7, where the preacher (another name for the author of Ecclesiastes) asks, in effect, "Why do the righteous suffer while the wicked seem to prosper?"

Question

Why do the righteous suffer while the wicked continue to prosper? (Chapter 7, verse 15)

Ecclesiastes 7:15

15 All *things* **have I seen in the days of my vanity: there is a just** *man* **that perisheth in his righteousness, and there is a wicked** *man* **that prolongeth** *his life* **in his wickedness.**

Answer (Chapter 7, verse 18)

> The answer can be seen only with an eternal perspective. With that perspective, you will see that in the eternities, the righteous prosper and the unrepentant wicked will suffer.

Ecclesiastes 7:18

18 *It is* good that thou shouldest **take hold of this** [*perhaps meaning the counsel about to be given*]; yea, also from this withdraw not thine hand: for **he that feareth God shall come forth of them all** [*in other words, those who honor God and live the gospel will rise above all others (exaltation) in the next life*].

> The above answer is confirmed in chapter 8.

Ecclesiastes 8:12–13

12 ¶ Though a sinner do evil an hundred times, and his *days* **be prolonged** [*even if the wicked live a long life*]**, yet surely I know that it shall be well with them that fear** [*respect, honor, obey*] **God, which fear before him:**

13 But it shall not be well with the wicked, neither shall he prolong *his* days, *which are* as a shadow [*which are fleeting, temporary*]; because he feareth not before God.

> The same message is again confirmed in the last chapter of Ecclesiastes.

Ecclesiastes 12:13–14

13 ¶ Let us hear the conclusion of the whole matter: Fear God, and keep his commandments: for this *is* the whole *duty* of man.

14 For God shall bring every *work* into judgment, with every secret thing, whether *it be* **good, or whether** *it be* **evil.**

> The false doctrines and beliefs of the natural man, who neither believes in God or in life after death, are exemplified in the following verses:

Ecclesiastes 9:5 & 10

5 For the living know that they shall die: but **the dead know not any thing,** neither have they any more a reward; for the memory of them is forgotten.

10 Whatsoever thy hand findeth to do, do *it* with thy might; for *there is* **no work, nor device, nor knowledge, nor wisdom, in the grave, whither thou goest** [*in other words, once you die, that is the end*].

> Some people use verses 5 and 10, above, taken out of context, to attempt to prove from the Bible that there is no life after death. This is what is known as "wresting the scriptures"—taking something in the scriptures out of context in order to attempt to prove a falsehood.
>
> We will now conclude our study of Ecclesiastes by examining chapters 11 and 12 verse-by-verse.

Keep in mind, as previously stated, that there is more than one way to look at what the "preacher" (probably Solomon) teaches. What we present in these last two chapters is just one approach.

ECCLESIASTES 11

Selection: all verses

ONE MESSAGE OF this chapter seems to be to plant wisely so that we have a good harvest, despite troubles and difficulties along the way. In other words, we should live wisely and keep the commandments of God as we move through mortality, in order to have a pleasant harvest as we stand before God on Judgment Day.

1 Cast thy bread upon the waters: for thou shalt find it after many days [*what you do now will come back to you in the future*].

2 Give a portion to seven, and also to eight; for thou knowest not what evil shall be upon the earth [*perhaps meaning that if you prepare well, future downturns will not be as damaging to you*].

3 If the clouds be full of rain, they empty *themselves* upon the earth [*what you fill your life with will come out in the end*]: **and if the tree fall toward the south, or toward the north, in the place where the tree falleth, there it shall be** [*when you* die, you will remain what you are at the time].

4 He that observeth the wind [*pays too much attention to the wind*] **shall not sow** [*will not plant*]; and **he that regardeth the clouds** [*is afraid there won't be enough rain to grow a newly-planted crop*] **shall not reap** [*a person who worries too much about planting will never get a harvest; in other words, a pessimist lives in fear of the future, therefore never gets anything done*].

> Verses 5-6, next, seem to be saying that even though there are many things we do not understand about life and about God, we should still proceed with planting and working toward goals.

5 As thou knowest not what *is the way of the spirit, *nor* how the bones *do grow* in the womb of her that is with child: even so thou knowest not the works of God who maketh all.

6 In the morning sow thy seed, and in the evening withhold not thine hand [*keep working*]: for **thou knowest not whether** [*which of your efforts or works*] **shall prosper,** either this or that, or whether they both *shall be* alike good.

> Among other things, verses 7-8, next, remind us that we run into both good and evil during our mortal lives.

7 ¶ Truly the light *is* sweet, and a **pleasant** *thing it is* **for the eyes to behold the sun** [*a beautiful day with sunlight is pleasant to see*]:

8 But if a man live many years, *and* rejoice in them all; yet let him remember **the days of darkness** [*there will be bad times too*]; for they shall be many. **All that cometh *is* vanity** [*passing, temporary*].

9 ¶ Rejoice, O young man, in thy youth; and let thy heart cheer thee in the days of thy youth, and walk in the ways of thine heart, and in the sight of thine eyes: but **know thou, that for all these *things* God will bring thee into judgment** [*remember, you will someday stand before God to account for your life*].

10 Therefore **remove sorrow from thy heart** [*be happy*], and **put away evil from thy flesh** [*avoid the sins common to mortals*]: for **childhood and youth *are* vanity** [*temporary, fleeting*].

ECCLESIASTES 12

Selection: all verses

AS MENTIONED EARLIER, verses 13 and 14 are "the conclusion of the whole matter" for the "preacher" (the author of Ecclesiastes, probably Solomon). Throughout the previous chapters of Ecclesiastes, he has asked many questions, emphasized the temporary nature of mortality, presented many things from the viewpoint of the "natural man," pointed out that there is much to be appropriately enjoyed here on earth, and taught that an eternal perspective is essential for us in order to make sense of mortal life.

Now, in this final chapter, he counsels us to be wise in our earlier mortal days, while future accountability before God is far off (verses 1–6). He teaches the doctrine that, upon our mortal deaths, our spirits return to God (verse 7), in other words, there is indeed life after death. He once again reminds us that mortality is temporary and fleeting (verse 8). After that, he adds a personal note, explaining that he has taught his people and given them many wise sayings, through much study on his part (verses 9–12). At the end of the chapter, he gives us his final conclusion and counsel about mortality (verses 13–14).

We will use **bold** to point these things out.

1 Remember now **thy Creator in the days of thy youth,** while the evil days come not [*before old age comes to you*], nor the years draw nigh, when thou shalt say, I have no pleasure in them [*before you get so old that you no longer find pleasure in the things of youth*];

2 While the sun, or the light, or the moon, or the stars, be not darkened [*while you are still young, before old age catches up to you and dims your senses*], nor the clouds return after the rain:

3 In the day when the keepers of the house shall tremble, and the strong men shall bow themselves, and the grinders cease because they are few, and those that look out of the windows be darkened,

4 And the doors shall be shut in the streets, when the sound of the grinding is low, and he shall rise up at the voice of the bird, and all the daughters of musick shall be brought low;

5 Also *when* they shall be afraid of *that which is* high, and fears *shall be* in the way, and the almond tree shall flourish, and the grasshopper shall be a burden [*just like the grasshopper—whose life is also temporary—finally grows old and drags slowly to his death*], and desire shall fail: because man goeth to his long home [*because he finally dies*], and the mourners go about the streets:

Verse 6, next, uses several different idiomatic sayings from the culture of ancient Israel, which in this context all say, in effect, the day eventually comes to all of us in which we will die. We have many such idiomatic phrases in our modern language that likewise refer to death. Some of them are, "We will all bite the dust," "kick the bucket," "give up the ghost," "cash in," or "our ticker will stop."

6 Or ever **the silver cord be loosed** [*death comes; mortal life comes to an end*], or **the golden bowl be broken**

[*death come*], or **the pitcher be broken** at the fountain [*mortal life comes to an end; the source of mortal life—the spirit—leaves*], or **the wheel broken** at the cistern [*the well of life ceases to sustain mortal life*].

7 Then shall the dust [*mortal body*] **return to the earth** as it was: **and the spirit shall return unto God who gave it.**

> The word "return" in the last half of verse 7, above, is an important doctrinal reminder that we did have a premortal life with Heavenly Father.

8 ¶ Vanity [*temporary*] of vanities, saith the preacher; **all** *is* **vanity** [*everything in mortality is temporary*].

> Next, the preacher adds a personal note about his attempts to share his knowledge and wisdom with his people.

9 And moreover [*in addition*], **because the preacher was wise, he** still **taught the people knowledge;** yea, he gave good heed, and sought out, *and* set in order **many proverbs** [*wise sayings*].

10 The preacher sought to find out acceptable words [*he worked hard to find the right words to communicate his wisdom*]: and *that which was* written *was* upright, *even* words of truth.

11 The words of the wise *are* as **goads** [*sharp-pointed sticks—see footnote 11a in your Bible; cattle prods*],

and **as nails fastened** *by* **the masters of assemblies** [*the words of the wise are like a collection of goads assembled by masters of wisdom*], **which** are **given from one shepherd** [*which ultimately come from one source*].

12 And further, **by these, my son, be admonished** [*allow yourself to be taught by these collections of wisdom*]: of making many books *there is* no end [*there is no end to the possibilities for writing wise sayings*]; and much study *is* a weariness of the flesh [*much study can make a body tired*].

> There is another possible interpretation of verse 12, above, that is quite different from the possibility we gave above. We will include it as a reminder that there are many disagreements as to how to correctly interpret ancient languages.

Verse 12, repeated

12 And further, **by these, my son, be admonished** [*"be warned about anything in addition to"—NIV Bible and German Bible (Martin Luther translation)*]: of making many books *there is* no end [*there is no end to the writing of books*]; and much study *is* a weariness of the flesh [*much study can make a body tired*].

The Conclusion (verses 13–14)

13 ¶ Let us hear the conclusion of the whole matter: **Fear** [*honor, respect, obey*] **God, and keep his commandments:** for this *is* the whole *duty* of man.

14 For **God shall bring every** *work* [*act, deed*] **into judgment,** with every secret thing, whether *it be* good, or whether *it be* evil [*we will all ultimately stand before God to account for our lives*].

THE SONG OF SOLOMON

THE SONG OF Solomon is thought by some to have been written by Solomon but many Bible scholars consider its authorship to be unknown. Some consider it to be a simple love song while others look at its imagery as being symbolic of the love that God has for His people.

Because of some of its content, some students wonder how such a book as this even made it into the Bible. In fact, over the ages, the Song of Solomon has generated quite a bit of controversy. A statement by the Prophet Joseph Smith is helpful. You will see a note in your Bible, after footnote 1a in chapter one of Song of Solomon, which quotes the manuscript for the Joseph Smith Translation of the Bible (the JST) as saying: "The Songs of Solomon are not inspired writings." As a result of the Prophet's statement, we will not do more with the Song of Solomon in this study guide.

ISAIAH

WE WILL INCLUDE every verse of Isaiah, with notes and commentary, in this study guide. Isaiah began his ministry about 740 BC (see chronology chart in the Bible Dictionary in the back of your LDS Bible). He continued until about 701 BC. He is one of the greatest prophets who ever lived. You can read a summary about him in the Bible Dictionary under "Isaiah." We will quote one portion of that summary here:

ISAIAH

"The Lord is salvation. Son of Amoz, a prophet in Jerusalem during 40 years, 740–701 BC He had great religious and political influence during the reign of Hezekiah, whose chief advisor he was. Tradition states that he was "sawn asunder" during the reign of Manasseh; for that reason he is often represented in art holding a saw."

The Savior quoted Isaiah more often than He quoted any other prophet in the Old Testament. This fact alone testifies of the importance of the writings and teachings of Isaiah. During the Savior's ministry to the Nephites on the American continent, He quoted Isaiah (in 3 Nephi 22) and then said (**bold** added for emphasis):

3 Nephi 23:1
1 AND now, behold, I say unto you, that **ye ought to search these things.** Yea, a commandment I give unto you that ye search these things diligently; for great are the words of Isaiah.

There are obviously many reasons that the teachings of Isaiah are vital to us. We will quote again from the Book of Mormon to see two major reasons to study Isaiah, according to Nephi. We will use **bold** to point out Nephi's reasons for quoting Isaiah to his people, including his wayward brothers Laman and Lemuel.

1 Nephi 19:23–24
23 And I did read many things unto them which were written in the books of Moses; but that I might **more fully persuade them to believe in the Lord their Redeemer** I did read unto them that which was written by the prophet Isaiah; for I did liken all scriptures unto us, that it might be for our profit and learning.
24 Wherefore I spake unto them, saying: Hear ye the words of the prophet, ye who are a remnant of the house of Israel, a branch who have been broken off; hear ye the words of the prophet, which were written unto all the house of Israel, and liken them unto yourselves, **that ye may have hope** as well as your brethren from whom ye have been broken off; for after this manner has the prophet written.

Thus we are taught that Isaiah's teachings can greatly strengthen our testimonies of Jesus Christ, our Redeemer, and provide wonderful hope and assurance in our hearts that we can be found among those who are saved.

Knowing what Isaiah can do for us is one thing, but for many members of the Church, understanding the writings of Isaiah is quite another thing. Many years ago when I first remember reading 3 Nephi 23:1 (quoted above), I thought to myself, "If the Savior says that the words of Isaiah are great, then there must be something wrong with me because I don't understand most of them. Perhaps I am not spiritual enough, or the Holy Ghost can't work with me, or whatever." At any rate, it was a concern to me that I found Isaiah so difficult to understand.

Several years later, I attended a summer class for seminary and institute of religion teachers that was being taught by Brother Ellis Rasmussen of the BYU religion department. With Brother Rasmussen's first words, Isaiah came alive for me. As I recall, he quoted the first line of Isaiah 53:1 where Isaiah says, "Who hath believed our report?" And then he explained that it is just another way of saying, "Who believes us prophets anyway?"

Just like that, the key for understanding Isaiah was turned for me. It was possible to understand it! I listened with rapt attention and made many tiny, short notes in my scriptures during Brother Rasmussen's classes.

My intent is to make Isaiah "easier," not necessarily "easy," for students of the scriptures. The notes provided are intentionally brief, for two main reasons. One: They allow you to read the actual Bible text, with minimal interruption, and get a quick threshold understanding of Isaiah's teachings. Two: You may wish to write some of these brief notes in your own scriptures.

In order to keep the notes brief and somewhat conversational, considerable license has been taken with respect to capitalization and punctuation. The explanations and interpretations provided are not intended to be the final word on Isaiah. I am hopeful that readers will begin to see many other possibilities for interpretation and application of this great prophet's words, for the symbolism and messages of Isaiah do indeed lend themselves to multiple interpretations in various settings.

By the way, the references for the notes in brackets that say "German" are a reference to the translation found in the Martin Luther edition of the German Bible.

We will now proceed with our study of Isaiah.

ISAIAH 1

Selection: all verses

CHAPTER 1 IS a preface to the whole book of Isaiah, much like Doctrine and Covenants, section one, is to the whole Doctrine and Covenants, or like the superscription at the beginning of First Nephi is, which says "An account of Lehi . . ."

1 The vision of Isaiah the son of Amoz, which he saw **concerning Judah and Jerusalem** in the days of Uzziah, Jotham, Ahaz, and Hezekiah, kings of Judah [*The kings mentioned above reigned from about 740 BC to 701 BC*].

Isaiah states the main problem, in verses 2–4, next.

2 Hear, O heavens, and give ear, O earth: for the Lord hath spoken, **I have nourished and brought up children, and they have rebelled against me.**

3 The ox knoweth his owner, and the ass his master's crib [*manger*]: but **Israel doth not know** [*know God*], my people doth not consider [*think seriously, Israel—animals are wiser than you are!*].

4 Ah **sinful nation**, a **people laden with iniquity** [*loaded down with wickedness*], a seed of evildoers, children that are **corrupters**: they **have forsaken the Lord,** they have provoked the Holy One of Israel unto anger, they **are gone away backward** [*retrogressing; they are "in the world" and "of the world"*].

5 ¶ Why should ye be stricken any more [*why do you keep asking for more punishment*]? ye will revolt more and more: **the whole head** [*leadership*] **is sick,** and the whole heart [*the people*] faint [*is diseased; in other words, the whole nation is spiritually sick*].

Isaiah continues the theme that the whole nation is riddled with wickedness and is thus spiritually sick. He uses repetition to drive home the point.

6 From the sole of the foot even unto the head there is no soundness in it [*you are completely sick*]; but **wounds, and bruises, and putrifying** [*filled with pus*] **sores** [*symbolically saying that the people are spiritually beaten and infected with sin*]: **they have not been closed, neither bound up, neither mollified with ointment** [*you are sick and you don't even care; you won't try the simplest first aid (the Atonement of Christ)*].

Old Testament prophets often spoke prophetically of the future as if it had already taken place. Isaiah uses this technique next, as he prophesies of the impending captivity of these wicked people.

7 Your country is desolate, your cities are **burned** with fire: your land, strangers [*foreigners*] devour it in your presence, and it is desolate as overthrown by strangers [*foreigners, specifically the Assyrians*].

8 And **the daughter of Zion** [*Israel*] **is left as a cottage** [*temporary shade structure built of straw and leaves*] in a vineyard, as a lodge [*same as cottage*] in a garden of cucumbers, as a besieged city [*you are about as secure as a flimsy shade shack in a garden*].

9 Except the Lord of hosts had left unto us a very small remnant [*if God hadn't intervened and saved a few of Israel*], **we should have been as Sodom**, and we should have been like unto Gomorrah [*completely destroyed*].

10 ¶ Hear the word of the Lord, ye rulers of Sodom [*"Listen up, you wicked leaders!"*]; **give ear unto the law of our God, ye people of Gomorrah** [*Sodom and Gomorrah symbolize total wickedness*].

11 To what purpose is the multitude of your sacrifices unto me [*what good are your insincere, empty rituals*]? **saith the Lord: I am full** [*"I've had it to here!"*] **of the burnt offerings of rams, and the fat of fed beasts; and I delight not in the blood of bullocks, or of lambs, or of he goats.**

12 When ye come to appear before me, who hath required this at your hand, to tread my courts [*who authorized you hypocrites to act religious and pretend to worship Me*]?

13 Bring no more vain [*useless*] **oblations** [*offerings*]; incense is an abomination unto me; the new moons [*special Sabbath ritual at beginning of month—see Bible Dictionary under "New Moon"*] and sabbaths, the calling of assemblies, I cannot [*"I can't stand it!"*] away with; it is iniquity, even the solemn meeting [*solemn assembly*].

14 Your new moons and your appointed feasts [*your hypocritical worship*] **my soul hateth: they are a trouble unto me; I am weary to bear them.**

15 And when ye spread forth your hands [*when you pray*], **I will hide mine eyes from you: yea, when ye make many prayers, I will not hear: your hands are full of blood** [*bloodshed; murder—see verse 21*].

Next, in spite of the gross wickedness of these people, as described by Isaiah, they are invited by a merciful Savior to repent and return to Him.

Major Message
If you want to repent but you think your sins have put you beyond the reach of the Savior's Atonement, think again.

16 ¶ Wash you [*be baptized*], make you clean; put away the evil of your doings from before mine eyes [*repent*]; cease to do evil;

17 Learn to do well [*don't just cease to do evil but replace evil with good in your lives*]; **seek judgment** [*be fair in your dealings with others*], **relieve the oppressed, judge the fatherless** [*be kind and fair to them*], **plead for** [*stand up for, defend*] **the widow.**

Verse 18, next, is among the most well-known of all quotes from Isaiah. With verses 1–15 as a backdrop, this verse wonderfully and clearly teaches the power of the Atonement of Jesus Christ to cleanse and heal completely.

18 Come now, and let us reason together, saith the Lord: **though your sins be as scarlet** [*cloth dyed with scarlet, a colorfast dye*], **they shall be as white as snow** [*even though you think your sins are "colorfast," the Atonement can cleanse you*]; **though they be red like crimson, they shall be as wool** [*a long process is required to get wool white, but it can be done*].

19 If ye be willing [*agency, choice*] **and obedient,** ye shall eat the good of the land [*you will prosper*]:

20 But if ye refuse and rebel, ye shall be devoured with the sword: for the mouth of the Lord hath spoken it.

The word "harlot" (or prostitute), in verse 21, next, is a play on the imagery of a husband whose wife commits adultery against him. In the symbolism of the Bible, the husband represents Christ, and the wife represents Israel. They are bound together by covenant, but Israel cheats on her husband by being loyal to false gods, including wickedness and self-indulgence.

21 ¶ How is [*did*] **the faithful city** [*Jerusalem*] **become an harlot** [*unfaithful to the Lord; a willful sinner*]! it was full of judgment [*justice*]; righteousness lodged in it; but now murderers.

22 Thy silver is become dross [*surface scum on molten metal*] thy wine mixed with water [*you are polluted!*]:

23 Thy princes [*leaders, rulers*] **are rebellious,** and companions of thieves: **every one loveth gifts** [*bribes*], and followeth after rewards: they judge not [*do not do justice to*] the fatherless, neither doth the cause of the widow come unto them [*never penetrates their hearts*].

24 Therefore saith the Lord, the Lord of hosts, the mighty One of Israel, Ah, **I will ease me of** [*be rid of*] **mine adversaries,** and avenge me of mine enemies [*in other words, the Lord will turn the wicked people of Israel over to the law of justice, since they have chosen to become His enemies*]:

25 ¶ And **I will turn my hand upon thee** [*repeatedly chastise you*], and purely purge away thy dross, and take away all thy tin [*slag; I will refine thee; in other words, put you through the refiner's fire to burn your impurities and sins out of you*]:

26 And **I will restore thy judges as at the first** [*among other things, a reference to the future when the gospel is restored by Joseph Smith*], and thy counsellors as at the beginning: **afterward thou shalt be called, The city of righteousness, the faithful city** [*the future gathering of Israel*].

27 **Zion shall be redeemed** [*a prophetic fact*] with judgment, and her converts with righteousness [*message of hope*].

28 **And the destruction of the transgressors and of the sinners shall be together** [*at the same time*], and they that forsake the Lord shall be consumed [*at the Second Coming*].

29 For **they shall be ashamed of** [*put to shame because of*] **the oaks** [*trees and gardens used in their idol worship*] which ye have desired, and **ye shall be confounded for the** [*because of the*] **gardens** [*used in idol worship*] that ye have chosen.

30 For **ye shall be as an oak whose leaf fadeth, and as a garden that hath no water** [*drought; destruction will come upon you because of your wickedness*].

31 And **the strong** [*the mighty wicked among you*] **shall be as tow** [*as a tuft of inflammable fibers*], and the maker of it as a spark, and **they shall both burn together, and none shall quench them** [*destruction of the wicked is sure to happen*].

ISAIAH 2

Selection: all verses

CHAPTERS 2, 3, and 4 go together. Chapter 2 is a multifaceted prophecy of the latter-day gathering to the tops of the Rocky Mountains (Salt Lake City), the building of latter-day temples, the Millennium, and the destruction of the wicked at the Second Coming. Isaiah saw these things in vision (as stated in verse 1).

1 **The word that Isaiah the son of Amoz saw** concerning Judah and Jerusalem.

2 And it shall come to pass **in the last days,** that **the mountain** of the Lord's house shall be established in the top of the mountains [*"high place"—temples will be established; also, the Church will be established in the tops of the mountains in the last days*], and shall be exalted above the hills [*symbolism: you can get higher, closer to God in the temples than on the highest mountains*]; and **all nations shall flow unto it** [*the gathering of Israel in the last days, coming to the true gospel, with headquarters in the "top of the mountains"*].

3 And **many people shall go and say, Come ye, and let us go up to the mountain of the Lord,** to the house [*temples*] of the God of Jacob; and **he will teach us of his ways, and we will walk in his paths:** for out of Zion shall go forth the law,

and the word of the Lord from Jerusalem [*"law" and "word" are synonyms; this seems to be a reference to the Millennium, when there will be two headquarters of Christ's kingdom, Zion (the New Jerusalem), built in Independence, Missouri, and Old Jerusalem; the Lord's word will go out from both cities*].

Verse 4, next, is a direct reference to the Millennium.

4 And he [*Christ*] **shall judge** [*rule*] **among the nations,** and shall rebuke many people: and **they shall beat their swords into plowshares, and their spears into pruninghooks** [*there will be peace*]: **nation shall not lift up sword against nation, neither shall they learn war any more** [*Millennium*].

Isaiah now switches from the future back to his own time and people. It is a common practice (and somewhat confusing to us) for Isaiah to switch from the future to the past, or the present, and then back and forth, with no notice. It is part of "the manner of prophesying among the Jews" (2 Nephi 25:1).

Having told the people what will happen to their descendants in the far-distant future, and given them a glimpse of the beautiful peace and joy of living with the Savior during the Millennium, he now invites them to repent and prepare themselves to be worthy of living with Him forever.

5 O house of Jacob [*another name for Israel*], **come ye, and let us walk in the light of the Lord.**

Next, Isaiah reminds these wicked people why they are not currently enjoying the blessings of the Lord.

6 Therefore [*this is why*] thou [*the Lord*] hast forsaken thy people the house of Jacob [*the Israelites*], **because they be replenished from the east** [*they are adopting false eastern religions*], **and are soothsayers** [*are into witchcraft, sorcery, and so forth*] like the Philistines, and **they please themselves in the children of strangers** [*are mixing with and marrying foreigners, people not of covenant Israel*].

7 Their land also is full of silver and gold, neither is there any end of their treasures [*they have become materialistic*]; **their land is also full of horses,** neither is there any end of their **chariots** [*horses and chariots represent armaments of war*]:

8 Their land also is full of idols; they worship the work of their own hands, that which their own fingers have made [*Isaiah is pointing out how absurd worshiping idols is*]:

The Book of Mormon adds a very important word in two places in verse 9, next. The Book of Mormon passages of Isaiah came from the brass plates and were thus of much earlier date and accuracy than the manuscripts from which our Old Testament is taken.

9 And the **mean man** [*poor, low in social status*] **boweth** [*not, see 2 Nephi 12:9*] **down, and the great** [*high in social status and influence*] **man humbleth himself** [*not*]: therefore forgive them not [*no one is humble*].

The main message in verse 10, next, is that it is impossible to hide from God.

10 **Enter into the rock** [*go ahead and try to find a place to hide from the Lord in the rocks, you wicked people*], **and hide thee in the dust,** for fear of the Lord and for [*2 Nephi 12:10 does not have "for"*] the glory of his majesty [*2 Nephi 12:10 adds "shall smite thee"*].

One other thing we learn from verse 10, above, with the Book of Mormon additions, is that the wicked will be destroyed by the glory of the coming Savior, at the time of the Second Coming (compare with Doctrine & Covenants 5:19).

11 **The lofty looks of man** [*pride*] **shall be humbled,** and the haughtiness of men shall be bowed down, and **the Lord alone shall be exalted in that day** [*the Lord will demonstrate power over all things at the Second Coming*].

Verse 12, next, is yet another reminder to you that Isaiah uses repetition to emphasize a point he wishes to make.

12 **For the day of the Lord of hosts** [*Second Coming*] **shall be upon** [*against*] **every one that is proud** and lofty, and upon [*against*] every one that is lifted up [*full of pride*]; and he shall be brought low [*humbled*]:

Trees are often used by Isaiah and other Old Testament prophets to represent people. We see this technique in verse 13, next.

13 And **upon all the cedars** [*people*] of Lebanon, **that are high and lifted up**, and upon all the oaks [*people*] of Bashan,

14 And upon all the high mountains, and upon all the hills that are lifted up,

15 And upon every high tower, and upon every fenced wall [*man-made defenses*],

16 And **upon all the ships of Tarshish** [*symbolic of materialism and earthly power; noted for ability to travel long distances and carry large cargoes, and for their strength as warships*], **and upon all pleasant pictures** [*pleasure craft upon which the wealthy traveled*].

17 And **the loftiness** [*pride*] **of man shall be bowed down**, and the haughtiness of men shall be made low: and **the Lord alone shall be exalted in that day** [*at the time of the Second Coming*].

18 And **the idols he shall utterly abolish.**

The terror in the hearts of the wicked at the time of the Second Coming is depicted in verses 19 and 21, next.

19 And **they** [*the wicked*] **shall go into the holes of the rocks** [*caves*], and into the caves of the earth, **for fear of the Lord, and for the glory of his majesty,** when he ariseth to shake terribly the earth [*at the time of the Second Coming*].

20 In that day [*Second Coming*] a man shall cast his idols of silver, and his idols of gold, which they made each one for himself to worship [*a reminder that idol worship is completely absurd*], **to the moles and to the bats** [*a play on words, pointing out that wicked people live in "darkness" also*];

21 To go into the clefts of the rocks, and into the tops of the ragged rocks, for fear of the Lord, and for the glory of his majesty, when he ariseth to shake terribly the earth [*at the time of the Second Coming*].

22 Cease ye from man [*stop trusting in man*], **whose breath is in his nostrils** [*who is mortal*]: **for wherein is he to be accounted of** [*in other words, why trust in man rather than God*]?

ISAIAH 3

Selection: all verses

IN THIS CHAPTER Isaiah describes the downfall of Jerusalem because of wickedness. In a significant way, it is a pattern that applies to any nation or society in which personal sin and wickedness become a way of life for the majority of citizens.

Beginning with verse 16 and continuing to the end of the chapter, Isaiah points out, in effect, that women are generally the last stronghold against the downfall of a nation, and that when they also turn to pride and personal wickedness as a lifestyle, the nation is doomed.

We will be introduced to an ancient writing technique in this chapter called "chiasmus." It is a writing form in which the author says certain things and then intentionally repeats them in reverse order for emphasis.

Chiasmus was not discovered by scholars until after the time the Book of Mormon was published. This is significant because the Book of Mormon has several passages in which chiasmus is used (for example, 2 Nephi 29:13, Mosiah 3:18–19, and Alma 36). Such use of chiasmus as a writing style in the Book of Mormon is strong evidence that it is of ancient origin, which of course it is. We will include one example from the Book of Mormon. You will in fact see two short chiastic structures within this one verse. In this case, the structure consists of **A B C C' B' A,'** and it is repeated twice.

<u>2 Nephi 29:13</u>

13 And it shall come to pass that the **Jews** [A] shall have the **words** [B] of the **Nephites** [C], and the **Nephites** [C'] shall have the **words** [B'] of the **Jews** [A]; and the **Nephites and the Jews** [A] shall have the **words** [B] of the **lost tribes of Israel** [C]; and the **lost tribes of Israel** [C] shall have the **words** [B'] of the **Nephites and the Jews** [A'].

Often, but not necessarily always, the pivot point or midpoint of the chiasmus is the main message. For example, in the chiasmus used by Isaiah here in the first eight verses, the main message is found in verse 5, where he emphasizes that when a society collapses because of wickedness, everyone is persecuted and oppressed by everyone else.

We will now proceed with this chapter. The chiastic structure begins in verse 1 and ends at the beginning of verse 8. You may wish to read only the words of the chiasmus (in **underlined bold**), and then come back and read the complete verses. It will help you get the feel of a chiasmus.

1 For, behold, the Lord, the Lord of hosts, doth **take away from Jerusalem** [A] and from Judah the stay [*supply*] and the staff [*support*], the whole stay of **bread** [B], and the whole stay of water [*the Lord is going to pull the props out and the whole thing will collapse*],

2 The **mighty man** [C] [*the powerful leader*], and the man of war [*your military power will crumble*], the judge, and the prophet, and the prudent, and the ancient,

3 The captain of fifty, and **the honourable man, and the counsellor** [D] [*no competent leaders*], and the cunning artificer [*skilled craftsman*], and the eloquent orator [*all the stable, dependable people who are the mainstays of a stable society will be gone*].

4 And I will give **children to be their princes** [E] [*leaders*], and babes [*immature people*] shall rule over them [*immature, irresponsible leaders will take over*].

5 And **the people shall be oppressed, every one by another** [F], [*this is the pivot point of this chiasmus*] and every one by his neighbour [*anarchy*]: the **child shall behave himself proudly against the ancient** [E'], and the base [*crude and rude*] against the honourable [*no respect for authority; public acceptance of coarseness, crudeness, rudeness*].

Economic conditions will become so bad that people will be asked to serve as leaders if they happen to have a decent set of clothes.

6 When a man shall take hold of his brother of the house of his father, saying, **Thou hast clothing, be thou our ruler** [D'], and let [*let not; see 2 Nephi 13:6*] this ruin be

under thy hand [*be our leader, don't let this happen to us*]:

7 In that day shall he [*the man asked to be the leader in verse 6, above*] swear [*protest*], saying, **I will not be an healer** [**C'**] [*I can't lead you and fix your problems!*]; for in my house is neither **bread** [**B'**] nor clothing: make me not a ruler of the people [*I can't solve your problems. I've got my own problems*].

8 For **Jerusalem is ruined** [**A'**], and Judah is fallen: because their tongue and their doings are against the Lord, to provoke the eyes of his glory [*in word and actions, the people are completely against the Lord*].

> Next, Isaiah tells us that the faces of the truly wicked and evil "radiate" their wickedness to all.

9 ¶ The shew of their countenance doth witness against them; and they declare their sin as Sodom, they hide it not [*blatant sin; they show no embarrassment nor shame for what they are doing*]. **Woe unto their soul!** for they have rewarded evil unto themselves [*they are sinning against themselves, preparing an evil harvest for themselves*].

> Next, the Lord assures the righteous among the wicked that they will reap the sweet harvest of their goodness.
>
> The **bolded** text in verses 10 and 11, next, summarizes a major message found throughout Isaiah's teachings.

10 **Say ye to the righteous, that it shall be well with him;** for they shall eat the fruit of their doings [*righteousness will pay off*].

11 **Woe unto the wicked! it shall be ill with him:** for the reward of his hands shall be given him. [*"As ye sow, so shall ye reap."*]

12 ¶ As for my people, **children are their oppressors, and women rule over them** [*breakdown of traditional family; men are weak leaders, women have to fill in; can also reflect the deep bitterness and powerful influence of many women when they turn wicked*]. O my people, **they which lead thee cause thee to err,** and destroy the way of thy paths [*leadership without basic gospel values can be devastating*].

13 **The Lord standeth up to plead** [*to try your case as in a court of law; implying that the evidence is against you*], and standeth to judge the people.

14 **The Lord will enter into judgment** [*in effect, you will stand before the Lord to answer for your behaviors*] with the ancients of his people, and the princes [*leaders*] thereof: for **ye have eaten up the vineyard; the spoil of** [*things you have taken from*] **the poor is in your houses** [*you were supposed to protect them but instead you preyed on them*].

15 What mean ye [*what have you got to say for yourselves*] that **ye beat my people to pieces, and grind the faces of the poor?** saith the Lord God of hosts.

> Isaiah now says that society is lost when women also turn to evil. From this we can better understand the devil's strategy in our day as he works to convince women to join in the evils of men and pull away from home and family.

16 ¶ Moreover the Lord saith, **Because the daughters of Zion** [*women of the Church particularly, and women in general*] **are haughty** [*full of pride*], and **walk with stretched forth necks** [*prideful*] and **wanton eyes** [*lustful*], walking and **mincing as they go** [*walking in such a way as to attract men's lustful thoughts*], and **making a tinkling with their feet** [*a reference to wearing expensive, high-fashion shoes (in Isaiah's day) with little bells on them to attract attention to their wealthy status*]:

17 Therefore [*for these reasons*] **the Lord will smite with a scab the crown of the head** [*will take away their beauty*] of **the daughters of Zion**, and the Lord will discover [*uncover*] their secret parts [*expose their evil deeds*].

> Scholars do not always agree on the nature of the female ornaments mentioned in verses 18–23, next. We will supply definitions from a variety of sources, realizing that many of them are simply best guesses.

18 In that day [*when destruction comes*] **the Lord will take away** the bravery [*beauty*] of their tinkling **ornaments** about their feet, and their **cauls**, and their **round tires like the moon** [*possibly crescent-shaped necklaces*],

19 The chains, and the **bracelets**, and the **mufflers** [veils],

20 The bonnets, and the **ornaments** of the legs, and the *head-bands*, and the **tablets** [*perfume boxes*], and the **earrings**,

21 The rings, and **nose jewels**,

22 The changeable suits of apparel [*beautiful clothing*], and the *mantles*, and the **wimples** [*shawls*], and the crisping pins [*money purses*],

23 The glasses [*see-through clothing; see Isaiah 3:23, footnote a in your Bible*], and the **fine linen**, and the **hoods** [*turbans*], and the **vails**. [*Isaiah has described female high-society fashions, accompanied by arrogance and materialism, in terms of such things in his day.*]

24 And it shall come to pass, that instead [*in place of*] **of sweet smell there shall be stink** [*from corpses of people killed by invading armies*]; **and instead of a girdle** [*high-fashion clothing*] **a rent** [*torn clothing, rags*], **and instead of well set hair baldness**

[*invading armies customarily shaved the heads of captives whom they enslaved for the purposes of humiliation, identification, and sanitation*]; and instead of a **stomacher** [*nice robe*] a girding of sackcloth [*coarse clothing worn by slaves and the poor class*]; and burning [*branding; conquerors often branded their slaves*] instead of [*in the place of*] beauty.

25 Thy men shall fall by the sword, and thy mighty in the war [*invasion*].

> The above-mentioned slaughter of men will set the stage for the plural marriage mentioned in Isaiah 4:1. With so few men left, the widows and other women in Jerusalem will plead with men to marry several wives, so that they can have a proper place in society. They will offer to pay their own way so they will not become a financial burden on their husbands. Remember that plural marriage was common in that culture at the time.

26 And her [*Jerusalem's*] **gates shall lament and mourn; and she** being desolate [*empty, defeated*] **shall sit upon the ground** [*a sign of defeat and humility*].

ISAIAH 4

Selection: all verses

BOTH THE JOSEPH Smith Translation and the Hebrew Bible put verse one of chapter 4 at the end of chapter 3, which puts it in the context of Jerusalem's destruction and the scarcity of men resulting from the war prophesied in Isaiah 3:25-26. Footnote 4:1a in your Bible, says "because of scarcity of men due to wars. See 3:25." Footnote b likewise refers the reader to chapter 3.

Verses 2-6 deal with the Millennium.

1 And in that day [*the time of the destruction of Jerusalem spoken of in Isaiah 3:25–26*] **seven women shall take hold of one man, saying,** We will eat our own bread, and wear our own apparel [*we will pay our own way*]: only let us be called by thy name [*please marry us*], to take away our reproach [*the stigma in that society of being unmarried and childless*].

> Verse 2, next, starts a new topic, namely, conditions during the Millennium.

2 In that day [*Millennium*] **shall the branch of the Lord** [*Christ— see Jeremiah 23:5*] **be beautiful and glorious,** and the fruit of the earth shall be excellent and comely [*pleasant to look at*] for them that are escaped of Israel [*for those who have escaped wickedness—the righteous remnant of Israel*].

3 And it shall come to pass, that he that is left in Zion, and he that remaineth in Jerusalem, shall be called holy, even every one that is written among the living [*those saved by approval of the Messiah*] in Jerusalem:

4 When the Lord shall have washed away the filth of the daughters of Zion [*after the Lord has cleansed the earth of the wicked at the Second Coming*], and shall have purged the blood of Jerusalem from the midst thereof by the spirit of judgment, and by the spirit of burning [*earth will be cleansed by fire*].

> The angel Moroni quoted verses 5 and 6 to Joseph Smith in reference to the last days. (See Messenger and Advocate, April 1835, page 110.) The imagery in verse five can symbolize the presence of the Lord in the meetings of the saints as well as upon the homes of the righteous in the last days, as well as the presence of the Lord on earth during the Millennium.

> It is very encouraging to know that, in spite of the gross wickedness upon the earth in the final days before the Second Coming, the righteous can be assured of having the presence of the Lord in their homes and in their church meetings.

5 And the Lord will create upon every dwelling place [*homes*] of mount Zion [*faithful covenant people*], and upon her assemblies [*meetings, sacrament meetings, stake conferences, mission conferences, general conferences, and so forth*], a cloud and smoke by day [*represent the presence of the Lord as in Exodus 19:16–18*], and the shining of a flaming fire by night: for upon all the glory shall be a defence.

6 And there shall be a tabernacle [*shelter*] for a shadow [*shade*] in the daytime from the heat, and for a place of refuge, and for a covert [*protection*] from storm and from rain [*peace and protection*].

ISAIAH 5

Selection: all verses

IN THIS CHAPTER we will see Isaiah's marvelous intellect and poetic talent at work as he composes a song or poetic parable of a vineyard, symbolizing God's mercy and Israel's unresponsiveness to Him.

1 Now will I sing [*compose a song or poetic parable*] to my wellbeloved a song of my beloved [*Christ*] touching his vineyard [*Israel—see verse 7*]. My wellbeloved hath a vineyard in a fruitful hill [*in a place where they have great potential to grow and produce the desired fruit*]:

2 And he fenced it, and gathered out the stones thereof [*took away the stumbling blocks and obstacles to progression*], and planted it with the choicest vine [*the men of Judah—see verse 7; symbolic of His covenant people*], and built a tower [*set prophets*] in the midst of it, and also made a winepress therein [*planning for a good harvest*]: and he looked that it should bring forth grapes [*the desired product, faithful people*], and it

brought forth wild grapes [*apostasy*].

3 And now, O inhabitants of Jerusalem, and men of Judah, **judge, I pray you, betwixt me and my vineyard** [*I'll give you the facts; you be the judge*].

4 **What could have been done more** to my vineyard, **that I have not done** in it [*the main question—compare with Jacob 5:47, 49*]? **wherefore** [*why*], when I looked [*planned*] that it should bring forth grapes [*the desired result, faithful people*], **brought it forth wild grapes** [*wicked people; apostasy*]?

5 And now go to; **I will tell you what I will do to my vineyard** [*Israel*]: **I will take away the hedge** [*divine protection*] thereof, **and it shall be eaten up** [*destroyed*]; and **break down the wall** [*protection*] thereof, **and it shall be trodden down** [*by enemies*]:

6 And **I will lay it waste: it shall not be pruned** [*will not have sins, false doctrines, and so forth pruned out of the lives of its people by living prophets*], **nor digged** [*nourished; the Spirit withdraws, no prophets*]; **but there shall come up briers and thorns** [*apostate doctrines and behaviors*]: I will also command the clouds that they rain **no rain** upon it [*famine*].

Next, in verse 7, Isaiah defines some of the symbolism in this parable.

7 For **the vineyard** of the Lord of hosts **is the house of Israel, and the men of Judah his pleasant plant: and he looked for judgment** [*fairness, honesty, and so forth*], **but behold oppression; for righteousness, but behold a cry** [*found riotous living instead*].

Verse 8, next, has actually been misinterpreted on occasions to mean that building row houses and condominiums is sinful. Of course, such is not the meaning but it is interesting how far astray things can go.

8 ¶ **Woe unto them** [*the powerful, wealthy*] **that join house to house** [*cheat the poor and unfortunate out of their homes and take them from them*], **that lay field to field, till there be no place, that they** [*the poor*] **may be placed alone in the midst of the earth** [*those in power push the poor farmers off their land by unscrupulous means*].

9 In mine ears said the Lord of hosts, Of a truth **many houses shall be desolate,** even great and fair [*the homes and palaces of the great and powerful wicked*], without inhabitant [*troubles are coming because of your wickedness*].

Next, Isaiah uses stark imagery to prophesy that a famine is coming.

10 Yea, **ten acres of vineyard shall yield one bath** [*about 8¼ U.S. gallons*], and **the seed of an homer** [*6½ bushel of seed*] **shall yield an ephah**

[½ bushel of harvest; in other words, famine is coming].

Next, we see a warning against riotous living, which generally accompanies sin and wickedness in society.

11 ¶ Woe unto them that rise up early in the morning, that they may follow strong drink; that continue until night, till wine inflame them!

Next, in verse 12, Isaiah points out that these people "go to church" and go through all the motions of the true religion (Law of Moses, for them), but they are hypocrites and do not live the gospel in their daily lives.

12 And the harp, and the viol [lyre], the tabret [drums], and pipe [instruments associated with worship of the Lord in Bible times], and wine, are in their feasts: but they regard not the work of the Lord [their worship is empty, hypocritical], neither consider the operation of his hands [they do not actually acknowledge God].

Next, Isaiah speaks prophetically of the future as if it has already happened. This way of speaking is quite common in Old Testament prophecies.

13 ¶ Therefore [that is why] my people are gone into captivity, because they have no knowledge [Amos 8:11–12 famine of hearing words of the Lord]: and their honourable men are famished, and their multitude dried up with thirst [the prophesied destructions and famine have taken their toll].

14 Therefore [that is why] hell hath enlarged herself [they've had to add on to hell to make room for you], and opened her mouth without measure [more than anyone thought possible]: and their glory, and their multitude, and their pomp, and he that rejoiceth [in wickedness and riotous living], shall descend into it.

15 And the mean [poor] man shall be brought down [humbled], and the mighty man shall be humbled, and the eyes of the lofty shall be humbled [everyone needs humbling]:

16 But the Lord of hosts shall be exalted in judgment [you will see that the Lord is correct], and God that is holy shall be sanctified in righteousness [the Lord will triumph].

17 Then [after the destruction that is coming to Israel] shall the lambs feed [graze where the Lord's vineyard once stood—destruction is complete] after their manner, and the waste places [ruins] of the fat ones [the former prosperous inhabitants] shall strangers [foreigners] eat [in other words, foreign enemies will take over your land].

Next, in verse 18, Isaiah uses yet another image to describe the bondage of sin among the covenant people of Israel.

18 Woe unto them that draw iniquity with cords of vanity, and sin as it were with a cart rope [*you are tethered to your sins; they follow you like a cart follows the animal pulling it*]:

19 That say, Let him [*the Lord*] make speed, and hasten his work, that we may see it [*it is up to God to prove to us that He exists*]: and let the counsel [*plans*] of the Holy One of Israel [*the Lord*] draw nigh and come [*come to pass*], that we may know it [*if He wants us to know Him, He will have to be more obvious about His existence*]!

Verse 20, next, is well-known and often used in our lessons and sermons. We see much of this switching of things around in the world today.

20 ¶ Woe unto them that call evil good, and good evil; that put darkness for light, and light for darkness; that put bitter for sweet, and sweet for bitter!

21 Woe unto them that are wise in their own eyes [*full of evil pride*], and prudent in their own sight!

22 Woe unto them that are mighty to drink wine, and men of strength to mingle strong drink:

23 Which justify the wicked for reward [*bribes, corrupt judicial system*], and take away the righteousness of the righteous from him [*ruin the good reputations of righteous people*]!

Next, in verse 24, Isaiah describes serious ultimate consequences of rebellion and sin.

24 Therefore as the fire devoureth the stubble, and the flame consumeth the chaff, so their root shall be as rottenness, and their blossom shall go up as dust [*shall not bear fruit, shall have no posterity in the next life and destruction of many in this life*]: because they have cast away the law of the Lord of hosts, and despised the word of the Holy One of Israel.

The unfathomable depth of the love and mercy that the Savior has for us is brought out at the end of verse 25, next. In this we see the power of the Atonement of Jesus Christ to cleanse and heal. You may wish to reread Isaiah 1:18 as you read this verse.

25 Therefore [*for these reasons*] is the anger of the Lord kindled against his people [*covenant Israel*], and he hath stretched forth his hand against them, and hath smitten them: and the hills did tremble, and their carcases were torn in the midst of the streets [*great destruction is coming*]. For all this [*because of all this wickedness*] his anger is not turned away, but his hand is stretched out still [*you can still repent—compare with Jacob 6:4*].

In verses 26–30, next, we see a prophecy of the gathering of

Israel in the last days. We see modern transportation bringing members and new converts great distances to gather together as Saints. Isaiah's imagery shows us that none will stop the work of the Lord and the gathering of Israel in these marvelous times. Surely, we are witnessing this in our day.

26 ¶ And **he will lift up an ensign** [*flag, rallying point; the true gospel*] **to the nations from far,** and will hiss [*whistle; a signal to gather*] unto them from the end of the earth: and, behold, **they shall come with speed swiftly** [*modern transportation*]:

27 **None shall be weary nor stumble** among them; **none shall slumber nor sleep;** neither shall the girdle of their loins be loosed [*change clothes*], nor the latchet of their shoes be broken [*they will travel so fast that they won't need to change clothes or even take their shoes off*]:

28 **Whose arrows are sharp, and all their bows bent** [*perhaps describing the body of a sleek airliner, like an arrow, and the swept back wings like a bow*], **their horses' hoofs shall be counted like flint** [*making sparks like the wheels on a train?*], and their wheels like a whirlwind [*airplanes, trains?*]:

29 **Their roaring shall be like a lion** [*the noise of airplanes, trains, and so on?*], they shall roar like young lions: yea, they shall roar, and **lay hold of the prey** [*take in their passengers?*], **and shall carry it away safe, and none shall deliver it** [*the converts—none will stop the gathering of Israel in the last days*].

30 **And in that day** [*the last days*] they shall roar against them like the roaring of the sea: and **if one look unto the land, light is darkened in the heavens thereof** [*conditions in the last days: war, smoke, pollution, spiritual darkness?*].

ISAIAH 6

Selection: all verses

CHAPTER 6 CONTAINS rich Atonement symbolism, especially verses 6 and 7. Without an understanding of symbolism, these two verses seem strange and mysterious. With it, they show the wonderful power of the Atonement of Christ to cleanse and heal, and to enable us to accept difficult callings with assurance and faith.

Most scholars agree that this chapter is an account of Isaiah's call to serve as a prophet of the Lord. Some feel that it is a later calling to a major assignment. Either way, Isaiah feels completely inadequate and overwhelmed (verse 5).

Verse 1 identifies the date of this revelation to Isaiah.

1 **In the year that king Uzziah died** [*about 740 BC*] **I** [*Isaiah*] **saw**

also **the Lord** [*Jesus—see footnote 6c in your Bible*] **sitting upon a throne, high and lifted up** [*exalted*], **and his train** [*skirts of his robe; authority; power. Hebrew: wake, light*] **filled the temple** [*symbolic of heaven—see Revelation 21:22, where the celestial kingdom does not need a temple but, in effect, is a temple itself*].

2 Above it [*the throne*] **stood the seraphims** [*angelic beings*]: **each one had six wings** [*wings are symbolic of power to move, act, and so forth, in God's work—see Doctrine & Covenants 77:4*]; **with twain** [*two*] **he covered his face** [*symbolic of a veil, which shows reverence and respect toward God in biblical culture*], **and with twain he covered his feet, and with twain he did fly.**

3 And one cried unto another, and said, Holy, holy, holy, is the Lord of hosts [*a word repeated three times forms the superlative in Hebrew, meaning the very best*]: **the whole earth is full of his glory.**

4 And the posts of the door moved [*shook*] **at the voice of him that** cried, **and the house was filled with smoke** [*shaking and smoke are symbolic of God's presence in biblical culture, as at Sinai, Exodus 19:18*].

Next, Isaiah tells us that he was completely overwhelmed by the experience of seeing the Savior.

5 ¶ Then said I, Woe is me! for I am **undone** [*completely overwhelmed*]; because **I am a man of unclean lips** [*I am so imperfect*], **and I dwell in the midst of a people of unclean lips: for mine eyes have seen the King, the Lord of hosts.**

6 Then flew one of the seraphims unto me, having a live coal [*symbolic of the Atonement; also symbolic of the Holy Ghost who guides us to the Atonement; we often say that the Holy Ghost "cleanses by fire"*] **in his hand,** which he had taken with the tongs **from** off **the altar** [*the "altar cross," representing the Savior's sacrifice for our sins*]:

7 And he laid it [*the Atonement*] **upon my mouth** [*inadequacies, sins, imperfections*], **and said, Lo, this** [*the Atonement*] **hath touched thy lips** [*Isaiah's sins and imperfections—see verse 5, above*]; and **thine iniquity is taken away, and thy sin purged** [*the results of the Atonement*].

Watch now as the blessings of the Atonement give Isaiah confidence to accept his mission from the Lord. It can do the same for us in our callings.

8 Also [*then*] **I heard the voice of the Lord, saying, Whom shall I send, and who will go for us? Then said I** [*Isaiah*], **Here am I; send me** [*the cleansing power of the Atonement and help of the Spirit gave Isaiah the needed confidence to accept the call*].

Next, in verses 9–12, the Savior gives Isaiah an idea of the kinds of people he will be working with as a prophet. It will be a tough assignment. We will use a quote from Isaiah in the Book of Mormon to help with verse 9.

9 ¶ And he [*the Lord*] **said, Go** [*this is the official call*], **and tell this people, Hear** ye indeed, but understand not; **and see** ye indeed, but perceive not.

The Book of Mormon makes significant changes to the above verse of Isaiah.

2 Nephi 16:9

9 And he said: Go and tell this people—Hear ye indeed, but they understood not; and see ye indeed, but they perceived not [*Isaiah's task will not be easy with that kind of people*].

In verse 10, next, (*which contains a chiasmus—see notes in chapter 3 of this study guide*) the Lord gives Isaiah some additional insights as to the type of people he will be preaching to. In effect, the Savior appears to be telling him to imagine this type of people in his mind's eye.

10 [*In your imagination*] Make the **heart** [**A**] of this people fat [*unfeeling, insulated from truth*], and make their **ears** [**B**] heavy [*deaf to spiritual matters*], and shut their **eyes** [**C**] [*spiritually blind*]; lest they see with their **eyes** [**C'**], and hear with their **ears** [**B'**], and understand with their **heart** [**A'**], and convert, and be healed.

There is a quote in Matthew in which the Savior basically quoted the above verse of Isaiah.

Note that Matthew records that the people have refused to hear the gospel message.

Matthew 13:15

15 For this people's heart is waxed gross, and their ears are dull of hearing, and their eyes **they have closed**; lest at any time they should see with their eyes, and hear with their ears, and should understand with their heart, and should be converted, and I should heal them.

The Lord's description of the people with whom Isaiah would be working appears to have startled and concerned him somewhat, causing him to ask the following question:

11 Then said I, Lord, how long [*will people be like this*]? And **he answered**, Until the cities be wasted without inhabitant, and the houses without man, and the land be utterly desolate [*in other words, as long as people are around*],

12 And the Lord have removed men far away [*people are gone*], and there be a great forsaking [*many deserted cities*] in the midst of the land.

In verse 13, next, Isaiah is assured that the time will never come when there are no more people, as mentioned in the scenario given in verses 11–12, above. Instead, a remnant of Israel will survive and will be pruned by the Lord and gathered.

13 ¶ But yet in it [*the land*] shall be a tenth [*a remnant*], and it [*Israel*] shall return [*includes the concept of repenting*], and shall be eaten [*in other words, pruned—as by animals eating the limbs, leaves, and branches; in other words, the Lord "prunes" his vineyard or cuts out old apostates, false doctrines, and so forth; He destroys old unrighteous generations so new may have a chance to grow*]: as a teil [*lime?*] tree, and as an oak, whose substance [*sap*] is in them, when they cast their leaves [*trees that shed the old, non-functioning leaves and look dead in winter but are still alive*]: so the holy seed shall be the substance thereof [*Israel may look dead, but there is still life in it*].

ISAIAH 7

Selection: all verses

IN THIS CHAPTER, we see a plot by Israel (the northern ten tribes who became the "lost ten tribes," also known as "Ephraim" at this time in history) and Syria to attack Judah (Jerusalem and the surrounding area). Their plan is to conquer Judah and place a puppet king on the throne in Jerusalem who will be loyal to them.

You will see different names used to refer to Syria, the northern kingdom (Israel) and the southern kingdom (Judah), and this can be confusing. We will list some of these plus the names of kings, to help you keep things straight:

SYRIA
- Damascus (the capital city of Syria)
- Rezin (the king)

ISRAEL (the ten tribes)
- Ephraim
- Samaria (the capitol city of Israel)
- Pekah (the king)

JUDAH (the tribes of Judah and Benjamin)
- House of David
- Jerusalem
- Ahaz (the king)

In verse 1, next, we are told that this plot took place about 734 BC, which is about twelve years before the Assyrians conquered Israel and carried them away captive (thus they became the lost ten tribes).

1 And it came to pass in the days of Ahaz [*about 734 BC*] the son of Jotham, the son of Uzziah, king of Judah, that Rezin the king of Syria, and Pekah the son of Remaliah, king of Israel [*the ten tribes in northern Israel*], went up toward Jerusalem to war against it, but could not prevail against it [*didn't win, but they did kill 120,000 men of Judah and take 200,000 captives in one day; see 2 Chronicles 28:6–15*].

Next, in verse 2, we learn that the inhabitants of Judah found out about the plot against them.

2 And it was told the house of David [*Judah, Jerusalem*], saying, Syria is confederate [*joining forces*]

with Ephraim [*Israel, the northern ten tribes*]. **And his** [*King Ahaz's*] **heart was moved** [*shaken*], **and the heart of his people, as the trees of the wood are moved with the wind** [*they were "shaking in their boots"; scared*].

Next, the Lord sends Isaiah to wicked King Ahaz to tell him not to worry about the plot, because it will not amount to anything.

3 Then said the Lord unto Isaiah, Go forth now to meet Ahaz [*king in Jerusalem*], **thou, and Shear-jashub** [*Hebrew: "the remnant shall return"*] **thy son, at the end of the conduit of the upper pool in the highway of the fuller's field** [*where the women wash clothes—Ahaz is hiding among the women*];

4 And say unto him, Take heed, and **be quiet** [*settle down*]; **fear not,** neither be fainthearted [*don't worry about continued threats from Syria and Israel*] **for** [*because of*] **the two tails of these smoking firebrands** [*these two kings who think they are really something but are nothing but smoldering stubs of firewood*], for [*because of*] the fierce anger of Rezin with Syria, and of the son of Remaliah [*referring to Pekah, king of Israel*].

5 Because Syria, Ephraim [*the ten tribes*], **and the son of Remaliah** [*the ten tribes' king*], **have taken evil counsel** [*have evil plans*] **against thee, saying,**

6 Let us go up against Judah, and vex [*cause trouble for*] it, **and let us** make a breach therein for us, and **set a king in the midst of it** [*set up our own king in Jerusalem*], even the son of Tabeal [*the name of the fellow they had in mind to install as a puppet king*]:

7 Thus saith the Lord God, It shall not stand, neither shall it come to pass [*the plot will fail, so don't worry about it*].

8 For the head [*capital city*] **of Syria is Damascus, and the head** [*leader*] **of Damascus is Rezin;** and **within threescore and five years** [*sixty-five years*] **shall Ephraim** [*the ten tribes*] be **broken,** that it be not a people [*in sixty-five years, the ten tribes will be lost; apparently it took several years after Assyria captured the ten tribes (about 722 BC) until they were lost to the knowledge of other people*].

9 And the head [*capital city*] **of Ephraim is Samaria, and the head** [*leader*] **of Samaria is Remaliah's son** [*Pekah; apparently Isaiah had such disdain for Pekah that he refused to use his name, preferring instead to call him "Remaliah's boy"*]. **If ye** [*Ahaz and his people, the tribe of Judah*] **will not believe** [*in the Lord*], surely **ye shall not be established** [*not be saved by the Lord's power*].

Next, the Lord has Isaiah invite King Ahaz to ask for a sign to prove that what Isaiah has told him about the plot is true. Watch how this weak king reacts to this rare invitation from the Lord.

10 ¶ Moreover the Lord spake again unto Ahaz, saying,

11 Ask thee a sign [*to strengthen your faith*] **of the Lord** thy God; ask it either in the depth, or in the height above [*ask anything you want*].

12 But Ahaz said, I will not ask, neither will I tempt [*test*] **the Lord** [*refuses to follow prophet's counsel; he is deliberately evasive, and is already secretly depending on Assyria for help*].

13 And he [*Isaiah*] **said, Hear ye now, O house of David** [*Ahaz and his people, Judah*]; Is it a small thing for you to weary men, but **will ye weary my God also** [*try the patience of God*]?

Next, Isaiah prophesies of the coming of Jesus Christ in the meridian of time—see heading to chapter 7 in your Bible. Verse 14 emphasizes that because of their wickedness, these people desperately need the Savior.

14 Therefore [*because of your disobedience*] the Lord himself shall give you a sign; Behold, **a virgin shall conceive, and bear a son, and shall call his name Immanuel** [*the day will come when the Savior will be born*].

15 Butter and honey [*curd and honey, the only foods available to the poor at times*] **shall he eat, that he may know to refuse the evil, and choose the good.**

Next, in verse 16, Isaiah explains that in the same number of years it will take the future Savior to grow from an infant to the point of being able to choose between right and wrong, the kings of Syria and Israel will fall from power.

16 For before the child shall know to refuse the evil, and choose the good [*before he is old enough to choose right from wrong—in just a few years*], **the land** [*both Israel and Syria*] **that thou abhorrest** [*that causes you fear*] **shall be forsaken of both her kings.**

17 The Lord shall bring upon thee [*Ahaz*], **and upon thy people, and upon thy father's house** [*the royal family*], days that have not come [*trouble like never before*], from the day that Ephraim departed from Judah [*when the ten tribes comprising Israel split into the northern kingdom under Jeroboam I, and the tribes of Judah and Benjamin under Rehoboam, about 975 BC*]; even **the king of Assyria** [*the king of Assyria and his armies will come upon you*].

18 And it shall come to pass in that day, that the Lord shall hiss [*signal, call for*] **for the fly** [*associated with plagues, troubles and so forth*] **that is**

in the uttermost part of the rivers of Egypt, and for the bee that is in the land of Assyria.

19 And they shall come, and shall rest all of them in the desolate valleys, and in the holes of the rocks, and upon all thorns, and upon all bushes [*you will have enemies in your land like flies; they will overrun the land*].

> Verse 20, next, says, in effect, that the people of Judah will become slaves.

20 In the same day shall the Lord shave with a razor [*fate of captives, slaves—who are shaved for humiliation, sanitation, identification*] that is hired [*Assyria will be "hired" to do this to Judah*], namely, by them beyond the river, by the king of Assyria, the head, and the hair of the feet: and it shall also consume the beard [*they will shave you clean— conquer you; beards were a sign of dignity in ancient Israel*].

> The imagery used by Isaiah in verses 21–25, next, shows us that, after the conquering enemy armies have done their work, the land will be relatively empty of inhabitants.

21 And it shall come to pass in that day [*after much devastation in Judah*], that a man shall nourish a young cow, and two sheep;

22 And it shall come to pass, for the abundance of milk that they [*the domestic animals*] shall give he shall eat butter: for butter and honey shall every one eat that is left in the land [*not many people left, so a few animals can supply them well*].

23 And it shall come to pass in that day, that every place shall be, where there were a thousand vines at a thousand silverlings [*worth a thousand pieces of silver*], it shall even be for briers and thorns [*uncultivated land where it used to be cultivated and productive; symbolic of apostasy*].

24 With arrows and bows shall men come thither; because all the land shall become briers and thorns [*previously cultivated land will become wild and overgrown so hunters will hunt wild beasts there*].

25 And on all hills that shall be digged [*that were once cultivated*] with the mattock [*hoe*] there [*you*] shall not come thither [*because of*] the fear of briers and thorns: but it shall be for the sending forth [*pasturing*] of oxen, and for the treading of lesser cattle [*sheep or goats*].

ISAIAH 8

Selection: all verses

WE MENTIONED IN Isaiah 7:12 that King Ahaz was secretly planning on alliances and treaties for protection, rather than repenting and turning to the Lord for help. In this chapter, we will see the Lord warn Judah against such alliances.

Isaiah will have the uncomfortable and very unpopular role of telling the people that such treaties will do no good, and that they should repent instead and thus qualify for the help of the Lord.

Isaiah will also prophesy of the coming destruction of Syria and Israel (verse 4).

As the chapter begins, we see Isaiah's use of imagery and symbolism to carry his message. In verse 1, he is told that he and Sister Isaiah will have a son. They are to give him a name (verse 3) that means that enemy armies will carry swift destruction upon the cities of Judah (except Jerusalem).

1 Moreover **the Lord said unto me, Take thee a great** [*large*] **roll** [*scroll*], **and write in it** with a man's pen **concerning Maher-shalal-hash-baz** [*"to speed to the spoil, he hasteneth the prey"—see footnote 1d in your Bible*].

> Isaiah invites two men to witness this prophecy, as it is written upon the scroll.

2 And I [*Isaiah*] took unto me faithful **witnesses** to record, **Uriah** the priest, and **Zechariah** the son of Jeberechiah.

3 And I went unto the prophetess [*Isaiah's wife*]; and she conceived, and bare a son. **Then said the Lord to me, Call his name Maher-shalal-hash-baz.**

4 For **before the child shall have knowledge to cry, My father, and my mother** [*before their son is old enough to talk*], **the riches of Damascus** [*Syria*] and **the spoil** [*wealth*] **of Samaria** [*northern Israel; the ten tribes*] **shall be taken away before the king of Assyria** [*before Isaiah's son is old enough to say "Daddy," "Mommy," Assyria will attack and ravage northern Israel and Syria*].

> Now the topic turns to the people of Judah, with Jerusalem as their capital city.

5 The Lord spake also unto me again, saying,

6 **Forasmuch as** [*since*] **this people** [*Judah, Jerusalem*] **refuseth the waters of Shiloah** [*the gentle help of Christ, John 4:14*] **that go softly, and rejoice in Rezin** [*heed Syria instead of the Lord*] **and Remaliah's son** [*northern Israel's king*];

7 Now **therefore**, behold, **the Lord bringeth up upon them the waters of the river, strong** [*terrifying*] **and many** [*armies and so forth*], even the king of Assyria, and all his glory [*pomp fanfare and ceremony of coming enemy armies*]: and **he shall come up over all his channels, and go over all his banks** [*you'll be "flooded" with Assyrians*]:

8 And he [*Assyria*] **shall pass through Judah;** he shall overflow

and go over, he shall reach even to the neck [*to Jerusalem*]; and the stretching out of his wings shall fill the breadth of thy land, O Immanuel [*or, the land of the future birth of Christ*].

9 ¶ Associate yourselves [*if you form political alliances for protection rather than turning to God*], **O ye people, and ye shall be broken in pieces; and give ear, all ye of far countries** [*listen up, foreign nations who might rise against Judah*]: **gird yourselves** [*prepare for war against Judah*], **and ye shall be broken in pieces;** gird yourselves, and ye shall be broken in pieces [*note that "broken in pieces" is repeated three times for emphasis; repeating something three times indicates the Hebrew superlative*].

Perhaps you have noticed that Isaiah makes considerable use of repetition as a means of emphasizing his messages. This is a common part of the "manner of prophesying among the Jews" (2 Nephi 25:1). We see an example of this type of repetition in verse 10, next.

10 Take counsel together, and it shall come to nought [*your plans to destroy Judah will not succeed ultimately*]; **speak the word** [*make decrees*]**, and it shall not stand: for** God **is with us** [*Judah won't be destroyed completely*].

Next, beginning with verse 11, Isaiah is given the difficult task of taking a stand opposite to that

which was popular among the people. It was politically popular among the people at this time to advocate making alliances for safety with other nations, especially Assyria. Isaiah tells them this is a mistake.

11 ¶ For the Lord spake thus to me [*Isaiah*] **with a strong hand** [*firmly*]**, and instructed me that I should not walk in the way of this people** [*that I should not go along with popular opinion among the people of Judah*]**, saying,**

12 Say ye not, A confederacy [*be allies with Assyria*]**, to all them to whom this people shall say, A confederacy; neither fear ye their fear, nor be afraid.** [*"Isaiah, don't endorse Judah's plan for confederacy with Assyria. Don't tell them what they want to hear."*]

13 Sanctify the Lord of hosts himself; and let him be your fear, and let him be your dread. [*"Isaiah, you rely on the Lord, not public approval."*]

14 And he [*the Lord*] **shall be for a sanctuary** [*for you, Isaiah*]**; but for a stone of stumbling and for a rock of offence to** [*the Lord will stand in the way of*] **both the houses of Israel** [*Israel (the northern ten tribes) and Judah*]**, for a gin** [*a trap*] **and for a snare to the inhabitants of Jerusalem.**

Note Isaiah's great skill with words as he describes the downfall of Judah with hammer-like driving force, next, in verse 15.

15 And many among them [*Judah*] shall **stumble**, and **fall**, and be **broken**, and be **snared**, and be **taken**.

16 Bind up the testimony [*record your testimony against these wicked people, Isaiah*], seal the law among my disciples [*followers*].

Next, in verses 17-18, Isaiah pledges his loyalty to the Lord, in the face of much public opposition.

17 And I [*Isaiah*] **will wait upon the Lord** [*I will trust the Lord*], **that hideth his face from the house of Jacob** [*who has had to withdraw His blessings from the house of Israel*], and I will look for him [*will watch for His blessings and guidance in my life*].

18 Behold, I and the children whom the Lord hath given me are for signs and for wonders in Israel from the Lord of hosts, which dwelleth in mount Zion [*in other words, Isaiah and his family serve as a witness of the Lord among these Israelites*].

Many people turn to the occult for messages from beyond the veil. It seems to be easier to do this than to repent and gain revelation from the Lord. Isaiah speaks of this turning to the dark side in verse 19, next.

19 ¶ And when they [*the wicked*] **shall say unto you, Seek unto them** [*spiritualists, mediums, and so forth*]

that have familiar spirits, and unto wizards that peep [*into their crystal balls and so forth*], **and that mutter: should not a people seek unto their God?** for the living to the dead [*why consult the dead on behalf of the living*]?

20 To the law and to the testimony [*the scriptures*]: **if they** [*sorcerers, wizards, mediums, and so forth*] **speak not according to this word** [*the scriptures*], it is because there *is no light in them.*

Next, Isaiah foretells what will happen to these people if they continue in the direction they are heading.

21 And they [*Israel, who will be taken into captivity*] **shall pass through it** [*the land*], **hardly bestead** [*severely distressed*] **and hungry:** and it shall come to pass, that when they shall be hungry, **they shall fret themselves** [*become enraged*], **and curse their king and their God, and look upward** [*be cocky, defiant; not humbled by their troubles*].

22 And they shall look unto the earth [*will look around them*]; **and behold** [*see only*] **trouble and darkness, dimness of anguish** [*gloom*]; **and they shall be driven to darkness** [*thrust into utter despair; spiritual darkness as the result of wickedness*].

ISAIAH 9

Selection: all verses

THIS IS A continuation of the topic in chapter 8. King Ahaz of Judah ignored the Lord's counsel and made an alliance with Assyria anyway. Symbolism here can include that Assyria would represent the devil and his evil, prideful ways. King Ahaz could symbolize foolish and wicked people who make alliances with the devil or his evil ways and naively think that they are thus protected from destruction spiritually and often physically.

In this chapter, Isaiah gives one of the most famous and beautiful of all his messianic prophecies. He prophesies that Christ will come. Handel's "Messiah" puts some of this chapter to magnificent music. You will likely recognize verse 6.

Verse 1 is positioned as the last verse of chapter 8 in the Hebrew Bible. It serves as a transition from the end of chapter 8 to the topic of the Savior's mortal mission, in chapter 9.

Verse 1 is somewhat complex and basically prophesies that the Savior will come to earth and prepare a way for people to escape from spiritual darkness and despair. It helps to know that two of the twelve tribes of Israel, the tribes of Zebulun and Naphtali, were located in what became known as Galilee in the Savior's day. Thus, verse 1 says that the humbling of haughty Israel, which took place when the Assyrians swept down upon them, will someday be softened when the Savior walks and teaches there during His mortal mission.

1 Nevertheless the dimness [*the despair and spiritual darkness referred to in 8:22*] **shall not be such as was in her vexation** [*distress*], **when at the first** [*Assyrian attacks in Isaiah's day*] **he lightly afflicted** [*NIV: "humbled"*] **the land of Zebulun** [*in northern Israel*] **and the land of Naphtali** [*in northern Israel*], **and afterward did more grievously afflict** [*Hebrew: gloriously bless; German: bring honor to*] **her** [*NIV: Galilee*] by the way of the sea, beyond Jordan, **in Galilee** of the nations [*blessed her via Jesus walking and teaching in Galilee*].

Next, Isaiah speaks prophetically of the future as if it has already happened. As we mentioned before, this was a common form of prophesying among the Jews.

2 The people that walked in darkness [*apostasy and captivity*] **have seen a great light** [*the Savior and His teachings*]: they that dwell in the land of the shadow of death, **upon them hath the light shined.**

3 Thou hast multiplied the nation, and not [*"not" is a mistake in translation and doesn't belong here; see 2 Nephi 19:3 where it is rendered correctly in this chapter of Isaiah as found in the Book of Mormon*] **increased the joy:** they joy before thee according to the joy in harvest, and as men rejoice when they divide the spoil [*Christ and His faithful followers will ultimately triumph*].

4 For thou hast broken the yoke of his burden [*Thou hast set them free*], **and the staff of his shoulder, the rod** [*symbolic of power*] **of his oppressor, as in the day of Midian** [*just like with Gideon and his three hundred; Judges 7:22*].

Next, Isaiah looks ahead to the destruction of the wicked at the time of the Second Coming and points out that their destruction will be different than that found in a normal battle.

5 For every battle of the warrior [*of man against man*] **is with confused noise, and garments rolled in blood** [*normal battles involve much noise and bloodshed*]; **but this** [*the final freedom from the wicked*] **shall be with burning** and fuel of fire [*the burning at the Second Coming*].

6 For unto us a child [*Christ*] **is born, unto us a son is given: and the government shall be upon his shoulder: and his name shall be called Wonderful, Counsellor, The mighty God, The everlasting Father, The Prince of Peace.**

7 Of the increase of his government and peace there shall be no end, upon the throne of David [*during the Millennium, Christ will rule on earth*], and upon his kingdom, to order it, and to establish it with judgment [*fairness*] and with justice from henceforth even for ever. The zeal [*energy, power*] of the Lord of hosts will perform this.

The topic now switches back to Isaiah's day as he prophesies of the pride and wickedness that will continue to plague the northern ten tribes, often referred to at this point in history as "Israel" or "northern Israel." You will see that Isaiah uses several different ways of referring to the ten tribes.

8 The Lord sent a word into Jacob [*Israel*], and it hath lighted upon Israel.

9 And all the people shall know, even Ephraim [*northern Israel*] and the inhabitant of Samaria [*northern Israel*], **that say in the pride and stoutness of heart,**

Next, in verse 10, Isaiah points out how full of pride rebellious Israel is. In effect, they boast that God's punishments won't humble them. They don't need God and they are not afraid of Him. They are basically saying to the Lord, "Go ahead and tear down our cities. We will simply rebuild them and with better materials than ever!"

10 The bricks are fallen down, but we will build with hewn stones [*boastful northern Israel claims they can't be destroyed but would simply rebuild with better materials than before*]: **the sycomores are cut down, but we will change them into cedars** [*we will rebuild with better wood than before*].

11 Therefore the Lord shall set up the adversaries of Rezin [*Syria*] **against him** [*Israel*], and join his enemies together [*the enemies of Syria will also come against Israel*];

One of the most important and consistent messages of Isaiah is that the wicked can still repent. We see this sweet message at the end of verse 12, next.

Major Message

The wicked can still repent. It is not too late for these wicked Israelites.

12 The Syrians before [*on the east*], and **the Philistines behind** [*on the west*]; **and they shall devour Israel with open mouth.** For all this his anger is not turned away, **but his hand is stretched out still** [*the Lord will still let you repent if you will turn to Him. Compare with Jacob 6:4–5*].

Sadly, as Isaiah prophesies next, these people refuse the offer of freedom through repentence.

13 ¶ For **the people turneth not unto him** [*the Lord*] that smiteth them [*who is punishing them*], **neither do they seek the Lord of hosts.**

14 Therefore the Lord **will cut off from Israel head** [*leaders*] and **tail** [*false prophets*], **branch** [*palm branch, meaning triumph and victory in Hebrew culture*] and **rush** [*reed, meaning people low in social status in the Hebrew culture*], in one day [*it will happen fast*].

Next, Isaiah defines some of the terms he used in verse 14, above, which were familiar to people in his day but not to us.

15 The ancient and honourable, he is the head; and the [*false*] prophet that teacheth lies, he is the tail.

16 For **the leaders of this people cause them to err; and they that are led of them are destroyed.**

Verse 17, next, shows us that the entire society was corrupt through and through.

17 Therefore the Lord shall have **no joy** [*pleasure, satisfaction*] in their **young men, neither shall have mercy on their fatherless and widows** [*all levels of society have gone bad*]: for **every one is an hypocrite** and an **evildoer,** and **every mouth speaketh folly** [*evil, corruption*]. For all this his anger is not turned away, but **his hand is stretched out still** [*please repent!*].

18 For **wickedness burneth as the fire** [*wickedness destroys like wildfire*]: it shall devour the **briers and thorns** [*the people of apostate Israel*], and **shall kindle in the thickets of the forest** [*destroy the people*], and they shall mount up like the lifting up of smoke.

19 Through the wrath of the Lord **of hosts is the land darkened** [*awful conditions*], and the people shall be as the fuel of the fire: **no man shall spare his brother.**

Wickedness inevitably destroys a society and nation. Verse 20, next, describes the desperate conditions that eventually overtake a wicked people.

20 And **he** [*the wicked*] **shall snatch on the right hand, and be hungry;** and he shall eat on the left hand, and **they shall not be satisfied: they shall eat every man the flesh of his own arm** [*the wicked will turn on each other*]:

> Verse 21, next, speaks of the civil wars between the northern ten tribes and the people of Judah, which Isaiah has been discussing.

21 Manasseh, Ephraim [*Israel, the ten tribes*]; **and Ephraim, Manasseh: and they together shall be against Judah.** For all this his anger is not turned away, **but his hand is stretched out still** [*you can still repent; please do!*]

ISAIAH 10

Selection: all verses

IN THE HEADING to chapter 10 in your Bible, you find the phrase, *"Destruction of Assyria is a type of destruction of the wicked at the Second Coming."* The word "type" means something that is symbolic of something else. For example, both Joseph who was sold into Egypt and Isaac were "types" of Christ; in other words, many things that happened to them were symbolic of the Savior. The following charts show some of the ways in which these great prophets were "types" of Christ:

Joseph in Egypt	Christ
Was sold for the price of a common slave	Was sold for the price of a common slave
Was thirty years old when he began his mission as prime minister to save his people	Was thirty years old when He began His formal mission to save His people
Gathered food for seven years to save his people	Used seven "days" to create the earth in which to offer salvation to us
Forgave his persecutors	Forgave His persecutors

Isaac	Christ
Was the only begotten of Abraham and Sarah	Is the Only Begotten of the Father
Was to be sacrificed by his father	Was allowed to be sacrificed by His Father
Carried the wood for his sacrifice	Carried the cross for His sacrifice
Volunteered to give his life (Abraham was too old to restrain him.)	Gave His life voluntarily

ANOTHER EXAMPLE OF a "type" of Christ is found in Leviticus 14 where the priest is a "type" of Christ as he presents the privilege of being cleansed to the leper (who is a "type" of all sinners—that is to say, the leper can be symbolic of the need we all have to be cleansed from sin). We will include Leviticus 14:1–9 here as a brief lesson on the power of understanding the use of "types" in the scriptures.

Leviticus 14:1–9

1 And the LORD spake unto Moses, saying,

2 This shall be **the law of the leper** [*the rules for being made clean; symbolic of serious sin and great need for help and cleansing*] **in the day of his cleansing** [*symbolic of the desire to be made spiritually clean and pure*]: **He shall be brought unto the priest** [*authorized servant of God; bishop, stake president, who holds the keys of authority to act for God*]:

3 And **the priest shall go forth out of the camp** [*the person with leprosy did not have fellowship with the Lord's people and was required to live outside the main camp of the children of Israel; the bishop symbolically goes out of the way to help sinners who want to repent*]; and **the priest shall look, and, behold, if the plague of leprosy be healed in the leper** [*the bishop serves as a judge to see if the repentant sinner is ready to return to full membership privileges*];

4 Then shall the priest command to take for him that is to be cleansed [*the person who has repented*] **two birds** [*one represents the Savior during His mortal mission, the other represents the person who has repented*] alive *and* clean, and **cedar wood** [*symbolic of the cross*], and **scarlet** [*associated with mocking Christ before his crucifixion, Mark 15:17*], and **hyssop** [*associated with Christ on the cross, John 19:29*]:

5 And the priest shall command that **one of the birds** [*symbolic of the Savior*] be **killed in an earthen vessel** [*Christ was sent to earth to die for us*] **over running water** [*Christ offers "living water," the gospel of Jesus Christ—John 7:37–38—which cleanses us when we come unto Him*]:

6 **As for the living bird** [*representing the person who has repented*], he [*the priest; symbolic of the bishop, stake president, one who holds the keys of judging*] **shall take it** [*the living bird*], **and the cedar wood, and the scarlet, and the hyssop** [*all associated with the Atonement*], **and shall dip them and the living bird in the blood of the bird** *that was* **killed over the running water** [*representing the cleansing power of the Savior's blood, which was shed for us*]:

7 And he shall **sprinkle upon him that is to be cleansed from the leprosy** [*symbolically, being cleansed from sin*] **seven times** [*seven is the number that, in biblical*

numeric symbolism, represents completeness, perfection], **and shall pronounce him clean** [*he has been forgiven*], **and shall let the living bird** [*the person who has repented*] **loose into the open field** [*representing the wide open opportunities again available in the kingdom of God for the person who truly repents*].

8 And **he that is to be cleansed shall wash his clothes** [*symbolic of cleaning up your life from sinful ways and pursuits— compare with Isaiah 1:16*], and **shave off all his hair** [*symbolic of becoming like a newborn baby; "born again;" fresh start*], and **wash himself in water** [*symbolic of baptism*], **that he may be clean** [*cleansed from sin*]: and **after that he shall come into the camp** [*rejoin the Lord's covenant people*], and shall tarry abroad out of his tent seven days.

9 But it shall be on the seventh day, that he shall shave all his hair off his head and his beard and his eyebrows, even all his hair he shall shave off [*symbolic of being "born again"*]: and he shall wash his clothes [*clean up his life*], also he shall wash his flesh in water [*symbolic of baptism*], and he shall be clean [*a simple fact, namely that we can truly be cleansed and healed by the Savior's Atonement*].

HAVING CONSIDERED

THE use of "types" (sometimes called "types and shadows") in the scriptures, we will now proceed with chapter 10

and watch as Assyria is used as a "type" of the destruction of the wicked at the Second Coming.

1 **Woe unto them that decree unrighteous decrees** [*unrighteous laws*], **and that write grievousness** [*oppression*] **which they have prescribed;**

2 **To turn aside the needy from judgment** [fair treatment], **and to take away the right from the poor of my people, that widows may be their prey** [victims], **and that they may rob the fatherless!**

3 And **what will ye do in the day of visitation** [*punishment*], and in the desolation which shall come from far [*from Assyria*]? to whom will ye flee for help? and where will ye leave your glory [*wealth and so forth*]?

4 **Without me** [*the Lord*] **they shall bow down under the prisoners** [*huddle among the prisoners*], and **they shall fall under the slain.** For all this his anger is not turned away, but **his hand is stretched out still** [*you can still repent*].

> Have you noticed how often, in Isaiah's writings, the Lord says that "His hand is stretched out still"? It means that they can still repent. This is one of the major themes in the Lord's teachings through His prophet, Isaiah. We will quote from the Book of Mormon to verify that this is the meaning of that phrase:

<u>Jacob 6:4–5</u>

4 And how merciful is our God unto us, for he remembereth the house of Israel, both roots and branches; and **he stretches forth his hands unto them all the day long**; and they are a stiffnecked and a gainsaying people [*always opposing God*]; but as many as will not harden their hearts shall be saved in the kingdom of God.

5 Wherefore, my beloved brethren, I beseech of you in words of soberness that ye would **repent,** and come with full purpose of heart, and cleave unto God as he cleaveth unto you. And **while his arm of mercy is extended towards you** in the light of the day, harden not your hearts.

5 ¶ **O Assyrian, the rod of mine anger** [*the tool of destruction used by the Lord to "hammer" Israel*], and the staff in their hand is mine indignation.

6 **I will send him** [*Assyria*] **against an hypocritical nation** [*Israel*], and against the people of my wrath will I give him a charge, to take the spoil, and **to take the prey, and to tread them** [*Israel*] **down** like the mire of the streets.

7 **Howbeit** [*however*] **he meaneth not so,** neither doth his heart think so [*king of Assyria doesn't realize he is a tool in God's hand, thinks he's very important on his own*]; but it is in his heart to destroy and cut off nations not a few.

Isaiah depicts the boasting and bragging of the prideful king of Assyria, in verse 8, next.

8 For **he** [*Assyrian king*] **saith** [*brags*], Are not my princes [*commanders*] altogether kings [*just like kings in other countries*]?

Next, Isaiah depicts the king boasting about cities his armies have already conquered.

9 Is not **Calno** as **Carchemish?** is not **Hamath** as **Arpad?** is not **Samaria** as **Damascus?** [*Assyria has already taken these cities.*]

Next, the king boastfully declares that the gods of the above cities were powerless to save them, and they were more powerful than the God of Judah and Israel.

10 As my hand hath found the kingdoms of **the idols, and** whose **graven images did excel** [*were more powerful than*] **them of Jerusalem and of Samaria;**

11 **Shall I not, as I have done unto Samaria and her idols, so do to Jerusalem and her idols** [*a boast; I'll do the same to Jerusalem*]?

In verse 12, next, Isaiah explains what the Lord will do to the king of Assyria and his armies, when He is through using him to punish His rebellious covenant people.

12 Wherefore it shall come to

pass, that **when the Lord hath performed his whole work upon mount Zion and on Jerusalem, I will punish** the fruit of the stout heart of **the king of Assyria,** and the glory of his high looks [*when I'm through using Assyria against Israel, then Assyria will get its just punishments*].

13 For he [*Assyrian king*] **saith, By the strength of my hand I have done it,** and by my wisdom; for I am prudent: and I have removed the bounds of the people, and have robbed their treasures, and I have put down the inhabitants like a valiant man [*bragging*]:

14 And my hand hath found as a nest the riches of the people: and as one gathereth eggs that are left, have I gathered all the earth; and **there was none that moved the wing, or opened the mouth, or peeped** [*everybody is afraid of me!*].

15 Shall the axe [*Assyria*] **boast itself against him** [*the Lord*] **that heweth therewith** [*is it reasonable for the ax to claim that it swings itself*]? or shall the saw magnify itself against him that shaketh it [*uses it*]? as if the rod should shake itself against them that lift it up, or as if the staff should lift up itself, as if it were no wood [*how foolish for people to say they don't need the Lord*].

16 Therefore shall the Lord, the Lord of hosts, send among his fat ones [*Assyria's powerful armies*] **leanness** [*trouble is coming*]; and under his [*Assyria's*] glory **he** [*Christ*] **shall kindle a burning like the burning of a fire** [*the fate of Assyria*].

17 And **the light of Israel** [*Christ*] **shall be for a fire,** and his Holy One [*Christ*] for a flame: and **it shall burn and devour his** [*Assyria's*] **thorns and his briers** [*armies*] **in one day** [*Example: 185,000 Assyrians died of devastating sickness in one night as they prepared to attack Jerusalem; see 2 Kings 19:35–37*];

18 And shall consume the glory of his forest [*symbolic of his armies, people*], and of his fruitful field, both soul and body: and they shall be **as when a standardbearer fainteth** [*as when the last flag-carrying soldier falls and the flag with him, the Assyrians will waste away, be destroyed*].

Next, Isaiah uses an interesting image to foretell that the Assyrians will be reduced to few people, so few that a small child who is just learning how to count and write numbers could count them and write the number down.

19 And the rest of the trees [*people*] **of his forest shall be few, that a child may write them.**

Attention now turns to the remnant of Israel remaining after the Assyrians are through with them. It is a prophecy of the gathering of Israel in the last days.

20 ¶ And it shall come to pass **in that day** [*the last days*], that **the remnant of Israel**, and such as are escaped of the house of Jacob [*Israel*], **shall no more again stay** [*depend*] **upon him** [*Assyria; symbolic of Satan and his evil front organizations*] that smote them; **but shall stay upon the Lord, the Holy One of Israel, in truth.**

21 **The remnant shall return,** even the remnant of Jacob, **unto the mighty God** [*1. A remnant remains in the land after Assyrian destruction. 2. A future righteous remnant*].

22 For though thy people Israel be as the sand of the sea, yet **a remnant of them shall return**: the consumption decreed [*at end of the world*] shall overflow with righteousness [*Christ; the glory of the Savior will consume the wicked at the Second Coming; see Doctrine & Covenants 5:19; 2 Nephi 12:10*].

23 **For the Lord God of hosts** [*Jehovah, Jesus Christ*] **shall make a consumption,** even determined, in the midst of all the land.

The topic now turns again to the fate of the Assyrians.

24 ¶ Therefore thus saith the Lord God of hosts, O my people that dwellest in Zion, **be not afraid of the Assyrian: he shall smite thee** with a rod, and shall lift up his staff against thee, after the manner of Egypt [*like Egypt did in earlier times*].

25 **For yet a very little while**, and the indignation shall cease, and mine anger in their destruction [*then the Assyrian kingdom will fall via the anger of the Lord*].

26 And **the Lord of hosts shall stir up a scourge for him** according to the slaughter of Midian at the rock of Oreb: and as his rod was upon the sea [*the parting of the Red Sea*], so shall he lift it up after the manner of Egypt [*God will stop Assyria like he stopped the Egyptians*].

27 And it shall come to pass **in that day,** that **his burden** [*Assyria's rule; Satan's oppression*] **shall be taken away from off thy shoulder,** and his yoke from off thy neck, and **the yoke shall be destroyed because of the anointing** [*the Savior*].

Beginning with verse 28, next, Isaiah foretells how the Assyrian armies will gobble up city after city, and will come right up to the gates of Jerusalem, and then will be stopped in their tracks by the Lord. What remains of their army will then go home.

Isaiah speaks of the future as if it has already happened. He is a master at building dramatic tension.

28 He [*Assyria*] **is come to Aiath,** he is passed **to Migron: at Michmash**

he hath laid up his carriages [*horses and chariots are symbolic of military might in biblical symbolism*].

29 They are gone over the passage: they have taken up their lodging at **Geba; Ramah** is afraid; **Gibeah** of Saul is fled.

30 Lift up thy voice, O daughter of **Gallim:** cause it to be heard unto **Laish,** O poor **Anathoth** [*Jeremiah's hometown; see Jeremiah 1:1*].

31 Madmenah is removed; the inhabitants of **Gebim** gather themselves to flee.

32 As **yet shall he** [*Assyria*] **remain at Nob** that day [*Assyria will take city after city, getting closer and closer to Jerusalem until they come to Nob, just outside Jerusalem*]: **he shall shake his hand** [*threaten*] **against** the mount of the daughter of Zion [*Jerusalem*], the hill of **Jerusalem.**

33 Behold, the Lord, the Lord of hosts, shall lop [*cut off*] **the bough with terror** [*when the Assyrian armies get right to Jerusalem, the Lord will "trim them down to size," "clip their wings," and stop them in their tracks*]: **and the high ones of stature** [*leaders of Assyrian armies*] **shall be hewn down, and the haughty shall be humbled.**

34 And he shall cut down the thickets of the forest [*the Assyrians*] **with iron** [*an axe*], and Lebanon

shall fall by a mighty one [*see 2 Kings 19:32*].

ISAIAH 11

Selection: all verses

JOSEPH SMITH RECORDED that Moroni quoted this chapter, saying that it was about to be fulfilled. We find this statement in the Pearl of Great Price, Joseph Smith–History, as follows:

Joseph Smith–History 1:40

40 In addition to these, **he quoted the eleventh chapter of Isaiah, saying that it was about to be fulfilled.** He quoted also the third chapter of Acts, twenty-second and twenty-third verses, precisely as they stand in our New Testament. He said that that prophet was Christ; but the day had not yet come when "they who would not hear his voice should be cut off from among the people," but soon would come.

In Isaiah, chapter 11, we are taught that powerful leaders will come forth in the last days to lead the gathering of Israel. We are instructed in Christlike qualities of leadership. We will be shown the peace that will abound during the Millennium and Isaiah will also teach about the gathering of Israel in the last days.

1 And **there shall come forth a rod**

[Hebrew: *twig or branch; Doctrine & Covenants 113:3–4 defines this "rod" as "a servant in the hands of Christ"*] **out of the stem** [*root*] **of Jesse** [*Christ—see heading to this chapter in your Bible*], **and a Branch shall grow out of his roots:**

Perhaps, the imagery here in verse 1 grows out of the last two verses of chapter 10, where the wicked leaders end up, in effect, as "stumps" and have been destroyed. In the last days, new, righteous, powerful leaders will be brought forth to replace the "stumps" of the past and will have their origins in the "roots" of Christ. Roots can symbolically represent being solid and firmly rooted in God.

Next, we see a description of Christlike qualities of leadership.

2 And the spirit of the Lord shall rest upon him, the spirit of wisdom and **understanding,** the spirit of **counsel** and **might,** the spirit of **knowledge** and of the **fear of** [*respect, honoring of*] **the Lord;**

3 And shall make him of quick understanding in the fear of the Lord: and he shall not judge after the sight of his eyes, neither reprove after the hearing of his ears:

Verse 4, next, makes a transition into describing powers held exclusively by the Savior.

4 But with righteousness shall he judge the poor, and reprove with equity for the meek of the earth:

and he shall **smite the earth** with the rod of his mouth, and with the breath of his lips shall he **slay the wicked.**

5 And righteousness shall be the girdle of his loins [*He will be clothed in righteousness*], and faithfulness the girdle of his reins [*desires, thoughts*].

Next, we are taken into the Millennium, where we are shown conditions of peace.

6 The wolf also shall dwell with the lamb, and **the leopard shall lie down with the kid** [*young goat*]; and **the calf and the young lion** and the fatling together; **and a little child shall lead** [*herd*] **them** [*Millennial conditions*].

7 And the cow and the bear shall feed [*graze*]; their young ones shall lie down together: and **the lion shall eat straw like the ox.**

8 And the sucking [*nursing*] **child shall play on the hole of the asp** [*viper*], **and the weaned child shall** put his hand on the cockatrice' [*venomous serpent's*] den.

9 They shall not hurt nor destroy in all my holy mountain [*throughout the earth*]: for **the earth shall be full of the knowledge of** [Hebrew: "*devotion to*"] **the Lord,** as the waters cover the sea.

10 And in that day there shall be a root of Jesse [*probably Joseph*

Smith—see *Doctrine and Covenants Student Manual for Institutes of Religion of the Church, page 284*], **which shall stand for an ensign** [*a rallying point for gathering*] of the people; **to it shall the Gentiles seek:** and his rest shall be glorious.

11 And it shall come to pass in that day, that **the Lord shall set his hand again the second time** [*dual meaning: after Babylonian captivity; also last days*] **to recover** [*gather*] **the remnant of his people,** which shall be left, from Assyria, and from Egypt, and from Pathros, and from Cush, and from Elam, and from Shinar, and from Hamath, and from the islands of the sea [*in other words, Israel will be gathered throughout the earth*].

12 And **he shall set up an ensign** [*the Church in the last days*] for the nations, **and shall assemble the outcasts of Israel, and gather together the dispersed of Judah** from the four corners of the earth.

13 The envy also of Ephraim shall depart, and the adversaries of Judah shall be cut off: **Ephraim shall not envy Judah, and Judah shall not vex Ephraim** [*the United States and others will work with the Jews*].

14 But they [*the Jews with Ephraim's help*] **shall fly upon the shoulders of the Philistines toward the west** [*will attack the western slopes that*

were *Philistine territory*]; **they shall spoil them of the east** together: they shall lay their hand upon Edom and Moab; and the children of Ammon shall obey them [*the Jews will be powerful in the last days rather than easy prey for their enemies*].

15 And the Lord shall utterly destroy the tongue of the Egyptian sea [*perhaps meaning that the productivity of the Nile River will be ruined; see Isaiah 19:5–10*]; **and with his mighty wind shall he shake his hand over the river** [*perhaps the river referred to in Revelation 16:12; symbolically, the Euphrates, representing preparation for the Battle of Armageddon*], and shall smite it in the seven streams, and make men go over dryshod.

16 And **there shall be an highway** [*God will prepare a way for them to return; gathering*] **for the remnant of his people,** which shall be left, from Assyria; like as it was to Israel in the day that he came up out of the land of Egypt.

ISAIAH 12

Selection: all verses

THIS SHORT BUT beautiful chapter refers to the Millennium. It describes the faithful who survive the destruction at the Second Coming of Christ as praising the Lord and rejoicing at the salvation that has come to them.

1 And **in that day** [*during the Millennial reign of the Savior*] **thou** [*Israel*] **shalt say,** O Lord, I will praise thee: though thou wast angry with me [*in times past, because of my rebellions*], thine anger is turned away, and thou comfortedst me.

2 Behold, God is my salvation; I will trust, and not be afraid: for **the Lord JEHOVAH** [*Jesus Christ*] **is my strength and my song**: he also is become my salvation.

3 Therefore [*because Christ is your King during the Millennium*] **with joy shall ye draw water** [*"living water"; see John 4:10, 7:38–39*] **out of the wells of salvation.**

4 And **in that day shall ye say, Praise the Lord,** call upon his name, declare his doings among the people, make mention that his name is exalted.

5 Sing unto the Lord; for he hath done excellent things: this is known in all the earth [*knowledge of the gospel will permeate the whole earth during the Millennium*].

6 Cry out [*sing it out with great joy*] **and shout,** thou inhabitant of Zion [*the people who dwell on earth during the Millennium*]: **for great is the Holy One of Israel** [*Christ*] **in the midst of thee** [*the Savior will be on*

earth among the people during the Millennium].

ISAIAH 13

Selection: all verses

IN CHAPTER 10, the destruction of Assyria was described as a "type" of (meaning "symbolic of") the destruction of the wicked at the Second Coming of Christ. We discussed the definition of "type" in the notes at the beginning of that chapter. In this chapter, the destruction of Babylon is likewise a "type" of the destruction of Satan's kingdom at the time of the Second Coming.

It will be helpful for you to understand that the ancient city of Babylon was a huge city full of wickedness and evil. Over time, Babylon has come to symbolize the wickedness of the world. A brief description of Babylon is given in your Bible Dictionary under "Babylon" as follows (**bold** added for emphasis):

BIBLE DICTIONARY: BABYLON

The capital of Babylonia. According to Gen. 10:8–10 it was founded by Nimrod, and was one of the oldest cities of the land of Shinar; in 11:1–9 we have the record of the Tower of Babel and the "Confusion of Tongues." (See Ether 1:3–5, 34–35.) During the Assyrian supremacy (see *Assyria*) it became part of that empire, and was destroyed by Sennacherib. After the downfall of Assyria, Babylon became Nebuchadnezzar's capital. He built an enormous city, of which the ruins still remain. The city was square, and the Euphrates ran through the middle of it. According to Herodotus **the walls were 56 miles in circumference, 335 feet high, and 85 feet wide.** A large part of the city consisted of beautiful parks and gardens. The chief building was the famous temple of Bel. Inscriptions that have been recently deciphered show that the Babylonians had accounts of the Creation and the Deluge in many ways similar to those given in the book of Genesis. Other inscriptions contain accounts of events referred to in the Bible histories of the kingdoms of Israel and Judaea, and also give valuable information as to the chronology of these periods.

You can find a brief sketch of the history of the Babylonian empire in the Bible Dictionary, under "Assyria."

In verse 1, Isaiah tells us that this prophecy is essentially a message of doom to Babylon, which he saw in vision. It applies to ancient Babylon, as a nation, and to the "Babylon" of evil in the last days before the Second Coming.

1 The burden of Babylon [*message of doom to Babylon*], **which Isaiah the son of Amoz did see.**

In verses 2–5, next, Isaiah explains that The Lord will gather his righteous forces (as stated in verse 4) in the last days to do battle with the forces of evil (Babylon).

2 Lift ye up a banner upon the high mountain [*raise up an ensign to the righteous*], **exalt** [*raise*] **the voice unto them** [*the righteous*], **shake the hand** [*wave to them; signal to them*], **that they may go into the gates of the nobles** [*gather with the righteous*].

Next, Isaiah speaks of the future as if it had already happened. The Book of Mormon makes a significant change to verse 3, next.

3 I have commanded my sanctified ones [*the righteous who are worthy to be in the presence of the Lord*], **I have also called my mighty ones for mine anger** [*2 Nephi 23:3 adds "is not upon them"*], **even them that rejoice in my highness** [*exalted and glorious status*].

4 The noise of a multitude in the mountains [*gathering*], **like as of a great people; a tumultuous noise of the kingdoms of nations gathered together: the Lord of hosts mustereth the host of the battle** [*the Lord rallies the righteous together to do battle with evil*].

5 They come from a far country, from the end of heaven, even the Lord, and the weapons of his indignation, to destroy the whole land [*the wicked*].

Next, in effect, Isaiah suggests that the wicked in the last days would do well to begin practicing their howling and screaming in preparation for the Second Coming.

6 ¶ **Howl ye** [*the wicked*]; **for the day of the Lord** [*the Second Coming*] **is at hand** [*is getting close*]; it shall come as a destruction from the Almighty.

7 **Therefore shall all hands be faint** [*hang limp*], **and every man's heart shall melt** [*wicked men's courage will falter*]:

8 And **they shall be afraid:** pangs and sorrows shall take hold of them; they shall be in pain as a woman that travaileth [*like a woman in labor, they can't get out of it now*]: **they shall be amazed** [*will look in fear*] one at another; **their faces shall be as flames** [*burn with shame at the thought of facing the Lord*].

9 **Behold, the day of the Lord** [*Second Coming*] **cometh, cruel** [*as viewed by the wicked*] both with wrath and fierce anger, to lay the land desolate: **and he shall destroy the sinners thereof out of it** [*a purpose of the Second Coming*].

Next, Isaiah mentions a few signs of the times, which will precede the Second Coming.

10 For **the stars of heaven** and the constellations thereof **shall not give their light: the sun shall be** darkened in his going forth, and **the moon shall not** cause her light to **shine.**

11 And **I will punish the world for their evil,** and the wicked for their iniquity; and **I will cause the arrogancy of the proud to cease,** and will lay low the haughtiness of the terrible [*will humble the tyrants; typical Isaiah repetition to drive home a point*].

12 **I will make a man** [*survivor of the burning at the Second Coming*] **more precious** [*scarce*] **than fine gold;** even a man than the golden wedge of Ophir [*a land rich in gold, possibly in southern Arabia; in other words, there will be relatively few survivors of the Second Coming because of widespread wickedness at the time*].

13 **Therefore** [*because of gross wickedness on earth*] **I will shake the heavens, and the earth shall remove out of her place,** in the wrath of the Lord of hosts, and in the day of his fierce anger.

In verse 14, next, Isaiah turns his attention back to the nation of Babylon in ancient times. But the prophecy can also refer to the wicked in general. Huge numbers of the wicked, including foreigners, had gravitated to Babylon because of the opportunity for wickedness there.

14 **And it** [*dual meaning: Babylon; also the wicked in general*] **shall be**

as the chased roe [hunted deer], and as a sheep that no man taketh up [no shepherd, no one defending them]: they shall every man turn to his own people, and flee every one into his own land [foreigners who have had safety in Babylon because of Babylon's great power will return back to their homelands because Babylon is no longer powerful and safe].

15 Every one that is found ["everyone that is proud," 2 Nephi 23:15] shall be thrust through [with the sword]; and every one that is joined unto them [who has gathered with the wicked in Babylon] shall fall by the sword.

16 Their children also shall be dashed to pieces before their eyes [refers only to conditions in Babylon and among the wicked before the Second Coming, not at the Second Coming; young children will not be harmed by the Second Coming of the Savior]; their houses shall be spoiled, and their wives ravished [the fate of Babylon; conditions among the wicked in the last days].

Next, Isaiah prophesies that the Medes will be the army that conquers the ancient city of Babylon.

17 Behold, I will stir up the Medes against them [a specific prophecy; Medes from Persia conquered Babylon easily in 538 BC], which shall not regard silver; and as for gold, they

shall not delight in it [you Babylonians will not be able to bribe the Medes not to destroy you].

18 Their bows also shall dash the young men to pieces; and they shall have no pity on the fruit of the womb [babies]; their eye shall not spare children.

19 And Babylon [a huge city with 335-foot high walls; see Bible Dictionary, under "Babylon"], the glory of kingdoms, the beauty of the Chaldees' excellency [Babylonian's pride], shall be as when God overthrew Sodom and Gomorrah [Babylon will be completely destroyed and never inhabited again].

20 It shall never be inhabited, neither shall it be dwelt in from generation to generation: neither shall the Arabian pitch tent there; neither shall the shepherds make their fold there.

21 But wild beasts of the desert shall lie there; and their houses [the ruins of ancient Babylon] shall be full of doleful creatures [lonely, solitary creatures]; and owls shall dwell there, and satyrs [male goats; can also mean demons—see footnote 21b in your Bible] shall dance [leap about] there.

Have you noticed that whenever Isaiah desires to communicate the complete destruction of a city, people, or nation, he describes the ruins that are left as places where owls live? Owls tend to prefer to live in lonely places, away from human habitation.

22 And the wild beasts of the islands [NIV: "hyenas"] **shall cry** [howl] **in their desolate houses** [the ruins], and dragons [hyenas, wild dogs, jackals] in their pleasant [in their once-pleasant] palaces: and **her time is near to come, and her days shall not be prolonged** [Babylon's time is nearly up, her days are almost over].

The rest of verse 22, above, was apparently left out of the Bible. We will turn to the Book of Mormon for it.

<u>2 Nephi 23:22</u>
22 And the wild beasts of the islands shall cry in their desolate houses, and dragons in their pleasant palaces; and her time is near to come, and her day shall not be prolonged. **For I will destroy her speedily; yea, for I will be merciful unto my people, but the wicked shall perish.**

ISAIAH 14

Selection: all verses

IN THIS CHAPTER, Isaiah uses colorful style and imagery as he prophesies concerning the future downfall of the King of Babylon and, symbolically, the downfall of Satan's kingdom. Verse 12 is a particularly well-known verse.

There are several possible fulfillments of verse 1, next.

1 For the Lord will have mercy on Jacob [Israel], and will yet choose Israel [bless Israel; another definition of "choose" is to "elect for eternal happiness"; see 1828 Noah Webster's Dictionary, under "choose"], **and set them in their own land** [One historical fulfillment was when Cyrus the Great of Persia allowed captives in Babylon to return in 538 BC; another group returned in 520 BC. This is also being fulfilled in our day.]: **and the strangers shall be joined with them** [foreigners will live with them], and they shall cleave to the house of Jacob [possibly meaning that Gentiles will join with Israel in the last days].

2 And the people [many nations who will help Israel return] **shall take them** [Israel], **and bring them to their place:** and **the house of Israel shall possess them** [nations who used to dominate Israel] in the land of the Lord for servants and handmaids: **and they** [Israel] **shall take them** [nations who used to dominate Israel] **captives,** whose captives they [Israel] were; **and they shall rule over their oppressors** [the tables will be turned in the last days].

In verse 3, next, we are taught that righteous Israel will finally have peace during the Millennium.

3 And it shall come to pass in the

day ["*in that day,*" *2 Nephi 24:3*] **that the Lord shall give thee rest from thy sorrow, and from thy fear, and from the hard bondage** wherein thou wast made to serve [*Israel will finally be free from subjection by foreigners and enemies during the Millennium*],

Several of the verses that follow now can be considered as dual in meaning. Many of them can refer to the king of Babylon. And they can also refer to Satan, as his kingdom comes to an end for a thousand years at the time of the Second Coming.

Verse 4 is a continuation of verse 3, with Isaiah holding forth the thought to Israel, in order to make a point, that when they are set free by the fall of Babylon, and ultimately by the fall of Satan and his kingdom, they will be in a position to taunt their former adversaries. The message is that ultimately, the righteous will triumph over all their enemies, because they have sided with the Lord.

4 That **thou shalt take up this proverb** [*a taunting*] against the king of Babylon [*dual: literally King of Babylon. Refers to Satan also, plus any wicked leader*], **and say, How hath the oppressor ceased** [*what happened to you!*]! the golden city ceased [*your unconquerable city, kingdom, is gone!*]!

The answer to the question in verse 4, above, is found in verse 5, next. One of the important doctrines in the answer is

that God has power over Satan and any members of his evil kingdom.

5 **The Lord hath broken the staff of the wicked**, and the sceptre [*power*] of the rulers.

6 **He** [*Babylon; Satan*] **who smote the people in wrath with a continual stroke** [*constantly*], **he that ruled the nations in anger, is persecuted** [*punished*], **and none hindereth** [*nobody can stop it*].

7 **The whole earth is at rest, and is quiet: they break forth into singing** [*during the Millennium*].

8 Yea, **the fir trees** [*cyprus trees; symbolic of people*] **rejoice** at thee, and the cedars [*people*] of Lebanon, saying, **Since thou art laid down** [*since you got chopped down; compare with Isaiah 10:33–34*], **no feller** [*tree cutter; destruction*] **is come up against us.**

9 Hell [*spirit prison*] **from beneath is moved for thee** [*is getting ready to receive you*] to meet thee at thy coming: it stirreth up the dead for thee, even all the chief ones of the earth [*wicked leaders*]; it hath raised up from their thrones all the kings of the nations.

In verses 9 and 10, Isaiah creates a scene in our minds wherein all the wicked leaders of the earth (who by the time this vision is foretelling are in spirit prison) are taunting the devil and the king of Babylon at the time they arrive in hell.

10 All they shall speak and say unto thee, Art thou also become weak as we [*What happened to your power, Satan; king of Babylon*]? **art thou become like unto us** [*how is it that you are no better off than we are*]?

11 Thy pomp is brought down to the grave [*was destroyed with you*], and the noise of thy viols [*royal harp music*]: **the worm is spread under thee, and the worms cover thee** [*your dead body is covered with maggots just like ours were; you're no better off here in hell than we are, so ha, ha, ha! (refers to the king of Babylon, since Satan has no physical body)*].

12 How art thou fallen from heaven, O Lucifer [*what happened to you; how were you dethroned*], **son of the morning** [*one who was high in authority—compare with Doctrine & Covenants 76:25–26*]! **how art thou cut down to the ground, which didst weaken the nations** [*how did you get cut down to this; you used to destroy nations, now your power is destroyed*]!

Next, in verses 13–14, Isaiah explains to us Lucifer's motives that led to his rebellion.

13 For thou hast said in thine heart [*these were your motives*], **I will ascend into heaven, I will exalt my throne above the stars of God** [*I will be the highest*]: **I will sit also upon the mount of the congregation,** in the sides of the north [*mythical mountain in the north where gods assemble*]:

14 I will ascend above the heights of the clouds; **I will be like the most High** [*as described in Moses 4:1–3*].

We will quote from the scene given in Moses, in the Pearl of Great Price, in which Lucifer rebelled, and will add **bold** to point things out:

Moses 4:1–3

1 And I, the Lord God, spake unto Moses, saying: That **Satan**, whom thou hast commanded in the name of mine Only Begotten, is the same which was from the beginning, and he **came before me, saying**—Behold, here am I, **send me, I will be thy son** [*the Redeemer*], and I will redeem all mankind, that one soul shall not be lost, and surely I will do it; **wherefore give me thine honor.**

2 But, behold, my Beloved Son, which was my Beloved and Chosen from the beginning, said unto me—Father, thy will be done, and the glory be thine forever.

3 Wherefore, because that **Satan** rebelled against me, and **sought** to destroy the agency of man, which I, the Lord God, had given him, and also, **that I should give unto him mine own power;** by the power of mine Only Begotten, I caused that he should be cast down;

We will now continue with Isaiah's teaching as to what will become of Satan when his kingdom (referred to as "the kingdom of the devil" in 1 Nephi 22:22) is brought down by the power of God.

15 Yet thou [*Lucifer*] **shalt be brought down to hell, to the sides of the pit** [*to the lowest part of the world of the dead, outer darkness*].

16 They [*the residents of hell*] **that see thee** [*Lucifer; King of Babylon*] **shall narrowly look upon thee** [*look at you with contorted faces and sneers*], and **consider thee, saying** [*with sarcasm*], **Is this the man that made the earth to tremble, that did shake kingdoms;**

17 That made the world as a wilderness, and destroyed the cities thereof; that opened not the house of his prisoners [*who never freed his prisoners*]?

18 All the kings of the nations, even all of them, **lie in glory, every one in his own house** [*all other kings have magnificent tombs*].

19 But thou [*dual meaning: King of Babylon literally; Satan figuratively because he doesn't even have a physical body*] **art cast out of thy grave like an abominable branch** [*cut off and walked upon*], and as the raiment of those that are slain, thrust through with a sword [*ruined and discarded*], that go down to the stones of the pit [*the very bottom*]; as a carcase trodden under feet.

20 Thou [*King of Babylon/Satan*] **shalt not be joined with them in burial** [*you will not have a magnificent tomb like they do. Satan will not get a tomb because he does not have a physical body*], because thou hast destroyed thy land, and slain thy people: the seed of evildoers shall never be renowned [*none of your (king of Babylon) evil family will survive*].

21 Prepare slaughter for his [*king of Babylon's*] **children for** [*because of*] **the iniquity of their fathers** [*parents and ancestors*]; that they do not rise, nor possess the land, nor fill the face of the world with cities [*none of your children will rule the earth like you have*].

22 For I will rise up against them, saith the Lord of hosts, **and cut off from Babylon the name, and remnant, and son, and nephew** [*I will destroy Babylon completely; Satan's kingdom on earth completely*], saith the Lord.

23 I will also make it [*Babylon*] **a possession for the bittern** [*owls*], and pools of water: and I will sweep it with the besom [*broom*] of destruction [*a "clean sweep"*], saith the Lord of hosts.

Next, beginning with verse 24, Isaiah begins a new topic. It is a prophecy concerning the fate of Assyria. Remember that Isaiah served as a prophet from about 740 BC to 701 BC, which means that he was still alive when the Assyrians attacked and conquered the northern ten tribes (known as Israel during this period of history) in about 722 BC. The Assyrian army will suffer a major defeat in Judah about 701 BC.

His prophecy about the downfall of Babylon (the first part of this chapter) was for future fulfillment (about 538 BC).

24 The Lord of hosts hath sworn [*covenanted, promised*], **saying,** Surely as I have thought [*planned*], so shall it come to pass [*here is something else I will do*]; and as I have purposed, so shall it stand [*it will happen*]:

25 That **I will break the Assyrian** [*the Assyrian army*] **in my land** [*Judah*], **and upon my mountains** [*the mountains of Judah*] **tread him** [*the Assyrians*] **under foot:** then shall his yoke [*bondage*] **depart from off them** [*my people*], and his burden depart from off their shoulders [*dual meaning: the Assyrian downfall in Judah in 701 BC; the forces of the wicked will be destroyed at the Second Coming and again, after the final battle at the end of the Millennium, when Satan and his followers will be cast out permanently; see Doctrine & Covenants 88:111–15*].

26 This is the purpose [*the plan*] **that is purposed upon the whole earth:** and this is **the hand** [*the hand of the Lord*] **that is stretched out upon all the nations** [*the eventual fate of all wicked nations*].

27 For the Lord of hosts hath purposed, and who shall disannul it [*prevent it*]**? and his hand is stretched out, and who shall turn it back?**

Beginning with verse 28, next, the topic again changes, this time to the fate of the Philistines, who have also been enemies to the Lord's people.

28 In the year that king Ahaz died [*about 720 BC*] **was this burden** [*prophetic message of doom to the Philistines*].

29 Rejoice not [*don't start celebrating*], whole Palestina [*Philistia*], **because the rod** [*power*] **of him** [*Shalmaneser, King of Assyria from 727–722 BC*] **that smote thee is broken: for out of the serpent's root** [*"snakes lay eggs"—from the same source, Assyria*] **shall come forth a cockatrice** [*one "snake" is dead (Shalmaneser) and a worse one will yet come (Sennacherib, King of Assyria, 705–687 BC). The Philistines rejoiced when Sargon, King of Assyria from 722–705 BC took over at Shalmaneser's death. Sargon was not as hard on them as his predecessor was.*], **and his**

[Sennacherib's] **fruit shall be a fiery flying serpent.**

> Next, in verse 30, the Lord describes the two options that are before the Philistines at this point.

30 And the firstborn of the poor shall feed, and the needy shall lie down in safety *[if you Philistines will repent and join with the Lord, you too can enjoy peace and safety, otherwise . . .]*: **and I will kill thy** *[Philistines']* **root with famine, and he shall slay thy remnant** *[you will be utterly destroyed, if you don't repent].*

> Next, Isaiah speaks prophetically of the future, as if it had already happened.

31 Howl, O gate; cry, O city; thou whole Palestina *[Philistia]*, **art dissolved** *[reduced to nothing]*: **for there shall come from the north a smoke** *[cloud of dust made by an enemy army]*, **and none shall be alone in his appointed times** *[the enemy army will have no cowards in it].*

32 What shall one then answer the messengers of the nation *[Philistia—what will one say when people ask, "What happened to the Philistines"?]* *[Answer:]* **That the Lord hath founded Zion, and the poor of his people shall trust in it** *[the Lord is the one who caused the destruction of the wicked and established Zion].*

ISAIAH 15

Selection: all verses

NEXT, WE SEE a message of doom to the country of Moab, located east of the Dead Sea and named after the son of Lot's oldest daughter. There was constant warfare between the Moabites and the Israelites.

One of the major messages of these chapters of "doom" for the enemies of Israel is that all enemies of the Lord and His covenant people will ultimately fall. In other words, all members of Satan's kingdom, whose ultimate goal it is to destroy righteousness and the agency of others, will be overcome by the power of the Lord.

1 The burden *[message of doom]* **of Moab** *[descendants of Lot and his eldest daughter; see Genesis 19:37].* **Because in the night** *[suddenly? unexpectedly?]* **Ar of Moab** *[a city in Moab]* **is laid waste, and brought to silence; because in the night, Kir** *[another city]* **of Moab is laid waste, and brought to silence;**

2 He *[Moab, the country east of the Dead Sea]* **is gone up to Bajith** *[a city]*, **and to Dibon,** *[a city]*, **the high places** *[pagan places of worship]*, **to weep: Moab shall howl** over Nebo *[Mt. Nebo, north of Moab]*, and over Medeba *[a city]*: **on all their heads shall be baldness** *[symbolic of slavery, captivity, and mourning]*, **and**

every beard cut off [disgrace, *slavery, captivity, and mourning*].

3 In their streets they shall gird [*dress*] **themselves with sackcloth** [*symbolic of deep tragedy and mourning*]: **on** the tops of their houses [*flat-roofed buildings used like we use decks, etc.*], **and in their streets, every one shall howl, weeping abundantly.**

4 And Heshbon [*a city in Moab*] **shall cry, and Elealeh** [*a city*]: their voice shall be heard even unto Jahaz [*a city*]: therefore [*for this reason*] **the armed soldiers of Moab shall cry out;** his life shall be grievous [*miserable*] unto him.

5 My heart shall cry out for Moab; his fugitives shall flee unto Zoar [*a border city just south of the Dead Sea*], an heifer [*young cow*] of three years old [*Moab, including Zoar, is being destroyed in its prime*]: for by the mounting up of Luhith [*where you start climbing up to get to Luhith*] **with weeping shall they go** it up; for in the way of Horonaim they shall raise up a cry of destruction.

6 For the waters of Nimrim shall be desolate [*dried up*]: for **the hay is withered away, the grass faileth, there is no green thing** [*there will be a drought and resulting famine*].

7 Therefore the abundance they have gotten, and that which they have laid up, shall they carry away to the brook of the willows [*probably the border between Moab and Edom—land directly south of Moab*].

Again, as previously mentioned several times in this study guide, Isaiah is speaking of the future as if it had already happened. This is part of "the manner of prophesying among the Jews" mentioned by Nephi in 2 Nephi 25:1.

8 For the cry is gone round about the borders of Moab [*they are completely surrounded*]; the howling thereof unto Eglaim, and the howling thereof unto Beer-elim.

9 For the waters of Dimon shall be full of blood: for **I will bring more upon Dimon, lions upon him that escapeth of Moab,** and upon the remnant of the land [*those who manage to escape the enemy armies will be destroyed by other means, including lions.*]

ISAIAH 16

Selection: all verses

A MOOD CHANGE NOW occurs. Isaiah indicates the time will come when Moab will come under the protection of Jerusalem, probably symbolic of the Savior, during the Millennium (verses 1–5).

1 Send ye the lamb [*send an appeal for help*] to the ruler of the land from

Sela [*about sixty miles south of the Dead Sea*] to the wilderness, unto the mount of the daughter of Zion [*Jerusalem*].

2 For it shall be, that, **as a wandering bird cast out of the nest, so the daughters of Moab shall be** at the fords of Arnon [*a river on the northern border of Moab. Moab will have gone through some rough times.*]

Isaiah now prophesies that Moab will appeal to Judah for help. Their plea to Judah for help is given in verse 3, next. This could take place at a future time when harmony exists between them.

3 Take counsel, execute judgment [*kindness and fairness*]; make thy shadow [*symbolic of protection and help*] as the night in the midst of the noonday; **hide the outcasts** [*protect the inhabitants of Moab*]; bewray [*betray*] not him that wandereth.

4 **Let mine outcasts dwell with thee, Moab** [*should say "Judah"; NIV: "Let the Moabite fugitives stay with you"*]; **be thou a covert** [*protection*] **to them** [*Moab's inhabitants*] from the face of the spoiler [*German: destroyer*]; **for the extortioner** [*persecutor*] **is at an end, the spoiler ceaseth, the oppressors are consumed out of the land** [*thanks to help from Judah. Could also refer to destruction of wicked at Second Coming.*].

5 And **in mercy shall the throne be established: and he** [*Christ—see heading to this chapter in your Bible*] **shall sit upon it in truth in the tabernacle of David, judging, and seeking judgment, and hasting righteousness.** [*Conditions during the Millennium. Could also refer to Judah in the last days.*]

Isaiah now returns to troubles to come upon Moab back then.

6 **We have heard of the pride of Moab; he is very proud**; even of his **haughtiness**, and his **pride**, and his **wrath**: but his **lies** shall not be so. [*Moab's unfounded boasts of strength and well-being will not work out in fact.*]

In the background notes accompanying Isaiah chapter 3 in this study guide, we introduced a writing technique called "chiasmus." You may wish to go back and reread those notes, because Isaiah uses chiastic structure again here, in verses 7 through 11. In this case, he lists several cities in order and then lists them in reverse order (the basic structure of a chiasmus). The last two cities of the chiasmus are out of order, but it still works.

7 Therefore [*because of these sins listed in verse 6*] shall Moab howl for <u>**Moab**</u> [**A**], every one shall howl: for the foundations of <u>**Kir-hareseth**</u> [**B**] shall ye mourn; surely they are stricken.

8 For the fields of **Heshbon** [C] languish, and the vine of **Sibmah** [D]: the lords of the heathen [*enemy nations—Assyrians*] have broken down the principal plants thereof [*the Assyrians ruined terraced vineyards when they attacked Moab*], they are come even unto **Jazer** [E], they wandered through the wilderness: her branches are stretched out, they are gone over the sea.

9 ¶ Therefore [*this is why*] I will bewail with the weeping of **Jazer** [E'] the **vine** of **Sibmah** [D']: I will water thee with my tears, O **Heshbon** [C'], and Elealeh: for the shouting for thy summer fruits and for thy harvest is fallen.

10 And gladness is taken away, and joy out of the plentiful field; and in the vineyards there shall be no singing, neither shall there be shouting [*in other words, there will be great sadness*]: the treaders shall tread out no wine in their presses [*because the grapes and vines have been destroyed by the enemy soldiers*]; I have made their vintage shouting to cease.

11 Wherefore my bowels [*symbolic in Hebrew of the center of feeling and emotion*] shall sound like an harp for **Moab** [A'], and mine inward parts for **Kir-haresh** [B'].

12 ¶ And it shall come to pass, when it is seen that Moab is weary on the high place [*places of worshipping idols and false gods*], that **he shall come to his sanctuary to pray; but he shall not prevail** [*won't get the help he needs from his false gods*].

13 This is the word that the Lord hath spoken concerning Moab since that time [*the Lord has warned Moab through past prophets too*].

14 But now the Lord hath spoken, saying, **Within three years**, as the years of an hireling, and **the glory of Moab shall be contemned** [*scorned*], with all that great multitude; **and the remnant shall be very small and feeble** [*in three years, there won't be much left of Moab*].

ISAIAH 17

Selection: all verses

ISAIAH NOW TELLS what will happen to Syria and says a few more things about Israel.

1 **The burden** [*message of doom*] **of Damascus** [*a major city in Syria*]. Behold, **Damascus is taken away from being a city, and it shall be a ruinous heap** [*worthless pile of rubble*].

Isaiah is speaking prophetically of the future as if it had already taken place.

2 **The cities of Aroer** [*area near Damascus*] **are forsaken**: they shall be for flocks, which shall lie down, and

none shall make them afraid [*animals will graze where cities now stand*].

3 The fortress [*fortified city*] **also shall cease from Ephraim** [*northern Israel, the northern ten tribes*], and the kingdom from Damascus, and the remnant of Syria: **they shall be as the glory of the children of Israel** [*will be cut down like Israel will be*], saith the Lord of hosts.

> The topic now turns to Israel's coming troubles.

4 And in that day it shall come to pass, that **the glory of Jacob** [*Israel*] **shall be made thin**, and the fatness of his flesh [*his prosperity*] shall wax lean [*bad times are coming*].

5 And **it shall be as when the harvestman gathereth the corn** [*grain*], and reapeth the ears with his arm; and it shall be as he that gathereth ears in the valley of Rephaim [*a fertile valley northwest of Jerusalem well-known for good harvests—Israel will be "harvested," plucked up*].

6 ¶ **Yet gleaning grapes shall be left in it** [*a small remnant will be left after Assyria's attack on Israel*], as the shaking of an olive tree, two or three berries [*olives*] in the top of the uppermost bough, four or five in the outmost fruitful branches thereof, saith the Lord God of Israel [*remnants scattered here and there*].

7 At that day shall a man look to

his **Maker** [*people will repent*], **and his eyes shall have respect to the Holy One of Israel** [*Jesus*].

8 **And he shall not look to the altars** [*of false gods*], **the work of his hands** [*idols he has made*], neither shall respect [*worship*] that which his fingers have made, either the groves [*locations used for idol worship*], or the images [*idols*]. [*This probably refers also to the last days and into the Millennium.*]

9 ¶ **In that day shall his** [*Syria's*] **strong cities be as a forsaken bough** [*limb*], and an uppermost branch, which they left because of the children of Israel: and there shall be desolation [*in Syria*].

10 **Because** [*this is why you have these problems*] **thou hast forgotten the God of thy salvation**, and hast not been mindful of the rock of thy strength [*the Lord*], therefore shalt thou plant pleasant plants [*continue idol worship*], and shalt set it with strange slips [*cuttings for grafting, symbolic of imported gods or idols*]:

11 **In the day** [*while things are going well*] **shalt thou make thy plant to grow** [*continue worshiping idols*], and in the morning shalt thou make thy seed to flourish: **but the harvest** [*results of idol worship*] **shall be a heap** [*worthless*] in the day of grief and of desperate sorrow [*your false gods will not help you*].

12 Woe to the multitude of many people [*nations, including Assyria, who attack the Lord's people*], **which make a noise like the noise of the seas** [*powerful*]; **and to the rushing of nations, that make a rushing like the rushing of mighty waters!**

13 The nations shall rush like the rushing of many waters: but God shall rebuke them [*will stop them*], **and they shall flee far off, and shall be chased as the chaff of the mountains before the wind, and like a rolling thing** [*tumbleweeds, etc.*] **before the whirlwind** [*wicked enemy nations are nothing compared to God's power; when the time is right, the Lord will stop them*].

14 And behold at eveningtide trouble; and before the morning [*unexpected, sudden disaster*] **he is not** [*the wicked are gone, destroyed; can refer to the destruction at the time of the Second Coming also*]. **This is the portion** [*the lot; in other words, they will get what is coming to them*] **of them that spoil us** [*the Lord's people*], **and the lot of them that rob us.**

ISAIAH 18

Selection: all verses

THIS CHAPTER USES symbolism to depict the gathering of Israel in the last days. You will see the missionaries (verse 2) going forth throughout the world, inviting all people to gather into the gospel fold. This is, in effect, the final pruning (verse 5) before the Second Coming.

As we begin with verse 1, we see a mistranslation with the first word.

1 Woe [*this is a mistranslation in the King James Version. The Hebrew word means "hark" or "greetings" and has no negative connotation—see footnote 1a in your Bible*] **to the land** [*most likely America*] **shadowing** [*overshadowed with God's protecting Spirit*] **with wings** [*wings often represent shelter or protection, as in the hen gathering her chicks under her wings in Matthew 23:37, and so forth. Wings also represent power in Doctrine & Covenants 77:4; Also, North and South America look somewhat like wings*], **which is beyond the rivers of Ethiopia** [*America is beyond the "rivers" or oceans beyond Africa*].

2 That sendeth ambassadors [*missionaries*] **by the sea, even in vessels of bulrushes upon the waters, saying, Go, ye swift** [*modern transportation?*] **messengers, to a nation scattered** [*scattered Israel*] **and peeled, to a people terrible from their beginning hitherto** [*German: once powerful, perhaps meaning once righteous*]; **a nation meted out and trodden down** [*scattered Israel*], **whose land the rivers** [*symbolic of enemy nations in Isaiah 8:7, 17:12*] **have spoiled!**

3 All ye inhabitants of the world, and dwellers on the earth, see ye [*pay attention*], **when he** [*the Lord*] **lifteth up an ensign** [*a signal to gather; the restored gospel*] **on the mountains** [*can symbolize Church headquarters; see Isaiah 2:2; also can symbolize temples*]**; and when he bloweth a trumpet** [*a clear, unmistakable sound, easy to distinguish from other sounds—the gospel message*]**, hear ye.**

4 For so the Lord said unto me [*Isaiah*]**, I will take my rest, and I will consider in my dwelling place like a clear heat** [*nourishing rays of light and truth*] **upon herbs, and like a cloud of dew** [*nourishing water*] **in the heat of harvest** [*right when it is needed*]**.**

5 For afore [*before*] **the harvest** [*at the time of the Second Coming*]**, when the bud is perfect, and the sour grape** [*immature grape*] **is ripening in the flower, he** [*the Lord*] **shall both cut off the sprigs with pruning hooks, and take away and cut down the branches** [*just before the millennial harvest, a final "pruning" will take place—the wicked will be destroyed, pruned away so the righteous can develop to their full potential*]**.**

6 They [*the wicked*] **shall be left together** [*completely*] **unto the fowls of the mountains** [*birds of prey*]**,** and to the beasts of the earth: and the fowls shall summer upon them, and all the beasts of the earth shall winter upon them.

> Isaiah now prophesies that the remnant, scattered Israel, will be gathered and brought back to the Lord, a righteous nation.

7 ¶ In that time [*probably the last days*] **shall the present** [*gift, gathered Israel*] **be brought unto the Lord** of hosts of a people scattered and peeled, and from a people terrible from their beginning hitherto; a nation meted out and trodden under foot, whose land the rivers have spoiled [*see verse 2*], to the place of the name of the Lord of hosts, the mount Zion [*the remnant, scattered Israel, will be gathered and brought back to the Lord a righteous nation; see verse 1*].

ISAIAH 19

Selection: all verses

THIS CHAPTER CONTAINS a rather detailed prophecy about Egypt, including civil war (verse 2). Of particular interest to us in modern times is the prophecy of the destruction that will occur against the productivity of the Nile River in the last days (verses 5–10). The building of the Aswan Dam, beginning in 1960, may be a substantial contributor to the fulfilling of this prophecy, because of the severe problems it caused downstream.

A beautiful prophecy, beginning with verse 18, informs us that the day will come when our Egyptian brothers and sisters will have the gospel of Jesus Christ, and that Egypt and Assyria will join together with Israel as covenant people of the Lord.

1 **The burden** [*message of doom*] **of Egypt.** Behold, the Lord rideth upon a swift cloud [*trouble coming quickly*], and shall come into Egypt: and the idols [*false religions*] of Egypt shall be moved at his presence, and the heart [*courage*] of Egypt shall melt in the midst of it [*they will be terrified*].

2 And **I will set the Egyptians against the Egyptians** [*civil war*]: and they shall fight every one against his brother, and every one against his neighbor; city against city, and kingdom against kingdom.

3 And **the spirit of Egypt shall fail** [*great despair*] in the midst thereof; and I will destroy the counsel [*plans*] thereof: and **they shall seek to the idols** [*they will seek help from their false gods*], and to the charmers, **and to them that have familiar spirits** [*spiritualists who claim to contact the dead*], and to the wizards [*the occult*].

4 And **the Egyptians will I give over into the hand of a cruel lord** [*hard masters*]; and **a fierce king shall rule over them** [*we don't know who this is or was*], saith the Lord, the Lord of hosts.

5 And the waters shall fail from the sea, and **the river shall be wasted** and dried up [*the Nile River will be ruined*].

6 And **they** [*the Egyptians*] **shall turn the rivers far away** [*will ruin their own rivers*]; and the brooks of defence shall be emptied and dried up: the reeds and flags shall wither.

7 **The paper reeds** [*papyrus*] by the brooks, by the mouth of the brooks, **and every thing sown** [*planted*] **by the brooks, shall wither,** be driven away, and be no more [*the papyrus industry, crops, and so forth will be devastated*].

8 **The fishers also shall mourn,** and all they that cast angle [*fish-hooks*] into the brooks shall lament, **and they that spread nets upon the waters shall languish** [*fishing industry will be ruined*].

9 Moreover [*in addition*] **they that work in fine flax** [*linen fabric is made from flax plant fibers*], **and they that weave networks** [*fine linen*], **shall be confounded** [*stopped; in other words, the textile industry will be ruined*].

10 And they shall be broken in the purposes [*will have no success*] thereof, all **that make sluices** [*dams*] **and ponds for fish.**

11 Surely the princes [*nobles; leaders*] of Zoan [*Tanis, ancient capital of*

the Nile Delta] **are fools**, the **counsel** of the wise counsellors of Pharaoh **is become brutish** [*absurd; Pharaoh has received bad counsel from those who are supposed to be wise*]: **how say ye unto Pharaoh, I am the son of the wise, the son of ancient kings** [*how do you counselors to Pharaoh dare to claim to be wise*]?

12 Where are they? **where are thy wise men** [*to whom you have turned instead of the Lord*]? and **let them tell thee now**, and let them know what the Lord of hosts hath purposed upon [*against*] Egypt.

13 The princes [*leaders*] **of Zoan are become fools**, the princes of Noph [*Memphis, capital of northern Egypt*] are deceived; **they have also seduced Egypt** [*led her astray*], even they that are the stay [*support*] of the tribes thereof.

14 The Lord hath mingled [*has allowed, because of agency*] a perverse spirit in the midst thereof: and **they have caused Egypt to err in every work thereof**, as a drunken man staggereth in his vomit.

15 Neither shall there be any work for Egypt, which the head [*leaders, high society*] or tail [*poor, low society*], branch [*palm branch, high society*] or rush [*papyrus reed, low society, poor*], may do.

16 In that day [*the last days*] **shall**

Egypt be like unto women [*the worst insult in Egyptian culture of that day*]: **and** it [*Egypt*] **shall be afraid and fear because of the shaking of the hand of the Lord** of hosts, which he shaketh over it.

Next, in verse 17, Isaiah tells us that, in the last days, the Jews will become a terror to Egypt. This is the exact opposite of what the situation has been throughout history, where the Egyptians were a terrifying power in the eyes of the Jews.

17 And the land of Judah shall be a terror unto Egypt [*a complete turnabout; tremendous prophecy!*], every one that maketh mention thereof shall be afraid in himself, because of the counsel [*plan*] of the Lord of hosts, which he hath determined against it [*Egypt*].

Next, Isaiah prophesies that the day will come when relations will improve between Egypt and Israel. He also foretells the day in which the Egyptians will have the true gospel and will make covenants with the Lord.

18 In that day [*last days*] **shall five** [*several*] **cities in the land of Egypt speak the language of Canaan** [*Israel; a prophecy of greatly improved relationship between Egypt and Judah in the last days*], **and swear** [*make covenants*] **to the Lord of Hosts** [*make covenants with Jesus Christ*]; one shall be called, The city of destruction [*not a good translation; could be "city of the sun"*].

Verse 19, next, tends to make us think that there will someday be a temple to the Lord built in Egypt.

19 In that day [last days] **shall there be an altar** [a temple?] **to the Lord in the midst of the land of Egypt,** and a pillar [symbolic of a temple] at the border thereof to the Lord.

20 And it [the altar and the pillar] **shall be for a sign and for a witness** [reminder] **unto** [of] **the Lord of hosts in the land of Egypt:** for they [Egyptians] shall cry [pray] unto the Lord because of the oppressors, and **he shall send them a saviour,** and a great one, **and he shall deliver them** [the Egyptians will hear and live the gospel].

21 And the Lord shall be known to Egypt, and the Egyptians shall know the Lord in that day [the last days], and shall do sacrifice [3 Nephi 9:20; broken heart and contrite spirit] and oblation [Doctrine & Covenants 59:12]; yea, **they shall vow a vow** [make covenants] **unto the Lord, and perform it** [and will be faithful to them].

Often, the Lord has to first humble people and then heal them. Otherwise they won't listen to Him. We see this in verse 22, next.

22 And the Lord shall smite Egypt: he shall smite **and heal it** [first humble it, then heal it]: **and they shall return even to the Lord,** and he shall be intreated [prayed to] of [by] them, and shall heal them [wonderful blessings are in store for Egypt].

23 ¶ In that day shall there be a highway out of Egypt to Assyria [Iraq?], and the Assyrian shall come into Egypt, and the Egyptian into Assyria, and **the Egyptians shall serve** [the Lord; see verse 25] **with the Assyrians.**

24 In that day [the last days] **shall Israel be the third with Egypt and with Assyria** [all three will be allied, with Israel as a blessing in the midst of them], even a blessing in the midst of the land:

25 Whom the Lord of hosts shall bless, saying, **Blessed be Egypt my people, and Assyria the work of my hands, and Israel mine inheritance** [all three nations will worship the true God and be part of the Lord's people].

ISAIAH 20

Selection: all verses

ISAIAH 20 SEEMS to have no particular references to the future. It deals with ancient Egypt and is a prophecy that Assyria will overrun Egypt.

1 In the year [about 711 BC] **that Tartan** [an Assyrian general] **came**

unto **Ashdod** [*when Sargon the king of Assyria sent him, Ashdod was a coastal city about forty miles west of Jerusalem*] **and fought against Ashdod** [*the center of a revolt against Assyria*], **and took it;**

> In verse 2, next, Isaiah uses a rather dramatic method of communicating what is in store for Egypt, when the Assyrians attack them.

2 At the same time [*about 711 BC—see verse 1*] **spake the Lord by Isaiah** the son of Amoz, **saying, Go and loose the sackcloth** [*symbolic of mourning already*] **from off thy loins, and put off thy shoe from thy foot. And he did so, walking naked** [*without an upper garment; symbolic of slavery and exile; see verse 4*] **and barefoot** [*like a slave*].

3 And the Lord said, Like as my servant Isaiah hath walked naked [*stripped to the waist*] **and barefoot three years** [*we don't know whether this means constantly during the three years, or occasionally during the three years to remind the people of the message*] **for a sign and wonder upon Egypt and upon Ethiopia** [*symbolic of what will happen to Egypt and Ethiopia*];

4 So shall the king of Assyria lead away the Egyptians prisoners, and the Ethiopians captives, young and old, naked and barefoot, even with their buttocks [*upper thighs*]

uncovered, to the shame of Egypt.

> The Jews at this time had been depending on Egypt and Ethiopia for protection from Assyria, rather than repenting and turning to the Lord for help, as counseled by their prophets. In verse 5, next, the Lord tells them that their hopes are in vain.

5 And they [*Judah*] **shall be afraid and ashamed of** [*disappointed by*] **Ethiopia their expectation** [*hope*], **and of Egypt their glory** [*as mentioned above, Judah was hoping for protection from Egypt and Ethiopia, rather than repenting and turning to God*].

6 And the inhabitant of this isle [*nation; in other words, Jerusalem, Judah*] **shall say in that day, Behold, such is our expectation** [*our hope is destroyed!*], **whither we flee for help to be delivered from the king of Assyria: and how shall we escape** [*if that can happen to Ethiopia and Egypt, our "protection" from Assyria, what do we do now*]?

ISAIAH 21

Selection: all verses

THIS CHAPTER IS another prophecy about the destruction of Babylon. As mentioned in verses 2–4, this was a particularly difficult vision for Isaiah to watch.

1 The burden [*message of doom*] **of**

the desert of the sea [*Babylon*]. As whirlwinds [*which are devastating in the desert*] in the south pass through; so it cometh from the desert, from a terrible land.

2 A grievous vision is declared unto me [*Isaiah; this was extra hard for Isaiah to watch*]; the treacherous dealer dealeth treacherously, and the spoiler spoileth. Go up, O Elam [*a country east of Babylon*]: besiege [*attack*], O Media [*a country northeast of Babylon; the Medes conquered Babylon in about 538 BC*]; all the sighing thereof [*groaning Babylon has caused*] have I [*the Lord*] made to cease.

3 Therefore are my [*Isaiah's*] loins [*whole being*] filled with pain: pangs have taken hold upon me, as the pangs of a woman that travaileth [*is in labor*]: I was bowed down at the hearing of it [*the vision*]; I was dismayed at the seeing of it [*this vision of the destruction of Babylon overwhelmed Isaiah*].

4 My heart panted [*faltered*], fearfulness affrighted me [*made me tremble*]: the night of my pleasure hath he turned into fear unto me [*I can't get to sleep at night*].

5 Prepare the table, watch in the watchtower, eat, drink: arise, ye princes, and anoint the shield [*oil your shields, get ready for action*].

6 For thus hath the Lord said unto me [*Isaiah*], Go, set a watchman, let him declare what he seeth.

7 And he saw a chariot with a couple of horsemen, a chariot of asses, and a chariot of camels; and he hearkened diligently with much heed [*paid close attention to what he saw*]:

8 And he cried, A lion: My lord, I stand continually [*day after day*] upon the watchtower in the daytime, and I am set in my ward whole nights [*I am keeping watch constantly like You told me to*]:

9 And, behold, here cometh a chariot of men, with a couple of horsemen [*messengers*]. And he answered and said, Babylon is fallen, is fallen [*dual meaning: Babylon has fallen; Satan's kingdom will likewise eventually fall*]; and all the graven images of her gods he hath broken unto the ground [*the Medes joined the Persians and Elamites and conquered Babylon, about 538 BC*].

10 O my threshing [*O my crushed one*], and the corn [*grain*] of my floor [*the son of my threshing floor, that is, the Israelites who will survive Babylon's downfall*]: that which I have heard of the Lord of hosts, the God of Israel, have I declared unto you.

It seems that no wicked nation is escaping Isaiah's prophecies of destruction. Next, we see the message of doom to the Edomites in Dumah.

11 The burden of Dumah [*message of doom to the Edomites who live in Dumah, a desert oasis about 250 miles southeast of the Dead Sea*]. **He calleth to me out of Seir** [*mountain range southeast of the Dead Sea*], **Watchman, what of the night** [*how long until daylight? In other words, how long will this oppression last*]? Watchman, what of the night?

12 The watchman said, **The morning cometh, and also the night** [*the end of Babylonian captivity will come but another oppressor will follow*]: if ye will enquire, enquire ye [*ask for more information later*]: return, come.

13 The burden upon Arabia [*difficulties caused Arabia by the Babylonian conquests*]. In the forest [*oasis*] in Arabia shall ye lodge, O ye travelling companies of Dedanim [*an area about 150 miles east of the Sea of Galilee*].

14 The inhabitants of the land of Tema [*about 250 miles south of Jerusalem, in the Arabian Desert*] **brought water to him** [*Kedar, that is, refugees from Kedar*] **that was thirsty, they prevented** [*met; "prevent" is used seventeen times in King James Version, always in the obsolete sense of "go before," "meet," "precede," and so forth. See Psalm 119:147,*

where *"prevented" means "got up before dawn." See also Matthew 17:25, where Jesus spoke first, before Peter spoke*] **with their bread him that fled** [*refugees from Kedar fleeing the Babylonians, Dedan and Tema need to prepare to take care of later refugees from Kedar*].

15 For they [*refugees from Kedar*] **fled from the swords**, from the drawn sword, and from the bent bow, and from the grievousness of war.

16 For thus hath the Lord said unto me [*Isaiah*], **Within a year**, according to the years of an hireling [*a wage earner, who can be fired for poor performance just as Kedar, in one year, will be "fired" for poor performance with respect to God*], and **all the glory of Kedar shall fail.**

17 And **the residue of the number of archers, the mighty men** of the children of Kedar, **shall be diminished** [*Kedar will be devastated and have few warriors left*]: **for the Lord God of Israel hath spoken it.**

ISAIAH 22

Selection: all verses

THIS PROPHECY DEALS with the wicked inhabitants of Jerusalem. If you read the heading to this chapter in your Bible, you see that it prophesies of the coming captivity of the Jews. It also deals with the power of Christ to free captives from sin.

1 The burden of the valley of vision [*message of doom to Jerusalem*]. **What aileth thee now, that thou art wholly gone up to the house-tops** ["*What's wrong with you! Can't you see what's coming? How can you be so insensitive, always partying when your future is so bleak!*"]?

2 Thou that art full of stirs [*noise*], **a tumultuous city, a joyous city** [*always partying; false sense of security*]: **thy slain men are not slain with the sword,** nor dead in battle [*are easily captured and killed*].

> Remember, as in many cases previously pointed out in this study guide, Isaiah is speaking prophetically of the future as if it has already taken place. We see that the partying and lack of vigilance on the part of the Jewish soldiers has made it easy for the enemy to capture them.

3 All thy rulers are fled together, they are bound by the archers [*captured easily; tied up by the archers, who don't normally do the actual hand-to-hand combat and capturing*]: **all that are found in thee are bound together, which have fled from far.**

4 Therefore said I [*this is the reason Isaiah said*], **Look away from me** [*don't try to get me to party with you*]; **I will weep bitterly, labour not to comfort me** [*don't try to comfort me*

because I see what's coming], **because of the spoiling of the daughter of my people** [*Jerusalem*].

5 For it is a day of trouble, and of treading down, and of perplexity by the Lord God of hosts in the valley of vision [*Jerusalem*], breaking down the walls, and of crying to the mountains.

6 And Elam bare the quiver with chariots [*symbolic of war*] **of men and horsemen** [*horse is symbolic of conquering, victory*], **and Kir uncovered the shield** [*Jerusalemites hope the soldiers of Elam and Kir—on the main road between Elam and Babylon—will defeat the Assyrians before they reach Jerusalem*].

> Isaiah is pointing out the futility of the efforts of the Jews to defend themselves against these enemies. They have been weakened by wickedness and riotous living. Their only effective defense is to repent and turn to the Lord (verse 11).

7 ¶ And it shall come to pass, that thy choicest valleys shall be full of chariots, and the horsemen shall set themselves in array at the gate [*enemy soldiers will be everywhere in your land*].

8 And he discovered [*stripped off*] **the covering** [*defense*] **of Judah,** and thou didst look in that day to the armour of the house of the forest [*Jerusalem's* *defense is inadequate].*

9 Ye have seen also the breaches [*cracks, breaks in the wall*] **of the city of David** [*Jerusalem*]**, that they are many** [*Isaiah points out weaknesses in Jerusalem's defenses*]**: and ye gathered together the waters of the lower pool** [*Hezekiah's tunnel; you dug a tunnel to bring water into the city during siege*].

10 And ye have numbered [*taken stock of things*] **the houses of Jerusalem, and the houses have ye broken down to fortify the wall** [*dismantled houses for stone to fortify city walls and so forth*].

11 Ye made also a ditch between the two walls for the water of the old pool: but ye have not looked unto the maker thereof [*the Lord*]**, neither had respect unto him that fashioned it long ago** [*you have not turned to the Lord and repented, wherein your only reliable protection lies*].

Verse 12 again reminds them that humility and repentance are the only way out of the coming destruction.

12 And in that day did the Lord God of hosts call to weeping, and to mourning, and to baldness, and to girding with sackcloth [*God said, "Repent, humble yourselves!"*]**:

13 And behold [*instead of repenting and humbly turning to the Lord for protection, the people continued in*]

joy and gladness [*partying*]**, slaying oxen, and killing sheep, eating flesh, and drinking wine: let us eat and drink; for to morrow we shall die** [*people ignore God, don't repent, continue riotous living*].

14 And it was revealed in mine ears by the Lord of hosts, Surely this iniquity shall not be purged from you till ye die, saith the Lord God of hosts [*the way you're heading, you will die in your sins*].

Next, Isaiah illustrates the negative influence that foreign lifestyles, philosophies and religions, and so forth, are having upon the Lord's people at this time.

15 Thus saith the Lord God of hosts, Go, get thee unto [*go see*] **this treasurer, even unto Shebna** [*leader of the king's court, probably a foreigner; perhaps symbolic of foreign religions, lifestyles, and so forth, taking hold of Jews but eventually driven out by the Messiah; see verses 19–20*]**, which is over the house, and say,**

16 What hast thou here? and whom hast thou here, that thou hast hewed thee out a sepulchre here [*foreign influences attempting to become permanent; Shebna is a vain man carving out a great monument to himself*]**, as he that heweth him out a sepulchre on high, and that graveth an habitation for himself in a rock?**

17 Behold, the Lord will carry thee

away with a mighty captivity, and will surely cover thee [*you won't be famous*].

18 He will surely violently turn and toss thee like a ball into a large country: there shalt thou die [*you will die in a foreign land (likely Assyria—see footnote 18a in your Bible), symbolic of the fate of Jerusalem's inhabitants as they are carried away into a foreign land*], and there the chariots of thy glory shall be the shame of thy lord's house.

19 And I will drive thee from thy station, and from thy state shall he pull thee down.

20 And it shall come to pass in that day, that **I will call my servant Eliakim** [*a real person in Jerusalem, symbolic of the Messiah—see footnote 20a in your Bible*] the son of Hilkiah:

21 And I will clothe him with thy robe, and strengthen him with thy girdle [*he will take your place*], **and I will commit thy government into his hand**: and he [*Messiah*] shall be a father to the inhabitants of Jerusalem, and to the house of Judah.

22 And the key of the house of David will I lay upon his shoulder; so he shall open, and none shall shut; and he shall shut, and none shall open [*symbolic of Christ's power*].

23 And I will fasten him as a nail in a sure place [*the Messiah is absolutely reliable*]; and he shall be for a glorious throne to his father's house [*dual meaning: Eliakim's family depends on him for their temporal salvation; we depend on Christ for our spiritual salvation*].

24 And they shall hang upon him all the glory of his father's house, the offspring and the issue, all vessels of small quantity, from the vessels of cups, even to all the vessels of flagons [*dual meaning: Eliakim's relatives, small and great, depend on him; Christ carries all mankind, small and great, upon the cross; Atonement*].

The symbolism in verse 25, next, does not apply to the Savior, rather, only to Eliakim.

25 In that day, saith the Lord of hosts, shall the nail that is fastened in the sure place be removed, and be cut down, and fall; and the burden that was upon it shall be cut off: for the Lord hath spoken it [*Eliakim will eventually fall from office and his family with him*].

ISAIAH 23

Selection: all verses

THIS IS THE last of the set of prophecies against foreign nations that began with chapter 13.

1 The burden [*prophecy of doom*] **of Tyre** [*located about 120 miles north of Jerusalem, on the coast of the Mediterranean Sea; a leading sea power of Isaiah's time*]. **Howl, ye ships of Tarshish** [*large ships of trade*]; **for it** [*Tyre*] **is laid waste**, so that there is no house, no entering [*harbor*] in: from the land of Chittim [*Cyprus*] it is revealed to them.

2 Be still [*stunned*], ye inhabitants of the isle [*seaport of Tyre or Cyprus?*]; thou whom the merchants of Zidon, that pass over the sea, have replenished [*made rich*].

3 And by great waters the seed [*grain from the Nile*] of Sihor [*city in Egypt*], the harvest of the river, is her revenue; and she is a mart [*marketplace*] of nations.

4 Be thou ashamed [*German: terrified—Sidon's commerce will be interrupted via Tyre's downfall*], **O Zidon:** for the sea hath spoken, even the strength of the sea, saying, I travail not, nor bring forth children, neither do I nourish up young men, nor bring up virgins [*Tyre is not producing anymore*].

5 As at the report concerning Egypt [*as the report comes to Egypt*], **so shall they** [*the Egyptians*] **be sorely pained at the report of Tyre** [*Egypt will be in anguish upon hearing what has happened to Tyre*].

6 Pass ye over to Tarshish [*probably in Spain*]; howl, ye inhabitants of the isle.

7 Is this your joyous [*riotous*] **city**, whose antiquity is of ancient days? **her own feet shall carry her afar off to sojourn** [*she creates her own downfall like we do when we go against God*].

8 Who hath taken this counsel [*who is planning this*] **against Tyre**, the crowning city, whose merchants are princes [*mighty leaders*], whose traffickers [*traders*] are the honourable [*famous*] of the earth?

> Verse 9, next, has the answer to the question posed by Isaiah, in verse 8, above.

9 The Lord of hosts hath purposed [*planned*] **it**, to stain the pride of all glory, and to bring into contempt [*to humble*] all the honourable [*unrighteous famous*] of the earth.

10 Pass through thy land as a river, O daughter of Tarshish : **there is no more strength** [*you are ruined*].

11 He [*the Lord*] **stretched out his hand over the sea, he shook the kingdoms: the Lord hath given a commandment against the merchant city** [*Tyre*], **to destroy the strong holds thereof** [*merchandising networks; Tyre is doomed*].

12 And he said, **Thou shalt no more rejoice**, O thou oppressed virgin [*unconquered until the fulfillment of this prophesy*], daughter of Zidon: arise, pass over to Chittim [*Cyprus*]; **there also shalt thou have no rest** [*Tyre's downfall ruins other economies too*].

13 Behold [*look at*] **the land of the Chaldeans** [*Babylon*]; **this people was not, till** [*was not ruined, until*] **the Assyrian founded it** [*set it up*] **for them** [*desert creatures*] **that dwell in the wilderness** [*the Assyrians destroyed Babylon to the point that it is now nothing more than a place for desert creatures to live*]: **they set up the towers** [*siege towers*] **thereof, they raised** [*razed; destroyed*] **up the palaces thereof; and he** [*Assyria*] **brought it to ruin.**

14 Howl, ye ships of Tarshish: for your strength is laid waste [*via Tyre's downfall*].

15 And it shall come to pass in that day, that Tyre shall be forgotten seventy years, according to the days of one king: **after the end of seventy years shall Tyre sing as an harlot** [*will "prostitute" the ways of God again*].

16 Take an harp, go about the city, thou harlot that hast been forgotten; make sweet melody, sing many songs, that thou mayest be remembered.

17 And it shall come to pass after the end of seventy years, that the Lord will visit **Tyre,** and she **shall turn** [*return*] **to her hire** [*wicked ways*], **and shall commit fornication** [*symbolic of intense and total disloyalty to God; see Bible Dictionary, under "Adultery"*] **with all the kingdoms of the world upon the face of the earth** [*Tyre will be an evil influence to many nations*].

18 And her merchandise and her hire shall be holiness to the Lord [*perhaps referring to the future when the wicked will be gone and the good things and wealth of the earth will be for the righteous and the building up of the kingdom of God*]: **it shall not be treasured nor laid up; for her merchandise shall be for them that dwell before the Lord** [*the righteous*], **to eat sufficiently, and for durable clothing** [*righteousness blesses people for eternity*].

ISAIAH 24

Selection: all verses

IN THE FIRST part of this chapter, Isaiah emphasizes the consequences of wickedness. The punishment for sin (if they don't repent) will eventually come upon all, regardless of social status (verse 3). Isaiah will again use chiasmus (see notes in the background for chapter 3 in this study guide) as a means of providing emphasis. It will be a simple chiasmus, consisting of **A, B, C, B,' A.'**

Other messages in this chapter also include the seriousness of breaking covenants (beginning with verse 5), and the burning of the wicked at the time of the Second Coming.

We will begin our study now by noting the chiasmus, which begins in verse 1.

1 Behold, **the Lord** [A] maketh the **earth empty** [B], and maketh it waste, and turneth it upside down, and scattereth abroad the inhabitants thereof.

2 And it shall be, as with the **people** [C], so with the priest; as with the servant, so with his master; as with the maid, so with her mistress; as with the buyer, so with the seller; as with the lender, so with the borrower; as with the taker of usury [*interest on loans*], so with the giver of usury to him [*no one who is wicked will escape, regardless of social status*].

3 The **land shall be utterly emptied** [B'], and utterly spoiled: for **the Lord** [A'] hath spoken this word.

> Verse 4, next, reminds us that pride is a devastating sin for individuals and nations.

4 The earth mourneth and fadeth away, **the world languisheth** [*wastes away*] and fadeth away, **the haughty** [*prideful*] **people of the earth do languish.**

> The main problem that is causing the people of the world (verse 4) to waste away is described by Isaiah in verse 5.

5 **The earth** also **is defiled** under the inhabitants thereof; **because they have transgressed the laws, changed the ordinance, broken the everlasting covenant** [*they have gone into apostasy*].

> In verse 6, next, Isaiah explains that apostasy with its accompanying personal and national wickedness will be the cause of the burning at the Second Coming.

6 **Therefore** [*this is why*] **hath the curse** [*the punishments of God*] **devoured the earth,** and they that dwell therein are desolate: **therefore** [*this is why*] **the inhabitants of the earth are burned, and few men left** [*at the Second Coming*].

> The glory of the Lord will be the source of the burning at the Second Coming, according to Doctrine & Covenants 5:19 and 2 Nephi 12:10, 19, and 21.

> In verses 7–12, next, Isaiah uses several different ways to say, in effect, that the party is over for the wicked.

7 **The new wine mourneth** [*fails, runs out*], the vine languisheth [*fails*], **all the merryhearted do sigh** ["*the party's over!*"].

8 **The mirth** [*merriment*] **of tabrets** [*drums; tambourines*] **ceaseth,** the noise of them that rejoice [*party, revel in riotous living*] endeth, the joy of the harp ceaseth.

9 **They shall not drink wine with a**

song [drunken singing]; strong drink shall be bitter to them that drink it.

10 The city of confusion is broken down [towns are broken down]: **every house is shut up, that no man may come in.**

11 There is a crying for wine in the streets [people still want their wicked lifestyle]; **all joy is darkened, the mirth of the land is gone.**

12 In the city is left desolation, and **the gate is smitten with destruction** [Isaiah has "painted" a verbal picture that the "party" is very over, in verses 7–12. This is an excellent example of his inspired brilliance and use of repetition in his prophesying].

13 When thus it shall be in the midst of the land among the people [nations], **there shall be as the shaking of an olive tree, and as the gleaning grapes when the vintage is done** [a few righteous will be separated, or gleaned from the wicked].

14 They [the relatively few righteous] **shall lift up their voice, they shall sing** [praises] **for the majesty of the Lord,** they shall cry aloud from the sea.

15 Wherefore glorify ye the Lord in the fires [probably should say "islands," see footnote 15a in your Bible], **even the name of the Lord God of Israel in the isles of the sea** [nations of the earth; a few righteous,

a remnant, are scattered throughout the earth].

16 From the uttermost part of the earth have we heard songs, even glory to the righteous. But I [Isaiah] **said, My leanness, my leanness** [my inability to change things!], **woe unto me! the treacherous dealers have dealt very treacherously; yea, the treacherous dealers have dealt treacherously** [wickedness continues despite Isaiah's efforts to warn them and get them to change].

17 Fear [terror], **and the pit** [a trap], **and the snare** [a trap], **are upon thee, O inhabitant** [wicked people] **of the earth.**

In verse 18, next, Isaiah teaches that, ultimately, there is no escape for the wicked.

18 And it shall come to pass, that he who fleeth from the noise of the fear shall fall into the pit [as stated in verse 17, above]; **and he that cometh up out** [escapes] **of the midst of the pit shall be taken in the snare** [sometimes the wicked think that they have escaped the justice of God, but they haven't]: **for the windows from on high are open** [heaven is watching], **and the foundations of the earth do shake.**

19 The earth is utterly broken down, the earth is clean dissolved, the earth is moved exceedingly [will "reel to and fro"; see verse 20].

20 **The earth shall reel to and fro like a drunkard**, and shall be removed like a cottage [*flimsy temporary shade structure built in a garden; see Isaiah 1:8*]; and the transgression thereof shall be heavy upon it; and it shall fall, and not rise again [*German: not remain standing*].

21 And it shall come to pass **in that day, that the Lord shall punish the host of the high ones** [*wicked, proud*] that are on high, and the kings of the earth upon the earth [*the wicked will be punished*].

> The doctrine of missionary work in the postmortal spirit world prison is clearly taught in verse 22, next.

22 And **they shall be gathered together, as prisoners are gathered in the pit** [*spirit prison—see footnotes 22a and 22b in your Bible*], and shall be shut up in the prison, **and after many days shall they be visited** [*by missionaries who come to the spirit prison; see Doctrine & Covenants 138*].

> Next, in verse 23, Isaiah explains to us that the glory of the Savior, as He comes to earth at the time of His Second Coming, will be beyond anything we have ever experienced.

23 **Then the moon shall be confounded, and the sun ashamed** [*moon and sun's majesty are nothing compared to radiant glory and majesty of Christ when He comes; see Doctrine & Covenants 133:49*],

when the Lord of hosts shall reign in mount Zion, and in Jerusalem [*during the Millennium*], and before his ancients gloriously.

ISAIAH 25

Selection: all verses

ONE OF THE major messages in this chapter is that it is worth being righteous. Those who are worthy to be with the Savior will receive the very best of blessings and enjoy the results of their righteous efforts.

As we begin, we see the righteous praising God for the plan of salvation.

1 **O Lord, thou art my God**; I will exalt thee, **I will praise thy name**; for thou hast done wonderful things; **thy counsels of old** [*plans made in Council in Heaven*] are faithfulness and truth.

> Next, the righteous praise and acknowledge the Lord for His power over the wicked. This is an important doctrine, since some people are of the opinion that the forces of evil, with Satan at the helm, have a chance to ultimately triumph over the Savior. They don't.

2 **For thou hast made of a** [*wicked*] **city an heap** [*pile of rubble*]; **of a defenced city a ruin: a palace of strangers** [*symbolic of kingdoms of the wicked*] **to be no city**; it shall never be built [*rebuilt; symbolic of the*

fall of Babylon, and the eventual fall of Satan's kingdom].

3 Therefore shall [*this is why*] **the strong** [*powerful wicked*] **people glorify** [*acknowledge*] **thee**, the city of the terrible [*tyrant; German: powerful Gentile*] nations shall fear thee [*God has power over the wicked*].

4 For thou hast been a strength to the poor, a strength to the needy in his distress, a refuge from the storm, a shadow [*shade; protection*] **from the heat, when the blast of the terrible ones** [*the wicked*] **is as a storm against the wall** [*you have helped the righteous poor and needy*].

5 Thou shalt bring down [*humble*] **the noise** [*unrighteous revelry*] of strangers [*foreigners; people whose lifestyle is "foreign" to the gospel*], as the heat in a dry place [*strangers who have been fierce like the heat in the desert against the righteous*]; even the heat with the shadow [*shade*] of a cloud [*God subdues the wicked like He subdues desert heat with clouds*]: **the branch** [*German Bible: victory song of tyrants*] **of the terrible ones** [*tyrants*] **shall be brought low** [*humbled*].

6 ¶ And in this mountain [*mount Zion—see heading to this chapter in your Bible; probably a reference to the Millennium—see Doctrine & Covenants 133:56*] **shall the Lord of hosts make unto all people**

[*nations; the righteous*] **a feast of fat things** [*the best*], a feast of wines on the lees [*thickest, best part of the wine, in other words, the best blessings of the gospel are made available to the righteous*], of fat things full of marrow, of wines on the lees well refined.

7 And he will destroy in this mountain the face of the covering [*veil*] cast over all people, and **the vail that is spread over all nations** [*veil of spiritual darkness will be taken away*].

> We see the blessed and happy state of the righteous, because of the resurrection and Atonement of Jesus Christ, highlighted in verse 8, next.

8 He [*Christ*] **will swallow up death in victory** [*the resurrection*]; **and the Lord God will wipe away tears from off all faces** [*through the Atonement come happiness and eternal life for the righteous; sharp contrast with the fate of wicked in verses 2, 10, 11, 12, and so forth*]; and the rebuke [*troubles, persecutions, problems*] of his people shall he take away from off all the earth: for **the Lord hath spoken it** [*it will happen!*].

9 And it shall be said in that day [*future*], **Lo, this is our God; we have waited for him, and he will save** [*has saved*] **us: this is the Lord; we have waited for him, we will be** [*are*] **glad** and rejoice in his salvation.

In verses 10–12, next, Isaiah yet again emphasizes the fact that the Lord will triumph over the wicked.

10 For in this mountain shall the hand of the Lord rest, and Moab [*symbolic of the wicked*] **shall be trodden down under him,** even as straw is trodden down for the dunghill [*fate of the wicked*].

11 And he shall spread forth his hands in the midst of them [*the wicked*], as he that swimmeth spreadeth forth his hands to swim: and **he shall bring down their pride** together with the spoils of their hands [*He will humble the wicked and take away their ill-gotten gain*].

12 And the fortress of the high fort [*supposedly invincible domains of the wicked*] of thy walls **shall he** [*the Lord*] **bring down, lay low, and bring to the ground, even to the dust** [*kingdoms of the wicked destroyed completely!*].

ISAIAH 26

Selection: all verses

THIS CHAPTER CON-SISTS of a message of encouragement to the righteous and a warning against wickedness. It depicts the righteous singing and praising Jehovah.

1 In that day [*last days*] **shall this song** [*of praise to the Lord*] **be sung in the land of Judah;** We have a strong city; **salvation will God appoint for walls and bulwarks** [*"salvation is all around us"*].

2 Open ye the gates [*several possible meanings: implies peaceful times when the city gates can be left open; can mean the gates of heaven; "gate" can also mean baptism*], **that the righteous nation** [*the righteous people*] **which keepeth the truth may enter in.**

3 Thou wilt keep him [*the righteous nation; individual*] **in perfect peace, whose mind is stayed** [*based, supported, supplied by*] **on thee:** because he trusteth in thee.

4 Trust ye in the Lord for ever: for in the Lord JEHOVAH [*the Savior*] **is everlasting strength.**

5 ¶ For he [*JEHOVAH in verse 4, above*] **bringeth down** [*humbles*] **them that dwell on high** [*the "high and mighty," that is, the proud wicked*]; **the lofty city, he layeth it low; he layeth it low, even to the ground; he bringeth it even to the dust** [*will completely destroy the wicked*].

6 The foot shall tread it [*the lofty city, that is, the wicked*] **down,** even the feet of the poor, and the steps of the needy [*the tables are turned; the oppressed now triumph and the wicked get their just dues*].

7 The way of the just [*righteous*] is uprightness: **thou, most upright** [*Christ*], **dost weigh the path of the just** [*make the path smooth, bless the righteous*].

8 Yea, **in the way of thy judgments, O Lord, have we waited for thee** [*we've been living righteously*]; **the desire of our soul is to thy name** [*our hearts are right; see Doctrine & Covenants 64:22*], and to the remembrance of thee.

9 **With my soul have I desired thee in the night; yea, with my spirit within me will I seek thee early** [*I seek Thee day and night, in other words, always*]; for when thy judgments [*teachings and commandments*] are in the earth, the inhabitants of the world will learn righteousness.

Next, in verse 10, Isaiah points out to us that the problem with the wicked is that they do not want to do right.

10 **Let favour be shewed to the wicked, yet will he not** [*does not want to*] **learn righteousness:** in the land of uprightness [*among the righteous*] will he deal unjustly [*the wicked are always looking for ways to cheat the righteous*], and **will not** [*does not want to*] **behold the majesty of the Lord** [*even when the Lord shows kindness to the wicked, they don't repent because they don't desire righteousness; their hearts are not right*].

11 **Lord, when thy hand is lifted up** [*when Your power and existence are obvious*], **they** [*the wicked*] **will not see** [*don't want to see*]: **but they shall see** [*every knee shall bow and every tongue confess; see Doctrine & Covenants 76:110*], **and be ashamed** [*put to shame*] for their envy at the people [*because of thy zeal for thy people*]; yea, **the fire of** [*reserved for*] **thine enemies shall devour them** [*the wicked; Second Coming*].

12 ¶ Lord, thou wilt ordain peace for us: for **thou also hast wrought all our works in us** [*all we have is from Thee; gratitude—compare with Doctrine & Covenants 59:21*].

13 O Lord our God, **other lords** [*secular leaders, including wicked rulers*] beside thee **have had dominion over us: but by thee only will we make mention of thy name** [*Thou only do we honor and worship*].

Next, Isaiah speaks of the fact that the wicked will not be resurrected with the righteous. He speaks of the future as if it had already happened.

14 **They** [*the wicked rulers*] **are dead, they shall not live** [*until the resurrection of the wicked at the end of the Millennium—see Doctrine & Covenants 88:101*]; they are deceased, **they shall not rise** [*their power is ended*]: **therefore** [*because of their wickedness*] **hast thou visited** [*punished*] **and destroyed them,** and

made all their memory to perish.

15 Thou hast increased the nation [*the righteous—see verse 2*], **O Lord, thou hast increased the nation: thou art glorified: thou hadst** [*hast*] **removed** [*spread*] **it far unto all the ends of the earth** [*there will be a tremendous increase in the number of righteous during the Millennium*].

16 Lord, in trouble have they [*the righteous*] **visited thee** [*come unto thee*]**, they poured out a prayer when thy chastening was upon them** [*the righteous turn to God in times of trouble*].

17 Like as a woman with child, that draweth near the time of her delivery, is in pain, and crieth out in her pangs: so have we been in thy sight, O Lord [*when unavoidable trouble came, we turned to thee*].

> Next, Israel, in effect, confesses that they have not always acted like the Lord's covenant people, which includes the responsibility of blessing others with the gospel and taking the gospel and the priesthood to all the world (see Abraham 2:9–11).

18 We have been with child [*we have had pain and suffering as part of our mortal probation*]**, we have been in pain, we have as it were brought forth wind** [*nothing—sometimes we have turned from Thee, and pain and suffering have not produced desired results, fruits of righteousness in our lives*]**, we have not wrought any deliverance in the earth** [*we have not brought salvation to people of the earth like we were called to do as Thy covenant people*]**; neither have the inhabitants of the world fallen** [*been humbled*].

> Next, in verse 19, the Savior teaches that the righteous, who have died before His resurrection, will be resurrected with Him (see also Doctrine & Covenants 133:54–55).

19 Thy dead men shall live [*be resurrected*]**, together with my** [*Christ's*] **dead body shall they arise** [*they will be resurrected with Christ*]**. Awake and sing, ye that dwell in dust** [*lie in graves*]**: for thy dew is as the dew of herbs, and the earth shall cast out the dead** [*resurrection*].

20 ¶ Come, my people [*the righteous, Isaiah 19:25*]**, enter thou into thy chambers, and shut thy doors about thee: hide thyself as it were for a little moment, until the indignation** [*cleansing of the earth*] **be overpast.** [*This verse is full of Passover symbolism. The Israelites closed their doors and put lamb's blood (symbolic of the Atonement) on doorposts, which provided them safety from the Lord's destruction among the Egyptians. Through righteous homes where the gospel is lived and the Atonement used, we can be spared God's punishments. God punishes* *only those who merit punishment.*]

21 For, behold, the Lord cometh out of his place [*heaven*] **to punish the inhabitants of the earth for their iniquity** [*the destruction of the wicked at the Second Coming as well as many destructions of the wicked previous to that time*]: **the earth also shall disclose her blood, and shall no more cover her slain** [*the bloodshed and crimes of the wicked will be exposed and punishment given out*].

ISAIAH 27

Selection: all verses

THIS CHAPTER IS a prophecy of the gathering of Israel in the last days. The Church will flourish and spread throughout the earth (verse 6), as prophesied in Daniel 2:35, 44–45. The "kingdom of the devil" spoken of in 1 Nephi 22:22, will ultimately be destroyed by Christ.

1 In that day [*spoken of in chapter 26, above*] **the Lord with his sore** [*hard, fierce*] **and great and strong sword shall punish leviathan** [*Satan; can also include all forces of evil, all who serve Satan*] **the piercing serpent, even leviathan that crooked serpent** [*the devil—see Revelation 12:9*]; **and he shall slay the dragon** that is in the sea [*Leviathan was a legendary sea monster representing evil*].

2 In that day sing ye unto her [*Israel*], **A vineyard of red wine** [*symbolizing a productive people to the Lord*].

3 I the Lord do keep it [*my vineyard, Israel*]; **I will water it every moment: lest any hurt it, I will keep it night and day** [*so that it will flourish as described in verse 6*].

4 Fury is not in me: who would set the briers and thorns [*the wicked*] **against me in battle** [*who dares to fight against the Lord*]? **I would go through them, I would burn them together** [*all of them*].

5 Or let him [*Israel*] **take hold of my strength** [*repent and come unto Me*], **that he may make peace with me; and he shall make peace with me** [*prophetic!*].

6 He [*God*] **shall cause them** [*Israel*] **that come of Jacob** [*the father of the twelve sons who became the twelve tribes of Israel*] **to take root** [*Israel will be restored*]: **Israel shall blossom and bud, and fill the face of the world with fruit** [*the blessings of righteousness and salvation*].

Without help, the pronouns in verse 7, next, can be quite confusing.

7 ¶ Hath **he** [*God*] smitten **him** [*Israel*], as **he** [*God*] smote **those** [*Israel's enemies*] that smote **him** [*Israel*]? or is **he** [*Israel*] slain according to [*like*] the slaughter of **them** [*Israel's enemies*] that are slain by him [God]? [Has God been as hard on his people, Israel, as on her enemies? Answer: No!]

8 In measure [moderation], **when it** [Israel] **shooteth forth, thou wilt debate with it** [prune it, discipline it]: **he** [God] **stayeth his rough wind in the day of the east wind** [God could destroy you with a really "rough" wind, but instead he sends the terrible east wind, a hot, dry wind off the Arabian Desert that devastates crops and helps humble you. In German, this says "You mete to them what is needed to set them straight so You can set them free." Jeremiah 30:11 in the King James Version says the same thing and is much clearer than the King James translation of verse 8, above.]

> We will include Jeremiah 30:11 here, so you can read it along with verse 8, above:
>
> **Jeremiah 30:11**
> 11 **For I** *am* **with thee**, saith the LORD, to save thee: though I make a full end of all nations whither I **have scattered thee, yet will I not make a full end of thee** [you will not be destroyed completely]: but I **will correct** [discipline] **thee in measure**, and will not leave thee altogether unpunished.

9 By this [the rough times, refiner's fire referred to in verse 8] **therefore shall the iniquity** [wickedness] **of Jacob** [Israel] **be purged** [rooted out]; **and this is all the fruit** [the product of Israel's wickedness—the

consequences designed by God to purge wickedness out of them] **to take away his** [Israel's] **sin; when he** [God] **maketh all the stones of the altar** [used in idol worship] **as chalkstones that are beaten in sunder** [into pieces], **the groves** [used in idol worship] **and images** [used in idol worship] **shall not stand up** [your false religions, upon which you have relied, will crumble].

10 Yet [the time will come that] **the defenced city** [established wickedness] **shall be desolate**, and the habitation forsaken [abandoned], and left like a wilderness: **there shall the calf feed** [in effect, where you once lived will become a place for animals to live], and there shall he [the calf] lie down, and consume the branches thereof [nothing will be left of you and your wickedness].

11 When the boughs thereof are withered, they shall be broken off: the women come, and set them on fire [women will use what is left for cooking fires; symbolically, wickedness will be destroyed completely by fire]: for **it is a people of no understanding** [of the gospel, because they don't want it]: **therefore** [that is why] **he that made them will not have mercy on them**, and he [God] that formed them will shew them no favour.

> Isaiah now switches topics somewhat, and prophesies

of the latter-day gathering of Israel, "one by one."

12 ¶ And it shall come to pass in that day [*the last days*], **that the Lord shall beat** [*glean*] **off from the channel of the river** [*from Mesopotamia*] **unto the stream of Egypt** [*the Nile River; gather Israel out of the whole world*], **and ye shall be gathered one by one, O ye children of Israel** [*the righteous shall be gathered to Christ from the whole earth*].

13 And it shall come to pass in that day, that the great trumpet shall be blown [*to signal the gathering*], **and they shall come which were ready to perish in the land of Assyria** [*symbolic of the wicked world*], **and the outcasts in the land of Egypt** [*the righteous, who have been "outcasts" in the wicked world*], **and shall worship the Lord in the holy mount at Jerusalem** [*in the holy temples*].

ISAIAH 28

Selection: all verses

ISAIAH SPEAKS TO Israel (the northern ten tribes in his day, also referred to as "Ephraim") in verses 1–4. This message came probably somewhere around 724 BC, before the ten tribes were taken captive by the Assyrians in 722 BC.

1 Woe to the crown of pride [*the haughty Ephraimites at Samaria,*

capital city of Israel, who have not yet come under Assyrian control and have boasted about their invincibility], **to the drunkards of Ephraim** [*northern Israel is "drunk," out of control with wickedness*], **whose glorious beauty is a fading flower** [*on the way out*], **which are on the head of the fat valleys** [*rich, productive land area in Samaria*] **of them that are overcome with wine** [*you are out of control with wickedness*]!

2 Behold, the Lord hath a mighty and strong one [*Shalmaneser, the Assyrian king and his armies*], **which as a tempest of hail and a destroying storm, as a flood of mighty waters overflowing** [*compare with Isaiah 8:7*], **shall cast down** to the earth with the hand [*the Assyrians will flood your land and conquer you*].

3 The crown of pride, the drunkards of Ephraim, shall be trodden under feet [*Israel, the northern ten tribes, will be destroyed; this happens in 722 BC via Assyria*]:

We have mentioned several times that one of the techniques used by ancient prophets was repetition. We are seeing another example of that in the verses that follow.

4 And the glorious beauty, which is on the head of the fat valley, shall be a fading flower, and as the hasty fruit [*early fruit; the first ripe fruit on the tree*] **before the summer;**

which when he that looketh upon it seeth, while it is yet in his hand he eateth it up [*it doesn't last long once someone has spotted it, in other words, you will be "gobbled up" quickly like the first ripe fruit of the season*].

5 In that day [*last days or Millennium*] shall the Lord of hosts be for a crown of glory, and for a diadem [*crown*] of beauty, unto the residue [*the righteous who are left*] of his people [*the Savior will lead you, as opposed to the proud, haughty drunkards referred to in verse 1*],

6 And for a spirit of judgment to him that sitteth in judgment, and for strength to them that turn the battle to the gate [*Christ will provide strength to overcome all enemies and "push them back to where they came from"*].

7 ¶ But they [*Israel's leaders*] also have erred through wine, and through strong drink are out of the way; the [*false*] priest and the [*false*] prophet have erred through strong drink, they are swallowed up of wine, they are out of the way through strong drink; they err in vision, they stumble in judgment [*apostasy; out of control literally and symbolically*].

8 For all tables are full of vomit and filthiness, so that there is no place clean [*apostasy has completely penetrated the nation*].

9 ¶ Whom shall he [*the Lord*] teach knowledge [*of the gospel*]? and whom shall he make to understand doctrine? [*answer:*] them that are weaned from the milk, and drawn from the breasts [*toddlers; in other words, start teaching them while very young*].

Verse 10, next, is a rather well-known quote from Isaiah.

10 For precept must be upon precept, precept upon precept; line upon line, line upon line; here a little, and there a little [*a lifelong process starting very young*]:

11 For with stammering [*not understandable*] lips and another tongue [*a tongue "foreign" to the wicked; in other words, through the Holy Ghost*] will he speak to this people.

12 To whom he said, This is the rest [*peace of God*] wherewith ye may cause the weary to rest; and this is the refreshing [*available from God through righteous living*]: yet they [*Israel*] would not [*didn't want to*] hear [*in verse 10, the Lord tells them how he would help them bit by bit, not overwhelm them, but they don't want to hear such stuff*].

Next, in verse 13, Isaiah repeats again that the stubborn people of the northern ten tribes (Israel) had plenty of opportunity to hear and understand the gospel. They were given the opportunity so that they would be accountable for the consequences when they rebelled. This is the law of justice in action.

Remember that at this point in history, the northern ten tribes are called "Israel," and the southern two tribes (Judah and Benjamin) are called "Judah."

13 But **the word of the Lord was unto them precept upon precept,** precept upon precept; **line upon line,** line upon line; here a little, and there a little; **that they might go, and fall backward** [*apostasy isn't just "falling"; it is retrogressing—falling backward*], and **be broken,** and **snared,** and **taken** [*by Satan; in other words, when ignored, the word of God condemns*].

Next, Isaiah turns his attention to the haughty people of Judah.

14 ¶ **Wherefore hear the word of the Lord, ye scornful men** [*scoffers*], **that rule this people** which is in Jerusalem [*Isaiah now speaks to the people in Jerusalem in his day*].

15 **Because ye have said** [*boasted*], **We have made a covenant with death, and with hell are we at agreement** [*we have an "agreement" with death and hell*]; **when the overflowing scourge** [*that all the prophets keep saying will come*] **shall pass through, it shall not come unto us: for we have made lies our refuge** [*we have found that wickedness does pay!*], **and under falsehood have we hid ourselves** [*we will live wickedly and get away with it!*]:

16 ¶ **Therefore** [*because of your wickedness, boasting, and so forth*] **thus saith the Lord God, Behold, I lay in Zion for a foundation a stone** [*the Savior*], **a tried** [*proven reliable*] **stone, a precious corner stone** [*Ephesians 2:20*], **a sure foundation** [*the Lord is the only one with whom you can strike agreements and have guaranteed results*]: **he that believeth shall not make haste** [*will not flee; he that lives righteously will not have to flee before the face of the Lord*].

17 **Judgment also will I lay to the line** [*carpenter's line, used to build straight and true*], **and righteousness to the plummet** [*plumb bob (carpenter's tool used to build precisely); symbolic of the fact that all things about the Savior and His gospel are exact and true*]: **and the hail shall sweep away the refuge of lies** [*in other words, you won't get away with your boast in verse 15*], **and the waters** [*can refer to the Assyrians, see 8:7; could also refer to Christ as "living water," as in John 4:10*] **shall overflow the hiding place** [*of the wicked*].

18 ¶ And **your covenant with death** [*verse 15*] **shall be disannulled** [*cancelled*], **and your agreement with hell shall not stand;** when the overflowing scourge [*referred to boastfully in verse 15*] shall pass through, then **ye shall be trodden down by it** [*the wicked will be destroyed*].

19 From the time that it [*the punishment of God*] **goeth forth it shall take you: for morning by morning shall it pass over, by day and by night** [*continuously*]: **and it shall be a vexation** [*pure terror*] **only to understand the report** [*God's judgments*].

Isaiah now refers to the proud boast in verse 15 that they could be comfortable and protected in sin. He uses the imagery of a bed that is too short for the person trying to sleep in it.

20 For **the bed is shorter than that a man can stretch himself on it** [*you can't ever get completely comfortable in the bed of sin you've made for yourselves to lie in*]: **and the covering** [*the blanket of lies you made for yourselves*] **narrower than that he can wrap himself in it** [*you can't get completely comfortable in your blanket of sin!*].

21 For **the Lord shall rise up as in mount Perazim** [*David attacked and smote the Philistines there, with the Lord's help*], **he shall be wroth as in the valley of Gibeon** [*where the Lord killed Joshua's enemies, the Amorites, with huge hailstones*], **that he may do his work, his strange work; and bring to pass his act, his strange** [*unusual*] **act.**

Next, Isaiah issues a strong warning to these arrogant people.

22 Now therefore **be ye not mockers** [*don't scoff at God's word*], **lest your bands be made strong** [*lest you be totally enslaved by wickedness*]: **for I** [*Isaiah*] **have heard from the Lord God of hosts a consumption, even determined upon the whole earth** [*I've heard God will annihilate the wicked*].

23 ¶ **Give ye ear, and hear my voice; hearken, and hear my speech.**

24 **Doth the plowman** [*farmer; symbolic of God*] **plow all day to sow** [*getting ready to plant*]: **doth he open and break the clods of his ground** [*continuously*]? [*Does the Lord just keep plowing, preparing and preparing the ground forever, or does he go on to the next steps, planting, harvesting, and so forth? In other words, "Do you think Judgment Day will never come, that the Lord will never get around to harvest time?"*]

Isaiah answers his own question in verse 25, next.

25 **When he** [*the farmer*] **hath made plain the face thereof** [*has the ground plowed and leveled*], **doth he not cast abroad** [*plant, throw the seeds by hand*] **the fitches** [*dill seeds*], **and scatter the cummin, and cast in the principal wheat** [*the main crop*] **and the appointed** [*planned on*] **barley and the rie in their place** [*doesn't the farmer plan carefully and then work his plan*]?

26 For **his** [*the plowman's*] **God doth instruct him to discretion, and doth teach him.**

Next, Isaiah uses some different methods of harvesting used in his day to illustrate that the Lord carefully applies differing harvesting methods to harvest His people, depending on their personalities.

27 For **the fitches** [*a plant producing small seeds that were harvested and used like we use pepper*] **are not threshed with a threshing instrument, neither is a cart wheel** [*used in harvesting larger grain seeds such as wheat*] **turned about** [*around and around*] **upon the cummin** [*very small seeds*]; but the fitches are beaten out with a staff, and the cummin with a rod [*God will use appropriate methods to "harvest" all the righteous out from the wicked, according to their personalities, aptitudes, talents, and so forth*].

28 Bread corn [*cereal grain*] is bruised [*ground in a mill*]; because he will not ever [*forever*] be threshing it, nor break it with the wheel of his cart, nor bruise it with his horsemen. [*In the Martin Luther German Bible, this verse says basically that cereal grain is ground to make bread, not threshed to the point of destruction when it is threshed with wagon wheels and horses.*]

29 **This also cometh forth from the Lord of hosts** [*this is how the Lord goes about harvesting the righteous*], **which is wonderful in counsel** [*who is wonderful in how He plans His work; see Isaiah 19:3, 25:1*], and **excellent in working** [*German: carries it out wonderfully*].

ISAIAH 29

Selection: all verses

THIS CHAPTER COMPARES with 2 Nephi 27 in the Book of Mormon. The Book of Mormon rendition provides many changes for this chapter in the Bible. We will draw heavily from it as we proceed.

This prophecy was given by Isaiah about 700 BC, near the end of his ministry. It deals with the last days, including the restoration of the gospel through the Prophet Joseph Smith, giving many specific details about the coming forth of the Book of Mormon. It is a chapter of scripture that bears extra strong witness of the truthfulness of prophecies given by the Lord through His chosen servants, such as Isaiah.

Isaiah begins by prophesying about the out-of-control wickedness that will prevail among all peoples upon the earth in the last days.

1 Woe to Ariel [*Jerusalem; Zion in 2 Nephi 27:3*], to Ariel, **the city where David dwelt!** add ye year to year; let them kill sacrifices [*keep right on going as you are with your wickedness and empty rituals; it will do you no good!*].

2 Yet I will [*I will continue to*]

distress Ariel, and there shall be heaviness and sorrow: and **it shall be unto me as Ariel** [*it shall become a proper Zion*].

3 And **I will camp against thee** [*the Lord will humble his rebellious covenant people*] round about, and will lay siege against thee with a mount [*mound of dirt*], and I will raise forts against thee [*as is the case in a planned military action; in other words, you will be chastened until you repent*].

4 **And thou** [*Ariel*] **shalt be brought down** [*humbled*], and shalt speak out of the ground, and **thy speech shall be low out of the dust**, and **thy voice shall be, as of one** that hath a familiar spirit [*a dead relative speaking from the spirit world*], **out of the ground**, and thy speech shall whisper out of the dust [*the Book of Mormon came "out of the ground" and in it, the Nephites, our dead Israelite "relatives" who came from Ariel; in other words, Jerusalem, speak to us as from the dust*].

5 Moreover **the multitude of thy strangers** [*the number of your enemies*] **shall be like small dust** [*countless*], and the multitude of the terrible ones [*tyrants*] shall be as chaff that passeth away [*that blows away in the wind, in other words, countless*]: yea, **it shall be at an instant suddenly** [*the things that humble you; see

first part of verse 4; will catch you off guard so that you will hardly be able to believe they are happening so rapidly and nobody is stopping them].

6 **Thou shalt be visited of** [*disciplined or punished by*] **the Lord** of hosts with thunder, and with earthquake, and great noise, with storm and tempest, and the flame of devouring fire.

In verses 7–8, next, Isaiah describes the ultimate failure and frustration of the wicked who fight against the work of the Lord.

7 ¶ And the multitude of **all the nations that fight against Ariel** [*the Lord's people; Zion, 2 Nephi 27:3*], even all that fight against her and her munition, and that distress her, **shall be as a dream of a night vision.**

8 It [*their persecution of the Saints*] **shall even be** [*unto them, 2 Nephi 27:3—enemy nations*] **as when an hungry man dreameth, and, behold, he eateth; but he awaketh, and his soul is empty** [*he is still hungry*]: or as when a thirsty man dreameth, and, behold, he drinketh [*in his dream*]; but he awaketh, and, behold, he is faint, and his soul hath appetite: **so shall the multitude of all the nations be, that fight against mount Zion** [*persecutors of the Saints never feel satisfied, are still "hungry and thirsty" for more, can't leave us alone*].

9 ¶ Stay yourselves, and wonder [*you wicked people, stop and think*]; cry ye out, and cry: they [*the wicked, 2 Nephi 27:4*] are drunken [*out of control*], but not with wine; they stagger [*stumble around*], but not with strong drink [*in other words, they are "drunk" with wickedness, out of control because they have no prophets to lead them, as mentioned in verse 10, next*].

> The Book of Mormon makes an important doctrinal correction to the Bible, in verse 10, next. It is not the Lord who causes spiritual darkness to come upon people; rather, it is the people themselves who close their eyes to truth and light and who are the cause of spiritual darkness.

10 For the Lord hath poured out upon you the spirit of deep sleep [*spiritual darkness*], and hath closed [**"ye have closed,"** *2 Nephi 27:5*] your eyes: the prophets and your rulers, the seers hath he covered [*"because of your iniquity," 2 Nephi 27:5*].

> Next, Isaiah begins a marvelous prophecy about the coming forth of the Book of Mormon in the last days. He gives an amazing amount of specific detail, which, as you will see, was fulfilled.

11 And the vision of all [*German: the vision of all the prophets, in other words, all of the scripture*] is become unto you [*Israelites who are spiritually dead*] as the words of a book [*Book of Mormon—see footnote 11a*]

in your Bible] that is sealed [*because you refuse to hearken to the scriptures, they might just as well be sealed and unreadable to you, like the copy of characters from the Book of Mormon plates*], which men [*Martin Harris, with the help of Joseph Smith*] deliver to one that is learned [*Professor Charles Anthon of Colombia College in New York City, February 1828*], saying, Read this, I pray thee: and he [*Charles Anthon*] saith, I cannot; for it is sealed:

> You can read the account of Martin Harris and Charles Anthon, prophesied above, in the Pearl of Great Price, Joseph Smith—History 1:63–65.

12 And the book [*the gold plates*] is delivered to him [*Joseph Smith*] that is not learned [*educated, like Professor Anthon*], saying, Read this, I pray thee: and he saith, I am not learned [*I can't translate it without God's help*].

13 ¶ Wherefore the Lord said, Forasmuch as this people draw near me with their mouth, and with their lips do honour me, but have removed their heart far from me [*they are spiritually dead*], and their fear toward me is taught by the precept [*traditions*] of men [*people have gone far astray from truth*]:

14 Therefore, behold, I will proceed to do a marvellous work among this people, even a

marvellous ["*astonishing*" *as used in Old Testament Hebrew*] **work and a wonder** [*the Restoration of the gospel*]: **for the wisdom of their wise men shall perish** [*revealed truth cuts through falsehood*], **and the understanding of their prudent men shall be hid** [*false philosophies and false scientific conclusions fade away in light of truth*].

15 Woe unto them [*the wicked*] **that seek deep to hide their counsel** [*plans*] **from the Lord, and their works are in the dark, and they say, Who seeth us? and who knoweth us?** [*We can get away with wickedness without getting exposed—typical thinking of wicked people.*]

16 Surely your turning of things upside down [*foolish perversion of the truth*] **shall be esteemed as** [*is the same as*] **the potter's clay: for shall the work** [*the pot*] **say of him that made it** [*the potter*], **He made me not? or shall the thing framed say of him that framed it, He had no understanding?** [*He doesn't know me; I have successfully hidden from God. In other words, you wicked are just as foolish as the potter's clay that claims it made itself into a pot and has no responsibility to its maker.*]

Next, beginning with verse 17, Isaiah tells us that the coming forth of the Book of Mormon will be the key event signaling the beginning of the Restoration of the gospel in the last days and the fulfilling of the many prophecies that will culminate with the Second Coming. Included in these prophecies are the gathering of the Jews and their establishment as a nation again in the Holy Land.

17 Is it not yet a very little while [*after the Book of Mormon comes forth*], **and Lebanon** [*the Holy Land*] **shall be turned into a fruitful field, and the fruitful field shall be esteemed as a forest?** [*In other words, Israel will blossom with forests and in other ways (including eventual spiritual conversion) after the Restoration.*]

18 ¶ And in that day [*the time of the Restoration of the gospel, with the Book of Mormon leading the way*] **shall the** [*spiritually*] **deaf hear the words of the book, and the eyes of the** [*spiritually*] **blind shall see out of obscurity, and out of darkness** [*as a result of the Book of Mormon and the Restoration, the spiritually deaf and blind will be healed*].

19 The meek also shall increase their joy in the Lord, and the poor among men shall rejoice in the Holy One of Israel [*the righteous will know the Savior again*].

20 For the terrible one [*tyrant*] **is brought to nought, and the scorner** [*scoffer*] **is consumed, and all that watch for iniquity are cut off** [*the restored truth will expose wickedness and eventually overthrow it*]:

In verse 21, next, Isaiah describes the crippling corruption in governments and judicial systems in the last days.

21 That make a man an offender for a word [*via unjust lawsuits, corrupt judicial system, and so forth*], **and lay a snare for him that reproveth in the gate** [*try to eliminate honest people in government, and those who try to expose corruption in government*], **and turn aside the just for a thing of nought** [*destroy the effectiveness of honest government and judicial leaders; replace truth and honesty with lies*].

Next, Isaiah uses his great skill as a writer to create in our minds a picture of a rather embarrassed Jacob (the father of the twelve sons who became the twelve tribes of Israel). In the past, he has been embarrassed by the behaviors of his posterity, rebellious Israel. However, because of the restoration of the gospel in the last days and the gathering of Israel, they will finally become a righteous people. He is no longer embarrassed to be their "father;" rather, he is humbly proud of them.

22 Therefore thus saith the Lord, who redeemed Abraham, **concerning the house of Jacob** [*Israel; implies "I redeemed Abraham and I can and will redeem you."*], **Jacob shall not now be ashamed, neither shall his face now wax pale** [*Father Jacob, Israel, will no longer have to be embarrassed by the behavior of his posterity*].

23 But when he [*Jacob*] **seeth his children** [*his posterity*], **the work of mine hands** [*who are now finally righteous—"My people"*], **in the midst of him, they shall sanctify my name, and sanctify the Holy One of Jacob** [*the Savior*], **and shall fear** [*respect*] **the God of Israel.** [*Isaiah here has said, in many ways, that in the last days Israel will return to God.*]

In concluding this vision, Isaiah summarizes the marvelous effects of the Book of Mormon and the Restoration of the gospel through the Prophet Joseph Smith.

24 They also that erred in spirit shall come to understanding, and they that murmured shall learn doctrine [*through the Book of Mormon and the Restoration of the Church of Jesus Christ*].

ISAIAH 30

Selection: all verses

IN THIS CHAPTER, we will see the scattering of Israel because they rejected their prophets. Then we will see the gathering and eventual coming of the Savior and the destruction of the wicked.

The historical setting is 705–701 BC. King Sargon II, of Assyria, has died. Judah joins the Philistines and Phoenicians in rebellion against Assyria. Judah makes a treaty for protection with Egypt (which sometimes is used to symbolize Satan's kingdom in Old Testament writings).

In verse 1, Isaiah points out that Judah has turned to political alliances for protection from her enemies, rather than repenting and turning to God for protection.

1 Woe to the rebellious children, saith the LORD, that take counsel [make political plans], but not of me; and that cover with a covering [alliance], but not of my spirit [not approved by God], that they may add sin to sin [add insult to injury; make things worse]:

2 That walk to go down into Egypt [turn to Egypt for help], and have not asked at my mouth [haven't asked My permission]; to strengthen themselves in the strength of Pharaoh, and to trust in the shadow [protection] of Egypt!

3 Therefore [because you have done this] shall the strength of Pharaoh be your shame [downfall], and the trust in the shadow [protection] of Egypt your confusion [your pact with Egypt will lead to your ruin; you should have turned to God rather than man for help].

4 For his [Pharaoh's] princes [leaders] were at Zoan [Tanis], and his ambassadors came to Hanes [leaders from one end of Egypt to the other worked out the treaty with Judah].

5 They [Judah] were [will be] all ashamed of [disappointed by] a people [Egypt] that could not [can not] profit them, nor be an help nor profit, but a shame, and also a reproach [this deal with Egypt will bring shame and scorn to Judah].

6 The burden of [message of doom for those of Judah who travel with loads of gifts on animals toward Egypt, verses 2–7] the beasts of the south: into the land of trouble and anguish, from whence come the young and old lion, the viper and fiery flying serpent, they [Judah] will carry their riches upon the shoulders of young asses, and their treasures upon the bunches of camels, to a people [Egypt] that shall not profit them.

7 For the Egyptians shall help in vain, and to no purpose: therefore have I cried concerning this, Their strength is to sit still [Egypt won't help you at all!].

Next, the Lord instructs Isaiah to be sure to write this prophecy and warning down as a written witness against these wicked people.

8 ¶ Now go, write it before them in a table, and note it in a book [which will eventually become scripture], that it may be for the time to come for ever and ever [write this down as a witness against Judah]:

9 That this [Judah] is a rebellious people, lying children, children

that will not hear the law of the LORD:

10 Which say to the seers, See not; and to the prophets, Prophesy not unto us right things, speak unto us smooth things [comfortable false doctrines], prophesy deceits:

11 Get you out of the way, turn aside out of the path, cause the Holy One of Israel to cease from before us [tell God to quit bothering us].

12 Wherefore thus saith the Holy One of Israel, Because ye despise [spurn, intentionally ignore] this word, and trust in oppression [German: wickedness] and perverseness, and stay [depend] thereon:

13 Therefore this iniquity shall be to you as a breach [broken section in a protective wall] ready to fall, swelling [bulging] out in a high wall, whose breaking cometh suddenly at an instant [you are living on borrowed time; you have broken the covenant that could protect you like a wall by making covenants with Egypt rather than God].

14 And he [Christ] shall break it as the breaking of the potters' vessel that is broken in pieces; he shall not spare: so that there shall not be found in the bursting of it a sherd [fragment] to take fire from the hearth, or to take water withal

out of the pit [there won't be a piece big enough left to take a fire start from the fireplace or to dip a little water from the well; nothing usable remains].

Next, the Lord tells these rebellious people how they could be saved from the fate just described.

15 For thus saith the Lord GOD, the Holy One of Israel; In returning [to God] and rest shall ye be saved [German: you could be saved]; in quietness [peacefulness] and in confidence [faith in God] shall be your strength: and ye would not.

16 But ye said [bragged], No; for we will flee [into battle against Assyria] upon horses [symbolize victory]; therefore [because of your rebellion] shall ye flee [from Assyria's armies]: and, We will ride upon the swift [Judah bragged]; therefore shall they [Assyrians] that pursue you be swift [it will be exactly opposite of what you brag, Judah].

17 One thousand [of Judah] shall flee at the rebuke of one [Assyrian]; at the rebuke of five [Assyrians] shall [German: all of you] ye flee: till ye be left as a beacon upon the top of a mountain, and as an ensign on an hill [lonely, nobody left, scattered].

18 ¶ And therefore will the LORD wait [because of your wickedness, the Lord will have to wait], that he may

be gracious unto you [*at a future time*], and therefore will he be exalted, that he may have mercy upon you: for the LORD is a God of judgment [*justice*]: **blessed are all they that wait for** [*German: trust in*] **him.**

> Isaiah now describes the ultimate in paradisiacal conditions for those who do trust in the Lord.

19 For the people shall dwell in Zion at Jerusalem: **thou shalt weep no more: he will be very gracious unto thee at the voice of thy cry; when he shall hear it, he will answer thee.**

20 And **though the Lord give you the bread of adversity, and the water of affliction** [*even though you go through some trying times*], yet shall not thy teachers [*thy teacher, the Lord*] be removed into a corner any more, **but thine eyes shall see thy teachers:**

21 And **thine ears shall hear a word behind thee, saying, This is the way, walk ye in it**, when ye turn to the right hand, and when ye turn to the left [*you will be surrounded with guidance and truth*].

22 **Ye shall defile** [*cease to worship*] **also the covering of thy graven images of silver** [*your graven images covered with silver*], and the ornament of thy molten images of gold: thou shalt cast them away as a menstruous cloth [*they will be totally repulsive to you*]; thou shalt say unto it, Get thee hence [*you will shudder at the thought of idol worship*].

23 **Then shall he give the rain of thy seed, that thou shalt sow the ground withal** [*you will prosper*]; and bread of the increase of the earth, and it shall be fat and plenteous: in that day shall thy cattle feed in large pastures [*things will go well when Israel repents and is gathered*].

24 **The oxen likewise and the young asses that ear the ground** [*work the ground in agriculture*] shall eat clean provender [*hay*], which hath been winnowed with the shovel and with the fan.

25 And **there shall be** upon every high mountain, and upon every high hill, **rivers and streams of waters** in the day of the great slaughter, when the towers fall [*when your enemies have been destroyed*].

26 **Moreover the light of the moon shall be as the light of the sun, and the light of the sun shall be sevenfold, as the light of seven days** [*everything will be better than you can imagine*], in the day that the LORD bindeth up the breach of his people, and healeth the stroke of their wound [*Christ heals when people repent*].

27 ¶ Behold, the name of **the LORD**

cometh from far, burning with his anger, and the burden thereof is heavy: his lips are full of indignation, and his tongue as a devouring fire [the wicked are destroyed]:

28 And his breath, as an overflowing stream [flood], shall reach to the midst of the neck, to sift [German: destroy] the nations [the wicked] with the sieve of vanity [German: until they are all filtered out, destroyed, gone]: and there shall be a bridle in the jaws of the people, causing them to err [they have allowed wickedness to take control of them; that's why they are destroyed].

29 Ye [the righteous survivors] shall have a song, as in the night when a holy solemnity is kept; and gladness of heart, as when one goeth with a pipe [German: flute] to come into the mountain of the LORD, to the mighty One of Israel [the Savior].

30 And the LORD shall cause his glorious voice to be heard, and shall shew the lighting down of his arm [will come crashing down upon the wicked], with the indignation of his anger, and with the flame of a devouring fire, with scattering, and tempest, and hailstones.

31 For through the voice [power] of the LORD shall the Assyrian [the enemy now threatening Judah] be beaten down, which smote [Israel] with a rod.

32 And in every place where the grounded staff shall pass [every stroke of the rod of punishment], which the LORD shall lay upon him [Assyria], it shall be with tabrets and harps: and in battles of shaking [several "waves" of battle] will he fight with it.

33 For Tophet [the "Place of Burning," hell] is ordained of old [was planned for in the beginning]; yea, for the king [of Assyria] it is prepared; he [God] hath made it deep and large [there is plenty of room in hell for the Assyrians and all other wicked]: the pile thereof is fire and much wood [plenty of fuel to burn them]; the breath of the LORD, like a stream of brimstone [fiery molten sulfur], doth kindle it [the Lord is prepared to destroy the wicked].

ISAIAH 31

Selection: all verses

IN CHAPTER 30, we learned that the nation of Judah had determined to turn to Egypt for help against Assyria. In this chapter, Isaiah continues to warn them about this mistake.

1 Woe to them [Judah] that go down to Egypt for help; and stay [rely] on horses, and trust in chariots [the military might of Egypt], because they [Egyptian soldiers] are many; and in horsemen, because they are very strong; but

they look not unto the Holy One of Israel, neither seek the LORD [*Judah should turn to the Lord instead of Egypt for help*]!

2 Yet he [*the Lord*] also **is wise, and will bring evil** [*calamity upon the wicked*], **and will not call back** [*retract*] **his words: but will arise against the house of the evildoers, and against the help** [*helpers*] **of them that work iniquity.**

3 **Now the Egyptians are men, and not God;** and their horses flesh, and not spirit. When the LORD shall stretch out his hand, both he that helpeth shall fall, and he that is holpen [*helped*] shall fall down, and they all shall fail together [*Egypt and Judah will both fail*].

> Next, Isaiah reminds the Jews that the Lord does indeed have power to protect them against their enemies.

4 For **thus hath the LORD spoken unto me** [*Isaiah*], **Like as the lion** and the young lion roaring on his prey, **when a multitude of shepherds is called forth against him,** he will not be afraid of their voice, nor abase himself for the noise of them: **so shall the LORD of hosts come down to fight for mount Zion, and for the hill thereof** [*the Lord will be as unstoppable among the wicked as a lion among sheep*].

5 **As birds flying** [*hovering over their young, protecting them*], **so will the LORD of hosts defend Jerusalem;** defending also he will deliver it; and passing over he will preserve it.

6 **Turn ye unto him** [*the Lord*] from whom the children of Israel have deeply revolted [*please repent*].

7 For **in that day** [*if and when you repent*] **every man shall cast away his idols of silver, and his idols of gold,** which your own hands have made unto you for a sin [*turn away from your sinful idol worship*].

8 ¶ **Then shall the Assyrian fall** with the sword, not of a mighty man; and the sword, not of a mean [*poor*] man, shall devour him: but he shall flee from the sword, and his young men shall be discomfited [*put in slavery; God, not men, will overthrow Assyria*].

9 **And he shall pass over to his strong hold for fear** [*will retreat in fear*], **and his princes shall be afraid of the ensign,** saith the LORD, whose fire is in Zion, and his furnace in Jerusalem [*the power of the Lord can protect Zion, Jerusalem*].

ISAIAH 32

Selection: all verses

IN THIS CHAPTER, Isaiah prophesies that the day will come when Jesus Christ will rule and reign, but in the meantime, until the restoration of the gospel and the gathering of Israel, the land of Israel will be a wilderness.

1 Behold, **a king** [*Jesus*] **shall reign in righteousness, and princes** [*His leaders*] **shall rule in judgment** [*justice, fairness*].

2 **And a man** [*Jesus*] **shall be as an hiding place from the wind, and a covert** [*protection*] **from the tempest;** as rivers of water in a dry place, as the shadow of a great rock in a weary land [*Jesus will be our refuge and protection*].

> Next, Isaiah teaches what the effects of the Savior and His gospel will be upon those who listen, who have previously been spiritually blind and deaf.

3 **And the eyes of them that see shall not be dim** [*the spiritual eyes of those who see the gospel, who were previously spiritually blind, shall no longer be dim*], **and the ears of them that hear shall hearken** [*people will be blessed with understanding and discernment*].

4 **The heart** [*mind*] **also of the rash** [*impulsive*] **shall understand** knowledge [*have good judgment*], **and the**

tongue of the stammerers shall be ready to speak plainly [*those who previously could not explain the purposes of life according to the gospel will now discuss the gospel plainly*].

5 **The vile person** [*villain*] **shall be no more called liberal** [*noble*], **nor the churl** [*miser; cruel financier*] **said to be bountiful** [*people will be recognized for what they really are, not what they appear to be*].

> In verses 6–8, Isaiah describes what the motives of people alluded to in verse 5 really are like.

6 For **the vile person will speak villany,** and his heart **will work iniquity,** to practise **hypocrisy,** and to **utter error against the LORD,** to make empty the soul of the hungry [*oppress the poor and needy*], and he will cause the drink of the thirsty to fail.

7 **The instruments** [*devices*] **also of the churl** [*wicked moneylenders*] **are evil: he deviseth wicked devices to destroy the poor with lying words** [*trickery*], even when the needy speaketh right [*is in the right*].

8 But **the liberal** [*noble*] **deviseth liberal** [*honorable, righteous*] **things;** and by liberal things shall he stand [*German: he will hold to honorable thoughts and actions*].

> Next, Isaiah warns the women against the spiritual dangers that confront them.

9 ¶ Rise up, ye women [German: proud women] that are at ease [overconfident about their safety; see 2 Nephi 28:24]; hear my voice, ye careless daughters [overconfident, complacent, too secure to change your ways]; give ear unto my speech [message].

10 Many days and years shall ye be troubled, ye careless women: for the vintage [vineyard] shall fail [not produce], the gathering [harvest] shall not come [famine].

11 Tremble, ye women that are at ease; be troubled, ye careless ones: strip you [of pride], and make you bare, and gird sackcloth upon your loins [humble yourselves].

In verses 12–14, Isaiah tells of a long period of destruction soon to come upon unsuspecting Israelites.

12 They shall lament for the teats [beat upon the breast in mourning], for the pleasant fields, for the fruitful vine [they will long for the good times].

13 Upon the land of my people shall come up thorns and briers; yea, upon all the houses of joy in the joyous city [rough times are coming because of wickedness]:

14 Because the [your] palaces shall be forsaken; the multitude of the city shall be left [deserted]; the forts and towers shall be for dens [places of habitation for wild beasts] for ever, a joy of wild asses, a pasture of flocks [you will be scattered and your lands left lonely and desolate];

Isaiah now mentions the peaceful conditions to come upon Israel in a future day of righteousness.

15 Until the spirit be poured upon us from on high, and the wilderness be [become] a fruitful field, and the fruitful field be counted for a forest.

16 Then judgment [justice, fairness] shall dwell in the wilderness [in formerly apostate Israel], and righteousness remain in the fruitful field.

17 And the work [result] of righteousness shall be peace; and the effect [result] of righteousness quietness [lack of turmoil] and assurance [security] for ever.

18 And my people shall dwell in a peaceable habitation, and in sure [safe] dwellings, and in quiet resting places [German: splendid peace];

19 When it shall hail [destruction upon the wicked], coming down on the forest [wicked people?]; and the city [probably the proud and wicked] shall be low in a low place [brought down, humbled].

20 Blessed [happy] are ye [the

righteous] **that sow beside all waters** [German: everywhere], that send forth thither [everywhere] the feet of the ox and the ass [perhaps saying that there will be peace everywhere for the righteous].

ISAIAH 33

Selection: all verses

ISAIAH WILL NOW prophesy of great wickedness before the Second Coming of the Lord. Israel will be gathered. There will be great destruction among the wicked. The wicked will ultimately be destroyed by fire and the Savior will rule as our King during the Millennium.

The issue in verse 1 is that it seems as though the wicked often get away with sin without consequences. They don't.

1 Woe to thee [probably Sennacherib, king of Assyria, Isaiah 36:1; symbolic of all wicked who seem to get away with wickedness] **that spoilest, and thou wast not spoiled; and dealest treacherously, and they dealt not treacherously with thee!** when thou shalt cease to spoil, **thou shalt be spoiled;** and when thou shalt make an end to deal treacherously, they shall deal treacherously with thee [after the Lord is through using you to punish other wicked nations, you will get your just reward].

2 O LORD, be gracious unto us [Israel]; **we have waited for thee: be thou their** [our] **arm** [symbolic of power in biblical language] **every morning, our salvation also in the time of trouble.**

3 At the noise of the tumult the people fled [flee]; at the lifting up of thyself [Christ] the nations were [are] scattered.

4 And your spoil [Israel's remnants] **shall be gathered** [by missionaries] like the gathering of the caterpiller: as the running to and fro of locusts [perhaps describing missionaries going everywhere in the last days] shall he [they] run [collect] upon them [Israel].

5 The LORD is exalted; for he dwelleth on high: he hath filled Zion with judgment and righteousness.

Next, Isaiah teaches that the restored gospel will provide stability in the lives of those who embrace it.

6 And **wisdom and knowledge shall be the stability of thy times, and strength of salvation:** the fear of the LORD is his treasure [results of the Restoration].

Verses 7–9 refer back to the Assyrian attack.

7 Behold, their [wicked Israel's] **valiant ones** [wicked heroes] **shall cry without** [outside of Zion]: **the ambassadors of peace shall weep bitterly.**

8 The highways lie waste, the wayfaring man ceaseth [there are no more travelers]: he hath broken the covenant, he hath despised the cities, he regardeth no man.

9 The earth mourneth and languisheth: Lebanon is ashamed [the Holy Land is severely distressed] and hewn down: Sharon is like a wilderness; and Bashan and Carmel shake off their fruits.

10 Now will I rise, saith the LORD; now will I be exalted; now will I lift up myself [the time will come when God will take over from the wicked].

11 Ye shall conceive chaff, ye shall bring forth stubble [the end result of wicked lifestyles is nothing of value]: your breath, as fire, shall devour you [sow evil, harvest misery].

12 And the people shall be as the burnings of lime: as thorns cut up [as useless branches cut up for burning] shall they be burned in the fire.

13 ¶ Hear, ye that are far off [everybody in the whole world, listen up and acknowledge], what I have done; and, ye that are near, acknowledge my might [in the future the whole world will know God].

14 The sinners in Zion are afraid; fearfulness hath surprised [seized] the hypocrites. Who among us shall dwell with the devouring fire? who among us shall dwell with everlasting burnings [who will not be burned, destroyed—who can survive the presence of God]?

In verses 15–22, plus 24, next, Isaiah answers the question he posed in verse 14, above.

15 He that walketh righteously, and speaketh uprightly; he that despiseth the gain of oppressions [unrighteous profit at the expense of others], that shaketh his hands from holding of bribes [refuses bribes], that stoppeth his ears from hearing of blood, and shutteth his eyes from seeing evil [does not participate in evils];

16 He [the righteous] shall dwell on high: his place of defence shall be the munitions [fortress] of rocks: bread shall be given him; his waters shall be sure [reward to the righteous].

17 Thine eyes shall see the king [the Savior] in his beauty: they shall behold the land that is very far off [heaven?].

18 Thine heart shall meditate [soften, put down] terror. Where is the scribe [Assyrian tallyman, conqueror]? where is the receiver? where is he that counted the towers [Assyrian army? In other words, where are the wicked now?]?

19 Thou shalt not see a fierce

people [*foreign invaders*], a people of a deeper speech than thou canst perceive; of a stammering tongue, that thou canst not understand [*enemies who speak foreign languages*].

20 Look upon Zion, the city of our solemnities: **thine eyes shall see Jerusalem a quiet habitation,** a tabernacle that shall not be taken down; not one of the stakes thereof shall ever be removed, neither shall any of the cords thereof be broken [*the future has glorious things in store for the righteous*].

21 But there the glorious LORD will be unto us a place of broad rivers and streams; wherein shall go no galley [*enemy ships*] with oars, neither shall gallant ship pass thereby.

22 For the LORD is our judge, the LORD is our lawgiver, the LORD is our king; he will save us.

In verse 23, next, Isaiah describes the shutting down of the power of the wicked and compares it to the stopping of a ship.

23 Thy [*the wicked's*] **tacklings** [*ship's rigging*] **are loosed; they could not well strengthen their mast, they could not spread the sail** [*the wicked will be shut down*]: then is the prey of a great spoil divided; **the lame** [*the righteous; the wicked have considered the righteous to be lame, weak*] **take the prey** [*the wicked*].

24 And the inhabitant shall not say, I am sick: **the people that dwell therein shall be forgiven their iniquity.**

ISAIAH 34

Selection: all verses

THIS CHAPTER SPEAKS of the Second Coming and the destruction of the wicked. It contains Isaiah's harshest words against the wicked. It is a review of earlier chapters and is a companion chapter to chapter 35.

1 **Come near, ye nations** [*speaking to the whole world*], **to hear;** and hearken, ye people: let the earth hear, and all that is therein; the world, and all things that come forth of it.

Isaiah now speaks of the future as if it has already happened.

2 For **the indignation** [*righteous anger*] **of the LORD is upon all nations** [*all the wicked*], and his fury upon all their armies: **he hath utterly destroyed them,** he hath delivered them to the slaughter [*future; ultimate fate of the wicked*].

3 Their slain also shall be cast out, and their stink shall come up out of their carcases, and **the mountains shall be melted** [*soaked*] **with their blood.**

4 And all the host [*stars?*] of heaven shall be dissolved, and **the heavens shall be rolled together as a scroll** [*compare with Doctrine & Covenants 88:95, which speaks of the Second Coming*]: and all their host [*starry host?*] shall fall down, as the leaf falleth off from the vine, and as a falling fig from the fig tree [*perhaps goes with Doctrine & Covenants 133:49 and 88:95; Second Coming*].

5 For **my sword shall be bathed in heaven** [*bathed in blood*]: behold, **it shall come down upon Idumea** [*Edom; the world, see Doctrine & Covenants 1:36; connotes the wicked world*], and **upon the people of my curse** [*upon the wicked*], to judgment.

6 **The sword of the LORD is filled with blood** [*bathed in blood*], it is made fat with fatness [*covered with fat like a knife used in animal sacrifices*], and with the blood of lambs and goats, with the fat of the kidneys of rams: for the LORD hath a sacrifice in Bozrah [*the capital of Edom, a kingdom south of the Dead Sea*], and a great slaughter in the land of Idumea [*the wicked world; the sword of the Lord is going to come crashing down on the wicked of the world*].

7 And the unicorns [*wild oxen*] shall come down with them, and the bullocks [*bull calves*] with the bulls; and

their land shall be soaked with blood, and their dust [*land*] made fat with fatness [*covered with fat trimmed away by sword of justice*].

8 For **it is the day of the LORD's vengeance** [*it is time for the law of justice to take over*], and the year of recompences [*deserved rewards*] for the controversy [*German: avenging*] of Zion [*a day of avenging the wrongs done against Zion throughout the history of the world*].

9 **And the streams thereof** [*of Edom, the wicked*] **shall be turned into pitch** [*goes up in flames easily*], **and** the dust thereof into **brimstone** [*burning sulfur*], **and the land thereof shall become burning pitch** [*the wicked of the world will be destroyed by fire*].

10 **It shall not be quenched night nor day** [*no one can stop the destruction of the wicked*]; the smoke thereof shall go up for ever: from generation to generation it shall lie waste; none shall pass through it for ever and ever [*wickedness will be destroyed completely*].

> Isaiah often uses the imagery that now follows to emphasize the theme that the wicked will all be gone.

11 But the cormorant and the bittern [*lonely desert creatures*] **shall possess it; the owl also** and the raven shall dwell in it: and he [*the

Lord] shall stretch out upon it the line [*measuring tape*] of confusion, and the stones [*plumb line*] of emptiness [*Edom, the wicked, will not "measure up."*].

12 They shall call the nobles [*leaders*] thereof to the kingdom, **but none shall be there**, and all her [*Edom's*] princes [*leaders*] shall be nothing [*German: they will be people without a kingdom, will have nothing to rule over*].

13 And **thorns shall come up in her palaces**, nettles and brambles in the fortresses thereof: and **it shall be an habitation of dragons** [*jackals*], **and a court** [*home*] **for owls** [*none of the wicked will remain*].

14 The wild beasts of the desert shall also meet with the wild beasts [*hyenas*] of the island [*in other words, the wicked will all be gone, and the ruins where they once lived will be inhabited by creatures that don't like to live around people*], and the satyr [*wild goat*] shall cry to his fellow; the screech owl also shall rest there, and find for herself a place of rest.

15 There shall the great owl make her nest, and lay, and hatch, and gather under her shadow: there shall the vultures also be gathered, every one with her mate [*each of the animals mentioned above were considered unclean by the Israelites*].

16 ¶ Seek ye out of the book of the LORD, and read [*this is the word of God*]: no one of these [*unclean creatures*] shall fail, none shall want [*lack*] her mate: for my mouth it hath commanded, and his spirit it hath gathered them.

17 And he hath cast the lot [*voted*] **for them, and his hand hath divided it unto them by line: they shall possess it for ever, from generation to generation shall they dwell therein** [*If the Lord takes such good care of these "unclean" creatures, think how much more the righteous will get; a transition to chapter 35*].

ISAIAH 35

Selection: all verses

THIS CHAPTER IS a continuation of the prophecy in chapter 34 (see background note for chapter 34). However, in this, we are given a prophetic picture of the beauty and peace that the righteous will receive.

1 The wilderness and the solitary place shall be glad for them [*the righteous who return*]; and **the desert shall rejoice, and blossom as the rose** [*a paradise awaits the righteous*].

2 It shall blossom abundantly, and rejoice even with joy and singing: the glory of Lebanon [*the Holy*

Land; *symbolic of anywhere the righteous gather*] **shall be given unto it, the excellency of Carmel and Sharon, they shall see the glory of the LORD, and the excellency of our God.**

The Lord will strengthen the righteous, who have become weary in fighting evil.

3 ¶ Strengthen ye the weak [*German: tired*] **hands, and confirm** [*German: revive*] **the feeble** [*German: stumbling*] **knees.**

4 Say to them [*the righteous*] **that are of a fearful** [*German: discouraged*] **heart, Be strong, fear not: behold, your God will come with vengeance** [*upon the wicked*], **even God with a recompence; he will come and save you** [*the righteous*].

5 Then the eyes of the [*spiritually*] **blind shall be opened, and the ears of the** [*spiritually*] **deaf shall be unstopped** [*the restored gospel heals spiritual blindness and deafness*].

6 Then shall the lame man leap as an hart [*deer*], **and the tongue of the dumb** [*people who can't talk; symbolic of those who didn't know the gospel previously*] **sing: for in the wilderness shall waters break out, and streams in the desert** [*literal; also symbolic of "living water," the gospel*].

7 And the parched ground [*symbolic of apostate Israel; see Isaiah 53:2,* Mosiah 14:2] **shall become a pool, and the thirsty land springs of water** [*through the Restoration of the gospel*]: **in the habitation of dragons** [*jackals; Isaiah has used this imagery before (see Isaiah 13:22; 34:13–15) to depict the barrenness left when the wicked are destroyed. Here, he depicts the barrenness, apostate "wilderness," and so forth, being replaced with lush growth symbolizing the Restoration of the gospel*] **where each lay, shall be grass with reeds and rushes** [*restored productivity*].

8 And an highway [*perhaps literal highways upon which various groups have returned or will return; symbolically, the path to God—the gospel, "strait and narrow" way, temple covenants, baptismal covenants, and so forth*] **shall be there, and a way, and it shall be called The way of holiness; the unclean** [*the wicked*] **shall not pass over it; but it shall be for those: the wayfaring men, though fools** [*JST (Joseph Smith Translation of the Bible): "though they are accounted fools"—though men might consider the righteous to be fools*], **shall not err therein.**

9 No lion shall be there, nor any ravenous beast [*enemies of Israel's return; forces of evil*] **shall go up thereon, it shall not be found there** [*perhaps looking ahead to millennial conditions*]; **but the redeemed shall walk there:**

10 And the ransomed of the LORD [*those who have been redeemed by the Lord's Atonement*] **shall return, and come to Zion** with songs and ever-lasting joy upon their heads: **they shall obtain joy and gladness, and sorrow and sighing shall flee away** [*see Revelation 21:4; 7:17; the final state of the righteous*].

ISAIAH 36

Selection: all verses

MANY OF THE chapters of Isaiah we have studied so far have dealt with the future. This chapter is an account of what happened when the Assyrians approached Judah with the goal of conquering Jerusalem and the cities of Judah. This took place near the end of Isaiah's service as a prophet.

1 Now it came to pass **in the fourteenth year** [*about 701 BC*] **of king Hezekiah** [*righteous king of Judah*], that **Sennacherib king of Assyria came up against all the defenced cities of Judah, and took them** [*perhaps as many as forty-six cities*].

Having conquered many cities in Judah, the Assyrian king now sends one of his chief officers to the outskirts of Jerusalem to harass King Hezekiah and his people in preparation for conquering them.

2 And **the king of Assyria sent Rabshakeh** [*a title meaning "chief of the officers"—see footnote 2a in your Bible*] from Lachish [*about thirty-five miles southwest of Jerusalem*] **to Jerusalem unto king Hezekiah with a great army.** And he [*Rabshakeh*] stood by the conduit of the upper pool in the highway of the fuller's field [*where fullers bleached cloth*].

Next, righteous King Hezekiah sends some trusted leaders to engage in talks with Rabshakeh.

3 Then came forth unto him [*Rabshakeh*] **Eliakim** [*prime minister of Judah*], **Hilkiah's son, which was over the house, and Shebna** the scribe, **and Joah,** Asaph's son, the recorder.

4 ¶ And Rabshakeh said unto them, Say ye now to Hezekiah, Thus saith the great king [*sarcastically mimicking "Thus saith the Lord"*], **the king of Assyria, What confidence is this wherein thou trustest?** [*you are fools to trust Egypt for protection*]

5 I say, sayest thou, [*but they are but vain words*] **I have counsel** [*plans with Egypt*] **and strength for war** [*Egypt is our ally*]: **now on whom dost thou** [*Hezekiah/Judah*] **trust, that thou rebellest against me** [*Assyria*]?

6 Lo, thou trustest in the staff [*"scepter," power*] **of this broken reed** [*"broken broom straw"*], **on Egypt;**

whereon if a man lean, it will go into his hand, and pierce it ["*Egypt is so weak, so thin that if you were to lean on it with your hand it would poke right through*"]: **so is Pharaoh king of Egypt to all that trust in him** [*Egypt never could protect anyone*].

Next, Rabshakeh takes a poke at the worship of God, which Hezekiah has centralized in Jerusalem.

7 But if thou say to me, We trust in the LORD our God: is it not he [*the Lord*], **whose high places and whose altars** [*places of worship*] **Hezekiah hath taken away** [*King Hezekiah did away with local sites of worship and required the Jews to worship at the temple in Jerusalem*], **and said to Judah and to Jerusalem, Ye shall worship before this altar** [*worship at the temple in Jerusalem*]?

8 Now therefore give pledges ["*Let's make a bet.*"], **I pray thee, to my master the king of Assyria, and I will give thee two thousand horses, if thou be able on thy part to set riders upon them** ["*if I give you two thousand horses, I'll bet you can't find two thousand able-bodied soldiers in all of Judah to ride them*"].

9 How then wilt thou turn away the face of one captain of the least of my master's servants, and put thy trust on Egypt for chariots and for horsemen [*you'll get no help from puny Egypt!*]?

Next, in verse 10, Rabshakeh claims that the God of Israel, Jehovah, sent him to conquer Jerusalem.

10 And am I now come up without the LORD against this land to destroy it? **the LORD said unto me, Go up against this land, and destroy it** [*"your God told me to come up and destroy you!" A lie, but sometimes an effective intimidation strategy*].

Next, the emissaries sent by King Hezekiah timidly ask Rabshakeh to speak in a language all the public, who have gathered on the wall of Jerusalem to hear, can't understand.

11 Then said Eliakim and Shebna and Joah unto Rabshakeh, Speak, I [*we*] pray thee [*please*], **unto thy servants** [*us, King Hezekiah's representatives*] **in the Syrian language; for we understand it: and speak not to us in the Jews' language, in the ears of the people that are on the wall.** [*"Can't we discuss this in a language our citizens don't understand? This is too embarrassing."*]

12 But Rabshakeh said, Hath my master sent me to thy master and to thee to speak these words? hath he not sent me to the men that sit upon the wall, that they may eat their own dung, and drink their own piss with you [*Before Assyria is through with you, you'll be that bad off*]?

13 Then Rabshakeh stood, and cried with a loud voice in the Jews' language [*intentionally so the citizens could easily hear*], and said, **Hear ye the words of the great king, the king of Assyria.**

14 Thus saith the king, **Let not Hezekiah deceive you: for he shall not be able to deliver you.**

15 **Neither let Hezekiah make you trust in the LORD, saying, The LORD will surely deliver us:** this city shall not be delivered into the hand of the king of Assyria.

16 **Hearken not to Hezekiah:** for **thus saith the king of Assyria, Make an agreement with me** by a present [*via a payment*], and **come out to me** [*surrender*]: and eat ye every one of his vine, and every one of his fig tree, and drink ye every one the waters of his own cistern [*in effect, stay on your own land for a while in peace, until I make arrangements to transport you elsewhere—see verse 17, next*];

17 **Until I come and take you away to a land like your own land,** a land of corn [*grain*] and wine, a land of bread and vineyards [*you'll like where I take you*].

18 **Beware lest Hezekiah persuade you** [*don't let your foolish king fast-talk you into resisting us Assyrians*], **saying, The LORD will deliver us.**

Hath any of the gods of the nations delivered his land out of the hand of the king of Assyria? [*no other gods in other lands have been able to stop us and yours won't either!*]

19 **Where are the gods of Hamath** [*part of modern Syria*] and **Arphad** [*part of modern Syria*]? where are the gods of **Sepharvaim** [*part of modern Syria*]? and have they delivered **Samaria** [*headquarters for the ten tribes, which the Assyrians conquered about twenty-one years earlier, in 722 BC*] out of my hand?

> Next, Rabshakeh says, in effect, if the gods of all these other places could not hold us back from conquering them, what makes you think your Jehovah could possibly stop us?

20 **Who are they among all the gods of these lands, that have delivered their land out of my hand** [*which of their gods stopped us*]**, that the LORD should deliver Jerusalem out of my hand?**

21 But they [*Hezekiah's three men*] **held their peace, and answered him not a word:** for the king's commandment was, saying, Answer him not.

22 Then came **Eliakim**, the son of Hilkiah, that was over the household, **and Shebna** the scribe, **and Joah**, the son of Asaph, the recorder, **to Hezekiah with their clothes**

rent [torn; a sign in their culture that they were very distraught], **and told him the words of Rabshakeh.**

ISAIAH 37

Selection: all verses

THIS CHAPTER IS a continuation of the tense situation reported in chapter 36. Righteous King Hezekiah will send to Isaiah the prophet, for counsel as to how to deal with the situation.

1 And it came to pass, **when king Hezekiah heard it** [the report from his emissaries in Isaiah 36:22], that **he rent** [tore] **his clothes** [as a sign of extreme worry], **and covered himself with sackcloth, and went into the house of the LORD** [the temple].

> Have you noticed that the word "LORD" (end of verse 1, above, and elsewhere), as printed in your King James version of the Bible, is spelled with a large capital "L" and small caps "ORD"? This is the King James Version of the Bible's way of pointing out that it is "Jehovah" about whom they are speaking. We know from Isaiah 43:1-3, 11, 14, and elsewhere that Jehovah is the premortal Jesus Christ, who is the God of the Old Testament.

2 **And he sent Eliakim** [his prime minister], who was over the household, **and Shebna** the [royal] scribe, **and the elders** [older priests] of the priests covered with sackcloth [a sign of deep distress and mourning in their culture], **unto Isaiah** the prophet the son of Amoz.

3 **And they said unto him,** Thus saith Hezekiah, **This day is a day of trouble, and of rebuke** [we're in big trouble], **and of blasphemy** [the Assyrians speak totally disrespectfully of the Lord]: for the children are come to the birth, and there is not strength to bring forth [we're doomed, like when a woman is in hard labor, but the baby doesn't come].

4 **It may be the LORD thy God will hear** [has heard] **the words of Rabshakeh** [Assyria's representative], whom the king of Assyria his master hath sent to reproach [blaspheme] the living God, **and will reprove the words** [of Rabshakeh] which the LORD thy God hath heard [we hope the Lord will not let them get away with such talk]: wherefore lift up thy prayer for the remnant that is left.

5 So the servants of king Hezekiah came to Isaiah.

6 ¶ And **Isaiah said** unto them, Thus shall ye **say unto your master,** Thus saith the LORD, **Be not afraid of the words that thou hast heard,** wherewith the servants of the king of Assyria have blasphemed me [the Lord].

7 **Behold, I** [*the Lord*] **will send a blast upon him** [*I will change his frame of mind, make him nervous*], and **he shall hear a rumour** [*bad news from home*], **and return to his own land; and I will cause him to fall by the sword in his own land.**

8 ¶ **So Rabshakeh returned, and found the king of Assyria warring against Libnah** [*southwest of Jerusalem*]: **for he** [*Rabshakeh*] **had heard that he** [*the King of Assyria*] **was departed from Lachish.**

9 **And he** [*the Assyrian King*] **heard** say **concerning Tirhakah king of Ethiopia** [*the Egyptian army*], **He is come forth to make** war with thee. **And when he** [*King of Assyria*] **heard it, he sent messengers to Hezekiah, saying** [*the King of Assyria, worried about approaching Egyptian armies, now presses King Hezekiah for quick surrender*],

10 Thus shall ye speak to Hezekiah king of Judah, saying, **Let not thy God, in whom thou trustest, deceive thee, saying, Jerusalem shall not be given into the hand of the king of Assyria** [*your God can't help you; you will be powerless before the Assyrians*].

11 Behold, **thou hast heard what the kings of Assyria have done to all lands by destroying them utterly; and shalt thou be delivered** [*what makes you think you'll be different*]?

12 **Have the gods of the nations delivered** them which my fathers have destroyed, as **Gozan** [*Iraq*], and **Haran** [*Turkey*], and **Rezeph** [*Iraq*], and the children of Eden which were in **Telassar** [*Iraq*]?

13 Where is the king of **Hamath** [*Syria*], and the king of Arphad [*Syria*], and the king of the city of **Sepharvaim** [*Syria*], **Hena** [*unknown*], and **Ivah** [*unknown*]?

14 And **Hezekiah received the letter** from the hand of the messengers, and read it: **and Hezekiah went up unto the house of the LORD, and spread it before the LORD.**

15 **And Hezekiah prayed unto the LORD, saying,**

16 O LORD of hosts, God of Israel, that dwellest between [*German: above*] the cherubims, **thou art the God, even thou alone,** of all the kingdoms of the earth: **thou hast made heaven and earth.**

17 **Incline thine ear, O LORD, and hear;** open thine eyes, O LORD, and see: and **hear all the words of Sennacherib** [*King of Assyria*], **which hath sent to reproach** [*blaspheme*] **the living God.**

18 Of a truth [*it is true*], LORD, the

kings of Assyria have laid waste all the nations, and their countries [*just as the letter in verse 14 says*],

19 And have cast their gods [*idols*] into the fire: for they were no gods [*weren't real gods*], but the work of men's hands, wood and stone: **therefore they have destroyed them** [*that's why Assyria was able to conquer those cities and nations*].

20 Now therefore, O LORD our God, save us from his hand, that all the kingdoms of the earth may know that thou art the LORD, even thou only.

> Next, the Lord answers Hezekiah's prayer through Isaiah, the prophet. This is often the case today, as the Lord answers many of our prayers through our living prophets.

21 ¶ Then Isaiah the son of Amoz sent unto Hezekiah, saying, Thus saith the LORD God of Israel, Whereas thou hast prayed to me against Sennacherib king of Assyria:

22 This is the word which the LORD hath spoken concerning him [*this is the answer to Sennacherib*]; **The virgin, the daughter of Zion** [*the unconquered people of Jerusalem*], **hath despised thee, and laughed thee to scorn;** the daughter of Jerusalem hath shaken her head at thee [*not afraid of you Assyrians*].

23 **Whom hast thou reproached and blasphemed?** and against whom hast thou exalted thy voice, and lifted up thine eyes on high? even against the Holy One of Israel [*you chose the wrong one to offend this time; you have mocked the true God*].

24 **By thy servants** [*including Rabshakeh—see Isaiah 36:4*] **hast thou reproached** [*blasphemed*] **the Lord**, and hast said [*bragged*], By the multitude of my chariots am I come up to the height of the mountains, to the sides [*west*] of Lebanon; and I will [*have*] cut down the tall cedars thereof, and the choice fir trees thereof: and I will enter [*have entered*] into the height of his border, and the forest of his Carmel.

25 **I have digged** [*wells*], **and drunk water** [*in many a conquered land*]; and with the sole of my feet have I dried up all the rivers of the besieged places [*end of quoting the Assyrian King's boasts*].

26 Hast thou [*King of Assyria*] not heard long ago ["*Haven't you heard by now?*"], how I [*the Lord*] have done [*allowed*] it; and of ancient times, that I have formed it? now have I brought it to pass, that thou shouldest be to lay waste defenced cities into ruinous heaps [*I, the Lord, allowed you to do these things, otherwise you would never have had such power*].

27 Therefore [*that is why*] **their inhabitants were of small power** [*were weak before your armies*], **they were dismayed and confounded: they were as the grass of the field, and as the green herb, as the grass on the housetops, and as corn** [*grain*] **blasted before it be grown up.**

28 But I [*the Lord*] **know thy abode** [*I know you well*], **and thy going out, and thy coming in, and thy rage against me.**

29 Because thy rage against me, and thy tumult, is come up into mine ears, therefore will I put my hook in thy nose [*such as a ring in the nose of a wild animal with which to control it*], **and my bridle in thy lips** [*I will control you, King of Assyria*], **and I will turn thee back by the way** [*road*] **by which thou camest** [*I will stop you cold*].

> The topic now turns to the word of the Lord to Hezekiah and his people, who have been worrying because of the siege against them by the Assyrians.

30 And this shall be a sign unto thee [*Hezekiah and his people*], **Ye shall eat this year such as groweth of itself** [*because of the Assyrian siege, you have not had time to plant crops normally, yet you will harvest some "volunteer" crops from plants that grew from seeds spilled during last year's harvest; in other words, you'll be okay food wise*]; **and the second year that which springeth of** the same: **and in the third year sow ye, and reap, and plant vineyards, and eat the fruit thereof** [*you'll be back to normal planting and harvesting by the third year from now*].

31 And the remnant that is escaped of the house of Judah shall again take root downward, and bear fruit upward [*a remnant of Judah will flourish again*]:

32 For out of Jerusalem shall go forth a remnant, and they that escape out of mount Zion: the zeal of the LORD of hosts shall do this [*a remnant will flourish again via God's intervention*].

> Verse 33 is a specific prophecy and most comforting to King Hezekiah. The Assyrians, despite their boasting, will not shoot so much as one arrow into Jerusalem!

33 Therefore thus saith the LORD concerning the king of Assyria, **He shall not come into this city, nor shoot an arrow there, nor come before it with shields, nor cast a bank** [*a mound of dirt around it thrown up from trenches dug in order to lay siege*] **against it.**

34 By the way [*road*] **that he** [*the Assyrian king and his armies*] **came, by the same shall he return** [*he will retreat*], **and shall not come into this city, saith the LORD.**

35 For I will defend this city to

save it for mine own sake, and for my servant David's sake.

> Next, we see how the Lord stopped the Assyrian armies dead in their tracks.

36 Then [*after the Assyrian armies had come to the outskirts of Jerusalem and were ready to attack*] **the angel of the LORD went forth, and smote in the camp of the Assyrians a hundred and fourscore and five thousand:** and when they [*the few survivors*] arose early in the morning, behold, **they were all dead corpses** [*185,000 Assyrians were dead the following morning*].

37 ¶ So Sennacherib king of Assyria departed, and went and returned, and dwelt at Nineveh [*went home to his headquarters*].

38 And it came to pass, as he was worshipping in the house of Nisroch his god, that **Adrammelech and Sharezer his sons smote** [*killed*] **him with the sword;** and they escaped into the land of Armenia: and Esar-haddon his son reigned in his stead [*this happened about twenty years after his retreat from Jerusalem*].

ISAIAH 38

Selection: all verses

CHAPTERS 38 AND 39 fit historically before chapters 36 and 37 and could be considered "flashbacks" to 705–703 BC.

Isaiah was the prophet during Hezekiah's reign. At one point, righteous King Hezekiah was sick and on his deathbed.

1 In those days [*about 705–703 BC*] **was Hezekiah sick unto death.** And **Isaiah** the prophet the son of Amoz **came unto him, and said** unto him, Thus saith the LORD, **Set thine house in order** [*get ready*]: **for thou shalt die, and not live.**

2 Then Hezekiah turned his face toward the wall, and **prayed unto the LORD,**

3 And said, **Remember** now, O LORD, I beseech thee, **how I have walked before thee in truth and with a perfect heart, and have done that which is good** in thy sight [*in other words, I have lived a good life*]. And Hezekiah wept sore [*bitterly*].

4 ¶ Then came the word of the LORD to Isaiah, saying,

5 Go, and say to Hezekiah, Thus saith the LORD, the God of David thy father [*ancestor*], **I have heard**

thy prayer, I have seen thy tears: behold, I will add unto thy days fifteen years [*I will add fifteen years to your life*].

Major Message

When it is in harmony with the will of the Lord, the mighty prayers of the faithful can change the plan temporarily.

6 And I will deliver thee and this city out of the hand of the king of Assyria: and I will defend this city [*this would seem to place Hezekiah's illness sometime during the Assyrian threats to Jerusalem as described in chapters 36 and 37*].

7 And this shall be a sign unto thee from the LORD, that the LORD will do this thing that he hath spoken;

8 Behold, I will bring again the shadow of the degrees [*the shadow on the sundial*], which is gone down in the sun dial of Ahaz, ten degrees backward. So the sun returned ten degrees, by which degrees it was gone down [*the sun came back up ten degrees; in other words, time was turned backward*].

Hezekiah was healed and now gives thanks and praise to the Lord for his miraculous recovery.

9 ¶ The writing [*psalm*] of Hezekiah king of Judah, when he had been sick, and was recovered of his sickness [*after he had been sick and had recovered*]:

Righteous King Hezekiah now tells us what he said, expressing the thoughts of his heart, when he was blessed with another fifteen years of life by the Lord.

First, he tells us what was going through his mind when he knew he was going to die.

10 I [*Hezekiah*] said in the cutting off of my days [*when I was on my deathbed*], I shall go to the gates of the grave [*I am doomed*]: I am deprived of the residue [*remainder*] of my years [*I am too young to die*].

11 I said, I shall not see the LORD, even the LORD, in the land of the living [*I am about to leave this mortal life*]: I shall behold man no more with the inhabitants of the world [*I won't be around anymore to associate with my fellow men*].

12 Mine age is departed [*German Bible: my time is up*], and is removed from me as a shepherd's tent [*they are taking down my tent*]: I have [*Thou hast*] cut off like a weaver my life [*Thou hast "clipped my threads" like a weaver does when the rug is finished*]: he will cut me off with pining sickness [*fatal illness is how the Lord is sending me out of this life*]: from day even to night wilt thou make an end of me [*I will die shortly*].

13 I reckoned till morning [*German: I thought, If I could just live until morning*], that, as a lion, so will he break all my bones [*I can't stop the*

Lord if He wants me to die any more than I could stop a lion]: from day even to night wilt thou make an end of me [I'm doomed; my time is short].

14 Like a crane or a swallow, so did I chatter [German: whimper]: I did mourn as a dove: mine eyes fail with looking upward [falter as I look up to heaven]: O LORD, I am oppressed [German: suffering]; undertake [German: soothe, moderate my condition] for me [be Thou my help, security].

> Next, Hezekiah tells us how he felt when he found out he was not going to die.
>
> The Joseph Smith Translation of the Bible helps us considerably with verses 15-17, next.

15 **What shall I say** [how can I express my gratitude]? he hath both spoken unto me, and himself hath done it [JST: healed me]: I shall go softly [German: in humility] all my years [JST: that I may not walk] in the bitterness of my soul.

16 O Lord, by these things men live, and in all these things is the life of my spirit [JST: "thou who art the life of my spirit, in whom I live"]: so wilt thou recover [heal] me, and make me to live [JST: "and in all these things I will praise thee"].

17 Behold, for peace I had great bitterness [JST: "Behold, I had great bitterness instead of peace"]: but thou hast in love to my soul delivered it [JST: "saved me"] from the pit of corruption [from rotting in the grave]: for thou hast cast all my sins behind thy back [the effect of the Atonement].

18 For the grave cannot praise [German: hell does not praise] thee, death can not celebrate thee: they [people in spirit prison] that go down into the pit [hell; see Isaiah 14:15] cannot hope for thy truth [see Alma 34:32–34].

19 The living, the living, he shall praise thee, as I do this day [I am very happy to still be alive]: the father to the children shall make known thy truth [I will testify to my family and others of Thy kindness to me].

20 The LORD was ready to save me: therefore we [I and my family] will sing my songs to the stringed instruments [we will put my words of praise to music] all the days of our life in the house of the LORD.

> Next, Hezekiah refers to something Isaiah instructed him to do in order to be healed.

21 **For Isaiah had said, Let them take a lump of figs, and lay it for a plaister** [plaster] **upon the boil, and he shall recover** [perhaps the lump of figs served the same purpose as the lump of clay to heal the blind man in John 9:6–7; faith obedience].

22 Hezekiah also had said, What is the sign that I shall go up to the

house of the LORD? [*This verse fits after verse 6. See 2 Kings 20:8.*]

ISAIAH 39

Selection: all verses

AS YOU HAVE perhaps noticed, these chapters are not particularly in chronological order. This chapter records events that took place before chapters 36–37. It appears that King Hezekiah, King of Judah with headquarters in Jerusalem, as a gesture of good faith, showed emissaries from Babylon the great treasures in the temple and in the palace at Jerusalem (verse 2). In about one hundred years, Babylon will be an enemy to Judah and will carry them away into captivity.

1 At that time [*about 705–703 BC*] **Merodach-baladan,** the son of Baladan, **king of Babylon, sent letters and a present to Hezekiah: for he had heard that he had been sick,** and was recovered.

2 And Hezekiah was glad of them, and **shewed them** [*the Babylonian delegation who brought the letters and present*] **the house of his precious things,** the silver, and the gold, and the spices, and the precious ointment, and all the house of his armour, and all that was found in his treasures: **there was nothing in his house, nor in all his dominion, that Hezekiah shewed them not.**

Next, Isaiah comes to Hezekiah and expresses concern about what he has shown to the delegation from Babylon. It sets the stage for a prophecy about the future Babylonian captivity of the Jews.

3 ¶ Then came Isaiah the prophet unto king Hezekiah, and said unto him, What said these men? and from whence came they unto **thee? And Hezekiah said, They are come from a far country unto me, even from Babylon.**

4 Then said he [*Isaiah*], **What have they seen in thine house?** And **Hezekiah answered, All that is in mine house have they seen:** there is nothing among my treasures that I have not shewed them.

5 Then said Isaiah to Hezekiah, Hear the word of the LORD of hosts:

6 Behold, **the days come, that all that is in thine house,** and that which thy fathers [*ancestors*] have laid up in store until this day, **shall be carried to Babylon:** nothing shall be left, saith the LORD [*prophecy regarding Babylonian captivity, which will take place in about a hundred years*].

7 And of thy sons that shall issue from thee, which thou shalt beget, **shall they take away; and they shall be eunuchs** [*servants; they will be made unable to father children—see Bible Dictionary, under "Eunuch"*] **in**

the palace of the king of Babylon.

8 Then said Hezekiah to Isaiah, Good is the word of the LORD which thou hast spoken. He said moreover, For there shall be peace and truth in my days.

Some scholars are critical of Hezekiah's response in verse 8, above, but he remained loyal to God and did much good for his people during his reign. Perhaps he did mourn for his people in the future and it is just not recorded here. See 2 Kings 20:19–20. It is possible to be happy and at peace with God despite others' wickedness. For instance, see Mormon in Mormon 2:19 and Lehi in 2 Nephi 1:15.

ISAIAH 40

Selection: all verses

THIS CHAPTER CON-TAINS a number of prophecies about the Messiah, and includes a description of the role of John the Baptist. Chronologically, it seems to move around quite a bit, including prophecies of the Savior's mortal mission as well as of His Second Coming. It is a chapter of comfort and witness about the Savior, and teaches beautifully that none on earth can compare to Him.

Isaiah will also point out the absurdity of idol worship, in view of the true power of the true God.

1 Comfort ye, comfort ye my people, saith your God.

Verse 2, next, seems to refer to the last days and on into the Millennium.

2 Speak ye comfortably [German: in a friendly manner; Hebrew: tenderly] to Jerusalem, and cry unto her, that her warfare [time of service] is accomplished, that her iniquity is pardoned [through repentance and the Atonement]: for she hath received of the LORD's hand double for all her sins [has paid a heavy penalty for wickedness].

3 ¶ The voice of him that crieth in the wilderness, Prepare ye the way of the LORD, make straight in the desert a highway for our God. [This fits John the Baptist as described in Matthew 3:1–3. Other "Eliases," or "preparers" and prophets, also fit this passage in the last days as they prepare us for the Second Coming.]

4 Every valley shall be exalted [raised], and every mountain and hill shall be made low: and the crooked shall be made straight, and the rough places [mountains] plain [changes in the earth at the Second Coming; also can be symbolic of wickedness, being "straightened out" at the Second Coming]:

5 And the glory of the LORD shall be revealed, and all flesh shall see it together [at the same time at the

Second Coming]: for the mouth of the LORD hath spoken it.

> Verse 6, next, is a course in perspective. Man's power is insignificant compared to that of God. See also verse 18.

6 The voice said, Cry [preach]. And he said, What shall I cry [preach]? [Answer:] All flesh [people] is [are like] grass, and all the goodliness thereof is as the flower of the field: [Mortality is temporary; not that we are not significant and important—Christ gave His life for us—but just a reminder that God is way ahead of us and we would be wise to follow and obey Him completely. We are nothing, at this point, compared to Him.]:

7 The grass withereth, the flower fadeth: because the spirit of the LORD bloweth upon it: surely the people is grass [man's power and wisdom pale against the Lord's].

8 The grass withereth, the flower fadeth: but the word of our God shall stand for ever [trust in God, not in the "arm of flesh"].

9 O Zion, that bringest good tidings [the gospel], get thee up into the high mountain; O Jerusalem, that bringest good tidings, lift up thy voice with strength; lift it up, be not afraid; say unto the cities of Judah, Behold your God!

> Next, Isaiah bears witness of the Second Coming.

10 Behold, the Lord GOD will come with strong hand [German: with power], and his arm [symbolic of power] shall rule for him [He will rule on earth; Second Coming and Millennium]: behold, his reward is with him [He will reward the righteous and the wicked, according to what they have earned], and his work before him [German: reward precedes Him; that is, Second Coming, Revelation 22:12].

11 He shall feed his flock like a shepherd [He knows each of us by name; Millennial reign]: he shall gather the lambs with his arm, and carry them in his bosom, and shall gently lead those that are with young [peaceful conditions during the Millennium].

> The "course in perspective" concerning the greatness of God continues, leading to verse 18.

12 ¶ Who hath measured the waters in the hollow of his hand, and meted out heaven with the span, and comprehended the dust of the earth in a measure, and weighed the mountains in scales, and the hills in a balance? [Who else do you know who can create worlds and design oceans, continents, mountains, heavens, and so forth?]

13 Who hath directed [taught] the Spirit of the LORD [the Holy Ghost], or being his counsellor hath taught him [what mortal could teach God anything!]?

14 With whom took he [God] counsel [from whom does God seek counsel, advice], and who instructed him, and taught him in the path of judgment, and taught him knowledge, and shewed to him the way of understanding [the answer "no one" is implied]?

15 Behold, the nations [of this earth] are as a drop of [in] a bucket [compared to God's domain], and are counted as [like] the small dust of the balance [are about as significant as a small speck of dust on a scale]: behold, he taketh up the isles as a very little thing [German: the continents are like the tiniest speck of dust to Him].

16 And Lebanon [sometimes used to represent all of Palestine] is not sufficient to burn, nor the beasts thereof sufficient for a burnt offering [all the wood and all the animals in Lebanon wouldn't even begin to make a sacrifice worthy of who God really is].

17 All nations before [compared to] him are as nothing; and they are counted [compared] to him less than nothing, and vanity.

Verse 18, next, serves as a transition to the topic of how absurd and foolish it is to use idols as substitutes for God.

18 ¶ To whom then will ye liken [compare] God? or what likeness [idol] will ye compare unto him?

19 The workman [craftsman] melteth [uses molten metal to form] a graven image, and the goldsmith spreadeth [covers] it over with gold, and casteth [makes] silver chains [foolish people make idols and then compare them to God].

20 He that is so impoverished that he hath no oblation [German: so poor that he can give only the smallest offering] chooseth a tree that will not rot [selects wood for an idol]; he seeketh unto him a cunning workman [he hires a skilled craftsman] to prepare a graven image [idol], that shall not be moved [German: becomes a permanent fixture].

21 Have ye not known [German: Do you not know?]? have ye not heard? hath it not been told you from the beginning? have ye not understood from the foundations of the earth [don't you understand!]?

22 It is he [the Lord] that sitteth upon the circle of the earth [is above all], and the inhabitants thereof are as grasshoppers [compared to God; continues the theme of verse 17]; that stretcheth out [creates] the heavens as a curtain, and spreadeth them out as a tent to dwell in [the Lord is the Creator]:

23 That bringeth the princes [leaders] to nothing; he maketh the

judges [*rulers*] of the earth as vanity [*nothing*].

24 Yea, they [*the wicked rulers and leaders*] shall not be planted [*German: shall be as if they hadn't even been planted*]; yea, they shall not be sown: yea, their stock shall not take root in the earth: and he [*the Lord*] shall also blow upon them, and they shall wither, and the whirlwind shall take them away as stubble [*they are nothing compared to God*].

25 To whom then will ye liken me, or shall I be equal? saith the Holy One [*Jehovah: Jesus Christ; same question as in verse 18*].

26 Lift up your eyes on high [*look all around you*], and behold [*see*] who hath created these things [*God's creations*], that bringeth out their host by number: he calleth them all by names [*He knows every one of them*] by [*because of*] the greatness of his might [*German: ability*], for that he is strong in power; not one faileth [*His creations all obey him*].

27 Why sayest thou, O Jacob [*you Israelites*], and speakest, O Israel, My way is hid from the LORD [*why do you think that you can hide your wickedness from God*], and my judgment [*cause*] is passed over from [*is unknown by*] my God?

28 ¶ Hast thou not known? hast thou not heard [*haven't you heard by now*], that the everlasting God, the LORD, the Creator of the ends of the earth, fainteth not [*German: is not weak*], neither is weary? there is no searching of his understanding [*you can't comprehend His understanding*].

29 He giveth power to the faint; and to them that have no might he increaseth strength [*Ether 12:27*].

30 Even the youths [*with lots of energy*] shall [*may grow*] faint and be weary, and the young men shall utterly fall [*all mortals have their limitations*]:

31 But they that wait [*base their hopes*] upon the LORD shall renew their strength; they shall mount up with wings as eagles [*be renewed like molting eagles are as they lose their old feathers each year, then get new ones*]; they shall run, and not be weary; and they shall walk, and not faint [*in pursuing exaltation. See context of Doctrine & Covenants 89:20–21; the righteous receive extra strength on earth, have a glorious resurrection, and receive the strength of the Lord as joint heirs with Christ*].

ISAIAH 41

Selection: all verses

CHAPTERS 41–44 REFER

mainly to the last days.

There are many different opinions among scholars concerning the meaning of some verses in this chapter. In such cases, I have used the *Old Testament Student Manual* (Institute of Religion, Religion 302), as the authority for interpretive notes in brackets. I have also made considerable use of the Martin Luther version of the German Bible for clarifications.

1 Keep silence before me [*hush, and let me teach you*], **O islands** [*all land masses where scattered Israel live*]; **and let the people renew their strength** [*as mentioned in Isaiah 40:31*]: let them come near; then let them speak: let us come near together to judgment. [*German: dispute, see who is right—see who is more powerful, God or your idols; similar to Elijah and priests of Baal in I Kings 18*];

> In verse 2, next, Isaiah asks the question, "Who is more powerful, your idols or our God?"

2 Who raised up the righteous man from the east [*the Savior Himself fits this description, coming in from the east wilderness at age thirty to begin His ministry; could also refer to many prophets, including Abraham, who have come from the "East"—on assignment from the Lord, and assisted in "calling the generations from the beginning," verse 4*], **called him to his foot** [*German: to go forth*], **gave** [*him power over*] **the nations before him, and made him rule over kings?** he gave them

[*kings*] as the dust to his sword [*they couldn't stop his sword (power) anymore than dust particles could*], and as driven stubble to his bow [*nations and kings couldn't stop him*].

3 He pursued them, and passed safely; even by the way that he had not gone with his feet [*German: without wearying of his errand, assignment; perhaps ties back to Isaiah 40:31*].

4 Who hath wrought and done it [*the things referred to above*], **calling the generations** [*German: calling all people*] **from the beginning?** [*Answer to the question put in verse 2:*] **I the LORD, the first, and with the last; I am he.**

5 The isles [*scattered Israel*] **saw it, and feared** [*respected it, responded positively*]; **the ends of the earth were afraid, drew near, and came** [*people from all parts of the earth responded; the gathering of Israel*].

6 They helped every one his neighbour; and every one said to his brother, Be of good courage.

7 So [*yet, nevertheless*] **the carpenter encouraged the goldsmith, and he that smootheth with the hammer him that smote the anvil, saying,** It [*an idol*] is ready for the sodering: and he fastened it with nails, that it should not be moved [*yet, many foolishly continued with their making and worshipping of idols*].

Next, those who want to be the faithful covenant people of the Lord are encouraged to remember who they are and to remain loyal to God.

8 But thou, Israel, art my servant, Jacob whom I have chosen, the seed of Abraham my friend.

9 Thou whom I have taken [*gathered*] **from the ends of the earth,** and called thee from the chief men thereof, and said unto thee, Thou art my servant; I have chosen thee, and not cast thee away [*I have not left you*].

Verse 10, next, reminds us of the third verse of our hymn, "How Firm a Foundation" (*Hymns*, 85).

10 Fear thou not; for I am with thee: be not dismayed; for I am thy God: I will strengthen thee; yea, I will **help thee;** yea, I will **uphold thee with the right hand of my righteousness.**

Verse 11, next, reminds us that the wicked will someday face the consequences of their fighting against the Saints.

11 Behold, all they that were incensed [*German: prejudiced; angry*] **against thee shall be ashamed** [*shamed*] **and confounded** [*German: humiliated*]: they shall be as nothing; and they that strive with [*fight against*] thee shall perish [*ultimately, your enemies will not succeed against you*].

12 Thou shalt seek them [*your enemies*], **and shalt not find them,** even them that contended with thee: they that war against thee shall be as nothing, and as a thing of nought [*eventually, the wicked will all be gone*].

13 For I the LORD thy God will hold thy right hand [*covenant hand; in other words, I will strengthen you with covenants*], **saying unto thee, Fear not; I will help thee.**

Have you noticed that most Christians do not believe that Jesus is the God of the Old Testament (under the Father's direction)? Verse 14, next, teaches correct doctrine on this matter. It uses the word "redeemer" in reference to the Lord (the premortal Christ) who is directing Israel in Old Testament times. We will see additional strong evidence in chapter 43 of this doctrine.

14 Fear not, thou worm [*meek, humble*] **Jacob, and ye men of Israel; I will help thee, saith the LORD, and thy redeemer, the Holy One of Israel** [*Jesus*].

15 Behold, I will make thee [*German: into*] **a new sharp threshing instrument having teeth** [*capable of much destruction*]: **thou shalt thresh the mountains** [*your former strong enemies*], **and beat them small,** and shalt make the hills as chaff. [*Israel will triumph over her enemies. Perhaps this verse could also* *remind us that Israel, as a "sharp threshing instrument," will help gather the wheat—scattered Israel—and separate it from the "chaff," or the wicked.*]

16 Thou shalt fan [*German: scatter; as in the threshing process of throwing wheat up into the wind so the chaff is blown away while the wheat drops back to the threshing floor*] **them, and the wind shall carry them away, and the whirlwind shall scatter them: and thou shalt rejoice in the LORD, and shalt glory in the Holy One of Israel** [*Israel will once again become righteous and give glory to God*].

17 When the poor and needy seek water, and there is none, and their tongue faileth for thirst, I the LORD will hear them, I the God of Israel will not forsake them [*I will help you. I have not left you; see verse 9*].

18 I will open rivers in high places, and fountains in the midst of the valleys: I will make the wilderness a pool of water, and the dry land springs of water [*geographical changes will help Israel; could also be symbolic of "living water" (John 4:10), or the gospel, bringing forth new life in an apostate wilderness and satisfying the thirst mentioned in verse 17*].

19 I will plant in the wilderness the cedar, the shittah [*acacia*] **tree, and the myrtle, and the oil tree; I will set in the desert the fir** [*cypress*] **tree, and the pine** [*ash*], **and the box tree together** [*Hebrew prophets often use trees to represent people, for example, Isaiah 2:13; Ezekiel 31:3; thus various types of trees in this verse could be symbolic of the gospel's going to all races of people in the last days*]:

20 That they may see, and know, and consider, and understand together, that the hand of the LORD hath done this, and the Holy One of Israel hath created it.

21 Produce your cause [*present your case*], **saith the LORD; bring forth your strong reasons** [*arguments against the Lord*], **saith the King of Jacob** [*Christ, Jehovah, the King of Israel*].

22 Let them [*idol worshippers*] **bring them** [*their idols*] **forth, and shew us what shall happen** [*predict the future*]: **let them** [*idols*] **shew the** former things [*the past*], what they be, that we may consider them, and know the latter end [*the final outcome*] of them; or declare us things for to come [*predict the future*].

23 Shew the things that are to come hereafter, that we may know that ye are gods [*let's see if your idols can predict the future like God can; in other words, prove that your idols are gods*]: **yea, do good, or do evil, that we may be dismayed** [*surprised, startled*], **and behold it together** [*just *do anything, good or bad, to demonstrate your power to us].*

24 Behold, ye [*idols*] **are of nothing, and your work of nought** [*you are worthless and do absolutely nothing*]: **an abomination is he** [*the wicked who worship idols*] **that chooseth you** [*idols*].

25 I have raised up one [*perhaps meaning Christ, referring back to verse 2*] from the north [*possibly meaning coming from Nazareth, north of Jerusalem*], **and he shall come: from the rising of the sun** shall he call upon my name: **and he shall come upon** [*descend upon, destroy*] **princes** [*wicked leaders of nations*] as upon morter, and as the potter treadeth clay [*He will tread upon the wicked and none will stop Him; Doctrine & Covenants 133:50–51*].

26 Who [*which of your idols*] **hath declared** [*prophesied this*] **from the beginning, that we may know?** and beforetime, that we may say, He is righteous? yea, there is none that sheweth, yea, there is none that declareth, yea, there is none that heareth your words [*none of your idols do a thing!*].

27 The first shall say to Zion [*the Lord will prophesy it*], Behold, behold them: and I [*the Lord*] will give to Jerusalem one that bringeth good tidings.

28 For I beheld, and there was no man; even among them, and **there was no counsellor, that, when I asked of them, could answer a word** [*idol worship has reduced them to a completely confused people*].

29 Behold, they are all vanity [*false*]; their works are nothing: their molten images [*idols*] are wind and confusion.

ISAIAH 42

Selection: all verses

IN THIS CHAPTER, ISAIAH CONTINUES to prophesy about the Messiah. Considerable emphasis is given to the Restoration of the gospel in the last days and the taking of the gospel to all the world.

1 Behold my servant [*Christ—see Matthew 12:18; perhaps in a dual sense could also include the whole house of Israel—see Isaiah 41:8*], **whom I uphold; mine elect** [*Christ; those set apart as a chosen people; Israelites*], **in whom my soul delighteth**; I have put my spirit upon him: he shall bring forth judgment to the Gentiles.

2 He shall not cry, nor lift up, nor cause his voice to be heard in the street [*Christ was low-key, designed His preaching to not make great disturbances, often said to those healed, "tell no one"*].

The tenderness of the Savior is described beautifully by Isaiah in verse 3, next.

3 A bruised reed shall he not break [*he came to help the weak, the "bruised," not to crush them more*], **and the smoking flax** [*the glowing candle wick that still has a tiny spark of light in it*] **shall he not quench** [*he came to gently fan the spark within into a flame of belief and testimony, not to snuff it out*]: he shall bring forth judgment unto truth [*victory, see Matthew 12:20*].

4 He shall not fail [*falter, stop, quit; see Doctrine & Covenants 19:19*] **nor be discouraged** [*German: unable to finish*], till he have set judgment in the earth: and the isles [*all continents, nations*] shall wait for [*trust in*] his law.

5 ¶ Thus saith God the LORD, he that created the heavens, and stretched them out; he that spread forth the earth, and that which cometh out of it; he that giveth breath unto the people upon it, and spirit to them that walk therein [*the Creator of all*]:

Verse 6, next, seems to apply mainly to Israel. See Israel's responsibility and mission in Abraham 2:9–11.

6 I the LORD have called thee in righteousness, and will hold thine hand, and will keep thee, **and give thee for a covenant of the people, for a light of** [*German: unto*] **the Gentiles;**

7 To open the blind eyes, to bring out the prisoners from the prison, and them that sit in darkness out of the prison house [*what Christ and his righteous servants can do*].

8 I am the LORD: that is my name: and my glory will I not give to another [*you are still My chosen people*], neither my praise to graven images [*idols*].

9 Behold, the former things [*truth and keys from former days— the Restoration of the gospel*] **are come to pass, and new things** [*new knowledge in dispensation of fulness of times*] **do I declare:** before they spring forth I tell you of them [*they have been prophesied*].

10 Sing unto the LORD a new song, and his praise from the end of the earth [*to all the world*], ye that go down to the sea, and all that is therein; the isles, and the inhabitants thereof [*restored gospel will be preached to all the world*].

11 Let the wilderness [*dual meaning: literal wilderness; apostate Israel*] **and the cities thereof lift up their voice,** the villages that Kedar [*nomadic tribe in the wilderness east of Sea of Galilee; Kedar was a grandson of Abraham through Ishmael, see Genesis 25:13*] doth inhabit: let the inhabitants of the rock [*Sela, a desert town south of the Dead Sea*] sing, let them shout from the top of the mountains [*even remote places like Kedar and Sela will receive the gospel and be able to rejoice in it*].

12 Let them give glory unto the LORD, and declare his praise in the islands [*everybody will hear the gospel in the last days*].

13 The LORD shall go forth as a mighty man, he shall stir up jealousy [*with zeal*] like a man of war: he shall cry, yea, roar; **he shall prevail against his enemies** [*the Lord will ultimately triumph*].

14 I [*the Lord*] **have long time holden my peace** [*I have been patient*]; I have been still, and refrained myself [*I have been patient and not shown forth great power*]: now will I cry like a travailing woman [*woman in labor; in other words, delivery time for Israel has come; the restored gospel will go forth with great power that none can stop*]; I will destroy and devour at once.

15 I will make waste mountains and hills, and dry up all their herbs; and I will make the rivers islands, and I will dry up the pools [*after the gospel is restored, there will be great destruction, drought, and so forth as the Lord preaches "sermons" via the forces of nature as a way of getting people's attention in the*

last days—see Doctrine & Covenants 88:87–90].

16 And I will bring the blind [*the spiritually blind scattered of Israel*] **by a way** [*the restored gospel*] **that they knew not; I will lead them in paths** [*truths and covenants of the restored gospel*] **that they have not known: I will make darkness light before them,** and crooked things straight [*effects of the Restoration*]. **These things will I do unto them, and not forsake them.**

17 ¶ They shall be turned back, **they shall be greatly ashamed, that trust in graven images,** that say to the molten images, Ye are our gods [*idol worship will not pay off*].

18 Hear, ye deaf; and look, ye blind, that ye may see [*open your eyes and ears to the truth*].

The Joseph Smith Translation makes many changes in verses 19 through 25. We will first examine these verses as they stand in our Bible, and then provide the JST with explanatory notes added to the JST.

19 Who *is* blind, but my servant? or deaf, as my messenger *that* I sent? who *is* blind as *he that is* perfect, and blind as the LORD's servant?

20 Seeing many things, but thou observest not; opening the ears, but he heareth not.

21 The LORD is well pleased

for his righteousness' sake; he will magnify the law, and make *it* honourable.

22 But this *is* a people robbed and spoiled; *they are* all of them snared in holes, and they are hid in prison houses: they are for a prey, and none delivereth; for a spoil, and none saith, Restore.

23 Who among you will give ear to this? *who* will hearken and hear for the time to come?

24 Who gave Jacob for a spoil, and Israel to the robbers? did not the LORD, he against whom we have sinned? for they would not walk in his ways, neither were they obedient unto his law.

25 Therefore he hath poured upon him the fury of his anger, and the strength of battle: and it hath set him on fire round about, yet he knew not; and it burned him, yet he laid *it* not to heart.

JST Isaiah 42:19–25
19 For I will send my servant unto you who are blind; yea, a messenger to open the eyes of the blind, and unstop the ears of the deaf;

20 And they [*those who listen and repent*] shall be made perfect [*the power of the Atonement; 2 Nephi 25:23*] notwithstanding their blindness, if they will hearken unto the messenger, the Lord's servant.

21 Thou [*Israel*] art a people, seeing many things, but thou observest not [*you don't obey*]; opening the ears to hear, but thou hearest not [*you don't want to hear the truth*].

22 The Lord is not well pleased with such a people, but for his righteousness' sake he will magnify the law and make it honorable.

23 Thou art a people robbed and spoiled; thine enemies, all of them, have snared thee in holes, and they have hid thee in prison houses; they have taken thee for a prey, and none delivereth; for a spoil, and none saith, Restore [*consequences of Israel's wickedness*].

24 Who among them [*Israel's enemies in verse 23*] will give ear unto thee [*Israel*], or hearken and hear thee for the time to come? and who gave Jacob for a spoil, and Israel to the robbers [*who turned Israel over to her enemies*]? did not the Lord, he against whom they have sinned [*the Lord did, because of Israel's wickedness*]?

25 For they [*Israel*] would not walk in his ways, neither were they obedient unto his law; therefore [*that is why*] he [*the Lord*] hath poured upon them the fury of his anger, and the strength of battle; and they [*Israel's enemies*] have set them [*Israel*] on fire round about [*have caused terrible destruction*], yet they [*Israel*] know not [*won't acknowledge that they are being punished*], and it burned them, yet they laid it not to heart [*refused to repent*].

ISAIAH 43

Selection: all verses

THIS CHAPTER CONTAINS clear doctrine that Jesus Christ, our Savior and Redeemer, is the God of the Old Testament—see, for example, verses 3, 11 and 14.

Having pointed out the foolishness of idol worship and the wisdom of being loyal to the true God, the Savior now reaches out to covenant Israel, inviting them to be gathered to Him. Everyone on earth can become a member of covenant Israel through being baptized, living the gospel, and making and keeping the additional covenants available to faithful members of the Church.

1 But now **thus saith the LORD that created thee, O Jacob,** and he that formed thee, **O Israel** [*emphasis on the words "created" and "formed" as used in Genesis 1:27 and 2:7; in other words, the true God is your Creator as described by Moses; these words will again be repeated for emphasis in verse 7*], Fear not: for **I have redeemed thee, I have called thee by thy name; thou art mine** [*the Savior will succeed in redeeming a remnant of Israel despite their coming problems as described in Isaiah 42:22–25*].

2 **When thou passest through the waters, I will be with thee; and through the rivers, they shall not overflow thee** [*referring to the parting of the Red Sea and Jordan River; in other words, I helped you then and the same power and help is still available to you*]: **when thou walkest through the fire, thou shalt not be burned; neither shall the flame kindle upon thee.** [*Perhaps referring to how He will help Shadrach, Meshach, and Abed-nego survive the fiery furnace (Daniel 3). I want to protect and bless you too.*]

3 For **I am** the LORD thy God, the Holy One of Israel, **thy Saviour:** I gave Egypt for thy ransom, Ethiopia and Seba [*a people in southern Arabia*] for thee [*I will ransom you from your enemies—sin, Satan—represented by Egypt. I will pay the price that you might go free. Applies literally also, in terms of protection from physical enemy nations, see Isaiah 45:14*].

4 **Since thou wast** [*art, are*] **precious in my sight,** thou hast been honourable [*honored by me*], and **I have loved thee: therefore will I give men for thee** [*prophets' lives have been sacrificed for us, for our benefit*], **and people for thy life** [*many have given their lives for the benefit of others. Most especially, Christ's Atonement works for us*].

5 **Fear not: for I am with thee:** I

will bring thy [Israel's] seed from the east, and gather thee from the west [the gathering of Israel];

6 I will say to the north, Give up [give up the Israelites you're holding back from the Lord]; and to the south, Keep not back: bring my sons from far, and my daughters from the ends of the earth [the gathering of Israel is worldwide];

7 Even every one that is called by my name [that is willing to make and keep covenants]: for I have created him for my glory, I have formed him; yea, I have made him [carries the connotation of redemption through the Atonement via repentance—being "born again" as discussed in Alma 5. That is how the Savior "creates" us as new people spiritually].

8 ¶ Bring forth the blind people that have eyes, and the deaf that have ears [spiritually blind and deaf who have ignored prophets' messages and turned to other gods—see verse 9].

9 Let all the nations be gathered together, and let the people be assembled: who among them can declare this [the true gospel], and shew us former things [such as premortal life details]? let them bring forth their witnesses [their false gods, sorcerers, and so forth], that they may be justified [let's see their false gods, sorcerers, etc., do the kinds of things the true God of Israel can do]:

or let them hear, and say, It [Israel's message as given in verses 11–13] is truth.

10 Ye [Israel] are my witnesses, saith the LORD, and my servant whom I have chosen [to carry the gospel to all the world, see Abraham 2:9]: that ye may know and believe me, and understand that I am he: before me there was no God formed, neither shall there be after me [no idols ever have, nor ever will, take My place].

11 I [Jesus], even I, am the LORD; and beside me there is no saviour. [This is the message!]

12 I have declared, and have saved, and I have shewed, when there was no strange god [idol] among you [I have greatly blessed you when you were not worshipping idols]: therefore ye [Israel] are my witnesses [our calling, responsibility], saith the LORD, that I am God.

13 Yea, before the day was I am he [I was God before time began for you and will continue to be God]; and there is none that can deliver out of my hand: I will work [perform the Atonement and bless you with the gospel], and who shall let [JST: "hinder"] it?

14 ¶ Thus saith the LORD, your redeemer, the Holy One of Israel; For your sake I have sent to [I will

triumph over] **Babylon** [*dual meaning: Symbolically Satan's kingdom; literally Israel's enemies in the nation of Babylon*], **and have brought** [*will bring*] **down all their nobles, and the Chaldeans** [*inhabitants of southern Babylon; symbolic of the wicked in all nations*], **whose cry is in the ships** [*German: whose shouting will turn to lamenting as I hunt them in their ships; in other words, freedom from your enemies comes through the Savior*].

Verse 15, next, summarizes the main point of this chapter.

15 I am the LORD, your Holy One, the creator of Israel, your King.

16 Thus saith the LORD, which maketh a way in the sea [*parted the Red Sea*], **and a path in the mighty waters;**

17 Which bringeth forth [*German: puts down, dismantles*] **the chariot and horse, the army and the power; they** [*your enemies*] **shall lie down** [*die*] **together, they shall not rise: they are extinct, they are quenched as tow** [*snuffed out like a smoldering candle*].

In verse 18, next, we see, among other things, that the gospel of Jesus Christ allows us to leave the past behind us and put all our energy into the present in order to have a glorious future. This is the essence of the Atonement of Christ.

18 Remember ye not the former things, neither consider the things of old [*forget the past troubles and oppressions; they are now behind you*].

19 Behold, I will do a new thing [*the Restoration of the gospel; the gathering of Israel*]; **now it shall spring forth; shall ye not know it** [*you will see it plainly*]? **I will even make a way in the wilderness, and rivers in the desert** [*perhaps dual meaning, referring to physical changes in the earth to help Israel's gathering, and also symbolic of effects of "living water," gospel, bringing life to apostate Israel (referred to as "dry ground" in Isaiah 53:2; 44:3) as water does to the wilderness, desert*].

20 The beast of the field shall honour me, the dragons and the owls [*jackals and ostriches—see footnote 20a in your Bible; in other words, even "unclean" animals and fowls will honor Me*]: **because I give waters in the wilderness, and rivers in the desert,** to give drink [*"living water" also; John 7:37–38*] to my people, my chosen.

21 This people have I formed [*German: prepared*] **for myself; they** shall shew forth my praise [*definite, strong prophecy that Israel will return to the Lord and be gathered*].

Next, the topic turns to Israel's past performance, which has not been good.

22 ¶ But thou hast not called upon

me, O Jacob; but thou hast been weary of me, O Israel [*you have a poor "track record," a history of disloyalty to Me*].

23 Thou hast not brought me the small cattle [*lambs or young goats*] of thy burnt offerings; neither hast thou honoured me with thy sacrifices. I have not caused thee to serve with an offering [*German: I have not been pleased with your offerings of the first fruits, Numbers 18:12*], nor wearied thee with incense [*German: nor taken pleasure in your incense*].

24 Thou hast bought me no sweet cane [*spices used in making anointing oil for use in the tabernacle; Exodus 30:23–25*] with money, neither hast thou filled [*satisfied*] me with the fat of thy sacrifices [*your sacrifices are empty ritual*]: but thou hast made me to serve [*burdened me; German: made work for me*] with thy sins, thou hast wearied me [*German: caused me trouble and pains*] with thine iniquities.

Next, in verse 25, we see another clear statement that Jesus Christ is the God of the Old Testament, in other words, the one who is speaking and teaching in the Old Testament. Here He teaches about His Atonement.

25 I [*the Savior*], even I, am he that blotteth out thy transgressions for mine own sake [*I desire very much to forgive you and save you; Moses 1:39, Isaiah 1:18*], and will not remember thy sins [*if you truly repent; Doctrine & Covenants 58:42–43*].

26 Put me in remembrance [*remember me*]: let us plead together [*German: debate as in a court of law; in other words, let us look at the facts*]: declare thou [*state your point of view*], that thou mayest be justified [*go ahead, try to justify your wicked behavior*].

27 Thy first father [*ancestors; early Israel, the children of Israel under Moses—see footnote 27a in your Bible*] hath sinned, and thy teachers [*priests and ministers*] have transgressed against me.

28 Therefore [*for this reason*] I have profaned the princes [*priests and ministers; considered them to be worldly, not acceptable to Me*] of the sanctuary [*probably meaning the tabernacle or the temple in Jerusalem*], and have given Jacob [*Israel*] to the curse [*German: excommunication, cut off*], and Israel to reproaches [*German: become the object of scorn*].

ISAIAH 44

Selection: all verses

VERSES 1-8 DEAL mostly with Christ's role in redeeming Israel. Verses 9-20 deal mainly with pagan idol worship.

1 Yet now hear, O Jacob [*another word for Israel*] my servant; and

Israel, whom I have chosen [*in other words, Israel constitutes the Lord's "chosen people"*]:

There are many things one could say about the word "chosen" in verse 1, above. For example, Israel is chosen to carry the gospel and blessings of the priesthood to all the world (see Abraham 2:9–11). Israel is chosen to carry heavy burdens of persecution and scorn, from time to time. Israel (which can include anyone who is willing to join the Church through baptism and afterwards keep the commandments) is chosen to be exalted. Israel is chosen "to stand as witnesses of God at all times and in all things, and in all places" (Mosiah 18:9). And the list of meanings for the word "chosen" goes on and on.

The thing that "chosen" does not imply is that God arbitrarily chooses some people over others to be saved.

Notice that "Jacob" and "Israel" are often used interchangeably in the scriptures. That is because they are both names of the father of the twelve sons who became the heads of the twelve tribes of Israel.

2 Thus saith the LORD that made thee, and formed thee from the womb, which will help thee [*I have been helping you from the beginning and will continue to do so*]; **Fear not, O Jacob, my servant; and thou, Jesurun** [*those who are righteous, Deuteronomy 33:26, footnote 26a*], **whom I have chosen.**

3 For I will pour water [*dual meaning: literal; also "living water" (the gospel of Jesus Christ), 2 Nephi 9:50*] **upon him that is thirsty, and floods upon the dry ground** [*apostate Israel; Isaiah 53:2*]**: I will pour my spirit upon thy seed** [*descendants*], **and my blessing upon thine offspring** [*the "blessings of Abraham, Isaac, and Jacob;" Abraham 2:9–11*]:

4 And they shall spring up as among the grass, as willows by the water courses [*there will be righteous Israelites all over the place; Isaiah 49:21, 1 Nephi 21–21*]

5 One shall say, I am the LORD's; and another shall call himself by the name of Jacob [*they have both converted to the Lord and are loyal to Him; compare with 19:25*]**; and another shall subscribe with his hand** [*make covenants*] **unto the LORD, and surname himself by the name of Israel** [*take upon himself the name of Christ and become part of righteous covenant Israel*].

6 Thus saith the LORD the King of Israel, and **his** [*Israel's*] **redeemer** the LORD of [*heavenly*] **hosts; I am the first, and I am the last** [*Jesus was chosen at the first, in the premortal existence, to be our Redeemer, and He will be around at the last, to be our Judge—see John 5:22*]**; and beside me there is no God** [*there are no idols that are actually gods*].

7 And who [*what idols; compare*

with Isaiah 40:25], **as I, shall call, and shall declare it, and set it in order for me, since I appointed** *[established]* **the ancient people** *[my people]?* **and the things that are coming** *[future events]*, **and shall come, let them** *[your idols, false gods]* **shew unto them** *[foretell for you; in other words, this whole verse is a challenge for apostate Israel to have their idols do as well as the Lord in leading them and prophesying the future]*.

8 Fear ye not, neither be afraid *[trust in me]*: **have not I told thee from that time** *[from the ancient times from the beginning; see verse 7]*, **and have declared it? ye are even my witnesses** *[Israel's calling, stewardship]*. **Is there a God beside me** *[is there an idol that is a god like Me]? yea, there is no God; I know not any.**

Verses 9–20 will now deal primarily with the apostate practice of worshiping idols.

9 They that make a graven image *[an idol]* **are all of them vanity** *[German: vain, conceited, won't take counsel from God]*; **and their delectable** *[German: precious]* **things shall not profit** *[will do them no good]*; **and they are their own witnesses; they see not, nor know** *[those who worship idols are as blind and empty-headed as the idols they worship]*; **that they may be ashamed** *[may be put to shame]*.

10 Who hath formed a god, or

molten a graven image that is profitable for nothing *[good for nothing; in other words, who would do such a foolish thing]?*

11 Behold, all his fellows *[fellow idol worshipers]* **shall be ashamed:** **and the workmen, they are of men** *[are mere mortals]*: **let them all be gathered together, let them stand up; yet they shall fear, and they shall be ashamed together** *[no matter how many worship idols, it does no good; they will all be put to shame]*.

12 The smith *[blacksmith]* **with the tongs both worketh in the coals, and fashioneth it** *[an idol]* **with hammers, and worketh it with the strength of his arms: yea, he is hungry** *[the craftsman is a mere mortal]*, **and his strength faileth: he drinketh no water, and is faint** *[the craftsmen who make idols for you are mere mortals themselves]*.

13 The carpenter stretcheth out his rule; he marketh it *[the idol he is making]* out with a line; he fitteth it with planes, and he marketh it out with the compass *[your craftsmen exercise great care and skill in manufacturing your idols]*, and maketh it after the figure of a man, according to the beauty of a man; that it may remain in the house *[your craftsmen put great care into making your idols; implication: if you were as careful worshipping God as you are in making idols . . .]*.

14 He heweth him down cedars, and taketh the cypress and the oak, which he strengtheneth [*cultivates and grows*] for himself among the trees of the forest: he planteth an ash [*tree*], and the rain doth nourish it.

15 Then shall it be for a man to burn: for he will take thereof, and warm himself; yea, he kindleth it, and baketh bread; yea, he maketh a god, and worshippeth it [*you use most of the tree's wood for normal daily needs; how can you possibly turn around and worship wood from the same tree in the form of idols!*]; he maketh it a graven image, and falleth down thereto.

16 He burneth part thereof in the fire; with part thereof he eateth flesh; he roasteth roast, and is satisfied: yea, he warmeth himself, and saith, Aha, I am warm, I have seen the fire [*normal uses*]:

17 And **the residue thereof** [*with the rest of the tree*] **he maketh a god**, even his graven image: **he falleth down unto it, and worshippeth it**, and prayeth unto it, and saith, Deliver [*save*] me; for thou art my god [*Isaiah is saying how utterly ridiculous it is to assign part of a tree to have powers over yourselves*].

18 They [*idol worshipers; see Isaiah 45:20*] **have not known** [*German: know nothing*] **nor understood** [*German: understand nothing*]: for he hath shut their eyes [*German: they are blind*], that **they cannot see** [*are spiritually blind*]; and **their hearts, that they cannot understand** [*they are as blind and unfeeling, insensitive, as the idols they make and worship*].

19 And **none considereth in his heart** [*if idol worshipers would just stop and think*], **neither is there knowledge nor understanding** [*they don't have enough common sense*] **to say, I have burned part of it** [*the tree spoken of in verse 14*] **in the fire; yea, also I have baked bread upon the coals thereof; I have roasted flesh, and eaten it: and shall I make the residue thereof an abomination** [*is it reasonable to make the leftover portion into an abominable idol*]? **shall I fall down to the stock of a tree** [*is it rational to worship a chunk of wood*]?

20 He [*the idol worshiper*] **feedeth on ashes** [*German: takes pleasure in ashes, perhaps referring to ashes left over from some forms of idol worship*]: a [*German: his own*] **deceived heart hath turned him aside** [*German: leads him astray*], **that he cannot deliver** [*save*] **his soul, nor say** [*wake up and think*], **Is there not a lie in my right hand** [*covenant hand—am I not making covenants with false gods*]?

21 ¶ Remember these, O Jacob and Israel; for thou art my servant: I

have formed thee [the exact opposite of idol worshipers who form their
gods]; thou art my servant: O
Israel, thou shalt not be forgotten
of me.

Next, in verse 22, the Savior
assures Israel that their sins can
be blotted out completely by His
Atonement.

22 I have blotted out, as a thick
cloud, thy transgressions, and, as
a cloud, thy sins [the Atonement can
still work for you]: return unto me;
for I have redeemed thee [I have
paid the price of your sins; therefore,
please repent].

In verse 23, next, all things in
nature are invited to praise the
Lord for what He has done for
Israel.

23 Sing, O ye heavens; for the
LORD hath done it: shout, ye
lower parts of the earth [German:
O earth below]: break forth into
singing, ye mountains, O forest,
and every tree therein: for the
LORD hath redeemed Jacob, and
glorified himself in Israel [speaking
of the future].

24 Thus saith the LORD, thy
redeemer, and he that formed
[German: prepared] thee from the
womb, I am the LORD that maketh
all things; that stretcheth forth
the heavens alone; that spreadeth
abroad the earth by myself [I created heaven and earth; no idols helped
Me!];

One of the evil things rebellious
Israelites had done was to go to
fortune-tellers, witches, sorcerers, and so forth for "revelation,"
rather than repenting and going
to God for revelation. Verse 25,
next, addresses this issue.

25 That frustrateth [causeth
to fail] the tokens [signs] of the
liars [German: fortune tellers], and
maketh diviners [people who deal
in the occult] mad [German: absurd];
that turneth [so-called] wise men
backward, and maketh their
knowledge [German: business of
fortune-telling] foolish;

26 [I am the Lord] That confirmeth
the word of his servant, and per-
formeth the counsel of his messengers [I support My servants, whereas
idols don't support theirs]; that saith
to Jerusalem, Thou shalt be inhabited; and to the cities of Judah, Ye
shall be built, and I will raise up
the decayed places thereof [when I
command, things obey; idols can't command and aren't obeyed]:

27 [I am the Lord] That saith to
the deep [the sea, such as the Red Sea
when the Israelites crossed through it],
Be dry, and I will dry up thy rivers [as in the case of the Jordan River
when the Israelites crossed through
it into the promised land; see Joshua
3:17]:

28 That saith of Cyrus [the Persian],
He is my shepherd [a tool in my
hand], and shall perform all my

pleasure: even saying to Jerusalem, Thou shalt be built; and to the temple, Thy foundation shall be laid. [*A specific prophecy! Cyrus conquered Babylon about 538 BC, who had conquered Jerusalem about fifty years earlier in 588 BC. In 537 BC, Cyrus issued a decree to let the Jews return home to Palestine to rebuild Jerusalem and the temple. See 538 BC on the chronology chart in the Bible Dictionary at the back of your LDS Bible*].

ISAIAH 45

Selection: all verses

THIS CHAPTER CONTAINS a prophecy about Cyrus the Persian, who conquered Babylon in about 538 BC and subsequently (about 537 BC) allowed the Jews to return to Jerusalem to build up the city again and rebuild the temple. One of the lessons we learn here is that the Lord often uses "nonmember" leaders and individuals to accomplish His purposes. For example, the British helped the Jews return to their homeland in 1948 and establish their own nation.

1 Thus saith the LORD to his anointed, **to Cyrus**, whose right hand I have holden [*strengthened*], to subdue nations before him; and I will loose the loins of kings [*German: take the sword of kings away from them*], to open before him the two leaved gates [*main city gates*];

and the gates shall not be shut [*the Lord will open the way for Cyrus and none will stop him*];

2 I will go before thee, and make the crooked places straight [*German: will take out the bumps*]: I will break in pieces the gates of brass, and cut in sunder [*cut through*] the bars of iron:

3 And **I will give thee** the **treasures** of darkness, and hidden riches of secret places [*hidden treasures, probably referring to Babylon*], that thou mayest know that I, the LORD, which call thee [*Cyrus*] by thy name, am the God of Israel.

> Remember, "Jacob" and "Israel," as used in verse 4, next, are the same thing. In "the manner of prophesying among the Jews" (2 Nephi 25:1), it is common for prophets such as Isaiah to say the same thing in succession, for emphasis. If you don't understand this, you might think that Jacob and Israel are two separate groups in this verse.

4 For Jacob my servant's sake, and Israel mine elect, I have even called thee [*Cyrus*] **by thy name: I have surnamed thee, though thou hast not known me** [*although you don't know Me and do not realize that I am using you to fulfill My purposes, I will use you to free the Jews*].

5 I am the LORD, and there is none else, there is no God beside me: I girded thee [*dressed you for war* and strengthened you], **though thou hast not known me:**

6 That they may know from the rising of the sun, and from the west [from east to west—everywhere], **that there is none beside me** [that I am the only true God; in other words, idols and man-made deities are not gods]. **I am the LORD, and there is none else.**

7 I form the light, and create darkness: I make peace, and create evil [cause calamity, as in 3 Nephi 9:3–12]: **I the LORD do all these things.**

8 Drop [drip; rain] **down, ye heavens, from above, and let the skies pour down righteousness: let the earth open** [produce], **and let them** [heaven and earth] **bring forth salvation** [the main purpose of creating the earth], **and let righteousness spring up together** [with it]; **I the LORD have created it** [let the purposes of creating heaven and earth be wonderfully fulfilled].

9 Woe unto him that striveth with [fights against] **his Maker! Let the potsherd** [vessel of clay; shard, broken piece of pottery] **strive with the potsherds of the earth** [German: a shard like other mortal shards—how foolish of a mere mortal to quarrel with his Creator]. **Shall the clay say to him that fashioneth it, What makest thou?** or thy work, **He hath no hands** [an insolent question, asking,

in effect, "Who do you think you are, God?"; compare with Isaiah 29:16]?

10 Woe unto him that saith unto his father, What begettest thou? or to the woman [his mother], **What hast thou brought forth** [what do you think you're doing; being sassy]?

11 Thus saith the LORD, the Holy One of Israel [Jehovah, Jesus Christ], and his [Israel's] Maker, **Ask me of things to come** [about the future] concerning my sons, and concerning the work of my hands **command** [German: acknowledge me as the Creator] **ye me** [ask Me, I'll tell you].

12 I have made the earth, and created man upon it: I, even my hands, have stretched out [created] the heavens, and all their host have I commanded [I am the Creator].

Having borne strong witness of the fact that none of the pagan gods are real gods, the Lord returns now to the prophecy that He will use a leader named Cyrus (verse 1) to free the Jews from Babylon so that they can return to Jerusalem. Since Isaiah served as a prophet from about 740 BC to 701 BC, and since Cyrus the Persian conquered Babylon in about 538 BC and decreed the Jews' freedom about 537 BC, this prophecy is given by Isaiah over 160 years before it takes place!

13 I have raised him [Cyrus—see verse 1] **up in righteousness** [I will use him to fulfill My righteous purposes], **and I will direct all his ways: he shall**

build my city [rebuild Jerusalem], and he shall let go my captives [the Jews], not for price nor reward [the hand of the Lord is in it], saith the LORD of hosts.

14 Thus saith the LORD, The labour of **Egypt**, and merchandise of **Ethiopia** and of **the Sabeans** [a people in southeastern Arabia], men of stature, shall come over unto thee, and they **shall be thine:** they shall come after thee [behind you]; in chains they shall come over, and they shall fall down unto thee, they shall make supplication unto thee, saying, Surely God is in thee; and there is none else, there is no God [all nations will recognize that the Lord is with Cyrus and Israel].

15 Verily **thou art a God that hidest thyself** [in other words, can't be seen physically on a daily basis like idols can], O God of Israel, the Saviour.

16 They [nations of the world] **shall be ashamed** [put to shame because of their wickedness and corruption], and also confounded, all of them: they shall go to confusion together **that are makers of idols** [results of idol worship].

17 But Israel shall be saved in the LORD with an everlasting salvation: ye shall not be ashamed nor confounded world without end [throughout eternity; results of righteousness].

18 **For thus saith the LORD** [in answer to the insolent question in verses 9 and 10] **that created the heavens;** God himself that formed **the earth** and made it; he hath established it, he created it not in vain, he formed it to be inhabited: **I am the LORD; and there is none else.**

19 **I have not spoken in secret, in a dark place of the earth** [I have not hidden from you, played "hard to get." I have been open and direct with you.]: **I said not unto the seed of Jacob** [the covenant people, Israel], **Seek ye me in vain:** I the LORD speak righteousness, I declare things that are right.

20 **Assemble yourselves and come;** draw near together, **ye that are escaped** [survivors] of the nations: they [idol worshippers, Isaiah 44:18] **have no knowledge** [see notes for Isaiah 44:18] that set up the wood of their graven image, and pray unto a god [idol] that cannot save.

21 **Tell ye** [spread the word], and **bring them** [idol worshippers] **near;** yea, **let them take counsel** [plot] together: **who hath declared** [explained] **this from ancient time** [since time began]? who hath told it from that time? **have not I the LORD? and there is no God else beside me; a just God and a Saviour;** there is none beside me [there is no comparison between idols and the true God!].

Next, the Lord invites all people everywhere to repent.

22 Look unto me [*German: turn to me; in other words, repent*], **and be ye saved,** all the ends of the earth [*the Atonement applies to all*]: for I am God, and there is none else.

Next, in verse 23, we are taught that every person who has ever been born or who will be born, will someday acknowledge that Jesus is the Christ.

23 I have sworn [*covenanted, promised*] **by myself** [*in My own name*], the word is gone out of my mouth in righteousness, and shall not return [*see Doctrine & Covenants 1:38*], **That unto me every knee shall bow, every tongue shall swear** [*acknowledge Christ; does not mean that everyone will repent and be righteous; for example this phrase refers to inhabitants of the telestial glory as used in Doctrine & Covenants 76:110*].

24 Surely, shall one say, in the LORD have I righteousness and strength: even to him shall men come; **and all that are incensed** [*angry*] **against him shall be ashamed** [*put to shame; disappointed, disconcerted*].

25 In the LORD [*Christ*] **shall** [*can*] **all the seed of Israel be justified** [*brought into harmony with God's ways, thus be approved to dwell with God*], **and shall glory** [*in the Lord, 1 Corinthians 1:31*].

It is interesting to note that the word "justified," seen in verse 25 above, is used in current word processing terminology to mean "lined up," as in "justify the margins." In scriptural language, "justified" likewise means "lined up"—in other words, "lined up with God's will," or in harmony with God's commandments and thus worthy to be ratified and approved by the Holy Ghost, the Holy Spirit of Promise, to live with God forever.

ISAIAH 46

Selection: all verses

THIS CHAPTER CONTINUES the comparison of Jehovah with the false gods and idols worshiped by so many people in Isaiah's day. The point is that there is no comparison!

Verse 1 introduces us to two prominent false gods in Isaiah's day. Bel and Nebo were chief gods in Babylon. Ancient cultures such as Babylon believed that each "god" had a territory, and when a city or country was defeated in battle by enemies, it meant that their gods (such as Bel and Nebo) had been defeated by the enemy's gods. Chapter 46 ties in with chapters 13 and 14 concerning Babylon's downfall, and with chapters 40–45 concerning Jehovah's power as compared to the lack of power of idols.

1 Bel boweth down [*German: has been defeated*], **Nebo stoopeth, their idols were upon the beasts, and upon the cattle** [*the idols are* powerless; they can't move by themselves and have to be transported upon beasts of burden]: your carriages were heavy loaden; they [the idols] are a burden to the weary beast [the message, by implication, is that Bel and Nebo are burdens to those who "created" them, in contrast to the true God of Israel, who lightens the burdens of those He created, who worship Him].

2 They [Bel and Nebo] **stoop, they bow down together** [German: they are both defeated]; **they could not deliver** [German: remove] **the burden** [they couldn't do the job], **but themselves are gone into captivity** [they have failed their worshippers and couldn't even save themselves].

3 Hearken unto me, O house of Jacob, and all the remnant of the house of Israel, which are borne by me [note that I the Lord carry you, help you, am not a burden] **from the belly** [from the womb, or from the beginning], **which are carried from the womb** [I have carried you from the beginning, contrasted to idol worshippers who have to transport their "gods"]:

4 And even to your old age [throughout your entire life] **I am he** [the true God]; **and even to hoar** [gray] **hairs will I carry you: I have made** [German: I want to do it], **and I will** [German: desire to] **bear; even I will**

carry, and will **deliver** you [I want to help, support and bless you throughout your entire life; I want to be your Redeemer!].

5 To whom will ye liken me, and make me equal, and compare me, that we may be like [who among your false gods can compare to Me]? [Same question as in 40:18, 25.]

> Next, in verses 6–7, Isaiah again points out how ridiculous it is to make and then worship idols.

6 They [idol worshippers] **lavish gold** out of the bag, **and weigh silver** in the balance [on the scales; in other words, you pay out much money for your worthless idols], **and hire a goldsmith; and he maketh it a god** [turns it into an idol]: **they fall down, yea, they worship.**

7 They [idol worshippers] **bear him** [their idol] **upon the shoulder, they carry him, and set him in his place** [put the idol in the room or place they want it to stay], **and he standeth; from his place shall he not remove** [the idol can't even move from the place the people put it]: **yea, one shall cry** [pray] **unto him** [the idol], **yet can he** [the idol] **not answer, nor save him** [the idol worshiper] out of his trouble [idols are totally worthless!].

8 Remember this, and shew yourselves men [think about this and prove that you are man enough to face the truth]: **bring it again to mind, O**

ye transgressors [*face the issue, you sinners!*].

9 Remember the former things of old [*the many miracles I performed for you in the past*]: **for I am God, and there is none else; I am God, and there is none like me,**

10 Declaring the end from the beginning [*prophesying the future*], **and from ancient times the things that are not yet done** [*things prophesied anciently that are yet in the future*], **saying, My counsel shall stand, and I will do all my pleasure** [*everything I have said will happen; this message is also given in Doctrine & Covenants 1:38*]:

11 Calling a ravenous bird from the east [*a bird of prey; in other words, Cyrus from Persia—see 45:1*], **the man that executeth** [*carries out*] **my counsel** [*plans*] **from a far country** [*Persia*]: **yea, I have spoken it, I will also bring it to pass; I have purposed** [*planned*] **it, I will also do it.**

12 Hearken unto me, ye stout-hearted [*hardhearted*], **that are far from righteousness** [*as mentioned in verse 8*]:

13 I bring near my righteousness [*victory, triumph*]; **it shall not be** [*German: is not*] **far off, and my salvation shall not tarry** [*will not be late*]: **and I will place salvation in Zion for Israel my glory** [*I will*

succeed in bringing salvation and glory to Israel, and you can be a part of it if you repent*].

ISAIAH 47

Selection: all verses

THIS CHAPTER IS a prophecy about the downfall of Babylon. Remember that Babylon was an actual large city (56 miles around with walls 335 feet high and 85 feet wide—see Bible Dictionary, under "Babylon"), but that Babylon is also used often in the scriptures to symbolize Satan's kingdom.

1 Come down [*be humbled*], **and sit in the dust** [*a sign of humiliation in eastern cultures; see Isaiah 3:26, Lamentations 2:10*], **O virgin** [*unconquered*] **daughter of Babylon** [*the Babylonian Empire*], **sit on the ground** [*humiliation*]: **there is no throne** [*Babylon was to be conquered, overthrown; this prophecy was fulfilled literally by Cyrus the Persian in 538 BC and will be fulfilled symbolically as Christ overthrows Satan's kingdom*], **O daughter of the Chaldeans** [*inhabitants of southern Babylonia, part of the Babylonian Empire*]: **for thou shalt no more be called tender and delicate** [*German: desirable*].

Using imagery to illustrate a conquered Babylon, Isaiah now describes conditions and tasks of slaves, according to the culture of his day.

2 Take the millstones, and grind meal [*flour*]: **uncover thy locks** [*take off your veil, like slaves do*], **make bare the leg, uncover the thigh** [*tie up your skirts and expose your legs so you can get around easily to do the work required of slaves*], **pass over the rivers** [*you'll have to wade through canals to get from one field to another as you do the work of slaves*].

3 Thy nakedness shall be uncovered [*dual meaning: sexual abuse suffered by slaves; also the "true colors"—in other words, the wickedness of Babylon will be uncovered, exposed*], **yea, thy shame shall be seen: I** [*the Lord*] **will take vengeance, and I will not meet thee** [*Babylon and all things represented by Babylon*] **as a man** [*you won't be able to stop Me because I'm not a mortal man*].

4 As for [*German: thus doeth*] **our redeemer,** the LORD **of hosts is his name, the Holy One of Israel.**

5 Sit thou [*Babylon*] **silent, and get thee into darkness, O daughter of the Chaldeans** [*Babylon*]: **for thou shalt no more be called, The lady of kingdoms** [*you've been conquered*].

Next, in verse 6, the Lord explains why He allowed Babylon to conquer the Jews (the main portion of Israel affected by this prophecy). Remember that Isaiah is prophesying of the future as if it had already happened. The events foretold here didn't actually take place until over one hundred years later.

6 I [*God*] **was wroth** [*angry*] **with my people, I have polluted** [*German: disowned*] **mine inheritance** [*wicked Israel*], **and given them** [*prophecy of future*] **into thine** [*Babylon's*] **hand: thou didst shew them** [*Israel, especially the Jews*] **no mercy; upon the ancient hast thou very heavily laid thy yoke** [*in other words, you abused the power I allowed you to have over Israel*].

7 And thou [*Babylon*] **saidst** [*boasted*], **I shall be a lady** [*German: a queen*] **for ever: so that thou didst not lay these things to thy heart** [*you didn't take My warnings seriously*], **neither didst remember the latter end of it** [*you didn't stop to consider the consequences of your behavior*].

8 Therefore hear now this, thou [*Babylon*] **that art given to pleasures** [*lustful and riotous living*], **that dwellest carelessly** [*NIV: "lounging in your security"*], **that sayest in thine heart, I am, and none else beside me** [*I am the most powerful of all!*]; **I shall not sit as a widow** [*have my kingdom taken away from me*], **neither shall I know the loss of children** [*Babylon boasts she will never be conquered; however, she will be depopulated and her king destroyed*]:

9 But these two things [*the loss of your king and your inhabitants*] **shall**

come to thee in a moment [*suddenly*] **in one day, the loss of children,** and **widowhood:** they shall come upon thee in their perfection [*in full measure*] for [*despite*] the multitude of thy sorceries, and for [*despite*] the great abundance of thine enchantments [*the so-called "magic" of your false religions will not save you*].

10 For thou hast trusted in [*relied on*] **thy wickedness:** thou hast said, None seeth me [*I can get away with it*]. Thy wisdom and thy knowledge, it hath perverted thee [*German: has led you astray*]; and thou hast said in thine heart, I am, and none else beside me [*I am all-powerful*].

11 Therefore [*because of the things mentioned above*] **shall evil come upon thee;** thou shalt not know [*German: expect it*] from whence it riseth [*the source of your demise will surprise you*]: and mischief [*ruin*] shall fall upon thee; thou shalt not be able to put it off [*German: atone for it via sacrifices to false gods; see verse 12*]: and **desolation shall come upon thee suddenly,** which thou shalt not know [*foresee*].

12 Stand now with thine enchantments, and with the multitude of thy sorceries, wherein thou hast laboured from thy youth [*like you've done all your lives*]; if so be thou shalt be able to profit, if so be thou mayest prevail [*go ahead, try to stop this destruction with your false gods and enchantments; see if they help or not*].

13 Thou art wearied in the multitude of thy counsels [*you have spent many boring hours with your counselors, stargazers, and so forth*]. **Let now the astrologers,** the **stargazers,** the monthly **prognosticators** [*those who predict the future*], **stand up, and save thee from these things that shall come upon thee** [*call their bluff*].

14 Behold, they [*your religious leaders, soothsayers, wizards, and so forth, as mentioned in verse 13*] **shall be as stubble; the fire shall burn them;** they shall not deliver themselves from the power of the flame: there shall not be a coal to warm at, nor fire to sit before it [*your soothsayers are utterly powerless to save themselves, let alone you*].

The whole message of this chapter, that no one can save Babylon, is summarized in verse 15, next.

15 Thus [*like straw in a fire*] **shall they be unto thee** with whom thou hast laboured, even thy merchants [*religious leaders*], from thy youth: they shall wander every one to his quarter; **none shall save.**

ISAIAH 48

Selection: all verses

IN THIS CHAPTER, "Babylon" is used in the symbolic sense. It means wickedness and evil, in other words, Satan's kingdom. This is one of the two chapters of Isaiah that Nephi read to his people in First Nephi, including his rebellious brothers, Laman and Lemuel (1 Nephi 20 and 21). Nephi explained to us why he chose to read these words of Isaiah. He said (**bold** added for emphasis):

1 Nephi 19:23–24
23 And I did read many things unto them which were written in the books of Moses; but **that I might more fully persuade them to believe in the Lord their Redeemer I did read unto them that which was written by the prophet Isaiah;** for I did liken all scriptures unto us, that it might be for our profit and learning.

24 Wherefore I spake unto them, saying: Hear ye the words of the prophet, ye who are a remnant of the house of Israel, a branch who have been broken off; hear ye the words of the prophet, which were written unto all the house of Israel, and liken them unto yourselves, **that ye may have hope** as well as your brethren from whom ye have been broken off; for after this manner has the prophet written.

EVERY VERSE OF 1 Nephi, chapter 20, has at least one thing that is different than what we will read here in Isaiah, chapter 48. This is a reminder that the Book of Mormon text of Isaiah was translated from the Brass Plates of Laban, which Lehi and his family had obtained. The Isaiah passages found in the Book of Mormon come from records much closer to the original source (Isaiah only lived about one hundred years before Lehi's departure from Jerusalem). In contrast, Isaiah in the Bible is derived from sources much farther removed from the original. Therefore, we will use 1 Nephi chapter 20 often for clarification as we study this chapter.

AS WE BEGIN, we see that Isaiah is pointing out the empty worship and hypocrisy of Israel. After doing so, he issues an invitation from the Lord for these people to repent, to flee from Babylon (wickedness), and come unto Him. He finishes with a stern warning that there is no peace for the wicked.

1 Hear ye this, O house of Jacob [*the twelve tribes of Israel*], **which are called by the name of Israel** [*who are known as the Lord's covenant people*], **and are come forth out of the waters of Judah** [*waters of baptism, 1 Nephi 20:1*], **which swear by the name of the LORD** [*who make covenants in the name of Jesus Christ*], **and make mention of the God of Israel, but not in truth, nor in righteousness** [*you make covenants but don't live the gospel; empty worship is the problem*].

2 For they call themselves of the holy city [*they claim to be the Lord's people*], **and stay themselves upon** [*pretend to rely upon*] **the God of Israel;** The LORD of hosts [*Jehovah*] is his name.

> In the next several verses, the Lord reminds Israel that there is no lack of evidence that He exists.

3 I have declared the former things from the beginning [*I've had prophets prophesy*]; **and they** [*their prophecies*] **went forth out of my mouth, and I shewed them** [*fulfilled them, so you would have solid evidence that I exist*]; I did them suddenly, and they came to pass [*so you can know I am God; Isaiah 42:9*].

4 Because I knew that thou art obstinate, and thy neck is an iron sinew [*your necks won't bend; you are not humble*], **and thy brow brass** [*you are thickheaded; can't get things through your skulls*];

5 I have even from the beginning declared it [*prophecies*] **to thee; before it** [*prophesied events*] **came to pass I shewed it thee:** lest thou shouldest say, Mine idol hath done them, and my graven image, and my molten image, hath commanded them [*so you couldn't claim your idols, false gods, did it*].

6 Thou hast heard, see all this; **and will not ye declare it** [*acknowledge it*]? **I have shewed thee new things** from this time, even hidden things, and **thou didst not know them** [*German: that thou hadst no way of knowing*].

7 They [*the prophesied events*] **are created** [*happening*] **now,** and not from the beginning; even before the day when thou heardest them not [*without my prophecies, you couldn't have known in advance*]; lest thou shouldest say, Behold, I knew them [*I did it this way so you would have obvious evidence that I exist*].

8 Yea, **thou heardest not;** yea, thou knewest not; yea, from that time that **thine ear was not opened** [*you wouldn't listen*]: for **I knew that thou wouldest deal very treacherously** [*the Lord knew right from the start that it would be hard to "raise" us. Great potential for good inherently has great potential for evil, but it was worth the risk!*], **and wast called a transgressor from the womb** [*I've had trouble with you Israelites right from the start*].

9 For my name's sake [*because I have a reputation to uphold—mercy, patience, love, and so forth*] **will I defer mine anger,** and for my praise will I refrain for thee, that I cut thee not off [*I will not cut you off completely*].

> In verse 10, next, the Lord is speaking of the future as if it has already happened. The message

is that He will yet have a people who are righteous and worthy of celestial glory. They will have gone through the refiner's fire to get there, just as pure gold must go through the refiner's fire in order to be set free from the impurities of the ore in which it is found.

10 Behold, I have refined thee, but not with [*German: "as"*] silver [*"but not with silver" is deleted in 1 Nephi 20:10. Perhaps this phrase in the Bible implies that we are not being refined to be "second-best"—in other words, silver—but rather to be gold, the best, celestial. See Revelation 4:4*]; **I have chosen thee** [*German: I will make you*] **in the furnace of affliction.**

11 For mine own sake, even for mine own sake, will I do it: for how should my name be polluted [*German: lest My name be slandered for not keeping My promise*]? and I will not give my glory unto another [*the Lord will stick with Israel*].

12 Hearken unto me, O Jacob and Israel, my called [*chosen people*]; **I am he; I am the first, I also am the last** [*I am the Savior*].

13 Mine hand also hath laid the foundation of the earth [*I am the Creator*], **and my right hand** [*the covenant hand; the hand of power*] **hath spanned** [*spread out; created*] **the heavens:** when I call unto them, they stand up together.

14 All ye, assemble yourselves, and hear; which among them hath declared these things? The LORD hath loved him [*Israel*]: **he** [*God*] **will do his pleasure on** [*will punish*] **Babylon,** and his arm shall be on the Chaldeans [*southern Babylon*].

15 I, even I, have spoken; yea, I [*Jesus speaking for Heavenly Father?*] **have called him** [*Jesus?*]: **I have brought him, and he shall make his way prosperous.**

16 Come ye near unto me, hear ye this; I have not spoken in secret [*I have been open about the gospel*] **from the beginning; from the time that it was** [*declared, 1 Nephi 20:16*], **there am I** [*from the time anything existed, I have spoken*]: and now the Lord GOD, and his Spirit, hath sent me.

17 Thus saith the LORD, thy Redeemer, the Holy One of Israel [*Jesus*]; **I am the LORD thy God** which teacheth thee to profit [*German: for your profit, benefit*], **which leadeth thee by the way that thou shouldest go.**

18 O that thou [*Israel*] **hadst hearkened** [*if you had just listened and been obedient*] **to my commandments! then had thy peace been as a river** [*you would have had peace constantly flowing unto you*], **and thy righteousness as the waves of the sea** [*you would have been steady, constant*]:

19 Thy seed also had been as the sand [*your posterity could have been innumerable; exaltation*], **and the offspring of thy bowels like the gravel thereof** [*like the sand of the seashore*]; **his name should not have been cut off nor destroyed from before me** [*Israel could have had it very good and would not have been conquered*].

Next, in verse 20, the Lord invites all people to flee from wickedness. Remember, Babylon is often used in the scriptures to mean wickedness.

20 Go ye forth of Babylon [*quit wickedness*], **flee ye from the Chaldeans** [*Babylonians*], **with a voice of singing** [*be happy in your righteousness*] **declare ye, tell this, utter it even to the end of the earth; say ye, The LORD hath redeemed his servant Jacob** [*spread the word everywhere you go that the Atonement of Christ works*].

Next, the Savior reminds Israel that just as He brought forth water for the children of Israel in the desert, so also He can provide the refreshing living water of the gospel for all who are willing to partake.

21 And they thirsted not when he led them through the deserts [*perhaps symbolic of the results of drinking "living water" (the gospel) as you follow the Savior through the barren world of the wicked*]: **he caused the waters to flow out of the rock** [*Exodus 17:6; symbolic of the Savior*]

for them: he clave the rock also, and the waters gushed out.

One of the major messages of Isaiah's writings is summarized in verse 22, next.

22 There is no peace, saith the LORD, unto the wicked.

ISAIAH 49

Selection: all verses

1 NEPHI 21 IS the Book of Mormon version of this chapter of Isaiah. As was the case with Isaiah 48, we will draw heavily from the Book of Mormon as we study Isaiah 49, here.

Isaiah continues his prophecy about the Messiah, and of the gathering of Israel in the last days. The prophecy includes the fact that the governments of many nations will assist in this gathering. In the last days, Israel will finally do the work she was originally called to do but failed to accomplish.

This particular chapter contains one of my personal favorite verses, verse 16, which contains beautiful Atonement symbolism. Beginning with verse 1, we will be taught about the foreordination of covenant Israel and the responsibilities we have as the Lord's chosen people. Remember that "chosen" includes the concept that we are chosen to carry whatever burdens are necessary in order to spread the gospel and the priesthood throughout the earth.

Isaiah sets the stage for this prophecy

by having us think of Israel as a person who is thinking about her past and feels like she has been a failure as far as her calling and mission from the Lord is concerned. Then she is startled by her success in the last days. Note that Isaiah says the same thing twice in a row, using different words, several times in this chapter. In verse 1, for example, he says "**Listen**, O isles unto me; and **hearken** . . ." As previously mentioned in this study guide, this was typical repetition for emphasis in biblical culture.

1 Listen, O isles [*"isles" means "continents and nations throughout the world;" symbolic of scattered remnants of Israel throughout the world—see 1 Nephi 21:1*], **unto me; and hearken, ye people, from far; The LORD hath called me** [*Israel; see verse 3*] **from the womb** [*before I was born; foreordination*]; **from the bowels of my mother** [*from my mother's womb*] **hath he made mention of my name** [*Israel was foreordained in premortality to assist the Lord in His work*].

2 And he hath made my mouth like a sharp sword [*Israel is to be an effective instrument in preaching the gospel; the imagery of a sharp sword implies that the gospel is hard on the wicked but helps the righteous by cutting through falsehood*]; **in the shadow** [*protection*] **of his hand hath he hid me, and made me a polished shaft; in his quiver hath he hid me** [*Israel has been refined and prepared*

by the Lord to fulfill its calling];

3 And said unto me, Thou art my servant, O Israel, in whom I will be glorified [*a prophecy that Israel will yet fulfill its stewardship*].

In verses 4–12, Isaiah portrays Israel's loneliness and regrets because of rebellion and apostasy in times past. The prophecy also shows us the glorious blessings and responsibilities that await her as she repents.

In order to better appreciate what Isaiah is doing to portray Israel to us, you might picture an actor, representing Israel, dressed in black, sitting all alone on stage, with a single spotlight on her, speaking to the audience as she discusses her past failure to fulfill the mission the Lord gave her.

4 Then I [*Israel*] **said** [*to myself*], **I have laboured in vain, I have spent my strength for nought, and in vain** [*uselessly, in apostasy, false religions, and so on*]: **yet surely my judgment is with the LORD** [*German: the case against me is in God's hands*], **and my work** [*German: my office, my calling*] **with my God** [*German: is from God*].

5 And now, saith the LORD that formed [*foreordained*] **me** [*Israel, Abraham's posterity through Isaac*] **from the womb to be his servant, to bring Jacob** [*Israel*] **again to him, Though Israel be not gathered, yet shall I be glorious in the eyes of**

the LORD, and my God shall be my strength [*those who try valiantly to convert and gather Israel will be blessed, whether or not Israel responds; similar to Nephi with respect to Laman and Lemuel in 1 Nephi 2:18–21*].

Next, in verse 6, Israel tells us that the Lord not only wants her to bring the gospel to the scattered remnants of Israel, but to the whole world also.

6 And he said, It is a light thing [*German: not enough of a load*] **that thou shouldest be my servant** to raise up the tribes of Jacob [*Israel*], and **to restore the preserved** [*remnants or survivors*] **of Israel: I will also give thee for a light to the Gentiles** [*you must also bring the gospel to everyone else; quite a prophecy in Isaiah's day when almost any enemy nation could walk all over Israel*], **that thou mayest be my salvation unto the end of the earth** [*the responsibility of members of the Church today; compare with Abraham 2:9–11*].

7 Thus saith the LORD, the Redeemer of Israel, and [*"and" is deleted in 1 Nephi 21:7*] his [*Israel's*] Holy One, **to him** [*Israel*] **whom man despiseth, to him whom the nation abhorreth** [*German: to the people despised by others*], **to a servant of rulers** [*you have been servants and slaves to many nations*], **Kings shall see** [*the true gospel as you fulfill your stewardship*] **and arise** [*out of respect for God*], **princes** [*leaders of nations*]

also shall worship [*German: fall down and worship*], **because of the LORD** that is faithful, and the Holy One of Israel, **and he shall choose thee** [*German: who chose you*].

Next, Isaiah speaks prophetically of the future as though it had already happened. We are watching this prophecy being fulfilled.

8 Thus saith the LORD, In an acceptable time [*when the time is right, beginning with Joseph Smith and the Restoration*] **have I heard thee, and in a day of salvation have I helped** thee: and I will preserve thee, and give thee for a covenant of the people, **to establish the earth** [*to establish the gospel on the earth again*], **to cause to inherit the desolate heritages** [*the spiritual wildernesses caused by apostasy, in other words, the Lord will gather Israel and help Israel fulfill its stewardship as described in verse 6 above*];

9 That thou mayest say to the prisoners [*including the living and the dead in spiritual darkness*], **Go forth** [*Go free*]; to them that are in darkness, Shew yourselves [*German: Come out!*]. They shall feed in the ways, and their pastures shall be in all high places [*they will have it good when they repent and follow the true God*].

10 They shall not hunger nor thirst; neither shall the heat nor sun smite them: **for he** [*Christ*] **that hath**

mercy on them **shall lead them,** even by the springs of water shall he guide them [*benefits of accepting and living the gospel*].

11 And **I will make all my mountains a way, and my highways shall be exalted** [*the high road of the gospel will be available to all; "mountains" could symbolize temples in the last days and during the Millennium, where the Lord teaches us the plan of salvation and provides ordinances of exaltation*].

12 Behold, **these** [*remnants of scattered Israel*] **shall come from far:** and, lo, these from the north and from the west [*the gathering will be from all parts of the world*]; and these from the land of Sinim [*perhaps China but not certain; see Bible Dictionary, under "Sinim"*].

13 Sing, O heavens; and be joyful, O earth; and break forth into singing, O mountains: for **the LORD hath comforted his people, and will have mercy upon his afflicted** [*the Lord will eventually redeem Israel*].

With verse 14, next, Isaiah takes us back to Israel, who says, in effect, "Don't waste your effort trying to comfort me. I have failed and the Lord has given up on me."

14 But Zion said [*Israel hath said*], **The LORD hath forsaken me, and my Lord hath forgotten me** [*wicked Israel's complaint; 1 Nephi 21:14*

adds "*but he will show that he hath not*" to this verse].

Next, Isaiah says, in effect, "You think that a mother's bond to her nursing child is strong, but that is nothing compared to how much the Lord cares for Israel."

15 Can a woman forget her sucking [*nursing*] **child,** that she should not have compassion on the son of her womb? yea, **they** [*Israel*] **may forget, yet will I** [*the Lord*] **not forget thee** [*Israel*].

Verse 16, next, contains beautiful Atonement symbolism and demonstrates how much the Savior cares for all of us.

16 Behold, **I have graven thee upon the palms of my hands** [*In effect, I will be crucified for you. Just as a workman's hands bear witness of his profession, his type of work, so shall nail prints in My hands bear witness of My love for you.*]; **thy walls are continually before me** [*I know where you live, see you continuously, and I will not forget you*].

17 Thy children [*descendants*] **shall make haste;** [*"haste against," 1 Nephi 21:17*] **thy destroyers and they that made thee waste shall go forth of** [*flee from*] **thee** [*the tables will be turned in the last days*].

18 Lift up thine eyes round about, and behold [*look into the future*]: **all these** [*Israelites*] **gather themselves together, and come to thee** [*you *thought you had no family left, but look at all your descendants in the future].* **As I live** [*the strongest Hebrew oath or promise possible was to promise by the Living God*], **saith the** LORD, **thou shalt surely clothe thee with them all, as with an ornament, and bind them on thee, as a bride doeth** [*a bride puts on her finest clothing for the occasion; in other words, Israel will have many of her finest descendants in the last days*].

19 For thy waste and thy desolate places, and the land of thy destruction [*where you've been trodden down for centuries*], **shall even now be too narrow by reason of the inhabitants** [*you will have so many Israelites, you'll seem to be running out of room for them all; latter-day gathering of Israel*], **and they** [*your former enemies*] **that swallowed thee up shall be far away.**

20 The children [*converts to the true gospel*] **which thou shalt have, after thou hast lost the other** [*child; through apostasy, war and so on*], **shall say again in thine ears, The place is too strait for me: give place to me that I may dwell** [*there is not enough room for us all*].

We see evidence of the rapid growth of the Church, as prophesied in these verses, in the ever expanding need for new chapels, temples, MTC's, etc. in our day.

21 Then shalt thou [*Israel*] **say in thine heart, Who hath begotten me these, seeing I have lost my children** [*where in the world did all these Israelites come from*], **and am desolate, a captive, and removing to and fro** [*scattered all over*]? **and who hath brought up these? Behold, I was left alone** [*I thought I was done for*]; **these, where had** [*have*] **they been?**

In verses 22–26, next, the Lord answers the question asked in verse 21, above, as to where all these future faithful Israelites will come from. The answer is simple and powerful. The Lord will use His power to gather them.

22 Thus saith the Lord GOD, Behold, I will lift up mine hand to the Gentiles, and set up my standard [*the true Church, gospel*] **to the people: and they** [*the Gentiles or non-Jews*] **shall bring thy sons in their arms, and thy daughters shall be carried upon their shoulders** [*the Lord will open the way and inspire people everywhere to help in gathering Israel*].

23 And kings shall be thy nursing fathers, and their queens thy nursing mothers [*leaders of nations will help gather Israel; for instance, as mentioned previously, Great Britain sponsored the return of the Jews to Palestine in 1948*]: **they shall bow down to thee with their face toward the earth, and lick up the dust of thy feet** [*the tables will be turned and they will show* respect for you]; and **thou shalt know that I am the LORD: for they shall not be ashamed** [*disappointed*] **that wait for** [*trust in*] **me.**

24 Shall the prey be taken from the mighty, or the lawful [*the Lord's covenant people*] **captive delivered** [*Israel asks how they can be freed from such powerful enemies*]?

25 But thus saith the LORD, Even the **captives** [*Israel*] **of the mighty** [*Israel's powerful enemies*] **shall be taken away** [*from the enemy*], **and the prey** [*victims*] **of the terrible** [*tyrants*] **shall be delivered** [*set free*]: **for I** [*the Lord*] **will contend with him that contendeth with thee, and I will save thy children** [*the covenant people; see 2 Nephi 6:17*].

26 And I will feed them that oppress thee with their own flesh [*your enemies will turn on each other and destroy themselves*]; **and they shall be drunken with their own blood, as with sweet wine: and all flesh shall know that I the LORD am thy Saviour and thy Redeemer,** the mighty One of Jacob.

ISAIAH 50

Selection: all verses

THIS CHAPTER CAN be compared with 2 Nephi 7. As with many other portions of Isaiah, this chapter speaks of the future as if it had already taken place.

A major question here is who has left whom when people apostatize and find themselves far away from God spiritually. Another question that Isaiah asks is, essentially, "Why don't you come unto Christ? Has He lost His power to save you?"

It is in this chapter that we learn that one of the terrible tortures inflicted upon the Savior during His trial and crucifixion was the pulling out of His whiskers (see verse 6).

At the beginning of verse 1, the Lord asks, in effect, "Did I leave you, or did you leave Me?"

1 Thus saith the LORD, Where is the bill of your mother's divorcement, whom I have put away [*where are the divorce papers, decreeing that I left you? In other words, do you think I would divorce you (break My covenants with you) and send you away from Me like a man who divorces his wife*]? **or which of my creditors is it to whom I have sold you** [*was it I who sold you into slavery*]? **Behold, for your iniquities have ye sold yourselves** [*the real cause*], **and for your transgressions is your mother put away** [*you brought it upon yourselves*].

2 Wherefore [*why*], **when I** [*Jesus*] **came** [*to save My people*], **was there no man** [*who accepted Me as Messiah; in other words, why did My people reject Me*]? **when I called** [*"Come unto Me"*], **was there**

none to answer [*German: no one answered*]? **Is my hand shortened at all, that it cannot redeem? or have I no power to deliver** [*have I lost My power*]? **behold, at my rebuke** [*command*] **I dry up the sea** [*as with the parting of the Red Sea*], **I make the rivers a wilderness: their fish stinketh, because there is no water, and dieth for thirst** [*no, I have not lost My power!*].

3 I clothe the heavens with blackness, and I make sackcloth [*a sign of mourning*] **their covering** [*I can cause the sky to be dark during the day, as if it were mourning the dead (which it will do at Christ's death; see Matthew 27:45)*].

4 The Lord GOD [*the Father*] **hath given me** [*Jesus*] **the tongue of the learned** [*Father taught Me well*], **that I should know how to speak a** [*strengthening*] **word in season to him** [*Israel; see 2 Nephi 7:4*] **that is weary: he wakeneth morning by morning, he wakeneth mine ear to hear as the learned** [*German: the Father is constantly communicating with Me and I hear as His disciple*].

5 The Lord GOD [*the Father*] **hath opened mine ear, and I was not rebellious, neither turned away back** [*I was obedient and did not turn away from accomplishing the Atonement*].

In verses 6–7, next, Isaiah

prophesies some details surrounding Christ's crucifixion. In verse 6, especially, He speaks of the future as if it is past.

6 I gave my back to the smiters [*allowed Himself to be flogged; see Matthew 27:26*], **and my cheeks to them that plucked off the hair** [*pulled out the whiskers of My beard*]: **I hid not my face from shame and spitting** [*see Matthew 26:67*].

Here is a quote from Bible scholar Edward J. Young, (not a member of the Church) concerning the plucking of the beard, in verse 6, above:

"In addition the servant [*Christ, in Isaiah 50:6*] gave his cheeks to those who pluck out the hair. The reference is to those who deliberately give the most heinous and degrading of insults. The Oriental regarded the beard as a sign of freedom and respect, and to pluck out the hair of the beard (for *cheek* in effect would refer to a beard) is to show utter contempt." (*Book of Isaiah*, vol. 3, page 300.)

7 For the Lord GOD [*the Father*] **will help me; therefore shall I not be confounded** [*I will not be stopped*]: **therefore have I set my face like a flint** [*I brace Myself for the task*], **and I know that I shall not be ashamed** [*I know I will not fail*].

8 He [*the Father*] **is near that justifieth me** [*approves of everything I do*]; **who will** [*dares to*] **contend**

with me? let us [*Me and those who would dare contend against Me*] stand together [*go to court, as in a court of law—go ahead and present your arguments against Me*]: who is mine adversary? let him come near to me [*face Me*].

9 Behold, the Lord GOD [*the Father*] will help me [*the Savior*]; who is he that shall condemn me? lo, they [*those who contend against Me*] all shall wax old as a garment; the moth shall eat them up [*the wicked will have their day and then fade away and reap the punishment*].

> Next, in verse 10, the question is asked, in effect, "Who is loyal to the Lord and is not supported by Him?" The answer, as you will see, is no one.

10 Who is among you that feareth [*respects*] the LORD, that obeyeth the voice of his servant, that walketh in darkness, and hath no light? [*Answer: No one, because the Lord blesses His true followers with light.*] let him trust in the name of the LORD, and stay upon [*be supported by*] his God.

> Verse 11, next, addresses all who decide that they can get along fine without God.

11 Behold, all ye that kindle a fire, that compass [*surround*] yourselves about with sparks: walk in the light of your fire [*try to live without God, according to your own*] philosophies], and in the sparks that ye have kindled [*rather than Christ's gospel light*]. This shall ye have of mine hand [*German: you will get what you deserve*]; ye shall lie down in sorrow [*misery awaits those who try to live without God*].

ISAIAH 51

Selection: all verses

THE LORD NOW speaks to the righteous in Israel. Compare with 2 Nephi 8.

One of Satan's goals is to get people to believe that they have no basic worth, that they are simply a biological accident that has somehow developed an ability to think and move about. He teaches that there is no God and that when people die, that is the absolute end of them. In this chapter, Isaiah begins with an invitation for us to consider our origins, the marvelous heritage we have from Abraham and Sarah, and the reality of the hand of the Lord in our lives.

1 Hearken to me, ye that follow after righteousness, ye that seek the LORD: look unto the rock whence [*from whence; 2 Nephi 8:1*] ye are hewn [*look at the top-quality stone from which you originate*], and to the hole of the pit [*the rock quarry*] whence ye are digged [*consider your origins; you come from the finest stock*].

2 Look unto Abraham your father, and unto Sarah [*note that Abraham and Sarah are of equal importance*] that bare you [*your ancestors; in other words, your heritage is the finest*]: for I called him alone [*of his family, to renew the covenant line*], and blessed him [*see Abraham 2:9–11*], and increased him.

3 For the LORD shall comfort Zion: he will comfort all her waste places; and he will make her wilderness like Eden, and her desert like the garden of the LORD [*the Garden of Eden*]; joy and gladness shall be found therein, thanksgiving, and the voice of melody [*wonderful reward for the righteous*].

4 Hearken unto me, my people; and give ear unto me, O my nation: for a law shall proceed from me, and I will make my judgment to rest for a light of the people [*My laws will bring light to the nations*].

5 My righteousness [*triumph; ability to save*] is near [*is available to you*]; my salvation is gone forth, and mine arms shall judge the people [*I will personally rule over the nations*]; the isles [*nations of the world*] shall wait [*trust; rely*] upon me, and on mine arm [*My power*] shall they trust.

6 Lift up your eyes to the heavens, and look upon the earth beneath: for the heavens shall vanish away like smoke, and the earth shall wax old like a garment, and they that dwell therein shall die in like manner: but my salvation [*the salvation I bring*] shall be for ever [*will last forever*], and my righteousness [*triumph*] shall not be abolished [*compare Doctrine & Covenants 1:38*].

7 Hearken unto me, ye that know righteousness [*you who are righteous*], the people in whose heart is my law [*you who have taken My gospel to heart*]; fear ye not the reproach [*insults*] of men, neither be ye afraid of their revilings [*stinging criticism*].

8 For the moth shall eat them [*the wicked who revile against the righteous*] up like a garment, and the worm shall eat them like wool [*they are just like moth-eaten clothing that will disintegrate and disappear*]: but my righteousness [*salvation and deliverance*] shall be [*will last*] for ever, and my salvation from generation to generation [*throughout eternity*].

The righteous now reply and invite the Lord's blessings and help in their lives, leading to salvation.

9 Awake, awake [*German: Now then, come, Lord*], put on strength, O arm [*symbolic of power*] of the LORD; awake, as in the ancient days, in the generations of old [*please, Lord, use Thy power to save us like You did in olden days*]. Art

181

thou not it that hath cut Rahab [German: the proud; hath trimmed the proud down to size. Rahab can refer to the sea monster, Leviathan, in Isaiah 27:1, which represents Satan and any who serve him, such as Egypt when the Israelites escaped them via the Red Sea.], and wounded the dragon [in other words, defeated Satan, see Revelation 12:7–9]?

10 Art thou not it which hath dried the sea [the Red Sea], the waters of the great deep; that hath made the depths of the sea a way [a path] for the ransomed [the children of Israel, whom the Lord ransomed from Egypt] to pass over?

> Next, Isaiah prophesies about the gathering of Israel in the last days.

11 Therefore [because of the Lord's power] the redeemed of the LORD [Israel; those who will be saved] shall return [the gathering of Israel in the last days], and come with singing unto Zion; and everlasting joy shall be upon their head: they shall obtain gladness and joy; and sorrow and mourning shall flee away [the results of righteousness].

> Now the Lord speaks to righteous Israel, responding to their plea for help and reminding them again that He is their God and the One who will help them return.

12 I, even I, am he that comforteth you: who art thou, that thou shouldest be afraid of a man that shall die [mortal men], and of the son of man [mortal men] which shall be made as grass [short-lived glory of evil mortal men; fear God, not man];

13 And forgettest the LORD thy maker, that hath stretched forth the heavens, and laid the foundations of the earth [how could you forget Me, your Creator!]; and hast feared continually every day because of the fury of the oppressor, as if he were ready to destroy [why should you live in fear of mortal men]? and where is the fury of the oppressor [the day will come when their fury won't be able to touch you]?

14 The captive exile hasteneth that he may be loosed, and that he should not die in the pit, nor that his bread should fail [the day will come when Israel will be set free, no more to die in captivity, and will have plenty].

15 But I am the LORD thy God, that divided the sea [parted the Red Sea], whose waves roared: The LORD of hosts is his name [is My name, 2 Nephi 8:15].

16 And I have put my words in thy mouth [I have given you My teachings], and I have covered thee in the shadow [protection] of mine hand, that I may plant the heavens, and lay the foundations of the earth [I created heaven and earth for you], and

say unto Zion, Thou art my people [you are My covenant people].

17 Awake, awake, stand up, O Jerusalem, which hast drunk at the hand of the LORD the cup of his fury; thou hast drunken the dregs [the bitter, coarse stuff that settles in the bottom of the cup] of the cup of trembling, and wrung them out [you have "paid through the nose" for your wickedness].

Next, we are reminded that in times of apostasy, the people lose direction.

18 There is none to guide her among all the sons whom she [Israel] hath brought forth [you have spent many years without prophets]; neither is there any that taketh her by the hand of all the sons that she hath brought up.

The Book of Mormon provides much-needed help for understanding verse 19, next.

19 These two things are come unto thee; who shall be sorry for thee [2 Nephi 8:19 changes this line considerably: "These two sons are come unto thee, who shall be sorry for thee"]? desolation, and destruction, and the famine, and the sword: by whom shall I comfort thee? [This verse in the Book of Mormon seems to refer to the two prophets in the last days who will keep the enemies of the Jews from totally destroying them. See Revelation 11.]

20 Thy sons [your people] have fainted [German: are on their last leg, save these two, 2 Nephi 8:20], they lie at the head of all the streets, as a wild bull in a net [your wicked people are being brought down like a wild animal by a net of wickedness]: they are full of the fury of the LORD [they are catching the full fury of the Lord], the rebuke of thy God [the consequences of sin have caught up with them].

21 Therefore hear now this, thou afflicted, and drunken [out of control], but not with wine [rather with wickedness]:

22 Thus saith thy Lord the LORD, and thy God that pleadeth the cause of his people [I have not deserted you], Behold, I have taken out of thine hand the cup of trembling [I suffered the Atonement for you; see Doctrine & Covenants 19:15–19], even the dregs of the cup of my fury; thou shalt no more drink it again [Christ will save the Jews in the last days, see 2 Nephi 9:1–2]:

23 But I will put it [the cup of his fury in verse 22] into the hand of them [your enemies] that afflict thee; which have said to thy soul [have said to you], Bow down, that we may go over [lie down so we can walk on you]: and thou hast laid thy body as the ground [you did], and as the street, to them that went over [*you have been walked all over, treated like dirt*].

ISAIAH 52

Selection: all verses

MOST OF THIS chapter is essentially contained in 3 Nephi 20:30–44, although in different order. It is an invitation to come unto Christ and be gathered to Him with His covenant people, Zion. It begins with a focus on the gathering of the Jews to Jerusalem. The imagery is that of clothing oneself in the gospel of Jesus Christ.

1 **Awake, awake; put on thy strength** [*repent and take Christ's name upon you*], **O Zion; put on thy beautiful garments** [*return to proper use of the priesthood; see Doctrine & Covenants 113:7–8*], **O Jerusalem,** the holy city: for henceforth there shall no more come into thee the uncircumcised and the unclean [*the wicked*].

2 **Shake thyself from the dust; arise** [*from being walked on, Isaiah 51:23*], **and sit down** [*in dignity, redeemed at last*], **O Jerusalem: loose thyself from the bands of thy neck** [*come forth out of spiritual bondage*], **O captive daughter of Zion.**

Next, we get a brief review of why Israel has had troubles in the past.

3 For thus saith the LORD, **Ye have sold yourselves for nought** [*for*

nothing of value; in other words, apostatized*]; **and ye shall be redeemed without money** [*the hand of the Lord is in it*].

4 For thus saith the Lord GOD [*Jehovah*], **My people went down aforetime** [*a long time ago*] **into Egypt to sojourn** [*live*] **there; and the Assyrian oppressed them without cause** [*were not justified in how they treated Israel; they abused their power as did Babylon; see 47:6*].

Verse 5, next, emphasizes the need for redemption.

5 Now therefore, **what have I here,** saith the LORD, **that my people is taken away for nought** [*why have My people sold themselves into spiritual bondage for such worthless things (such as pride, wickedness, worshiping false gods, materialism)*]? **they that rule over them make them to howl,** saith the LORD; **and my name continually every day is blasphemed.**

Verse 6, next, foretells the day when Israel, including the Jews, will return to the Lord.

6 Therefore **my people shall know my name:** therefore they shall know in that day [*in the last days*] that I am he that doth speak: behold, it is I.

7 [**"And then shall they say,"** *3 Nephi 20:40, referring to the last days*] **How beautiful upon the mountains are the feet of him that bringeth good**

tidings, that publisheth peace; that bringeth good tidings of good, that publisheth salvation; that saith unto Zion, Thy God reigneth [*missionary work, gathering, etc.*]!

8 [*Compare with 3 Nephi 20:32*] Thy watchmen [*prophets, leaders*] shall lift up the voice; with the voice together shall they sing: for they shall see eye to eye, <u>when the LORD shall bring again Zion.</u> [*The underlined phrase is replaced in 3 Nephi 20:33 with "Then will the Father gather them together again and give unto them Jerusalem for the land of their inheritance."*]

9 [*"Then shall they," 3 Nephi 20:34*] Break forth into joy, sing together, ye waste places of Jerusalem: for the LORD hath comforted his people, he hath redeemed Jerusalem [*will likely occur in the last days, near or at the beginning of the Millennium*].

10 The LORD [*the Father, 3 Nephi 20:35*] hath made bare his holy arm [*shown forth His power*] in the eyes of all the nations; and all the ends of the earth shall see the salvation [*the power to save and redeem*] of our God [*"of the Father; and the Father and I are one." 3 Nephi 20:35*].

Verse 11, next, provides direction for being among those who are gathered to the Father through the Savior.

11 [*And then shall a cry go forth*, 3 Nephi 20:41; *referring to the last days*] Depart ye, depart ye, go ye out from thence [*from among the wicked, Doctrine & Covenants 38:42*], touch no unclean thing; go ye out of the midst of her [*Babylon, or wickedness*]; be ye clean, that bear the vessels of the LORD [*a major message of Isaiah*].

12 For ye shall not go out with haste, nor go by flight [*the gospel brings calmness*]: for the LORD will go before you; and the God of Israel will be your rereward [*rearward, protection; see Doctrine & Covenants 49:27*].

13 Behold, my servant [*could be Joseph Smith Jr. (3 Nephi 21:10–11; page 428 of Religion 121 Book of Mormon Student Manual); or Christ; or modern servants and prophets of God; or all of the above working together to fulfill verse 15*] shall deal prudently, he shall be exalted and extolled, and be very high.

14 As many were astonied [*astonished*] at thee; his visage was so marred more than any man [*the Savior as well as most prophets are highly praised by some, see verse 13, and much maligned by others*], and his form more than the sons of men:

15 So shall he sprinkle [*JST: gather*] many nations; the kings shall shut their mouths at him: for that which had not been told them shall

they see; and that which they had not heard shall they consider [see 3 Nephi 21:8; kings (powerful leaders) will not be able to stop the Lord's work in the last days].

ISAIAH 53

Selection: all verses

THIS CHAPTER COM-PARES with Mosiah 14 in the Book of Mormon. It is a wonderful chapter, showing that a dominant part of the work of Old Testament prophets was teaching and prophesying about Christ.

Isaiah gives specific details about the Savior's mortal mission and gives a beautiful description of the blessings of the Atonement for each one of us. Among other insights, he teaches us that Jesus Himself derived great personal satisfaction in having performed the Atonement for us (verse 11).

Isaiah starts out with a bit of frustration over how few people take him and his fellow prophets seriously.

1 Who hath believed our report [German: Who listens to us prophets anyway]? and **to whom is the arm of the LORD revealed** [who sees God's hand in things]?

Beginning with the last part of verse 2, next, Isaiah speaks prophetically about the future, as if it has already taken place.

2 For he [Jesus] **shall grow up before**

him [possibly referring to the Father but could also refer to mankind as implied in the last phrase of verse 1] **as a tender plant** [a new plant, a restoration of truth], **and as a root out of a dry ground** ["dry ground" symbolizes apostate Judaism]: **he** [Jesus] **hath no form nor comeliness** [no special, eye-catching attractiveness]; **and when we shall see him, there is no beauty that we should desire him** [normal people couldn't tell He was the Son of God just by looking at Him].

3 He [Jesus] **is despised and rejected of men; a man of sorrows** [sensitive to people's troubles and pain], **and acquainted with grief** [He endured much suffering and pain]: **and we hid as it were our faces from him** [wouldn't even look at Him]; **he was despised, and we** [people in general] **esteemed him not** [German: paid no attention to him; even his own brothers rejected him at first; see John 7:5].

4 Surely he hath borne our griefs, and carried our sorrows [the Atonement]: **yet we did esteem him stricken, smitten of God, and afflicted** [we didn't recognize Him as the Great Atoner; we rather thought He was just another criminal receiving just punishment from God].

5 But he was wounded for our transgressions [He suffered for our sins; see 2 Nephi 9:21], **he was bruised for our iniquities** [He suffered for our sins (double empha-sis)]: **the chastisement of** [required for] **our peace was upon him** [He was punished so that we could have peace]; and **with his stripes** [wounds and punishments] **we are healed** [from our sins, upon repentance].

6 All we like sheep **have gone astray; we have turned every one to his own way** [every one of us has sinned; we all need the Atonement]; **and the LORD** [the Father] **hath laid on him** [the Savior] **the iniquity of us all** [2 Nephi 9:21].

Isaiah continues to speak prophetically as if the future events he is foretelling have already taken place, thus empha-sizing the fact that they will take place.

7 He [Christ] **was oppressed, and he was afflicted, yet he opened not his mouth** [for instance, He wouldn't even speak to Pilate; see Mark 15:3]: **he is brought as a lamb to the slaughter, and as a sheep before her shearers is dumb** [doesn't speak], **so he openeth not his mouth.**

8 He was taken from prison and from judgment [He was refused fair treatment]: **and who shall declare his generation? for he was cut off out of the land of the living: for the transgression of my people was he stricken** [He was punished for our sins].

9 And he made his grave with the wicked [He died with convicted crimi-nals], **and with the rich in his death** [a rich man (Joseph of Arimathaea) donated his tomb; see John 19:38–42]; **because he had done no vio-lence** [German: no wrong], **neither was any deceit in his mouth** [Christ was perfect].

10 Yet it pleased the LORD to bruise him [it was the Father's will to allow the Atonement to be performed by His Son]; **he hath put him to grief: when thou** [He, Christ] **shalt make** [makes] **his soul** [German: life] **an offering for sin, he shall see his seed** [His loyal followers, suc-cess; see Mosiah 15:10–12], **he shall prolong his days, and the pleasure of the LORD** [the Father's plan] **shall prosper in his hand** [will suc-ceed through Christ's mission and Atonement].

11 He [Jesus] **shall see** [the results] **of the travail** [suffering] **of his soul, and shall be satisfied** [shall have joy—the Savior will have personal joy because of having performed the Atonement for us]: **by his knowledge** [by the knowledge He brings] **shall my righteous servant** [Christ] **justi-fy** [save; prepare them to be approved by the Holy Ghost, sealed by the Holy Spirit of Promise] **many; for he shall bear their iniquities.**

12 Therefore will I divide him

a portion with the great [*He will receive His reward*], and **he shall divide the spoil** [*share the reward, in other words, we can be joint heirs with Him; see Romans 8:17*] **with the strong** [*the righteous*]; **because he hath poured out his soul unto death** [*laid down His life*]: **and he was numbered with the transgressors; and he bare the sin of many, and made intercession for the transgressors.**

ISAIAH 54

Selection: all verses

THIS CHAPTER DEALS with the last days and compares with 3 Nephi 22. A major message of this chapter is that in the last days, Israel will finally be righteous and successful.

1 Sing, O barren [*one who has not produced children; Israel, who has not produced righteous children*], **thou that didst not bear; break forth into singing, and cry aloud, thou that didst not travail** [*go into labor*] **with child** [*in former days, you did not succeed in bringing forth righteous children, loyal to Christ*]: **for more are the children** [*righteous converts*] **of the desolate** [*perhaps meaning scattered Israel*] **than the children of the married wife** [*perhaps meaning Israelites who remained in the Holy Land; in other words, now in*] the last days, you've got more righteous Israelites than you ever thought possible, with almost all the converts coming from outside the land of Israel], saith the LORD.

2 Enlarge the place of thy tent [*make more room*], **and let them stretch forth the curtains of thine habitations: spare not, lengthen thy cords, and strengthen thy stakes** [*the Church will greatly expand in the last days as righteous Israel is gathered*];

3 For thou shalt break forth on the right hand and on the left [*righteous Israel will show up everywhere*]; **and thy seed shall inherit the Gentiles, and make the desolate cities** [*cities without the true gospel*] **to be inhabited** [*Church membership will grow throughout the world*].

4 Fear not; for thou shalt not be ashamed [*you will not fail in the last days*]: **neither be thou confounded; for thou shalt not be put to shame: for thou shalt forget the shame of thy youth, and shalt not remember the reproach of thy widowhood any more** [*you can forget the failures of the past when Israel was apostate; the once "barren" Church is going to bear much fruit in the last days*].

5 For thy Maker is thine husband [*you have returned to your Creator in the last days*]; **the LORD of hosts is his name; and thy Redeemer** the

Holy One of Israel; The God of the whole earth shall he be called.

6 For the LORD hath called thee as a woman forsaken and grieved in spirit [*Israel has been through some very rough times*], **and a wife of youth, when thou wast refused** [*when you didn't bear righteous children*], saith thy God.

7 For a small moment have I forsaken thee [*because you apostatized*]; **but with great mercies will I gather thee** [*in the last days*].

8 In a little wrath I hid my face from thee for a moment [*when you rejected me*]; but **with everlasting kindness will I have mercy on thee**, saith the LORD thy Redeemer.

9 For **this** [*your situation*] **is as the waters of Noah** unto me: **for as I have sworn** [*promised*] **that the waters of Noah should no more go over the earth; so have I sworn that I would not be wroth with thee, nor rebuke thee** [*just as I promised not to flood the earth again, so I have promised to accept you back as you return to Me in the last days*].

10 For the mountains shall depart, and the hills be removed; but **my kindness shall not depart from thee**, neither shall the covenant of my peace be removed, saith the LORD that hath mercy on thee. [*Isaiah reminds us here of the true*

nature of God, a very kind and merciful God indeed! Unfortunately, many people have not been correctly taught this truth.]

> Next, the Lord promises to prepare fine accommodations for righteous Israel in the last days, as well as in the celestial kingdom.

11 O thou [*Israel*] **afflicted, tossed with tempest, and not comforted** [*you have been through some very rough times*], behold, **I will lay thy stones with fair colours** [*I will use the finest "materials" for the Restoration of the gospel in the last days and to build your "celestial homes"*], and lay thy foundations with sapphires [*precious gemstones*].

12 And I will make thy windows [*German: battlements*] of agates [*gemstones*], and thy gates of carbuncles [*bright, glittering gemstones*], and all thy borders of pleasant stones [*similar to the description of the celestial city in Revelation 21; you Israelites will have it very good, even better than you can imagine, when you repent and return unto Me to dwell*].

13 And **all thy children shall be taught of the LORD; and great shall be the peace of thy children** [*likely referring to the Millennium; see Doctrine & Covenants 45:58–59*].

14 In righteousness shalt thou be established: thou shalt be far from oppression; for thou shalt not fear:

and from terror; for it shall not come near thee [*seems to refer to millennial conditions*].

15 Behold, they [*enemies of righteousness*] shall surely gather together, but not by me: **whosoever shall gather together against thee shall fall for thy sake** [*I will protect you, you will finally have peace*].

16 Behold, **I have created the smith** that bloweth the coals in the fire, and that bringeth forth an instrument for his work; **and I have created the waster** [*German: the Destroyer*] **to destroy** [*I created all things and have power over Satan. I can control all things; you are safe with Me*].

17 **No weapon that is formed against thee shall prosper;** and every tongue that shall rise against thee in judgment thou shalt condemn. **This is the heritage of the servants of the LORD,** and their righteousness is of me, saith the LORD [*there is safety for the righteous with Me*].

ISAIAH 55

Selection: all verses

THE LORD HERE invites all to come partake of the bounties of the gospel (which are equally available to all, either here on earth or afterward in the spirit world), and to enjoy eternity with Him.

1 **Ho** [*German: come now!*], **every one that thirsteth, come ye to the waters** [*the "living water"; in other words, Christ; see John 4:14, 7:37–38*], **and he that hath no money; come ye, buy** [*with your good works, keeping the commandments, and so forth*], **and eat; yea, come, buy wine and milk without money and without price** [*the gospel is available to all without regard to economic status*].

2 **Wherefore** [*why*] **do ye spend money for that which is not bread** [*not of true value*]? **and your labour for** *that which* **satisfieth not** [*why are you so materialistic*]? **hearken diligently unto me** [*the Lord*], **and eat ye that which is good** [*that which comes of Christ*], and **let your soul delight itself in fatness** [*the best; in other words, the richness of the gospel*].

3 **Incline your ear** [*listen carefully*], and **come unto me** [*Christ*]: **hear, and your soul shall live** [*you will receive salvation*]; and **I will make an everlasting covenant** [*the fulness of the gospel; see Doctrine & Covenants 66:2*] **with you, even the sure mercies of David** [*German: the mercies and pardons of Christ spoken of by David; "David" is often used symbolically for Christ—see Isaiah 22:22; hence, "sure mercies of David" can mean the "sure mercies of Christ"*].

4 Behold, I have given him [*Christ*] **for a witness to the people,** a leader and commander to the people.

There could be many different interpretations of verse 5, next. One possibility is presented here.

5 Behold, thou [*Christ*] **shalt call a nation that thou** [*Israel*] **knowest not, and nations** [*the true Church in the last days*] **that knew not thee** [*weren't personally acquainted with ancient Israel*] **shall run unto thee** [*shall gather Israel*] **because of the LORD** thy God [*under the direction of the Lord*], and for the Holy One of Israel; **for he** [*Israel*] **hath glorified thee** [*God*]. [*In the last days, Israel will be gathered, will return to God, and be saved.*]

Verses 6–7, next, are an invitation to repent and return to a kind, merciful God.

6 Seek ye the LORD while he may be found, call ye upon him while he is near:

7 Let the wicked forsake his way, and the unrighteous man his thoughts: and let him return unto the LORD, and he [*the Lord*] **will have mercy upon him; and to our God, for he will abundantly pardon.**

Next, in verses 8–9, Isaiah again uses chiasmus in order to make a point. You may wish to read the background notes accompanying Isaiah chapter 3 in this study guide for some insights

about chiasmus. In this case, the chiastic structure is brief, consisting of **A, B, C, C,' B,' A.'** You'll notice that **C** and **C'** are not the same; rather, they are related ideas, and thus still work in a chiasmus.

8 For my thoughts [A] are not your thoughts, neither are your **ways [B]** my ways, saith the LORD.

9 For as the heavens [C] are higher than the **earth [C']**, so are my **ways [B']** higher than your ways, and my **thoughts [A']** than your thoughts [*come unto Me and live as I do, which way of life is much more satisfying than you can possibly comprehend*].

10 For as the rain cometh down, and the snow from heaven, and returneth not thither, but watereth the earth, and maketh it bring forth and bud, that it may give seed to the sower, and bread to the eater:

11 So shall my word be [*designed to bring forth exaltation*] **that goeth forth out of my mouth: it shall not** return unto me void, but **it shall accomplish that which I please,** and it shall prosper in the thing whereto I sent it [*My gospel will ultimately succeed; can also mean that those who receive the gospel into their lives will be greatly blessed*].

12 For ye shall go out [*from premortality to earth*] **with joy, and be led forth** [*to return home to God*] with peace: the mountains and the hills shall break forth before you into singing, and all the trees of the field shall clap their hands [*God's creations rejoice as their role in helping man achieve exaltation is fulfilled*].

13 Instead of the thorn shall come up the fir tree, and instead of the brier shall come up the myrtle tree [*the earth will eventually be celestialized; see Doctrine & Covenants 130:9*]: and it [*the earth and many of its inhabitants' achieving celestial glory*] shall be to the LORD for a name [*will increase God's glory and dominion*], for an everlasting sign [*that God's promises are fulfilled and that man can achieve exaltation*] that shall not be cut off [*that will never end*].

ISAIAH 56

Selection: all verses

VERSES 1-8 EXTEND the invitation (given in chapter 55) to exaltation to all, including Gentiles.

1 Thus saith the LORD, **Keep ye judgment, and do justice** [*be righteous*]: for my salvation is near to come, and my righteousness to be revealed.

2 **Blessed is the man that doeth this** [*the good mentioned in verse 1*], **and the son of man that layeth**

hold on it [*who follows My counsel to live righteously*]; **that keepeth the Sabbath from polluting it, and keepeth his hand from doing any evil.**

3 **Neither let the son of the stranger** [*the Gentiles*], **that hath joined himself to the LORD** [*that has joined the Church, accepted and follows Christ*], **speak, saying, The LORD hath utterly separated me from his people** [*the Lord has made me a second-class citizen forever*]: **neither let the eunuch** [*see Bible Dictionary, under "eunuch"*] **say, Behold, I am a dry tree** [*I will never have children; eunuchs were not allowed into the congregation of Israel; see Deuteronomy 23:1*].

4 **For thus saith the LORD unto the eunuchs** [*symbolically represent a class of people that the Israelites despised and would never consider to be potential citizens of heaven*] **that keep my sabbaths, and choose the things that please me** [*keep my commandments*], **and take hold of my covenant** [*make and keep covenants of exaltation with Me*];

5 **Even unto them will I give in mine house** [*temple; celestial kingdom*] **and within my walls** [*perhaps dual, meaning temples or heavenly home*] **a place and a name** [*King Benjamin promised his people a "name" in Mosiah 1:11; in other*

words, the name of Christ, Mosiah 5:8] **better than of sons and of daughters** [they will have more honor and glory in exaltation than they would have had from having sons and daughters on earth]: **I will give them an everlasting name** [a new name (see Revelation 2:17, Doctrine & Covenants 130:11), symbolic of covenants of exaltation], **that shall not be cut off** [eunuchs and all "outcasts" can be exalted too!].

6 Also the sons of the stranger [Gentiles], **that join themselves to the LORD** [make covenants], **to serve him, and to love the name of the LORD, to be his servants, every one that keepeth the Sabbath from polluting it, and taketh hold of my covenant** [all Gentiles can receive exaltation if they keep the commandments];

7 Even them will I bring to my holy mountain [God's kingdom], **and make them joyful in my house** of prayer: their burnt offerings and their sacrifices shall be accepted upon mine altar; for mine house shall be called an house of prayer for all people [celestial exaltation is available for all people who make covenants with the Lord and keep His commandments].

8 The Lord GOD which gathereth the outcasts of Israel [the gathering of scattered Israel] **saith, Yet will**

I gather others [Gentiles] **to him** [Israel], **beside those** [Israelites] **that are gathered unto him** [Israel].

Isaiah switches topics now to the Gentile "beasts" who will come to "devour" (destroy) the wicked of Israel.

9 All ye beasts [Gentile armies] **of the field, come to devour** [come to devour Israel], **yea, all ye beasts in the forest.**

10 His watchmen [Israel's wicked leaders] **are blind: they are all ignorant** [of the dangers of wickedness], **they are all dumb dogs** [not doing their job of warning the people of danger], **they cannot bark** [they won't sound the alarm]; **sleeping, lying down, loving to slumber** [they are asleep on the job].

11 Yea, they are greedy dogs which can never have enough [are never satisfied], **and they are shepherds that cannot understand** [leaders who don't understand the seriousness of the situation]: **they all look to their own way** [look only after their own interests], **every one for his gain,** from his quarter.

12 Come ye, say they, I will fetch wine, and we will fill ourselves with strong drink ["Let's party!"]; **and to morrow shall be as this day, and much more abundant** ["And tomorrow we will have even a bigger and better party!"].

ISAIAH 57

Selection: all verses

IN THIS CHAPTER, Isaiah gives comfort to the righteous and a warning to the wicked. In verse 1, he addresses the issue that the righteous often suffer and no one seems to care. In verse 2, Isaiah gives counsel and comfort to the righteous.

1 The righteous perisheth [*the righteous suffer when the wicked rule; see Doctrine & Covenants 98:7*], and no man layeth it to heart [*no one seems to care*]: and merciful men are taken away, none considering that the righteous is taken away from the evil to come.

2 He [*the righteous*] shall enter into peace: they shall rest in their beds [*or on their couches*], each one walking in his uprightness [*personal righteousness leads to inner peace here and peace in eternity*].

Beginning with verse 3, next, Isaiah addresses the wicked.

3 But draw near hither, ye sons of [*followers of*] the sorceress [*people who live wickedly*], the seed of [*followers of*] the adulterer and the whore [*gross wickedness; used in 1 Nephi 22:14 to represent Satan's kingdoms*].

4 Against whom do ye sport yourselves [*whom are you mocking*]? against whom make ye a wide mouth [*making faces*], and draw out the tongue [*sticking your tongues out*]? are ye not children of transgression [*totally caught up in sin*], a seed of falsehood [*a bunch of liars*],

5 Enflaming yourselves [*sexually arousing yourselves*] with idols under every green tree [*German: You run to your gods with sexual arousal, referring to the use of prostitutes as part of pagan worship*], slaying the [*your*] children in the valleys under the clifts of the rocks [*killing your children as human sacrifices*]?

6 Among the smooth stones of the stream [*used for building altars for idol worship*] is thy portion [*German: you base your whole existence on your false gods, idols*]; they, they are thy lot [*you have chosen them over Me, therefore, you will have to depend on them for your reward*]: even to them hast thou poured a drink offering [*part of idol worship that was originally revealed for worship of the true God—see Exodus 29:40; they have perverted proper worship ceremonies over to their idol worship*], thou hast offered a meat offering [*to your idols; see Exodus 29:41*]. Should I receive comfort in these [*do you expect Me to be happy about such perversions of true worship*]?

In verses 7 and 8, the Lord chastises Israel for breaking the seventh commandment literally by having sexual intercourse with temple prostitutes as part of pagan worship services. Symbolically, the Lord is the husband and Israel is the bride in the covenant relationship, symbolized by marriage. In these next verses, Isaiah uses the imagery of a wife being unfaithful to her husband and committing adultery.

7 Upon a lofty and high mountain hast thou set thy bed: even thither wentest thou up to offer sacrifice.

8 Behind the doors also and the posts hast thou set up thy remembrance [German: *statue*]: **for thou hast discovered** [*uncovered, exposed, undressed*] **thyself to another than me** [*you have "stepped out on Me," been unfaithful to Me*], **and art gone up; thou hast enlarged thy bed** [*made room for many false gods in your life*], **and made thee a covenant with them** [*you have given your loyalty to many false gods*]; **thou lovedst their bed where thou sawest it.**

9 And thou wentest to the king [*Molech, a large, brass idol with a hollow fire-pit stomach, used for sacrificing children*] **with ointment, and didst increase thy perfumes** [*you have worshipped the idol, Molech, with ointment and perfumes*], **and didst send thy messengers far off, and didst debase thyself even unto hell.** [*"You have traveled all the way to hell to find new and worse ways to commit sin!"; the Lord implies that they have made covenants with Satan himself.*]

10 Thou art wearied in the greatness of thy way [*you got tired trying to find worse ways to sin*]; **yet saidst thou not, There is no hope** [*but you didn't give up; rather, you said to yourself, "There has got to be something more wicked we can do!"*]: **thou hast found the life of thine hand** [*renewal of strength*]; **therefore thou wast not grieved** [*you kept striving for worse wickedness against all odds*].

11 And of whom hast thou been afraid or feared, that thou hast lied [*why have you respected false gods instead of Me*], **and hast not remembered me, nor laid it to thy heart** [*you don't even seem to be aware of Me*]? **have not I held my peace even of old, and thou fearest me not** [*have I been too kind and gentle with you*]?

12 I will declare [German: *point out*] **thy** [*so-called*] **righteousness, and thy works; for they shall not profit thee** [*I will expose your so-called righteousness and good works; they won't save you*].

13 When thou criest [*cry out for help when you are in trouble*], **let thy companies** [*of idols*] **deliver** [*save*] **thee;** but the wind shall carry them all away [*your idols and false gods are no more secure and stable than a tumbleweed in the wind*]; vanity shall take them [*a puff of breath will blow them away*]: **but he that putteth his**

trust in me shall possess the land, and shall inherit my holy mountain [*I do have power to save you and can give you great blessings*];

14 And [*I, the Lord*] **shall say**, Cast ye up, cast ye up [*German: make a highway, make a highway*], prepare the way [*clear the way*], take up the stumbling block out of the way of my people [*prepare the way for the return of My people—certainly foreshadowing the Restoration*].

15 For thus saith the high and lofty One [*the Lord*] that inhabiteth eternity, whose name is Holy; **I dwell in the high and holy place, with him also that is of a contrite and humble spirit** [*the contrite and humble will find safety and security with Me*], **to revive** [*German: refresh*] **the spirit of the humble, and to revive the heart of** [*give new courage to*] **the contrite ones.**

> The word "contrite," used at the end of verse 15, above, not only means "humble," but also carries with it the connotation of "desiring to be corrected as needed."

16 For I will not contend [*against you*] **for ever**, neither will I be always wroth [*angry*]: for the spirit should fail before me [*if I did, all mankind would perish*], and the souls [*people*] which I have made [*no one would survive*].

17 For the iniquity [*because of the wickedness*] **of his** [*Israel's*]

covetousness [*wicked greediness*] **was I wroth, and smote him:** I hid me [*I withdrew My spirit*], and was wroth, and he [*Israel*] went on frowardly in the way of his heart [*kept right on in his wicked ways*].

18 I have seen his ways [*probably referring to Israelites who repent with a contrite and humble spirit as mentioned in verse 15*], **and will heal him:** I will lead him also, and restore comforts [*comfort him*] unto him and to his mourners [*those Israelites who mourn for their sins, who repent*].

19 I create the fruit of the lips [*speech; German: I will create fruit of the lips that preaches:*]; **Peace, peace to him** [*the righteous*] **that is far off,** and to him that is near, saith the LORD; and I will heal him [*the repentant, anywhere he is found*].

20 But the wicked are like the troubled sea, when it cannot rest, whose waters cast up mire and dirt.

21 There is no peace, saith my God, to the wicked [*a major message from the Lord through Isaiah*].

ISAIAH 58

Selection: all verses

VERSES 1-3 IMPLY that the people have been complaining about not getting the blessings they want from the Lord, even though they keep the letter-of-the-law ordinances. The Lord responds in verses 4–5.

VERSES 6-12 ARE some of the most beautiful found anywhere in scripture regarding the purposes of fasting and detailing some of the blessings of fasting as the Lord intends it to be.

VERSES 13-14, LIKEWISE, describe the desired attitude about keeping the Sabbath holy.

1 Cry aloud, spare not, lift up thy voice like a trumpet, and shew my people their transgression, and the house of Jacob their sins [go ahead, Isaiah, tell the people why they aren't getting the desired blessings; tell them of their sins].

2 Yet they seek me daily [are going through the motions, doing all the rituals], and [appear to] delight to know my ways, as a nation that did righteousness, and forsook not the ordinance of their God [German: as if they were a nation who had not forsaken the ordinances of their God]: they ask of me the ordinances of justice [German: they demand their rights]; they take delight in approaching to God [German: want to debate with God and demand their rightful blessings].

3 Wherefore [why] have we fasted, say they, and thou seest not [You don't seem to notice]? wherefore have we afflicted our soul [why do we put our bodies through this pain], and thou takest no knowledge [You ignore it]? [God now answers their question:] Behold, in the day of your fast ye find pleasure [German: you do what you desire], and exact all your labours [German: make your employees work].

4 Behold, ye fast for strife and debate [your way of fasting causes contention], and to smite with the fist of wickedness: ye shall not fast as ye do this day, to make your voice to be heard on high [you cannot expect the Lord to bless you for such hypocritical fasting].

5 Is it such a fast that I have chosen [do you really think such fasting pleases Me]? a day for a man to afflict his soul [German: do evil to his body]? is it to bow down his head as a bulrush, and to spread sackcloth and ashes under him? wilt thou call this a fast, and an acceptable day to the LORD [do you really think outward appearance is everything]?

Next, in verses 6–12, we are taught principles of true fasting.

6 Is not this the fast that I have chosen [let Me tell you the real purpose of the fast]? to loose the bands of wickedness [to help you grow in righteousness], to undo the heavy burdens [including those that are brought on by sin], and to let the oppressed [by sin] go free, and that ye break every yoke

[*break loose from every burden*]?

7 Is it not to deal thy bread to the hungry [*to feed the hungry*], and that thou bring the poor that are cast out to thy house [*to take care of the homeless*]? when thou seest the naked, that thou cover him [*to clothe the naked*]; and that thou hide not thyself from thine own flesh [*to help your own family and relatives*]?

8 Then [*when you do the above*] shall thy light break forth as the morning, and thine health shall spring forth speedily: and thy righteousness shall go before thee; the glory of the LORD shall be thy rereward [*rear guard; protection*].

9 Then shalt thou call, and the LORD shall answer; thou shalt cry [*pray*], and he shall say, Here I am. If thou take away from the midst of thee the yoke [*root out the evils from among you*], the putting forth of the finger [*pointing in a gesture of scorn*], and speaking vanity [*maliciously*];

10 And if thou draw out thy soul [*German: heart*] to the hungry [*help the hungry*], and satisfy the afflicted soul [*help the afflicted*]; then shall thy light rise in obscurity [*shine in the darkness*], and thy darkness be as the noonday [*instead of darkness, you will have light*]:

11 And the LORD shall guide thee continually, and satisfy thy soul in drought, and make fat thy bones [*strengthen you*]: and thou shalt be like a watered garden, and like a spring of water, whose waters fail not [*never cease*].

12 And they that shall be of thee shall build the old waste places [*German: and through you shall the old waste places be built*]: thou shalt raise up the foundations of many generations; and thou shalt be called, The repairer of the breach, The restorer of paths to dwell in [*perhaps indicating that as Israel returns to the Lord and does the things prescribed in verses 6 and 7, then they will be the means of restoring the Church*].

Next we are taught the proper attitude about keeping the Sabbath day holy.

13 If thou turn away thy foot from the Sabbath, from doing thy pleasure on my holy day [*if you will do My will rather than your will on the Sabbath*]; and call the Sabbath a delight [*have a good attitude about the Sabbath*], the holy of the LORD, honourable; and shalt honour him [*the Lord*], not doing thine own ways, nor finding thine own pleasure, nor speaking thine own words:

14 Then shalt thou delight thyself in the LORD [*then you will have*

joy in the Lord]; **and I will cause thee to ride upon the high places of the earth, and feed thee with the heritage of Jacob thy father** [*you will receive the Lord's choicest blessings, the blessings of Abraham, Isaac, and Jacob*]: for the mouth of the LORD hath spoken it [*this is a promise!*].

ISAIAH 59

Selection: all verses

IN THIS CHAPTER Isaiah teaches us a lesson on the behaviors of the wicked and the motives and thought processes found in their minds and hearts. Then he teaches us about the Messiah and His role in intervening for our sins, if we choose to repent. Isaiah concludes by strongly emphasizing that the Lord will indeed save those who repent from their sins (verse 20).

Verse 1 explains that the Lord has not lost His power to save, and verses 2–8 explain that the Israelites have put distance between themselves and the Lord by their wicked behaviors.

1 Behold, **the LORD's hand is not shortened, that it cannot save;** neither his ear heavy [*deaf*], that it cannot hear [*the Lord has not lost His power to save, perhaps referring back to the people's questions in Isaiah 58:3*]:

2 But **your iniquities have separated between you and your God, and your sins have hid his face from** you, that he will not hear [*your wickedness has separated you from God*].

3 For **your hands are defiled with blood** [*perhaps referring to their killing the prophets and others as implied in verse 7*], **and your fingers with iniquity** [*you've got your hands in all kinds of wickedness*]; **your lips have spoken lies** [*you are dishonest*], **your tongue hath muttered perverseness** [*German: unrighteousness; you are wicked through and through*].

4 **None calleth** [*seeks*] **for justice, nor any pleadeth for** [*desires; advocates*] **truth: they trust in vanity** [*man rather than God*], **and speak lies** [*are dishonest*]; **they conceive mischief** [*they are constantly dreaming up more ways to sin*], **and bring forth iniquity** [*their desires are to do evil continually*].

5 **They hatch cockatrice' eggs** [*they "hatch" all kinds of wickedness, like hatching poisonous snake eggs in their minds*], **and weave the spider's web** [*design entanglements in sin*]: **he that eateth of their eggs dieth, and that which is crushed breaketh out** [*hatches*] **into a viper** [*they are creating a menu for spiritual death and going from bad to worse*].

6 **Their webs** [*the things they've surrounded themselves with*] **shall not become garments** [*they cannot clothe themselves comfortably in wickedness*], **neither shall they**

cover themselves ["insulate" themselves] with their works [they will not "insulate" themselves from consequences of wickedness; they can't get completely comfortable in wickedness; see Isaiah 28:20]: their works are works of iniquity, and the act of violence is in their hands.

7 Their feet run to evil [they are anxious to sin], and they make haste to shed innocent blood [they are anxious to kill their true prophets and others of the righteous]: their thoughts are thoughts of iniquity [evil desires are constantly on their minds]; wasting and destruction are in their paths [they are wasting away their lives, heading for disaster].

8 The way of peace they know not; and there is no judgment [justice] in their goings: they have made them [for themselves] crooked paths [they have created a very wicked and perverse lifestyle for themselves]: whosoever goeth therein shall not know peace [there is no peace for the wicked; compare with Isaiah 57:21].

In verses 9–15, Israel admits guilt and faces the issue that they are behaving wickedly, like Alma the Younger did as described in Alma 36:13–14. This paves the way for the Atonement to work in their lives.

9 Therefore [for this reason] is judgment [fairness, integrity in our dealings with others] far from us, neither doth justice [charity, righteousness]

overtake us: we wait for [look forward to] light, but behold obscurity [darkness]; for brightness, but we walk in darkness [because of our wickedness].

10 We grope for the wall like the blind, and we grope as if we had no eyes [we are stumbling around in the dark (spiritual darkness)]: we stumble at noonday as in the night; we are in desolate places as dead men [we are as good as dead, we've about had it].

11 We roar all like bears [we are fierce], and mourn sore [plaintively] like doves [and have our sorrows]: we look for judgment [pleasant treatment], but there is none; for salvation, but it is far off from us [we are a long way away from God].

12 For [because we are so wicked] our transgressions are multiplied before thee, and our sins testify against us: for our transgressions are with us [we are dragging our sins around with us]; and as for our iniquities, we know [German: feel] them [we are aware of and acknowledge our sins];

13 In transgressing and lying against the LORD [making and then breaking covenants], and departing away from our God, speaking oppression and revolt, conceiving and uttering from the heart words of falsehood [our hearts have not been right before God].

14 And **judgment is turned** away backward, and **justice standeth afar off**: for truth is fallen in the street [*our lifestyle is completely out of line*], and **equity** [*honesty*] **cannot enter** [*into our lives the way we are living them now*].

15 Yea, **truth faileth** [*is lacking*]; and **he that departeth from evil maketh himself a prey** [*When a person repents and turns from evil, he is mocked and becomes a victim in a wicked society. From here to the end of verse 21, Isaiah says that the Lord can now start redeeming Israel, because they have faced guilt, verses 9–15, and are turning from transgression, verse 20.*]: **and the LORD saw it, and it displeased him that there was no judgment.**

16 And **he saw that there was no man** [*no one besides Christ could do the job of redeeming Israel; similar to Revelation 5:3–4*], **and wondered that there was no intercessor: therefore his** [*the Lord's*] **arm brought salvation unto him** [*German: himself, Christ had the power within Himself; see Isaiah 63:5*]; **and his** [*Christ's personal*] **righteousness, it sustained him** [*Christ*].

17 For he [*Christ*] **put on righteousness** as a breastplate, and an helmet of salvation upon his head [*breastplate and helmet are armor and imply intense attacks by the enemies*

of righteousness]; and he put on the garments of vengeance for clothing [*Christ can save us through His righteousness and power of salvation (the law of mercy), or punish us (according to the law of justice, sometimes referred to as "vengeance"), depending on our deeds as stated in verse 18*], and was clad with zeal as a cloke [*Christ is completely able to be the Intercessor desired in verse 16*].

18 According to their deeds, accordingly he will repay [*the law of the harvest*], fury to his [*Christ's*] adversaries, recompence [*Alma 41:4*] to his enemies; to the islands [*all continents, nations*] he will repay recompence [*emphasis is on "recompence," or giving them what they have earned*].

19 So shall they fear [*includes the idea of respect, reverence*] the name of the LORD from the west, and his glory from the rising of the sun [*from east to west, everywhere*]. When the enemy [*German: the Lord*] shall come in like a flood [*the judgments of God will come quickly to the whole earth, "islands" in verse 18*], the Spirit of the LORD shall lift up a standard against him [*the enemies; the wicked in verse 18*].

20 And **the Redeemer shall come to Zion, and unto them that turn from** [*repent from*] **transgression** in Jacob [*among the house of*

Israel], saith the LORD [*the righteous will live with Christ; implies Millennium*].

21 As for me [*the Lord*], **this is my covenant with them** [*those who have turned away from sin, verse 20*], saith the LORD; **My spirit** that **is upon thee**, and **my words** [*the fulness of the gospel*] which I have put in thy mouth, **shall not depart out of thy mouth**, nor out of the mouth of thy seed, nor out of the mouth of thy seed's seed, saith the LORD, from henceforth and for ever [*an everlasting covenant which will see ultimate fulfillment with those who attain exaltation in the celestial kingdom*].

ISAIAH 60

Selection: all verses

ISAIAH NOW PROPHESIES that in the last days the Church of Jesus Christ will arise, shine forth, and be a light to the nations as taught in Isaiah 5:26, as well as other places. Ultimately, all those who have chosen to join with the Lord and become part of covenant Israel will enjoy celestial glory with Him forever.

1 Arise, shine; for thy light is come [*the time for the Restoration of the gospel through the Prophet Joseph Smith has come*], **and the glory of the LORD is risen upon thee.**

2 For, behold, the darkness [*spiritual darkness in the last days, see* Teachings of the Prophet Joseph Smith, *page 47*] **shall cover the earth,** and gross darkness the people: **but the LORD shall arise upon thee, and his glory shall be seen upon thee** [*the restored Church; Zion in the last days*].

3 And the Gentiles shall come to [*German Bible: walk in*] **thy light, and kings to the brightness of thy rising** [*German: to the brightness that has come upon you*].

4 Lift up thine eyes round about, and see: all they gather themselves together, they come to thee [*Israel, Zion*]: **thy sons** [*converts*] **shall come from far, and thy daughters** [*converts*] **shall be nursed at thy side** [*people will gathered to Zion from far and near, and will be nourished by the true gospel of Jesus Christ*].

5 Then thou shalt see, and flow together [*be radiant, be happy*], **and thine heart shall fear** [*German: be surprised, thrill*], **and be enlarged** [*swell; rejoice*]; because the abundance of the sea [*multitude*] shall be converted unto thee [*Zion*], the forces [*wealth*] of the Gentiles shall come unto thee.

In these verses, we see, among other things, that the restored Church will become prosperous in the last days.

6 The multitude of camels shall

cover thee, the dromedaries [*young camels*] of Midian and Ephah [*parts of Jordan and Saudi Arabia*]; all they from Sheba [*part of Saudi Arabia*] shall come: **they shall bring gold and incense** [*similar to when the Wise Men came to Christ; perhaps symbolic of when people come to Christ*]; **and they shall shew forth the praises of the LORD** [*people from these Arabic countries will come unto Christ; symbolic of people from all nations coming to Christ in the last days*].

7 All the flocks [*perhaps symbolic of converts*] of Kedar [*Syria*] shall be gathered together unto thee, the rams [*strong men, leaders, chiefs*] of Nebaioth shall minister unto thee [*Israel in the last days*]: **they** [*people out of all nations*] **shall come up with acceptance on mine altar** [*shall become acceptable to Me*], and I will glorify the house of my glory.

8 **Who are these that fly as a cloud**, and as the doves to their windows [*who are these people who flock into the Church from over the sea (the gathering)*]?

9 Surely **the isles** [*nations*] **shall wait** [*German: trust in; look forward eagerly*] **for me**, and the ships of Tarshish first, to bring thy sons [*converts*] from far, **their silver and their gold with them**, unto the name of the LORD thy God, and

to the Holy One of Israel, because he hath glorified thee [*Israel; the true Church*].

10 **And the sons of strangers** [*foreigners*] **shall build up thy walls** [*will help build up Zion*], and **their kings shall minister unto thee** [*leaders of foreign governments will help the spread of the Church in the last days*]: for in my wrath I smote thee [*in times past, I've had to severely discipline you*], but in my favour have I had mercy on thee [*but in the last days as you (Israel) return to Me, you will partake of My mercy*].

11 **Therefore thy gates** [*as in city gates, closed as needed for defense*] **shall be open continually** [*you will not fear attack by enemies*]; they shall not be shut day nor night; that men may bring unto thee the forces [*wealth*] of the Gentiles, and that their kings may be brought [*German: that their kings may be brought to you also*].

12 For **the nation and kingdom that will not serve thee** [*Zion, in the last days, and as the Millennium begins*] **shall perish**; yea, those nations shall be utterly wasted.

Remembering that Isaiah often uses trees to symbolize people is helpful in understanding verse 13, next.

13 **The glory** [*the best of*] **of Lebanon** [*the Holy Land*] **shall come unto thee**,

the fir tree, the pine tree, and the box together, to beautify the place of my sanctuary [temple]; and I will make the place of my feet [footstool, earth, temple] glorious.

14 The sons also of them [your former enemies] **that afflicted thee shall come bending unto thee;** and all they that despised thee shall bow themselves down at the soles of thy feet [your former enemies and oppressors will humbly respect you]; **and they shall call** [acknowledge] **thee, The city of the LORD, The Zion of the Holy One of Israel.**

15 Whereas thou hast been forsaken and hated [in the past], so that no man went through thee [people hated you and avoided you], **I will make thee an eternal excellency, a joy of many generations.**

16 Thou shalt also suck the milk of [be nourished and assisted by] **the Gentiles, and** shalt suck the breast of [be nourished and assisted by] **kings: and thou shalt know that I the LORD am thy Saviour and thy Redeemer,** the mighty One of Jacob [in other words, the God of Abraham, Isaac, and Jacob].

> The basic message of verse 17, next, is that the gospel of Jesus Christ brings the very best into our lives.

17 For [instead of] **brass I will bring gold,** and for [instead of] **iron**

I will bring **silver,** and for [instead of] wood brass, and for [instead of] stones iron [you will prosper]: **I will also make thy officers** [leaders] **peace, and thine exactors** [rulers] **righteousness** [righteous leaders will bless our lives in the Church in the last days; also, during the Millennium, Christ will be assisted by the righteous Saints as leaders and rulers; see Revelation 20:4].

18 Violence shall no more be heard in thy land, wasting nor destruction within thy borders [wonderful peace awaits the righteous]; but thou shalt call thy walls Salvation [you will be surrounded with peace and salvation], and thy gates Praise.

19 The sun shall be no more thy light by day; neither for brightness shall the moon give light unto thee: but **the LORD shall be unto thee an everlasting light,** and thy God thy glory [some conditions in New Jerusalem will be similar to conditions in the celestial glory as described in Revelation 21:23 and 22:5].

20 Thy sun shall no more go down; neither shall thy moon withdraw itself: for the LORD shall be thine everlasting light, and **the days of thy mourning shall be ended** [your earthly sorrows will be over].

> Next, we are taught that the righteous will inherit the earth forever. We know that this earth will be celestialized and become

the celestial kingdom for those from our world who are worthy of it (see Doctrine & Covenants 130:9).

21 Thy people also shall be all righteous: they shall inherit the land [earth] for ever [Doctrine & Covenants 88:17–20; 130:9], the branch of my planting, the work of my hands [the righteous], that I may be glorified.

22 A little one [a seemingly unimportant, insignificant person] shall become a thousand, and a small [insignificant] one a strong nation [perhaps referring to "a continuation of the seeds (children) forever," Doctrine & Covenants 132:19; eternal posterity for those who gain exaltation]: I the LORD will hasten it [act quickly] in his [My] time [the Lord will act quickly to bestow these blessings when the time is right].

ISAIAH 61

Selection: all verses

ISAIAH HERE DESCRIBES Christ's authority, power, and the purposes of His earthly ministry. The Savior quoted verse 1 and the first phrase of verse 2 in Luke 4:18–19 as He stood and read from Isaiah, identifying Himself as the Messiah to those assembled in the synagogue at Nazareth. They were incensed and attempted to throw Him off a cliff.

1 The Spirit of the Lord GOD [Jehovah—see footnote 1b in your Bible] is upon me; because the LORD hath anointed me [My mission, calling, is] to preach good tidings [the gospel] unto the meek; he hath sent me to bind up [apply first aid; to heal] the brokenhearted, to proclaim liberty to the captives [those in spiritual bondage here and in spirit prison], and the opening of the prison [spirit prison; spiritual blindness] to them that are bound;

2 To proclaim the acceptable year [the time designated by the Father for Me to perform My earthly missions—see Bruce R. McConkie, Doctrinal New Testament Commentary, vol. 1, page 161] of the LORD, and the day of vengeance of our God; [this phrase refers to the destruction of the wicked at the Second Coming] to comfort all that mourn;

3 To appoint [extend compassion] unto them that mourn in Zion, to give unto them beauty for [in place of] ashes, the oil of joy for [in place of] mourning, the garment of praise for [in the place of] the spirit of heaviness [depression]; that they might be called trees of righteousness, [righteous people in the Lord's garden] the planting [people, work] of the LORD, that he might be glorified [that He might bring people to live in exaltation with Him eternally; compare with Moses 1:39].

4 And they [*the righteous in the last days*] shall build the old wastes, they shall raise up the former desolations, and **they shall repair the waste cities, the desolations of many generations** [*in the last days Zion will be built up again*].

5 **And strangers** [*foreigners, your former enemies*] **shall stand and feed your flocks,** and the sons of the alien [*foreigner*] shall be your plowmen and your vinedressers [*the tables are turned, former enemies will be your servants now*].

6 **But ye shall be named the Priests of the LORD:** [*make covenants leading to exaltation*] men shall call you **the Ministers of our God:** [*you will have priesthood authority*] ye shall eat the riches of the Gentiles, and in their glory [*wealth*] shall ye boast [*German: enjoy*] yourselves.

7 **For** [*in place of*] **your shame** [*German: humiliation in times past*]; **ye shall have double** [*a reference to the birthright blessing; in other words, exaltation; see Doctrine & Covenants 132:20*]; **and for** [*in place of*] **confusion they** [*righteous Israel in the last days and beyond*] **shall rejoice in their portion** [*reward*]: therefore in their land they shall possess the double [*birthright blessing; see Deuteronomy 21:17*]: **everlasting joy shall be unto them.**

8 **For I the LORD love judgment** [*justice, righteousness*], **I hate robbery** [*plundering*] **for** [*in place of*] **burnt offering** [*I hate hypocrisy, evil lifestyles, combined with empty worship rituals with which people try to look righteous*]; and **I will direct their work in truth, and I will make an everlasting covenant with them.**

9 And their seed [*the righteous*] shall **be known among the Gentiles** [*the gospel will spread to all nations*], and their offspring among the people: **all that see them shall acknowledge** [*recognize*] **them, that they are the seed which the LORD hath blessed** [*they are the people of the Lord, those who receive the blessings of Abraham as promised in Abraham 2:8–11*].

Next, in verses 10–11, we see rejoicing and singing songs of praise to the Lord. This can have dual or triple or quadruple meaning, which is typical of Isaiah's words. For example, it can be Isaiah who is rejoicing, or Zion, or any of the righteous in the last days, or anyone who attains exaltation. And, no doubt, you can come up with additional possibilities.

10 I [*Isaiah or Zion or other*] **will greatly rejoice in the Lord, my soul shall be joyful in my God; for he hath clothed me with the garments of salvation** [*2 Nephi 4:33–35, similar to Nephi's rejoicing in the Lord*], **he hath covered me with the robe**

of righteousness, as a bridegroom decketh himself with ornaments [German: priestly clothing; Hebrew: mitre or cap; see Exodus 39:28 footnote b], and as a bride adorneth herself with her jewels.

Reference to garments, robes, priestly "ornaments" or cap, in verse 10, above, points one's mind to ordinances of exaltation in temples today.

11 For as the earth bringeth forth her bud, and as the garden causeth the things that are sown in it to spring forth; so the Lord GOD will cause righteousness [victory of Zion] and praise [of Zion, Israel] to spring forth before [among] all the nations [the Lord will restore Israel and will again make the blessings of exaltation available in the last days].

ISAIAH 62

Selection: all verses

THIS CHAPTER DEALS with the gathering of Israel in the last days, and the fact that the earth will have true prophets of God again. The gathering will be the result of the preaching of the gospel throughout the world. People will once again become part of the covenant people of the Lord, which is another way of saying that they will be saved.

1 For Zion's sake will I not hold my peace [remain silent], and for Jerusalem's sake I will not rest [remain silent], until the righteousness thereof [victory of Zion] go forth as brightness [very noticeable, beautifully conspicuous], and the salvation thereof as a lamp that burneth [flaming torch; in other words, the restored gospel will be a light for all who chose to come unto Christ].

2 And the Gentiles shall see thy [Zion's] righteousness, and all kings [world leaders] thy glory: and thou shalt be called by a new name [symbolic of having made covenants with God, which, when kept, lead to life in celestial glory; see Doctrine & Covenants 130:11; Revelation 2:17], which the mouth of the LORD shall name.

3 Thou shalt also be a crown of glory [symbolic of exaltation; see Revelation 4:4; 2 Timothy 4:8] in the hand of the LORD, and a royal diadem [crown, symbolic of royal power and authority] in the hand of thy God.

4 Thou shalt no more be termed Forsaken [you will never again be forsaken]; neither shall thy land any more be termed Desolate: but thou shalt be called Hephzi-bah [JST: delightful], and thy land Beulah [the married wife; you will belong to the Lord and the Lord to you]: for the LORD delighteth in thee, and thy land shall be

married [you will belong to the Lord; you will be His covenant people].

5 For as a young man marrieth a virgin, so shall thy sons [JST: God] marry thee: and as the bridegroom rejoiceth over the bride, so shall thy God rejoice over thee.

Remember that Isaiah is speaking prophetically of the future as if it has already happened.

6 I have set watchmen [latter-day prophets] upon thy walls, O Jerusalem, which shall never hold their peace [remain silent] day nor night [in other words, there will again be continuous revelation]: ye that make mention of the LORD [you who pray and worship the Lord], keep not silence,

7 And give him [the Lord] no rest [don't stop praying], till he [the Lord] establish, and till he [the Lord] make Jerusalem [Zion, the Lord's covenant people in the last days] a praise in the earth [highly respected throughout the earth].

Verses 8–9, next, appear to describe conditions during the Millennium.

8 The LORD hath sworn by his right hand [has covenanted], and by the arm of his strength, Surely I will no more give thy corn [crops] to be meat [food] for thine enemies; and the sons of the stranger [foreigners, Gentiles] shall not drink thy wine, for the which thou hast laboured [in other words, you will live in peace with Me]:

9 But they that have gathered [harvested] it shall eat it, and praise [give thanks to] the LORD; and they that have brought it [made it] together shall drink it in the courts of my holiness [you will enjoy the fruits of your labors in peace in My holy kingdom].

10 Go through, go through the gates [come to Zion, via the gates—baptism and other gospel ordinances, coupled with righteous living]; prepare ye the way of the people; cast up, cast up the highway [the highway to Zion, the way to God, will be built up]; gather out the stones [remove the stumbling blocks]; lift up a standard [ensign, or the restored gospel of Jesus Christ] for the people.

11 Behold, the LORD hath proclaimed unto the end of the [all of the] world, Say ye to the daughter of Zion [Jerusalem, the righteous], Behold, thy salvation [your Deliverer] cometh; behold, his [Christ's] reward [He brings your reward with Him when He comes] is with him, and his work before him.

12 And they shall call them [the righteous will be referred to as], The holy people, The redeemed of

the LORD: and thou [*righteous Israel*] shalt be called, Sought out, A city not forsaken [*chosen by the Lord to be blessed and enjoy His help*].

ISAIAH 63

Selection: all verses

THIS IS ONE of the better-known chapters of Isaiah, particularly because it informs us that the Savior will wear red (either literally or symbolically) when He comes at the time of the Second Coming (see verses 1–2). The red represents the blood of the wicked, who are destroyed at His coming. Verses 3–6 continue the theme of the destruction of the wicked at that time.

Isaiah is a master at using comparison and contrast for teaching purposes. Thus, beginning with verse 7, he contrasts the horror of the wicked, depicted in the first six verses, with the blessed state of the righteous, who will receive the promised blessings of peace and safety when the Lord returns.

1 Who is this [*Christ*] **that cometh** [*the Second Coming*] **from Edom** [*from the east; travelers from the east to Jerusalem usually came north past the Dead Sea and then west to Jerusalem. From Edom could also mean from the east, or heaven; see Doctrine & Covenants 133:46*], **with dyed** [*red—see verse 2*] **garments** [*clothing*] from Bozrah [*the capital*

city of Edom]? this **that is glorious in his apparel** [*Christ comes in glory*], **travelling in the greatness of his strength** [*Christ comes in great power at the Second Coming*]? **I** [*Christ; "It is I," the Savior*] **that speak in righteousness, mighty to save** [*the repentant*].

2 Wherefore [*why*] **art thou red in thine apparel** [*what is the red spattered all over Your clothing; see Doctrine & Covenants 133:51*], **and thy garments like him that treadeth in the winefat** [*Hebrew: press, in other words, the wine press and the vat for collecting the juice of the grapes or olives*]?

> Next, the Savior answers the question posed in verses 1–2, above, as to who He is.

3 I have trodden the winepress alone [*I was the only one capable of doing the Atonement*]; **and of the people there was none with me** [*I had to do it alone*]: **for** [*the reason that My clothing is red is that*] **I will tread them** [*the wicked*] **in mine anger, and trample them in my fury; and their blood** [*the blood of the wicked—see Doctrine & Covenants 133:51*] **shall be sprinkled upon my garments, and I will stain all my raiment** [*judgment will be thorough*].

4 For the day of vengeance is in mine heart [*German: is part of My task, My responsibility*], **and the year**

of my redeemed is come [*the time has come for the righteous to be set free from the cares of a wicked world, perhaps referring to the Millennium*].

Another way to look at the phrase "the day of vengeance is in mine heart," in verse 4, above, is to say "the law of justice is also in My heart"; in other words, the law of justice is a vital part of the plan of salvation (see Alma 42:25).

5 And I looked, and there was none to help [*no mortal; no one could help Me do the Atonement*]; and I wondered that there was none to uphold [*I had to do it alone—see Matthew 27:46*]: therefore mine own arm [*the power was within Me*] brought salvation unto me; and my fury [*My own divine strength*], it upheld me.

6 And I will tread down the people [*the wicked*] in mine anger, and make them drunk in my fury [*judgment, the law of justice, will fall upon the wicked*], and I will bring down their strength to the earth [*I will humble the wicked*].

Isaiah now switches topics and turns to the kindness and blessings of the Lord to the righteous. In so doing, he will review some of Israel's rebellious past.

7 I will mention the lovingkindnesses of the LORD, and the praises of the LORD, according to all that the LORD hath bestowed on us, and the great goodness toward the house of Israel, which he hath bestowed on them according to his mercies, and according to the multitude of his lovingkindnesses.

8 For he said, **Surely they are my people,** children that will not lie [*German: people of integrity*]: **so he was their Saviour.**

9 **In all their affliction he was afflicted** [*He suffered and paid for their sins*], **and the angel of his presence saved them** [*the Lord rescued the children of Israel from Egypt*]: in his love and in his pity **he redeemed them; and he bare them, and carried them all the days of old** [*see Doctrine & Covenants 133:53–55, referring to righteous*].

10 **But they** [*the children of Israel*] **rebelled, and vexed his holy Spirit: therefore he was turned to be their enemy, and he fought against them.** [*He had to discipline them severely*]

11 **Then he remembered,** [*His people remembered—see footnote 11a in your Bible*] **the days of old, Moses, and his people, saying, Where is he that brought them** [*us*] **up out of the sea** [*the parting of the Red Sea*] **with the shepherd** [*leaders— see footnote 11c in your Bible*] **of his flock? where is he that put his holy Spirit within him?** [*within them— see footnote 11e in your Bible*];

Isaiah is reminding the people

that they had been greatly blessed by the Lord in times past (verses 11–14), in contrast to wicked Israel's punishments in Isaiah's day and for centuries since then.

12 That led them by the right hand of Moses with his glorious arm, dividing the water [*parting the Red Sea*] before them, to make himself an everlasting name?

13 That led them [*children of Israel*] **through the deep** [*Red Sea*], **as** [*easily as a*] **an horse in the wilderness** [*walks along in the desert*], **that they should not stumble** [*be stopped*]?

14 As a beast goeth [*as cattle walk easily*] **down into the valley, the Spirit of the LORD caused him** [*them, the Israelites*] **to rest:** so didst thou lead thy people, to make thyself a glorious name [*You led Your people and became famous among surrounding nations as a result*].

Next, Isaiah pleads with the Lord to bless Israel.

15 Look down from heaven, and behold from the habitation of thy holiness [*German: from Your heavenly home*] **and of thy glory: where is thy zeal and thy strength, the sounding of thy bowels** [*Thy tenderness*] **and of thy mercies toward me? are they restrained?**

16 Doubtless thou art our father, though Abraham be ignorant of us, and Israel acknowledge us not [*Abraham is long since dead, can't help us. Jacob is long since dead, can't help us*]: **thou, O LORD, art our father, our redeemer;** thy name is from everlasting [*German: You have been our Redeemer since the beginning*].

17 O LORD, why hast thou made [*JST: "suffered," (allowed)*] **us to err from thy ways, and hardened** [*allowed us to harden*] **our heart from thy fear** [*German: to the point that we no longer feared You*]? **Return for thy servants' sake, the tribes of thine inheritance** [*let us be Thy people again*].

18 The people of thy holiness [*covenant Israel*] **have possessed it** [*the temple*] **but a little while:** our adversaries have trodden down thy sanctuary [*the temple, Doctrine & Covenants 64:11; in other words, enemies have possessed the temple more than we have through the ages*].

19 We are thine: thou never barest rule over them [*German: we have become just like people over whom You have never ruled*]; **they were not called by thy name** [*like people who are not Your covenant people, not bearing Your name*].

ISAIAH 64

Selection: all verses

ISAIAH CONTINUES THE theme of 63:15, desiring that the Lord would come down now and rule over Israel. Isaiah, in effect, has Israel pleading with the Lord to come again, as promised (the Second Coming—see heading to this chapter in your Bible).

1 Oh that thou wouldest rend the heavens, that thou wouldest **come down**, that the mountains might flow down at thy presence [*the Second Coming*],

2 As when the melting fire burneth, the fire causeth the waters to boil, **to make thy name known to thine adversaries** [*the wicked*], that the nations may tremble at thy presence!

3 When thou didst terrible things [*German: because of the miracles you do*] which we looked not for [*German: which we didn't expect*], **thou camest down, the mountains flowed down at thy presence.**

4 For since the beginning of the world **men have not heard, nor perceived by the ear, neither hath the eye seen, O God, beside thee, what he hath prepared for him that waiteth for him** [*trusts in Him; no one can even imagine the blessings the Lord has in store for the righteous*].

The JST makes significant changes in verse 5, next. We will give it as it stands in the King James Version of the Bible and then give it from the Joseph Smith Translation of the Bible.

5 Thou meetest [*guidest*] him that rejoiceth and worketh righteousness, those that remember thee in thy ways: behold, thou art wroth; for we have sinned: in those is continuance, and we shall be saved.

JST Isaiah 64:5

5 Thou meetest him that worketh righteousness, and rejoiceth him that remembereth thee in thy ways; in righteousness there is continuance, and such shall be saved.

6 But [*JST: "we have sinned"*] **we are all as an unclean thing,** and all our righteousnesses are as filthy rags [*the few things we do right are of little value because of our gross wickedness*]; **and we all do fade as a leaf** [*we are fading away as a covenant people because of wickedness*]; and **our iniquities**, like the wind, **have taken us away** [*our wickedness has separated us from Thee*].

7 And **there is none that calleth upon thy name** [*no one turns to the Lord*], that stirreth up himself to take hold of thee: for **thou hast hid thy face from us, and hast consumed us, because of our iniquities** [*we have separated ourselves from You*].

8 But now [and yet], O LORD, thou art our father; we are the clay, and thou our potter [our Maker]; and we all are the work of thy hand.

9 Be not wroth very sore [please don't be too angry with us], O LORD, neither remember [our] iniquity for ever [please forgive us]: behold, see, we beseech thee, we are all thy people.

10 Thy holy cities are a wilderness, Zion is a wilderness, Jerusalem a desolation [much destruction has come to us already because of our wickedness].

11 Our holy and our beautiful house [the temple in Jerusalem], where our fathers praised thee, is burned up with fire: and all our pleasant [German: beautiful-to-look-at] things are laid waste.

12 Wilt thou refrain thyself for these things [will You continue to withhold blessings despite our pleas], O LORD? wilt thou hold thy peace [keep silent], and afflict us very sore [continue to punish us severely— please have mercy on us!]?

ISAIAH 65

Selection: all verses

THIS CHAPTER SUM-MARIZES the reasons the Lord rejected ancient Israel and explains in some detail the consequences of rejecting the Lord. In contrast, it also gives some details about the Millennium and the blessings for the righteous at that time, including the fact that mortals then living will live to be one hundred years old (verse 20).

The JST makes several changes in verses 1, 2, 4, and 20. We will point these out as we go along.

Verse 1 in the JST seems to answer the question in Isaiah 64:12, namely, how long the Lord will remain silent and keep punishing rebellious Israel.

1 I am sought of them that asked not for me [JST: "I am found of them who seek after me. I give unto all them that ask of me"]; I am [JST: "I am not"] found of them that sought me not [JST: "or that inquireth not after me"]: I said [JST: "unto my servant" (probably meaning Isaiah)], Behold me, behold me [JST: "look upon me; I will send you"], unto a nation that was not called by my name [JST: "is not called after my name"]; [that has not taken upon them My name].

2 I have spread out my hands [invited them to come unto me—compare with Jacob 6:4–5] all the day [constantly] unto a rebellious people, which walketh in a way that was not good, after their own thoughts [they are rebellious and wicked];

JST Isaiah 65:2
2 For I have spread out my

hands all the day to a people who walketh not in my ways, and their works are evil and not good, and they walk after their own thoughts.

3 A people that provoketh me to anger continually to my face [in other words, blatantly disobey God]; that sacrificeth in gardens, and burneth incense upon altars of brick [the Israelites were commanded in Exodus 20:25 to use unhewn (uncut) stones in making altars; in other words, they just won't obey God];

4 Which remain [German: sit] among the graves [implies that they were breaking the commandment in Leviticus 19:31: they were attempting to commune with spirits of the dead], and lodge in the monuments [German: hang around the graveyards overnight], which eat swine's flesh [strictly forbidden by Mosaic law], and broth of abominable [unclean] things is in their vessels [they are breaking every rule in the book];

JST Isaiah 65:4
4 Which remain among the graves, and lodge in the monuments; which eat swine's flesh, and broth of abominable beasts, and pollute their vessels;

5 Which say, Stand by thyself [stay away from me], come not near to me; for I am holier than thou. These are a smoke in my nose

[such hypocrites are a constant source of irritation], a fire that burneth all the day.

6 Behold, it is written before me [it is written in the scriptures]: I will not keep silence, but will recompense [pay back, reward], even recompense into their bosom [drop their sins right back into their own laps; they will be held accountable for their wickedness],

7 Your iniquities, and the iniquities of your fathers [ancestors] together [along with yours], saith the LORD, which have burned incense upon the mountains [worshiped idols], and blasphemed me upon the hills [worshiped false gods]: therefore will I measure their former work into their bosom [I will drop their sins right back into their laps].

8 Thus saith the LORD, As the new wine [fresh grape juice] is found in the cluster [of grapes; there is still potential for good in Israel], and one saith, Destroy it not; for a blessing is in it [Israel still has potential]: so will I do for my servants' sakes, that I may not destroy them all [a remnant of Israel will remain].

9 And I will bring forth a seed [descendants; a remnant] out of Jacob [Israel], and out of Judah [the Jews] an inheritor of my mountains [God's kingdom and blessings]: and

mine elect shall inherit it, and my servants shall dwell there.

10 And Sharon [*part of the Holy Land*] shall be a fold of flocks [*a peaceful place*], and the valley of Achor [*a part of the Holy Land, near Jericho*] a place for the herds to lie down in, for my people that have sought me [*the righteous will receive wonderful peace and blessings*].

11 But ye are they that forsake the LORD, that forget my holy mountain [*the gospel*], that prepare a table for that troop [*Gad, an idol of fortune—see footnote 11a in your Bible*], and that furnish the drink offering unto that number [*Meni, an idol of fate or destiny—see footnote 11b in your Bible*].

12 Therefore [*because of your wickedness*] will I number you [*turn you over*] to the sword, and ye shall all bow down to the slaughter [*great destruction will come upon you*]: because when I called, ye did not answer; when I spake, ye did not hear; but did evil before mine eyes, and did choose that [*wickedness*] wherein I delighted not.

Isaiah now contrasts rewards for the righteous with punishments for the wicked.

13 Therefore thus saith the Lord GOD, Behold, my servants [*the righteous*] shall eat, but ye [*the wicked*] shall be hungry: behold, my servants shall drink, but ye shall be thirsty: behold, my servants shall rejoice, but ye shall be ashamed [*put to shame, devastated*]:

14 Behold, my servants shall sing for joy of heart, but ye shall cry for sorrow of heart, and shall howl for vexation of spirit.

15 And ye [*the wicked*] shall leave your name for a curse unto my chosen [*it is you, the wicked, who will be cursed*]: for the Lord GOD shall slay thee [*you will be destroyed*], and call his servants by another name [*a new name; see Isaiah 62:2, Doctrine & Covenants 130:11, Revelation 2:17; symbolic of celestial glory*]:

16 That he who blesseth himself [*asks for blessings from the Lord*] in the earth shall bless himself in the God of truth [*will pray to God, not idols*]; and he that sweareth [*makes covenants*] in the earth shall swear by the God of truth [*rather than idols*]; because the former [*past*] troubles are forgotten [*over*], and because they are hid from mine eyes [*your troubles will then be over, gone*].

17 For, behold, I create new heavens and a new earth [*paradisiacal conditions during the Millennium— see footnote 17c in your Bible*]: and the former shall not be remembered, nor come into mind [*because past troubles will be completely overshadowed by the beauties of millennial life*].

18 But be ye glad and rejoice for ever in that which I create: for, behold, **I create Jerusalem a rejoicing, and her people a joy** [*the Jews in Jerusalem will become a righteous covenant people of the Lord during the Millennium*].

19 And **I will rejoice in Jerusalem, and joy in my people: and the voice of weeping shall be no more heard in her,** nor the voice of crying [*millennial conditions*].

20 There shall be no more thence [*during the Millennium*] an infant of days [*German: an infant who lives just a few days*], **nor an old man that hath not filled his days** [*lived out his years completely*]: for **the child shall die an hundred years old;** but the sinner being an hundred years old shall be accursed.

<u>JST Isaiah 65:20</u>
20 In those days there shall be no more thence an infant of days, nor an old man that hath not filled his days; for **the child shall not die, but shall live to be an hundred years old; but the sinner, living to be an hundred years old, shall be accursed.**

Elder Joseph Fielding Smith taught the following about the age of mortals during the Millennium (**bold** added for emphasis):

"When Christ comes the Saints who are on the earth will be quickened and caught up to meet him. This does not mean that those who are living in mortality at that time will be changed and pass through the resurrection, for mortals must remain on the earth until after the thousand years are ended. A change, nevertheless, will come over all who remain on the earth; they will be quickened so that they will not be subject unto death until they are old. **Men shall die when they are one hundred years of age**, and the change shall be made suddenly to the immortal state. Graves will not be made during this thousand years, and Satan shall have no power to tempt any man. Children shall grow up 'as calves of the stall' unto righteousness, that is, without sin or the temptations that are so prevalent today. Even the animal kingdom shall experience a great change, for the enmity of beasts shall disappear, as we have already stated, 'and they shall not hurt nor destroy in all my holy mountain: for the earth shall be full of the knowledge of the Lord, as the waters cover the sea.'—Isaiah 11:9." (*The Way to Perfection*, pages 298–99)

21 And **they shall build houses, and inhabit them; and they shall plant vineyards, and eat the fruit of them** [*no one will attack and take things away during the Millennium*].

22 They shall not build, and another inhabit; they shall not plant, and another eat: for as the days [*age; see Doctrine & Covenants 101:30*] of a tree [*one hundred years,*

Isaiah; see 65:20] **are the days of my people, and mine elect shall long enjoy the work of their hands.**

23 They shall not labour in vain, nor bring forth [German: bear children] **for trouble** [into a world of trouble]; **for they** [the children you bring forth during the Millennium] **are the seed** [children] **of the blessed** [you, the righteous] **of the LORD, and their offspring** [descendants] **with them.**

24 And it shall come to pass, that before they call, I will answer; and while they are yet speaking, I will hear [conditions during the Millennium will be even better than you can imagine].

25 The wolf and the lamb shall feed together, and the lion shall eat straw like the bullock: and dust shall be the serpent's meat [food]. **They shall not hurt nor destroy in all my holy mountain, saith the LORD** [peace will abound during the Millennium].

ISAIAH 66

Selection: all verses

THE LORD NOW says that everything He has created is designed for the purpose of developing humble, righteous people.

1 Thus saith the LORD, The heaven is my throne, and the earth is my footstool: where is the house that ye build unto me? and where is the place of my rest?

2 For all those things hath mine hand made, and those things [everything I have created] have been [created], saith the LORD: but **to this man** [the humble, righteous person] **will I look** [with this type of person I am pleased], even **to him that is poor** [humble] **and of a contrite spirit, and trembleth at my word** [takes God's word seriously].

Isaiah now switches topics and speaks of hypocrites.

3 He [the type of person who wants to look good by offering sacrifices to God, yet intentionally lives in sin] **that killeth an ox is as if he slew a man** [is like a murderer]; **he that sacrificeth a lamb, as if he cut off** [German: broke] **a dog's neck** [see Exodus 13:13; his efforts are useless, just as an animal with a broken neck is useless]; **he that offereth an oblation** [a grain offering], **as if he offered swine's blood; he that burneth incense, as if he blessed** [worshipped] **an idol.** Yea, **they have chosen** [they have their agency] **their own ways, and their soul delighteth in their abominations** [they are wicked and like to be so].

4 I also will choose [they have "chosen" to have the Lord "choose" to punish them] **their delusions** [punishments], and will bring their fears [German: that which they dread] upon them; because when I called, none did answer; when I spake, they did not hear [they have been intentionally disobedient]: but they did evil before mine eyes, and chose that in which I delighted not [they chose wickedness].

5 Hear the word of the LORD, ye [the righteous] that tremble at his word [that take His word seriously]; your brethren [your own people] that hated you, that cast you out for my name's sake [that persecuted you because you obeyed Me], said, Let the LORD be glorified [let the Lord come and show His power—we're not afraid; the haughty attitude of the wicked]: but he [the Lord] shall appear to your joy [to the joy of the righteous], and they [the wicked] shall be ashamed [put to shame, devastated].

6 A voice of noise from the city, a voice from the temple, a voice of the LORD that rendereth recompence to his enemies [the punishments spoken of will surely come upon the wicked].

Verses 7 and 8 seem to parallel Isaiah 49:21, "Who hath begotten me these . . .?" In other words, "Where in the world did all these Israelites come from?" Isaiah is describing the rapid growth of Zion as the earth is prepared for the Millennium (see verse 22, near the end of this chapter).

7 Before she travailed [went into labor], she brought forth [her child was born]; before her pain [labor pains] came, she [perhaps the Church of God (see JST Revelation 12:7); in other words, the Church brings forth the kingdom of God very rapidly upon the earth in the last days and on into the Millennium] was delivered of a man child [the kingdom of God (see JST Revelation 12:7); in other words, the kingdom of God will grow much faster than expected].

8 Who hath heard such a thing? who hath seen such things? Shall the earth be made to bring forth in one day [it will seem to happen overnight!]? or shall a nation [righteous Israel] be born at once? for as soon as Zion travailed, she brought forth her children [can refer to rapid progress of the work of the Lord in the last days, or the righteousness brought suddenly by the Second Coming, or both].

9 Shall I bring to the birth, and not cause to bring forth [would the Lord get everything ready and then not follow through with what He has revealed]? saith the LORD: shall I cause to bring forth, and shut the womb [stop it at the last moment]? saith thy God.

10 Rejoice ye with Jerusalem [the Lord's people], and be glad with her,

all ye that love her [the Lord's kingdom]: **rejoice for joy with her,** all ye that mourn for her [the day will come when joy and peace will reign supreme]:

> Isaiah now describes wonderful blessings that will come to those who join Zion and seek nourishment from the Lord therein.

11 That ye may suck, and be satisfied with the breasts of her consolations; that ye may milk out, and **be delighted with the abundance of her glory.**

12 For thus saith the LORD, Behold, I will extend peace to her [Zion, the righteous] **like a river** [a constant supply], and the glory [wealth] of the Gentiles like a flowing stream: **then shall ye suck** [the righteous will be nourished], ye shall be borne upon her sides [German: in her arms], **and be dandled** [German: held happily] **upon her knees.**

13 As one whom his mother comforteth, so will I comfort you [the righteous will feel right at home with the Savior; millennial conditions]; and ye shall be comforted in Jerusalem [God's kingdom].

14 And when ye [the righteous] **see this, your heart shall rejoice, and your bones shall flourish like an herb** [German: you will green up like lush grass]: and the hand of the LORD shall be known toward his servants [great blessings will come to the righteous], and his indignation toward his enemies [but the wicked will be punished].

15 For, behold, the LORD will come with fire, and with his chariots like a whirlwind, **to render his anger with fury, and his rebuke with flames of fire** [the destruction of the wicked at the Second Coming].

16 For by fire and by his sword will the LORD plead with all flesh [judge all people]: **and the slain of the LORD shall be many** [there will be large numbers of wicked in the last days, and they will be destroyed at His coming].

> Isaiah now refers again to forbidden practices among the wicked of Israel, as already mentioned in verse 3.

17 They [the wicked] **that sanctify themselves, and purify themselves in the gardens** behind one tree in the midst [attempting to make themselves holy via false gods, idol worship located in groves of trees, and so on], **eating swine's flesh** [strictly forbidden], and the abomination, **and the mouse** [a forbidden food; see Leviticus 11:29], **shall be consumed together** [suddenly, at the same time, at the Second Coming], saith the LORD.

18 For I know their [the wicked] **works and their thoughts** [and that is why they will be destroyed]: [Isaiah *begins a new topic now, namely the gathering of Israel in the last days and on into the Millennium]* **it shall come, that I will gather all nations and tongues; and they shall come, and see my glory.**

19 And I will set a sign *[ensign (see Isaiah 5:26); the true gospel, certainly including the Book of Mormon as explained in 3 Nephi 21:1–7]* **among them** *[the remnant of Israel]*, **and I will send those that escape of them** *[a righteous remnant of Israel; see Isaiah 37:32; missionary work]* **unto the nations, to Tarshish** *[Spain?]*, **Pul** *[Lybia]*, **and Lud, that draw the bow** *[famous for skilled archers]*, **to Tubal** *[Turkey]*, **and Javan** *[Greece; Isaiah has thus described basically all the commonly known world in his day]*, **to the isles** *[continents]* **afar off** *[to all nations]*, **that have not heard my fame, neither have seen my glory; and they shall declare my glory among the Gentiles** *[the gospel will be preached to all nations]*.

20 And they *[the missionaries; the true Church]* **shall bring all your brethren** *[Israelites; the gathering]* **for an offering** *[righteous lives; see 1 Samuel 15:22]* **unto the LORD out of all nations upon horses, and in chariots** *[with great power—compare with Jeremiah 23:3]*, **and in litters, and upon mules, and upon**

swift beasts, **to my holy mountain Jerusalem** *[to the true gospel]*, **saith the LORD, as the children of Israel bring an offering in a clean vessel into the house of the LORD.**

21 And I will also take of them for priests and for Levites, **saith the LORD** *[the priesthood will be restored to men in the last days]*.

22 For as the new heavens and the new earth *[can refer to millennial earth, Doctrine & Covenants 101:25; and celestial earth, Doctrine & Covenants 130:9; 88:18, 19, 25, 26]*, **which I will make, shall remain** *[will be eternal]* **before me, saith the LORD, so shall your seed** *[families]* **and your name** *[symbolic of celestial glory, Doctrine & Covenants 130:11]* **remain** *[you and your families can be with Me forever]*.

23 And it shall come to pass, that from one new moon *[special Sabbath ritual among the Israelites at the beginning of the month; see Bible Dictionary, under "New Moon"]* **to another, and from one Sabbath to another, shall all flesh come to worship before me, saith the LORD** *[the righteous are those who will be completely consistent and faithful during the Millennium and beyond]*.

24 And they *[the righteous]* **shall go forth, and look upon the carcases**

of the men that have transgressed against me [*they will be aware that the judgments of God did finally come upon the wicked*]: **for their worm shall not die** [*"Worm" refers to a scarlet dye that was made from the dried body of a certain type of female worm (Coccus ilicis). Scarlet was considered a "colorfast" dye—permanent, lasting. Hence, "their worm shall not die" implies that, even though their dead bodies can be seen, the "permanent" part of them (spirit up until the resurrection of the wicked, then their resurrected bodies) will live forever and they will thus face the consequences of their wicked choices.*] **neither shall their fire be quenched; and they shall be an abhorring unto all flesh** [*a final warning from Isaiah that wickedness does not pay at all*].

JEREMIAH

JEREMIAH IS A well-known prophet in the Old Testament. There are at least sixty-two prophecies given in his writings. The book of Jeremiah has almost twenty-two thousand words, making it somewhat longer than Isaiah, and making it the second longest book in the Old Testament (only Psalms is longer). Just so you know, if you were to count the pages of Jeremiah and Isaiah in our LDS Bible, in English, you would come up with more pages for Isaiah than for Jeremiah. That is because there is more space taken up for footnotes in Isaiah. In a page count in a King James Bible without footnotes, Jeremiah is several pages longer than Isaiah.

The book of Jeremiah can be divided roughly into the following sections:

Chapters 1–25
Prophecies about Judah and Jerusalem

Chapters 26–35
Prophecies about the restoration of Israel and Judah

Chapters 36–45
History and life story of Jeremiah

Chapters 46–51
Prophecies against foreign nations

Chapter 52
Basically an appendix giving some details of the Babylonian captivity of Jerusalem and wicked King Zedekiah's downfall, including the carrying of the Jews into Babylon.

JEREMIAH WAS BORN

into a priestly family in the Levite town of Anathoth (see Jeremiah 1:1 and Bible Dictionary under "Jeremiah"), which was located about three miles northeast of Jerusalem and is known today as Anata. According to the Bible Dictionary in our LDS English edition of the Bible, he served as a prophet in Jerusalem for over forty years, from about 626 BC to 586 BC. After the fall of Jerusalem to Babylonian captivity in about 587 BC, a group of Jews who escaped into Egypt took Jeremiah with them (Jeremiah 43:5–7), and, according to tradition, later stoned him to death.

Jeremiah was a contemporary of Lehi and several other prophets who preached during the same time period when the wickedness of the people in and around Jerusalem was setting the stage for the Babylonian captivity of Jerusalem, in about 587 BC, when the Jews were carried captive to Babylon. Babylon was a very large city located about fifty miles south of modern-day Bagdad, Iraq. It was nearly six hundred miles directly east of Jerusalem, across the desert, and was about nine hundred miles away from Jerusalem by land travel routes. As you will perhaps recall, Lehi and his family fled Jerusalem in 600 BC, as directed by the Lord, and journeyed to the promised land of America.

In 1 Nephi 1:4, Nephi mentions "many prophets" who prophesied at the time Lehi, his father, was prophesying and preaching. You might wish to go to the Chronology in your Bible Dictionary (in the back of your LDS Bible) and note several of these prophets in the "Internal History" column, beginning with 642 BC. You will see Nahum (with a ?), Jeremiah, Zephaniah, Obadiah (with a ?), and Habakkuk, as well as Daniel and Ezekiel who prophesied while in Babylonian captivity.

Jeremiah was one of the few ancient prophets who prophesied destruction for the people and then saw the fulfillment of his prophecies during his own lifetime. In a way, he was a lot like Mormon, in the Book of Mormon, who was called by the Lord to work with a people for whom there was little hope, because of their extreme wickedness (see Mormon 2:15, 19; 3:12; 5:2).

Jeremiah ministered as a prophet during the reign of the last five kings of Judah, which kingdom came to an end in 587 BC with the final wave of the Babylonian captivity. Remember that the kingdom of Israel (the northern ten tribes) had previously been carried away into captivity by the Assyrians about 722 BC, and had thus become the "lost ten tribes." The two remaining tribes, Judah and part of Benjamin, were known collectively as "Judah," with headquarters in Jerusalem.

Three of these last kings of Judah are mentioned in Jeremiah 1:2–3. A more detailed study of biblical history shows that there were actually five kings who reigned during Jeremiah's ministry, but two of them ruled for only three months apiece. They were Jehoahaz, who reigned for three months before being exiled to Egypt in 609 BC, and Jehoiachin, who ruled three months before he was exiled to Babylon in 598 BC.

Of these kings, all but King Josiah were wicked, and led their people deeper into depravity and toward destruction. The last, King Zedekiah, is probably most familiar to members of the Church because Nephi mentions him as being the king in Jerusalem when Lehi began preaching (see 1 Nephi 1:4). Zedekiah was twenty-one years old at the time he began ruling as king (see 2 Kings 24:18), and reigned for eleven years before his captivity. One of his sons, Mulek, somehow escaped captivity and was brought by the Lord to America (see Helaman 6:10; 8:21). We know his descendants in the Book of Mormon as Mulekites.

We will provide a quote used in the *Old Testament Student Manual: 1 Kings–Malachi*, for the Church's institutes of religion (page 235) that describes the conditions under which Jeremiah served as a prophet:

> "With the exception of Josiah, all of the kings of Judah during Jeremiah's ministry were unworthy men under whom the country suffered severely. Even during the reign of an earlier king, the wicked Manasseh, the Baal cult was restored among the Jews, and there was introduced the worship of the heavenly planets in accordance with the dictates of the Assyro-Babylonian religion. Jeremiah therefore found idolatry, hill-worship, and heathen religious practices rampant among his people. Heathen idols stood in the temple (Jeremiah 32:34),

children were sacrificed to Baal-Moloch (7:31; 19:5; 32:35), and Baal was especially invoked as the usual heathen deity. The worship of the 'queen of Heaven' ought also to be mentioned (7:18; 44:19). The corruption of the nation's religious worship was, of course, accompanied by all manner of immorality and unrighteousness, against which the prophet had continually to testify. The poor were forgotten. Jeremiah was surrounded on all sides by almost total apostasy. But professional prophets there were aplenty. Says Dr. H. L. Willett:

> "'He was surrounded by plenty of prophets, but they were the smooth, easy-going, popular, professional preachers whose words awakened no conscience, and who assured the people that the nation was safe in the protecting care of God. This was a true message in Isaiah's day, but that time was long since past, and Jerusalem was destined for captivity. Thus Jeremiah was doomed to preach an unwelcome message, while the false prophets persuaded the people that he was unpatriotic, uninspired, and pessimistic (14:13, 14).' " (Sidney B. Sperry, *The Voice of Israel's Prophets*, page 153.)

As you study Jeremiah's writings, you will see much symbolism and imagery (as is the case with studying Isaiah). For example, we will look ahead at three verses that describe the people of Judah during Jeremiah's time as hardened clay, no longer moldable by the Lord. This image basically sums up the description of Judah given by Brother Sperry in the above quote. We will use **bold**, as usual, to point things out to you.

Selection: Jeremiah 19:1, 10–11

1 THUS saith the LORD, Go and get a potter's **earthen bottle** [*a hardened clay jar, no longer moldable; symbolic of the people of Judah who are no longer willing to be molded and shaped by the hands of the Lord*], and *take* of the ancients of the people, and of the ancients of the priests;

10 Then shalt thou **break the bottle** [*symbolic of the fact that Judah will soon be "broken" by the Babylonian captivity—see verse 11, next*] in the sight of the men that go with thee,

11 And shalt say unto them, **Thus saith the LORD of hosts; Even so will I break this people** [*the kingdom of Judah*] **and this city** [*Jerusalem*]**, as one breaketh a potter's vessel** [*a clay jar*]**, that cannot be made whole again:** and they shall bury *them* in Tophet [*a location south of Jerusalem where human sacrifices were offered*], till *there be* no place to bury.

During King Zedekiah's wicked rule, Jeremiah spent much time in prison. The king kept him in a dismal dungeon with deep mud, bringing him out of the dungeon from time to time to see if he had anything new to say or had changed his mind about the things he had prophesied concerning the kingdom of Judah. We read especially about these most difficult conditions for this humble prophet in Jeremiah, chapters 38–39.

Jeremiah was probably a relatively young man when he began his ministry (in approximately 628–626 BC, depending on which historical sources used), preaching and prophesying about the rampant evils of society among the people of Judah. We read about his call in chapter 1. One of the major doctrines taught in this chapter is that of premortal life. Few, if any, Christian denominations teach that we lived before we were born on earth, even though it is so clearly taught in Jeremiah 1:5.

We will now proceed with chapter 1.

JEREMIAH 1

Selection: all verses

IN THIS CHAPTER, Jeremiah records his call to serve as a prophet. He records his feelings of inadequacy. His call as a true prophet is immediately apparent as he teaches the doctrine of premortality and tells us of two visions he was given.

1 THE words of Jeremiah the son of Hilkiah, of the priests that *were* in Anathoth [*a town about three miles northeast of Jerusalem*] in the

land of Benjamin [*the area given to the tribe of Benjamin when the twelve tribes of Israel arrived in the land of Canaan*]:

Next, in verse 2, Jeremiah, without additional explanation, humbly and simply tells us that he was called by the Lord to be a prophet in the thirteenth year of the reign of Josiah, king of Judah, which, according to most sources, would be approximately 627 BC (about twenty-seven years before Lehi and his family left Jerusalem).

Jeremiah's Call

2 To whom the word of the LORD came in the days of Josiah the son of Amon king of Judah, in the thirteenth year of his reign.

Next, in verse 3, Jeremiah states, in effect, that he continued to receive and deliver the word of the Lord to the people of Judah, as a prophet, for over forty years, until Jerusalem was taken captive by Babylon at the end of King Zedekiah's reign.

3 It [*the word of the Lord to Jeremiah*] **came also in the days of Jehoiakim** the son of Josiah king of Judah, **unto the end of the eleventh year of Zedekiah** the son of Josiah king of Judah, unto the carrying away of Jerusalem captive in the fifth month.

Few if any other Christian churches teach the doctrine of premortality as a vital part of the plan of salvation. Perhaps you have been surprised or even amazed that they do not teach it, since Jeremiah teaches it clearly here in verses 4-5.

Doctrine

We lived in premortality before we were born into mortality.

4 Then the word of the LORD came unto me, saying,

5 Before I [*the Lord*] **formed thee in the belly** [*before you were conceived and grew in your mother's womb; in other words, in the premortal life*] **I knew thee; and before thou camest forth out of the womb I** sanctified thee, *and* **I ordained thee a prophet unto the nations** [*Before Jeremiah was born, he was foreordained to be a prophet*].

Doctrine

In addition to the doctrine of premortality in verse 5, we also see the doctrine of foreordination.

Verse 5, above, tells us that Jeremiah was "ordained," in other words, "foreordained" to be a prophet on earth, while he was yet in his premortal existence. He was no doubt one of the "noble and great ones" spoken of in Abraham 3:22–23.

Being foreordained does not imply loss of agency, nor does it mean "predestined." Rather, it means that we were set apart or ordained in our premortal lives to accomplish certain tasks in the work of the Lord here on earth. Joseph Smith explained this. He taught:

"Every man who has a calling to minister to the inhabitants of the world was ordained to that very purpose in the Grand Council of heaven before this world was. I suppose I was ordained to this very office in that Grand Council" (*Teachings of the Prophet Joseph Smith*, page 365).

Foreordination is very similar in concept to patriarchal blessings. Direction is given and potential to do good and fulfill specific work in the Lord's plan is revealed, yet agency is preserved.

Jeremiah was overwhelmed by this call from the Lord, as has been the case with countless others throughout the ages who have been called to fulfill the Lord's will in unexpected ways. This would include Moses (see Exodus 3:11), Isaiah (see Isaiah 6:5), Enoch (Moses 6:31), and Mary (Luke 1:34). You have very likely experienced similar feelings. We see Jeremiah's reaction to the call in verse 6, next, and the Lord's response to his concerns, in verses 7–9.

6 Then said I, **Ah, Lord GOD! behold, I cannot speak** [*perhaps meaning "I am speechless." Could also mean "I am not old enough to be taken seriously by the people"*]: **for I** *am* **a child.**

7 ¶ But the LORD said unto me, Say not, I *am* a child: for thou shalt go to all that I shall send thee, and

whatsoever I command thee thou shalt speak.

8 **Be not afraid** of their faces: **for I** *am* **with thee** to deliver thee, saith the LORD.

Next, the Lord (the premortal Jesus Christ, who is the God of the Old Testament—see for example Ether 3:6 and 14) gives Jeremiah the gift of speaking the mind and will of God clearly.

9 Then **the LORD put forth his hand, and touched my mouth.** And the LORD said unto me, Behold, I **have put my words in thy mouth.**

This scene with Jeremiah is very similar to the scene with Enoch at the time he was called to preach the gospel. We will take a moment to read two verses about Enoch's call from the book of Moses:

Moses 6:31–32
31 And **when Enoch had heard these words** [*his call from the Lord*], **he** bowed himself to the earth, before the Lord, and **spake** before the Lord, saying: Why is it that **I** have found favor in thy sight, and **am but a lad,** and all the people hate me; for **I am slow of speech;** wherefore [*why*] am I thy servant?

32 **And the Lord said** unto Enoch: Go forth and do as I have commanded thee, and no man shall pierce thee. **Open thy mouth, and it shall be filled, and I will give thee utterance,** for all flesh is in my

hands, and I will do as seemeth me good.

Next, the Savior describes the scope of Jeremiah's mission for him.

10 See, I have this day set thee over the nations and over the kingdoms, to root out [*to expose and destroy evil*], and to **pull down,** and to **destroy,** and to **throw down** [*to destroy wickedness and the wicked—see Jeremiah 12:17 and 18:7*], to **build** [*righteousness*], and to **plant** [*including planting the seeds of the gospel in peoples' lives*].

Next, the Lord shows Jeremiah two visions, one described in verses 11–12, and the other in verses 13–16.

Vision

11 ¶ Moreover the word of the LORD came unto me, saying, Jeremiah, **what seest thou? And I** said, **I see a rod of an almond tree** [*the first tree to blossom in the spring in the Jerusalem area of Jeremiah's day*].

12 Then said the LORD unto me, Thou hast well seen: for **I will hasten my word to perform it** [*perhaps meaning that the Lord will fulfill Jeremiah's prophecies about coming destruction of Judah sooner than expected*].

Vision

13 And the word of the LORD came unto me the second time, saying, **What seest thou? And I** said, **I see a seething pot** [*a boiling cauldron*]**; and the face thereof is toward the north** [*the invading Babylonian armies will come from Babylon (about six hundred miles across the desert directly east of Jerusalem). But their route will be the trade route which will bring them northwest up over the Arabian Desert and then west and then south, down to Jerusalem; therefore, the "seething pot" would likely symbolize the conquering enemy armies of Babylon who will come from the north as they swoop down on the wicked people of Judah*].

14 Then the LORD said unto me, Out of the north an evil [*probably referring to the Babylonian armies, which will come upon the people of Judah in about forty years*] **shall break forth upon all the inhabitants of the land.**

15 For, lo, I will call all the families of the kingdoms of the north [*most likely the Babylonians*], saith the LORD; and **they shall come,** and they **shall set every one his throne at the entering of the gates** [*symbolic of conquering a city*] of Jerusalem, and against all the walls thereof round about, and against all the cities of Judah.

16 And I will utter my judgments [*the punishments of God*] **against them** [*the people of Judah*] touching all their wickedness, **who have forsaken me**, and have **burned incense unto other gods** [*who have turned to idol worship*], and **worshipped the works of their own hands** [*idols, which they have made with their own hands*].

> Verses 17-19, next, appear to be a repetition of the Lord's instructions to Jeremiah in verses 7-8, above, with a bit more detail as to how the Lord will enable him to accomplish his mission, if he exercises faith.

17 ¶ Thou therefore **gird up thy loins** [*prepare for action*], and **arise**, and **speak unto them** [*the inhabitants of the kingdom of Judah*] **all that I command thee: be not dismayed at their faces**, lest I confound thee before them [*if you falter in faith, you will not be blessed to succeed*].

18 For, behold, **I have made thee this day a defenced city**, and **an iron pillar**, and **brasen walls** [*in other words, the Lord will defend Jeremiah*] against the whole land, against the kings of Judah, against the princes [*leaders*] thereof, against the priests thereof, and against the people of the land.

> Next, in verse 19, the Savior prophesies that Jeremiah will face much opposition during his ministry.

19 And **they shall fight against thee; but they shall not prevail** [*win*] **against thee; for I** *am* **with thee**, saith the LORD, **to deliver thee**.

> One of the important messages for us in verse 19, above, is that, with the Lord on our side, our enemies cannot ultimately triumph over us spiritually. Such was the case with Jeremiah. Although he was subjected to much physical misery during mortality, his enemies did not win against him spiritually. And that is everything, as we view things from the perspective of the eternal truths given in the plan of salvation.

JEREMIAH 2

Selection: all verses

IN THIS CHAPTER, Jeremiah basically says that the Lord loves His people and that they once had a loyal, tender relationship with Him. But now they have deserted Him and are worshipping false gods. The prophet rebukes the people, describing their apostasy in some detail.

1 MOREOVER **the word of the LORD came to me** [*Jeremiah*], **saying,**

> Next, in verses 2-3, Jeremiah speaks for the Lord, reminding the people of the Lord's love for them and of good times in the past when the Israelites kept the commandments and were close to Him.

2 Go and cry in the ears of Jerusalem [*the people of Judah*], saying, Thus saith the LORD; I remember thee,

the kindness of thy youth [*the love and tenderness of the earlier days of our relationship*], the love of thine espousals [*when you made covenants of loyalty to Me*], when thou wentest after me in the wilderness [*when you followed Me in the wilderness, a cloud by day and a pillar of fire by night*], in a land *that was* not sown [*in the unplanted wilderness, when I provided manna for you*].

3 Israel *was* holiness unto the LORD, *and* the firstfruits of his increase [*you belonged to Me and were dedicated to being My covenant people*]: all that devour him shall offend; evil shall come upon them, saith the LORD [*it was said at that time that any enemies who came upon Israel were held guilty by the Lord and disaster came upon them*].

The implication in verse 3, above, is that the Lord protected covenant Israel in times past, but now, because of their wickedness, He will allow their enemies (Babylon) to come upon them. In other words, disastrous punishments will no longer come upon Judah's enemies, rather, they will be allowed to conquer and humble Judah, because of wickedness among her people.

Perhaps you've noticed that we keep using the terms "Israel," "Judah," "Israelites," and other terms somewhat interchangeably. This can be a bit confusing. Let's have a brief review:

"Israel" is a general term for the twelve tribes of Israel. These twelve tribes were descendants of the twelve sons of Jacob (son of Isaac and grandson of Abraham), whose name was later changed to "Israel." The Lord made a covenant with Abraham (see Abraham 2:9–11). Part of the covenant was that he and his descendants, through Isaac, were to carry the gospel and the blessings of the priesthood to all the world. Thus, the descendants of Abraham, through Isaac and Jacob, are often referred to as "the covenant people of the Lord." They are also referred to as "Israel." Likewise, they are "Israelites," and were also called "the children of Israel," especially when Moses was leading them in the wilderness.

"Judah" was one specific group of Israelites, headquartered in Jerusalem. When Joshua led the children of Israel across the Jordan River and into the promised land (the land of Canaan), he divided the land up among the twelve tribes. Eventually, these twelve tribes broke up and formed two nations, one consisting of ten tribes and the other consisting of two tribes. The ten tribes, with Ephraim as the dominant tribe, became known as the "Northern Kingdom" and retained the name, "Israel." The other two tribes, with Judah as the dominant tribe, became known as the "Southern Kingdom," or "Judah," and were headquartered in Jerusalem.

In about 722 BC, the Assyrians conquered the northern ten tribes, headquartered in Samaria, and carried most of them away into captivity. They became the "lost ten tribes of Israel."

The two remaining tribes, Judah and Benjamin, known collectively as "Judah," remained. Jeremiah was sent to warn them and preach to them. He continued to preach and prophesy to Judah until the Babylonians conquered them in about 587 BC.

Remember that the people of Judah are from the "house of Jacob," in other words they are descendants of Jacob (Israel), and, therefore, are Israelites. Thus, in verse 4, next, Jeremiah addresses them as the "house of Jacob." In verse 5 the Lord will ask these wicked people what wickedness they have found in Him that has caused them to leave Him.

Details of Israel's apostasy (Verses 4–13)

4 Hear ye the word of the LORD, O house of Jacob [*Israel*]**, and all the families of the house of Israel:**

5 ¶ Thus saith the LORD, What iniquity have your fathers [*ancestors*] **found in me** [*the Lord*]**, that they are gone far from me** [*that has given them a reason to have left Me, apostatized*]**, and have walked after vanity** [*things that have no value—see verse 11*]**, and are become vain** [*have lost their value as a covenant people of the Lord*]**?**

One of the causes of apostasy is not remembering past blessings from the Lord. This is pointed out in verses 6-8, next.

6 Neither said they, Where *is* **the**

LORD that brought us up out of the land of Egypt, that **led us through the wilderness,** through a land of **deserts** and of **pits,** through a land of **drought,** and of the **shadow of death,** through a land [*the deserts of Sinai*] that no man passed through, and **where no man dwelt?**

7 And **I brought you into a plentiful country** [*Canaan, the promised land*]**, to eat the fruit thereof and the goodness thereof;** but when ye entered, **ye defiled my land** [*polluted the promised land with wickedness*]**, and made mine heritage an abomination** [*you polluted your inheritance given to you by Me*]**.**

8 The priests said not, Where *is* **the LORD?** [*In other words, were not faithful to God.*] and **they that handle the law knew me not** [*your priests and leaders led you astray*]**: the pastors also transgressed against me,** and **the prophets prophesied by Baal** [*you accepted and followed false religious leaders and prophets who led you to worship Baal, a major false religion of the day*]**, and walked after** *things that* **do not profit.**

The word "plead," in verse 9, next, means "to bring charges against" as in a formal court of law. In other words, sadly, Israel is guilty of leaving God and turning instead to false gods and the abominable practices associated with their worship. The Lord, operating under the law of justice, is, in effect, formally charging wicked Judah with apostasy.

9 ¶ Wherefore [*this is the reason*] **I will yet plead with you** [*bring charges against you*], **saith the LORD, and with your children's children will I plead.**

10 For pass over the isles of Chittim [*Cyprus and beyond*], and see; and send unto Kedar [*in the Arabian Desert*], and consider diligently, and **see if there be such a thing** [*look far and wide and see if you can find such a thing as people changing gods*].

11 Hath a nation changed *their* **gods,** which *are* yet no gods [*can you find a nation who has changed their false gods, who have no power at all*]? **but my people** [*Israel*] **have changed their glory** [*have exchanged the glory and blessings of their God, who does have power*] **for that which doth not profit.**

12 Be astonished, O ye heavens, **at this, and be horribly afraid,** be ye very desolate, saith the LORD.

13 For **my people have committed two evils; they have forsaken me** [*Jehovah, Jesus Christ*] the fountain of living waters [*the source of the true gospel—see John 4:10, 14*], *and* hewed them out cisterns, broken cisterns, that can hold no water [*and have replaced Me with leaky containers (false gods) that are incapable of holding "living water," in other words, that cannot save*].

Next, in verse 14, the Lord asks why Israel is being so foolish. What could possibly lead the covenant people to abandon their True God and worship powerless false gods? What reasons could they have?

14 ¶ *Is* **Israel a servant?** *is* he **a homeborn** *slave* [*does he not stand a chance of "promotion" to exaltation*]? **why is he spoiled** [*why has Israel become easy prey for their enemies*]?

Perhaps you have noticed that ancient prophets among the Israelites often spoke of the future as if it had already taken place. This is part of the "manner of prophesying among the Jews" (2 Nephi 25:1) spoken of by Nephi which is difficult for many modern students of the scriptures to grasp. We see examples of this in the next verses as the Lord speaks of coming destruction upon Israel because of wickedness, as if it had already taken place.

15 The young lions [*symbolic of terrible destruction*] **roared upon him** [*Israel*], *and* **yelled, and they made his land waste: his cities are burned without inhabitant.**

16 Also **the children of Noph** [*the men of Memphis, an ancient city in Egypt not far south of modern Cairo*] **and Tahapanes** [*in Egypt*] **have broken the crown of thy head** [*have cracked your skull*].

17 Hast thou not procured this unto thyself [*did you not ask for this*], **in that**

thou hast forsaken the LORD thy God, when he led thee by the way [*in spite of the fact that He led you in safety in times past*]?

Next, in verse 18, the Lord refers to the fact that Israel has adopted the wicked practices common in the world, symbolized by Egypt and Babylon. In other words, they have sunk to the level of spiritual depravity that existed in that day in these nations.

Have you noticed that Egypt and especially Babylon are often used elsewhere in the scriptures to symbolize worldly wickedness?

18 And now **what hast thou to do in the way of Egypt, to drink the waters of Sihor** [*the Nile River; in other words, can the Nile (symbolic of Egypt) provide you with "living water—verse 13*]? **or what hast thou to do in the way of Assyria, to drink the waters of the river** [*why have you turned to the spiritually lifeless waters of idolatrous Babylon*]?

Major Message (verse 19)

We are often punished "by" our sins as well as "for" them.

19 **Thine own wickedness shall correct** [*punish*] **thee, and thy backslidings shall reprove thee: know therefore and see that** *it is* **an evil** *thing* **and bitter, that thou hast forsaken** [*abandoned*] **the LORD thy God, and that my fear** [*respect, reverence, awe before God*] *is* **not in thee,** saith the Lord GOD of hosts.

A scathing rebuke of Judah (Verses 20–37)

20 ¶ **For of old time** [*in days gone by*] **I** [*the Lord*] **have broken thy yoke,** *and* **burst thy bands** [*I set you free from the bondage of Egypt (symbolic of being set free from the bondage of sin)*]; **and thou saidst, I will not transgress; when upon every high hill and under every green tree thou wanderest, playing the harlot** [*you promised to keep the commandments while at the same time you were engaging in worshiping false gods*].

"Under every green tree," in verse 20, above, has reference to sexual immorality engaged in with temple prostitutes used in the worship of idols of the day, especially in Baal worship. The phrase "playing the harlot" refers to "spiritual adultery" in the sense that the people, who had made covenants of loyalty to God, were "stepping out on Him" as they worshipped false gods.

21 **Yet I had planted thee a noble vine, wholly a right seed** [*I gave you the best possible start, as My covenant people with the true gospel*]: **how then art thou turned into the degenerate plant of a strange vine unto me** [*how could you possibly leave Me and become an apostate people, producing bitter fruit*]?

In verse 22, next, the word "nitre" means lye, carbonate of soda—see footnote 22b in your LDS Bible. It was a strong cleansing agent used in ancient times. The point is that the people of Judah cannot continue in wickedness and hope to still be clean.

22 For though thou wash thee with nitre, and take thee much soap, *yet* **thine iniquity** [*wickedness*] **is marked before me,** saith the Lord GOD.

23 How canst thou say [*claim*]**, I am not polluted, I have not gone after Baalim** [*I have not worshiped Baal*]**? see thy way in the valley** [*look back at your tracks*]**,** know what thou hast done: *thou art* a swift dromedary traversing her ways;

> We will quote from the *Old Testament Student Manual: 1 Kings–Malachi* for the explanation of the "dromedary" (camel) in verse 23, above, and the wild ass in verse 24, next.
>
> "The imagery indicates that as a camel or a wild ass in heat runs back and forth during the mating season, so did Israel run after false gods" (*Old Testament Student Manual*, page 236).

24 A wild ass used to the wilderness, *that* **snuffeth up the wind at her pleasure; in her occasion** [*when she is in heat*] **who can turn her away?** all they that seek her will not weary themselves; in her month they shall find her.

> The JST (Joseph Smith Translation of the Bible) of verse 24, above, changes the position of "not," implying that the wicked wear

themselves out in evil pursuits, but do not ultimately find satisfaction.

<u>JST Jeremiah 2:24</u>
24 A wild ass used to the wilderness, *that* snuffeth up the wind at her pleasure; in her who can turn her away? all they that seek her will weary themselves; in her month they shall **not** find her.

The imagery in verse 25, next, is that of people so anxious to get on with the sinful life of worshipping false gods that they won't even take time to put on shoes or get a drink of water to slake their thirst before they run out of their houses to pursue idolatry.

25 Withhold thy foot from being unshod [*at least take time to put on your shoes*]**, and thy throat from thirst** [*at least get a drink*]**: but thou saidst, There is no hope** [*I am hopeless*]**: no; for I have loved strangers** [*I am an idol worshiper*]**, and after them will I go** [*and that is what I want to keep doing*]**.**

> We see from verse 26, next, that Judah is corrupt, through and through.

26 As the thief is ashamed [*put to shame, disgraced*] **when he is found** [*caught*]**, so is the house of Israel ashamed; they, their kings,** their **princes, and their priests,** and their **prophets** [*their false prophets*]**,**

> In verses 27–28, Jeremiah points out how ridiculous idol worship is.

27 Saying to a stock [*a piece of wood which they have carved into an idol*], **Thou art my father**; and **to a stone** [*an idol*], **Thou hast brought me forth** [*you are my creator*]: for **they** [*Judah*] **have turned their back unto me** [*have rejected the Lord*], and not *their* face: **but in the time of their trouble they will say, Arise, and save us** [*Israel has a track record of turning to the Lord only in times of trouble*].

28 But where are thy gods that thou hast made thee? **let them** arise, if they can **save thee in the time of thy trouble**: for *according to the number of thy cities are thy gods* [*you have as many idols, false gods, as you have cities*], O Judah.

It was common practice for each city to have its own god, represented by a specific idol. And when one city prevailed over another, it was thought that their god was more powerful than the losing city's god.

The Lord goes on in verse 29 to ask, in effect, what complaint Judah has against Him which caused the people to turn to other gods.

29 Wherefore [*why*] **will ye plead** [*quarrel, argue—see footnote 29a in your LDS Bible*] **with me?** ye all have transgressed against me, saith the LORD.

Next, in verse 30, the Lord tells Judah that it has not done a bit of good for Him to punish Israelites, such as the northern ten tribes, who are gone now. Judah has not repented at all.

30 In vain have I smitten your [*Israel's*] **children; they received no correction**: your own sword hath devoured your prophets [*you have destroyed the prophets I have sent to correct you*], like a destroying lion.

31 ¶ O generation, see ye the word of the LORD. **Have I been a wilderness unto Israel** [*have I not blessed Israel abundantly*]? a land of darkness? **wherefore say my people, We are lords; we will come no more unto thee** [*why do My people arrogantly say that they will no longer consider Me to be their God*]?

32 Can a maid forget her ornaments, or a bride her attire [*her wedding gown, her finest clothing; in other words, have you ever known a bride to forget to prepare for her wedding? Symbolic of covenant Israel keeping covenants in preparation to meet the Groom (the Savior)*]? yet **my people have forgotten me days without number** [*they have a long track record of forgetting Me*].

33 Why trimmest thou thy way to seek love [*why do you demonstrate such skill in pursuing false gods*]? **Therefore** [*because of your skill in evil ways*] **hast thou also taught the wicked ones thy ways** [*even the most wicked can learn more evil from you*].

34 Also **in thy skirts is found the blood of the souls of the poor innocents** [*your guilt against the righteous is obvious, is written all over you*]: **I have not found it by secret search, but upon all these.**

> Verse 35, next, is very applicable today. The wicked claim that what they are doing is not against God's will. Therefore, they are innocent, and thus God's punishments will not come upon them.
>
> In the second half of the verse, the Lord says that He will indeed bring them to accountability and punishment for their wickedness.

35 Yet thou [*Judah*] **sayest, Because I am innocent, surely his anger shall turn from me.** Behold, I [*the Lord*] **will plead with thee** [*will bring charges against you*], **because thou** sayest, I have not sinned.

36 Why gaddest thou about so **much to change thy way** [*why do you go back and forth so much, constantly changing your loyalties*]? **thou also shalt be ashamed of Egypt** [*Egypt will provide no protection for you*], **as thou wast ashamed of Assyria** [*just as Assyria was no protection for your brethren of the Northern Kingdom, when they tried to make alliances with them for protection*].

37 Yea, **thou shalt go forth from him, and thine hands upon thine head** [*you will be enslaved*]: for **the LORD hath rejected thy**

confidences [*your trust in other gods*], **and thou shalt not prosper in them.**

JEREMIAH 3

Selection: all verses

IN THIS CHAPTER, Jeremiah uses the imagery of a wife being unfaithful to her husband and divorcing him to represent Judah's apostasy from the Lord. In other words, the wife is symbolic of Judah (and Israel in general), and the husband is symbolic of the Lord. The phrase "played the harlot" (in verse 1) is a phrase that means "committed adultery." In this case, it is used to mean "spiritual adultery," in other words, breaking covenants made with the Lord through personal and national wickedness. Actual physical sexual immorality is a major player in the spiritual adultery committed by Israel and Judah against the Lord.

In spite of the extreme wickedness of the people in Jeremiah's day, you will see an invitation to repent and return to God in several verses within the chapter, thus reminding us of the tender love of the Savior and His desire to have sinners return to Him and thus to His Father. It is also a reminder of the power of the Atonement to cleanse and heal.

In this chapter, you will also see a prophecy that Israel will be gathered again in the last days, some one at a time, and sometimes just a few members of a family at a time. They will be brought into the latter-day Zion through the restored gospel of Jesus Christ.

Watch now as Jeremiah points out the wickedness of Judah and the open invitation, still in place, for them to repent.

1 THEY say, If a man put away his wife [*it is said that if a man divorces his wife (implying that she has been unfaithful to him)*], **and she go from** [*leave*] **him, and become another man's** [*symbolic in this case of worshipping idols*], **shall he return unto her again** [*do you think he would ever take her back (answer: No, according to the Law of Moses—see Deuteronomy 24:3–4)*]? **shall not that land be greatly polluted** [*wouldn't that ruin that nation*]? **but thou** [*Judah specifically, Israel in general*] **hast played the harlot with many lovers** [*you have worshiped many false gods; you have broken covenants made with God*]; **yet return again to me,** saith the LORD [*please return, it is not too late*].

Next, in verse 2, Jeremiah invites the people of wicked Judah to look all around them to see obvious evidence of their apostasy. The "high places" are the mountains and groves of trees on them where idolatry typically takes place, including literal adultery with temple prostitutes as a part of idol worship, especially Baal worship.

2 Lift up thine eyes unto the high places, and see where thou hast not been lien with [*see if you can find any places where idol worship and associated adultery has not taken place; symbolically, look all around you and see if you can find any people of Judah who have not been involved in idolatry*]. **In the ways hast thou sat for them** [*you have waited by the side of the road for idols to worship just like a harlot waits along the path for potential lovers*], **as the Arabian in the wilderness** [*as is the common practice*]; **and thou hast polluted the land** [*the promised land*] **with thy whoredoms** [*unfaithfulness to God*] **and with thy wickedness.**

We will quote from the Bible Dictionary (in the back of your LDS Bible) for a general statement on the subject of sexual immorality commonly associated with idol worship. We will use **bold** for emphasis:

Bible Dictionary: Idol
Among the nations of Canaan and W. Syria Baal was the sun god or source of life, and Ashtoreth was the corresponding female deity. In addition each nation had its own peculiar god to whom it ascribed its prosperity and misfortunes (see *Chemosh; Molech*). The idolatry into which the Israelites so often fell consisted either in making images that stood for Jehovah, such as the calves of Jeroboam (1 Kgs. 12:28); or in worshipping, in addition to Jehovah, one of the gods of the heathen nations around them (1 Kgs. 11:7, 33; 2 Kgs. 21:3–6; 23:10; Jer. 7:31; Ezek. 20:26–49), **such idolatry** being some form of nature worship, which **encouraged as a rule immoral practices.**

Next, in verse 3, the Lord tells the people that their wickedness is the cause of drought in their land. Then, He points out that the people of Judah are not even ashamed of their wickedness.

3 Therefore [*because you have "played the harlot"*] **the showers have been withholden,** and there hath been no latter rain [*the spring rains have been withheld by the Lord*]; and **thou hadst a whore's forehead** [*you advertised your wickedness like a prostitute marks her forehead (a cultural practice of that day) to attract lovers*], **thou refusedst to be ashamed** [*and you weren't even embarrassed at your public display of wickedness*].

4 Wilt thou not from this time cry unto me, My father, thou *art* the guide of my youth [*won't you please return to Me and seek guidance from Me as in times past*]?

Next, the people ask, in effect, how long the Lord will be angry with them. Jeremiah then points out their shallowness and hypocrisy, noting that even while they are asking the question about the Lord's anger, they continue in their evil ways.

5 Will he [*the Lord*] **reserve** [*keep*] *his anger for ever?* **will he keep** *it* **to the end?** Behold, thou [*Judah*] hast spoken [*asked the above questions*] **and done evil things as thou couldest** [*the people ask how long the Lord will be angry with them but they keep*

right on being wicked].

Next, Jeremiah tells the people what the Lord had called his attention to previously during the reign of King Josiah. Jehovah had used Israel (the ten tribes who were carried away captive by the Assyrians about one hundred years ago, in 722 BC) as an example of what happens to covenant people who get completely caught up in wickedness. Judah should look at what happened to Israel, wake up and repent.

6 ¶ The LORD said also unto me in the days of Josiah the king, **Hast thou seen** *that* **which backsliding Israel hath done?** she is gone up upon every high mountain and under every green tree, and there hath played the harlot [*apostate Israel was deeply involved with idol worship before their destruction by the Assyrians*].

The Lord points out that in spite of Israel's wickedness, He had still invited them to repent. But they refused.

7 And I said after she [*Israel—the northern ten tribes*] **had done all these** *things,* **Turn thou unto me. But she returned not.** And her treacherous sister Judah saw *it.*

In verses 8–11, next, the Lord continues to point out that the people of Judah have not learned a lesson from what happened to their fellow Israelites, the northern ten tribes (referred to as "Israel" in this context).

8 And I [*the Lord*] **saw, when for all the causes whereby backsliding Israel committed adultery** [*broke her covenants with Me*] **I had put her away, and given her a bill of divorce** [*I rejected her and let her be carried away into Assyrian captivity*]; **yet her treacherous sister Judah feared not, but went and played the harlot also** [*Judah did not learn from what happened to Israel, rather, continued breaking covenants*].

As has been previously stated, the word, "adultery," as used in verse 8, above, often means "apostasy." We will quote from the Bible Dictionary on this subject (**bold** added for emphasis):

Bible Dictionary: Adultery
While adultery is usually spoken of in the individual sense, **it is sometimes used to illustrate the apostasy of a nation or a whole people from the ways of the Lord,** such as Israel forsaking her God and going after strange gods and strange practices (Ex. 20:14; Jer. 3:7–10; Matt. 5:27–32; Luke 18:11; Doctrine & Covenants 43:24–25).

9 And it came to pass through the lightness of her whoredom [*she did not consider her disloyalty to God to be a serious matter*], **that she defiled the land, and committed adultery with stones and with stocks** [*she committed spiritual adultery by worshiping idols of rock and wood*].

10 And yet for all this [*in view of all this evidence*] **her treacherous sister Judah hath not turned unto me** with her whole heart, but feignedly [*merely pretended*], saith the LORD.

11 And the LORD said unto me [*Jeremiah*], **The backsliding Israel hath justified herself more than treacherous Judah** [*even apostate Israel was not as wicked as Judah has become*].

Unless we realize that verses 12–18, next, are a prophecy about the future, we can become confused. As we read verse 12, we might think, "Wait a minute. Israel is gone. The Assyrians took the people away over one hundred years ago. How can Jeremiah talk to them?" But when we understand that it is a prophecy about the future gathering of Israel (see heading to this chapter in your Bible), it makes sense. And we realize that we are watching a major portion of the fulfillment of this prophecy in our day.

12 ¶ Go and proclaim these words toward the north [*address this message to Israel*]**, and say,** Return, thou backsliding Israel, saith the LORD; *and* I will not cause mine anger to fall upon you: for **I** *am* **merciful, saith the LORD,** *and* I will not keep *anger* for ever.

In verses 13–14, next, the Lord explains in the simplest terms how Israel will someday be enabled to return to Him.

13 Only **acknowledge thine iniquity, that thou hast transgressed against the LORD thy God,** and hast scattered thy ways to the strangers [*you have joined the ways of the world, participated in their evil ways*] under every green tree [*a reference to the immoral practices associated with ancient idol worship*], and ye have not obeyed my voice [*the problem*], saith the LORD.

14 **Turn, O backsliding children, saith the LORD**; for I am married unto you [*I am your God; you can be My covenant people again*]: **and I will take you** [*gather you*] **one of a city, and two of a family, and I will bring you to Zion:**

> In times past, wicked priests and false prophets led Israel astray. Verse 15, next, prophesies that in conjunction with the gathering of Israel in the last days, we will once again have righteous leaders whose hearts are in tune with God. They will nourish us with correct doctrine.

15 **And I will give you pastors** [*leaders*] **according to mine heart** [*whose hearts are in harmony with the Lord's heart*], **which shall feed you with knowledge and understanding.**

> Verse 16, next, appears to be saying that, in the last days when the gospel is restored and Israel is being gathered, the focus will no longer be on the Law of Moses, with the ark of the covenant, etc. Rather the emphasis will be on the restored gospel of Jesus Christ.

16 **And it shall come to pass, when ye be multiplied and increased in the land, in those days** [*when Israel is gathered in the last days*], saith the LORD, **they shall say no more, The ark of the covenant** of the LORD: neither shall it come to mind: neither shall they remember it; **neither shall they visit** *it*; neither shall *that* be done any more [*the people will no longer live by the Law of Moses*].

> Verse 17, next, appears to refer to the Millennium, when the Savior will be "KING OF KINGS AND LORD OF LORDS" (Revelation 19:16) as He rules and reigns on earth during the Millennium. During the one thousand years of peace, there will be two headquarters of the Church on earth, one in Zion (Independence, Jackson County, Missouri) and one in Old Jerusalem. We will say a bit more about this and give a reference for it, after verse 17.

17 **At that time** [*during the Millennium*] **they shall call Jerusalem the throne of the LORD** [*Jerusalem will be a headquarters for the Savior during the Millennium*]; **and all the nations** [*people from all nations*] **shall be gathered unto it, to the name of the LORD, to Jerusalem: neither shall they walk any more after the imagination of their evil heart** [*the people will not be wicked*].

> Joseph Fielding Smith (who

became the tenth president of the Church) taught about the two cities that would become headquarters of the kingdom of God during the Millennium. He said:

"ZION AND JERUSALEM: TWO WORLD CAPITALS. When Joseph Smith translated the Book of Mormon, he learned that America is the land of Zion which was given to Joseph and his children and that on this land the City Zion, or New Jerusalem, is to be built. He also learned that Jerusalem in Palestine is to be rebuilt and become a holy city. **These two cities, one in the land of Zion and one in Palestine, are to become capitals for the kingdom of God during the millennium"** (*Doctrines of Salvation*, vol. 3, page 71).

Verse 18, next, contains an additional prophecy. As you perhaps recall, after settling in the Holy Land, the twelve tribes of Israel eventually broke up into two nations, Israel (ten tribes) and Judah (two tribes). This happened after King Solomon's death. There was much hatred and animosity between the two nations. Verse 18 foretells the day when Judah and Israel will once again be united in peace and harmony.

18 In those days **the house of Judah shall walk with the house of Israel,** and they shall come together out of the land of the north to the land that I have given for an inheritance unto your fathers.

Verse 19, next, gives a simple

answer as to how Israel and Judah can someday live in peace and be the Lord's covenant people.

19 But I said, How shall I put thee among the children, and give thee a pleasant land, a goodly heritage of the hosts of nations? and I said, **Thou shalt call me, My father; and shalt not turn away from me** [*they will accept the gospel of Jesus Christ and remain faithful to Him*].

Verses 20–22, next, review once again what got these people into such a mess and the invitation to repent is given yet again.

20 ¶ Surely *as* **a wife treacherously departeth from her husband, so have ye dealt treacherously with me, O house of Israel,** saith the LORD.

21 A voice was heard upon the high places, weeping *and* supplications of **the children of Israel: for they have perverted their way,** *and* **they have forgotten the LORD their God.**

22 Return, ye backsliding children, *and* **I will heal** your backslidings. Behold, we come unto thee; for thou *art* the LORD our God.

The last half of verse 22, above, and verses 23–25, next, may be understood to be Israel's reply to the Lord, in the last days, as they repent and return to Him, affirming that He is the only one who can provide salvation.

23 Truly in vain *is* **salvation hoped**

for **from the hills** [*salvation is not available through the worship of false gods*], *and* **from** the multitude of mountains: **truly in the LORD our God** *is* **the salvation of Israel.**

24 For shame hath devoured the labour of our fathers from our youth [*we have long since apostatized from the foundations laid by our ancestors*]; **their flocks and their herds, their sons and their daughters.**

25 We lie down in our shame, and our confusion covereth us: for we have sinned against the LORD our God, we and our fathers, from our youth even unto this day, and have not obeyed the voice of the LORD our God.

JEREMIAH 4

Selection: all verses

IN HELAMAN IN the Book of Mormon we are informed that Jeremiah prophesied of the destruction of Jerusalem. We read:

Helaman 8:20

20 And behold, also Zenock, and also Ezias, and also Isaiah, and Jeremiah, (**Jeremiah** being that same prophet who **testified of the destruction of Jerusalem**) and now we know that Jerusalem was destroyed according to the words of Jeremiah. O then why not the Son of God come, according to his prophecy?

We read one of Jeremiah's many prophecies of Jerusalem's coming destruction, starting with verse 7 here in chapter 4 and going through chapter 5, verse 13. But first, beginning with verse 1, we read another invitation to repent. You will see that the first requirement for returning to God is a desire to repent.

1 IF thou wilt [*if you have a desire to*] **return, O Israel, saith the LORD, return unto me** [*just do it*]: **and if thou wilt put away thine abominations out of my sight** [*if you will stop being wicked; this is the next step*], then shalt thou not remove [*then you will remain My covenant people*].

The next step, as given in verse 2, is for the people to sincerely and seriously commit to Jehovah as their God.

2 And thou shalt swear [*pledge, commit*], **The LORD liveth, in truth, in judgment, and in righteousness; and the nations shall bless themselves in him, and in him shall they glory.**

Did you notice the phrase in verse 2, above, which says, in effect, that we are doing ourselves a tremendous favor when we are loyal to the Lord? It is "the nations shall bless themselves in him."

Verses 3 and 4, next, appear to be an invitation to the men of Judah, with headquarters in Jerusalem, to repent and become clean. The Lord uses considerable symbolism to get the message across.

3 ¶ For thus saith the LORD to the men of Judah and Jerusalem, **Break up your fallow** [*unplowed*] **ground** [*perhaps meaning you have yet another chance to become productive as the Lord's covenant people*], and **sow** [*plant*] **not among thorns** [*don't try to mix the gospel and wickedness together in your lives*].

4 **Circumcise yourselves to the LORD** [*dedicate yourselves to the Lord*], and **take away the foreskins of your heart** [*dedicate your hearts to the Lord*], ye men of Judah and inhabitants of Jerusalem: **lest my fury come forth like fire,** and burn that none can quench *it,* [*otherwise, the punishments of the Lord will come upon you and none will stop them*] because of the evil of your doings.

5 Declare ye in Judah, and publish in Jerusalem [*spread the word throughout the people of Judah*]; and say, Blow ye the trumpet in the land: cry, gather together, and say, Assemble yourselves, and let us go into the defenced [*fortified*] cities [*in other words, spread the word that we must gather to the Lord for protection against the enemies*].

6 Set up the standard [*sound the alarm, raise the flag, signaling to gather*] toward Zion [*symbolic of returning to the Lord*]: retire, stay not [*don't hesitate*]: for I will bring evil from the north [*the Babylonians are coming*], and a great destruction.

Next, Jeremiah uses fearsome images to warn the people of Judah of the destruction that is coming if they don't repent.

7 **The lion** [*the King of Babylon and his armies; symbolic of Satan and his evil hosts*] **is come up from his thicket** [*has come out of hiding*], and the destroyer of the Gentiles [*the Babylonian armies have destroyed many Gentile cities*] is on his way; he is gone forth from his place to make thy land desolate; *and* thy cities shall be laid waste, without an inhabitant.

8 For this [*because of this*] **gird you with sackcloth** [*clothe yourselves with course, uncomfortable cloth to symbolize that you are going into mourning*], **lament and howl:** for the fierce anger of the LORD is not turned back from us [*we are still in trouble with the Lord, (because, as a nation, they have not repented)*].

9 And **it shall come to pass at that day** [*when the punishments and destructions come*], saith the LORD, **that the heart** [*courage*] **of the king shall perish, and the heart of the princes** [*the leaders of the land will lose courage*]; and the priests shall be astonished [*the false priests will be horrified*], and the prophets shall wonder [*the false prophets will be appalled*].

Verse 10, next, is a problem as it stands. Surely, Jeremiah would not say such a thing to the Lord.

Either something is missing or the translation is wrong. Let's read the verse and then look at an alternate translation.

10 Then said I, Ah, Lord GOD! surely thou hast greatly deceived this people and Jerusalem, saying, Ye shall have peace; whereas the sword reacheth unto the soul.

The Martin Luther translation of the German Bible may provide some help for us regarding verse 10, above. It has Jeremiah saying, in effect, "Lord, thou has allowed these people and Jerusalem to be led far astray, because their false prophets and priests said to them that they would have peace [*in spite of their wickedness*], whereas in reality the sword is about to destroy their souls."

Verses 11–20, next, carry on the prophetic theme of coming destruction.

11 At that time [*when destruction comes to Judah and Jerusalem*] shall it be said to this people and to Jerusalem, **A dry wind** [*symbolic of destruction*] of the high places in the wilderness **toward the daughter of my people** [*Jerusalem*], not to fan, nor to cleanse [*not a pleasant, cleansing breeze*],

12 Even **a full wind** [*a very devastating destruction*] from those *places* shall come unto me: now also will I give sentence against them.

13 Behold, he shall come up as clouds, and his chariots *shall be* as **a whirlwind**: his horses are swifter than eagles. Woe unto us! for we are spoiled.

14 O Jerusalem, **wash thine heart from wickedness** [*repent and be baptized*], that thou mayest be saved. **How long shall thy vain thoughts lodge within thee** [*how long will your wicked and foolish thinking stay with you*]?

Joseph Fielding Smith indicated that verse 14, above, is a reference to baptism. Speaking of the fact that the Jews were not surprised by the baptisms performed by John the Baptist, because it was a common Old Testament ordinance, he said:

"John stood forth in the spirit of the prophets of old to preach his baptism of repentance symbolized by cleansing with water. (See Jer. 4:14; Ezek. 36:25; Zech. 13:1.)" (*Answers to Gospel Questions*, vol. 2, page 68)

It is helpful for understanding verse 15, next, to know that the land of Dan was the farthest north among the inheritances of the twelve tribes when they arrived in the promised land.

15 For a voice declareth from Dan [*the news of destruction is coming from the north*], and publisheth affliction from mount Ephraim.

16 Make ye mention to the nations [*spread the news*]; behold, publish against Jerusalem, *that* **watchers** [NIV: "*a besieging army*"] come from a far country [*Babylon*], and **give out**

their voice against [are enemies to] the cities of Judah.

17 As keepers of a field, are they against her round about [they will surround Judah]; because she hath been rebellious against me, saith the LORD.

18 Thy way and thy doings have procured these *things* unto thee [you have brought this destruction upon yourselves]; this *is* thy wickedness, because it is bitter, because it reacheth unto thine heart [you are wicked through and through (ripe in iniquity)].

Verse 19, next, can describe the terror that will engulf the wicked inhabitants of Judah as the Babylonian armies descend upon them. However, it can also describe the deep anguish and sorrow in Jeremiah's heart as he sees the vision of coming destruction upon the wicked people of Judah.

19 ¶ My bowels, my bowels [a phrase meaning "deepest anguish"]! I am pained at my very heart [deepest agony]; my heart maketh a noise in me [my heart is pounding]; I cannot hold my peace [I cry out], because thou hast heard, O my soul, the sound of the trumpet, the alarm of war.

20 Destruction upon destruction is cried; for **the whole land is spoiled** [ruined, ravaged]: suddenly are my tents spoiled, *and* my curtains [dwelling places] in a moment.

21 How long shall I see the standard, *and* hear the sound of the trumpet [how long do I have to look at this scene of horror, this scene of battle and destruction]?

It appears that verse 22, next, could represent the feelings of the Lord about Judah at this time.

22 For **my people** *is* **foolish**, they have not known me [they have apostatized, left Me]; they *are* sottish [senseless; do not think] children, and they have none understanding: **they** *are* **wise to do evil, but to do good they have no knowledge.**

Verses 23–29 seem to describe the devastation and desolation that will come upon Judah and Jerusalem when the invading Babylonian armies finish with them.

23 I beheld the **earth, and, lo,** *it* *was* **without form, and void** [the land was "empty and desolate"—see Abraham 4:2]; and the heavens, and **they** *had* **no light** [perhaps meaning that the dust from the battles obscured the sunlight; could also symbolize that the light of the gospel is gone].

24 I beheld the mountains, and, lo, they trembled, and all the hills moved lightly.

25 I beheld, and, lo, *there was* no man [the people were slaughtered or taken away into captivity], and all the

birds of the heavens were fled.

26 I beheld, and, lo, **the fruitful place** [*the once-beautiful Jerusalem and surrounding area*] *was* **a wilderness,** and all the cities thereof were broken down at the presence of the LORD, *and* **by his fierce anger.**

In verse 27, next, the Lord says that the land will be desolate, but the Jews will not be completely destroyed.

27 For thus hath the LORD said, The whole land shall be desolate; **yet will I not make a full end.**

In the context of this chapter and prophecy, verse 28, next, states emphatically that unless the people of Judah repent (verse 14), the destruction will come as described.

By the way, since the Lord is sinless, He has no need to repent. Thus, the word "repent" in this verse is not a good translation in view of the normal use of the word.

28 For this [*because of this destruction*] shall the earth mourn, and the heavens above be black: because **I have spoken** *it,* **I have purposed** *it,* **and will not repent** [*relent nor change My mind*], **neither will I turn back from it.**

29 **The whole city** [*Jerusalem*] **shall flee** for [*because of*] the noise of the horsemen and bowmen [*the Babylonian armies*]; they shall go into thickets, and climb up upon the

rocks: **every city** [*of Judah*] **shall be forsaken** [*deserted*], and not a man dwell therein.

Verses 30–31 conclude this chapter with the question, "What will you do when all this happens?" And the basic answer is that Judah will still seek help from her false gods, her idols. Verse 30 is a description of a harlot attempting to make herself attractive for her lovers. The imagery is that Judah (the "harlot," symbolic of "stepping out on God," in other words, disloyalty to her covenants with Jehovah) attempts to get help from her false gods and gets none.

30 And *when* **thou** *art* **spoiled** [*ruined by the Babylonians*], **what wilt thou do?** Though thou clothest thyself with crimson, though thou deckest thee with ornaments of gold, though thou rentest thy face with painting [*use makeup to make your eyes look bigger—see footnote 30b, in your LDS Bible*], in vain shalt thou make thyself fair [*your attempts to make yourself look attractive won't work*]; **thy lovers** [*false gods*] **will despise thee,** they will seek thy life [*they will not help you at all against your enemies*].

Part of the imagery in verse 31, next, is that there is no way (in Jeremiah's day) to stop childbirth labor once it starts. So also, once the coming armies descend upon Jerusalem, there will be no way to stop them. The pain and anguish of a woman having her first child is compared to the anguish of the people of Judah, as the stark reality of their destruction hits them.

31 For **I have heard a voice as of a woman in travail** [*childbirth labor*], *and* the **anguish** as of her that bringeth forth her first child, the voice of the daughter of Zion [*Jerusalem*], *that* **bewaileth herself,** *that* spreadeth her hands, *saying,* **Woe** *is* **me now!** for my soul is wearied because of murderers [*my life is in the hands of murderers*].

JEREMIAH 5

Selection: all verses

IN THIS CHAPTER, Jeremiah describes the corruption that has permeated every facet of society by this point in the history of Judah.

We will move rather quickly through this chapter, using **bold** to let the scriptures themselves point out this corruption to you. The hope is that you will gain more skill and confidence in capturing the basic meaning of Jeremiah's writing without having to understand every detail. We will intentionally add very few notes in this chapter. Try going through first, just reading the **bolded** words and phrases. Remember, we are looking for various types of corruption that can ruin society and lead to downfall and destruction, as well as the consequences of such behavior, as described by Jeremiah.

1 RUN ye to and fro through the streets of Jerusalem, and see now, and know, and seek in the broad places thereof, **if ye can find a man,** if there be *any* that executeth judgment, **that seeketh the truth;** and I will pardon it.

2 And **though they say, The LORD liveth; surely they swear falsely** [*break covenants and contracts; don't keep their word*].

3 O LORD, *are* not thine eyes upon the truth? **thou hast stricken them, but they have not grieved; thou hast consumed them,** *but* **they have refused to receive correction:** they have made their faces harder than a rock; **they have refused to return.**

4 Therefore I said, Surely these *are* poor; they are foolish: for **they know not the way of the LORD,** *nor* the judgment of their God.

5 I will get me unto the great men, and will speak unto them; for they have known the way of the LORD, *and* the judgment of their God: but **these have altogether broken the yoke** [*the covenants that bind them to Jehovah*], *and* burst the bonds.

6 Wherefore a lion out of the forest **shall slay them,** *and* **a wolf** of the evenings **shall spoil them,** a leopard shall watch over their cities: every one that goeth out thence shall be torn in pieces [*the Lord will allow their destruction*]: **because their transgressions are many,** *and* their backslidings are increased.

7 ¶ **How shall I pardon thee for this?** **thy children have forsaken me,** and **sworn by** *them that are* **no gods** [*have worshiped idols*]: when I had fed them to the full, they then **committed adultery,** and **assembled themselves by troops in the harlots' houses.**

8 **They were** *as* **fed horses** in the morning: **every one neighed after his neighbour's wife** [*sexual immorality is rampant throughout society*].

9 **Shall I not visit** [*punish*] **for these** *things?* **saith the LORD:** and shall not my soul be avenged on such a nation as this?

10 ¶ Go ye up upon her walls, and destroy; but make not a full end: take away her battlements; for they *are* not the LORD's.

11 **For the house of Israel and the house of Judah have dealt very treacherously against me,** saith the LORD.

12 **They have belied** [*lied about*] **the LORD,** and said, *It is* not he; neither shall evil come upon us; neither shall we see sword nor famine:

13 And **the prophets shall become wind, and the word** *is* **not in them** [*the prophecies against us will not be fulfilled*]: thus shall it be done unto them.

14 Wherefore thus saith the LORD God of hosts, **Because ye speak this word** [*verse 13*], behold, **I will make my words in thy mouth fire,** and this people wood, **and it shall devour them.**

15 Lo, **I will bring a nation upon you from far,** O house of Israel, saith the LORD: **it** *is* **a mighty nation, it** *is* **an ancient nation, a nation whose language thou knowest not, neither understandest what they say.**

16 Their quiver *is* as an open sepulchre, **they** *are* **all mighty men.**

17 And **they shall eat up thine harvest, and thy bread,** *which* thy sons and thy daughters should eat: they shall eat up **thy flocks and thine herds:** they shall eat up **thy vines and thy fig trees:** they shall impoverish thy fenced cities, wherein thou trustedst, with the sword.

18 **Nevertheless** in those days, saith the LORD, **I will not make a full end with you** [*I will preserve a remnant of Judah*].

19 ¶ And it shall come to pass, when ye shall say, Wherefore [*why*] doeth the LORD our God all these *things* unto us? then shalt

thou answer them, Like as **ye have forsaken me**, and served strange gods in your land, **so shall ye serve strangers in a land** *that is* **not yours** [*you will be taken into slavery to a foreign country (Babylon)*].

20 Declare this in the house of Jacob [*Israel*], and **publish it in Judah**, saying,

21 Hear now this, **O foolish people**, and without understanding; which have eyes, and see not; which have ears, and hear not:

22 Fear ye not me? saith the LORD: **will ye not tremble at my presence**, which have placed the sand *for* the bound of the sea by a perpetual decree, that it cannot pass it: and though the waves thereof toss themselves, yet can they not prevail; though they roar, yet can they not pass over it?

23 But **this people hath a revolting and a rebellious heart**; they are revolted and gone.

24 Neither say they in their heart, Let us now fear the LORD our God, that giveth rain, both the former and the latter, in his season: he reserveth unto us the appointed weeks of the harvest.

25 ¶ Your iniquities have turned away these *things*, **and your sins have withholden good** *things* **from you.**

26 For **among my people are found wicked** *men:* they lay wait, as he that setteth snares; they set a trap, they catch men.

27 As a cage is full of birds, so *are* **their houses full of deceit:** therefore they are become great, and waxen rich.

28 They are waxen fat [*they have grown rich on corruption*], they shine: yea, **they overpass** [*ignore*] **the deeds of the wicked:** they judge not the cause, the cause of the fatherless, yet they prosper; and the right of the needy do they not judge.

29 Shall I not visit [*punish*] **for these** *things?* saith the LORD: shall not my soul be avenged on such a nation as this?

30 ¶ A wonderful [*astonishing*] and **horrible thing is committed in the land;**

31 The prophets [*false prophets*] **prophesy falsely**, and the priests bear rule by their means [*take authority unto themselves; are not authorized by God*]; and **my people love** *to have it* **so:** and what will ye do in the end thereof?

How did you do? This approach to reading the Old Testament can be quite helpful. Even though you may not understand everything, you get the big picture and can benefit much from the major messages.

JEREMIAH 6

Selection: all verses

THIS CHAPTER CONTINUES the theme of the destruction of Jerusalem by the Babylonians, because of gross wickedness among the covenant people. We will add a few more notes here than we did for chapter 5, in hopes that you will continue to get a better feel for the "manner of prophesying among the Jews" (2 Nephi 25:1), including the use of words and symbolism to create pictures in the minds of the readers.

1 O YE children [*descendants*] **of Benjamin** [*remember that the tribes of Judah and Benjamin stayed together at the time the twelve tribes split into two nations, after King Solomon died; they became known as "Judah"*], gather yourselves to **flee out of the midst of Jerusalem**, and blow the trumpet [*sound the alarm*] in Tekoa [*a Judean city, about six miles south of Bethlehem, which is about five miles southwest of Jerusalem*], and set up a sign of fire in Beth-haccerem: **for evil appeareth out of the north, and great destruction.**

Next, the siege of Jerusalem by Babylon is described.

2 I have likened [*compared*] the **daughter of Zion** [*Jerusalem*] to a comely [*beautiful*] and delicate woman.

3 The shepherds [*the Babylonians*] with their flocks shall come unto her; they **shall pitch** *their* **tents against her round about;** they shall feed every one in his place.

4 Prepare ye war against her [*Jerusalem*]; arise, and let us [*Babylon*] go up at noon [*let's attack Jerusalem at noon*]. Woe unto us! for the day goeth away [*the daylight is fading*], for the shadows of the evening are stretched out [*are getting longer*].

5 Arise, and let us go by night [*let us also attack Jerusalem at night*], and **let us destroy her palaces.**

6 ¶ For thus hath the LORD of hosts said, **Hew ye down trees, and cast a mount against Jerusalem** [*throw up a mound of dirt outside the walls of Jerusalem for the siege and build battlements*]: **this** *is* **the city to be visited** [*punished*]; she *is* wholly oppression in the midst of her [*Jerusalem is completely corrupt*].

Next, Jerusalem is described as a fountain of filthy water, spewing forth wickedness all around.

7 As a fountain casteth out her waters, so **she casteth out her wickedness:** violence and spoil is heard in her; before me continually *is* grief and wounds.

8 Be thou instructed [*heed the warnings*], O Jerusalem, lest my soul depart from thee; **lest I make thee desolate, a land not inhabited.**

The symbolism in verse 9, next, is that of being thoroughly harvested. The "gleaners" went through the vineyards again, after the main harvest was gathered, and completely stripped the vines of any remaining grapes. Thus, the inhabitants of Jerusalem and the surrounding cities of Judah are going to be thoroughly "gleaned" by their enemies.

9 ¶ Thus saith the LORD of hosts, They [*the* Babylonians] **shall thoroughly glean the remnant of Israel** [*Judah*] as a vine: turn back thine hand as a grapegatherer into the baskets.

Next, the question is, in effect, who is there in all of Judah to whom this urgent message might get through? Answer: nobody.

10 **To whom shall I speak, and give warning,** that they may hear? behold, **their ear** *is* **uncircumcised** [*they don't even recognize the word of God; they are wicked to the point that they are completely spiritually deaf*], and **they cannot hearken** [*they cannot obey because they cannot hear*]: behold, **the word of the LORD is unto them a reproach** [*they consider the word of the Lord to be a negative thing*]; **they have no delight in it.**

In verse 11, next, we are told that destruction will come upon all the inhabitants of Jerusalem, regardless of age and circumstance.

11 **Therefore** [*this is why*] **I am full of**

the fury of the LORD; I am weary with holding in [*holding it back*]: I will pour it [*the fury of the Lord*] out upon the children abroad [*playing in the streets*], and upon the assembly of young men together [*simultaneously*]: for even the husband with the wife shall be taken, the aged with *him that is* full of days [*those who are bent over with age*].

12 And their houses shall be turned unto others [*others will inhabit their homes*], *with their* fields and wives together: for I will stretch out my hand upon [*I will punish*] the inhabitants of the land, saith the LORD.

Perhaps you've noticed that Jeremiah is saying the same basic thing many different ways. This is typical of prophetic utterances of his day. Repetition for emphasis is typical of Isaiah's writings also, likewise with many other prophets in the Old Testament.

Next, Jeremiah again repeats that society in and around Jerusalem is completely riddled with corruption. (This is one of the reasons Lehi and his family were commanded to leave the Jerusalem area.)

13 For from the least of them even unto the greatest of them **every one** *is* **given to covetousness**; and from the prophet [*false prophet*] even unto the priest [*false, corrupt priest*] **every one dealeth falsely.**

14 **They** [*the false prophets and false*

priests supported by these corrupt peo-ple] **have healed also the hurt** *of the daughter* **of my people slightly** *[have superficially addressed the moral corruption and coming destruction and war]*, saying, Peace, peace; when *there is* no peace.

Next, in verse 15, we see that the people had lost their ability to blush and be embarrassed at wickedness. It had become so common and accepted among them that it was no longer a big deal.

15 Were they ashamed when they had committed abomination? **nay, they were not at all ashamed, neither could they blush:** therefore they shall fall among them that fall: at the time *that* I visit *[punish]* them they shall be cast down, saith the LORD.

Once again, in verse 16, next, the people are invited to repent. But they refuse.

16 Thus saith the LORD, Stand ye in the ways *[repent and stand in holy places; in other words, live righteously]*, and see, and **ask for the old paths** *[the old ways of truth and righteousness]*, where *is* the good way, **and walk therein, and ye shall find rest for your souls. But they said, We will not walk** *therein.*

Have you noticed that the Lord reminds us over and over that He has given these people plenty of warning? One of the great blessings in our lives is

that we hear the same warning messages time and time again in our lives, thus giving us many opportunities to repent and continually improve.

Once again, these wicked people of Judah refuse to listen to the warning.

17 Also **I set watchmen** *[prophets]* over you, *saying,* Hearken to the sound of the trumpet *[listen to the warning of approaching danger and destruction].* **But they** *[the people of Judah]* **said, We will not hearken.**

18 ¶ Therefore hear, ye nations, and know, O congregation, **what** *is* **among them** *[all nations are called to serve as witnesses against Judah].*

19 Hear, O earth: behold, **I will bring evil upon this people,** *even* the fruit *[product]* of their thoughts *[their evil thoughts have produced wicked deeds]*, **because they have not hearkened unto my words, nor to my law, but rejected it.**

As you can see, the main message of verse 20, next, is that empty ritual and empty worship is of no value. The incense and offerings mentioned were part of normal religious worship under the Law of Moses.

20 To what purpose cometh there to me incense from Sheba, and the sweet cane from a far country *[in other words, what good does your ritual and worship do]?* **your burnt offerings** *are* **not acceptable, nor your sacrifices sweet unto me.**

The theme of destruction continues in verse 21, next.

21 Therefore thus saith the LORD, Behold, I [*the Lord*] **will lay stumblingblocks** before this people, and **the fathers and the sons together shall fall upon them; the neighbour and his friend shall perish.**

More repetition. Remember, repetition for emphasis is a major component of the Jewish culture at the time of Jeremiah. Sometimes, "westerners" (including most of us) struggle a bit with such repetition, because we start thinking, "Wait a minute. He already said that. Is he saying something else here and I am missing it?" No. You are not missing it. It is just part of the manner of speaking and prophesying among the Jews.

22 Thus saith the LORD, Behold, **a people** [*the Babylonian armies*] **cometh from the north country,** and **a great nation** [*Babylon*] shall be raised **from the sides of the earth** [*the ends of the earth; in other words, from far away*].

23 They shall lay hold on bow and spear [*they will be well-armed*]; **they** *are* **cruel**, and have no mercy; their voice roareth like the sea; and they ride upon horses, set in array as men for war against thee, O daughter of Zion [*Jerusalem*].

24 We have heard the fame thereof: our hands wax feeble [*we get weak and faint just hearing about them*]: anguish hath taken hold of us, *and* pain, as of a woman in travail.

25 Go not forth into the field [*don't leave the house*], **nor walk by the way;** for the sword of the enemy *and* **fear** *is* **on every side.**

26 ¶ O daughter of my people, gird *thee* **with sackcloth** [*start mourning now*], and **wallow thyself in ashes** [*roll in ashes; putting ashes upon one's self was a sign of mourning in the Jewish culture of the day*]: **make thee mourning,** *as for* an only son, **most bitter** lamentation: for the spoiler [*Babylon*] shall suddenly come upon us.

Next, the Savior reassures Jeremiah of his calling to be a prophet (compare with Jeremiah 1:18).

27 I have set thee *for* **a tower** *and* a fortress among my people, that thou mayest know and try their way.

The imagery of the "tower," in verse 27, above, is that of the watchtowers which were built in those days. A person standing upon the watchtower could spot trouble coming a long way off. Our prophets, as inspired men of God, serve as "watchtowers" among us to spot coming danger and warn us of it while there is still time to prepare to defend ourselves from it.

Next, Jeremiah is reminded of the kind of people he is to serve, as one of the Lord's prophets shortly before the downfall of Jerusalem. The Lord uses the imagery of a refiner attempting to smelt precious metal from available ore to describe the wicked residents of Judah. In the normal refining process, the ore is placed in a crucible that is then heated with fire until the ore melts.

As the ore melts, the impurities float to the top and are removed as slag. The precious metal is heavier, so it sinks to the bottom of the crucible. The impurities are, in effect, burned out of the mix and all that remains is the precious metal, in other words, the desired product of the refiner's fire.

Symbolically, the Lord is the Refiner. We are the ore. We have many imperfections that need to be burned out of us in the "furnace of affliction." If we are willing, the "fire of the Holy Ghost" will burn the imperfections out of our souls. We can thus be cleansed by the Atonement of Christ, and become pure gold in the hands of the Refiner.

In the case of Israel, and Judah specifically in this example, they are not allowing the Refiner's fire to work on them successfully. They remain "brass and iron" (verse 28). In fact, they get "consumed" by the fire (verse 29), rather than refined. It is an agency choice whether to be purged and cleansed by the refiner's fire, or destroyed by it. The people of Judah have chosen to be destroyed at this time in their history.

28 They *are* all grievous revolters,** walking with slanders: *they are* brass and iron; they *are* all corrupters.**

29 The bellows are burned [*the bellows of the refiner's fire blow fiercely; see footnote 29a in your LDS Bible*], **the lead is consumed of [***by***] the fire** [*in effect, the Jews have decided they want to be "lead" rather than gold (symbolic of godliness) and thus are destroyed by the refiner's fire*]; **the founder melteth in vain** [*the Lord works in vain to redeem these people*]: for **the wicked are not plucked away** [*the imperfections are not purged out of the people; in other words, there are not just a few wicked people of Judah, rather, the whole nation is corrupt; therefore, if the Lord takes out the "impurities," there will be almost no one left in Judah*].

30 Reprobate [*rejected*] silver shall *men* call them, because **the LORD hath rejected them.**

JEREMIAH 7

Selection: all verses

CHAPTERS 7 THROUGH 10 go together. Chapter 26 contains the same basic prophecy but is somewhat shorter. In these chapters, sometimes called "the temple sermon" or "the temple prophecy" by scholars, Jeremiah is told by the Lord to stand in the gate of the temple in Jerusalem and deliver the messages that follow.

You will see that yet another invitation to repent is given to these wicked and foolish people. It is another reminder to all of us that it is not too late to repent, but can become so. The sweet message is that we can repent still. The sad fact is that these people opt to refuse to return to the Lord. Consequently, additional detail is provided regarding the coming destruction.

Perhaps you have noticed that it is often difficult to determine who is speaking here, Jeremiah or the Lord. Sometimes it is quite clear, but in many instances it is not. We won't worry too much about this because we are familiar with the quote from the Doctrine and Covenants which says (**bold** added for emphasis):

> <u>Doctrine & Covenants 1:38</u>
> 38 What I the Lord have spoken, I have spoken, and I excuse not myself; and though the heavens and the earth pass away, my word shall not pass away, but shall all be fulfilled, **whether by mine own voice or by the voice of my servants, it is the same.**

Again, we will make frequent use of **bold** for emphasis.

1 THE word that came to Jeremiah from the LORD, saying,

2 Stand in the gate of the LORD's house [*the temple in Jerusalem*], and proclaim there this word, **and say, Hear the word of the LORD,** all *ye of* Judah, that enter in at these gates to worship the LORD.

Did you notice that even though they are wicked, they are still "going to church," so to speak?

3 Thus saith the LORD of hosts, the God of Israel, **Amend your ways** and your doings, **and I will cause you to dwell in this place** [*and you can stay here*].

4 Trust ye not in lying words, saying, The temple of the LORD, The temple of the LORD, The temple of the LORD, *are these* [*don't trust in the physical temple, nor in going there to worship, to save you (unless you repent)*].

5 For **if ye thoroughly** [*through and through; genuinely*] **amend your ways and your doings;** if ye throughly execute judgment [*fairness; integrity*] between a man and his neighbour;

6 If ye oppress not the stranger, **the fatherless, and the widow,** and **shed not innocent blood** in this place, **neither walk after other gods** [*worship idols*] to your hurt:

7 Then will I cause you to dwell in this place, in the land that I gave to your fathers, **for ever and ever.**

8 ¶ Behold, ye trust in lying words, that cannot profit [*you trust in the words of false prophets and priests,* *corrupt leaders, etc., which do you no good*].

9 Will ye steal, murder, and commit adultery, and **swear falsely,** and **burn incense unto Baal,** and **walk after other gods** whom ye know not;

10 And come and stand before me in this house [*the temple in Jerusalem*], which is called by my name, and say, We are delivered to do all these abominations [*as long as we attend the temple, we are free to be wicked*]?

11 Is this house [*the temple*], which is called by my name, **become a den of robbers** in your eyes? Behold, even **I have seen** *it*, **saith the LORD.**

Next, the people are told to go to Shiloh and be reminded what happened there to wicked Israel. By way of quick review, after Joshua led the children of Israel into the promised land, the Tabernacle was set up in Shiloh (about twenty miles north of Jerusalem). Thus, Shiloh, in effect, was the site of their temple. Eventually, Israel became so wicked that they set up idols and worshipped them there (Judges 18:30–31). They lost the protection of the Lord and the Philistines conquered Shiloh and took the ark of the covenant (1 Samuel 4:10–12).

12 But go ye now unto my place which *was* **in Shiloh,** where I set my name at the first, **and see what I did to it for** [*because of*] **the wickedness of my people Israel.**

13 And now, because ye have done all these works, saith the LORD, and **I spake unto you,** rising up early and speaking, **but ye heard not** [*you would not listen*]; and **I called you, but ye answered not;**

14 Therefore will I do unto *this* **house** [*the temple in Jerusalem*], which is called by my name, wherein ye trust, and unto the place which I gave to you and to your fathers, **as I have done to Shiloh.**

15 And I will cast you out of my sight, as I have cast out all your brethren, *even* **the whole seed of Ephraim** [*Israel, the lost ten tribes, which were commonly referred to as "Ephraim"*].

Verse 16, next, is a dramatic way of saying that the people are so wicked that it is hopeless for Jeremiah to try to get the Lord to save them. This can remind us of the hopeless situation Mormon faced, when his people fell to the same spiritual low as Jeremiah's people here. Let's read what Mormon said about the Nephites of his day and then look at verse 16 in Jeremiah:

Mormon 5:2
2 But behold, **I was without hope,** for I knew the judgments of the Lord which should come upon them; for they repented not of their iniquities, but did

struggle for their lives without calling upon that Being who created them.

16 Therefore **pray not thou for this people,** neither lift up cry nor prayer for them, **neither make intercession to me: for I will not hear thee** [*in other words, in effect, the Lord will not be able to answer Jeremiah's prayers for them, because He cannot violate their agency; see also verse 27*].

17 ¶ Seest thou not what they do in the cities of Judah and in the streets of Jerusalem?

Verse 18, next, says, in effect, that everyone in Judah is participating in idol worship, including every member of every family. Various activities involved in preparing for and performing idol worship are described.

18 The **children gather wood** [*to be used in pagan sacrifices*], and the **fathers kindle the fire,** and the **women** knead *their* dough, to **make cakes to the queen of heaven** [*the goddess of fertility, such as Ishtar, whom the Babylonians worshiped—see footnote 18a in your LDS Bible*], and to **pour out drink offerings unto other gods,** that they may provoke me to anger.

19 Do they provoke me to anger? saith the LORD: *do they* not *provoke* themselves to the confusion of their own faces [*aren't they bringing shame and disgrace upon*

themselves by so doing—see footnote 19a in your LDS Bible]?

20 Therefore [*this is why*] thus saith the Lord GOD; Behold, **mine anger and my fury shall be poured out upon this place,** upon man, and upon beast, and upon the trees of the field, and upon the fruit of the ground; and it shall burn, and shall not be quenched.

Verses 21–24, next, say, in effect, that a major purpose of burnt offerings and sacrifices for the children of Israel under the Law of Moses was to teach obedience to God. The problem with Judah is that the people are continuing the ritual sacrifices of the Law of Moses but they are disobeying the Lord in their daily lives. Their ritual worship of Jehovah is empty and meaningless.

21 ¶ Thus saith the LORD of hosts, the God of Israel; **Put your burnt offerings unto your sacrifices, and eat flesh** [*go ahead and continue with your empty rituals, offering sacrifices and eating the meat from the animal sacrifices as always*].

22 For I spake not unto your fathers, nor commanded them in the day that I brought them out of the land of Egypt, concerning burnt offerings or sacrifices [*NIV: "I did not just give them commands about burnt offerings and sacrifices"*]:

23 But this thing commanded I them, saying, Obey my voice, and

I will be your God, and ye shall be my people: and walk ye in all the ways that I have commanded you, that it may be well unto you.

24 But they hearkened not, nor inclined their ear [*wouldn't listen*], but walked in the counsels *and* in the imagination of their evil heart, and went backward, and not forward.

> Next, the Savior reminds these people that He has constantly tried to save them.

25 Since the day that your fathers [*forefathers, ancestors*] came forth out of the land of Egypt unto this day I have even sent unto you all my servants the prophets, daily rising up early [*I have warned you constantly, ahead of the coming destruction*] and sending *them*:

26 Yet they hearkened not unto me, nor inclined their ear, but hardened their neck [*remained prideful*]: they did worse than their fathers [*they are worse than their ancestors—compare with Jeremiah 16:12*].

> Next, Jehovah reminds Jeremiah that the people will not listen to him and change their ways. He gives him more specific things to say to them.

27 Therefore thou shalt speak all these words unto them [*the call to repentance*]; but they will not hearken to thee: thou shalt also call unto them; but they will not answer thee [*respond positively*].

28 But thou shalt say unto them, This *is* a nation that obeyeth not the voice of the LORD their God, nor receiveth correction [*they refuse to repent*]: truth is perished, and is cut off from their mouth [*they no longer live truth nor speak it*].

> Verse 29, next, can well have several meanings. It is typical of Jeremiah, Isaiah, and others to embed several symbolic meanings into a word or phrase in their writings. For example, in verse 29, it says, in effect, that the Jews of Jeremiah's day should go into mourning now in anticipation of the coming destruction. It says for Jerusalem to cut off her hair. This can have many possible meanings:
>
> 1. Conquering armies of the day often shaved their prisoners bald, to identify them as slaves as well as to humiliate them (compare with Isaiah 3:24).
>
> 2. Shaving one's head was symbolic of grief as in Job 1:20.
>
> 3. In Jewish culture of the time, one's hair was considered to be a diadem, a crown symbolizing royalty and dignity. And having it cut off by an enemy was demeaning and a terrible insult.
>
> 4. In a religious sense, long hair could symbolize the vow of a Nazarite and his consecration to Jehovah (Numbers 6:2–8.) Intentionally cutting off one's hair could be symbolic of abandoning Jehovah and His commandments.

29 ¶ Cut off thine hair, O Jerusalem, and cast it away, and take up a lamentation [go into mourning] on high places; for the LORD hath rejected and forsaken the generation of his wrath [because you are no longer under the protection of the Lord].

Several reasons as to why the Lord can no longer bless and protect these wicked people are reviewed again in verses 30–31, next. Verse 31 informs us that they had gone so far as to sacrifice their children to their false gods.

30 For the children of Judah [the Jews] have done evil in my sight, saith the LORD: they have set their abominations in the house [they have placed idols in the temple at Jerusalem] which is called by my name, to pollute it.

31 And they have built the high places of Tophet, which is in the valley of the son of Hinnom, to burn their sons and their daughters in the fire; which I commanded them not, neither came it into my heart.

In verses 32–34, next, we see that the coming Babylonian armies will cause such slaughter that there will not be room to bury all the dead of Jerusalem and Judah.

32 ¶ Therefore, behold, the days come, saith the LORD, that it shall no more be called Tophet, nor the valley of the son of Hinnom [the

site where the Jews sacrificed their children to their false gods—see verse 31], but the valley of slaughter: for they shall bury in Tophet, till there be no place.

The Bible Dictionary gives us a bit of additional information about Tophet (verse 32, above).

Bible Dictionary: Tophet
A spot in the valley of the son of Hinnom, south of Jerusalem, where human sacrifices were offered to Molech (2 Kgs. 23:10; Isa. 30:33; Jer. 7:31 f.; 19:6, 13).

33 And the carcases of this people [the people of Judah and Jerusalem] shall be meat [food] for the fowls of the heaven, and for the beasts of the earth; and none shall fray [frighten] them away.

Verse 34, next, is a prophetic description of the devastating aftermath resulting from the Babylonian captivity of the Jews.

34 Then will I cause to cease from the cities of Judah, and from the streets of Jerusalem, the voice of mirth, and the voice of gladness, the voice of the bridegroom, and the voice of the bride: for the land shall be desolate.

JEREMIAH 8

Selection: all verses

JEREMIAH'S DESCRIP-
TION OF the destruction of
Judah and Jerusalem continues in
this chapter. Verses 1–2 describe one
of the ultimate insults heaped upon a
nation by its conquerors, namely the
desecration of their dead by the trium-
phant enemies.

1 AT that time [*when Jerusalem and
Judah are defeated*], saith the LORD,
they [*the enemies*] **shall bring out
the bones** of the kings of Judah,
and the bones of his princes, and the
bones of the priests, and the bones
of the prophets, and the bones of
the inhabitants of Jerusalem, **out of
their graves:**

2 And they shall spread them
before the sun, and the moon, and all
the host of heaven, whom they have
loved, and whom they have served,
and after whom they have walked,
and whom they have sought, and
whom they have worshipped: **they
shall not be gathered, nor be buried; they shall be for dung upon the
face of the earth.**

We will include a quote from the
Old Testament Student Manual
that helps us understand verses
1–2, above.

"In order to pour the utmost
contempt upon the land, the
victorious enemies dragged
out of their graves, caves, and

sepulchers, the bones of kings,
princes, prophets, priests, and
the principal inhabitants, and
exposed them in the open air; so
that they became, in the order of
God's judgments, a reproach to
them in the vain confidence they
had in the sun, moon, and the
host of heaven—all the planets
and stars, whose worship they
had set up in opposition to
that of Jehovah. This custom of
raising the bodies of the dead,
and scattering their bones about,
seems to have been general. It
was the highest expression of
hatred and contempt" (Adam
Clarke, *The Holy Bible . . . with a
Commentary and Critical Notes*,
4:276).

Verse 3, next, indicates that the
fate of those who survive the
slaughter will be worse than
death. They will desire to die
rather than to continue living in
such horrible conditions.

**3 And death shall be chosen rath-
er than life by all the residue of
them that remain of this evil family** [*Judah*], which remain in all the
places whither I have driven them,
saith the LORD of hosts.

From here to the end of the
chapter, we see the sins of
these people described. You will
no doubt see many parallels
between them and the world in
which we live.

In verses 4–5, next, the question
is asked, in effect, "Why don't
these people return to the
Lord?"

4 ¶ Moreover [*in addition*] **thou**
[*Jeremiah*] **shalt say unto them,**

Thus saith the LORD; **Shall they fall, and not arise** [*don't people normally get up after they fall*]? **shall he turn away, and not return?**

5 Why *then* **is this people of Jerusalem slidden back by a perpetual backsliding** [*why do these people live lives of continual apostasy*]? **they hold fast deceit** [*they hold on tightly to wickedness and evil, to self-deception*], **they refuse to return** [*repent*].

6 I hearkened and heard [*the Lord has listened carefully for them to ask for forgiveness*], **but they spake not aright** [*but they don't ask*]: **no man repented him of his wickedness, saying, What have I done?** every one turned to his course [*they all walk in their own paths*], **as the horse rusheth into the battle** [*like a horse running into battle*].

Next, in effect, we are told that creatures are wiser than these people. The creatures sense when to migrate, etc., and do it. But the covenant people of the Lord do not sense the coming destruction.

7 Yea, the stork in the heaven knoweth her appointed times; and the turtle and the crane and the swallow observe the time of their coming [*follow their migratory patterns*]; **but my people know not the judgment of the LORD.**

Next, in verse 8, we are told that

the scribes (who interpret the laws of God among these Jews) have led them astray with their false and evil interpretations of the law of the Lord.

8 How do ye say [*how can you say*], **We** *are* **wise, and the law of the LORD** *is* **with us** [*we have the law of God among us*]? Lo, certainly in vain made he *it*; **the pen of the scribes** *is* **in vain** [*the scribes have misinterpreted the Laws of Moses*].

9 The wise *men* **are ashamed** [*your supposedly wise men will be put to shame*], **they are dismayed and taken: lo, they have rejected the word of the LORD; and what wisdom** *is* **in them** [*why listen to them*]?

The message of verse 10, next, is that the wicked leaders of Jerusalem will be gone. Another message is that their society is completely corrupt. Greed is a major problem.

10 Therefore will I give their wives unto others, *and* **their fields to them** [*new owners*] **that shall inherit** *them*: **for every one from the least even unto the greatest is given to covetousness,** from the prophet [*false prophet*] even unto the priest [*corrupt priests*] **every one dealeth falsely.**

Next, we see that the leaders of the Jews at this point in their history have treated corruption and wickedness lightly, telling the people that destruction is not coming and that peace will continue. The imagery used is that of treating a serious wound as if it were just a scratch.

11 For they have healed the hurt of the daughter of my people slightly, saying, Peace, peace; when *there is* no peace.

Next, we see that one of the problems of this corrupt society is that nobody blushes at evil anymore.

12 Were they ashamed when they had committed abomination? nay, they were not at all ashamed, neither could they blush: therefore shall they fall among them that fall: in the time of their visitation [*punishment*] they shall be cast down, saith the LORD.

13 ¶ I will surely consume them, saith the LORD: *there shall be* no grapes on the vine, nor figs on the fig tree [*none will escape*], and the leaf shall fade; and *the things that* I have given them shall pass away from them [*the Lord's former blessings will disappear*].

Verses 14–16, next, appear to be the answer from the inhabitants of Jerusalem and Judah in response to what the Lord has said above about the coming destruction. Verses 15–16 seem to be in the future, as if the Babylonian captivity is already under way or is completed.

14 Why do we sit still [*why are we sitting here*]? **assemble yourselves, and let us enter into the defenced cities** [*let's all retreat into our fortified*

cities], **and let us be silent there** [*NIV: "and perish there"*]: for the LORD our God hath put us to silence [*NIV: "For the Lord our God has doomed us to perish"*], and given us water of gall [*bitter water*] to drink, **because we have sinned against the LORD.**

15 We looked for peace [*perhaps meaning that they looked for peace in wickedness*], **but no good** *came*; *and* for a time of health, and behold trouble!

16 The snorting of his horses [*the enemy armies; horses are symbolic of military might and power in Jewish symbolism*] was heard from Dan [*was heard in the far north*]: **the whole land trembled at the sound of the neighing of his strong ones;** for they are come, and **have devoured the land, and all that is in it; the city, and those that dwell therein.**

17 For, behold, I [*the Lord*] **will send serpents, cockatrices** [*poisonous serpents; vipers; symbolic of the coming enemy armies*], **among you, which** *will* **not** *be* **charmed** [*which you cannot talk out of destroying you*], and **they shall bite you,** saith the LORD.

Opinions vary among scholars as to whether verses 18–22 represent the Lord's words or Jeremiah's. We will use verse 19 to sway us to believe that they represent the mourning of the

Lord for His wayward people. But remember, it could represent Jeremiah's feelings too. We know from the record of Enoch in Moses that the Lord weeps for His people when they go astray.

Moses 7:28 (see also 28–44)
28 And it came to pass that the God of heaven looked upon the residue of the people, and he wept; and Enoch bore record of it, saying: How is it that the heavens weep, and shed forth their tears as the rain upon the mountains?

18 ¶ *When* I would comfort myself against sorrow, **my heart** *is* **faint in me** [*German Bible: "my heart is sick"*].

19 Behold the voice of **the cry of the daughter of my people** [*Jerusalem*] **because of them that dwell in a far country** [*apparently representing the future cries of the Jews far away in Babylonian captivity*]: *Is* not the LORD in Zion? *is* not her king in her? **Why have they provoked me to anger** with their graven images, *and* with strange vanities [*idol worship; pride, sin*]?

20 The harvest is past, the summer is ended, and we are not saved.

21 For [*because of*] the hurt [*suffering*] **of the daughter of my people** [*Judah and Jerusalem*] **am I hurt** [*I suffer*]; **I am black** [*gloomy—see footnote 21a in your Bible; I am heartbroken, in mourning*]; astonishment

hath taken hold on me.

You will see the phrase, "balm in Gilead," in verse 22, next. It is a reference to a healing gum or spice found in a large area east of the Jordan River, extending north of the Dead Sea. The balm was highly prized and was used, among other things, to heal wounds. It appears to be a reference to Christ and the healing power of His Atonement. You are probably familiar with this phrase because "balm of Gilead" is used in verse 3 of our hymn, "Did You Think to Pray," which begins with "Ere you left your room this morning" (*Hymns*, no. 140).

22 *Is there* no balm in Gilead [*is healing not available*]; *is there* no physician there [*can no one heal; is the Physician (the Savior) not available*]? **why then is not the health of the daughter of my people recovered** [*perhaps meaning why don't the people turn to the Savior and be healed*]?

JEREMIAH 9

Selection: all verses

VERSES 1-3 OF this chapter appear to be a continuation from chapter 8, bemoaning the coming destruction. Remember that the language of the Old Testament is often that of painting pictures and feelings with words. We see that here as the Lord (or possibly Jeremiah), as indicated in verse 3, expresses deep-felt sorrow for apostate Judah.

1 OH that my head were waters, and mine eyes a fountain of tears, that I might weep day and night for the slain of the daughter of my people [*Jerusalem and the cities of Judah*]!

2 Oh that I had in the wilderness a lodging place of wayfaring men [*a place where travelers could obtain temporary lodging*]; that I might leave my people, and go from them! for **they be all adulterers, an assembly of treacherous men.**

In addition to the rampant sexual immorality mentioned in verse 2, above, the people of Jerusalem and its surroundings were also filled with dishonesty. Their whole lifestyle was one of seeking greater and greater evil in which to participate, as indicated in verse 3, next.

3 And they bend their tongues *like* their bow *for* lies: but they are not valiant for the truth upon the earth; for **they proceed from evil to evil, and they know not me, saith the LORD.**

The next several verses point out more sins of these wicked people and give us a feel for what their wickedness has done to their society. As stated previously, this could be either the Lord or Jeremiah speaking or both. It is difficult to tell since they both share the same feelings, and also since a prophet can speak for the Lord as if the Lord were the one doing the talking (D&C 1:38).

The first thing that is pointed out is the distrust that permeates a dishonest society.

4 Take ye heed [*beware*] every one of his neighbour, and **trust ye not in any brother:** for every brother will utterly supplant [*deceive you at every opportunity to do so*], and every neighbour will walk with slanders [*gossips*].

5 And they will deceive every one his neighbour, and will not speak the truth: they have taught their tongue to speak lies, *and* weary themselves [*wear themselves out*] to commit iniquity.

6 Thine habitation *is* in the midst of deceit [*you are surrounded by deception*]; **through deceit they refuse to know me, saith the LORD.**

Verse 7, next, says, in effect, that the Lord will have to send them through the "refiner's fire" in order to once again have a pure people.

7 Therefore thus saith the LORD of hosts, Behold, **I will melt them** [*as a refiner does with gold ore in order to extract impurities and have pure gold as the end product of the refining process*], and try them; **for how shall I do for the daughter of my people** [*what else can I do in light of the sins of My people in Jerusalem*]?

8 Their tongue *is as* an arrow shot out; it speaketh deceit [*they are constantly shooting off their mouths with lies*]: *one* speaketh peaceably to his neighbour with his mouth, but in heart he layeth his wait [*he* *sets a trap for him; he says one thing but thinks another].*

9 ¶ Shall I not visit [*punish*] **them for these** *things?* **saith the LORD:** shall not my soul be avenged [*should not the law of justice take over*] on such a nation as this?

> Verses 10–11, next, prophesy emptiness and desolation, rubble and loneliness where a once-prosperous people lived.

10 For the mountains will I take up a weeping and wailing, and for the habitations of the wilderness a lamentation [*I will mourn for the mountains and wilderness where many people once lived and traveled*], because they are burned up [*they have become like a barren desert*], so that **none can pass through** *them;* neither can *men* hear the voice of **the cattle;** both **the fowl of the** heavens **and the beast** are fled; they **are gone.**

11 And I will make Jerusalem heaps [*a pile of rubble*], **and a den of dragons** [*a place where desert animals (jackals) live*]; **and I will make the cities of Judah desolate, without an inhabitant.**

12 ¶ Who *is* **the wise man, that may understand this** [*who is wise enough to get the picture*]*?* **and** *who is he* **to whom the mouth of the LORD hath spoken, that he may declare it** [*who can explain why this*

has happened], for what [*why*] the land perisheth *and* is burned up like a wilderness [*has become like a desert*], that none passeth through?

> In verse 12, above, the Lord asked a question, in effect, "Who can explain why this happened to Jerusalem?" In verses 13–16, He now answers His own question. In effect, He says, "I will tell you why."

13 And the LORD saith, Because they have forsaken my law which I set before them, and have not obeyed my voice, neither walked therein;

14 But have walked after the imagination of their own heart, and after Baalim [*Baal worship, an extremely wicked form of idol worship*], which their fathers taught them:

15 Therefore thus saith the LORD of hosts, the God of Israel; Behold, **I will feed them,** *even* this people, **with wormwood** [*extremely bitter*], and **give them water of gall to drink** [*in other words, the Lord will give them bitter medicine*].

16 I will scatter them also among the heathen [*foreign nations*], whom neither they nor their fathers have known: and I will send a sword after them, till I have consumed them.

> "Consumed," as used in verse 16, above, does not mean to become extinct. We will quote from the *Old Testament Student Manual* for clarification on this:

"To be consumed does not mean to become extinct. Being consumed and destroyed, in the context of the prophecies of the scattering of Israel, meant to be utterly disorganized and disbanded so that Israel's power, influence, and cohesiveness as a nation was gone. Moses, in Deuteronomy 4:26, told all Israel that they would 'utterly be destroyed.' Yet the verses following show that Israel still existed as homeless individuals" (*Old Testament Student Manual*, page 238).

Next, these unrepentant people are told to get ready to mourn.

17 ¶ Thus saith the LORD of hosts, Consider ye, and **call for the mourning women,** that they may come; and **send for cunning** *women* [*skilled mourners*], that they may come:

18 And let them make haste [*have them hurry, you will need them soon*], and **take up a wailing** [*mourning*] **for us,** that our eyes may run down with tears, and our eyelids gush out with waters [*tears*].

As stated previously, part of the "manner of prophesying among the Jews" (2 Nephi 25:1) was to speak of the future as if it had already taken place. Verse 19, next, is an example of this. It speaks of the coming destruction of Jerusalem as if it had already occurred.

19 For **a voice of wailing is heard out of Zion** [*Jerusalem and the other cities of Judah*], **How are we spoiled** [*see how completely we are ruined*]! **we are greatly confounded,** because we have forsaken the land, because our dwellings have cast *us* out.

20 Yet hear the word of the LORD, O ye women, and let your ear receive the word of his mouth, and **teach your daughters wailing,** and every one her neighbour lamentation.

21 For **death is come** up into our windows, *and* is entered into our palaces, to cut off the children from without, *and* the young men from the streets.

22 Speak, Thus saith the LORD, Even **the carcases of men shall fall as dung** [*animal droppings*] **upon the open field,** and as the handful [*the few remaining*] after the harvestman, and none shall gather *them.*

Do you know what the backward "P" at the beginning of verse 23, next, (and many other places throughout the King James Version of the Bible—the version we use in English) means? It indicates that the Bible is now turning to another topic or a new aspect of the topic already under consideration.

In this case, it is a very short course in how to avoid wickedness.

23 ¶ Thus saith the LORD, **Let not the wise** *man* **glory in his wisdom** [*avoid being prideful*], **neither let the mighty** *man* **glory in his might** [*let powerful people avoid pride*], **let not**

the rich *man* glory in his riches:

24 But let him that glorieth **glory in this, that he understandeth and knoweth me, that I *am* the LORD** which exercise lovingkindness, judgment, and righteousness, in the earth: for in these *things* I delight, saith the LORD.

> The topic now turns to hypocrisy, claiming to be the Lord's people through outward ordinances, but inwardly being the "natural man" (Mosiah 3:19). The Lord says that the day is coming when His people, who have been circumcised according to the Law of Moses (a token of loyalty and dedication to the Lord, from Abraham to the end of the Old Testament), will be punished by other wicked nations, referred to as "the uncircumcised" at the end of verse 25. The cause of this punishment is given at the end of verse 26.

25 ¶ **Behold, the days come, saith the LORD, that I will punish all** *them which are* **circumcised** [*who have entered into outward covenants with the Lord, but are wicked*] **with the uncircumcised;**

26 Egypt, and Judah, and Edom, and the children of Ammon, and Moab, and all *that are* in the utmost corners, that dwell in the wilderness: for **all** *these* **nations** *are* **uncircumcised, and all the house of Israel** *are* **uncircumcised in the heart** [*are not faithful to God*].

> The point in verses 25–26, above, seems to be that even though the people of Judah, as part of Israel, are outwardly the Lord's covenant people, they are in fact no better off than any other nation or people because they have broken their covenants with God.

JEREMIAH 10

Selection: all verses

IN THIS CHAPTER, the people are counseled to learn to distinguish between false gods and the true God. Jeremiah points out how absurd idol worship is and teaches the people to worship the Lord. We will quote from the *Old Testament Student Manual*:

"In a profound and yet simple chain of reasoning, Jeremiah showed the stupidity and sheer illogic of worshiping an idol. Men take such materials as wood and precious metals which they work and shape at their own will, making all kinds of objects of service. Then they take those same materials, make them into an idol by the work of their own hands, and suddenly expect the idol to be filled with supernatural power and be able to provide miraculous aid for the person who made it" (*Old Testament Student Manual*, pages 238–39).

1 HEAR ye the word which the LORD speaketh unto you, O house of Israel:

2 Thus saith the LORD, Learn

not the way of the heathen [*don't join with the heathen in their false religions, including idol worship*], and be not dismayed [*terrified*] at the signs of heaven [*at signs in the sky, such as eclipses and falling stars*]; for the heathen are dismayed at them.

Watch now as Jeremiah points out how ridiculous it is to make idols with their own hands and then worship them.

By the way, some have interpreted verse 3, next, to be a direct reference to Christmas trees in our day, and have thus come to the conclusion that the Bible is against them. Not so. The word of the Lord here is against idols, as a replacement for the true God. Trees were often cut down and idols made from the wood.

3 For the customs of the people *are* vain [*useless*]: for *one* cutteth a tree out of the forest, the work of the hands of the workman, with the axe.

4 They deck it with silver and with gold; they fasten it with nails and with hammers, that it move not [*so that it doesn't fall over*].

5 They [*the idols*] *are* upright as the palm tree, but speak not: they must needs be borne [*they have to be carried from place to place*], because they cannot go [*because they can't move themselves*]. Be not afraid of them; for they cannot do evil, neither also *is it* in them to do good.

Next, in verses 7-8, Jeremiah points out that neither idols nor the greatest among men can begin to compare with the true God.

6 Forasmuch as *there is* none like unto thee, O LORD; thou *art* great, and thy name *is* great in might.

7 Who would not fear [*revere and respect*] thee, O King of nations? for to thee doth it appertain [*reverence and honor are properly due You*]: forasmuch as among all the wise *men* of the nations, and in all their kingdoms, *there is* none like unto thee.

8 But they [*people who make and worship idols*] are altogether brutish [*are completely without sense*] and foolish: the stock [*the idol made from a portion of a tree trunk or limb*] *is* a doctrine of vanities [*is a worthless doctrine*].

9 Silver spread into plates is brought from Tarshish, and gold from Uphaz, the work of the workman, and of the hands of the founder: blue and purple *is* their clothing: they [*idols*] *are* all the work of cunning *men* [*skilled craftsmen*].

10 But the LORD *is* the true God, he *is* the living God, and an everlasting king: at his wrath the earth shall tremble, and the nations [*wicked nations*] shall not be able to abide his indignation.

11 Thus shall ye say unto them,

The gods [*idols and other false gods*] that have not made the heavens and the earth, *even* they **shall perish from the earth**, and from under these heavens.

12 He [*Jehovah; Jesus Christ*] **hath made the earth by his power**, he hath established the world by his wisdom, and hath stretched out the heavens by his discretion.

> Verse 13, next, gives a very brief summary of the creation. The point is that when the Living God speaks, He is obeyed by nature. Contrast this to the lack of power in idols, as described in verse 14.

13 When he uttereth his voice, *there is* a multitude of waters in the heavens [*see Genesis, chapter 1*], and he causeth the vapours to ascend from the ends of the earth; he maketh lightnings with rain, and bringeth forth the wind out of his treasures.

14 Every man is brutish [*behaving like an animal*] in *his* knowledge [*every man who makes and then worships an idol, is totally without common sense in applying knowledge*]: every founder [*goldsmith, silversmith, etc., who shapes precious metal overlays for idols*] is confounded [*put to shame*] by the graven image: for his molten image *is* falsehood [*the resulting idol is a lie*], and **there *is* no breath in them** [*idols*].

15 They *are* vanity [*worthless*], and

the work of errors [*the product of false doctrine*]: in the time of their visitation [*when God's punishments come*] they shall perish.

16 The portion of Jacob [*Jehovah, the God of Israel*] *is* **not like them** [*idols*]: for **he *is* the former** [*creator*] **of all *things*;** and Israel *is* the rod [*NIV: "tribe"*] of his inheritance: **The LORD of hosts *is* his name.**

> In verse 17, next, the people of Judah are told to gather their belongings in preparation for the coming siege. And in verse 18, they are told that after the siege (verse 17), they will be scattered.

17 ¶ Gather up thy wares out of the land, O inhabitant of the fortress [*the besieged city*].

18 For **thus saith the LORD**, Behold, **I will sling out the inhabitants of the land** at this once [*the Jews will be scattered by the Babylonians*], and will distress them, that they may find *it* so [*and will cause that they can be captured*].

> Verses 19–22, next, describe the mourning and devastation that will accompany the conquering and scattering of the Jews at this point in their history.

19 ¶ Woe is me for my hurt! **my wound is grievous:** but I said, Truly this *is* a grief, and I must bear it.

20 My tabernacle [*dwelling*] **is spoiled,** and all my cords [*the ropes* *that hold the tent up] are broken [in other words, economic and spiritual support are gone]:* **my children are gone forth of me** *[scattered]*, and they *are* not *[they are gone]: there is* none to stretch forth my tent any more, and to set up my curtains.

We will use verses 19–20, above, as a reminder that there is more than one way in which Jeremiah's writings can be interpreted. We will mention three possibilities for these verses. No doubt there are more.

One

If it is Jeremiah who is speaking, then we might interpret them as follows:

19 ¶ Woe is me [*Jeremiah*] for my hurt! my wound is grievous [*it makes me very sad to see this happen to my people*]: but I said, Truly this *is* a grief, and I must bear it.

20 My tabernacle is spoiled [*my home and homeland are ruined*], and all my cords are broken [*all the support for my people is gone*]: my children are gone forth of me [*my family and followers are scattered*], and they *are* not [*they are gone*]: there is none to stretch forth my tent any more, and to set up my curtains [*no one is left in the land*].

Two

These two verses could represent the mourning of the Lord for His people.

19 ¶ Woe is me [*the Lord*] for my hurt! my wound is grievous [*it makes Me very sad to see*

this happen to My people]: but I said, Truly this *is* a grief, and I must bear it.

20 My tabernacle is spoiled [*My temple in Jerusalem is ruined*], and all my cords are broken [*all the covenants with My people have been broken*]: my children are gone forth of me [*my people have been scattered*], and they *are* not [*they are gone*]: there is none to stretch forth my tent any more, and to set up my curtains [*there are none left in Jerusalem and the cities of Judah to establish My Church*].

Three

These two verses could even represent the mourning of Jerusalem for her people. Such personification of a city or land is often found in ancient writings.

19 ¶ Woe is me [*Jerusalem*] for my hurt! my wound is grievous [*it makes me very sad to see this happen to my people*]: but I said, Truly this *is* a grief, and I must bear it.

20 My tabernacle is spoiled [*my land is devastated*], and all my cords are broken [*I have fallen down, crumbled*]: my children are gone forth of me [*my inhabitants have been scattered*], and they *are* not [*they are gone*]: there is none to stretch forth my tent any more, and to set up my curtains [*no one is left in me*].

As you continue to read and study the writings of the Old Testament prophets, keep in mind that many of their writings can be understood in more than one way. Such is the beauty as well as the difficulty of writings that involve much use of symbolism.

We will continue now with some possible explanations of these next verses.

21 For **the pastors** are become brutish, and **have not sought the LORD** [*the leaders of the Jews are senseless and have not come to the Lord for guidance*]: **therefore they shall not prosper, and all their flocks shall be scattered** [*the scattering of the Jews*].

22 Behold, the noise of the bruit [*news*] is come [*the news of the coming armies has arrived*], and **a great commotion out of the north country, to make the cities of Judah desolate,** and a den of dragons [*jackals; in other words, jackals will move into the ruins of Jerusalem and Judah; symbolic of the desolation and emptiness left by the invading armies*].

Verse 23, next, says, in effect, that man, when he opts to do things on his own, without God, is not capable of governing himself successfully. Most scholars consider verses 23–25 to be Jeremiah speaking.

23 ¶ O LORD, I know that **the way of man is not in himself: it is not in man that walketh to direct his steps.**

Joseph Smith explained the principle in verse 23, above. He taught (**bold** added for emphasis):

"It has been the design of Jehovah, from the commencement of the

world, and is His purpose now, to regulate the affairs of the world in His own time, to stand as a head of the universe, and take the reins of government in His own hand. When that is done, judgment will be administered in righteousness; anarchy and confusion will be destroyed, and 'nations will learn war no more.' **It is for want of this great governing principle, that all this confusion has existed; 'for it is not in man that walketh, to direct his steps;'** this we have fully shown" (*Teachings of the Prophet Joseph Smith*, pages 250–51).

In verse 24, next, Jeremiah humbly requests that the Lord correct him as needed. This attitude is described by the word "contrite." It appears that what Jeremiah has seen in vision by way of the coming punishments that will come upon Jerusalem has caused him to be a bit concerned about the anger of the Lord. Thus, he asks that he not be punished in anger. We know that the Lord does not punish righteous people in anger, but it may be that Jeremiah is still learning.

24 O LORD, correct me, but with judgment [*justice; fairness*]; not in thine anger, lest thou bring me to nothing [*perhaps meaning "for fear that Thou destroy me too"*].

The enemies of Israel and Judah were cruel and wicked people themselves. In verse 25, next, Jeremiah invites the Lord to exercise punishment upon them too.

25 Pour out thy fury upon the

heathen [*referring to the enemies of Israel, in this context*] that know thee not, and upon the families that call not on thy name: for **they have eaten up Jacob** [*they have destroyed the house of Israel*], **and devoured him, and consumed him, and have made his habitation desolate.**

JEREMIAH 11

Selection: all verses

IN THIS CHAPTER we see emphasis on the fact that, anciently, Israel was chosen to be the Lord's covenant people, but they rejected Him and the covenant. Remember, the covenant involved being blessed themselves with the blessings of potential exaltation, and the responsibility of taking the priesthood and the blessings of the gospel to all people (Abraham 2:9–11).

As we begin, the people of Judah are reminded that they and their ancestors rejected the covenant through their wickedness. (Remember that the people of Judah, which includes part of the small tribe of Benjamin, are all that remain of the Israelites, as a group in the Holy Land, since the ten tribes were conquered and carried away captive about one hundred years ago at this point of Jeremiah's prophesying.)

1 THE word that came to Jeremiah from the LORD, saying,

2 Hear ye the words of this covenant, and **speak unto the men of Judah,** and to the inhabitants of Jerusalem;

3 And say thou unto them, Thus saith the LORD God of Israel; **Cursed** [*stopped in progression*] *be* **the man that obeyeth not the words of this covenant,**

The covenant (known to us as the Abrahamic covenant) is briefly described in verses 4–5, next.

4 Which I commanded your fathers [*ancestors*] in the day *that* I brought them forth out of the land of Egypt, from the iron furnace [*symbolic of affliction*], saying, **Obey my voice,** and do them [*keep the commandments—see verse 3, above*], according to all which I command you: **so shall ye be my people, and I will be your God:**

5 That I may perform the oath [*in other words, as you obey the commandments, you enable the Lord to keep His part of the bargain—compare with D&C 82:10*] which I have sworn [*promised*] unto your fathers, **to give them a land flowing with milk and honey** [*symbolic of prosperity on earth and eventual celestial exaltation*], as *it is* this day. **Then answered I** [*the children of Israel answered—compare with Deuteronomy 26:17; Exodus 6:7*], and said, **So be it, O LORD.**

We see yet another invitation to the wicked people of Judah to repent and renew their covenant, delivered through Jeremiah by the Lord, in verse 6, next.

6 Then the LORD said unto me, Proclaim all these words in the cities of Judah, and in the streets of Jerusalem, saying, **Hear ye the words of this covenant, and do them.**

Verse 7, next, reminds us that the Lord had given these rebellious Israelites many, many chances to repent and return to Him.

7 For **I earnestly protested** [*witnessed—see footnote 7a in your Bible*] **unto your fathers** [*ancestors*] in the day *that* I brought them up out of the land of Egypt, *even* **unto this day,** rising early and protesting, **saying, Obey my voice.**

8 **Yet they obeyed not,** nor inclined their ear, **but walked every one in the imagination of their evil heart:** therefore **I will bring upon them all the words of this covenant** [*they will be held accountable for breaking this covenant*], which I commanded *them* to do; but they did *them* not.

9 And the LORD said unto me [*Jeremiah*], **A conspiracy** [*deliberate disobedience*] **is found among the men of Judah,** and among the inhabitants of Jerusalem.

10 **They are turned back to the iniquities of their forefathers,** which refused to hear my words; and they **went after other gods** to serve them: **the house of Israel and the house of Judah have broken my covenant** which I made with their fathers.

11 ¶ **Therefore** thus saith the LORD, Behold, **I will bring evil upon them,** which they shall not be able to escape; and **though they shall cry unto me, I will not hearken unto them** [*it will get to the point that it is too late to be saved by the Lord from their enemies*].

12 **Then shall the cities of Judah and inhabitants of Jerusalem** go, and **cry unto the gods** [*their idols*] unto whom they offer incense: **but they shall not save them at all** in the time of their trouble.

Next, we see that Jewish society of the day was completely riddled with idolatry. They had idols for every city, with altars to them in every street. Baal was worshiped everywhere. Remember that Baal worship involved sexual immorality with temple prostitutes. Sexual immorality destroys societies as well as individuals.

13 For *according to* the number of thy cities were thy gods, O Judah; and *according to* the number of the streets of Jerusalem have ye set up altars to *that* shameful thing, *even* altars to burn incense unto Baal.

The hopelessness of Judah's situation is again symbolized by the Lord's requesting that Jeremiah no longer pray for these people.

14 Therefore pray not thou for this people, neither lift up a cry or prayer for them: for I will not hear *them* in the time that they cry unto me for their trouble.

15 What hath my beloved to do in mine house [*in effect, what is Judah thinking?*], *seeing* **she hath wrought lewdness** [*adultery*] **with many** [*in other words, has stepped out on God with spiritually illicit relationships with many false gods, as well as literal adultery*], and the holy flesh [*righteous, acceptable sacrifices—see footnote 15a in your Bible*] is passed from thee? **when thou doest evil, then thou rejoicest.**

Verses 16–17, next, remind us of the allegory of the tame and wild olive trees, taught by Zenos and quoted by Jacob in the Book of Mormon, in Jacob, chapter 5. We wonder in fact if Zenos lived before Jeremiah and these verses are a reference to his writings. We don't know the answer, but the question is interesting.

We will continue by giving one possible interpretation of verses 16–17, next.

16 The LORD called thy name, A green olive tree, fair, *and* **of goodly fruit** [*Judah is compared to an olive tree that once produced good people*]: **with the noise of a great tumult** [*with the coming destruction at the hands of the Babylonians*] **he** [*the Lord*] **hath kindled fire upon it** [*has destroyed Judah*], **and the branches of it are broken** [*the Jews are broken and scattered*].

17 For the LORD of hosts, that planted thee [*who established you as part of covenant Israel*], **hath pronounced evil against thee** [*the punishments of God are upon you*], **for** [*because of*] **the evil of the house of Israel and of the house of Judah,** which **they have done against themselves** to provoke me to anger in offering incense unto Baal [*they have brought great evil upon themselves because of their apostasy*].

Did you notice, in verse 17, above, that when we sin against God, we sin against ourselves?

Major Message
(Verse 17)

When we sin against God, we sin against ourselves.

Next, Jeremiah reports to us that the men of his hometown, Anathoth, hatched a plot to kill him. He was unaware of it until the Lord revealed it to him.

18 ¶ And the LORD hath given me knowledge *of it,* **and I know** *it:* **then thou shewedst me their doings** [*the plot devised by the men of Anathoth—see verse 21*].

19 But I *was* **like a lamb** *or* **an ox** *that* **is brought to the slaughter;** and **I knew not that they had devised devices against me,** *saying,* Let us destroy the tree with the fruit thereof, and let us cut him off from the land of the living, that his name may be no more remembered.

20 But, O LORD of hosts, that

judgest righteously, that triest the reins [*kidneys; symbolic, in Jewish culture of the day, of the deepest thoughts and feelings*] and the heart, let me see thy vengeance on them: for unto thee have I revealed my cause.

> Verse 21, next, tells us that the men of Jeremiah's hometown threatened to kill him if he did not stop prophesying.

21 Therefore thus saith the LORD of **the men of Anathoth**, that seek thy life, **saying, Prophesy not in the name of the LORD, that thou die not by our hand:**

22 Therefore **thus saith the LORD** of hosts, Behold, **I will punish them**: the young men shall die by the sword; their sons and their daughters shall die by famine:

23 And **there shall be no remnant of them** [*they will be wiped out*]: for **I will bring evil** [*punishment*] **upon the men of Anathoth**, *even* the year of their visitation [*the day of their punishment will come*].

JEREMIAH 12

Selection: all verses

IN THIS CHAPTER, Jeremiah asks a question that many people would like to hear the Lord's answer to. It is important to understand correct doctrine on this matter. The question is, in effect, why do the wicked prosper and the righteous suffer? (The same question is asked in Habakkuk, chapter 1, and answered in Habakkuk 2:1–4.)

We appreciate that Jeremiah's relationship with the Savior was such that he could be open about his concerns on this issue. In the heading to chapter 12, in your LDS Bible, you will note that the wording is "Jeremiah complains of the prosperity of the wicked." Let's dive right in and see how the Lord responds to his concerns about fairness.

1 RIGHTEOUS *art* thou, O LORD, when I plead with thee: **yet let me talk with thee of** *thy* **judgments** [*in effect, "I have a concern about how You are running things*]: **Wherefore** [*why*] **doth the way of the wicked prosper** [*why do the wicked prosper*]? **wherefore are all they happy that deal very treacherously** [*why are the wicked so happy*]?

2 **Thou hast planted them** [*You established them in this land*], yea, they have taken root: they grow, yea, **they bring forth fruit** [*they prosper*]: **thou** *art* **near in their mouth** [*they do lip service to You*], **and far from their reins** [*but You are far from their inner thoughts and desires*].

3 But thou, O LORD, knowest me: thou hast seen me, and tried [*tested*] mine heart toward thee: pull them out like sheep for the slaughter, and prepare them for the day of slaughter [*a prophecy of coming*

destruction for the wicked in Judah].

In verse 4, next, and also in verse 11, below, Jeremiah's concerns remind us of Enoch's witness of the earth's mourning because of the suffering she goes through due to the wickedness upon her.

Moses 7:48

48 And it came to pass that Enoch looked upon the earth; and he heard a voice from the bowels thereof, saying: Wo, wo is me, the mother of men; I am pained, I am weary, because of the wickedness of my children. When shall I rest, and be cleansed from the filthiness which is gone forth out of me? When will my Creator sanctify me, that I may rest, and righteousness for a season abide upon my face?

4 How long shall the land mourn, and the herbs of every field wither [*because of famine sent to punish the wicked*], for [*because of*] the wickedness of them that dwell therein? the beasts are consumed, and the birds; because they said, He shall not see our last end [*because the wicked say that God will not punish and destroy them*].

In verses 5–17, the Lord answers Jeremiah's question as to why the wicked seem to prosper. In effect, He says that punishment will come upon the wicked, in the Lord's due time. He also reminds Jeremiah that He does know what is going on.

5 ¶ If thou hast run with the footmen, and they have wearied thee, then how canst thou contend with horses [*perhaps saying to Jeremiah that he is getting in a bit over his head in wondering if the Lord is slipping up where the wicked are concerned*]? and if in the land of peace, *wherein* thou trustedst, *they wearied thee*, then how wilt thou do in the swelling of Jordan [*perhaps saying, in effect, to Jeremiah that if he is having trouble while peace is still upon the land, how will he handle it when the flood of enemies takes over the land*]?

6 For even thy brethren, and the house of thy father [*the members of your own family*], even they have dealt treacherously with thee; yea, they have called a multitude after thee [*it sounds like a mob came after Jeremiah*]: believe them not, though they speak fair words unto thee [*even though they try to convince you that you are in no danger from them*].

Next, it appears that the Lord is saying that Jeremiah is not the only one who has been deserted by his family. The Lord's people have likewise deserted Him, causing Him not to be able to bless them.

7 ¶ I have forsaken mine house, I have left mine heritage; I have given the dearly beloved of my soul into the hand of her enemies.

8 Mine heritage [*My people*] is unto me as a lion in the forest; it crieth

out against me [they cry loudly, like the roar of a lion, against Me]: therefore have I hated it [I could no longer bless them].

> When you see the phrase "the Lord hated them," or something to that effect in the scriptures, it often means "He could no longer bless them," rather than that He literally hates them.

> Have you ever seen birds, for example, baby chicks, peck at one that is odd or wounded, until they kill it? This seems to be the imagery used in verse 9, next, where the "speckled bird" (Judah, which should be different than other people because she is the covenant people of the Lord) is attacked by other birds (enemies).

9 Mine heritage [the Jews and the land of Judah] is unto me as a speckled bird, the birds round about are against her; come ye, assemble all the beasts of the field [symbolic of the armies of Babylon—see footnote 9a in your Bible], come to devour.

> Verse 10, next, points out the damage done to a society by false political and religious leaders.

10 Many pastors have destroyed my vineyard, they have trodden my portion under foot, they have made my pleasant portion [Jerusalem and the land of Judah] a desolate wilderness.

11 They have made it desolate, and being desolate it mourneth unto me; the whole land is made desolate, because no man layeth it to heart [no one pays attention—see footnote 11a in your Bible].

12 The spoilers [enemies] are come upon all high places through the wilderness: for the sword of the LORD shall devour from the one end of the land even to the other end of the land: no flesh shall have peace.

13 They have sown wheat, but shall reap thorns [they will harvest disappointment]: they have put themselves to pain [they work hard to be wicked], but shall not profit: and they shall be ashamed of your revenues [they will be put to shame because of the products of their wickedness] because of the fierce anger of the LORD [the law of justice].

> Next, in verses 14-17, we see a prophecy that the gospel will eventually be taught to all people, including the nations who attack the Lord's people. This reminds us that all people will have a completely fair chance to be taught the gospel, understand it, and accept it or reject it, before the day of final judgment.

14 ¶ Thus saith the LORD against all mine evil neighbours [all enemies of the Lord's covenant people], that touch the inheritance which I have caused my people Israel to inherit; Behold, I will pluck them out of their land, and pluck out the house of Judah from among them [the gathering of the Jews].

15 And it shall come to pass, after

that I have plucked them out **I will return, and have compassion on them**, and will bring them again, every man to his heritage, and every man to his land.

16 And it shall come to pass [*a prophecy*], **if they** [*all people in the world*] **will diligently learn the ways of my people** [*will learn the gospel of Jesus Christ*], to **swear by my name** [*make covenants with God*], The LORD liveth; as they taught my people to swear by Baal [*in place of the counterfeit covenants of false philosophies and false religions*]; **then shall they be built in the midst of my people** [*then they too will become the Lord's chosen people*].

17 But if they will not obey, I will utterly pluck up and destroy that nation, saith the LORD.

JEREMIAH 13

Selection: all verses

HAVE YOU NOTICED by now that the same basic messages are being repeated over and over in these chapters of Jeremiah? One of the benefits of studying some chapters in considerable detail is that it prepares you to understand the basic messages in other chapters, even though you may not understand all the details.

One of my friends recently observed

that although he did not understand everything he was listening to in Isaiah (on a portable recorder while walking), he discovered that he understood far more than he anticipated, just by paying attention to the main messages and words of the Lord and thinking how they might apply to him and the world today. This approach can be of great help to all of us as we study the writings of Old Testament prophets.

In this chapter, Israel and Judah are compared to a linen girdle or sash (verse 1) which is hidden or buried in a crevice of some rocks and later dug up (verse 7). Through this treatment, it becomes useless. We don't know if what the Lord commanded Jeremiah to do here, with respect to the linen sash, is literal, or if it is symbolic, a type of parable. Either way, the lesson is the same: Israel and Judah have become so marred by "hiding" from the Lord that they have basically become of no use as the covenant people.

1 THUS saith the LORD unto me [*Jeremiah*], **Go and get thee a linen girdle, and put it upon thy loins** [*put it around your waist*], **and put it not in water.**

2 So I got a girdle according to the word of the LORD, **and put** *it* **on my loins.**

3 And the word of the LORD came unto me the second time, saying,

4 Take the girdle that thou hast got, which *is* upon thy loins, **and arise, go to Euphrates, and hide it**

there in a hole of the rock.

It may be that "Euphrates," in verse 4, above, symbolizes Babylon, since a river by that name flows through that country. If so, this could symbolize the Babylonian captivity of Judah, which is just around the corner at this time in the history of the Jews.

5 So I went, and hid it by Euphrates, as the LORD commanded me.

6 And it came to pass after many days, that the LORD said unto me, Arise, go to Euphrates, and take the girdle from thence, which I commanded thee to hide there.

7 Then I went to Euphrates, and digged, and took the girdle from the place where I had hid it: and, behold, the girdle was marred, it was profitable for nothing [it was ruined, good for nothing].

8 Then the word of the LORD came unto me, saying,

The meaning of verses 1-7 is given in the next verses.

9 Thus saith the LORD, After this manner will I mar the pride of Judah, and the great pride of Jerusalem.

10 This evil people, which refuse to hear my words, which walk in the imagination of their heart [pridefulness, stubbornness], and walk after other gods, to serve them, and to worship them, shall even be as this girdle, which is good for nothing.

In verse 11, next, the Lord explains the symbolism. Just as a sash or girdle is wrapped around a man's waist, so also the house of Israel was invited to be the Lord's covenant people, and to "stick to Him" tightly, just as a girdle sticks tightly to the person wearing it. But when a girdle rots (see heading to this chapter in your Bible), it is of no use. Israel (the northern ten tribes in this context) and Judah (the tribes of Judah and Benjamin) could have been a glorious people, a credit to the Lord and to themselves, but they refused.

11 For as the girdle cleaveth to the loins of a man, so have I caused to cleave unto me the whole house of Israel and the whole house of Judah, saith the LORD; that they might be unto me for a people, and for a name, and for a praise, and for a glory: but they would not hear.

Verses 12-14, next, basically say that these people will become drunk with wickedness, in other words, out of control with wickedness, and will be destroyed.

12 ¶ Therefore thou shalt speak unto them this word; Thus saith the LORD God of Israel, Every bottle [symbolic of every person in Jerusalem and the other cities of Judah] shall be filled with wine: and they shall say unto thee, Do we not certainly

know that every bottle shall be filled with wine?

13 Then shalt thou say unto them, Thus saith the LORD, Behold, **I will fill all the inhabitants of this land, even the kings that sit upon David's throne, and the priests** [*false priests*]**, and the prophets** [*false prophets*]**, and all the inhabitants of Jerusalem, with drunkenness.**

14 And I will dash them one against another, even the fathers and the sons together, saith the LORD: I will not pity, nor spare, nor have mercy, but **destroy them.**

Next, the Lord issues yet another invitation to these people to repent, before it is too late and destruction comes upon them.

15 ¶ Hear ye, and give ear; **be not proud:** for the LORD hath spoken.

16 Give glory to the LORD your God, before he cause darkness, and before your feet stumble upon the dark mountains, and, while ye look for light, he turn it into the shadow of death, *and* make *it* gross darkness.

17 But if ye will not hear it, my soul shall weep in secret places for *your* pride; and **mine eye shall weep sore, and run down with tears, because the LORD's flock is carried away captive.**

18 Say unto the king and to the queen, **Humble yourselves,** sit

down: for your principalities shall come down, *even* the crown of your glory [*if you don't repent*].

19 The cities of the south shall be shut up, and none shall open *them:* **Judah shall be carried away captive all of it,** it shall be wholly carried away captive.

20 Lift up your eyes, and behold them [*the Babylonian armies*] that come from the north: where *is* the flock *that* was given thee, thy beautiful flock?

Verse 21, next, in effect asks the question "What will you have to say for yourselves, how will you explain your foolishness in ignoring the call from the Lord to repent, when all that is prophesied happens to you?"

21 What wilt thou say when he shall punish thee? for thou hast taught them *to be* captains, *and* as chief over thee: shall not sorrows take thee, as a woman in travail? [*In other words, unless you repent, the coming sorrows and destructions are as sure as the labor of a woman who is expecting a child.*]

22 ¶ And **if thou say in thine heart, Wherefore come these things upon me** [*why am I being punished*]**? For the** [*the answer is because of the*] **greatness of thine iniquity** are thy skirts discovered, *and* thy heels made bare [*you will be ravished and reduced to bondage*].

23 Can the Ethiopian change his skin, or the leopard his spots? *then may ye also do good, that are accustomed to do evil* [*in effect, if the impossible can happen, then people like you can do good who are completely caught up in wickedness*].

Next, we see another direct prophecy of the scattering of the Jews.

24 Therefore [*because of the above-mentioned wickedness*] **will I scatter them** as the stubble that passeth away by the wind of the wilderness.

25 This *is* thy lot [*this is what you have coming*], the portion of thy measures from me, saith the LORD; **because thou hast forgotten me, and trusted in falsehood.**

26 Therefore will I **discover thy skirts upon thy face** [*I will pull your skirts up over your face*], **that thy shame may appear** [*in effect, your protection, your false façade will be taken off and your sins will be exposed for all to see*].

Verse 27, next, contains a very brief summary of the sins of Judah, which will lead to Babylonian captivity. They are already spiritually in bondage to the devil.

27 I have seen thine **adulteries,** and thy **neighings** [*chasing after other men's wives—see Jeremiah 5:8*], the **lewdness** of thy **whoredom,** *and* thine **abominations on the hills** [*symbolic of idol worship*] in the fields. **Woe unto thee, O Jerusalem!** wilt thou not be made clean? **when *shall it once be*** [*when will the day finally come*]?

JEREMIAH 14

Selection: all verses

THIS CHAPTER DEALS with a devastating drought that will come to the Jerusalem area. Verses 1–6 describe how serious the drought will be and the famine that will ensue.

1 THE word of the LORD that came to Jeremiah **concerning the dearth** [*famine*].

2 **Judah mourneth,** and the gates thereof languish [*are wasting away*]; they are black [*dejected, discouraged*] unto the ground; and the cry of Jerusalem is gone up [*their desperate cry is heard everywhere*].

3 And their nobles have sent their little ones to the waters: they came to the pits [*wells*], *and* **found no water**; they returned with their **vessels empty;** they were ashamed [*dismayed*] and confounded [*in deep despair*], and covered their heads.

4 Because **the ground is chapt** [*cracked, parched*], for there was **no rain** in the earth, the plowmen were ashamed [*dismayed, desperate to know what to do*], they covered their heads.

5 Yea, **the hind** [*deer*] also **calved** [*had its baby*] in the field, **and forsook** *it* [*deserted its newborn fawn*], because there was **no grass.**

6 And the wild asses did stand in the high places, they snuffed up the wind [*pant*] like dragons [*jackals; wild dogs*]; their eyes did fail, because *there was* **no grass.**

In the next several verses, Jeremiah prays for his people, but is told that the Lord cannot answer his prayers because of the wickedness of Judah. In verse 7, it appears that Jeremiah humbly includes himself with his people.

7 ¶ **O LORD, though our iniquities testify against us, do thou** *it* [*please turn Thy wrath aside*] **for thy name's sake** [*for the sake of Your reputation as a merciful God*]: **for our backslidings are many; we have sinned against thee.**

8 O the **hope of Israel** [*another name for the Savior*], the **saviour thereof in time of trouble,** why shouldest thou be as a stranger in the land [*must You be far from us in our time of need*], and as a wayfaring [*traveling*] man *that* turneth aside to tarry for a night?

9 **Why shouldest thou be** as a man astonied [*astonished, paralyzed with surprise, unable to act*], **as a mighty man** *that* **cannot save** [*why can't You show your power for us*]? yet thou, O LORD, *art* in the midst of us, and we are called by thy name; **leave us not.**

Next, the Lord answers the questions raised above and explains why He cannot help them while they are wicked with no intent to repent.

10 ¶ Thus saith the LORD unto this people, **Thus have they loved to wander** [*in sin*], **they have not refrained their feet** [*they have not stopped wandering in the paths of sin*], **therefore the LORD doth not accept them;** he will now remember their iniquity, and visit [*punish*] their sins.

11 **Then said the LORD** unto me [*Jeremiah*], **Pray not for this people** for *their* good.

12 When they fast, **I will not hear their cry;** and when they offer burnt offering and an oblation, **I will not accept them:** but **I will consume them** by the sword, and by the famine, and by the pestilence.

13 ¶ Then said I, Ah, Lord GOD! behold, **the prophets** [*the false prophets among the Jews*] **say unto them, Ye shall not see the sword, neither shall ye have famine;** but I will give you assured peace in this place [*in effect, the false prophets have told the people that sin is not really sin and that there can be peace in wickedness*].

Sometimes we think of false prophets, such as those in verse 13, above, as being various religious leaders gone astray. But we would do well to think of political leaders, media idols, philosophers, teachers, in fact any who lead us away from the teachings of the gospel of Jesus Christ, as being false prophets also.

In verse 14, next, the Savior delivers a stern rebuke against such false prophets.

14 Then the LORD said unto me, **The prophets prophesy lies in my name** [*in other words, there are many who teach falsehoods in the name of God*]: **I sent them not,** neither have I commanded them, neither spake unto them: **they prophesy unto you a false vision** and divination, and a thing of nought, **and the deceit of their heart** [*they teach the wicked thoughts and intents of their own hearts as the word of God*].

15 Therefore thus saith the LORD concerning the prophets that prophesy in my name, and I sent them not [*in other words, concerning false prophets*], yet they say, Sword and famine shall not be in this land; **By sword and famine shall those prophets be consumed.**

16 And the people to whom they prophesy shall be cast out in the streets of Jerusalem because of the famine and the sword; and they shall have none to bury them, them, their wives, nor their sons, nor their daughters: **for I will pour their wickedness upon them.**

In verses 17–18, we see that the Lord weeps when His people become wicked.

17 ¶ Therefore thou shalt say this word unto them; **Let mine eyes run down with tears night and day,** and let them not cease: **for the virgin daughter of my people** [*Jerusalem*] **is broken with a great breach** [*is conquered*], with a very grievous blow.

18 If I go forth into the field, then **behold the slain** with the sword! and if I enter into the city, then **behold them that are sick with famine!** yea, both the prophet and the priest [*false prophets and priests*] go about into a land that they know not [*will be taken captive into a foreign land*].

Next, Jeremiah asks heartrending questions. He has the ability to love the wicked even though he has been told that they will be destroyed because of their rejecting the Lord.

19 Hast thou utterly rejected Judah? hath thy soul lothed [*loathed*] Zion? why hast thou smitten us, and *there is* no healing for us? we looked for peace, and *there is* no good; and for the time of healing, and behold trouble!

20 We acknowledge, O LORD,

our wickedness, *and* the iniquity of our fathers: for **we have sinned against thee.**

21 Do not abhor *us*, for thy name's sake, do not disgrace the throne of thy glory: remember, break not thy covenant with us.

22 Are there *any* among the vanities [*false gods*] **of the Gentiles that can cause rain?** or can the heavens give showers? *art* **not thou he, O LORD our God?** therefore we will wait upon thee: for thou hast made all these *things*.

JEREMIAH 15

Selection: all verses

THIS CHAPTER GIVES more prophetic detail about the destruction and scattering of the Jews in Jeremiah's day. Because of their intentional rebellion, there is no stopping the coming famine and captivity.

First, in verse 1, the Lord tells Jeremiah that even if the great prophets Moses and Samuel asked Him to stop the coming destruction upon Judah, it would not happen. We are seeing the law of justice in action. One of the lessons we are taught here is that mercy cannot "rob justice" (see Alma 42:25).

Major Message

Mercy cannot rob justice

1 THEN said the LORD unto me, **Though Moses and Samuel**

stood before me, *yet* **my mind** *could* **not** *be* **toward this people** [*in other words, He could not bless them*]: cast *them* out of my sight, and let them go forth [*they will be scattered*].

As mentioned several times already in this study guide, the "manner of speaking and prophesying among the Jews" is to repeat things many times for emphasis and to use words skillfully to paint pictures in our minds and create deep emotion in our hearts. We see this again in the next several verses.

2 And it shall come to pass, if they say unto thee, Whither shall we go forth [*if they ask you, "Where are we going"*]? **then thou shalt tell them,** Thus saith the LORD; Such as *are* for death, **to death;** and such as *are* for the sword, **to the sword;** and such as *are* for the famine, **to the famine;** and such as *are* for the captivity, **to the captivity.**

3 And I will appoint over them four kinds, saith the LORD: the sword to slay, and **the dogs to tear,** and **the fowls** [*carrion birds, such as vultures*] **of the heaven, and the beasts** of the earth, **to devour and destroy.**

4 And I will cause them to be removed into all kingdoms of the earth [*scattered to all nations of the earth*], because of Manasseh [*a very wicked king of Judah*] the son of Hezekiah king of Judah, for *that* which he did in Jerusalem.

5 For **who shall have pity upon thee, O Jerusalem?** or who shall bemoan thee? or who shall go aside to ask how thou doest?

6 **Thou hast forsaken me, saith the LORD,** thou art gone backward [*have gone away from the Lord*]: therefore will I stretch out my hand against thee, and destroy thee; **I am weary with repenting** [*since the Lord has no need to repent, this phrase is saying, in effect, I am tired of "relenting" and giving you chance after chance to repent; it doesn't do a bit of good*].

7 And **I will fan them with a fan** in the gates of the land [*I will scatter them, as a fan scatters chaff from wheat*]; I will bereave *them* of children [*they will lose their children*], **I will destroy my people, *since* they return not from their ways** [*since they refuse to repent*].

8 **Their widows are increased** to me above the sand of the seas [*there will be more widows than you can count*]: I have brought upon them against the mother of the young men **a spoiler at noonday** [*the enemy armies will be so powerful that they don't have to sneak up on you, rather, they can approach in broad daylight*]: I have caused *him* to fall upon it suddenly, and terrors upon the city.

9 She that hath borne seven languisheth [*grows weak*]: she hath given up the ghost [*has died*]; her sun is gone down while *it was* yet day [*all her hopes are suddenly dashed to pieces*]: she hath been ashamed and confounded [*confused and stopped*]: and the residue of them [*those who don't die of the famine*] will I deliver to the sword before their enemies, saith the LORD.

> Next, Jeremiah laments the fact that he was born to be such a focal point of contention to the wicked. Even though he has lived righteously, everyone hates him.

10 ¶ **Woe is me,** my mother, that thou hast borne me **a man of strife and a man of contention to the whole earth!** I have neither lent on usury, nor men have lent to me on usury [*in effect, I have faithfully kept the laws of God*]; **yet every one of them** [*the wicked*] **doth curse me.**

> Verse 11, next, could have several fulfillments. It could refer to Jeremiah, or it could be a prophecy that many of the Jews who are captured and carried away will be treated such that they survive. It could also be a prophecy about the return of the Jews from Babylonian captivity, or all of the above.
>
> If it refers to Jeremiah, then it can remind us of the words of the Lord to Joseph Smith when he was in Liberty Jail (D&C 121 and 122). He will eventually be delivered from his enemies. This can be literal on earth or literal in eternity.
>
> If it refers to the Jews and their eventual return, then it

prophesies that their captors will eventually take pity on them and allow them to return.

11 The LORD said, **Verily it shall be well with thy remnant;** verily I will cause the enemy to entreat thee *well* in the time of evil and in the time of affliction.

12 Shall iron break the northern iron and the steel?

The Martin Luther German Bible roughly translates verse 12, above, as saying, "Don't you know that such iron exists that can break iron and brass from the north?" Perhaps this could mean, in effect, that the Lord has power over the strong "iron hand" of nations (including Babylon who came from the north) who hold the Jews captive, and He can cause their captors to treat them well and eventually let them go free.

Verse 13, next, seems to refer to the Jews and be yet another reminder as to why many of them are to be slaughtered and the remainder carried away into captivity at this point of their history.

13 Thy substance and thy treasures will I give to the spoil without price, and *that* **for all thy sins,** even in all thy borders [*the whole nation of Judah is riddled with wickedness*].

Verse 14, next, tells Jeremiah that he too will be carried away captive into a foreign country. He was eventually taken by a group of Jews to Egypt as they escaped the conquerors of Jerusalem, and then, according to tradition, stoned to death by them. (See Bible Dictionary under "Jeremiah." It appears that Jeremiah is being reminded that the righteous also suffer when the wicked rule and incur the wrath of God [compare with D&C 98:9].)

14 And **I will make** *thee* **to pass with thine enemies into a land** *which* **thou knowest not:** for a fire is kindled in mine anger, *which* shall burn upon you.

Verse 15, next, reminds us of the words of the Prophet Joseph Smith in Liberty Jail, as he pled with the Lord. He said:

<u>D&C 121:5</u>
5 Let thine anger be kindled against our enemies; and, in the fury of thine heart, with thy sword **avenge us of our wrongs.**

15 ¶ O LORD, thou knowest: remember me, and visit [*bless*] me, and **revenge me of my persecutors;** take me not away in thy longsuffering: know that for thy sake I have suffered rebuke.

16 **Thy words were found** [*were given to me*], **and I did eat them** [*internalized them, made them a part of me*]; and **thy word was unto me the joy and rejoicing of mine heart:** for I am called by thy name, O LORD God of hosts.

17 I sat not in the assembly of the

mockers, nor rejoiced [*I did not join in wickedness and take pleasure in it with the wicked*]; **I sat alone** because of thy hand: for thou hast filled me with indignation [*against sin and wickedness*].

18 Why is my pain perpetual, and my wound incurable, *which* refuseth to be healed? wilt thou be altogether unto me as a liar, *and as* waters *that* fail [*perhaps meaning, in effect, "Are You not going to keep Your word? Why aren't Your promises of peace and protection and help fulfilled?"*]? [*Perhaps similar to Joseph Smith's pleading—see Doctrine and Covenants 121:1–6.*]

The Lord responds to Jeremiah's pleading.

19 ¶ Therefore thus saith the LORD, If thou return, then will I bring thee again, *and* **thou shalt stand before me:** and if thou take forth the precious from the vile, **thou shalt be as my mouth:** let them return unto thee; but return not thou unto them [*perhaps meaning for Jeremiah to stand firm, and if the people want the word of the Lord, let them come to him*].

The Lord's word to Jeremiah, in verses 20-21, next, seems to be that of being saved spiritually rather than physically. Spiritual salvation is the only thing that counts in the perspective of eternity.

20 And I will make thee unto this people a fenced brasen wall [*a fortified wall of brass or bronze*]: and **they shall fight against thee, but they shall not prevail against thee:** for I *am* with thee to save thee and to deliver thee, saith the LORD.

21 And I will deliver thee out of the hand of the wicked, and I will redeem thee out of the hand of the terrible.

JEREMIAH 16

Selection: all verses

THIS CHAPTER CONTAINS a prophecy that is quite often referred to in our lessons and talks on missionary work in the last days. It is verse 16. We will say more about it when we get there.

Verse 2, if taken literally, would mean that Jeremiah was told not to marry. As we proceed, we will take the viewpoint that this was symbolic, rather than literal. One possible message is that Jerusalem has become so polluted with wickedness that it is no longer a safe place to attempt to raise children. Another possible message is that the coming enemy armies from Babylon will show no mercy to the inhabitants, including children.

1 THE word of the LORD came also unto me, saying,

2 Thou shalt not take thee a wife, neither shalt thou have sons or

daughters in this place.

We will quote from the *Old Testament Student Manual* for help with verse 2, above (**bold** added for emphasis):

"Jeremiah's day was a sad one for Judah. To symbolize that truth, the Lord told his prophet three things that he was not to do:

"1. He was not to marry or father children (see Jeremiah 16:2). So universal was the calamity bearing down upon the people that God did not want children to suffer its outrage. **This commandment**, however, like the one to Hosea (see Hosea 10), who was commanded to take a wife of whoredoms, **was probably not a literal one; rather, it probably was allegorical, that is, Jeremiah was not to expect that his people would marry themselves to the covenant again, nor was he to expect to get spiritual children (converts) from his ministry.**

"2. He was not to lament those in Judah who died by the sword or famine (see Jeremiah 16:5), since they brought these judgments upon themselves.

"3. He was not to feast or eat with friends in Jerusalem (see verse 8), since feasting was a sign of celebration and eating together a symbol of fellowship.

"In addition, Jeremiah was commanded to explain very clearly to the people the reasons for his actions as well as the reasons for their coming punishment" (*Old Testament Student Manual*, page 241).

3 For thus saith the LORD concerning the sons and concerning the daughters that are born in this place, and concerning their mothers that bare them, and concerning their fathers that begat them in this land;

4 They shall die of grievous deaths; they shall not be lamented; **neither shall they be buried;** *but* they shall be as dung upon the face of the earth: and they shall be **consumed by the sword**, and by **famine**; and their carcases shall be **meat for the fowls of heaven, and for the beasts of the earth.**

Verse 5, next, is another reminder that if people do not repent, the law of mercy cannot take over from the law of justice.

5 For thus saith the LORD, Enter not into the house of mourning, neither go to lament nor bemoan them: for **I have taken away my peace from this people, saith the LORD,** *even* **lovingkindness and mercies.**

6 Both **the great** [*the famous and prominent in their society*] **and the small shall die in this land:** they shall **not be buried** [*implying a terrible slaughter*], neither shall *men* lament for them, **nor cut themselves, nor make themselves bald for them** [*signs of deep mourning and grief in their culture*]:

Verses 6 and 7, here, seem to indicate that everyone will be in such distress because of their own circumstances that they will not take time nor have inclination to mourn for others being ravished by the famines and conquering enemy armies.

7 Neither shall *men* tear *themselves* for them in mourning, to comfort them for the dead [*no one will comfort those who mourn*]; neither shall *men* give them the cup of consolation to drink for their father or for their mother.

8 Thou shalt not also go into the house of feasting, to sit with them to eat and to drink.

In verse 9, next, Jeremiah is told that these terrible devastations will come upon the Jews in his lifetime.

9 For thus saith the LORD of hosts, the God of Israel; Behold, I will cause to cease out of this place in your eyes, and **in your days,** the voice of mirth, and the voice of gladness, the voice of the bridegroom, and the voice of the bride.

Verse 10, next, warns Jeremiah that the wicked people against whom he preaches will act as if they are righteous and do not deserve such warnings and condemnation.

10 ¶ And it shall come to pass, when thou shalt shew this people all these words, and they shall say unto thee, **Wherefore** [*why*] **hath the LORD pronounced all this great evil against us?** or **what** *is* **our iniquity** [*what have we done wrong*]?

or what *is* our sin that we have committed against the LORD our God?

11 **Then shalt thou say** unto them, **Because your fathers** [*parents; ancestors*] **have forsaken me,** saith the LORD, and have walked after other gods, and have served them, and have worshipped them, and have forsaken me, **and have not kept my law;**

12 **And ye have done worse than your fathers;** for, behold, ye walk every one after the imagination of his evil heart, that they may not hearken unto me:

13 **Therefore will I cast you out of this land** into a land that ye know not, *neither* ye nor your fathers; and there shall ye serve other gods day and night; where I will not shew you favour [*I will not be able to bless you with the choicest gospel blessings*].

Next, we see a major prophecy concerning the gathering of Israel in the last days. The prophecy includes the fact that the deliverance of the children of Israel from Egypt, by the Lord, will no longer be the most spectacular event spoken of among the people. Rather, the gathering of Israel from all nations will become the focus of effort and conversation.

Major Prophecy

The Lord will gather scattered Israel in the last days.

14 ¶ Therefore, behold, **the days**

come, saith the LORD, that it shall no more be said, The LORD liveth, that brought up the children of Israel out of the land of Egypt;

15 But, The LORD liveth, that brought up the children of Israel from the land of the north, and from all the lands whither he had driven them: and I will bring them again into their land that I gave unto their fathers.

Notice the order of the missionary work in the last days, as given in verse 16, next. First, large numbers of converts will come into the Church, in various nations. This is represented by "fishers" who fish with nets and catch large numbers with them. These mass conversions are followed by missionaries who are depicted as "hunters" who search the once-fertile mission field for anyone else who will join the Church.

16 ¶ Behold, I will send for many fishers, saith the LORD, and they shall fish them; and after will I send for many hunters, and they shall hunt them [converts] from every mountain, and from every hill, and out of the holes of the rocks.

One example of "fishers," in verse 16, above, might be Wilford Woodruff and other early missionaries who baptized thousands of converts in England in the early days of the Church. Another example could

be the missionary work in South America in our day, where tens of thousands of converts are being baptized. Yet other examples might be found in any one of several countries or areas, including Africa, where initial missionary efforts have resulted in abundant baptisms in our day.

Now, though, in some areas of the world, convert baptisms are very few in number. The missionaries serving in such areas might be considered to be the "hunters," prophesied of by Jeremiah, who search everywhere for just a few who are willing to be taught the gospel.

Next, the topic turns to the fact that the Lord sees all, including the supposedly "secret" doings of the wicked.

17 For mine eyes are upon all their ways: they are not hid from my face, neither is their iniquity hid from mine eyes.

18 And first [before the great latter-day gathering] I will recompense [punish] their iniquity and their sin double; because they have defiled my land [polluted it with wickedness], they have filled mine inheritance with the carcases of their detestable and abominable things [such as idol worship].

Next, in verse 19, we see a prophecy that Gentiles from all nations will join the Church also in the last days.

19 O LORD, my strength, and

my fortress, and my refuge in the day of affliction, **the Gentiles shall come unto thee from the ends of the earth,** and **shall say, Surely our fathers have inherited lies, vanity, and** *things* **wherein** *there is* **no profit** [*these converts will discard the false traditions and beliefs of their parents and ancestors in order to join the Church*].

> Verse 20, next, is yet another reminder that it is completely ridiculous to make idols with one's own hands, and then worship them.

20 Shall a man make gods unto himself, and they *are* **no gods?**

> The Lord says, in verse 21, next, that through the coming punishments, the wicked will know once and for all that there is just one true God.

21 Therefore, behold, **I will this once cause them to know, I will** cause them to know mine hand and my might; and they shall know **that my name** *is* **The LORD** [*that I am the only true God, in other words, that their idols are not gods*].

JEREMIAH 17

Selection: all verses

THIS CHAPTER CONTINUES empha-sizing the sins that will lead to the destruction of Jerusalem and the cities of Judah as a nation in Jeremiah's day. Among other things, we are shown comparison and contrast between the lives of the wicked and the righteous.

First, in verse 1, we are told that they are hardened sinners, and that the deepest desire of their hearts is to be wicked.

1 THE sin of Judah *is* **written with a pen of iron,** *and* **with the point of a diamond** [*the fact that they are deeply wicked is irrefutable*]: *it is* **graven upon the table of their heart** [*the innermost desire of their heart is to be wicked*], and **upon the horns of your altars** [*their religions are dedicated to wickedness, rather than protection and blessings from the Lord*];

> The "horns of the altar," mentioned in verse 1, above, served as a place of protection and refuge for anyone who was being pursued by another. If they could get to the altar, and grab hold of one of the horns built on the four corners of it, they were safe from their enemy (see 1 Kings 1:50).

2 Whilst their children remember their altars and their groves by the green trees upon the high hills [*the children have been led astray by their idol-worshiping parents*].

> Verse 3, next, says, in effect, that everything the people of Judah treasure in their wicked hearts will be given to their enemies.

3 O my mountain in the field, **I will give thy substance** *and* **all thy treasures to the spoil** [*to your enemies*], *and* thy high places for sin, throughout all thy borders.

4 And **thou,** even thyself, **shalt discontinue from thine heritage that I gave thee** [*you will be taken from the Holy Land*]; and **I will cause thee to serve thine enemies in the land which thou knowest not:** for ye have kindled a fire in mine anger, *which* shall burn for ever.

5 ¶ Thus saith the LORD; **Cursed** *be* **the man that trusteth in man, and maketh flesh his arm, and whose heart departeth from the LORD.**

6 For **he shall be like the heath** [*juniper tree—see footnote 6a in your Bible*] **in the desert,** and shall not see when good cometh; but **shall inhabit the parched places in the wilderness,** *in* a salt land and not inhabited.

The "wilderness," spoken of in verse 6, above, is obviously literal, representing their trials in the land of Babylon. But it can also be symbolic of their apostasy, living in a "spiritual wilderness" without the gospel of Jesus Christ.

Verses 7–8, next, are a beautiful representation of the blessings of living the true gospel, in contrast to the devastations of apostasy depicted above.

7 Blessed *is* **the man that trusteth in the LORD, and whose hope the LORD is.**

8 **For he shall be as a tree planted by the waters, and** *that* **spreadeth out her roots by the river, and shall not see when heat cometh, but her leaf shall be green; and shall not be careful in the year of drought, neither shall cease from yielding fruit.**

Verse 9, next, is a reminder of how devastating a heart that is filled with wicked desires can be. A question is asked and an answer is given.

Question

9 ¶ The heart *is* deceitful above all *things*, and desperately wicked: **who can know it** [*who can tell what is in it*]?

Answer

10 **I the LORD search the heart,** *I* try the reins [*the innermost thoughts and feelings*], even to give every man according to his ways, *and* according to the fruit of his doings.

11 As the partridge sitteth *on eggs*, and hatcheth *them* not; *so* **he that getteth riches, and not by right** [*dishonestly*], shall leave them in the midst of his days, and at **his end shall be a fool.**

Next, Jeremiah praises the Lord.

12 ¶ **A glorious high throne from the beginning** *is* **the place of our**

sanctuary [*the Lord is above all and is the only safe refuge*].

13 O LORD, the hope of Israel, **all that forsake thee shall be ashamed** [*will come up empty; will be disappointed, put to shame*], *and* they that depart from me shall be written in the earth, **because they have forsaken the LORD, the fountain of living waters.**

14 Heal me, O LORD, and I shall be healed; save me, and I shall be saved: for thou *art* **my praise.**

In verses 15–18, next, Jeremiah stands firm and faithful before the Lord, and prays for protection from his enemies.

15 ¶ Behold, **they** [*Jeremiah's enemies*] **say unto me, Where** *is* **the word of the LORD** [*where are all the destructions you have prophesied*]? **let it come now.**

16 As for me, **I have not hastened from** *being* **a pastor** to follow thee [*I have been faithful to my calling*]: neither have I desired the woeful day [*the coming destruction*]; **thou knowest: that which came out of my lips was** *right* **before thee.**

17 Be not a terror unto me: thou *art* **my hope in the day of evil.**

18 Let them be confounded that persecute me, but let not me be confounded: let them be dismayed, but let not me be dismayed: bring upon

them the day of evil, and destroy them with double destruction.

Next, in verses 19–22, we are reminded of the importance of keeping the Sabbath holy.

<u>Major Message</u>
Keep the Sabbath Day holy.

19 ¶ Thus said the LORD unto me; **Go and stand in the gate** [*entrance*] of the children of the people, whereby the kings of Judah come in, and by the which they go out, and in **all the gates of Jerusalem** [*in other words, chose locations where everyone can hear your message*];

20 And say unto them, **Hear ye the word of the LORD,** ye kings of Judah, and all Judah, and **all the inhabitants of Jerusalem,** that enter in by these gates:

21 Thus saith the LORD; Take heed to yourselves, and **bear no burden on the sabbath day,** nor bring *it* in by the gates of Jerusalem;

22 Neither carry forth a burden out of your houses on the sabbath day, **neither do ye any work, but hallow ye the sabbath day,** as I commanded your fathers.

The reaction of the people to Jeremiah's message about the Sabbath is given in verse 23, next.

23 But they obeyed not, neither inclined their ear [*wouldn't listen*], but made their neck stiff [*they were* *full of pride, not humble enough to be taught]*, that they might not hear, nor receive instruction.

> Verses 24–26 explain the great blessings which could have come to these people, had they listened and repented.

24 And it shall come to pass, **if ye diligently hearken unto me, saith the LORD,** to bring in no burden through the gates of this city on the sabbath day, but **hallow the sabbath day, to do no work therein;**

25 Then shall there enter into the gates of this city kings and princes sitting upon the throne of David, riding in chariots and on horses, they, and their princes, the men of Judah, and the inhabitants of Jerusalem: and **this city shall remain for ever** [*in other words, great prosperity, protection and peace will be yours*].

26 **And they shall come** from the cities of Judah, and from the places about Jerusalem, and from the land of Benjamin, and from the plain, and from the mountains, and from the south, **bringing burnt offerings, and sacrifices, and meat offerings, and incense, and bringing sacrifices of praise, unto the house of the LORD.**

27 **But if ye will not hearken unto me to hallow the sabbath day,** and not to bear a burden, even

entering in at the gates of Jerusalem on the sabbath day; **then will I kindle a fire in the gates thereof, and it shall devour the palaces of Jerusalem, and it shall not be quenched.**

> Did you see the message in the above verses about the importance of keeping the Sabbath day holy? Among other things, when individuals and nations keep the Sabbath holy, it serves to remind them of God and the importance of keeping His commandments in their daily living. When people forget the Sabbath, they tend to forget God.

JEREMIAH 18

Selection: all verses

A PROBLEM COMES UP in this chapter where the King James version (the Bible we use for English-speaking areas of the Church) has the Lord repenting in verses 8 and 10. The Lord does not repent since He does not sin. As you will see, when you come to these two verses, the JST makes corrections in both instances.

This chapter starts out by using the symbolism of a potter creating a pot from clay on a potter's wheel. While the clay is pliable, he can form it according to his plans. He can even start over with the clay, if necessary. This symbolizes what the Lord (the Potter) desires to do with His people (the clay). He desires to mold and shape them to become His people.

Jeremiah is told to go to the potter's

house in his neighborhood where this message and lesson from the Lord can be demonstrated.

1 THE word which came to Jeremiah from the LORD, saying,

2 Arise, and go down to the potter's house, and there I will cause thee to hear my words.

3 Then I went down to the potter's house, and, behold, he wrought a work on the wheels [*the potter was making a clay pot on a potter's wheel*].

4 And the vessel that he made of clay was marred [*damaged; was not shaping according to plan*] in the hand of the potter: **so he made it again** another vessel [*so he started over with it and made another pot with it*], as seemed good to the potter to make *it*.

Next, the Lord explains the symbolism of the potter throwing (making) a pot.

5 Then the word of the LORD came to me, saying,

6 O house of Israel [*the twelve tribes of Israel; the Lord's covenant people*], cannot I do with you as this potter? saith the LORD. Behold, **as the clay *is* in the potter's hand, so *are* ye in mine hand,** O house of Israel.

Next, the Lord explains that He, as the Potter, will do whatever it takes to shape and form His covenant people, even if it means destroying them in order to

start over with them. If they will then use their agency to repent (see verse 8), He will be enabled to form them into a covenant people, in other words, a people whom He can bless with exaltation.

7 *At what* **instant** [*NIV: "if at any time"*] **I shall speak concerning a nation,** and concerning a kingdom, to pluck up, and to pull down, and **to destroy it** [*like a potter as he starts over with a failed pot by kneading it back into lump of clay*];

As mentioned in the background to this chapter, the idea that the Lord "repents" on occasions is not correct. We will first read verse 8, next, and will then use the JST to correct the translation.

(By the way, someone asked me recently where I get these JST quotes from, since they are not all in the footnotes or in the back of our LDS Bible. The answer is that there is not room in our LDS Bible to include all the JST corrections. You can see all of them in Joseph Smith's "New Translation" of the Bible, published by Herald Publishing House, Independence, Missouri. I use the 1970 edition. Most LDS bookstores have it or can get it for you.)

8 If that nation, against whom I have pronounced, turn from their evil, **I will repent** of the evil that I thought to do unto them.

JST Jeremiah 18:8
8 If that nation, against whom I have pronounced, turn from their evil, **I will withhold the**

evil that I thought to do unto them.

9 And *at what* **instant** [*whenever*] **I shall speak concerning a nation,** and concerning a kingdom, **to build and to plant** *it*;

10 If it do evil in my sight, that it obey not my voice, then **I will repent of the good,** wherewith I said I would benefit them.

JST Jeremiah 18:10

10 If it do evil in my sight, that it obey not my voice, then **I will withhold the good,** wherewith I said I would benefit them.

Next, in verse 11, the Lord instructs Jeremiah to once again invite these wicked people to repent.

Major Message

Even when it may appear that it is far too late to repent, there can still be hope.

11 ¶ Now therefore **go to, speak to the men of Judah, and to the inhabitants of Jerusalem,** saying, Thus saith the LORD; Behold, I frame evil against you, and devise a device against you [*your destruction looms before you*]: **return ye now every one from his evil way, and make your ways and your doings good** [*please repent*].

As we look at the phrase "there is no hope" in the context of verse 12, next, we understand that the people are not saying that there is no hope for them. Rather, they are saying, in effect, "Don't get your hopes up. There is no reason for us to repent. We like wickedness and we want to continue the way we are going."

12 And they said, There is no hope: but **we will walk after our own devices, and we will every one do the imagination of his evil heart.**

The basic question in verses 13–14, next, is "Have you ever heard of such a thing as a people leaving a God who has power to bless them?" Even the heathen are wiser than that!

13 Therefore thus saith the LORD; Ask ye now among the heathen, **who hath heard such things: the virgin of Israel** [*Jerusalem*] **hath done a very horrible thing.**

14 Will *a man* leave the snow of Lebanon *which cometh* from the rock of the field? *or* shall the cold flowing waters that come from another place be forsaken?

JST Jeremiah 18:14

14 Will you not leave the snow of the fields of Lebanon; shall not the cold flowing waters that come from another place from the rock, be forsaken?

It may be that verse 14, above, in the context of verse 13, is saying, in effect, "Would you not be better off not to leave a sure thing, like the God of Israel?"

The Lord goes on to describe the

"horrible thing" mentioned in verse 13.

15 Because **my people hath forgotten me**, they have **burned incense to vanity** [*idols*], and **they** [*their false gods and idols*] **have caused them to stumble in their ways** *from the* ancient paths, to walk in paths, *in a* way not cast up [*in a path which has not been graded and maintained*];

16 To make their land desolate [*their choices are setting up their land for destruction*], *and* a perpetual hissing; every one that passeth thereby shall be astonished, and wag his head [*there will be much negative and derisive gossip in the future about what happened to Judah and Jerusalem*].

17 I will scatter them as with an east wind [*symbolic of rapid and terrible devastation*] before the enemy: I will shew them the back, and not the face [*the Lord will turn His back to them*], in the day of their calamity.

The people don't like what Jeremiah is saying, so they plot to discredit him (verse 18). Verse 23 indicates that they plotted to kill him.

18 ¶ Then said they, **Come, and let us devise devices against Jeremiah;** for the law shall not perish from the priest, nor counsel from the wise, nor the word from the prophet [*the things he is prophesying will not come to pass*]. **Come, and let us smite him with the tongue,** and let us not give heed to any of his words.

Next, Jeremiah petitions the Lord for help and protection against his enemies. He asks that the Lord's punishments be upon them.

19 Give heed to me, O LORD, and hearken to the voice of them that contend with me [*be sure to hear the threats my enemies are giving out against me*].

20 Shall evil be recompensed for good? for **they have digged a pit for my soul.** Remember that I **stood before thee to speak good for them,** *and* **to turn away thy wrath from them** [*I have tried to save them*].

Verse 21, next, can serve to remind us of the application of the law of justice. It may also reflect the Lord's law of self-defense, as described in D&C 98.

21 Therefore deliver up their children to the famine, and pour out their *blood* by the force of the sword; and let their wives be bereaved of their children, and *be* widows; and let their men be put to death; *let* their young men *be* slain by the sword in battle.

22 Let a cry be heard from their houses, when thou shalt bring a troop suddenly upon them: for **they have digged a pit to take me, and hid snares for my feet.**

23 Yet, LORD, **thou knowest all**

their counsel against me to slay **me:** forgive not their iniquity, neither blot out their sin from thy sight, but **let them be overthrown before thee; deal** *thus* **with them in the time of thine anger.**

> As mentioned in our note before verse 21, above, D&C 98 may shed some light on verses 21–23, above. Jeremiah's life has been in danger and his enemies have tried to stop him a number of times by now. It may be that the "one, two, three" of D&C 98:23–27 have, in effect, been fulfilled, and he is now seeking to stop them, according to the law of self-defense that the Lord gave to the ancient prophets (D&C 98:32). We will quote some relevant verses from the Doctrine and Covenants, using **bold** for emphasis:
>
> <u>D&C 98:23–35</u>
> 23 Now, I speak unto you concerning your families— **if men will smite you, or your families, once,** and ye bear it patiently and revile not against them, neither seek revenge, ye shall be rewarded;
> 24 But if ye bear it not patiently, it shall be accounted unto you as being meted out as a just measure unto you.
> 25 And again, if your enemy shall smite you **the second time,** and you revile not against your enemy, and bear it patiently, your reward shall be an hundred fold.
> 26 And again, if he shall smite you **the third time,** and ye bear it patiently, your reward

shall be doubled unto you four-fold;
27 And these three testimonies shall stand against your enemy if he repent not, and shall not be blotted out.
28 And now, verily I say unto you, if that enemy shall escape my vengeance, that he be not brought into judgment before me, then ye shall **see to it that ye warn him in my name,** that he come no more upon you, neither upon your family, even your children's children unto the third and fourth generation.
29 And then, **if he shall come upon you or your children,** or your children's children unto the third and fourth generation, **I have delivered thine enemy into thine hands;**
30 And then if thou wilt spare him, thou shalt be rewarded for thy righteousness; and also thy children and thy children's children unto the third and fourth generation.
31 Nevertheless, thine enemy is in thine hands; and if thou rewardest him according to his works thou art justified; **if he has sought thy life, and thy life is endangered by him, thine enemy is in thine hands and thou art justified.**
32 Behold, **this is the law I gave unto my servant Nephi, and thy fathers, Joseph, and Jacob, and Isaac, and Abraham, and all mine ancient prophets and apostles.**

33 And again, this is the law that I gave unto mine ancients, that they should not go out unto battle against any nation, kindred, tongue, or people, save I, the Lord, commanded them.

34 And if any nation, tongue, or people should proclaim war against them, they should first lift a standard of peace unto that people, nation, or tongue; 35 And **if that people did not accept the offering of peace, neither the second nor the third time, they should bring these testimonies before the Lord;**

JEREMIAH 19

Selection: all verses

IN THIS CHAPTER, we see that the inhabitants of Jerusalem and the cities of Judah had arrived at the point where they were sacrificing their own children to idols. Such sacrifice is the ultimate blasphemy against the voluntary sacrifice of the Son of God for our sins.

Again, as in the case of the potter and the potter's wheel (chapter 18), Jeremiah is requested by the Lord to go to a certain place to obtain this message. This time, he is asked to pick up a clay jar and go to the "valley of the son of Hinnom" (verse 2), and await the word of the Lord. This valley was just south of Jerusalem and was the site of human sacrifices (see Bible Dictionary

under "Topheth.") These sacrifices included their own children (verse 5). The breaking (verse 10) of the clay jar (mentioned in verse 1) is symbolic of the destruction of Jerusalem.

1 THUS saith the LORD, **Go and get a potter's earthen bottle** [*a clay jar*], and *take* of the ancients of the people, and of the ancients of the priests [*take some of the city elders and old priests with you*];

2 And **go forth unto the valley of the son of Hinnom,** which *is* by the entry of the east gate, and proclaim there the words that I shall tell thee,

3 **And say,** Hear ye the word of the LORD, O kings of Judah, and inhabitants of Jerusalem; **Thus saith the LORD** of hosts, the God of Israel; Behold, **I will bring evil upon this place,** the which whosoever heareth, his ears shall tingle [*whoever hears about it will hardly believe their ears*].

4 **Because they have forsaken me, and have estranged this place** [*have desecrated this place; made it no longer a "Holy Land"*], and **have burned incense in it unto other gods** [*worshiped idols*], whom neither they nor their fathers have known, nor the kings of Judah, and **have filled this place with the blood of innocents** [*have offered human sacrifices, including children*];

5 They have built also the high

places of Baal [*they have built altars to Baal*], to **burn their sons with fire** *for* **burnt offerings unto Baal,** which I commanded not, nor spake *it*, neither came *it* into my mind:

> Verses 6–9 are yet another prophecy concerning the coming destruction of Jerusalem and the surrounding area.

6 Therefore [*because of gross wickedness*], **behold, the days come,** saith the LORD, **that this place shall no more be called** Tophet, **nor The valley of the son of Hinnom, but The valley of slaughter.**

7 And I will make void the counsel of Judah and Jerusalem in this place [*they will no longer have political clout*]; **and I will cause them to fall by the sword** before their enemies, and by the hands of them that seek their lives: **and their carcases will I give to be meat for the fowls of the heaven, and for the beasts of the earth.**

8 And I will make this city desolate, and an hissing [*an object of scorn and gossip*]; every one that passeth thereby shall be astonished and hiss [*deride them*] because of all the plagues thereof.

> Next, in verse 9, we see a frightful prophecy of cannibalism during the coming siege of Jerusalem.

9 And I will cause them to eat the flesh of their sons and the flesh of their daughters, and they shall eat

every one the flesh of his friend in the siege and straitness [*dire circumstances*], wherewith their enemies, and they that seek their lives, shall straiten them.

> The above prediction of hunger and cannibalism was fulfilled during the siege of Jerusalem by Nebuchadnezzar, king of Babylon. We read of it in Lamentations:
>
> Lamentations 4:8–10
> 8 Their visage is blacker than a coal; they are not known in the streets: their skin cleaveth to their bones; it is withered, it is become like a stick.
> 9 They that be slain with the sword are better than they that be slain with hunger: for these pine away, stricken through for want of the fruits of the field.
> 10 The hands of the pitiful women have sodden [boiled, cooked] their own children: they were their meat [*food*] in the destruction of the daughter of my people [during the destruction of Jerusalem].

> Next, Jeremiah is instructed to break the clay jar (representing the people of Judah) that he was instructed (in verse 1) to take with him to the site of human sacrifices.

10 Then shalt thou break the bottle [*symbolic of the "breaking" of Jerusalem and the scattering of the Jews in pieces—see verse 11*] **in the sight of the men** [*the city elders and leaders—see verse 1*] **that go with thee,**

11 And shalt **say unto them, Thus saith the LORD of hosts; Even so will I break this people and this city, as** *one* **breaketh a potter's vessel,** that cannot be made whole again: and they shall bury *them* in Tophet [*a spot in the Valley of Hinnon—see verse 2*], till *there be* no place to bury [*in other words, there will be a great slaughter of the Jews in that valley*].

12 **Thus will I do unto this place, saith the LORD,** and to the inhabitants thereof, and *even* make this city as Tophet [*a place of great slaughter*]:

> There is symbolism in the phrase "make this city as Tophet" in verse 12, above. As noted above, Tophet was a place in the valley, south of Jerusalem, where human sacrifice was practiced, including the sacrifice of children to the fire god Molech. (See Bible Dictionary under "Molech.") Therefore, to make Jerusalem like Tophet means that the wicked will be sacrificed to their wickedness, just like they wickedly sacrificed others to their false gods.

13 And **the houses of Jerusalem,** and the houses [*palaces*] of the kings of Judah, **shall be defiled as the place of Tophet,** because of all the houses upon whose roofs they have burned incense unto all the host of heaven [*all the false gods and idols imaginable*], and have poured out drink offerings unto other gods.

14 **Then came Jeremiah from Tophet,** whither the LORD had sent him to prophesy; **and he stood in the court of the LORD's house** [*the outer courtyard of the Jerusalem Temple*]; **and said to all the people,**

15 Thus saith the LORD of hosts, the God of Israel; **Behold, I will bring** upon this city and upon all her towns **all the evil that I have pronounced** [*prophesied*] against it, **because they have hardened their necks** [*refused to humble themselves*], **that they might not hear my words.**

JEREMIAH 20

Selection: all verses

IN THIS CHAPTER, Pashur, the senior officer or chief overseer of the temple in Jerusalem, vents his anger against Jeremiah because of the things he is teaching and prophesying about the wickedness of the Jews and their leaders (see, for example, Jeremiah 19:14–15). He beats Jeremiah (verse 2) and has him placed in the stocks.

1 NOW **Pashur** the son of Immer the priest, who *was* also **chief governor in the house of the LORD, heard that Jeremiah prophesied these things.**

2 **Then Pashur smote Jeremiah** the prophet, **and put him in the stocks** that *were* in the high gate of

Benjamin, which *was* by the house of the LORD.

We will quote from the *Old Testament Student Manual* for a description of being "put in the stocks." We will add **bold** for emphasis.

"Jeremiah 19:14–15 records Jeremiah's standing in the court of the temple, again reminding the people of the troubles that lay ahead because of their wickedness. When Pashur, the chief overseer of the temple, heard of the incident, he had Jeremiah beaten and placed in stocks. **Stocks were an instrument of torture by which the body was forced into an unnatural position, much as the wooden stocks of medieval times confined certain parts of the body, such as the arms, legs, or head, by means of wooden beams that locked the parts of the body into place**" (*Old Testament Student Manual*, page 245).

In verse 3, next, Jeremiah, under the direction of the Lord, uses the common technique (in their culture) of changing a person's name as a means of confirming a change in status, either good or bad. In this case, it is bad. "Pashur" means "free." But watch what the change of names denotes for Pashur's future, at the end of the verse.

3 And it came to pass **on the morrow** [*the next day*], that **Pashur brought forth Jeremiah out of the stocks.** Then said Jeremiah unto him, **The LORD hath not called thy name Pashur, but Magor-missabib**

["terror all around"—see footnote 3a in your Bible].

4 For thus saith the LORD, **Behold, I will make thee a terror to thyself, and to all thy friends: and they shall fall by the sword** of their enemies, and **thine eyes shall behold it** [*you will see this prophecy fulfilled*]: and **I will give all Judah into the hand of the king of Babylon, and he shall carry them captive into Babylon, and shall slay them with the sword.**

5 **Moreover** [*in addition*] **I will deliver all the strength of this city,** and all the labours thereof, and **all the precious things** thereof, and **all the treasures** of the kings of Judah will I give **into the hand of their enemies,** which shall spoil them, and take them, and carry them to Babylon.

6 **And thou, Pashur, and all that dwell in thine house shall go into captivity: and thou shalt come to Babylon, and there thou shalt die,** and shalt be buried there, thou, and all thy friends, to whom thou hast prophesied lies.

The scene in verse 6, above, reminds us of Abinadi in King Noah's court (Mosiah 17:16–18).

The word, "deceived," in verse 7, next, can be a problem. We will read it and then get some help on the matter.

7 ¶ O LORD, thou hast **deceived**

301

me, and I was deceived: thou art stronger than I, and hast prevailed: I am in derision daily, every one mocketh me.

"The great stress the prophetic calling caused Jeremiah is particularly discernible in Jeremiah 20:7-8, 14-18. The **Hebrew word translated in verse 7 as "deceived" means literally "enticed" or "persuaded."** The power that persuaded the prophet to continue to preach God's word at such great personal cost was 'as a burning fire shut up in [his] bones' (verse 9). It could not be stayed. Verses 14-18 reflect Jeremiah's despair over the lonely ministry he was given" (*Old Testament Student Manual*, page 245).

We will now repeat verse 7, above, and incorporate the helps given in the student manual. We catch a glimpse of Jeremiah's personality.

Jeremiah 20:7 (repeated)

❡ O LORD, thou hast deceived me [*persuaded me to serve as a prophet*], and I was deceived [*and I have been successfully persuaded*]: thou art stronger than I, and hast prevailed [*You win*]: I am in derision daily, every one mocketh me [*this is a most difficult calling*].

8 For since I spake, I cried out, I cried violence and spoil [*ever since I began to prophesy, I have had to say much about violence and devastation*]; because the word of the LORD was made a reproach unto me, and a derision, daily [*and it has caused me to be mocked and brought much personal pain*].

We continue to see insights into Jeremiah's personality. He is without guile and rather straightforward with the Lord. Next, he confesses that he considered not delivering the messages, but his burning testimony compelled him to be faithful to his calling as a prophet.

9 Then I said, I will not make mention of him, nor speak any more in his name [*I said to myself, "I will not do any more prophesying for the Lord"*]. But *his word* was in mine heart as a burning fire shut up in my bones, and I was weary with forbearing, and I could not stay [*I just could not hold back any more*].

Jeremiah continues, sharing his frustrations and confirming his absolute commitment to be true to the Lord. According to the first part of verse 10, next, it appears that there were many attempts to discredit Jeremiah through slander against his name. People were constantly watching to catch him in any kind of slip up.

10 ❡ For I heard the defaming [*slander*] of many, fear on every side [*paranoia everywhere*]. Report, say they, and we will report it. All my familiars [*close acquaintances*] watched for my halting [*watched, hoping to see me slip up*], saying, Peradventure he will be enticed

[*perhaps he will compromise his standards*], **and we shall prevail against him, and we shall take our revenge on him.**

11 But **the LORD** *is* **with me** as a mighty terrible one [*NIV: "like a mighty warrior"*]: **therefore my persecutors shall stumble, and they shall not prevail:** they shall be greatly ashamed [*disgraced*]; for **they shall not prosper:** *their* everlasting confusion shall never be forgotten.

> Again, we see Jeremiah plead with the Lord for help against his enemies, much the same as Joseph Smith did as recorded in D&C 121:2–5.

12 But, O LORD of hosts, that triest [*tests*] the righteous, *and* seest the reins and the heart [*and sees the innermost feelings and desires of the heart*], **let me see thy vengeance on them: for unto thee have I opened my cause.**

> Next, Jeremiah reaffirms his faith that the Lord has power to deliver him from the wicked.

13 Sing unto the LORD, praise ye the LORD: for **he hath delivered the soul of the poor** [*those in need*] **from the hand of evildoers.**

> This seems to be a low point in Jeremiah's life (understatement). We feel his discouragement and frustration in verses 14–18.

14 ¶ **Cursed** *be* **the day wherein I was born:** let not the day wherein my mother bare me be blessed.

15 Cursed *be* **the man who brought tidings to my father, saying, A man child is born unto thee;** making him very glad.

16 And let that man be as the cities which the LORD overthrew, and repented not: and **let him hear the cry in the morning, and the shouting at noontide** [*in other words, in effect, if the man who told my father that I was born could just hear what I hear everyday, he would be sorry he even announced my birth*];

17 Because he slew me not from the womb; **or that my mother might have been my grave, and her womb to be always great** *with* **me** [*if I could just not have been born; if my mother could have remained pregnant with me forever*].

18 Wherefore came I forth out of the womb [*why did I have to be born*] to see labour and sorrow, that my days should be consumed with shame [*perhaps meaning "that my life should be spent as a social outcast"*]?

⚓ JEREMIAH 21

Selection: all verses

AS MENTIONED IN the introduction to the Book of Jeremiah, in this study guide, Jeremiah served during the reigns of five different kings of Judah. The last king was Zedekiah. He was the wicked king who ruled when Lehi and his family left Jerusalem in 600 BC (see 1 Nephi 1:4).

In this chapter, wicked King Zedekiah (who was twenty-one years old when he began his reign and reigned for eleven years until the Babylonians took him prisoner) sends a servant to Jeremiah to see what the Lord has to say about the coming Babylonian armies.

1 THE word which came unto Jeremiah **from the LORD, when king Zedekiah sent unto him Pashur** [*not the same man as the "Pashur" in chapter 20, verse 1*] the son of Melchiah, and Zephaniah the son of Maaseiah the priest, **saying,**

2 Enquire, I pray thee, of the LORD for us; for Nebuchadrezzar king of Babylon maketh war against us; if so be that the LORD will deal with us according to all his wondrous works, that he may go up from us [*in other words, is there a possibility that the Lord will cause Nebuchadnezzar and his armies to go away without attacking Jerusalem?*].

> Perhaps you noticed a technical detail in verse 2, above. We usually refer to this powerful Babylonian king as "Nebuchadnezzar" (see, for example, Daniel 3:1–3), but in verse 2, it is spelled "Nebuchadrezzar" (with an "r" instead of an "n"). The spelling used in verse 2 is a Hebrew variation of the spelling.

Jeremiah's answer to the question of protection from the Lord, for this wicked king and his wicked people, is given in verses 3–14, next.

3 ¶ Then said Jeremiah unto them [*the messengers sent by king Zedekiah, of Jerusalem*], Thus shall ye say to Zedekiah:

4 Thus saith the LORD God of Israel; Behold, **I will turn back** [*make ineffective*] **the weapons of war that** *are* **in your hands,** wherewith ye fight against the king of Babylon, and *against* the Chaldeans [*another name for the Babylonians, in this context*], which besiege you without [*outside of*] the walls, and I will assemble them into the midst of this city [*I will bring your enemies right into the middle of Jerusalem*].

5 And I [*the Lord*] **myself will fight against you** with an outstretched hand and with a strong arm, even in anger, and in fury, and in great wrath.

6 And I will smite the inhabitants of this city, both man and beast: they shall die of a great pestilence.

7 And afterward, saith the LORD, I will deliver Zedekiah king of Judah, and his servants, and the people, and such as are left in this city from the pestilence, from the sword, and from the famine, **into the hand of Nebuchadrezzar king of Babylon,** and into the hand of their enemies, and into the hand of those that seek their life: and he shall smite them with the edge of the sword; **he shall not spare them, neither have pity, nor have mercy.**

In fulfillment of the above prophecy, King Zedekiah was captured by Nebuchadnezzar's armies, his sons (except for Mulek—see Helaman 6:10) were killed before his eyes, and then his eyes were put out and he was carried as a trophy of war to Babylon (see Jeremiah 52:8-11).

Next, the Lord instructs Jeremiah to tell the inhabitants of Jerusalem how they can avoid being killed by the invading armies.

8 ¶ And **unto this people thou shalt say,** Thus saith the LORD; Behold, **I set before you the way of life, and the way of death** [*you can either live or die in the coming siege*].

9 **He that abideth** [*remains*] **in this city** [*Jerusalem*] **shall die by the sword, and by the fam-ine, and by the pestilence: but he that goeth out** [*leaves the city*], **and falleth** [*surrenders*] **to the Chaldeans** [*Babylonian armies*] **that** besiege you, he **shall live, and his life shall be unto him for a prey** [*in other words, you will be taken captive and put in bondage—that's the condition under which you will remain alive*].

10 For **I have set my face against this city for** [*because of their*] **evil,**

and not for good, saith the LORD: **it shall be given into the hand of the king of Babylon, and he shall burn it with fire.**

Next, in verses 11-14, the Lord tells the royal family as well as the people that there is one way they can yet be preserved as a nation. It is if they will repent and turn to righteousness.

11 ¶ And **touching** [*concerning*] **the house of the king of Judah** [*the royal family*], *say,* Hear ye the word of the LORD;

12 O house of David, thus saith the LORD; **Execute judgment** [*be fair and righteous*] in the morning, and **deliver** *him that is* **spoiled out of the hand of the oppressor** [*conduct the business of the kingdom with integrity*], lest my fury go out like fire, and burn that none can quench *it,* because of the evil of your doings.

13 Behold, I *am* against thee, O inhabitant of the valley, *and* rock of the plain, saith the LORD; **which say,** Who shall come down against us [*who can conquer us*]? or who shall enter into our habitations [*what enemies could possibly come into our land*]?

14 But **I will punish you according to the fruit of your doings** [*according to your wicked deeds*], saith the LORD: and **I will kindle a fire in the forest thereof** [*in other words, the Lord will burn their trees; trees*

are often symbolic of people, in Old Testament symbolism], and it shall **devour all things round about it.**

JEREMIAH 22

Selection: all verses

IN THIS CHAPTER, Jeremiah is given yet another uncomfortable task. He is to go to the palace of the king and deliver a prophecy.

Verses 1–9 are a general invitation to the kings of Judah to repent and do right, and a warning about the ultimate consequences of their wickedness if they choose to continue doing evil.

1 THUS saith the LORD; **Go down to the house** [*palace*] **of the king of Judah, and speak there this word,**

2 And say, **Hear the word of the LORD, O king of Judah,** that sittest upon the throne of David [*who occupies the office of king, once held by King David*], **thou, and thy servants, and thy people** that enter in by these gates:

3 Thus saith the LORD; **Execute ye judgment and righteousness** [*be fair and exercise righteousness in your reign as king*], and **deliver the spoiled out of the hand of the oppressor** [*redeem the oppressed*]: and **do no wrong,** do no violence to the stranger [*foreigners*], the fatherless [*orphans*], nor the widow,

neither shed innocent blood in this place.

4 For **if ye do this thing** indeed, then shall there enter in by the gates of this house kings sitting upon the throne of David, riding in chariots and on horses, he, and his servants, and his people [*in other words, if you do what is right, the nation of Judah will continue and will thrive*].

5 **But if ye will not** hear these words, I swear by myself, saith the LORD, that **this house shall become a desolation** [*the royal family will be destroyed, along with its subjects*].

> For verse 6, next, it is helpful to know that "Gilead" had the richest soil in Israel, and "Lebanon" had the highest mountain and the finest trees in the surrounding area. Remember that trees often represent people in Old Testament symbolism. The message seems to be that Israel was planted in the best gospel soil (the promised land) and its people (the covenant people) were to be the very best "trees." The Lord knows their potential, and the stewardship of the kings of Judah was to foster righteousness and loyalty to God among their citizens.

6 For thus saith the LORD unto the king's house of Judah; **Thou *art* Gilead unto me, *and* the head of Lebanon** [*you have the potential to be the very best*]: **yet surely** [*if you don't repent*] **I will make thee a wilderness** [*I will cut down all your "trees"*],

and cities *which* are not inhabited.

7 And I **will prepare destroyers against thee**, every one with his weapons: and they shall cut down thy choice cedars [*your people*], and cast *them* into the fire.

8 And **many nations shall pass by this city** [*travelers from many nations will see the ruins of Jerusalem*], and **they shall say every man to his neighbour,** Wherefore hath the LORD done thus unto this great city [*what did they do to deserve such destruction*]?

9 Then they shall **answer,** Because they have forsaken the covenant of the LORD their God, and worshipped other gods, and served them.

Verses 10-12, next, are a very specific prophecy, directed to Jehoahaz, who succeeded his righteous father, King Josiah. Josiah reigned from about 641 BC to 610 BC, when he died of a wound received in the Battle of Megiddo. His wicked son, Jehoahaz became the next king of Judah, and ruled for just three months. People were mourning King Josiah's death at the time of this prophecy.

10 ¶ **Weep ye not for the dead** [*King Josiah*], neither bemoan him: *but* **weep sore for him** [*Jehoahaz*] **that goeth away: for he shall return no more, nor see his native country.**

After just three months as king,

Jehoahaz was captured and taken away to Egypt where he died.

11 For **thus saith the LORD touching Shallum** [*Jehoahaz*] the son of Josiah king of Judah, **which reigned instead of** [*in the place of*] **Josiah his father,** which went forth out of this place; **He shall not return thither any more** [*will never return to Jerusalem*]:

12 But he shall die in the place [*Egypt*] whither they have led him captive, and shall see this land no more.

In verses 13-19, next, Jeremiah rebukes Jehoiakim, also a son of righteous King Josiah, for his tyranny and self-centeredness as king. He ruled from about 609 BC to 598 BC

13 ¶ **Woe unto him** [*Jehoiakim—see verse 18*] **that buildeth his house by unrighteousness,** and his chambers by wrong; *that* **useth his neighbour's service without wages, and giveth him not for his work;**

14 That saith, **I will build me a wide house** [*a large palace*] and large chambers, and cutteth him out windows; and *it is* cieled [*paneled*] with cedar, and painted with vermilion [*bright red to red orange*].

15 Shalt thou reign, because thou closest *thyself* in cedar? **did not thy father** [*righteous King Josiah*] eat and drink, and **do judgment and**

justice, *and* then *it was* well with him?

16 He judged the cause of the poor and needy [*he was a righteous judge over his people*]; then *it was* well *with him: was* not this to know me [*isn't this what the gospel is all about*]? saith the LORD.

17 But thine eyes and thine heart *are* not but for thy covetousness [*you are self-centered and greedy*], and for **to shed innocent blood** [*you are a murderer*], and for **oppression**, and for **violence**, to do *it*.

18 Therefore thus saith the LORD concerning Jehoiakim the son of Josiah king of Judah; **They shall not lament for him,** *saying,* Ah my brother! or, Ah sister! they shall not lament for him, *saying,* Ah lord! or, Ah his glory!

19 He shall be buried with the burial of an ass [*a phrase in Jeremiah's day which meant to be dumped in an open field without burial*], **drawn and cast forth beyond the gates of Jerusalem** [*when he dies his carcass will be treated like that of a dead donkey, dragged outside the city and dumped*].

The Jewish historian, Josephus, recorded that Nebuchadnezzar killed Jehoiakim and commanded that he be thrown out without a burial. (See *Antiquities of the Jews*, 10.6.3.)

Lebanon and Bashan, in verse 20, next, are a prophetic description of the route of the captives of Judah as they were taken to Babylon.

20 ¶ Go up to Lebanon, and cry; and **lift up thy voice in Bashan, and cry from the passages** [*as you pass through that country*]: **for all thy lovers** [*false gods with whom you have committed spiritual adultery*] **are destroyed.**

21 I spake unto thee in thy prosperity; *but* thou saidst, I will not hear [*I invited you to repent when you were prosperous, but you refused*]. This *hath* been thy manner from thy youth, that thou obeyedst not my voice [*you have been this way for a long time*].

22 The wind [*the hot, dry east wind, symbolic of destruction*] **shall eat up all thy pastors** [*your wicked leaders*], **and thy lovers** [*false gods; also, sexual immorality was rampant among the Jews at this time in their history*] **shall go into captivity:** surely then shalt thou be ashamed and confounded for all thy wickedness.

Verse 23, next, can best be understood if you know that the cedars of Lebanon were often used as symbols of prideful people, in the vocabulary of the day. Here they represent the proud, rebellious leaders of Judah.

23 O inhabitant of Lebanon

[*Judah's proud, haughty leaders*], that makest thy nest in the cedars [*whose lives are filled with pride*], **how gracious shalt thou be when pangs** [*the pains of Babylonian captivity*] **come upon thee,** the pain as of a woman in travail [*which are as unavoidable now for you as the pains of a woman in labor*]!

> Next, Jeremiah turns his attention to Jehoiachin, another wicked king of Judah, whose wicked reign lasted only a few months. He and his mother will be carried captive into Babylon (verses 26–27) and none of his posterity will ever sit on the throne of King David (verses 28–30).

24 *As* **I live, saith the LORD, though** [*even if*] **Coniah** [*Jehoiachin*] the son of Jehoiakim king of Judah **were the signet** [*the signet ring*] **upon my right hand, yet would I pluck thee thence** [*I would take you off and throw you to Babylon*];

25 And **I will give thee into the hand** of them that seek thy life, and into the hand *of them* whose face thou fearest, even into the hand **of Nebuchadrezzar** [*another spelling of "Nebuchadnezzar"—see Jeremiah 27:8*] **king of Babylon,** and into the hand of the Chaldeans [*the Babylonians*].

26 And **I will cast thee out, and thy mother that bare thee, into another country** [*Babylon*], where ye were not born; and **there shall ye die.**

27 **But to the land whereunto they desire to return** [*Jerusalem and the land of Judah*], **thither** [*there*] **shall they not return.**

> Next, as a technique for emphasizing what has already been said, several questions are asked by Jeremiah about Jehoiachin (Coniah).

28 *Is* **this man Coniah a despised broken idol** [*is he like a despicable broken idol*]? *is he* **a vessel wherein** *is* **no pleasure** [*is he an empty vessel*]? **Wherefore** [*why*] **are they cast out** [*of Jerusalem*], he and his seed [*his posterity*], and are cast **into a land which they know not?**

29 O earth, earth, earth [*everyone listen up*], hear the word of the LORD.

30 Thus saith the LORD, **Write ye this man childless** [*consider this man to be childless, as far as ever having a son who will rule as king in Jerusalem*], a man *that* shall not prosper in his days: for **no man of his seed shall prosper, sitting upon the throne of David,** and ruling any more in Judah.

JEREMIAH 23 ·

Selection: all verses

FOR US, PROBABLY the most significant thing about this chapter is that it contains a marvelous prophecy of the gathering of Israel in the last days (verses 3–8). We are part of the fulfillment of that prophecy. The most important aspect of the "gathering" for each of God's children is to be converted to the gospel of Jesus Christ, to be baptized, and then to remain faithful to all covenants made in the Church. In other words, the top priority of the "gathering of Israel" is to "gather" each one of us to Christ, if we are willing.

The rest of the chapter lists and describes the terrible sins of the Jewish religious leaders, including false priests and false prophets of Jeremiah's day.

Jeremiah begins with a powerful denunciation of the wicked religious leaders of his day. This rebuke can apply to any, including political leaders, media personalities, and individuals, who lead people away from the Lord at anytime.

1 WOE be unto the pastors [*false religious leaders*] **that destroy and scatter the sheep** [*Israel*] of my pasture! saith the LORD.

2 Therefore thus saith the LORD God of Israel against the pastors that feed my people; **Ye have scattered my flock, and driven them away,** and have not visited [*taken good care of*] them: behold, **I will**

visit upon you the evil of your doings [*you will be punished for the evil you have done*], saith the LORD.

Next, in verse 3, we see a great prophecy concerning the gathering of Israel in the last days.

3 And I will gather the remnant of my flock [*Israel*] **out of all countries whither I have driven them,** and will bring them again to their folds [*various lands*]; and they shall be fruitful and increase.

4 And I will set up shepherds [*righteous religious leaders*] **over them which shall feed them:** and they shall fear no more, nor be dismayed, neither shall they be lacking [*because they will have the true gospel of Jesus Christ*], saith the LORD.

Elder Bruce R. McConkie explained the gathering, spoken of in the above verses. He taught:

"The gathering of Israel consists of receiving the truth, gaining again a true knowledge of the Redeemer, and coming back into the true fold of the Good Shepherd. In the language of the Book of Mormon, it consists of being 'restored to the true church and fold of God,' and then being 'gathered' and 'established' in various 'lands of promise.'" (2 Ne. 9:2; "Come: Let Israel Build Zion," *Ensign*, May 1977, p. 117)

President Spencer W. Kimball also instructed us on this important topic.

"He (the Lord) said through

Nephi, 'The house of Israel (sooner or later will) be scattered upon all the face of the earth.' (1 Nephi 22:3) And now He says, 'I will gather the remnant of my flock out of all countries whither I have driven them.' (Jeremiah 23:3)

"The gathering of Israel is now in progress. Hundreds of thousands of people have been baptized into the Church. Millions more will join the Church. And this is the way that we will gather Israel. The English people will gather in England. The Japanese people will gather in the Orient. The Brazilian people will gather in Brazil. So that important element of the world history is already being accomplished.

"It is to be done by missionary work. It is your responsibility to attend to this missionary work." (In Conference Report, Sao Paulo Brazil Area Conference, Feb.–Mar. 1975, p. 73)

Verses 5-6, next, prophesy of the millennial reign of the Savior (see footnote 5d in your Bible).

5 ¶ Behold, the days come, saith the LORD, that I will raise unto David a righteous Branch [*Christ*], and **a King shall reign and prosper** [*Jesus Christ will rule during the Millennium as King of kings and Lord of lords*"—*see Revelation 117:14*], **and shall execute judgment and justice in the earth.**

6 In his days Judah shall be saved, and Israel shall dwell safely: and this *is* his name whereby he shall

be called, THE LORD OUR RIGHTEOUSNESS.

Verses 7-8, next, prophesy more about the gathering of Israel in the last days, leading up to the Millennium. At that time, the much-talked-about event will no longer be the miraculous deliverance of the children of Israel from Egypt. Rather, the "buzz" will be about missionary work and the exciting gathering of Israel in all nations and lands.

7 Therefore, behold, **the days come, saith the LORD, that they shall no more say, The LORD liveth, which brought up the children of Israel out of the land of Egypt;**

8 But, **The LORD liveth**, which brought up and **which led the seed of the house of Israel** [*the descendants of scattered Israel*] out of the north country, and **from all countries whither I had driven them; and they shall dwell in their own land.**

From here to the end of the chapter, the main message is the terrible damage done by dishonest and wicked leaders of false religions among the Jews of Jeremiah's day.

9 ¶ **Mine heart within me is broken because of the** [*false*] **prophets;** all my bones shake; I am like a drunken man, and like a man whom wine hath overcome, because of the LORD, and because of the words of his holiness [*perhaps meaning that*

Jeremiah is heartbroken and almost out of his mind because of what he knows about the true gospel in contrast to what the false prophets among the Jews are teaching].

10 For **the land is full of adulterers**; for because of swearing [*because of the curse of the Lord*] **the land mourneth**; the pleasant places of the wilderness are dried up, and **their course is evil, and their force is not right** [*their influence leads people astray*].

11 For **both** [*false*] **prophet and** [*false*] **priest are profane** [*are not religious themselves—see footnote 11c in your Bible*]; yea, **in my house** [*in the temple in Jerusalem*] **have I found their wickedness**, saith the LORD.

12 Wherefore [*therefore*] **their way** [*their evil course in life*] **shall be unto them as slippery ways** [*will become treacherous*] in the darkness [*spiritual darkness*]: **they shall** be driven on, and **fall therein**: for I will bring evil upon them, *even* **the year of their visitation** [*the time when the Lord's punishment catches up with them*], saith the LORD.

By now you are probably quite used to seeing repetition as a means of driving home a particular point or message in Jeremiah's writing. We will see much of this repetition for emphasis in the next several verses.

The reason we bring this up is that occasionally students of the Old Testament will begin to wonder if perhaps they are missing something as they read such repetitions. They have already caught the message and wonder if maybe the prophet isn't saying something else instead of repeating and they are missing it. They are not.

Verse 13, next appears to refer specifically to the false prophets among the northern ten tribes (who were led away captive by Assyria about 722 BC) who led Israel away from the worship of Jehovah into the worship of Baal.

13 And **I have seen folly** [*wickedness*] in **the prophets of Samaria** [*the former capital of the ten tribes (Israel)*]; **they prophesied in Baal, and caused my people Israel to err.**

14 I have seen also in the [*false*] **prophets of Jerusalem** an horrible thing: they **commit adultery**, and **walk in lies**: they strengthen also the hands of evildoers [*they support wickedness*], that none doth return from his wickedness: **they are all of them unto me as Sodom, and the inhabitants thereof as Gomorrah** [*they have become just like the residents of Sodom and Gomorrah*].

15 Therefore thus saith the LORD of hosts **concerning the** [*false*] **prophets; Behold, I will feed them with wormwood** [*a terribly bitter herb—see Bible Dictionary under*

"Wormwood"], **and make them drink the water of gall** [in other words, these false prophets will have a bitter fate]: for from the prophets of Jerusalem is profaneness [lack of being truly religious] gone forth into all the land.

> Next, we see a warning to avoid heeding the words of false prophets. Remember, "false prophets" can be anyone, including religious leaders, politicians, media personalities, philosophers, atheists, gang leaders, and friends whose influence tends to lead people away from God.

16 Thus saith the LORD of hosts, **Hearken not unto the words of the** [false] **prophets that prophesy unto you:** they make you vain [they make you miss the truth]: they speak a vision of their own heart [they teach their own beliefs], and not out of the mouth of the LORD.

17 **They say** still **unto them that despise me,** The LORD hath said, **Ye shall have peace;** and they say unto every one that walketh after the imagination of his own heart, No evil shall come upon you [in other words, they teach that you can have peace in wickedness].

18 For **who** [which of these false prophets] **hath stood in the counsel of the LORD, and hath perceived and heard his word?** who hath marked his word [in his heart and daily life],

and heard it [in other words, which of these false prophets and teachers has embraced the true gospel and is attempting to live it]?

19 Behold, **a whirlwind** of [destruction from] the LORD is gone forth in fury, even a grievous whirlwind: it **shall fall grievously upon the head of the wicked.**

20 **The anger of the LORD shall not return** [turn away], **until he have executed, and till he have performed the thoughts of his heart** [until the prophesied destruction takes place]: in the latter days [NIV: "in days to come"] ye shall consider [understand] it perfectly.

21 **I have not sent these** [false] **prophets,** yet they ran [took over quickly]: I have not spoken to them, yet they prophesied.

22 But **if they had stood in my counsel** [if they had understood and followed My counsel], and had caused my people to hear my words, **then they should have turned them from their evil way,** and from the evil of their doings.

23 Am I a God at hand, saith the LORD, and not a God afar off [perhaps meaning "Am I not a God who knows all things, near and far—see verse 24]?

24 **Can any hide himself** in secret places **that I shall not see him?** saith

the LORD. **Do not I fill heaven and earth?** saith the LORD.

25 I have heard what the [*false*] **prophets said, that prophesy lies in my name,** saying, I have dreamed, I have dreamed [*the false prophets claim to have had dreams from God*].

26 How long shall *this* **be in the heart of the prophets that prophesy lies?** yea, *they are* prophets of the deceit of their own heart [*they teach according to the deceitfulness in their own hearts*];

27 Which think to cause my people to forget my name by their dreams which they tell every man to his neighbour, as their fathers [*ancestors*] have forgotten my name for [*because of*] Baal.

28 The [*true*] **prophet that hath a dream, let him tell a dream; and he** [*true prophets, such as Jeremiah and Lehi*] **that hath my word, let him speak my word faithfully.** What is the chaff to the wheat [*what is the word of false prophets compared to the true word of God*]? saith the LORD.

The power of the true word of God to burn out false doctrines and destroy the false philosophies of men is described in verse 29, next. We often see this power of the word described in scriptures as a two-edged sword, able to cut in all directions through falsehood and deception.

29 *Is* **not my word like as a fire?** saith the LORD; and **like a hammer** *that* **breaketh the rock in pieces?**

30 Therefore, behold, I *am* **against the prophets,** saith the LORD, **that steal my words every one from his neighbour** [*in other words, against the false prophets who borrow lies and falsehoods from one another to teach their followers*].

31 Behold, I *am* **against the** [*false*] **prophets,** saith the LORD, **that use their tongues, and say, He saith** [*who claim to be teaching the will of God*].

32 Behold, I *am* **against them that prophesy false dreams,** saith the LORD, and do tell [*preach*] **them,** and **cause my people to err by their lies,** and **by their lightness** [*failure to take the true words of God seriously*]; yet **I sent them not,** nor commanded them: therefore they shall not profit this people at all, saith the LORD.

The word, "burden," as used in the context of the next verses, basically means "prophesy," especially "message of doom." Thus, the Lord is telling Jeremiah what to say when people sarcastically come up to him and ask him what the next message of doom for them from God is.

33 ¶ And when this people, or the [*false*] **prophet, or a** [*false*] **priest,**

shall ask thee, saying, **What** *is* **the burden of the LORD?** **thou shalt then say** unto them, What burden? **I will even forsake you, saith the LORD.**

34 And *as for* the prophet, and the priest, and the people, that shall say, The burden of the LORD, **I will even punish that man and his house.**

> Next, in verse 35, Jeremiah is instructed to tell the wicked to spread the word that the Lord will forsake them (verse 33) because of their willful failure to repent.

35 Thus shall ye say every one to his neighbour, and every one to his brother, What hath the LORD answered [*what was the Lord's answer to our question [verse 33]*]? and, What hath the LORD spoken?

36 And the burden of the LORD shall ye mention no more: for every man's word shall be his burden [*you don't need to talk about the fact that the Lord has forsaken you, because you yourselves are your own worst enemies*]; for **ye have perverted** [*twisted and corrupted*] **the words of the living God,** of the LORD of hosts our God.

37 Thus shalt thou say to the [*false*] **prophet,** What hath the LORD answered thee? and, **What hath the LORD spoken** [*what has the Lord revealed to you*]?

38 But **since ye say, The burden of the LORD; therefore thus saith the LORD** [*since you claim to speak for the Lord*]; Because ye say this word, The burden of the LORD, and I have sent unto you, saying, **Ye shall not say, The burden of the LORD;**

39 Therefore, behold, I, even I, will utterly forget you, and **I will forsake you, and the city** that I gave you and your fathers, *and cast you out of my presence:*

> The phrase "I will utterly forget you," in verse 39, above, does not mean that the Lord actually forgets the wicked. Of course, His memory is perfect. It means that He will withdraw His blessings from them and will bring punishments upon them.

40 And I will bring an everlasting reproach upon you [*you will be looked down upon by other nations*], and a perpetual shame, which shall not be forgotten.

JEREMIAH 24

Selection: all verses

ULTIMATELY, AS PROPHESIED by Jeremiah, the Jews were taken captive into Babylon (sometimes referred to in these scriptures as "Chaldea"). After about seventy years, a remnant of them was allowed to return to Jerusalem to rebuild it.

In this chapter, Jeremiah has a vision of "two baskets of figs" (verse 1), one good and one bad (verse 2). The good figs represent the remnant of the Jews who will be brought back to Jerusalem by the Lord (verses 5–6) after seventy years.

The bad figs represent wicked King Zedekiah and the evil leaders of the Jews as well as many of their people (verses 8–10).

Jeremiah's vision in verse 1 shows the actual captivity of Jerusalem and the carrying of the captives into Babylon (roughly the location of modern Iraq). This is an interactive vision, where Jeremiah is asked questions and gives answers (starting with verse 3). In a way, it reminds us of Nephi's vision, beginning with 1 Nephi, chapter 11, where he is asked many questions as to what he sees in his vision.

1 THE LORD shewed me, and, behold, two baskets of figs *were* set before the temple of the LORD, **after** that **Nebuchadrezzar king of Babylon had carried away captive** Jeconiah the son of Jehoiakim king of Judah, and the princes [*leaders*] of Judah, with the carpenters and smiths [*in other words, with the skilled craftsmen*], from Jerusalem, **and had brought them to Babylon.**

2 One basket *had* **very good figs,** *even* like the figs *that are* first ripe: **and the other basket** *had* **very naughty figs,** which could not be eaten, they were so bad.

3 Then said the LORD unto me, **What seest thou, Jeremiah?** And I said, Figs; the good figs, very good; and the evil, very evil, that cannot be eaten, they are so evil.

Next, the Lord explains the meaning of the two baskets of figs. One thing we learn from this vision is that there were some good people among the Jews who were taken captive. It was not just the wicked that suffered because of the corrupt leaders who were among the people at this time.

4 ¶ Again **the word of the LORD came unto me, saying,**

5 Thus saith the LORD, the God of Israel; **Like these good figs, so will I acknowledge them that are carried away captive of Judah,** whom I have sent out of this place into the land of the Chaldeans **for** *their* **good.**

6 For I will set mine eyes upon them **for good,** and **I will bring them again to this land** [*Jerusalem and the surrounding territory of Judah*]: **and I will build them** [*they will rebuild Jerusalem and the surrounding country*], and not pull *them* down; and **I will plant them, and not pluck** *them* **up.**

7 And **I will give them an heart to know me, that I** *am* **the LORD:** and **they shall be my people,** and I will be their God: for **they shall return unto me with their whole heart.**

8 ¶ And as **the evil figs**, which cannot be eaten, they are so evil; surely thus saith the LORD, So will I give **Zedekiah the king of Judah, and his princes, and the residue of Jerusalem**, that remain in this land [*who are left behind*], and them that dwell in the land of Egypt:

9 And **I will deliver them to be removed** [*scattered*] **into all the kingdoms of the earth** for *their* hurt, **to be a reproach and a proverb, a taunt and a curse** [*to be looked down upon and disparaged*], **in all places whither I shall drive them.**

10 And **I will send the sword, the famine**, and the **pestilence**, among them, **till they be consumed from off the land** [*the Holy Land*] that I gave unto them and to their fathers [*ancestors; the children of Israel whom Joshua led into the promised land*].

JEREMIAH 25

Selection: all verses

IN THIS CHAPTER, we learn that the captives of Judah will serve in Babylon for seventy years (verse 11). At the end of that time, Babylon will be conquered and will serve other kings and nations (verses 12–14). The Lord also has Jeremiah prophesy against all wicked nations, warning them that all who are wicked and do not repent will eventually be punished by the Lord (verses 15–29).

The last part of the chapter "prophetically leaps forward to the time of the battle of Armageddon" in the last days (see *Old Testament Student Manual*, page 246).

In verse 1, Jeremiah identifies the time of this prophecy as about 605 BC Be aware that almost all dates given in Old Testament chronology are approximations. Thus, you will see slight variations in dates given for specific events, depending on the sources used.

The first part of this prophecy is directed at the people of Judah.

1 THE **word that came to Jeremiah concerning all the people of Judah in the fourth year of Jehoiakim** [*about 605* B.C.] **the son of Josiah king of Judah, that** *was* **the first year of Nebuchadrezzar king of Babylon;**

2 **The which Jeremiah the prophet spake unto all the people of Judah, and to all the inhabitants of Jerusalem,** saying,

In verse 3, next, Jeremiah tells us when he was first called to be a prophet. Remember, as stated above, dates vary a bit, depending on the sources. Thus, we often see anywhere from 628 to 626 BC given for the beginning of Jeremiah's service as a prophet.

3 **From the thirteenth year of Josiah** [*about 628* B.C.—*see chronology chart in Bible Dictionary*] the

son of Amon king of Judah, even **unto this day,** that *is* the three and twentieth year [*the twenty-third year that I have been serving as a prophet*], **the word of the LORD hath come unto me, and I have spoken unto you,** rising early and speaking; **but ye have not hearkened.**

> Next, in verse 4, Jeremiah informs us that the Lord sent many prophets to the people of Judah, including Jerusalem, at this time in history. This is confirmed in the Book of Mormon. We read (**bold** added for emphasis):
>
> **1 Nephi 1:4**
> 4 For it came to pass in the commencement of the first year of the reign of Zedekiah, king of Judah, (my father, Lehi, having dwelt at Jerusalem in all his days); and **in that same year there came many prophets,** prophesying unto the people that they must repent, or the great city Jerusalem must be destroyed.
>
> Included in these "many prophets" were Jeremiah, Lehi, Nahum, Habakkuk, Zephaniah, and perhaps Ezekiel.

4 And the LORD hath sent unto you all his servants the prophets, rising early and sending *them* [*sending them way ahead of your pending destruction*]; **but ye have not hearkened, nor inclined your ear to hear.**

5 They [*the true prophets*] **said, Turn ye again now every one from his evil way,** and from the evil of your doings [*in other words, repent*], and dwell in the land that the LORD hath given unto you and to your fathers for ever and ever:

6 And **go not after other gods to** serve them, and to worship them, and provoke me not to anger with the works of your hands [*idols*]; and I will do you no hurt.

7 Yet **ye have not hearkened unto me, saith the LORD;** that ye might provoke me to anger with the works of your hands [*including idols*] to your own hurt [*you are damaging yourselves*].

8 ¶ Therefore thus saith the LORD of hosts; **Because ye have not heard my words,**

> In verse 9, next, we see an illustration of something Mormon taught. He said:
>
> **Mormon 4:5**
> 5 But, behold, the judgments of God will overtake the wicked; and **it is by the wicked that the wicked are punished;** for it is the wicked that stir up the hearts of the children of men unto bloodshed.
>
> This principle applies to Nebuchadnezzar (spelled "Nebuchadrezzar" here), the wicked king whom the Lord uses to punish the wicked people of Judah.

9 Behold, **I will send and take all the families of the north** [*in other words, I will bring hordes of enemies upon you, and they will come in from the north*], saith the LORD, **and Nebuchadrezzar the king of Babylon,** my servant [*the instrument of destruction which the Lord will use against Judah*], **and will bring them against this land, and against the inhabitants thereof,** and against all these nations round about [*the Babylonians will conquer and devastate many surrounding nations also*], **and will utterly destroy them, and make them an astonishment** [*objects of startled horror*], and an **hissing** [*objects of scorn*], and perpetual **desolations** [*leave in ruins*].

10 **Moreover** [*in addition*] **I will take from them** the voice of **mirth** [*lighthearted pleasantness*], and the voice of **gladness** [*happiness*], the voice of the **bridegroom,** and the voice of the **bride,** the sound of the **millstones** [*grinding grain; in other words, economic well-being*], and the **light of the candle** [*pleasant evenings*].

11 And **this whole land shall be a desolation,** *and* an astonishment; and **these nations shall serve the king of Babylon seventy years.**

> Next, Jeremiah tells us what will happen when the seventy years of captivity and servitude are over.

12 ¶ And it shall come to pass, **when seventy years are accomplished** [*are over*], *that* **I will punish the king of Babylon, and that nation,** saith the LORD, **for their iniquity** [*for their wickedness*], and the land of the Chaldeans [*another name for Babylonia, sometimes used to refer to southeastern Babylon, where Abraham came from—see Abraham 1:1*], and will make it perpetual desolations.

> Verse 12, above, is rather important because it clears up any confusion about the phrase "the king of Babylon, my servant," reminding us that "servant," in this context, means an instrument used by the Lord to accomplish His purposes.

13 And **I will bring upon that land all my words which I have pronounced against it,** *even* all that is written in this book, **which Jeremiah hath prophesied against all the nations.**

14 For many nations and great kings shall serve themselves of them also: and **I will recompense** [*punish*] **them according to their deeds,** and according to the works of their own hands [*all the wicked will eventually be punished (unless they repent when given ample opportunity to do so)*].

> The "cup of fury" is commonly used imagery to represent the anger of the Lord, in other words, the law of justice as it descends upon the unrepentant

wicked. We see this imagery next, in verses 15-17, as the Lord tells Jeremiah to give the wicked nations what they have asked for.

15 ¶ For **thus saith the LORD God of Israel unto me** [*Jeremiah*]; **Take the wine cup of this fury at my hand, and cause all the nations, to whom I send thee** [*to whom you are called to prophesy*], **to drink it** [*in effect, "give them the punishments they have asked for from Me and have them drink them in"*].

16 And **they shall drink** [*the Lord's punishments will come upon them*], **and be moved** [*will stagger*], **and be mad** [*will be out of their mind with anguish*], **because of the sword** [*symbolic of destruction*] that I will send among them.

Next, Jeremiah testifies that he has obeyed the Lord and carried out His instructions. He is a witness against the wickedness of the people to whom he preaches.

17 Then took I the cup at the LORD's hand [*the cup of fury (the punishments of the Lord upon the wicked)*], **and made all the nations to drink, unto whom the LORD had sent me:**

As indicated in our note at the beginning of verse 18, next, "to wit" means "namely." In other words, Jeremiah is now going to list several of the nations implicated in his prophecy of punishment and destruction. He starts

out by naming Jerusalem, and then goes on to name several other nations and peoples who will eventually drink the "fury" of the Lord.

18 *To wit* [*namely—see footnote 18a in your Bible*], **Jerusalem,** and **the cities of Judah, and the kings** thereof, and **the princes** [*political and religious leaders*] thereof, to make them a desolation, an astonishment, an hissing, and a curse; as *it is* this day;

As pointed out previously, "princes" is a word that generally means "leaders." You will see this use of the word quite often in your Old Testament study.

19 Pharaoh king of **Egypt**, and his servants, and his princes, and all his people;

20 And all the mingled people, and all the kings of the land of **Uz**, and all the kings of the land of the **Philistines, and Ashkelon,** and **Azzah,** and **Ekron,** and the remnant of **Ashdod,**

21 Edom, and **Moab,** and the **children of Ammon,**

22 And all the kings of **Tyrus** [*NIV: "Tyre"*], and all the kings of **Zidon,** and the kings of the **isles** [*other nations*] **which** *are* **beyond the sea,**

23 Dedan, and **Tema,** and **Buz,** and **all** *that are* **in the utmost corners,**

24 And all the kings of **Arabia,** and

all the kings of **the mingled people** [*foreigners*] **that dwell in the desert,**

25 And all the kings of **Zimri,** and all the kings of **Elam,** and all the kings of the **Medes,**

26 And **all the kings of the north,** far and near, one with another, and **all the kingdoms of the world,** which *are* **upon the face of the earth:** and the king of **Sheshach** [*NIV: "Babylon"—see also Jeremiah 51:41*] shall drink after them [*NIV: "will drink it too"*].

No doubt you noticed that Jeremiah did not leave out any of the wicked anywhere. The message is clear: It is impossible for the wicked, who chose not to repent when given ample opportunity to do so, to escape the punishments of God.

Next, the fact that all have agency to choose is emphasized. Just like a person can choose to get drunk and throw up (verse 27), so also can nations and people choose to get drunk, or out of control with wickedness, where they lurch and stagger from one form of evil to another, until they fall and are destroyed.

27 Therefore thou shalt say unto them, Thus saith the LORD of hosts, the God of Israel; **Drink ye, and be drunken** [*symbolic of wickedness; in other words, you have agency to choose to be out of control with wickedness*], and **spue** [*NIV: "vomit"*], and **fall,** and **rise no more,** because of the sword [*destruction*]

which I will send among you.

Verse 28, next, reminds us that it is impossible for the unrepentant wicked to avoid the law of justice.

28 And it shall be, **if they refuse to take the cup at thine hand to drink** [*if they think they can stop the punishments of God*], then shalt thou **say unto them,** Thus saith the LORD of hosts; **Ye shall certainly drink.**

29 For, lo, **I begin to bring evil on the city which is called by my name** [*I am beginning even now to punish the inhabitants of Jerusalem*], and **should ye be utterly unpunished? Ye shall not be unpunished:** for I will call for a sword upon all the inhabitants of the earth [*none of the wicked anywhere will ultimately escape their punishment*], saith the LORD of hosts.

As mentioned in the background to this chapter in this study guide, the final verses here seem to point to the last days and eventually to the Battle of Armageddon. Evil and wickedness will spread throughout the earth, and nations will gather in a concerted effort against the work of the Lord and His people.

30 Therefore prophesy thou against them [*the wicked*] **all these words,** and say unto them, **The LORD shall roar** [*everyone will hear it; "roar" can also symbolize the destructive power of a lion when it falls upon its prey, as* mentioned in verse 38, below] from on high, and **utter his voice** from his holy habitation; he shall mightily roar upon his habitation; he shall give a shout, as they that tread *the grapes,* **against all the inhabitants of the earth.**

The imagery in the phrase "tread the grapes" in verse 30, above, can symbolize the destruction of the wicked. This symbolism is also used to represent the destruction of the wicked at the time of the Second Coming. The red on the Savior's clothing symbolizes the blood of the wicked as they are destroyed at His coming. We will quote from the Doctrine and Covenants:

Doctrine & Covenants 133:48–51
48 And **the Lord shall be red in his apparel,** and his garments **like him that treadeth in the wine-vat.**
49 And so great shall be the glory of his presence that the sun shall hide his face in shame, and the moon shall withhold its light, and the stars shall be hurled from their places.
50 And his voice shall be heard: I have trodden the wine–press alone, and have brought judgment upon all people; and none were with me;
51 And **I have trampled them** [*the wicked*] **in my fury,** and I did tread upon them in mine anger, and **their blood have I sprinkled upon my garments, and stained all my raiment** [*the blood of the wicked*

is symbolically spattered upon the Savior's clothing, dying it red]; for this was the day of vengeance which was in my heart [this was the execution of the law of justice, which is in His heart as a vital part of the Plan of Salvation].

31 A noise shall come *even* **to the ends of the earth;** for the LORD hath a controversy with the nations, he will **plead** with all flesh [*in effect,* "He will bring all people to His court of law]; **he will give them** *that are* **wicked to the sword,** saith the LORD.

32 Thus saith the LORD of hosts, Behold, **evil shall go forth from nation to nation,** and a great whirlwind shall be raised up from the coasts of the earth.

33 And **the slain of the LORD** [*the wicked who are destroyed*] **shall be at that day from** *one* **end of the earth even unto the** *other* end of the earth: they shall not be lamented, neither gathered, nor buried; they shall be dung upon the ground.

Next, Jeremiah targets the wicked leaders throughout the earth who lead the people astray.

34 ¶ Howl, ye shepherds, and cry; and **wallow yourselves** *in the ashes* [*a sign of great anguish and mourning in the culture of Jeremiah's day*], ye principal [*leaders*] of the flock: for the days of your slaughter and of your dispersions are accomplished [*the time for you to be punished has arrived*]; and ye shall fall like a pleasant vessel [*you will be shattered like fine pottery*].

35 And the shepherds shall have no way to flee, nor the principal of the flock to escape [*there is no escaping the Lord's punishments for you*].

> As you have no doubt noticed, Jeremiah is definitely using the technique of repetition for emphasis here.

36 A voice of **the cry of the shepherds** [*the anguish of the evil leaders*], and an **howling of the principal** [*leaders*] of the flock, *shall be heard:* **for the LORD hath spoiled their pasture.**

37 And **the peaceable habitations** [*the pleasant living conditions*] **are cut down because of the fierce anger of the LORD.**

38 He [*the Lord*] **hath forsaken his covert, as the lion** [*He has come out of hiding like a lion*]: for **their land is desolate** because of the fierceness of the oppressor, and because of his fierce anger.

JEREMIAH 26

Selection: all verses

IT IS HELPFUL to understand that the book of Jeremiah is not all arranged in chronological order. For example, chapter 25 fits in the fourth year of the reign of King Jehoiakim (see Jeremiah 25:1), whereas chapter 26 fits chronologically in the first year of his reign as king (see verse 1, next).

The JST makes important changes to seven verses in this chapter (verses 3, 5, 6, 13, 18, 19, and 20). We will include the JST text for each of these verses as we go along.

You have seen several prophecies about the destruction of Jerusalem so far in Jeremiah, and this chapter contains that same message. After he delivers this prophecy, Jeremiah will be arrested (verse 8) and tried in court for his life. The scene reminds us of Abinadi the prophet, arrested and tried in wicked King Noah's court because of the things he prophesied against the king and the people (Mosiah 12:9).

1 IN the beginning of the reign of Jehoiakim [*about 609 B.C.*] the son of Josiah king of Judah **came this word from the LORD** [*to Jeremiah*], saying,

2 Thus saith the LORD; Stand in the court of the LORD's house [*the outer courtyard of the temple in Jerusalem*], and **speak unto all the cities of Judah,** which come to worship in the LORD's house, **all**

the words that I command thee to speak unto them; diminish not a word [don't leave out a thing]:

> Verse 3, next, contains an invitation to the people to repent. And the JST makes an important correction, showing that it is the people who need to repent, not the Lord.

3 If so be they will hearken, and turn every man from his evil way [if they will repent], that I may repent me of the evil, which I purpose to do unto them because of the evil of their doings.

JST Jeremiah 26:3
3 If so be they will hearken, and turn every man from his evil way, **and repent, I will turn away the evil** which I purpose to do unto them because of the evil of their doings.

4 And thou shalt say unto them, Thus saith the LORD; **If ye will not hearken to me, to walk in my law,** which I have set before you,

5 To hearken to the words of my servants the prophets, whom I sent unto you, both rising up early, and sending *them*, **but ye have not hearkened;**

JST Jeremiah 26:5
5 To hearken to the words of my servants, the prophets, whom I sent unto you, **commanding them to rise up early**, and sending them;

In order to understand the comparison between the temple in Jerusalem and Shiloh, in verse 6, next, it helps to know that Shiloh (about twenty miles northeast of Jerusalem) was the final resting place for the tabernacle after the children of Israel settled in the promised land. Due to the eventual wickedness of the Israelites, the Lord allowed the Philistines to desecrate the tabernacle and destroy it. So also will the Lord allow the Babylonians to destroy the Jerusalem Temple and ravish Jerusalem.

6 Then will I make this house [*the temple in Jerusalem*] **like Shiloh, and will make this city a curse** to all the nations of the earth.

> The JST adds an important phrase to verse 6, above.

JST Jeremiah 26:6
6 Then will I make this house like Shiloh, and will make this city a curse to all the nations of the earth; **for ye have not hearkened unto my servants the prophets.**

7 So the priests and the prophets and all the people heard Jeremiah speaking these words in the house of the LORD.

8 ¶ Now it came to pass, **when Jeremiah had made an end of speaking** all that the LORD had commanded *him* to speak unto all the people, that **the priests and the** [*false*] **prophets and all the people**

took him [arrested him], saying, Thou shalt surely die.

9 Why hast thou prophesied in the name of the LORD, saying, This house shall be like Shiloh, and this city shall be desolate without an inhabitant? And all the people were gathered against Jeremiah in the house of the LORD.

> Next, beginning with verse 10, we see that a court was convened to try Jeremiah. The trial was held near the temple in a public place where large crowds could watch the proceedings.

10 ¶ When the princes [leaders] of Judah heard these things, then they came up from the king's house unto the house of the LORD, and sat down in the entry of the new gate of the LORD's house.

11 Then spake the priests and the prophets unto the princes and to all the people, saying, This man is worthy to die; for he hath prophesied against this city, as ye have heard with your ears.

12 ¶ Then spake Jeremiah unto all the princes and to all the people, saying, The LORD sent me to prophesy against this house and against this city all the words that ye have heard.

13 Therefore now amend your ways and your doings [in other words, repent], and obey the voice

of the LORD your God; and the LORD will repent [see JST changes, next] him of the evil that he hath pronounced against you.

JST Jeremiah 26:13
13 Therefore now, amend your ways and your doings, and obey the voice of the Lord your God, and repent, and the Lord will turn away the evil that he hath pronounced against you.

14 As for me, behold, I am in your hand: do with me as seemeth good and meet [appropriate] unto you.

15 But know ye for certain, that if ye put me to death, ye shall surely bring innocent blood upon yourselves, and upon this city, and upon the inhabitants thereof: for of a truth the LORD hath sent me unto you to speak all these words in your ears [compare with Abinadi's words in Mosiah 17:9–10].

> Next, we see that controversy arose concerning what to do with Jeremiah.

16 ¶ Then said the princes and all the people unto the [false] priests and to the [false] prophets; This man is not worthy to die: for he hath spoken to us in the name of the LORD our God.

17 Then rose up certain of the elders [older, wiser men] of the land, and spake to all the assembly of the people, saying,

18 Micah the Morasthite **prophesied** [see Micah, chapter 1] in the days of Hezekiah king of Judah, and spake to all the people of Judah, saying, Thus saith the LORD of hosts; **Zion shall be plowed like a field, and Jerusalem shall become heaps**, and the mountain of **the house** [Temple] as the high places of **a forest.**

JST Jeremiah 26:18
18 Micah the Morasthite prophesied in the days of Hezekiah king of Judah, and spake to all the people of Judah, saying, Thus saith the Lord of hosts; Zion shall be ploughed like a field, and Jerusalem shall become heaps, and the mountain of the house **of the Lord** as the high places of a forest.

19 Did Hezekiah king of Judah and all Judah put him at all to death [did they even come close to putting Micah to death for what he prophesied]? did he not fear the LORD, and besought the LORD, and the LORD repented him of the evil which he had pronounced against them? Thus might we procure great evil against our souls [we could lose our souls if we execute Jeremiah].

JST Jeremiah 26:19
19 Did Hezekiah, king of Judah, and all Judah put him at all to death? Did he not fear the Lord and beseech the Lord and repent? **and the Lord**

turned away the evil which he had pronounced against them. **Thus by putting Jeremiah to death** we might procure great evil against our souls.

Next, in verses 20–24, we catch a glimpse of how wicked King Jehoiakim was and thus understand that Jeremiah's life was indeed in danger. In these verses, a case from the past is brought up at Jeremiah's trial, detailing what had happened to Urijah, one of the Lord's prophets who had previously prophesied against the King and his wicked people.

20 And **there was also a man** that prophesied in the name of the LORD, **Urijah** the son of Shemaiah of Kirjath-jearim, **who prophesied against this city** and against this land according to all the words of Jeremiah [just like Jeremiah has done]:

You will see many changes made here by the Prophet Joseph Smith.

JST Jeremiah 26:20
20 But there was a man among the priests, rose up and said, that, Urijah the son of Shemaiah of Kirjath-jearim, prophesied in the name of the Lord, who also prophesied against this city, and against this land, according to all the words of Jeremiah;

21 And when Jehoiakim the king, with all his mighty men, and all the princes, heard his words, the king sought to put him to death: but when **Urijah** heard it, he was afraid, and **fled**, and went **into Egypt;**

22 And Jehoiakim the king sent men into Egypt, *namely,* Elnathan the son of Achbor, and *certain* men with him into Egypt.

23 And they fetched forth Urijah out of Egypt, and brought him unto Jehoiakim the king; who slew him with the sword [*King Jehoiakim personally killed Urijah*], **and cast his dead body into the graves of the common people.**

> The implication in verse 24, next, is that the officials of the court tried to turn Jeremiah over to the people to take him and kill him. But a man by the name of Ahikam protected him and saved his life. We will probably have to wait until we pass through the veil to get the rest of this story.

24 Nevertheless the hand of **Ahikam** the son of Shaphan **was with Jeremiah, that they should not give him into the hand of the people to put him to death.**

JEREMIAH 27

Selection: all verses

IN THIS CHAPTER, we see clearly that Judah is not the only nation that will be conquered by the coming armies of King Nebuchadnezzar of Babylon. We saw this same basic message in chapter 25.

As the Lord sends Jeremiah to deliver this message, He instructs him to use visual aids to help get the message across.

There appears to be a contradiction within the chapter as to when this prophecy was given. Verse 1 indicates that it came at the beginning of Jehoiakim's reign, but verses 3 and 12 suggest that it was given during King Zedekiah's reign several years later. We will quote from the *Old Testament Student Manual* for some helpful background.

"Ambassadors from several neighboring countries had come to Zedekiah with the proposal that unitedly they could defeat Babylon. **Jeremiah was instructed to take bonds and yokes and wear them to symbolize that it was the Lord's will that they submit to their would-be conquerors.** The message that they not try to change the decrees of God was also given by Jeremiah. Their lands were assigned to Babylon until that country ripened in iniquity and reaped its own reward. A specific promise to Judah was given in verse 11 that submission was their only hope of retaining their lands" (*Old Testament Student Manual*, page 247).

1 IN the beginning of the reign of Jehoiakim the son of Josiah [*should say "Zedekiah the son of Josiah"—see verse 3; also NIV, Jeremiah 27:1; this is probably an error made by a scribe somewhere along the way*] king of Judah came this **word unto Jeremiah from the LORD, saying,**

Can you imagine how unpopular Jeremiah's message of surrender was, which he gives in the next verses? He would be viewed as a coward and as a traitor.

2 Thus saith the LORD to me; **Make thee bonds and yokes, and put them upon thy neck** [*in other words, the Lord says for you to prepare to surrender*],

3 And send them to the king of Edom, and to the king of **Moab,** and to the king of the **Ammonites,** and to the king of **Tyrus** [*Tyre*], and to the king of **Zidon,** by the hand of the messengers [*the ambassadors*] which come to Jerusalem unto Zedekiah king of Judah;

4 And **command them to say unto their masters, Thus saith the LORD** of hosts, the God of Israel; Thus shall ye say unto your masters;

5 I have made the earth, the man and the beast that *are* upon the ground, by my great power and by my outstretched arm, **and have given it unto whom it seemed meet** [*good, appropriate*] unto me.

6 And **now have I given all these lands into the hand of Nebuchadnezzar the king of Babylon,** my servant [*an instrument temporarily in the hands of the Lord through whom to accomplish His*

purposes]; and the beasts of the field have I given him also to serve him.

7 And all [*these*] **nations shall serve him, and his son, and his son's son, until the very time of his land** [*JST "of their end"*] **come:** and then many nations [*JST "and after that many nations"*] and great kings shall serve themselves of him [*will conquer him and be served by him*].

8 And it shall come to pass, *that* **the nation and kingdom which will not serve** the same **Nebuchadnezzar** the **king of Babylon,** and **that will not put their neck under the yoke of the king of Babylon** [*those who will not surrender to him*], **that nation will I punish,** saith the LORD, with the sword, and with the famine, and with the pestilence, until I have consumed them by his hand.

When we combine verse 9, next, with verse 14, below, we come up with one scriptural definition of the term "false prophets."

9 Therefore **hearken not ye to your** [*false*] **prophets,** nor to your **diviners** [*fortune tellers who predict the future*], nor to your **dreamers,** nor to your **enchanters,** nor to your **sorcerers, which speak** unto you, **saying, Ye shall not serve the king of Babylon** [*who prophesy to you, saying that you will not come into bondage to Babylon*]:

10 For they **prophesy a lie unto**

you, to remove you far from your land; and that I should drive you out, and ye should perish.

11 But the nations that bring their neck under the yoke of [*voluntarily surrender to*] **the king of Babylon, and serve him, those will I let remain still in their own land, saith the LORD; and they shall till it, and dwell therein.**

Next, in verses 12–15, Jeremiah tells us that he personally delivered this message of surrender to King Zedekiah.

12 ¶ I spake also to Zedekiah king of Judah according to all these words, **saying, Bring your necks under the yoke of the king of Babylon, and serve him and his people, and live.**

13 Why will ye die, thou and thy people, by the sword, by the famine, and by the pestilence, **as the LORD hath spoken against the nation that will not serve the king of Babylon?**

14 Therefore hearken not unto the words of the [*false*] **prophets** [*such as those described in verse 9, above*] **that speak** unto you, **saying, Ye shall not serve** [*you will not come into bondage to*] **the king of Babylon: for they prophesy a lie** unto you.

15 For I have not sent them, saith the LORD [*in other words, they are*

false prophets], yet **they prophesy a lie in my name;** that I might drive you out, and that ye might perish, ye, and the prophets that prophesy unto you.

Next, Jeremiah reports that he has also delivered this same message to the false priests and to the people.

16 Also I spake to the priests and to all this people, saying, Thus saith the LORD; **Hearken not to the words of your** [*false*] **prophets** that prophesy unto you, saying, Behold, the vessels of the LORD's house shall now shortly be brought again from Babylon: **for they prophesy a lie unto you.**

Apparently, according to verse 16, above, some of the false prophets had told the people that the furnishings and adornments of the temple in Jerusalem would be taken to Babylon but would be returned to Jerusalem shortly thereafter.

17 Hearken not unto them; serve [*surrender to*] **the king of Babylon, and live:** wherefore should this city be laid waste?

Next, Jeremiah issues a challenge to the people to test their false prophets as to whether or not they are sent from God.

18 But if they *be* **prophets, and** if the word of the LORD be with them, **let them now make intercession to the LORD of hosts** [*let them use their influence with the true*

God], **that the vessels** [*the treasures*] which are left in the house of the LORD, and *in* the house of the king of Judah, and at Jerusalem, **go not to Babylon.**

Perhaps you sensed from the above verses that some of the Jews have already been taken to Babylon by this time. This is indeed the case. The conquest came in waves. For example, Daniel was taken to Babylon with many others in about 606 BC (see verse 20, below). The temple had not yet been completely looted, as indicated in verses 19–20, next.

19 ¶ For thus saith the LORD of hosts concerning the **pillars** [*of brass—see 2 Kings 25:13*], and concerning the **sea** [*the brass basin*], and concerning the **bases** [*stands*], and concerning the **residue of the vessels** [*furnishings, etc.*] that **remain in this city** [*Jerusalem*],

20 **Which Nebuchadnezzar king of Babylon took not, when he carried away captive Jeconiah** the son of Jehoiakim king of Judah from Jerusalem to Babylon, **and all the nobles of Judah and Jerusalem;**

We get a bit more information about the above-indicated wave of conquest from Daniel, which took place about 606 BC, including a definition of "the nobles of Judah" (verse 20, above).

Daniel 1:1–6

1 IN the third year of the reign of Jehoiakim king of Judah

came Nebuchadnezzar king of Babylon unto Jerusalem, and besieged it.

2 And the Lord gave Jehoiakim king of Judah into his hand, with **part of the vessels of the house of God:** which he carried into the land of Shinar [*Babylon*] to the house of his god; and he brought the vessels into the treasure house of his god.

3 ℂ And the king spake unto Ashpenaz the master of his eunuchs, that he should **bring** *certain* **of the children of Israel, and of the king's seed, and of the princes;**

4 **Children** in whom *was* no **blemish, but well favoured, and skilful in all wisdom, and cunning in knowledge, and understanding science, and such as** *had* **ability in them** to stand in the king's palace, and **whom they might teach the learning and the tongue of the Chaldeans.**

5 And the king appointed them a daily provision of the king's meat, and of the wine which he drank: so nourishing them three years, that at the end thereof they might stand before the king.

6 Now **among these were** of the children of Judah, **Daniel, Hananiah, Mishael, and Azariah** [*Shadrach, Meshach, and Abednego—see Daniel 3:12*]:

21 Yea, **thus saith the LORD of hosts, the God of Israel, concerning**

the vessels that remain *in* the house of the LORD, and *in* the house of the king of Judah and of Jerusalem;

22 They shall be carried to Babylon, and there shall they be until the day that I visit them [*bring the Jews back to Jerusalem, in about seventy years*], saith the LORD; then will I bring them up, and restore them to this place [*treasures will be brought back to Jerusalem*].

JEREMIAH 28

Selection: all verses

IN THIS CHAPTER we see Hananiah, a false prophet, go head-to-head with Jeremiah. It gets rather dramatic as Hananiah breaks the yoke (symbolic of slavery and forced labor—see Jeremiah 27:2) off of Jeremiah's neck and shoulders. In so doing, Hananiah emphasized his prophecy that those of Judah who had already been taken to Babylon would be back within two years, rather than in seventy years, as Jeremiah had prophesied (see Jeremiah 25:11).

Hananiah chooses a very public place to make his claim and challenge Jeremiah (verse 1). Let's see what happens.

1 AND it came to pass the same year, **in the beginning of the reign of Zedekiah** king of Judah, in the fourth year, *and* in the fifth month, *that* **Hananiah** the son of Azur the prophet, which *was* of Gibeon,

spake unto me [*Jeremiah*] in the house of the LORD, **in the presence of the priests and of all the people,** saying,

2 Thus speaketh the LORD of hosts, the God of Israel, saying, **I have broken the yoke of the king of Babylon.**

3 **Within two full years** will I bring again into this place **all the vessels** of the LORD's house, **that Nebuchadnezzar king of Babylon took away from this place,** and carried them to Babylon:

4 And **I will bring again to this place** Jeconiah the son of Jehoiakim king of Judah, **with all the captives of Judah,** that went into Babylon, saith the LORD: for **I will break the yoke** [*power*] **of the king of Babylon.**

Imagine the exited anticipation among the onlookers as Jeremiah responded to Hananiah's challenge.

5 ¶ **Then the prophet Jeremiah said unto the** [*false*] **prophet Hananiah** in the presence of the priests, and in the presence of all the people that stood in the house of the LORD,

6 Even the prophet **Jeremiah said, Amen: the LORD do so: the LORD perform thy words which thou hast prophesied,** to bring again the vessels of the LORD's house, and

all that is carried away captive, from Babylon into this place.

Did Jeremiah's response, above, catch you a little off guard? It might appear that he is giving in and agreeing with Hananiah, in front of the crowds of people. But he is not. The following quote helps us understand what is going on:

"In verse 6, **Jeremiah's 'Amen, the Lord do so,' is sarcastic**, a challenge to see whose prophecies would be fulfilled. Moses taught that one test of a true prophet is whether his words come to pass (see Deuteronomy 18:22). Jeremiah had prophesied destruction and captivity; Hananiah, return and restoration. Jeremiah's response was simply that the prophet whose words come to pass is the one chosen by the Lord (see verse 9)" (*Old Testament Student Manual*, page 247).

7 Nevertheless **hear thou now this word that I** [*Jeremiah*] **speak** in thine ears, and in the ears of all the people;

Next, Jeremiah points out that many true prophets of old have prophesied misery and destruction against wicked nations.

8 The **prophets** that have been before me and before thee **of old prophesied both against many countries, and against great kingdoms**, of war, and of evil, and of pestilence.

As mentioned above, the test of a true prophet is whether or

not his prophecies come true. Jeremiah points this out, next, in verse 9.

9 The prophet which prophesieth of peace, **when the word of the prophet shall come to pass,** *then* shall the prophet be known, that **the LORD hath truly sent him.**

Not yet satisfied, Hananiah next removes the wooden yoke, which Jeremiah is wearing around his neck (to symbolize the coming Babylonian captivity of the Jews and other nations), and breaks it in front of the crowd.

10 ¶ Then Hananiah the prophet took the yoke from off the prophet Jeremiah's neck, and brake it.

11 And Hananiah spake in the presence of all the people, saying, **Thus saith the LORD; Even so will I break the yoke of Nebuchadnezzar** king of Babylon from the neck of all nations **within the space of two full years.** And the prophet **Jeremiah went his way.**

12 ¶ Then the word of the LORD came unto Jeremiah *the prophet*, after that Hananiah the prophet had broken the yoke from off the neck of the prophet Jeremiah, saying,

13 Go and tell Hananiah, saying, Thus saith the LORD; **Thou hast broken the yokes of wood; but thou shalt make for them** [*in their*

place] **yokes of iron** [*in other words, the yokes of wood will be replaced with yokes of iron*].

14 For **thus saith the LORD** of hosts, the God of Israel; **I have put a yoke of iron** [*symbolizing something they cannot get away from*] **upon the neck of all these nations** [*some of whom are mentioned in Jeremiah 27:3*], **that they may serve Nebuchadnezzar** king of Babylon; **and they shall serve him** [*the emphasis is on "shall" as the Lord bears His own witness that this prophecy will come true*]: and I have given him the beasts of the field also.

15 ¶ Then said the prophet Jeremiah unto Hananiah the [*false*] **prophet, Hear now, Hananiah; The LORD hath not sent thee** [*you are not a true prophet*]; **but thou makest this people to trust in a lie.**

16 Therefore thus saith the LORD; Behold, I will cast thee from off the face of the earth: **this year thou shalt die,** because thou hast taught rebellion against the LORD.

17 So Hananiah the [*false*] **prophet died the same year in the seventh month.**

JEREMIAH 29

Selection: all verses

THIS CHAPTER CON-TAINS the words of a letter (see verse 1) that Jeremiah sent to the captives who had already been taken to Babylon (see note following Jeremiah 27:18 in this study guide), attempting to counteract the words of false prophets among the Jews there. He tells them not to fight against their captivity, rather to build homes, plant gardens, marry, raise families, support the Babylonians, pray for the Babylonians, and, in short, to prepare for many years in Babylon. The following quote sets the stage for understanding this chapter:

"As in Jerusalem, so too in Babylon the predictions of the false prophets fostered a lively hope that the domination of Nebuchadnezzar would not last long, and that the return of the exiles to their fatherland would soon come about. The spirit of discontent thus excited must have exercised an injurious influence on the fortunes of the captives, and could not fail to frustrate the aim which the chastisement inflicted by God was designed to work out, namely, the moral advancement of the people. Therefore Jeremiah makes use of an opportunity furnished by an embassy (ambassador) sent by King Zedekiah to Babel, to address a letter to the exiles, exhorting them to yield with submission to the lot God had assigned to them. He counsels them to prepare, by establishing their households there, for a long sojourn in Babel (Babylon), and to seek the welfare of that country as the necessary condition of their own. They must not let themselves be deceived by the false prophets' idle promises of a speedy return, since God will not bring them back and fulfil His glorious promises till after seventy years have passed (verses 4–14)" (C. F. Keil and F. Delitzsch, *Commentary on the Old Testament*, 8:1:408–9).

1 NOW **these** *are* **the words of the letter that Jeremiah the prophet sent from Jerusalem** unto the residue of the elders which were carried away captives, and to the priests, and to the prophets, and **to all the people whom Nebuchadnezzar had carried away captive from Jerusalem to Babylon** [*in the first wave or two of captives already taken to Babylon*];

Verse 1, above, will continue after a rather long parentheses (verse 2) and then yet another implied parentheses (verse 3). The last word of verse 3 continues, in effect, the substance of verse 1.

Verse 2, next, points out the common practice of first taking captives who were highly educated and capable of learning new languages and customs, skilled craftsmen, and so forth, in the initial waves of conquering a foreign country. This usually included those of the royal family, leaving a puppet king behind. In other words, they first carried off into captivity those who could make a significant contribution to the Babylonian economy.

2 (After that Jeconiah the king, and the queen, and the eunuchs, the princes of Judah and Jerusalem, and the carpenters, and the smiths, were departed from Jerusalem;)

3 By the hand of Elasah the son of Shaphan, and Gemariah the son of Hilkiah, (whom Zedekiah king of Judah sent unto Babylon to Nebuchadnezzar king of Babylon) saying,

4 Thus saith the LORD of hosts, the God of Israel, **unto all that are carried away captives,** whom I have caused to be carried away **from Jerusalem unto Babylon;**

5 Build ye houses [*prepare for many years (seventy years—see verse 10) in Babylonian captivity*], and dwell *in* them; and **plant gardens,** and eat the fruit of them;

6 Take ye wives, and **beget sons and daughters;** and **take wives for your sons,** and **give your daughters to husbands,** that they may bear sons and daughters; **that ye may be increased there** [*in Babylon*], and not diminished [*so that you do not die out as a people in captivity*].

7 And **seek the peace of the city** [*do things that contribute to the well-being of Babylon*] whither I have caused you to be carried away captives, and pray unto the LORD for it: **for in the peace thereof shall ye have peace**

[if the Babylonians have peace, you will have peace].

Next, Jeremiah warns the captives not to listen to the false doctrines and messages of false prophets among them. By the way, there were also true prophets among the captives, such as Daniel (see Daniel 1:1–6) and Ezekiel (see Ezekiel 1:1–3).

8 ¶ For thus saith the LORD of hosts, the God of Israel; Let not your [false] prophets and your diviners [soothsayers, fortune tellers, and the like], that be in the midst of you, deceive you, neither hearken to your dreams which ye cause to be dreamed [perhaps meaning don't give credibility to dreams which you dream in which you see yourselves free and back in Jerusalem].

9 For they [the false prophets among you] prophesy falsely unto you in my name: I have not sent them, saith the LORD.

10 ¶ For thus saith the LORD, That after seventy years be accomplished at Babylon I will visit [bless you] you, and perform my good word toward you, in causing you to return to this place [Jerusalem].

Verses 11–14, next, contain very tender and encouraging words of prophecy to the Jews who find themselves in Babylonian captivity at this time. They describe what will happen to the Jews after the seventy years in captivity.

11 For I know the thoughts that I think toward you, saith the LORD, thoughts of peace, and not of evil, to give you an expected end [freedom in Jerusalem again].

12 Then shall ye call upon me, and ye shall go and pray unto me, and I will hearken unto you.

13 And ye shall seek me, and find me, when ye shall search for me with all your heart.

14 And I will be found of you [and I will be available for you to find], saith the LORD: and I will turn away your captivity, and I will gather you from all the nations, and from all the places whither I have driven you, saith the LORD; and I will bring you again into the place [Jerusalem and Judah] whence I caused you to be carried away captive.

The prophets referred to in verse 15, next, are false prophets. Jeremiah counsels the captives about such deceivers and warns them not to follow them. Verses 15–19 prophetically inform the captives what is yet to happen to those Jews who are still at home in Jerusalem and Judah.

15 ¶ Because ye have said [claimed], The LORD hath raised us up prophets in Babylon [who are preaching lies to them, telling them that they will soon rejoin their friends and relatives back in Jerusalem];

16 Know that thus saith the LORD

of [*concerning*] **the king** that sitteth upon the throne of David [*the puppet king in Jerusalem*], **and of** [*about*] **all the people that dwelleth in this city,** *and* **of** [*about*] **your brethren that are not gone forth with you into captivity;**

17 Thus saith the LORD of hosts; Behold, **I will send upon them the sword,** the **famine,** and the **pestilence,** and will make them like vile figs [*that one throws away*], that cannot be eaten, they are so evil.

18 And **I will persecute them with the sword,** with the **famine,** and with the **pestilence,** and will deliver them to be **removed** [*scattered*] **to all the kingdoms of the earth,** to be a curse, and an astonishment, and an hissing, and a reproach [*to be disparaged and spoken of with contempt*], **among all the nations whither I have driven them:**

Verse 19, next, makes it sound like the Lord rises up early (which might falsely imply that, as a glorified, resurrected being, He still needs sleep). The JST straightens this out for us.

19 Because they have not hearkened to my words, saith the LORD, which I sent unto them by my servants the prophets, **rising up early and sending** *them*; but ye would not hear, saith the LORD.

<u>JST Jeremiah 29:19</u>

19 Because they have not hearkened to my words, saith the Lord, which I sent unto them by my servants the prophets, **commanding them to rise early, and sending them**; but ye would not hear, saith the Lord.

Next, Jeremiah warns specifically of two false prophets among the captives, one by the name of Ahab and one by the name of Zedekiah (both in verse 21).

20 ¶ Hear ye therefore the word of the LORD, **all ye of the captivity** [*all of you in Babylonian captivity*], whom I have sent from Jerusalem to Babylon:

21 Thus saith the LORD of hosts, the God of Israel [*in other words, Jehovah, the premortal Jesus Christ*], **of** [*about*] **Ahab the son of Kolaiah, and of** [*about*] **Zedekiah the son of Maaseiah, which prophesy a lie unto you in my name; Behold, I will deliver them into the hand of Nebuchadrezzar** [*usually spelled "Nebuchadnezzar"*] **king of Babylon;** and **he shall slay them before your eyes;**

Not only will these two false prophets among the Jews in Babylon be killed by the King of Babylon, but they will become the brunt of a saying which will become a popular way to wish death upon enemies.

22 And of them [*from what happens

to them] shall be taken up a curse [*a saying*] by all the captivity of Judah which *are* in Babylon [*among all the captive Jews in Babylon*], saying, The LORD make thee like Zedekiah and like Ahab, whom the king of Babylon roasted in the fire;

23 Because they [*Ahab and Zedekiah*] have committed villany [*vile deeds—see footnote 23a in your Bible*] in Israel [*among the Lord's people*], and have committed adultery with their neighbours' wives, and have spoken lying words in my name, which I have not commanded them; even I know, and *am* a witness, saith the LORD.

> Beginning with verse 24, next, Jeremiah responds (in his letter) to a man named Shemaiah, a man among the captives in Babylon, who has attempted to stir up trouble for Jeremiah by writing letters against him to people in Jerusalem. One letter, sent to a priest named Zephaniah in Jerusalem (verse 25) asks why he has done nothing to stop Jeremiah from prophesying. Among other things, Shemaiah suggests that Jeremiah be put in prison and in the stocks (verses 26–27).
>
> The Lord has instructed Jeremiah as to what to say to Shemaiah in this letter.

24 ¶ *Thus* shalt thou also speak to Shemaiah the Nehelamite, saying,

25 Thus speaketh the LORD of hosts, the God of Israel, saying,

Because thou hast sent letters in thy name unto all the people that *are* at Jerusalem, and to Zephaniah the son of Maaseiah the priest, and to all the priests, saying,

26 The LORD hath made thee priest in the stead of [*in place of*] Jehoiada the priest, that ye should be officers in the house of the LORD [*in other words, you are supposed to have authority and be in charge*], for every man *that is* mad, and maketh himself a prophet, that thou shouldest put him in prison, and in the stocks.

27 Now therefore why hast thou not reproved Jeremiah of Anathoth, which maketh himself a prophet to you [*who has set himself up as a false prophet*]?

> Next, Shemaiah complains to Zephaniah that Jeremiah has prophesied a long period of captivity for the Jews in Babylon, and instructed them to settle down as if permanent there. (This is in stark contrast to the false prophets' prophecies of a brief, no longer than two year period of captivity.)

28 For therefore he [*Jeremiah*] sent unto us *in* Babylon, saying, This *captivity is* long: build ye houses, and dwell *in them*; and plant gardens, and eat the fruit of them.

29 And Zephaniah the priest read this letter in the ears of Jeremiah the prophet.

30 ¶ Then came the word of the LORD unto Jeremiah, saying,

31 Send to all them of the captivity [*write to all the Jews in Babylonian captivity*]**, saying, Thus saith the LORD concerning Shemaiah the Nehelamite; Because that Shemaiah hath prophesied unto you, and I sent him not, and he caused you to trust in a lie** [*his own false prophecies*]**:**

32 Therefore thus saith the LORD; Behold, **I will punish Shemaiah the Nehelamite, and his seed:** he shall not have a man to dwell among this people; neither shall he behold [*live to see*] the good that I will do for my people, saith the LORD; **because he hath taught rebellion against the LORD** [*in other words, none of his posterity will return with the Jews in seventy years (about 537 BC—see chronology chart in Bible Dictionary), when Cyrus the Persian decrees that they can return and take the temple treasures back with them to Jerusalem*]*.*

JEREMIAH 30

Selection: all verses

WE WILL QUOTE from the *Old Testament Student Manual* for background for chapters 30–33.

"The prophet Jeremiah lived through one of the most troubled periods of history in the ancient Near East. He witnessed the fall of a great empire (Assyria) and the rising of another (Babylon). In the midst of this turmoil the kingdom of Judah was ruled by five kings, four of them deplorable. Jeremiah declared God's message for forty years, warning of coming disaster and appealing in vain to the nation to turn back to God.

"During Manasseh's long reign (687–642 BC), which was just before Jeremiah's time, Judah remained Assyria's vassal. This situation brought a resurgence of idolatry, in this case a mixture of belief in the Mesopotamian astrological gods and belief in the Canaanite fertility deities. As has been discussed, a great reformation was conducted by Josiah when the book of the law was discovered in the temple and its contents were made known to the people. Aside from this brief period of reform, Judah became increasingly insensitive to spiritual things during Jeremiah's time.

"The Lord showed Jeremiah a vision of the future that put the calamities he had witnessed into a perspective of hope. Like other prophets of his time (Isaiah, Ezekiel, Hosea, Amos, Micah, and Zechariah), Jeremiah was shown that scattered Israel would one day be gathered, that Judah would return to the lands of her possession, and that eventually all of Israel would become great. These visions and prophecies were recorded by Jeremiah and for centuries have provided hope to a nation of suffering people. They hold a very important place in the latter-day work of restoration" (*Old Testament Student Manual*, page 253).

Remember that "Israel," in an overall sense, refers to the Lord's covenant people, descendants of Abraham through Jacob (whose name was changed to Israel—see Genesis 32:28). It includes all who will make and keep covenants with the Lord, which will ultimately lead to exaltation in the highest degree of the celestial kingdom.

After Solomon's reign as King of Israel, the kingdom split into two nations, Judah and Israel. The tribes of Judah and Benjamin became known as Judah, and the northern ten tribes became known as Israel. The northern ten tribes became known as the lost ten tribes, after Assyria captured and carried them away, in about 722 BC Judah is being carried away into Babylonian captivity in waves, during Jeremiah's lifetime.

One of the great prophecies of the latter days is that Israel will be gathered and that the Lord will once again have a righteous covenant people. Jeremiah prophesied of this great gathering in many places, including these next three chapters.

In verses 1-2, next, Jeremiah is instructed by the Savior to record these prophecies of the future gathering of Judah and Israel.

1 THE word that came to Jeremiah from the LORD, saying,

2 Thus speaketh the LORD God of Israel, saying, Write thee all the words that I have spoken unto thee in a book.

3 For, lo, the days come, saith the LORD, that I will bring again the captivity of [*out of captivity*] **my people Israel and Judah,** saith the LORD: and I will cause them to return **to the land that I gave to their fathers,** and they shall possess it.

We understand verse 3, above, to refer both to the return of the captives after seventy years in Babylon and to the gathering of Israel in the last days (see heading to chapter 30 in your Bible). But the main emphasis in this chapter is on the restoration of the gospel and the gathering of Israel in the last days.

4 ¶ And these are the words that the LORD spake concerning Israel and concerning Judah.

Verses 5-7 seem to set the emotional stage for the latter-day gathering of Israel. They serve as reminders of the extreme agony and distress Israel and Judah have gone through throughout the centuries, because of their rebellion against their God.

5 For thus saith the LORD; We have heard a voice of trembling, of fear, and not of peace.

The picture "painted" by Jeremiah's words in verse 6, next, is, in effect, a scene in which strong men are trembling in agony, as if they were in childbirth labor. The message is that Israel and Judah have gone through terrible agony to get their attention and prepare them for redemption.

6 Ask ye now, and see whether a man doth travail with child [*have you ever heard of a man having labor pains*]? Wherefore [*why then*] do I see every man with his hands on his loins, as a woman in travail [NIV: "*with his hands on his stomach like a woman in labor*"], and all faces are turned into paleness?

7 Alas! for that day *is* great [*the punishments and pains of the past*], so that none *is* like it: it *is* even the time of Jacob's trouble [*Jacob (Israel) has gone through terrible pain*]; but he shall be saved out of it [*Israel will be gathered and saved in the last days*].

> The major message that now follows is that the gospel of Jesus Christ has power to redeem us out of the worst of conditions and spiritual bondage.

8 For it shall come to pass in that day [*in the last days*], saith the LORD of hosts, *that* I will break his yoke from off thy neck, and will burst thy bonds, and strangers shall no more serve themselves of him [*Israel will no more be in bondage (including the terrible bondage of sin—see footnote 8a in your Bible)*]:

9 But they shall serve the LORD their God, and David their king [*Christ—see heading to this chapter in your Bible*], whom I will raise up unto them.

10 ¶ Therefore fear thou not, O my servant Jacob, saith the LORD;

neither be dismayed, O Israel: for, lo, I will save thee from afar, and thy seed from the land of their captivity; and Jacob [*Israel*] shall return, and shall be in rest, and be quiet [*live in peace*], and none shall make *him* afraid.

11 For I *am* with thee, saith the LORD, to save thee: though I make a full end of all nations whither I have scattered thee, yet will I not make a full end of thee [*you will not be destroyed completely*]: but I will correct [*discipline*] thee in measure, and will not leave thee altogether unpunished.

> Without the help of the JST, verses 12, 13, and 15, next, would be completely negative. Whereas, with the JST, we see that there is still hope for these people.

12 For thus saith the LORD, Thy bruise *is* incurable, *and* thy wound *is* grievous.

<u>JST Jeremiah 30:12</u>
12 For thus saith the Lord, **Thy bruise is not incurable, although thy wounds are grievous.**

13 *There is* none to plead thy cause, that thou mayest be bound up: thou hast no healing medicines.

<u>JST Jeremiah 30:13</u>
13 **Is there none** to plead thy cause, that thou mayest be bound up? **Hast thou no healing medicines?**

14 All thy lovers [*false gods, idols*] **have forgotten thee; they seek thee not** [*they are not coming to help you out of trouble*]; for I have wounded thee with the wound of an enemy [*in effect, "I have punished you because you are an enemy of righteousness"*], with the chastisement of a cruel one, for [*because of*] the multitude of thine **iniquity**; *because* thy sins **were** increased [*you just keep getting more wicked*].

JST Jeremiah 30:14

14 **Have all thy lovers forgotten thee, do they not seek thee?** For I have wounded thee with the wound of an enemy, with the chastisement of a cruel one, for the multitude of thine **iniquities**; because thy sins **are** increased.

Next, in verse 15, the Lord again repeats the reason He has had to bring such calamities upon these people.

15 Why criest thou for [*because of*] thine affliction? **thy sorrow is incurable** for the multitude of thine iniquity: *because* thy sins **were** increased, I have done these things unto thee.

JST Jeremiah 30:15

15 Why criest thou for thine affliction? **Is thy sorrow incurable?** It was for the multitude of thine iniquities, and because thy sins **are** increased I have done these things unto thee.

16 Therefore all they that devour thee shall be devoured [*the wicked who conquer you will themselves be conquered*]; and all thine adversaries, every one of them, shall go into captivity [*for example, the Medes and the Persians eventually conquered the Babylonians*]; and they that spoil thee shall be a spoil [*shall become a prey to their own enemies*], and all that prey upon thee will I give for a prey.

JST Jeremiah 30:16

16 **But** all they that devour thee shall be devoured; and all thine adversaries, every one of them, shall go into captivity; and they that spoil thee shall be a spoil, and all that prey upon thee will I give for a prey.

It is interesting to note that all the foreign kingdoms in ancient times who conquered and persecuted the Jews have ceased to exist, but the Jews themselves still exist as a distinct people today.

Verse 17, next, prophesies that Israel will eventually be restored as the people of the Lord, and that their spiritual wounds will be healed.

17 For **I will restore health unto thee, and I will heal thee of thy wounds,** saith the LORD; because they called thee an Outcast, *saying,* This is Zion, whom no man seeketh after.

In verses 18–22, next, we see a prophecy of the conversion and restoration of Israel in the last days, including the establishment of their own political kingdoms. Remember, "Israel," in this context, is a collective term for all of the Lord's covenant people, including the Jews.

18 ¶ Thus saith the LORD; Behold, **I will bring again** [*restore*] **the captivity of Jacob's tents** [*the things lost during Israel's captivity*], **and have mercy on his dwellingplaces; and the city shall be builded upon her own heap** [*on the same site*], **and the palace shall remain after the manner thereof.**

19 And **out of them** [*the devastated cities and ruins*] **shall proceed thanksgiving and the voice of them that make merry:** and I will multiply them, and they shall not be few; **I will also glorify them, and they shall not be small** [*insignificant in world politics and influence*].

20 Their children also shall be as aforetime, and their congregation shall be established before me, and **I will punish all that oppress them.**

21 And **their nobles** [*governors, political leaders*] **shall be of themselves, and their governor shall proceed from the midst of them** [*in other words, they will no longer be governed and ruled over by foreigners, rather, will produce their own political leaders*]; and I will cause him to draw near, and **he shall approach unto me:** for who *is* this that engaged his heart to

approach unto me? saith the LORD.

22 And ye shall be my people, and I will be your God.

Verses 23–24, next, serve as a reminder that the punishments of God will continue to be poured out upon the wicked.

23 Behold, **the whirlwind of the LORD** goeth forth with fury, a continuing whirlwind: it **shall fall with pain upon the head of the wicked.**

24 **The fierce anger of the LORD shall not return** [*will not be pulled back*], until he have done *it*, and until he have performed the intents of his heart: **in the latter days ye shall consider it** [*fully understand it—see footnote 24b in your Bible*].

JEREMIAH 31

Selection: all verses

THIS CHAPTER CONTINUES with the theme of the gathering and restoration of Israel in the last days—see heading in your Bible.

Remember, the most important eternal aspect of the gathering of Israel is that each of us be gathered spiritually to the gospel of Jesus Christ. The physical gathering of Israel to various places, including stakes of Zion (D&C 109:39) is part of the plan which enables people to be gathered to Christ.

As we study this chapter, we will see the restoration of the gospel in the latter days, the role that Ephraim plays in the latter-day gathering, the renewal of the covenant with Israel, including Judah (verse 31), and the eventual coming of the Millennium (verse 34).

In verse 1, Jeremiah begins with the Restoration of the gospel to scattered Israel in the last days.

1 AT the same time [*referring to the "latter days," mentioned at the very end of chapter 30*], **saith the LORD, will I be the God of all the families of Israel, and they shall be my people.**

> Verse 2, next, speaks of the future as if it has already taken place. This is a common form of prophesying among Old Testament prophets.

2 Thus saith the LORD, The people *which were* **left of the sword** [*the remnant who survived the destruction and captivity*] **found grace** [*the favor of the Lord*] **in the wilderness** [*after they had been in apostasy*]; **even Israel, when I went to cause him to rest** [*when I restored the gospel to them*].

3 The LORD hath appeared of old [*in times past*] **unto me** [*Israel*], *saying,* **Yea, I have loved thee with an everlasting love: therefore with lovingkindness have I drawn thee** [*nourished and brought you forward*].

4 Again I will build thee [*beginning with the Restoration through Joseph Smith*], **and thou shalt be built, O**

virgin of Israel [*the Lord's covenant people*]: **thou shalt again be adorned with thy tabrets, and shalt go forth in the dances of them that make merry.**

5 Thou shalt yet plant vines upon the mountains of Samaria [*you will be restored to your lands*]: **the planters shall plant, and shall eat** *them* **as common things.**

> We will quote from the *Old Testament Student Manual* as background for verses 6–9, next:
>
> "The watchmen mentioned in verse 6 are the righteous prophets of the latter days (see also Ezekiel 3:16–21). In the last dispensation they shall cry to all people to join together in proper worship of the Lord (see D&C 1:1-2). Verse 8 speaks of gathered Israel coming from the north country (see D&C 110:11; 133:26) and from the coasts (ends) of the earth.
>
> "Elder LeGrand Richards said of this gathering: ' "I will bring them . . . a great company shall return thither." This was something the Lord was going to do. Note that Jeremiah does not say that they will return hither, or to the place where this prediction was made, but thither, or to a distant place. He understood that Joseph was to be given a new land in the "utmost bound of the everlasting hills" ' (See Genesis 49:22–26; Deuteronomy 33:13–17.)" (Israel! Do You Know? pp. 177-78).
>
> "Verse 9 refers to Israel returning with weeping. They will

weep because they will realize that the sufferings they have endured throughout the centuries came about because they rejected the Lord Jesus Christ, who shall lead them in the last days (see Jeremiah 50:4; Zechariah 12:10)" (*Old Testament Student Manual*, pages 254–55).

6 For **there shall be a day, *that* the watchmen** [*righteous latter-day prophets*] upon the mount Ephraim **shall cry,** Arise ye, and **let us go up to Zion unto the LORD our God.**

7 For thus saith the LORD; Sing with gladness for Jacob [*Israel*], and shout among the chief of the nations: publish ye, praise ye, **and say, O LORD, save thy people, the remnant of Israel.**

8 Behold, **I will bring them from the north country** [*when Israel (the lost ten tribes) were captured in about 722 B.C., the Assyrians took them to the north*], **and gather them from the coasts of the earth,** *and* with them the blind and the lame, the woman with child and her that travaileth with child together: **a great company shall return** thither.

The role of the birthright son in ancient times included the responsibility to take care of the rest of his father's children. We see this role for Ephraim, in verse 9, next.

9 They shall come with weeping, and with supplications will I lead them: I will cause them to walk by the rivers of waters in a straight way, wherein they shall not stumble: for **I am a father to Israel, and Ephraim *is* my firstborn** [*has the birthright and thus the first responsibility to shepherd the rest of the tribes to the safety of the gospel*].

The word, "isles," as used in the Old Testament, generally means continents and peoples throughout the earth, other than the Near East.

10 ¶ Hear the word of the LORD, O ye nations, and **declare *it* in the isles** [*continents*] **afar off** [*preach the gospel throughout the world*], and say, He that scattered Israel will gather him, and keep him, as a shepherd *doth* his flock.

11 For **the LORD hath redeemed Jacob** [*through the Restoration, the Lord will have redeemed Israel*], **and ransomed him from the hand of *him that was* stronger than he** [*and rescued him from his enemies*].

Note the beautiful descriptive language of Jeremiah as he describes the blessings of the Restoration and the blessings that come to people who allow the Lord to take care of them.

12 Therefore they shall come [*will be gathered*] and **sing** in the height of Zion, and shall **flow together to the goodness of the LORD,** for wheat, and for wine, and for oil, and for the young of the flock and of the herd: **and their soul shall be as a**

watered garden; and they shall not sorrow any more at all.

13 Then shall the virgin [*the faithful saints of Zion*] **rejoice in the dance, both young men and old together: for I will turn their mourning into joy, and will comfort them, and make them rejoice from their sorrow.**

14 And I will satiate [*completely satisfy*] **the soul of the priests** [*Church leaders*] **with fatness** [*the very best*], **and my people shall be satisfied** [*filled*] **with my goodness,** saith the LORD.

Next, we see the stage set emotionally for us to truly appreciate what it will mean for Israel to finally be gathered.

15 ¶ Thus saith the LORD; A voice was heard in Ramah [*a place in southern Israel, associated with Rachel's tomb, where the captives were gathered before being taken to Babylon—see BD, under "Ramah"*], **lamentation,** *and* **bitter weeping; Rahel** [*Rachel, the mother of Joseph, hence the grandmother of Ephraim*] **weeping for her children** refused to be comforted for her children, because they *were* not [*the descendants of Rachel, symbolically representing Israel, were carried away captive, both literally by enemies and figuratively by Satan into spiritual bondage*].

Verses 16–17, next, say, in effect,

"Cheer up! Look at the future and see the glorious restoration of the gospel and the gathering of Israel to the Lord in the last days."

16 Thus saith the LORD; **Refrain thy voice from weeping, and thine eyes from tears:** for thy work shall be rewarded, saith the LORD; and **they shall come again from the land of the enemy.**

17 And **there is hope** in thine end, saith the LORD, that **thy children shall come again** to their own border.

Using repetition, Jeremiah again drives home the point that Ephraim (another name for Israel or the northern ten tribes, with headquarters in Samaria before the Assyrians carried them away in 722 BC) has mourned his wickedness and apostasy and will repent in the last days.

18 ¶ I [*the Lord*] **have surely heard Ephraim bemoaning himself** *thus;* **Thou hast chastised me,** and I was chastised, as a bullock unaccustomed *to* the yoke [*the "yoke" of bondage settled me down and brought me under control*]: **turn thou me, and I shall be turned** [*please guide me now and I will follow*]; **for thou art the LORD my God.**

19 Surely after that I was turned, **I repented; and after that I was instructed,** I smote upon *my* thigh [*I mourned because of my past wickedness*]: I was ashamed, yea, even confounded, because I did bear the reproach of my youth [*I had to live with the disgrace of my past wickedness*].

> Next, the Lord assures Ephraim (Israel, in this context) that he can indeed repent and be gathered back to the Lord. The Lord will once again take delight in blessing him.

20 *Is* **Ephraim my dear son?** *is he* **a pleasant child** [*can he still be blessed*]? **for since I spake against him** [*punished him in times past*], **I do earnestly remember him still: therefore my bowels** [*My deepest feelings*] **are troubled for him** [*sympathize with him*]; **I will surely have mercy upon him,** saith the LORD.

> Next, the Lord encourages Israel to do everything in his power to turn around (from apostasy) and return home to God. Highway signs are used to symbolize his finding the right direction to return home.

21 **Set thee up waymarks** [*road-signs*], **make thee high heaps** [*rocks pointing the direction to return to God*]: **set thine heart toward the highway** [*turn your heart to Me*], **even the way** *which* **thou wentest: turn again** [*turn around from the apostate direction you've been going*], **O virgin of Israel, turn again to these thy cities** [*return home*].

> The "paragraph" mark (backward "P") at the beginning of verse 22 in your Bible (if it is a King James version) signals the change to a new topic. In this case, the Lord, having told them how wonderful it will be for them in the future, now asks Israel how long they are going to continue wandering in sin. Then, speaking of the future again, He tells them that a new experience (for them) will be available at that time, namely, "A woman shall compass a man" (end of verse 22).

22 ¶ How long wilt thou go about, O thou backsliding [*apostate*] **daughter? for the LORD hath created a new thing in the earth, A woman shall compass a man** [*see note, next*].

> The last phrase of verse 22, above, needs explaining. As you know, in the covenant relationship between Israel and the Lord, Israel is often referred to as the "bride" or wife, and the Lord (Jesus Christ or Jehovah) is referred to symbolically as the "bridegroom" or husband. The tender and intimate relationship between the husband and wife are symbolic of the closeness that should exist between the Lord and His people. We generally think of the Lord nourishing His people, but in the phrase above, the implication is that, in the last days, Israel will nourish the Lord and be tender toward Him. This can remind us that the Savior and our Father in Heaven both have joy when we are righteous.
>
> We will use a quote to further explain this:
>
> "In the verse (Jeremiah 31:22)

now before us (the Hebrew word which is translated as 'compass'), signifies to encompass with love and care, to surround lovingly and carefully,—the natural and fitting dealing on the part of the stronger to the weak and those who need assistance. And the new thing that God creates consists in this, that the woman, the weaker nature that needs help, will lovingly and solicitously surround the man, the stronger. Herein is expressed a new relation of Israel to the Lord, a reference to a new covenant which the Lord, ver. 31ff., will conclude with His people, and in which He deals so condescendingly toward them that they can lovingly embrace Him. This is the substance of the Messianic meaning in the words" (Keil and Delitzsch, *Commentary*, 8:2:30).

23 Thus saith the LORD of hosts, the God of Israel; **As yet** [*sometime in the future*] **they shall use this speech** [*phrase; saying*] **in the land of Judah and in the cities thereof,** when I shall bring again their captivity [*NIV: "When I bring them back from captivity"*]; **The LORD bless thee, O habitation of justice, and mountain of holiness** [*in other words, there will be peace and righteousness*] .

24 And there shall dwell in Judah itself, and in all the cities thereof together, husbandmen [*farmers*], and they *that* go forth with flocks.

Again, in verse 25, next, a future time of peace is spoken of

prophetically as if it had already come to pass.

25 For I have satiated [*satisfied*] the weary soul, and I have replenished [*renewed*] every sorrowful soul.

26 Upon this I awaked, and beheld; and my sleep was sweet unto me [*this is a sweet dream of the future which will someday be fulfilled*].

In verses 27–28, next, we see yet another form of the prophecy concerning the gathering and restoration of Israel and Judah in the last days.

27 ¶ Behold, **the days come,** saith the LORD, **that I will sow** [*plant*] **the house of Israel and the house of Judah with** the seed of **man, and with** the seed of **beast** [*whereas, in the past, Israel and Judah have been killed, reduced in population, and scattered, in the last days they will multiply and prosper*].

28 And it shall come to pass, *that* **like as I have watched over them, to pluck up,** and to **break down,** and to **throw down,** and to **destroy,** and to **afflict** [*just as I supervised their past punishments*]; **so will I watch over them, to build, and to plant,** saith the LORD.

Verse 29, next, is apparently a Jewish proverb in common use in Jeremiah's day, which says, in effect, that children are negatively affected by the sins of their parents.

29 In those days [*in the last days*]

they shall say no more [*the false doctrine will no longer be taught among the Lord's people*], The fathers have eaten a sour grape, and the children's teeth are set on edge [*the children are cursed by the sins of their parents*].

> Verse 30, next, says that when the gospel is restored, in the last days, the true doctrine will be taught, namely that we are accountable for our own transgressions, not for the sins of others.

30 But **every one shall die for his own iniquity**: every man that eateth the sour grape, his teeth shall be set on edge.

> When you read verse 30, above, did you think of the second Article of Faith? We will quote it here:
>
> Article of Faith 2
>
> 2 We believe that men will be punished for their own sins, and not for Adam's transgression.
>
> We learn more about the latter-day gathering of Israel and Judah and the important role of covenants associated with it beginning with verse 31, next.

31 ¶ Behold, the days come, saith the LORD, that I will make a new covenant with the house of Israel, and with the house of Judah:

32 Not according to [*not like*] the covenant that I made with their fathers [*ancestors—the children of Israel*] in the day *that* I took them by the hand to bring them out of the land of Egypt; which my covenant they brake, although I was an husband unto them [*even though I took good care of them*], saith the LORD:

> The covenant, or Law of Moses that the Lord gave the wayward children of Israel, included many laws and details that demanded strict obedience to detail. In verse 33, next, the Lord reveals that in the last days the covenants He will make with His people will require deep conversion and the heartfelt desire to live gospel principles, rather than the step-by-step demands of old.

33 But this *shall be* the covenant that I will make with the house of Israel; After those days, saith the LORD, I will put my law in their inward parts, and write it in their hearts; and will be their God, and they shall be my people.

> The peaceful and glorious conditions mentioned in verse 33, above, lead into verse 34, next, which alludes to the Millennium (see footnote 34a in your Bible).

34 And they shall teach no more every man his neighbour, and every man his brother, saying, Know the LORD: for they shall all know me [*during the Millennium*], from the least of them unto the greatest of them, saith the LORD; for I will forgive their iniquity, and I will remember their sin no more.

Verse 35, next, says, in effect, "Thus saith the Lord, the Creator of heaven and earth."

35 ¶ Thus saith the LORD, which giveth the sun for a light by day, *and* the ordinances [*orbits—see footnote 35c in your Bible*] of the moon and of the stars for a light by night, which divideth the sea when the waves thereof roar; The LORD of hosts *is* his name:

36 **If those ordinances** [*the ordinances contained in the covenant spoken of in verse 33, above*] **depart from before me,** saith the LORD, *then* **the seed of Israel also shall cease from being a nation before me for ever.**

We will quote from the *Old Testament Student Manual* to further explain verse 36, above:

"The Lord, who has worked so long and hard to establish his righteous people, said that if those saving and exalting priesthood ordinances cease to exist, then Israel also will cease to exist—forever. This statement surely indicates the importance of ordinances in the Lord's plan" (*Old Testament Student Manual,* page 256).

37 Thus saith the LORD; **If heaven above can be measured** [*which it cannot be by man*], **and the foundations of the earth searched out beneath, I will also cast off all the seed of Israel for** [*because of*] **all that they have done,** saith the LORD [*in other words, He will not reject Israel forever but will restore them through the use of covenants in the last days*].

In verses 38–40, next, we see a prophecy that Jerusalem will become an eternal city. It will become one of two cities (Old Jerusalem, in the Holy Land, and New Jerusalem, in Independence, Missouri) during the Millennium that will serve as headquarters for the Savior as He rules and reigns during the one thousand years. You can read a bit about these two cities in Ether 13:3–11.

38 ¶ Behold, **the days come, saith the LORD, that the city** [*Jerusalem*] **shall be built to the LORD** from the tower of Hananeel unto the gate of the corner.

39 And the measuring line shall yet go forth over against it upon the hill Gareb, and shall compass about to Goath.

40 And the whole valley of the dead bodies, and of the ashes, and all the fields unto the brook of Kidron, unto the corner of the horse gate toward the east, *shall be* **holy unto the LORD; it shall not be plucked up, nor thrown down any more for ever.**

JEREMIAH 32

Selection: all verses

AT THIS POINT in history, about 588 BC, wicked King Zedekiah has put Jeremiah in prison. The king is displeased with his prophecies about the impending Babylonian captivity of Jerusalem and the prophecy that the king will also be captured and will be taken to Babylon (verses 2–5). Daniel, along with Shadrach, Meshach, and Abednego (Daniel 3:12) have already been taken captive to Babylon with the first group of Jewish intellectuals and craftsmen in about 606 BC Lehi and his family left Jerusalem in 600 BC Ezekiel was taken to Babylon with another group of captives in about 598 BC He will serve as a prophet to the Jews in captivity for about twenty-two years, from 592–570 BC (see Bible Dictionary under "Ezekiel"). The final wave of Babylonian attacks and resulting captivity will soon take place.

It is the tenth year of the eleven-year reign of Zedekiah (see verse 1 coupled with Jeremiah 52:1), which puts the date of this chapter at about 588 BC Zedekiah is now about thirty-one years old, and Jeremiah has been serving as a prophet to the Jews for about thirty years.

As the heading to this chapter in your Bible states, Jeremiah will be instructed by the Lord to purchase some property as a means of symbolizing and prophesying that scattered Israel (including the Jews who are soon to be scattered) will be gathered by the Lord back to their land. The final gathering of Israel in the last days will be accomplished by means of covenants with the Lord, such as baptism and the covenants that follow among the faithful.

In verses 1–5, King Zedekiah has Jeremiah brought to him from prison and asks him why he has been so negative in his prophecies about the king and his kingdom.

1 THE word that came to Jeremiah from the LORD **in the tenth year** [*the tenth year of the reign*] **of Zedekiah** king of Judah, which *was* the eighteenth year of Nebuchadrezzar [*king of Babylon*].

2 For then the king [*Nebuchadnezzar (another biblical name for Nebuchadrezzar)*] of Babylon's army besieged Jerusalem: and **Jeremiah** the prophet **was shut up in** the court of the **prison,** which *was* in the king of Judah's house [*this prison was located in the king's palace*].

3 For **Zedekiah** king of Judah **had shut him up** [*put him in prison*], **saying, Wherefore** [*why*] **dost thou prophesy, and say, Thus saith the LORD, Behold, I will give this city** [*Jerusalem*] **into the hand of the king of Babylon,** and he shall take it;

4 **And Zedekiah** king of Judah **shall not escape** out of the hand of the Chaldeans [*another name for Babylonians*], but shall surely be

delivered into the hand of the king of Babylon, and shall speak with him mouth to mouth, and his eyes shall behold his eyes;

5 And he shall lead Zedekiah to Babylon, and there shall he be until I visit him, saith the LORD: though ye fight with the Chaldeans, ye shall not prosper [*will not win*].

> Next, beginning with verse 6, Jeremiah records that, at this point, the Lord told him to buy some property in Anathoth (Jeremiah's home town, about three miles north of Jerusalem). This purchase was to prophetically symbolize the return of Israel.

6 ¶ And Jeremiah said, The word of the LORD came unto me, saying,

7 Behold, Hanameel [*Jeremiah's cousin*] the son of Shallum thine uncle **shall come unto thee, saying, Buy thee my field that** *is* **in Anathoth:** for the right of redemption *is* thine to buy *it* [*you have the legal right to buy it before anyone else is given the option to purchase it*].

8 So Hanameel mine uncle's son **came to me in the court of the prison** according to the word of the LORD, **and said unto me, Buy my field,** I pray thee, that *is* in Anathoth, which *is* in the country of Benjamin: **for the right of inheritance** *is* **thine, and the redemption** *is* thine [*symbolic of the prophetic fact that Israel would someday be redeemed by the Savior*]; buy *it* for thyself. Then I knew that this *was* the word of the LORD.

9 And I bought the field of Hanameel my uncle's son, that *was* in Anathoth, and weighed him the money, *even* seventeen shekels [*NIV: about seven ounces*] of silver.

10 And I subscribed the evidence, and sealed *it* [*I signed and sealed the deed*], and **took witnesses,** and weighed *him* the money in the balances [*paid the bill*].

11 So I took the evidence of the purchase, *both* that which was sealed *according* to the law and custom, and that which was open:

12 And I gave the evidence of the purchase unto Baruch [*Jeremiah's personal scribe*] the son of Neriah, the son of Maaseiah, in the sight of Hanameel mine uncle's *son,* and **in the presence of the witnesses** that subscribed the book [*deed—see footnote 12b in your Bible*] of the purchase, **before** [*in the presence of*] **all the Jews that sat in the court of the prison.**

13 ¶ And I charged Baruch before them, saying,

14 Thus saith the LORD of hosts, the God of Israel; **Take these evidences** [*paper, documents*], this evidence **of the purchase**, both which is sealed, and this evidence which is open; **and put them in an earthen vessel** [*a clay jar*], that they may continue [*be preserved*] many days.

The prophetic symbolism of this transaction is explained in verse 15, next.

15 For thus saith the LORD of hosts, the God of Israel; **Houses and fields and vineyards shall be possessed again in this land** [*Israel, including the Jews, will return to their own lands*].

16 ¶ **Now when I had delivered the evidence of the purchase unto Baruch** the son of Neriah, **I prayed unto the LORD, saying,**

The words of Jeremiah's prayer are given in verses 17–25, next.

17 Ah Lord GOD! behold, thou hast made the heaven and the earth by thy great power and stretched out arm, *and* **there is nothing too hard for thee:**

18 Thou shewest lovingkindness unto thousands, **and recompensest** the **iniquity** of the fathers into the bosom of their children after them: the Great, the Mighty God, the LORD of hosts, *is* his name,

19 Great in counsel, and mighty in work: for **thine eyes** *are* **open upon** all the ways of the sons of men: **to give every one according to his ways,** and according to the fruit of his doings [*the law of the harvest*]:

20 Which **hast set signs and wonders in the land of** Egypt [*redeemed Israelites from Egyptian bondage; symbolic of being redeemed from the bondage of sin*], *even* unto this day, and in Israel, and among *other* men; and hast made thee a name, as at this day;

21 And **hast brought forth thy people Israel out of the land of Egypt** with signs, and with wonders [*miracles*], and with a strong hand, and with a stretched out arm, and with great terror;

22 And hast given them this land [*Palestine*], which thou didst swear [*covenant, promise*] to their fathers [*ancestors*] to give them, a land flowing with milk and honey [*a land of prosperity; symbolic of heaven*];

23 And they came in, and possessed it; but they obeyed not thy voice, neither walked in thy law; they have done nothing of all that thou commandedst them to do: **therefore thou hast caused all this evil** [*the Babylonian armies*] **to come upon them:**

24 Behold the mounts [*the mounds of dirt around Jerusalem, used by the Babylonians in the siege*], **they are come unto the city to take it;** and the city is given into the hand of the Chaldeans [*Babylonians*], that fight against it, because of the sword, and of the famine, and of the pestilence: **and what thou hast spoken** [*the prophecies of Jerusalem's downfall*] **is come to pass**; and, behold, thou seest *it*.

25 And thou hast said unto me [*Jeremiah*], O Lord GOD, **Buy thee the field for money, and take witnesses;** for the city is given into the hand of the Chaldeans.

> Beginning with verse 26, the Lord answers Jeremiah's prayer.

26 ¶ Then came the word of the LORD unto Jeremiah, saying,

27 Behold, I *am* **the LORD,** the God of all flesh: **is there any thing too hard for me?**

28 Therefore thus saith the LORD; Behold, **I will give this city** [*Jerusalem*] **into the hand of the Chaldeans,** and into the hand of Nebuchadrezzar king of Babylon, and he shall take it:

29 And the Chaldeans [*Babylonians*], that fight against this city, **shall come and set fire on this city,** and burn it with the houses, upon whose roofs they [*the Jews*] have offered incense unto Baal [*idol worship*], and poured out drink offerings unto other gods, to provoke me to anger.

30 For the children of Israel [*the northern ten tribes, who were taken captive by Assyria in about 722 B.C.*] **and the children of Judah** [*the Jews*] **have only done evil before me from their youth:** for the children of Israel have only provoked me to anger with the work of their hands [*such as idols*], saith the LORD.

31 For this city [*Jeremiah*] **hath been** to me as **a provocation of mine anger** and of my fury **from the day that they built it even unto this day;** that I should remove it from before my face,

32 Because of all the evil of the children of Israel and of the children of Judah, which they have done to provoke me to anger, they, their kings, their princes, their priests, and their [*false*] prophets, and the men of Judah, and the inhabitants of Jerusalem.

33 And they have turned unto me the back, and not the face [*they have rebelled against the Lord, and gone away from Him*]: though I taught them, rising up early and teaching *them* [*having My prophets teach and warn them constantly*], yet **they have not hearkened to receive instruction.**

34 But they set their abominations in the house, which is called by my name, **to defile it** [*they set up idols to worship in the temple in Jerusalem*].

35 And they built the high places

[*worship sites*] **of Baal**, which *are* in the valley of the son of Hinnom [*south and west of Jerusalem where idol worship included human sacrifices*], **to cause their sons and their daughters to pass through** *the fire* **unto Molech** [*Baal worship included idol worship, sexual immorality, and human sacrifice, including babies*]; which I commanded them not, neither came it into my mind, that they should do this abomination, to cause Judah to sin.

36 ¶ And **now therefore thus saith the LORD, the God of Israel, concerning this city** [*Jerusalem*], **whereof ye say** [*about which Jeremiah has prophesied*], **It shall be delivered into the hand of the king of Babylon** by the sword, and by the famine, and by the pestilence;

Verses 37–41, next, contain the marvelous prophecy of the gathering of Israel in the last days.

37 Behold, **I will gather them out of all countries, whither I have driven them** in mine anger, and in my fury, and in great wrath; **and I will bring them again unto this place, and I will cause them to dwell safely:**

38 And they shall be my people, and I will be their God:

39 And I will give them one heart, and one way [*they will be united in following the gospel of Jesus Christ*],

that they may fear [*respect and honor*] **me for ever, for the good of them** [*to their great benefit*], **and of their children after them:**

Next, in verses 40–41, we see the great value of making and keeping covenants with God.

40 And I will make an everlasting covenant with them, that I will not turn away from them, to do them good; but I will put my fear in their hearts, **that they shall not depart from me.**

41 Yea, I will rejoice over them to do them good, and I will plant them in this land assuredly with my whole heart and with my whole soul.

The return of Israel to the various lands of their inheritance in the last days is symbolic of the return of Israel to the Lord, which, as stated above, is accomplished through making and keeping covenants with Him.

42 For thus saith the LORD; Like as I have brought all this great evil upon this people, so will I bring upon them all the good that I have promised them.

The symbolism involved in having Jeremiah purchase land in his hometown is again explained in verses 43–44, next.

43 And fields shall be bought in this land, whereof ye say, It is desolate without man or beast; it is given into the hand of the Chaldeans.

Next, in verse 44, the Lord again explains the prophetic symbolism of having Jeremiah purchase land, having witnesses and proper documents to close the deal. It is prophesying the fact that the day will come in the future that the Jews will be gathered back to the Holy Land and be again able to buy land.

44 Men shall buy fields for money, and subscribe evidences, and seal *them*, and take witnesses in the land of Benjamin, and in the places about Jerusalem, and in the cities of Judah, and in the cities of the mountains, and in the cities of the valley, and in the cities of the south: **for I will cause their captivity to return** [*in the future, I will cause Israel to be gathered and return*], saith the LORD.

JEREMIAH 33

Selection: all verses

THIS CHAPTER CON-TINUES the prophetic theme of the gathering of Israel, including the Jews, in the last days. The most important aspect of the gathering is the gathering of people to Christ, regardless of what land they live in.

This prophecy was given to Jeremiah while he was in the king's personal prison in the palace.

1 MOREOVER **the word of the LORD came unto Jeremiah the second time, while he was yet shut up in the court of the prison,** saying,

2 **Thus saith the LORD** the maker thereof [*the Creator of the earth*], the LORD that formed it, to establish it; the LORD *is* his name;

3 **Call unto me, and I will answer thee, and shew thee great and mighty things,** which thou knowest not.

4 For thus saith the LORD, the God of Israel, **concerning** the houses of **this city** [*Jerusalem*], **and** concerning **the houses of the kings of Judah,** which are thrown down by the mounts [*the mounds of dirt used in laying siege to a city*], and by the sword;

Next, in verse 5, the Lord tells Jeremiah that any attempts by the Jews to successfully defeat the Babylonian armies who have laid siege to Jerusalem will be unsuccessful because of the wickedness of the people of Judah. In their rebellion against God, they plan to defeat the Babylonians without His help, but in reality, they are coming to fill the trenches dug by the enemy armies around Jerusalem with their own dead bodies.

5 **They** [*the people of Judah and Jerusalem*] **come to fight with the Chaldeans** [*Babylonians*]**, but** *it is* **to fill them with the dead bodies of men,** whom I have slain in

mine anger and in my fury, and for [*because of*] all whose wickedness I have hid my face from this city.

> Next, beginning with verse 6, the Lord speaks of the restoration of the gospel and the gathering of Israel, including the Jews in the last days. You have likely noticed that when Old Testament prophets speak and prophesy, they often jump directly from their day to the future without particularly announcing that they are doing so. We have an example of this in these verses.

6 Behold, I will bring it health and cure, and I will cure them, and will reveal unto them the abundance of peace and truth [*found in the true gospel of Jesus Christ*].

7 And I will cause the captivity of Judah and the captivity of Israel to return [*I will restore Judah and Israel*], and will build them, as at the first.

8 And I will cleanse them from all their iniquity, whereby they have sinned against me; and I will pardon all their iniquities, whereby they have sinned, and whereby they have transgressed against me.

9 ¶ And it [*Israel, the Lord's covenant people*] shall be to me a name of joy, a praise and an honour before all the nations of the earth, which shall hear all the good that I do unto them: and they shall fear and tremble [*have respect and admiration for the Lord*] for all the goodness and for all the prosperity that I procure unto it.

10 Thus saith the LORD; Again there shall be heard in this place, which ye say [*which Jeremiah has prophesied under the direction of the Lord*] shall be desolate without man and without beast, *even* in the cities of Judah, and in the streets of Jerusalem, that are desolate, without man, and without inhabitant, and without beast,

11 The voice of joy, and the voice of gladness, the voice of the bridegroom, and the voice of the bride, the voice of them that shall say, Praise the LORD of hosts: for the LORD *is* good; for his mercy *endureth* for ever: *and* of them that shall bring the sacrifice of praise into the house of the LORD. For I will cause to return the captivity of the land, as at the first, saith the LORD.

12 Thus saith the LORD of hosts; Again in this place, which is desolate without man and without beast, and in all the cities thereof, shall be an habitation of shepherds causing *their* flocks to lie down [*once again, the Holy Land will be inhabited in righteousness by the Lord's covenant people*].

13 In the cities of the mountains, in the cities of the vale, and in the cities of the south, and in the land

of Benjamin, and in the places about Jerusalem, and in the cities of Judah, shall the flocks pass again under the hands of him that telleth *them,* saith the LORD.

14 Behold, the days come, saith the LORD, that I will perform that good thing which I have promised unto the house of Israel and to the house of Judah.

Verses 15–16, next, remind us again that the source of the peace and prosperity spoken of above is the Savior.

15 ¶ In those days, and at that time, will I cause the Branch of righteousness [*Jesus Christ—see heading to this chapter in your Bible*] to grow up unto David; and he shall execute judgment and righteousness in the land [*in the earth—see footnote 15d in your Bible*].

16 In those days shall Judah be saved, and Jerusalem shall dwell safely: and this *is the name* wherewith she shall be called, The LORD our righteousness.

We will quote from the *Old Testament Student Manual* for additional clarification of verses 15–16, above:

"'The Branch of righteousness to grow up unto David' who will 'execute judgment and righteousness in the land' (verse 15) is Jesus Christ (see Isaiah 11:1; Jeremiah 23:5–6). When this millennial event occurs, the Jews will dwell safely in Jerusalem.

"The last part of verse 16 is not a particularly good translation since it implies that Jerusalem herself shall be called 'the Lord our righteousness.' According to Adam Clarke it should read: 'And this one who shall call to her is the Lord our Justification,' that is, Jesus Christ himself, the Branch of David (*The Holy Bible . . . with a Commentary and Critical Notes,* 4:344)" (*Old Testament Student Manual,* page 257).

17 ¶ For thus saith the LORD; David shall never want [*lack*] a man to sit upon the throne of the house of Israel [*when this time comes, there will be no lack of leadership for Israel*];

18 Neither shall the priests the Levites want [*lack*] a man before me to offer burnt offerings, and to kindle meat offerings, and to do sacrifice continually [*there will be no lack of authorized priesthood holders to carry on the work of salvation among the covenant people of the Lord*].

19 ¶ And the word of the LORD came unto Jeremiah, saying,

Next, in verses 20–22, the Lord says, in effect, that just as sure as day and night come and go, His promise to restore and redeem Israel someday in the future will be fulfilled.

20 Thus saith the LORD; If ye can break my covenant of the day, and my covenant of the night [*if you can stop the coming of day and night*], and

that there should not be day and night in their season;

21 *Then* may also my covenant [*given in verses 17–18, above*] be broken with David my servant, that he should not have a son to reign upon his throne; and with the Levites the priests, my ministers.

22 As the host of heaven cannot be numbered, neither the sand of the sea measured: so will I multiply the seed of David [*faithful members of the Lord's covenant people*] my servant, and the Levites that minister unto me [*innumerable hosts of Israel will yet be converted and gathered to the Father through Christ—compare with D&C 76:67*].

23 Moreover [*in addition*] the word of the LORD came to Jeremiah, saying,

24 Considerest thou not [*don't pay any attention to*] what this people [*the apostate Jews*] have spoken, saying, The two families [*Israel and Judah*] which the LORD hath chosen, he hath even cast them off? thus they have despised my people, that they should be no more a nation before them.

In verses 25–26, next, the Lord says, yet again, in effect, that just as sure as He is the Creator, He will keep His promise to restore Israel and Judah when the proper time arrives. He uses the opposite to emphasize the positive.

25 Thus saith the LORD; **If my covenant** *be* **not with day and night,** *and if* **I have not appointed the ordinances of heaven and earth** [*if I have not created the heaven and earth*];

26 **Then will I cast away the seed of Jacob** [*Israel*], **and David** [*symbolic of Judah*] **my servant,** *so* **that I will not take** *any* **of his seed** *to be* **rulers over the seed of Abraham, Isaac, and Jacob: for I will cause their captivity to return** [*I will cause them to return from captivity*], **and have mercy on them.**

JEREMIAH 34

Selection: all verses

IN THIS CHAPTER, Jeremiah foretells the captivity of Zedekiah, king of Jerusalem. As you have no doubt noticed thus far in your study of Jeremiah, the prophecy of the destruction of Jerusalem and the scattering and subsequent gathering of the Jews is often repeated in Jeremiah's writings.

In chapter 32, verses 4–5, we saw the prophecy that Zedekiah would be captured and taken to Babylon. Here, in chapter 34, we see it again. Chapter 52, verses 1–11, will tell of the fulfillment of this prophecy including the fact that Zedekiah was forced to watch as his sons were killed, then his eyes were put out and he was taken prisoner to Babylon.

It is a bit interesting, from an academic

standpoint, to note that here in verse 1, "Nebuchadnezzar" is spelled in the way that we normally think of it (not that many people worry a whole lot about how to spell it), rather than "Nebuchadrezzar," as was the case earlier in Jeremiah (example: 24:1).

1 THE word which came unto Jeremiah from the LORD, when Nebuchadnezzar king of Babylon, and all his army, and all the kingdoms of the earth of his dominion [*every nation under Nebuchadnezzar's subjection*]**, and all the people, fought against Jerusalem, and against all the cities thereof, saying,**

2 Thus saith the LORD, the God of Israel; **Go and speak to Zedekiah king of Judah, and tell him, Thus saith the LORD; Behold, I will give this city** [*Jerusalem*] **into the hand of the king of Babylon, and he shall burn it with fire:**

3 And thou shalt not escape out of his hand, but shalt surely be taken, and delivered into his hand; and thine eyes shall behold the eyes of the king of Babylon, and he shall speak with thee mouth to mouth, **and thou shalt go to Babylon.**

4 Yet hear the word of the LORD, O Zedekiah king of Judah; Thus saith the LORD of thee, **Thou shalt not die by the sword:**

5 *But* **thou shalt die in peace: and with the burnings of thy fathers** [*people will light funeral fires in honor of you, like they did for previous kings of Judah*]**,** the former kings which were before thee, so shall they burn *odours* for thee; **and they will lament thee,** *saying,* Ah lord [*in effect, hail to the king*]! for I have pronounced the word [*I, the Lord, have said it*], saith the LORD.

6 Then Jeremiah the prophet spake all these words unto Zedekiah king of Judah in Jerusalem,

7 When the king of Babylon's army fought against Jerusalem, and against all the cities of Judah that were left, against Lachish, and against Azekah: for these defenced cities remained of the cities of Judah.

The deceptiveness and dishonesty of King Zedekiah and his corrupt people is illustrated in verses 8–11, next. It is helpful to remember that the possession of slaves, including servants who had been put in bondage for a period of time to pay off personal or family debts, was a common part of the culture in this society at the time.

It appears that Zedekiah, for whatever reason, had proclaimed that all Hebrews who were in bondage to other Hebrews should be set free. After the people had carried out the king's orders, they simply turned around and put the freed Jews back into bondage.

8 ¶ *This is* **the word that came unto Jeremiah from the LORD,**

after that the king Zedekiah had made a covenant with all the people which *were* at Jerusalem, to proclaim liberty unto them;

9 That every man should let his manservant, and every man his maidservant, *being* an Hebrew or an Hebrewess, go free; that none should serve himself of them, *to wit* [*namely; for example*], of a Jew his brother.

10 Now when all the princes, and all the people, which had entered into the covenant, heard that every one should let his manservant, and every one his maidservant, go free, that none should serve themselves of them any more, then they obeyed, and let *them* go.

11 But afterward they turned, and caused the servants and the handmaids, whom they had let go free, to return, and brought them into subjection for servants and for handmaids.

Next, Jeremiah is told by the Lord to tell these Jews that they are hypocrites.

12 ¶ Therefore the word of the LORD came to Jeremiah from the LORD, saying,

13 Thus saith the LORD, the God of Israel; I made a covenant with your fathers in the day that I brought them forth out of the land of Egypt, out of the house of bondmen [*when I set them free from Egyptian bondage*], saying,

14 At the end of seven years let ye go every man his brother an Hebrew, which hath been sold unto thee; and when he hath served thee six years, thou shalt let him go free from thee: but your fathers [*ancestors*] hearkened not unto me, neither inclined their ear [*refused to listen to Me*].

15 And ye were now turned [*had reversed your position on holding slaves*], and had done right in my sight, in proclaiming liberty every man to his neighbour; and ye had made a covenant before me in the house which is called by my name [*in the temple at Jerusalem*]:

16 But ye turned and polluted my name [*violated your covenant*], and caused every man his servant, and every man his handmaid, whom ye had set at liberty at their pleasure, to return, and brought them into subjection, to be unto you for servants and for handmaids.

Verse 17, next, contains a very impactful message.

Major Message

When we set ourselves "free" from covenants we have made with the Lord, He is obligated by the law of justice to set us "free" from His blessings and protection.

17 Therefore thus saith the LORD;

Ye have not hearkened unto [obeyed] me, in proclaiming liberty, every one to his brother, and every man to his neighbour: behold, I proclaim a liberty for you, saith the LORD, to the sword, to the pestilence, and to the famine; and I will make you to be removed [scattered] into all the kingdoms of the earth.

18 And I will give the men that have transgressed my covenant, which have not performed the words of the covenant which they had made before me, when they cut the calf in twain, and passed between the parts thereof [a reference to a type of ritual associated with making covenants in the culture of the Jews at the time—compare with Genesis 15:8–10, 17],

19 The princes of Judah, and the princes of Jerusalem, the eunuchs, and the priests, and all the people of the land, which passed between the parts of the calf [who made a covenant and did not keep it—see note at end of verse 18, above];

20 I will even give them into the hand of their enemies, and into the hand of them that seek their life: and their dead bodies shall be for meat [food] unto the fowls of the heaven, and to the beasts of the earth.

21 And Zedekiah king of Judah and his princes will I give into the hand of their enemies, and into the hand of them that seek their life, and into the hand of the king of Babylon's army, which are gone up from you [who have temporarily gone away from you to do battle with an army which has come up from Egypt—see Jeremiah 37:5–10].

22 Behold, I will command, saith the LORD, and cause them to return [after temporarily leaving to defeat the Egyptians] to this city [Jerusalem]; and they shall fight against it, and take it, and burn it with fire: and I will make the cities of Judah a desolation without an inhabitant.

JEREMIAH 35

Selection: all verses

ACCORDING TO VERSE 1, the date of this chapter would be somewhere between 609 BC and 598 BC (see dates for Jehoiakim's reign on the chronology chart at the back of your Bible).

Some Bible scholars believe that the Rechabites, spoken of here, were descendants of Jethro, father-in-law to Moses. They are mentioned in 2 Kings 2:15, and were also known as Kenites (1 Chronicles 2:55). It is believed that they came into the Holy Land along with the children of Israel. They existed at various times in both the Northern Kingdom (Israel) and the Southern Kingdom (Judah).

The ancestors of these Rechabites had made a covenant long ago not to drink wine or other strong drink, and they were still faithful to that covenant, as shown in this chapter. The Lord holds them up as an example of people who keep their promises (as opposed to the Jews at this time in history), and, as you will see in this chapter, they are blessed because of this integrity.

1 THE word which came unto Jeremiah from the LORD **in the days of Jehoiakim** the son of Josiah **king of Judah** [*from 609–598 b.c.*], **saying,**

2 **Go unto** the house of **the Rechabites, and speak unto them, and bring them into the house of the LORD,** into one of the chambers, **and give them wine to drink.**

3 **Then I took** Jaazaniah the son of Jeremiah, the son of Habaziniah, and his brethren, and all his sons, and **the whole house of the Rechabites;**

4 **And I brought them into the house of the LORD** [*the temple in Jerusalem*], into the chamber of the sons of Hanan, the son of Igdaliah, a man of God, which *was* by the chamber of the princes, which *was* above the chamber of Maaseiah the son of Shallum, the keeper of the door:

Next, Jeremiah puts these Rechabites to the test, as instructed by the Lord, to see if they will keep their covenant not to drink wine or strong drink.

5 **And I set before the sons** [*descendants*] **of the house of the Rechabites pots full of wine, and cups, and I said unto them, Drink ye wine.**

6 **But they said, We will drink no wine:** for Jonadab the son of Rechab **our father** [*ancestor*] **commanded us, saying, Ye shall drink no wine,** *neither* ye, nor your sons for ever:

7 Neither shall ye build house [*they had also covenanted to live in tents*], nor sow seed, nor plant vineyard, nor have *any*: but all your days ye shall dwell in tents; that ye may live many days in the land where ye *be* strangers.

8 **Thus have we obeyed the voice of Jonadab the son of Rechab our father** in all that he hath charged us, **to drink no wine all our days, we, our wives, our sons, nor our daughters;**

9 Nor to build houses for us to dwell in: neither have we vineyard, nor field, nor seed:

10 **But we have dwelt in tents, and have obeyed, and done according to all that Jonadab our father commanded us.**

Next, in verse 11, these Rechabites explain why they are currently living in the city of Jerusalem instead of in their tents elsewhere.

11 But it came to pass, **when Nebuchadrezzar king of Babylon came** up into the land [*in earlier waves of siege and attack*], that **we said, Come, and let us go to Jerusalem** for fear of the army of the Chaldeans [*Babylonians*], and for fear of the army of the Syrians: **so we dwell at Jerusalem.**

12 ¶ Then came the word of the LORD unto Jeremiah, saying,

13 Thus saith the LORD of hosts, the God of Israel; **Go and tell the men of Judah and the inhabitants of Jerusalem, Will ye not receive instruction to hearken to my words?** saith the LORD. [*In other words, can't you be like the Rechabites and keep your word?*]

14 The words of Jonadab the son of Rechab, that he commanded his sons not to drink wine, **are performed;** for **unto this day they drink none, but obey their father's commandment:** notwithstanding I have spoken unto you, rising early and speaking [*having My prophets teach and preach to you from early each day—see verse 15*]; **but ye hearkened not unto me.**

Next, in verse 15, the Lord reminds the wicked people of Judah that He has sent many prophets (see 1 Nephi 1:4) to invite them to repent.

A very important message, repeated yet again by the Lord at this point in Jeremiah's teaching, is that in spite of their gross and repeated wickedness, these people are still invited to repent. They can still successfully return to the Lord. This is a most comforting testimony of the power of the Atonement of Jesus Christ to cleanse and heal all of us, if we will.

15 I have sent also unto you all my servants the **prophets,** rising up early [*and they have risen up early*] and **sending** *them,* saying, **Return ye now every man from his evil way, and amend your doings,** and go not after other gods [*idols*] to serve them, and ye shall dwell in the land which I have given to you and to your fathers: **but ye have not inclined your ear, nor hearkened unto me.**

16 Because the sons of Jonadab the son of Rechab [*the Rechabites*] **have performed the commandment of their father,** which he commanded them; **but this people** [*Judah*] **hath not hearkened unto me:**

17 Therefore thus saith the LORD God of hosts, the God of Israel; Behold, **I will bring upon Judah and upon all the inhabitants of Jerusalem all the evil that I have pronounced against them:** because I have spoken unto them, but they have not heard; and I have called unto them, but they have not answered.

18 ¶ And Jeremiah said unto the

house of the Rechabites, Thus saith the LORD of hosts, the God of Israel; Because ye have obeyed the commandment of Jonadab your father, and kept all his precepts, and done according unto all that he hath commanded you:

19 Therefore thus saith the LORD of hosts, the God of Israel; Jonadab the son of Rechab shall not want a man to stand before me for ever [*in other words, the Rechabites will be protected and preserved*].

JEREMIAH 36

Selection: all verses

BARUCH, JEREMIAH'S FAITHFUL scribe, had painstakingly written down the prophecies of Jeremiah so far, in order to have a written record of the words of the Lord given through him. After Baruch had read them in the temple at Jerusalem, King Jehoiakim ordered the writings of Jeremiah to be burned. He reaps the reward of his tyranny.

Afterward, Jeremiah dictates the prophecies again, and adds many additional revelations and teachings. This could remind us of the destruction by mobs of the original compilation of revelations through the Prophet Joseph Smith, known as the Book of Commandments, published in 1833. As the revelations were assembled again for publication, many more were added and it was named the Doctrine and Covenants,

published in 1835. It can also remind us of the loss of the 116 manuscript pages by Martin Harris, which were replaced by the translation of the small plates of Nephi, which contained more spiritual matters (see Doctrine & Covenants 10:30, 38–45).

As we proceed, we will remind you again that the chapters in Jeremiah are not necessarily compiled in chronological order.

1 AND it came to pass in the fourth year of Jehoiakim [*about 605 BC*] the son of Josiah king of Judah, *that* this word came unto Jeremiah from the LORD, saying,

2 Take thee a roll of a book [*NIV: "a scroll"*], and write therein all the words that I have spoken unto thee against Israel, and against Judah, and against all the nations, from the day I spake unto thee, from the days of Josiah, even unto this day [*over the last twenty-three years, since the time you were called (in about 628 BC) up to the present time (about 605 B.C.)*].

3 It may be that the house of Judah [*the Jews*] will hear all the evil [*the punishments*] which I purpose to do unto them; that they may return every man from his evil way [*repent*]; that I may forgive their iniquity and their sin.

4 Then Jeremiah called Baruch [*Jeremiah's scribe*] the son of Neriah:

and Baruch wrote from the mouth of Jeremiah [*as Jeremiah dictated*] all the words of the LORD, which he had spoken unto him, upon a roll of a book.

5 And Jeremiah commanded Baruch, saying, I *am* shut up [*I am under arrest—see footnote 5a in your Bible*]; I cannot go into the house of the LORD [*the temple in Jerusalem*]:

6 Therefore go thou, and read in the roll [*scroll*], which thou hast written from my mouth, the words of the LORD in the ears of the people in the LORD's house upon the fasting day [*a special day set aside for fasting and reading the scriptures together— see verse 9; also see Nehemiah 9:1–3*]: and also thou shalt read them in the ears of all Judah that come out of their cities [*who gather to the Jerusalem Temple from surrounding cities*].

7 It may be they will present their supplication before the LORD [*ask the Lord for forgiveness*], and will return [*repent*] every one from his evil way: for great *is* the anger and the fury that the LORD hath pronounced against this people.

8 And Baruch the son of Neriah did according to all that Jeremiah the prophet commanded him, reading in the book the words of the LORD in the LORD's house.

9 And it came to pass in the fifth year [*about 604 BC*] of Jehoiakim the son of Josiah king of Judah, in the ninth month, *that* they proclaimed a fast before the LORD to all the people in Jerusalem, and to all the people that came from the cities of Judah unto Jerusalem.

10 Then read Baruch in the book the words of Jeremiah in the house of the LORD, in the chamber of Gemariah the son of Shaphan the scribe, in the higher court, at the entry of the new gate of the LORD's house, in the ears of all the people.

11 ¶ When Michaiah the son of Gemariah, the son of Shaphan, had heard out of the book all the words of the LORD,

12 Then he went down into the king's house [*to the palace*], into the scribe's chamber: and, lo, all the princes [*leaders of the Jews*] sat there, *even* Elishama the scribe, and Delaiah the son of Shemaiah, and Elnathan the son of Achbor, and Gemariah the son of Shaphan, and Zedekiah the son of Hananiah, and all the princes.

13 Then Michaiah declared unto them all the words that he had heard, when Baruch read the book in the ears of the people.

Next, in verses 14–15, the princes (usually means "government leaders") send for Baruch and ask him to come to them and read Jeremiah's words to them.

14 Therefore all the princes sent Jehudi the son of Nethaniah, the son of Shelemiah, the son of Cushi, **unto Baruch, saying, Take in thine hand the roll** [*scroll*] **wherein thou hast read in the ears of the people, and come.** So Baruch the son of Neriah took the roll in his hand, and came unto them.

15 And they said unto him, Sit down now, and read it in our ears. So Baruch read *it* in their ears.

16 Now it came to pass, **when they had heard all the words, they were afraid** both one and other, **and said unto Baruch, We will surely tell the king of all these words.**

17 And they asked Baruch, saying, Tell us now, **How didst thou write all these words at his mouth** [*how did you end up writing all this; did he dictate it to you*]?

18 Then **Baruch answered** them, **He pronounced all these words unto me with his mouth** [*he dictated them to me*], **and I wrote *them* with ink in the book** [*scroll*].

19 Then said the princes unto Baruch, **Go, hide thee, thou and Jeremiah;** and let no man know where ye be.

20 ¶ And they went in to the king

into the court, but they laid up the roll [*put the scroll*] in the chamber of Elishama the scribe, **and told all the words in the ears of the king.**

21 So the king sent Jehudi to fetch the roll: and he took it out of Elishama the scribe's chamber. **And Jehudi read it in the ears of the king,** and in the ears of all the princes which stood beside the king.

22 Now **the king sat in the winterhouse** [*the winter apartment*] in the ninth month: **and *there was a fire on the hearth*** [*in the fireplace*] burning before him.

> Next, in verses 23–25, we see that the king became angry after hearing just three or four pages of the scroll, and cut it up with a knife and threw it into the fire, despite the objections from some of his men.

23 And it came to pass, *that* **when Jehudi had read three or four leaves, he** [*the king*] **cut it with the penknife, and cast *it* into the fire** that *was* on the hearth, **until all the roll was consumed** in the fire that *was* on the hearth.

24 Yet they were not afraid, nor rent their garments, *neither* the king, nor any of his servants that heard all these words [*they were not afraid of the prophecies of Jeremiah*].

25 Nevertheless **Elnathan and Delaiah and Gemariah** had made intercession to [had tried to intervene with] the king that he would not burn the roll: but he would not hear them.

> Next, in verse 26, the king commands that Baruch and Jeremiah be arrested, but the Lord hides them. It will be interesting someday to get the rest of this story.

26 But the king commanded Jerahmeel the son of Hammelech, and Seraiah the son of Azriel, and Shelemiah the son of Abdeel, to take Baruch the scribe and Jeremiah the prophet: but the LORD hid them.

> Next, in verses 27-32, the Lord commands Jeremiah to dictate the same words to Baruch to write again plus add many more words from the Lord.

27 ¶ Then the word of the LORD came to Jeremiah, after that the king had burned the roll, and the words which Baruch wrote at the mouth of Jeremiah, saying,

28 Take thee again another roll, and write in it all the former words that were in the first roll, which Jehoiakim the king of Judah hath burned.

29 And thou shalt say to Jehoiakim king of Judah, Thus saith the LORD; Thou hast burned this roll, saying, Why hast thou written therein, saying, The king of Babylon shall certainly come and destroy this land, and shall cause to cease from thence man and beast?

30 Therefore thus saith the LORD of Jehoiakim king of Judah; He shall have none to sit upon the throne of David [he shall have no posterity to take his place on the throne when he dies]: and his dead body shall be cast out in the day to the heat, and in the night to the frost [he will be despised and won't even get a burial].

31 And I will punish him and his seed and his servants for their iniquity; and I will bring upon them, and upon the inhabitants of Jerusalem, and upon the men of Judah, all the evil that I have pronounced against them; but they hearkened not.

32 ¶ Then took Jeremiah another roll, and gave it to Baruch the scribe, the son of Neriah; who wrote therein from the mouth of Jeremiah all the words of the book which Jehoiakim king of Judah had burned in the fire: and there were added besides unto them many like words.

JEREMIAH 37

Selection: all verses

THIS CHAPTER BEGINS at the start of Zedekiah's wicked reign over the kingdom of Judah, about 598 BC He is twenty-one years old (see 52:1) and will rule as king for eleven years.

The Babylonians have already begun the process of defeating the cities of Judah and Jerusalem. Daniel and others have already been taken captive to Babylon. Lehi and his family fled from the Jerusalem area in 600 BC and are likely still in the wilderness, journeying toward the ocean where Nephi will be commanded to build a ship.

Egyptian armies are coming up from Egypt to engage the Babylonian armies in battle, which will cause Nebuchadnezzar, king of Babylon to pull his armies away from Jerusalem temporarily in order to engage and defeat the Egyptians.

As we begin the chapter, we are given a brief description of King Zedekiah and his people.

1 AND king Zedekiah the son of Josiah **reigned instead of** [*in the place of*] **Coniah** the son of Jehoiakim, whom Nebuchadrezzar king of Babylon made king in the land of Judah.

2 But neither he, nor his servants, nor the people of the land, did hearken unto the words of the LORD, which he spake by the prophet Jeremiah.

Next, wicked King Zedekiah sends word to Jeremiah requesting him to pray for him and his people. The king has not yet arrested Jeremiah and put him in prison.

3 And Zedekiah the king sent Jehucal the son of Shelemiah and Zephaniah the son of Maaseiah the priest **to the prophet Jeremiah, saying, Pray now unto the LORD our God for us.**

4 Now Jeremiah came in and went out among the people [*he was still free to come and go as he pleased*]: **for they had not put him into prison.**

At this point in history, the Babylonian armies had already laid siege to Jerusalem. As you can see in verse 5, next, Egyptian armies had been sent up from Egypt by Pharaoh to engage the Babylonians in battle. It will prove to be merely a temporary distraction for Nebuchadnezzar's powerful Babylonian forces.

5 Then Pharaoh's army was come forth out of Egypt: and when the Chaldeans [*Babylonians*] that besieged Jerusalem **heard** tidings of them, **they departed from Jerusalem.**

The prophecy that Jeremiah now gives King Zedekiah is not well received by him and his people.

6 ¶ Then came the word of the

LORD unto the prophet Jeremiah, saying,

7 Thus saith the LORD, the God of Israel; **Thus shall ye say to the king** of Judah [*Zedekiah*], that sent you unto me to enquire of me; **Behold, Pharaoh's army, which is come forth to help you, shall return to Egypt into their own land.**

8 **And the Chaldeans shall come again, and fight against this city** [*Jerusalem*], and take it, and burn it with fire.

Remember that false prophets among the Jews at this time have repeatedly prophesied that the King of Babylon and his armies would not destroy Jerusalem—see verse 19. This made Jeremiah look bad as he prophesied the opposite.

9 Thus saith the LORD; **Deceive not yourselves, saying, The Chaldeans shall surely depart from us: for they shall not depart.**

As you can see by what the Lord says in verse 10, next, the Jews do not have any chance at all of defeating the Babylonians, when they focus again on the siege of Jerusalem after coming back from defeating the Egyptians.

10 **For though** [*even if*] **ye had smitten the whole army of the Chaldeans** [*the Babylonians*] that fight against you, **and there remained** *but* **wounded men among them, yet should they rise**

up every man in his tent, **and burn this city with fire.**

Next, beginning with verse 11, we are told what happened to Jeremiah during the temporary lull in the siege while the Chaldeans (Babylonian army) left to deal with the Egyptians.

11 ¶ And it came to pass, **that when the army of the Chaldeans was broken up from Jerusalem for fear of Pharaoh's army,**

12 Then **Jeremiah went** forth out of Jerusalem **to go into the land of Benjamin** [*in other words, as Jeremiah started to leave Jerusalem*], to separate himself thence in the midst of the people.

13 And **when he was in the gate of Benjamin** [*in other words, just as he was leaving Jerusalem*], **a captain** of the ward [*an officer in the king's army*] *was* there, whose name *was* Irijah, the son of Shelemiah, the son of Hananiah; and he **took** [*arrested*] **Jeremiah the prophet, saying** [*accusing him, saying*], **Thou fallest away to the Chaldeans** [*you are deserting to the Babylonians*].

14 **Then said Jeremiah, It** *is* **false; I fall not away to the Chaldeans.** But he [*the officer*] hearkened not to him: so Irijah took Jeremiah, and **brought him to the princes** [*the leaders of the Jews*].

15 Wherefore **the princes were**

wroth with Jeremiah, and smote him, and put him in prison in the house of Jonathan the scribe: for they had made that the prison.

16 ¶ When Jeremiah was entered into the dungeon, and into the cabins, and Jeremiah had remained there many days;

> Next, King Zedekiah secretly sends for Jeremiah and asks what the Lord has to say. He doesn't want anyone to know that he is asking such a question.

17 Then Zedekiah the king sent, and took him out [of the dungeon]: and the king asked him secretly in his house, and said, Is there any word from the LORD? And Jeremiah said, There is: for, said he, thou shalt be delivered into the hand of the king of Babylon.

18 Moreover Jeremiah said unto king Zedekiah, What have I offended against thee, or against thy servants, or against this people, that ye have put me in prison?

19 Where are now your [false] prophets which prophesied unto you, saying, The king of Babylon shall not come against you, nor against this land?

20 Therefore hear now, I pray thee, O my lord the king: let my supplication, I pray thee, be accepted before thee; that thou cause me not to return to the house of Jonathan the scribe, lest I die there.

> In response to Jeremiah's urgent request (verse 20, above) not to go back to the terrible conditions in the dungeon, Zedekiah has him put in the palace prison. As you can see, in verse 21, next, conditions of famine were already getting severe because of the Babylonian siege of Jerusalem.

21 Then Zedekiah the king commanded that they should commit Jeremiah into the court of the prison [a prison in the palace], and that they should give him daily a piece of bread out of the bakers' street, until all the bread in the city were spent. Thus Jeremiah remained in the court of the prison.

JEREMIAH 38

Selection: all verses

THIS CHAPTER CONTINUES the account of Jeremiah's imprisonment, which started in chapter 37. Our hearts go out to him as he is put in a miserable dungeon, where he sinks in the mud. A kindly Ethiopian, in the service of the king, is gentle with Jeremiah as he pulls him out of the mire, giving the prophet rags to put under his shoulders to pad the ropes used to pull him out so that they won't cut him (verses 11–13). It is apparently a dungeon that is accessed only by a hole in the ceiling. Prisoners are dropped in and must be hauled out with ropes.

As we begin reading this chapter, we soon discover that some influential government leaders are angry at what Jeremiah has prophesied concerning the destruction of Jerusalem by the Babylonians. They feel that his prophecies are demoralizing the Jewish soldiers assigned to protect Jerusalem and do battle against the Babylonians. They are particularly angry about Jeremiah's counsel from the Lord to them that they should surrender the city to Nebuchadnezzar's forces—see background to chapter 27 in this study guide. See also verse 2 here in chapter 38.

1 THEN Shephatiah the son of Mattan, and Gedaliah the son of Pashur, and Jucal the son of Shelemiah, and Pashur the son of Malchiah, heard the words that Jeremiah had spoken unto all the people, saying,

2 Thus saith the LORD, He that remaineth in this city shall die by the sword, by the famine, and by the pestilence: but he that goeth forth [surrenders] to the Chaldeans shall live; for he shall have his life for a prey, and shall live.

3 Thus saith the LORD, This city shall surely be given into the hand of the king of Babylon's army, which shall take it.

4 Therefore the princes [government leaders, rulers—see footnote 4a in your Bible] said unto the king, We beseech thee, let this man

[Jeremiah] be put to death: for thus he weakeneth the hands of the men of war [soldiers and defenders] that remain in this city, and the hands of all the people, in speaking such words unto them: for this man seeketh not the welfare of this people, but the hurt [Jeremiah is trying to undermine and hurt our people].

Next, in verse 5, we see the cowardly nature of King Zedekiah as he meekly claims he can do nothing to stop these men if they want to harm Jeremiah.

5 Then Zedekiah the king said, Behold, he is in your hand: for the king is not he that can do any thing against you.

6 Then took they Jeremiah, and cast him into the dungeon of Malchiah the son of Hammelech, that was in the court of the prison: and they let down Jeremiah with cords [ropes]. And in the dungeon there was no water, but mire: so Jeremiah sunk in the mire.

7 ¶ Now when Ebed-melech the Ethiopian, one of the eunuchs which was in the king's house [one of the king's servants], heard that they had put Jeremiah in the dungeon; the king then sitting in the gate of Benjamin [the king was conducting business in an area set aside for that purpose in a city gate];

8 Ebed-melech went forth out of the king's house, and spake to the king, saying,

9 My lord the king, these men have done evil in all that they have done to Jeremiah the prophet, whom they have cast into the dungeon; and he is like to die for hunger in the place where he is: for *there is* no more bread in the city [*the famine as a result of the Babylonian siege was getting very severe*].

10 Then the king commanded Ebed-melech the Ethiopian, saying, Take from hence thirty men with thee, and take up Jeremiah the prophet out of the dungeon, before he die.

11 So Ebed-melech took the men with him, and went into the house of the king under the treasury, and took thence old cast clouts [*threadbare, worn out clothes*] and old rotten rags, and let them down by cords into the dungeon to Jeremiah.

12 And Ebed-melech the Ethiopian said unto Jeremiah, Put now *these* old cast clouts [*discarded clothes*] and rotten rags under thine armholes [*armpits*] under the cords [*to pad the ropes*]. And Jeremiah did so.

13 So they drew up Jeremiah with cords, and took him up out of the dungeon: and Jeremiah remained in the court of the prison [*stayed in another prison in the palace*].

Beginning with verse 14, next, we watch as Zedekiah again calls for Jeremiah to be brought from prison in order to speak with him. He asks, in effect, that Jeremiah tell him exactly what the Lord has told him about the fate of Jerusalem and her king, and to withhold no information. You will see that this makes Jeremiah a bit nervous.

14 ¶ Then Zedekiah the king sent, and took Jeremiah the prophet unto him into the third entry that *is* in the house of the LORD: and the king said unto Jeremiah, I will ask thee a thing; hide nothing from me.

15 Then Jeremiah said unto Zedekiah, If I declare *it* unto thee, wilt thou not surely put me to death? and if I give thee counsel, wilt thou not hearken unto me [*and if I give you advice, isn't it true that you won't listen to me*]?

16 So Zedekiah the king sware [*promised*] secretly unto Jeremiah, saying, As the LORD liveth [*the strongest oath in Jewish culture of that day*], that made us this soul [*who gave us life*], I will not put thee to death, neither will I give thee into the hand of these men that seek thy life.

17 Then said Jeremiah unto Zedekiah, Thus saith the LORD, the God of hosts, the God of Israel;

If thou wilt assuredly go forth [surrender] unto the king of Babylon's princes [army commanders], then thy soul shall live, and this city shall not be burned with fire; and thou shalt live, and thine house [your wives and children also—see verse 23]:

18 But if thou wilt not go forth to the king of Babylon's princes, then shall this city be given into the hand of the Chaldeans, and they shall burn it with fire, and thou shalt not escape out of their hand.

19 And Zedekiah the king said unto Jeremiah, I am afraid of the Jews that are fallen to the Chaldeans [who have already deserted to the Babylonians—see footnote 19a in your Bible], lest they deliver me into their hand [lest the Babylonians turn me over to them], and they mock [abuse, mistreat] me.

20 But Jeremiah said, They shall not deliver thee [hand you over to the Jews who have surrendered]. Obey, I beseech thee, the voice of the LORD, which I speak unto thee: so it shall be well unto thee, and thy soul shall live.

21 But if thou refuse to go forth [surrender], this is the word that the LORD hath shewed me:

In order to understand verse 22, next, it is helpful to know that one of the worst insults in Jewish culture of the day was to be mocked in public by women. Jeremiah warns Zedekiah that this is exactly what will happen to him if he does not follow the Lord's counsel and surrender to the invading army.

22 And, behold, all the women that are left in the king of Judah's house [in other words, in the palace] shall be brought forth to the king of Babylon's princes [generals and leaders], and those women shall say [mock you, saying], Thy friends [German Bible: your trusted advisers] have set thee on [have misled you; i.e., you are gullible], and have prevailed against thee [have overruled you, the king]: thy feet are sunk in the mire [they have led you into a trap], and they are turned away back [your friends have deserted you].

23 So they shall bring out all thy wives and thy children to the Chaldeans [this indeed happened; and all of his sons (except Mulek) were killed before his eyes—see 52:10]: and thou shalt not escape out of their hand, but shalt be taken by the hand of the king of Babylon: and thou shalt cause this city to be burned with fire [it will be your fault that Jerusalem is burned].

Next, King Zedekiah tells Jeremiah that under penalty of death he is not to tell anyone about their secret conversation.

24 ¶ Then said Zedekiah unto

Jeremiah, **Let no man know of these words, and thou shalt not die.**

25 But if the princes hear that I have talked with thee, and they come unto thee, and say unto thee, Declare unto us now what thou hast said unto the king, hide it not from us, and we will not put thee to death; also what the king said unto thee:

26 Then thou shalt say unto them, I presented my supplication before the king, that he would not cause me to return to Jonathan's house [*which had been made into a prison— see 37:15*], to die there.

27 Then came all the princes unto Jeremiah, and asked him: and he told them according to all these words that the king had commanded. So they left off speaking with him; for the matter was not perceived [*they did not find out what Jeremiah and Zedekiah had discussed*].

> Verse 28, next, informs us that Jeremiah was kept in the royal palace prison until Jerusalem was captured.

28 So Jeremiah abode in the court of the prison until the day that Jerusalem was taken: and he was *there* when Jerusalem was taken.

JEREMIAH 39

Selection: all verses

THIS CHAPTER IS an account of the fall of Jerusalem, about 587 BC (see "Capture of Jerusalem" on the chronology chart in the Bible Dictionary at the back of your LDS Bible).

1 IN the ninth year of Zedekiah king of Judah, in the tenth month, came Nebuchadrezzar king of Babylon and all his army against Jerusalem, and they besieged it [*laid siege to it*].

2 And in the eleventh year of Zedekiah, in the fourth month, the ninth *day* **of the month, the city was broken up** [*the Babylonian soldiers broke through the city wall*].

3 And all the princes [*military leaders*] **of the king of Babylon came in,** and sat in the middle gate, *even* Nergal-sharezer, Samgar-nebo, Sarsechim, Rab-saris, Nergal-sharezer, Rab-mag, with all the residue of the princes [*other military leaders*] of the king of Babylon.

> Next we are told that King Zedekiah and some of his people made a futile attempt to escape and were captured near Jericho.

4 ¶ And it came to pass, *that* **when Zedekiah the king of Judah saw them, and all the men of war, then they fled, and went forth out of**

the city by night, by the way of the king's garden, by the gate betwixt the two walls: and he went out the way of the plain.

5 But the Chaldeans' army pursued after them, and overtook Zedekiah in the plains of Jericho: and when they had taken him, they brought him up to Nebuchadnezzar king of Babylon to Riblah [in northern Syria] in the land of Hamath, where he gave judgment upon him [where he sentenced him].

6 Then the king of Babylon slew the sons of Zedekiah in Riblah before his eyes: also the king of Babylon slew all the nobles of Judah.

We know from the Book of Mormon that one of Zedekiah's sons, Mulek, escaped, and was brought by the Lord to America. We will include two references from the Book of Mormon here:

Helaman 6:10
10 Now the land south was called Lehi and the land north was called Mulek, which was after the son of Zedekiah; for the Lord did bring Mulek into the land north, and Lehi into the land south.

Helaman 8:21
21 And now will you dispute that Jerusalem was destroyed? Will ye say that the sons of Zedekiah were not slain, all except it were Mulek? Yea, and do ye not behold that the seed of Zedekiah are with us,

and they were driven out of the land of Jerusalem? But behold, this is not all—

7 Moreover he put out Zedekiah's eyes, and bound him with chains, to carry him to Babylon.

8 ¶ And the Chaldeans burned the king's house [the palace in Jerusalem], and the houses of the people, with fire, and brake down the walls of Jerusalem.

Some groups of Jewish prisoners had already been taken to Babylon in earlier waves of the Babylonian conquest. Included in those groups of prisoners were Daniel and Ezekiel. Next, in verses 9–10, we see that many of the remaining Jews were taken to Babylon. However, many of the poor were left in the land of Judah and given land to farm.

9 Then Nebuzar-adan the captain of the guard [NIV: commander of the imperial guard] carried away captive into Babylon the remnant of the people that remained in the city, and those that fell away, that fell to him [who had deserted to the Babylonians—see footnote 9a in your Bible], with the rest of the people that remained.

10 But Nebuzar-adan the captain of the guard left of the poor of the people, which had nothing, in the land of Judah, and gave them vineyards and fields at the same time.

Next, in verses 11–14, we see

that King Nebuchadnezzar commanded that Jeremiah be set free from the prison he was in and be treated well.

11 ¶ Now **Nebuchadrezzar** king of Babylon **gave charge concerning Jeremiah** to Nebuzar-adan the captain of the guard, saying,

12 **Take him, and look well to him, and do him no harm; but do unto him even as he shall say unto thee.**

13 So Nebuzar-adan the captain of the guard sent, and Nebushasban, Rab-saris, and Nergal-sharezer, Rab-mag, and all the king of Babylon's princes;

14 Even **they sent, and took Jeremiah out of the court of the prison,** and committed him unto Gedaliah the son of Ahikam the son of Shaphan, **that he should carry him home:** so he dwelt among the people.

> Next, in verses 15–18, we find that before Jeremiah was set free, he had prophesied concerning the kind Ethiopian servant who threw him rags with which to pad his armpits with when he was pulled from the dungeon— see Jeremiah 38:7–13.

15 ¶ **Now the word of the LORD came unto Jeremiah, while he was shut up in the court of the prison,** saying,

16 **Go and speak to Ebed-melech the Ethiopian,** saying, Thus saith the LORD of hosts, the God of Israel;

Behold, I will bring my words upon this city for evil [all that has been prophesied concerning the destruction of Jerusalem will take place, because of wickedness], **and not for good; and they shall be** accomplished **in that day before thee.**

17 **But I will deliver thee** [the kind Ethiopian servant] **in that day, saith the LORD: and thou shalt not be given into the hand of the men of whom thou** art **afraid.**

18 **For I will surely deliver thee, and thou shalt not fall by the sword, but thy life shall be for a prey unto thee** [your life will be preserved]: **because thou hast put thy trust in me, saith the LORD.**

JEREMIAH 40

Selection: all verses

AFTER THE FALL of Jerusalem to the Babylonians, in about 587 BC, King Nebuchadnezzar's soldiers captured King Zedekiah, as detailed in chapter 39, verses 4–7. He then appointed a Jew named Gedaliah to serve as the governor over the remaining Jews who were left behind in Judah. It was Gedaliah's father, Ahikam, who had saved Jeremiah's life about twenty-two years earlier (see Jeremiah 26:24).

Jeremiah had been taken to Ramah, about five miles north of Jerusalem, in chains, with the other prisoners, but was set free by order of King

Nebuchadnezzar of Babylon to Nebuzar-adan, his captain of the guard (verse 1). (By the way, there were two towns called Ramah that were significant in Old Testament times. One was about twenty miles northwest of Jerusalem, and the other, mentioned here in verse 1, was about five miles north of Jerusalem.) After having been set free at Ramah, Jeremiah was allowed to choose whether to accompany the Jews being taken to Babylon or remain in Judah. In either case, he was to be treated well, by order of the king of Babylon. He stayed in Judah.

1 THE word that came to Jeremiah from the LORD, after that **Nebuzar-adan the captain of the guard had let him go** [*set him free*] **from Ramah**, when he had taken him being bound in chains among all that were carried away captive of Jerusalem and Judah, which were carried [*which were about to be carried*] away captive unto Babylon.

2 And the captain of the guard took Jeremiah, and said unto him, The LORD thy God hath pronounced this evil upon this place.

3 Now the LORD hath brought *it*, and done according as he hath said: because ye have sinned against the LORD, and have not obeyed his voice, therefore this thing is come upon you.

4 And now, **behold, I loose thee this day from the chains** which

were upon thine hand. **If it seem good unto thee to come with me into Babylon, come**; and I will look well unto thee: **but if it seem ill unto thee to come with me** into Babylon, forbear [*don't come*]: **behold, all the land** *is* **before thee: whither it seemeth good and convenient for thee to go, thither go** [*you may live wherever you desire in Judah*].

5 Now while he [*Jeremiah*] was not yet gone back [*before Jeremiah turned to go back*], he [*Nebuzar-adan*] *said*, **Go back** also **to Gedaliah** the son of Ahikam [*who had saved Jeremiah's life about twenty-two years ago*] the son of Shaphan, **whom the king of Babylon hath made governor** over the cities of Judah, **and dwell with him among the people: or go wheresoever it seemeth convenient unto thee to go.** So the captain of the guard gave him victuals [*a food allowance—see footnote 5b in your Bible*] and a reward, and let him go.

6 Then went Jeremiah unto Gedaliah the son of Ahikam to Mizpah; and dwelt with him among the people that were left in the land.

Next, in verses 7–11, we see that many Jews who had fled to open country to escape the Babylonians, or to neighboring nations, came back when things settled down and Gedaliah had been made governor.

7 ¶ Now when all the captains of

the forces [*Jewish army*] which *were* in the fields [*who had fled to open country*], *even* they and their men, heard that the king of Babylon had made Gedaliah the son of Ahikam governor in the land, and had committed unto him [*had put him in charge of*] men, and women, and children, and of the poor of the land, of them that were not carried away captive to Babylon;

8 Then they came to Gedaliah to Mizpah [*about ten miles north of Jerusalem*], even Ishmael the son of Nethaniah, and Johanan and Jonathan the sons of Kareah, and Seraiah the son of Tanhumeth, and the sons of Ephai the Netophathite, and Jezaniah the son of a Maachathite, they and their men.

Next, Governor Gedaliah assures these men that they will be safe if they submit to the Babylonian rule.

9 And Gedaliah the son of Ahikam the son of Shaphan sware unto them and to their men, saying, Fear not to serve the Chaldeans [*the Babylonians*]: dwell in the land, and serve the king of Babylon, and it shall be well with you.

10 As for me, behold, I will dwell at Mizpah to serve the Chaldeans, which will come unto us: but ye, gather ye wine, and summer fruits, and oil, and put *them* in your vessels, and dwell in your cities

that ye have taken [*in other words, settle down to farming in the cities you have occupied*].

11 Likewise when all the Jews [*other Jews who had fled to neighboring countries*] that *were* in Moab, and among the Ammonites, and in Edom, and that *were* in all the countries, heard that the king of Babylon had left a remnant of Judah, and that he had set over them Gedaliah the son of Ahikam the son of Shaphan;

12 Even all the Jews returned out of all places whither they were driven, and came to the land of Judah, to Gedaliah, unto Mizpah, and gathered wine and summer fruits very much [*and gathered an abundant harvest*].

Next, Governor Gedaliah is warned about a plot by the Ammonite king to assassinate him. The Ammonite nation was located east of the Jordan River, north of Jerusalem.

13 ¶ Moreover Johanan the son of Kareah, and all the captains of the forces that *were* in the fields, came to Gedaliah to Mizpah,

14 And said unto him, Dost thou certainly know that Baalis the king of the Ammonites hath sent Ishmael the son of Nethaniah to slay thee? But Gedaliah the son of Ahikam believed them not.

15 Then Johanan the son of Kareah spake to Gedaliah in Mizpah secretly, saying, Let me go, I pray thee, and I will slay Ishmael the son of Nethaniah, and no man shall know it: wherefore should he slay thee [why should he be allowed to assassinate you], that all the Jews which are gathered unto thee should be scattered, and the remnant in Judah perish?

16 But Gedaliah the son of Ahikam said unto Johanan the son of Kareah, Thou shalt not do this thing: for thou speakest falsely of Ishmael [you are falsely accusing Ishmael].

JEREMIAH 41

Selection: all verses

THE ASSASSINATION PLOT discussed in chapter 40 is carried out in this chapter. Jeremiah's friend, Gedaliah, who has been appointed governor of the remaining Jews in the land of Judah, by the king of Babylon, is murdered. As you found out near the end of chapter 40, Gedaliah was warned by friends about Ishmael's plot, but refused to believe that he would do such a thing to him.

As verse 1 indicates, Ishmael was a member of the Jewish royal family. He plotted with other former government leaders of the Jews to go visit Gedaliah at his headquarters at Mizpah, about ten miles north of Jerusalem, and kill him.

1 NOW it came to pass in the seventh month, that Ishmael the son of Nethaniah the son of Elishama, of the seed royal, and the princes of the king [who was of royal blood and who had been one of King Zedekiah's officers in his government], even ten men with him, came unto Gedaliah the son of Ahikam to Mizpah; and there they did eat bread together in Mizpah.

2 Then arose Ishmael the son of Nethaniah, and the ten men that were with him, and smote Gedaliah the son of Ahikam the son of Shaphan with the sword, and slew him, whom the king of Babylon had made governor over the land.

Next, in verse 3, we see that Ishmael and his men not only killed Governor Gedaliah and the Jews who were with him, but they also killed the Babylonian soldiers there, so that it took a couple of days before anyone found out about the assassination and slaughter.

3 Ishmael also slew all the Jews that were with him, even with Gedaliah, at Mizpah, and the Chaldeans that were found there, and the men of war [NIV as well as the Babylonian soldiers who were there].

Apparently, Gedaliah's stronghold was sufficiently isolated from the rest of Mizpah that no one immediately noticed the slaughter.

4 And it came to pass the second

day after he had slain Gedaliah, and **no man knew** *it*,

5 That **there came certain from Shechem, from Shiloh, and from Samaria** [*cities in the Holy Land*], **even fourscore men** [*eighty men*], having their beards shaven, and their clothes rent, and having cut themselves [*physical signs in that culture that they had made a vow, in this case to bring offerings to the temple no matter what*], **with offerings and incense** in their hand, **to bring** *them* **to the house of the LORD** [*on their way to the temple in Jerusalem*].

> Next, Ishmael and his henchmen set up an ambush for these Jews who were going to Jerusalem.

6 **And Ishmael** the son of Nethaniah **went forth from Mizpah to meet them, weeping all along** as he went: and it came to pass, **as he met them, he said** unto them, **Come to Gedaliah the son of Ahikam.**

7 **And** it was *so,* **when they came into the midst of the city,** that Ishmael the son of Nethaniah **slew them,** *and cast them* into the midst of the pit, **he, and the men that** *were* **with him.**

> Next, ten of the men who were ambushed persuade Ishmael not to kill them, in return for supplies of food.

8 But **ten men** were found among them that **said unto Ishmael, Slay us not: for we have treasures in the field, of wheat, and of barley, and of oil, and of honey.** So he forbare, and slew them not among their brethren.

9 Now the pit wherein Ishmael had cast all the dead bodies of the men, whom he had slain because of Gedaliah, *was* it which Asa the king had made for fear of Baasha king of Israel: *and* Ishmael the son of Nethaniah filled it with *them that were* slain.

10 **Then Ishmael carried away captive all the residue** [*the rest*] **of the people that** *were* **in Mizpah,** *even* [*including*] **the king's daughters, and all the people that remained in Mizpah,** whom Nebuzar-adan the captain of the guard had committed to Gedaliah the son of Ahikam: and **Ishmael the son of Nethaniah carried them away captive, and departed to go** [*intending to go*] **over to the Ammonites** [*an area east of the Jordan River and north of Jerusalem*].

11 ¶ **But when Johanan** the son of Kareah, **and all the captains of the forces that** *were* **with him, heard of all the evil that Ishmael** the son of Nethaniah **had done,**

12 Then **they took all the men, and went to fight with Ishmael** the son of Nethaniah, and found him by the great waters that *are* in Gibeon

[some pools of water, a bit northwest of Jerusalem].

Imagine the relief of the prisoners taken by Ishmael and his accomplices when they saw Johanan and the Jewish soldiers that were with him coming to rescue them!

13 Now it came to pass, *that* **when all the people which** *were* **with Ishmael saw Johanan** the son of Kareah, **and all the captains of the forces that** *were* **with him, then they were glad.**

14 So all the people that Ishmael had carried away captive from Mizpah **cast about** [*turned around*] **and returned,** and went unto Johanan the son of Kareah.

15 But Ishmael the son of Nethaniah **escaped from Johanan with eight men, and went to the Ammonites.**

Next, we see that Johanan and his men and the people with them were afraid of retaliation from the Babylonians, and so they decided to go to Egypt for safety.

16 Then took Johanan the son of Kareah, **and all the captains** of the forces that *were* with him, **all the remnant of the people whom he had recovered** [*rescued*] from Ishmael the son of Nethaniah, from Mizpah, after *that* he had slain Gedaliah the son of Ahikam, *even* mighty men of war, and the women, and the children, and the eunuchs, whom he had brought again from Gibeon:

17 **And they departed, and dwelt** in the habitation of Chimham, **which is by Beth-lehem, to go to enter into Egypt,**

18 Because of the Chaldeans: **for they were afraid** of them, **because Ishmael** the son of Nethaniah **had slain Gedaliah** the son of Ahikam, **whom the king of Babylon made governor in the land.**

JEREMIAH 42

Selection: all verses

THIS CHAPTER IS a continuation of the account in chapters 40–41. At the end of chapter 41, you saw Johanan and his soldiers, along with the Jews they had rescued from Ishmael, gather near Bethlehem, preparing to attempt an escape to Egypt.

They decided to go visit Jeremiah and ask for counsel from the Lord concerning their plans. Let's see what happens.

1 **THEN** all **the captains of the** forces [*the military officers*], **and Johanan** the son of Kareah, and Jezaniah the son of Hoshaiah, **and all the people** [*in Johanan's group*] from the least even unto the greatest, **came near** [*went and found Jeremiah*],

2 And said unto Jeremiah the prophet, Let, we beseech thee, our supplication be accepted before thee, and pray for us unto the LORD thy God, *even* for all this remnant; (for we are left *but* a few of many, as thine eyes do behold us [*we are a small enough group that you can see all of us before your eyes*]:)

3 That the LORD thy God may shew us the way wherein we may walk, and the thing that we may do.

4 Then Jeremiah the prophet said unto them, I have heard *you*; behold, I will pray unto the LORD your God according to your words; and it shall come to pass, *that* whatsoever thing the LORD shall answer you, I will declare *it* unto you; I will keep nothing back from you.

> Next, these refugees promise faithfully that they will follow the Lord's counsel exactly, no matter what He says.

5 Then they said to Jeremiah, The LORD be a true and faithful witness between us, if we do not even according to all things for the which the LORD thy God shall send thee to us.

6 Whether *it be* good, or whether *it be* evil, we will obey the voice of the LORD our God, to whom we send thee; that it may be well with us, when we obey the voice of the LORD our God.

7 ¶ And it came to pass after ten days, that the word of the LORD came unto Jeremiah.

8 Then called he Johanan the son of Kareah, and all the captains of the forces which *were* with him, and all the people from the least even to the greatest,

9 And said unto them, Thus saith the LORD, the God of Israel, unto whom ye sent me to present your supplication before him;

> Next, Jeremiah gives these men the answer from the Lord per their request (in verses 1 and 2). We will need the JST to clarify correct doctrine regarding the last phrase of verse 10.
>
> By the way, some have wondered why JST changes such as the one following verse 10 are not found in the footnotes in our LDS English edition of the Bible or at the back of it. The answer is that there was not enough room in our Bible to include them all. I use *Joseph Smith's "New Translation" of the Bible*, printed by Herald Publishing House, Independence, Missouri, 1970, which contains all of the Prophet's changes to the Bible as the source for these additional JST changes. It has been shown by LDS scholars to be reliable and true to the Prophet's original work on the Bible. Most LDS bookstores either carry books that have all of the JST changes to the Bible or can get it for you if you ask them to.

10 If ye will still abide in this land

[if you will stay here in Judah], **then will I build you, and not pull** *you* **down, and I will plant you, and not pluck** *you* **up** *[in other words, you will prosper if you stay in Judah in subjection to the Babylonians]*: for I repent me of the evil that I have done unto you.

JST Jeremiah 42:10

10 If you will still abide in this land, then will I build you, and not pull down; I will plant you, and not pluck up; **and I will turn away the evil that I have done unto you.**

11 Be not afraid of the king of Babylon, of whom ye are afraid; be not afraid of him, saith the LORD: **for I** *am* **with you to save you, and to deliver you from his hand.**

12 And I will shew mercies unto you, that he may have mercy upon you, and cause you to return to your own land.

13 ¶ But if ye say, We will not dwell in this land, neither obey the voice of the LORD your God,

14 Saying, No; but we will go into the land of Egypt, where we shall see no war, nor hear the sound of the trumpet *[the signal to battle for armies]*, nor have hunger of bread; and there will we dwell:

15 And now therefore hear the word of the LORD, ye remnant of Judah;

Thus saith the LORD of hosts, the God of Israel; **If ye wholly set your faces to enter into Egypt, and go to sojourn** *[remain]* **there;**

16 Then it shall come to pass, *that* **the sword,** which ye feared, shall overtake you there in the land of Egypt, **and the famine,** whereof ye were afraid, **shall follow close after you there in Egypt; and there ye shall die.**

17 So shall it be with all the men that set their faces to go into Egypt to sojourn there; **they shall die by the sword,** by the **famine,** and by the **pestilence** *[disease, plagues, disasters, and so forth]*: **and none of them shall remain or escape** from the evil that I will bring upon them.

18 For **thus saith the LORD** of hosts, the God of Israel; **As mine anger and my fury hath been poured forth upon the inhabitants of Jerusalem; so shall my fury be poured forth upon you, when ye shall enter into Egypt: and ye shall be an execration** *[people will curse and swear at you]*, **and an astonishment** *[horror]*, **and a curse, and a reproach** *[people will look down on you]*; **and ye shall see this place no more** *[you will never come back to Jerusalem and the land of Judah]*.

19 ¶ The LORD hath said concerning you, O ye remnant of Judah [fragment of the Jews]; **Go ye not into Egypt:** know certainly that I have admonished you this day [consider yourselves fairly warned].

> Next, Jeremiah warns these people, who were not being honest with themselves when they asked Jeremiah to get the word of the Lord to them, that they have made a fatal mistake by planning to ignore the Lord's counsel.

20 For ye dissembled in your hearts [you were not sincere in your request for counsel from the Lord], **when ye sent me unto the LORD** your God, saying, Pray for us unto the LORD our God; and according unto all that the LORD our God shall say, so declare unto us, and we will do it.

21 And now **I have this day declared** it **to you; but ye have not obeyed the voice of the LORD** your God, nor any thing for the which he hath sent me unto you.

22 Now therefore know certainly that ye shall die by the sword, by the famine, and by the pestilence, in the place whither ye desire to go [Egypt] and to sojourn [live].

JEREMIAH 43

Selection: all verses

THIS CHAPTER IS a continuation of the tense situation described at the end of chapter 42. In the end, Jeremiah and his faithful scribe, Baruch, will be kidnapped and taken by these rebels to Egypt.

1 And it came to pass, that **when Jeremiah had made an end of speaking unto all the people all the words of the LORD** their God [as recorded in chapter 42], for which the LORD their God had sent him to them, even all these words,

2 Then spake Azariah the son of Hoshaiah, **and Johanan** the son of Kareah, **and all the proud men,** saying unto **Jeremiah, Thou speakest falsely** [you are lying]: the LORD our God hath not sent thee to say, Go not into Egypt to sojourn there:

> Next, these rebellious men claim that Jeremiah's faithful scribe, Baruch, has prejudiced him against them and induced Jeremiah to give them a false revelation that will lead to their deaths or captivity.

3 But Baruch the son of Neriah **setteth thee on against us,** for to deliver us into the hand of the Chaldeans, that they might put us to death, and carry us away captives into Babylon.

4 So Johanan the son of Kareah, and all the captains of the forces, and all the people, obeyed not the voice of the LORD, to dwell in the land of Judah.

Next, we see that these rebels not only reject Jeremiah's words, but they kidnap Jeremiah and Baruch, and take them to Egypt with them.

5 But Johanan the son of Kareah, and all the captains of the forces, took all the remnant of Judah, that were returned from all nations, whither they had been driven, to dwell in the land of Judah;

6 Even men, and women, and children, and the king's daughters, and every person that Nebuzar-adan the captain of the guard had left with Gedaliah [the Jewish governor who was assassinated by Jewish rebels led by Ishmael—see chapter 41] the son of Ahikam the son of Shaphan, and Jeremiah the prophet, and Baruch the son of Neriah.

7 So they came into the land of Egypt: for they obeyed not the voice of the LORD: thus came they even to Tahpanhes [in Egypt, in the land of Goshen, where Joseph, his brothers, father and their families settled].

Next, the Lord uses drama as He has Jeremiah prophesy that the Babylonians will attack and overcome Egypt.

8 ¶ Then came the word of the LORD unto Jeremiah in Tahpanhes, saying,

9 Take great stones in thine hand, and hide them in the clay in the brickkiln, which is at the entry of Pharaoh's house in Tahpanhes, in the sight of the men of Judah;

10 And say unto them, Thus saith the LORD of hosts, the God of Israel; Behold, I will send and take Nebuchadrezzar the king of Babylon, my servant [the tool of the Lord to "hammer" Egypt], and will set his throne upon these stones that I have hid; and he shall spread his royal pavilion over them.

11 And when he cometh, he shall smite the land of Egypt, and deliver such as are for death to death; and such as are for captivity to captivity; and such as are for the sword to the sword.

12 And I will kindle a fire in the houses of the gods of Egypt; and he shall burn them, and carry them away captives: and he shall array himself with the land of Egypt, as a shepherd putteth on his garment; and he shall go forth from thence in peace.

13 He shall break also the images of Beth-shemesh, that is in the land of Egypt; and the houses of the gods of the Egyptians shall he burn with fire.

JEREMIAH 44

Selection: all verses

JEREMIAH AND BARUCH, his scribe, have now been taken captive into Egypt by a group of Jewish rebels, who believe they will find peace and safety from the Babylonians in Egypt. They won't. They have rebelled against the clear counsel of the Lord to them to stay in Judah (chapters 42–43). Jeremiah will prophesy that the group will all be destroyed, except for a small remnant.

1 THE word that came to Jeremiah concerning all the Jews which dwell in the land of Egypt, which dwell at Migdol [*in northern Egypt*], and at Tahpanhes [*in the eastern part of the Nile Delta*], and at Noph [*Memphis, capital of ancient Egypt, not far south of modern Cairo*], and in the country of Pathros [*upper Egypt*], saying,

2 Thus saith the LORD of hosts, the God of Israel; Ye have seen all the evil that I have brought upon Jerusalem, and upon all the cities of Judah; and, behold, this day they *are* a desolation, and no man dwelleth therein,

3 Because of their wickedness which they have committed to provoke me to anger, in that they went to burn incense, *and* to serve other gods [*worshiping false gods, including idol worship*], whom they knew not,

neither they, ye, nor your fathers.

The JST helps us with verse 4, next.

4 Howbeit I sent unto you all my servants the prophets, rising early and sending *them*, saying, Oh, do not this abominable thing that I hate.

JST Jeremiah 44:4

4 Howbeit I sent unto you all my servants the prophets, commanding them to rise early, and sending them, saying, Oh, do not this abominable thing that I hate.

5 But they hearkened not, nor inclined their ear to turn from their wickedness, to burn no incense unto other gods.

6 Wherefore my fury and mine anger [*the law of justice*] was poured forth, and was kindled in the cities of Judah and in the streets of Jerusalem; and they are wasted *and* desolate, as at this day.

Next, having reviewed the recent destruction of the Jews in the land of Judah, the Lord asks this rebellious colony of Jews in Egypt why they can't learn a lesson from what happened to their fellow Jews in the Holy Land. In effect, He asks them why they would want to get themselves likewise cut off from mortality.

7 Therefore now thus saith the LORD, the God of hosts, the

God of Israel; **Wherefore** [*why*] **commit ye** *this* **great evil against your souls** [*against yourselves*], to cut off from you man and woman, child and suckling, out of Judah, to leave you none to remain;

8 In that ye provoke me unto wrath with the works of your hands, burning incense unto [*worshiping*] **other gods in the land of Egypt,** whither ye be gone to dwell, **that ye might cut yourselves off,** and that ye might be a curse and a reproach among all the nations of the earth?

> Sometimes we tend to think mainly in terms of wicked men when it comes to the destruction of nations. However, as shown in verse 9, next, wicked women likewise play a major role in the downfall of nations. In fact, as described in Isaiah 3:16–26, when Satan succeeds in luring women as well as men into the paths of sin and evil, a nation and people are doomed. They are "ripe in iniquity."

9 Have ye forgotten the wickedness of your fathers [*ancestors*], **and** the wickedness of **the kings of Judah,** and the wickedness of **their wives,** and **your** own **wickedness, and the wickedness of your wives,** which they have committed in the land of Judah, and in the streets of Jerusalem?

10 They are not humbled *even* **unto this day,** neither have they feared, nor walked in my law, nor in my statutes, that I set before you and before your fathers [*those who were not slaughtered by the Babylonians still have not repented*].

11 ¶ Therefore thus saith the LORD of hosts, the God of Israel; Behold, **I will set my face against you for evil** [*because of wickedness*], and to cut off all Judah.

12 And I will take the remnant of Judah [*the group of rebel Jews*], **that have set their faces to go into the land of Egypt** to sojourn there, **and they shall all be consumed,** *and* fall in the land of Egypt; they shall *even* be consumed **by the sword** *and* **by the famine:** they shall die, from the least even unto the greatest, by the sword and by the famine: and they shall be an execration [*people will curse you and swear at you*], *and* an astonishment [*horror*], and a curse, and a reproach [*people will look down on you*].

13 For I will punish them that dwell in the land of Egypt, as I have punished Jerusalem, by the sword, by the famine, and by the pestilence:

14 So that none of the remnant of Judah, which are gone into the land of Egypt to sojourn there, shall escape or remain, that they should return into the land of Judah, to the which they have a desire to return to dwell there:

for **none shall return but such as shall escape** [*there will be a few Jews who will survive*].

> Next, these rebellious people blatantly reject the word of the Lord, knowing full well that they are guilty as stated. We see that the women were just as wicked as their husbands.

15 ¶ **Then all the men which knew that their wives had burned incense unto other gods, and all the women** that stood by, a great multitude, **even all the people** [*the Jews in this group*] that dwelt in the land of Egypt, in Pathros [*upper Egypt*], **answered Jeremiah, saying,**

16 *As for* the word that thou hast spoken unto us in the name of the LORD, **we will not hearken unto thee.**

> Next, these rebels proudly boast that they will go on doing what they have been doing.

17 **But we will certainly do whatsoever thing goeth forth out of our own mouth** [*we will do whatever we want*], **to burn incense unto the queen of heaven** [*a heathen female god*], and to pour out drink offerings unto her, **as we have done, we, and our fathers, our kings, and our princes, in the cities of Judah, and in the streets of Jerusalem:** for *then* had we plenty of victuals [*food*], and were well, and saw no evil [*in other words, we prospered under the false gods we were worshiping in the land of Judah*].

18 **But since we left off to burn incense to the queen of heaven** [*when we quit worshiping that female god*], and to pour out drink offerings unto her, **we have wanted** [*lacked*] **all *things*,** and have been consumed by the sword and by the famine.

19 **And when we** [*the women in the group are speaking now*] **burned incense to the queen of heaven,** and poured out drink offerings unto her, **did we make her cakes to worship her, and pour out drink offerings unto her, without our men?**

20 ¶ **Then Jeremiah said unto all the people,** to the men, and to the women, and to all the people which had given him *that* answer, saying,

21 **The incense that ye burned in the cities of Judah** [*as you worshiped your idols*], **and in the streets of Jerusalem,** ye, and your fathers, your kings, and your princes, and the people of the land, did not the LORD remember them, and came it *not* into his mind?

22 **So that the LORD could no longer bear, because of the evil of your doings,** *and* **because of the abominations which ye have committed;** therefore is your land [*Judah, including Jerusalem*] **a desolation,** and an astonishment, and a curse, without an inhabitant, as at this day.

23 Because ye have burned incense [*worshiped idols*], and because ye have sinned against the LORD, and have not obeyed the voice of the LORD, nor walked in his law, nor in his statutes, nor in his testimonies; therefore this evil is happened unto you, as at this day.

24 Moreover Jeremiah said unto all the people, and to all the women, Hear the word of the LORD, all Judah that *are* in the land of Egypt:

25 Thus saith the LORD of hosts, the God of Israel, saying; Ye and your wives have both spoken with your mouths, and fulfilled with your hand, saying, We will surely perform our vows that we have vowed, to burn incense to the queen of heaven, and to pour out drink offerings unto her: ye will surely accomplish your vows, and surely perform your vows.

26 Therefore hear ye the word of the LORD, all Judah that [*all of you Jews who*] dwell in the land of Egypt; Behold, I have sworn by my great name, saith the LORD, that my name shall no more be named in the mouth of any man of Judah in all the land of Egypt, saying, The Lord GOD liveth [*in other words, apostasy will be complete among the Jews who fled to Egypt at this time*].

27 Behold, I will watch over them for evil, and not for good [*punishments instead of blessings will come upon them*]: and all the men of Judah that *are* in the land of Egypt shall be consumed by the sword and by the famine, until there be an end of them.

28 Yet a small number that escape the sword shall return out of the land of Egypt into the land of Judah, and all the remnant of Judah, that are gone into the land of Egypt to sojourn there, shall know whose words shall stand, mine, or theirs [*in other words, these proud and haughty people will find out who is right, them or God*].

Verses 29–30, next, contain the last words of Jeremiah that we are aware of. It is a prophecy foretelling the death of Pharaoh in Egypt. He was killed during a rebellion in his own kingdom about 570 BC

29 ¶ And this *shall be* a sign unto you, saith the LORD, that I will punish you in this place, that ye may know that my words shall surely stand against you for evil:

30 Thus saith the LORD; Behold, I will give Pharaoh-hophra king of Egypt into the hand of his enemies, and into the hand of them that seek his life; as I gave Zedekiah king of Judah into the hand of Nebuchadrezzar king of Babylon, his enemy, and that sought his life.

NOTE

The remaining chapters in the Book of Jeremiah, except for chapter 52, are a compilation of prophecies given by Jeremiah. They appear to be added by someone as a sort of appendix to the main book, chapters 1–44. They are not given in chronological order and consist of chapter 45, which is a promise to Baruch, Jeremiah's faithful scribe; chapters 46–51, which are prophecies against several surrounding wicked nations; and chapter 52, a review of the conquest of Jerusalem and Judah by King Nebuchadnezzar in about 587 BC in which Zedekiah was taken captive.

JEREMIAH 45

Selection: all verses

BARUCH SERVED FAITHFULLY as Jeremiah's scribe throughout his ministry. The last we hear of him is in Egypt, where he continued to serve with Jeremiah. The prophecy and blessing for him, given in this chapter, was given about 605 BC

1 THE word that Jeremiah the prophet spake unto Baruch the son of Neriah, when he had written these words in a book at the mouth of Jeremiah, in the fourth year of Jehoiakim the son of Josiah king of Judah, saying,

2 Thus saith the LORD, the God of Israel, unto thee, O Baruch;

In verse 3, next, we are given to understand that it was a rough life for Baruch, as he faithfully remained loyal to Jeremiah through thick and thin.

3 Thou [*Baruch*] **didst say, Woe is me now! for the LORD hath added grief to my sorrow** [*it has been one thing after another*]; **I fainted in my sighing** [*I am constantly worn out and groaning under my burdens*], **and I find no rest.**

4 ¶ Thus shalt thou [*Jeremiah*] **say unto him** [*Baruch*], **The LORD saith thus; Behold,** *that* **which I have built will I break down, and that which I have planted I will pluck up, even this whole land.**

5 And seekest thou great things for thyself? seek *them* **not** [*don't set your heart on great things of the world*]: **for, behold, I will bring evil upon all flesh** [*mortality has its share of troubles*], **saith the LORD: but thy life will I give unto thee for a prey** [*your life will be preserved*] **in all places whither thou goest.**

JEREMIAH 46

Selection: all verses

THIS CHAPTER IS a prophecy against Egypt, foretelling that the Egyptian army will be conquered by Babylon. It also contains a prophecy about the scattering and gathering of Israel (verses 27–28). As mentioned in the note before

Jeremiah, chapter 45 in this study guide, this chapter is not in chronological sequence.

Verses 1–26 foretell the Babylonian conquest of Egypt in about 605 BC The Egyptian army had marched as far north as Carchemish (on the border between modern-day Turkey and Syria), and, as explained in verse 2, Pharaoh-necho (the king or Pharaoh of Egypt at the time) was defeated there by the Babylonians.

Jeremiah is a master at using lively language to describe his visions. For example, you will feel the Egyptians' optimistic rallying call to prepare for battle (verses 3–4) and then the sudden devastation among them as they realize defeat (verse 5).

1 THE word of the LORD which came to Jeremiah the prophet **against the Gentiles;**

2 Against Egypt, against the army of Pharaoh-necho king of Egypt, **which was by the river Euphrates in Carchemish, which Nebuchadrezzar king of Babylon smote** in the fourth year of Jehoiakim the son of Josiah king of Judah.

A vivid, prophetic description of the battle is seen in the next verses.

3 Order ye the buckler and shield, and draw near to battle.

4 Harness the horses; and get up, ye horsemen, and stand forth with *your* helmets; furbish the spears, *and* **put** on the brigandines [*armor*].

5 Wherefore [*why*] **have I seen them dismayed** *and* **turned away back** [*why are they retreating*]? and their mighty ones are beaten down, and are fled apace, and look not back: *for fear was* round about, saith the LORD.

6 Let not the swift flee away, nor the mighty man escape; they shall stumble, and fall toward the north by the river Euphrates.

7 [*Question*] **Who** *is* this *that* **cometh up as a flood,** whose waters are moved as the rivers [*what nation is behind this flood of soldiers*]?

8 [*Answer*] **Egypt** riseth up like a flood, and *his* waters are moved like the rivers; **and he saith, I will go up,** *and* **will cover the earth; I will destroy the city and the inhabitants thereof** [*Egypt plans to conquer the whole known world*].

Verse 9, next, shows us that the Egyptians had allies with them as they went north to "conquer the world."

9 Come up, ye horses; and rage, ye chariots; and **let the mighty men come forth; the Ethiopians** and the **Libyans,** that handle the shield; and the **Lydians,** that handle *and* bend the bow.

10 For this *is* the day of the Lord GOD of hosts, a day of vengeance, that he may avenge him of his adversaries: and **the sword shall devour, and it shall be satiate and made drunk with their blood: for the Lord GOD of hosts hath a sacrifice in the north country by the river Euphrates** [*Egypt will become a sacrifice to the Babylonians, along the Euphrates River*].

11 Go up into Gilead, and take balm, O virgin, the daughter of Egypt: **in vain shalt thou use many medicines** [*try different strategies to win the battle*]; *for* **thou shalt not be cured** [*you will be defeated, no matter what*].

> Next, Jeremiah prophetically describes the shame to be felt by the Egyptians when their mighty army is defeated.

12 **The nations have heard of thy shame,** and thy cry hath filled the land: for the mighty man hath stumbled against the mighty, *and* they are fallen both together.

13 ¶ **The word that the LORD spake to Jeremiah** the prophet, **how Nebuchadrezzar king of Babylon should come** *and* **smite the land of Egypt.**

> Several Egyptian cities are mentioned in verses 14–15, next, as Jeremiah describes the future destruction in Egypt by the Babylonians under King Nebuchadnezzar.

14 Declare ye in Egypt, and publish in **Migdol,** and publish in **Noph** and in **Tahpanhes:** say ye, Stand fast, and prepare thee; for **the sword shall devour round about thee.**

15 Why are thy valiant *men* swept away? they stood not, **because the LORD did drive them.**

16 **He made many to fall,** yea, one fell upon another: and they said, Arise, and let us go again to our own people, and to the land of our nativity, from the oppressing sword.

17 **They did cry there, Pharaoh king of Egypt** *is but* **a noise** [*does not have any power against the Babylonians*]; he hath passed the time appointed.

18 *As* **I live, saith the King** [*Jehovah*], whose name *is* the LORD of hosts, **Surely as Tabor** [*Mt. Tabor, just southwest of the Sea of Galilee*] *is* **among the mountains, and as Carmel by the sea** [*Mt. Carmel, by the Mediterranean Sea*], *so* **shall he come.**

19 **O thou daughter dwelling in Egypt** [*O you inhabitants of Egypt*], furnish thyself to go into captivity [*prepare yourselves for captivity*]: for Noph [*the capital of ancient Egypt, not far south of modern-day Cairo*] shall be waste and desolate without an inhabitant.

20 Egypt *is* like a very fair heifer [*a vulnerable young cow, that has not yet*

had a calf], but destruction cometh; it cometh out of the north [the direction from which the Babylonian army will come].

21 Also her hired men [the trained soldiers who intend to protect Egypt] are in the midst of her like fatted bullocks [ready to be sacrificed]; for they also are turned back, and are fled away together [will be forced to retreat and flee]: they did not stand [they will not stand their ground], because the day of their calamity was come upon them, and the time of their visitation [punishment for wickedness].

22 The voice thereof shall go like a serpent [they will be like a hissing snake as it retreats from danger]; for they [the Babylonians] shall march with an army, and come against her [Egypt] with axes, as hewers of wood [the Babylonians will chop down the Egyptians like an army of lumberjacks chopping down a forest].

23 They shall cut down her forest, saith the LORD, though it cannot be searched [even though the "forest" of Egyptians seems very dense]; because they [the Babylonian armies] are more than the grasshoppers, and are innumerable.

24 The daughter of [people of] Egypt shall be confounded [confused; stopped]; she shall be delivered into the hand of the people of the north [the Babylonians].

25 The LORD of hosts, the God of Israel, saith; Behold, I will punish the multitude of No [Thebes, the capital city of upper Egypt], and Pharaoh, and Egypt, with their gods, and their kings; even Pharaoh, and all them that trust in him [the Egyptians considered their Pharaoh to be a god and worshiped him as such]:

26 And I will deliver them into the hand of those that seek their lives [in other words, their enemies], and into the hand of Nebuchadrezzar king of Babylon, and into the hand of his servants: and afterward it shall be inhabited, as in the days of old, saith the LORD.

The last two verses are a prophecy about the scattering and gathering of Israel.

27 ¶ But fear not thou, O my servant [the Lord's covenant people] Jacob [Israel], and be not dismayed [discouraged], O Israel [Jacob]: for, behold, I will save thee from afar off [I will gather you from far away], and thy seed from the land of their captivity; and Jacob shall return, and be in rest and at ease, and none shall make him afraid [this will be fulfilled in the last days and into the Millennium].

28 Fear thou not, O Jacob my servant, saith the LORD: for I am with thee; for I will make a full end of all the nations [when the

Millennium comes—see D&C 87:6] whither I have driven thee: **but I will not make a full end of thee, but correct** [*discipline*] **thee in measure** [*appropriately*]; **yet will I not leave thee wholly unpunished** [*you still need some correction and discipline in order to fill your role as the Lord's covenant people*].

JEREMIAH 47

Selection: all verses

THIS CHAPTER IS a prophecy against the Philistines, a wicked nation at the time, located to the west of Jerusalem, down on the coast of the Mediterranean Sea.

1 THE word of the LORD that came to Jeremiah the prophet against the Philistines, before that Pharaoh smote Gaza.

2 Thus saith the LORD; Behold, waters rise up out of the north, and shall be an overflowing flood [*in other words, a "flood" of enemy soldiers is coming from the north, a reference to the army of Babylon*], **and shall overflow the land** [*you will be flooded, overrun with Babylonians*], **and all that is therein; the city, and them that dwell therein: then the men shall cry, and all the inhabitants of the land shall howl.**

Next, Jeremiah describes the sounds of war and battle, which will be heard when the Babylonians attack the Philistines.

3 At the noise of the stamping of the hoofs of his strong *horses*, **at the rushing of his chariots,** *and at the* **rumbling of his wheels, the fathers shall not look back to** *their* **children for feebleness of hands** [*NIV Fathers will not turn to help their children; their hands will hang limp*];

4 Because of the day that cometh to spoil all the Philistines, *and* **to cut off from Tyrus and Zidon every helper** [*ally*] **that remaineth: for the LORD will spoil** [*will cause the defeat of*] **the Philistines, the** remnant of the country of Caphtor.

5 Baldness [*humiliation, captivity—conquering nations often shaved their captives bald, for purposes of humiliation and identification*] **is come upon Gaza; Ashkelon** [*Gaza and Ashkelon were cities in southern Philistia*] **is cut off** *with* **the remnant** of their valley: **how long wilt thou cut thyself** [*how long will you keep bringing destruction upon yourselves through wicked living*]?

With great dramatic skill, Jeremiah poses a question in verse 6 and then gives the answer in verse 7. The "sword of the Lord" could be considered to be the law of justice, which cannot be sheathed until the unrepentant wicked are punished by justice. You may wish to read Alma 42 for a refresher course on the laws of mercy and justice.

6 O thou sword of the LORD, how long *will it be* ere thou be quiet? put up thyself into thy scabbard, rest, and be still.

7 How can it be quiet, seeing the LORD hath given it a charge against Ashkelon [*a charge or mission against the Philistines*], and against the sea shore [*the Philistines, many of whom lived along the coast of the Mediterranean Sea*]? there hath he appointed it [*the sword of justice still has work to do there*].

JEREMIAH 48

Selection: all verses

THIS CHAPTER CONTAINS a prophecy of destruction against Moab. You might wish to read Isaiah, chapters 15–16, as well as Ezekiel 25:8–11, for similar prophecies against this nation. Moab was a country immediately east of the Dead Sea. In fact, as recorded in the Book of Ruth, Naomi had been living in Moab because of the famine in the Holy Land (see Ruth 1:1–2) and returned to Bethlehem to live when the famine was over. Her daughter-in-law, Ruth, came with her.

The citizens of Moab were known for their materialism and contempt for Jehovah, the God of Israel. They were engulfed in idol worship, with its associated sexual immorality and debauchery.

The Babylonians conquered the land of Moab and took many of its people into captivity. The country never regained its status as an independent nation. The last verse of this chapter contains a message of hope for the people of that area and seems to say that they will receive the gospel of Jesus Christ in the last days.

As is often the case, Jeremiah specifies many cities and landmarks in Moab as he prophesies about it. Remember, Jeremiah is speaking of the future as if it had already taken place. He will use many words and phrases, along with much repetition to get his message across.

1 AGAINST Moab thus saith the LORD of hosts, the God of Israel; Woe unto Nebo [*a mountainous area in northern Moab, east of the Jordan River*]! for **it is spoiled** [*ruined*]: Kiriathaim [*a city in central Moab*] is **confounded** and taken: Misgab is confounded and **dismayed.**

2 *There shall be* no more praise of Moab [*Moab will cease to exist as a nation*]: in Heshbon [*a city to the northeast of Mt. Nebo, which originally was part of the country of Moab but eventually belonged to the Amorites and then to the Israelite tribes of Reuben and Gad*] they have devised evil against it; come, and **let us cut it off from** *being* a nation. Also **thou shalt be cut down, O Madmen; the sword shall pursue thee.**

3 A voice of **crying** *shall be* from Horonaim, **spoiling** and **great destruction.**

4 Moab is destroyed; her little ones have caused a cry to be heard.

5 For in the going up of Luhith **continual weeping** shall go up; for in the going down of Horonaim the enemies have heard a cry of **destruction.**

6 Flee, save your lives, and be like the heath [*juniper tree—see Jeremiah 17:6, footnote a in your Bible*] in the wilderness.

> Next, in verse 7, we see that materialism was a major cause of Moab's destruction. The worship of false gods was likewise a major cause of their demise.

7 ¶ For because thou hast trusted in thy works and in thy treasures, thou shalt also be taken: and **Chemosh** [*the god of the Moabites; Solomon introduced the worship of Chemosh at Jerusalem—see 1 Kings 11:7*] **shall go forth into captivity** *with* **his priests and his princes together** [*in other words, Chemosh, your false god, with all his false priests and servants will not protect you from destruction*].

8 And **the spoiler shall come upon every city, and no city shall escape:** the valley also shall perish, and the plain shall be destroyed, as the LORD hath spoken.

9 Give wings unto Moab, that it may flee and get away [*in order to escape this destruction, you would have to sprout wings and fly away*]: for the cities thereof shall be desolate, without any to dwell therein.

10 Cursed *be* **he that doeth the work of the LORD deceitfully** [*with hypocrisy*], **and cursed** *be* **he that keepeth back his sword from blood.**

> Next, in effect, Jeremiah says that Moab has had it so good for so long that they are not able to face reality or change their thinking and attitudes.

11 ¶ Moab hath been at ease from his youth, and he hath settled on his lees [*has relaxed his guard against danger—see footnote 11a in your Bible*], and hath not been emptied from vessel to vessel, neither hath he gone into captivity: **therefore his taste** [*for wickedness*] **remained in him, and his scent is not changed.**

12 Therefore, behold, the days come, saith the LORD, that I will send unto him wanderers [*enemies*], **that** shall cause him to wander, and **shall empty his vessels** [*enemies will tip you over and empty you out—compare with footnote 12a in your Bible*], **and break their bottles.**

13 And **Moab shall be ashamed of Chemosh** [*embarrassed, put to shame, by the inability of Chemosh, their false god, to save them*], **as the house of Israel** [*the northern ten tribes*] **was ashamed of Beth-el**

[a formerly sacred site selected by Jeroboam for setting up golden calf worship in place of worshiping God—see 1 Kings 12:28–29] their confidence [in which the Israelites had trusted].

14 ¶ How say ye, We are mighty and strong men for the war [how can you say you are powerful and strong and can defend yourselves just fine]?

15 Moab is [will be] spoiled, and gone up out of her cities, and his chosen young men are gone down to the slaughter, saith the King [the true God], whose name is the LORD of hosts.

16 The calamity of Moab is near to come, and his affliction hasteth fast [is rapidly approaching].

17 All ye that are about him, bemoan him; and all ye that know his name, say, How is the strong staff broken, and the beautiful rod [be startled at what will happen to a once-strong nation]!

18 Thou daughter that dost inhabit Dibon [you people of Dibon—a town in central Moab], come down from thy glory, and sit in thirst; for the spoiler of Moab [the coming Babylonian armies; they would be at least one fulfillment of this prophecy] shall come upon thee, and he shall destroy thy strong holds.

19 O inhabitant of Aroer [a town south of Dibon, in central Moab], stand by the way, and espy [watch]; ask him that fleeth, and her that escapeth, and say, What is done [prepare to ask what is going on]?

20 Moab is confounded [brought to a halt]; for it is broken down: howl and cry; tell ye it in Arnon [a river that formed the border between the Moabites and the Amorites to the north], that Moab is spoiled,

21 And judgment is come upon the plain country; upon Holon, and upon Jahazah, and upon Mephaath,

22 And upon Dibon, and upon Nebo, and upon Beth-diblathaim,

23 And upon Kiriathaim, and upon Beth-gamul, and upon Beth-meon,

24 And upon Kerioth, and upon Bozrah, and upon all the cities of the land of Moab, far or near.

25 The horn [power] of Moab is cut off, and his arm [power] is broken, saith the LORD.

26 ¶ Make ye him drunken [in your mind's eye, picture him drunk]: for he magnified himself [exhibited pride] against the LORD: Moab also shall wallow in his vomit, and he also shall be in derision [will be mocked by others].

27 For was not Israel a derision unto thee [didn't you make fun of Israel,

the Lord's people, and claim that their God, Jehovah, was not as powerful as your god, therefore you rebelled against Israel—see 2 Kings 3:5]? was he found among thieves? for since thou spakest of him [every time you ridiculed Israel], thou skippedst for joy.

> Jeremiah is a master at using imagery with which the people were familiar to illustrate his message. As he continues this rather lively and frightening prophecy of coming doom to Moab, he warns the inhabitants of that country to get out while they can.

28 O ye that dwell in Moab, **leave the cities, and dwell in the rock** [hide among the boulders], and **be like the dove that maketh her nest in the sides of the hole's mouth** [find caves to live in].

> Next, in verse 29, we are reminded that the Moabites were afflicted by the sin of pride, just as is the case with many today.

29 We have heard the pride of Moab, (he is exceeding proud) his **loftiness,** and his **arrogancy,** and his **pride,** and the **haughtiness of** his **heart.**

30 I know his wrath [anger at righteousness], saith the LORD; but **it shall not be so** [but it will not do him any good]; **his lies shall not so effect it** [his false beliefs and boasts against Jehovah will not turn back his destruction].

31 Therefore will I howl for Moab, and **I will cry out for all Moab;** **mine heart shall mourn** for the men of Kir-heres.

32 O vine of Sibmah, I will weep for thee with the weeping of Jazer [an Amorite town east of the Jordan River, which was conquered by the Israelites as they entered the promised land]: thy plants are gone over the sea, they reach even to the sea of Jazer: the spoiler [enemy] is fallen upon thy summer fruits and upon thy vintage.

33 And joy and gladness is taken from the plentiful field, and **from the land of Moab;** and I have caused wine to fail [become nonexistent] from the winepresses: none shall tread with shouting; their shouting shall be no shouting.

> Next, in verse 34, Jeremiah uses specific geography in Moab to illustrate the prophetic message that Moab will be devastated from north to south and east to west, in other words, completely.

34 From the cry of Heshbon [in the far northeast of Moab] even unto Elealeh [a bit farther northeast], and even unto Jahaz [in the northeast], have they uttered their voice, from Zoar [in the far southwest] even unto Horonaim [in south central Moab], as an heifer of three years old [symbolic of being in the prime of life; in other words, prosperous and haughty

Moab will be destroyed in the prime of life]: for **the waters also of Nimrim** [*a major source of water in far west central Moab*] **shall be desolate.**

35 Moreover I will cause to cease in Moab, saith the LORD, **him that offereth in the high places** [*locations used for idol worship*], **and him that burneth incense to his gods** [*idol worshipers will be destroyed*].

36 Therefore mine heart shall sound for Moab like pipes [*like sad music played on a flute*], and mine heart shall sound like pipes for the men of Kir-heres [*Kir-hareseth, the capital city, located in south central Moab*]: because **the riches** *that* **he hath gotten are perished.**

> Verse 37, next, describes symbolically as well as literally the fate of captives and slaves.

37 For every head *shall be* **bald,** and every **beard clipped**: upon all the hands *shall be* **cuttings** [*perhaps a reference to having marks cut into their hands which identify them as prisoners*], and upon the loins **sackcloth.**

38 *There shall be* **lamentation** generally [*everywhere*] upon all the housetops of Moab, and in the streets thereof: for I have broken Moab like a vessel wherein *is* no pleasure [*NIV: like a jar that no one wants*], saith the LORD.

39 They shall howl, *saying,* How is it broken down! how hath Moab turned the back with shame! so shall Moab be a derision and a dismaying [*a topic of gossip and a source of horror*] to all them about him.

40 For thus saith **the LORD;** Behold, he **shall fly as an eagle, and shall spread his wings over Moab** [*destruction is coming to Moab*].

41 Kerioth is taken, and the strong holds are surprised, and **the mighty men's hearts in Moab at that day shall be as the heart of a woman in her pangs** [*in labor*].

42 And **Moab shall be destroyed** from *being* a people [*as a nation*], **because he hath magnified** *himself* **against the LORD.**

43 Fear, and the pit, and the snare, *shall be* **upon thee,** O inhabitant of Moab, saith the LORD.

> Note how Jeremiah emphasizes that the wicked in Moab cannot escape from the Lord, in verse 44, next. The imagery is that of a hunted animal, running away in fear, who escapes from one trap only to be caught in another.

44 He that fleeth from the fear shall fall into the pit; and he that getteth up out of the pit shall be taken in the snare: for I will bring upon it, *even* upon Moab, the year of their visitation [*when the time for punishment is right*], saith the LORD.

Remember, as mentioned previously, Jeremiah is speaking prophetically of the future as if it has already taken place. This is illustrated in the first phrase of verse 45, next.

45 They that fled stood under the shadow of Heshbon because of the force [*those who try to flee from Moab will be helpless*]: but a fire shall come forth out of Heshbon, and **a flame** from the midst of Sihon, and **shall devour** the corner of **Moab**, and the crown of the head of the tumultuous ones [*the noisy boasters*].

46 Woe be unto thee, O Moab! the people of Chemosh perisheth [*the people who worship Chemosh will perish*]: **for thy sons are taken captives, and thy daughters captives.**

As mentioned in the background to this chapter in this study guide, verse 47, next, is the one bright spot in this message of doom to Moab. It is a reminder that all people will be given a completely fair chance, before final Judgment Day, to understand and then accept or reject the gospel of Jesus Christ. The great missionary work in the last days, the marvelous missionary work now being done in spirit prison, and the temple work done during the Millennium, will afford this opportunity to everyone. No one will be missed.

47 ¶ Yet will I bring again the captivity of Moab [*the people of Moab will have their opportunity to come unto Christ*] **in the latter days,** saith

the LORD. Thus far *is* the judgment of Moab.

JEREMIAH 49

Selection: all verses

THIS CHAPTER CONTAINS prophecies of judgment and destruction directed at several different nations and peoples, the Ammonites (verses 1–6), Edom (verses 7–22), Damascus (verses 23–27), Kedar and Hazor (verses 28–33), and Elam (verses 34–39). Many Bible scholars believe that this set of prophecies was given after the downfall of Jerusalem.

All people have a certain degree of accountability to choose right and avoid wrong. Every person in the nations to whom this chapter was directed had the light of Christ (see John 1:9), which is a conscience and much more, a constant influence persuading each person born on earth to choose right and avoid wrong. Without this understanding, we might think it not fair for such stinging prophecies of doom and punishment to be directed at them. With this understanding, the reality of accountability for all people beyond age eight looms large.

Thus, one of the major messages we can derive from each of these prophecies directed at heathen nations is the fact that all people should do right and treat each other well. They have the conscience necessary to do so and are accountable to God when they go against it. We will take just another moment before we start this chapter and read a quote from the Bible Dictionary describing the light of Christ. We will add bold for teaching purposes.

Bible Dictionary: Light of Christ

"The light of **Christ is** just what the words imply: **enlightenment, knowledge, and an uplifting, ennobling, persevering influence that comes upon mankind because of Jesus Christ.** For instance, Christ is 'the true light that lighteth every man that cometh into the world' (D&C 93:2; John 1:9) . . . 'the light that quickeneth' man's understanding (see D&C 88:6–13, 41). In this manner, the light of Christ is related to man's conscience and tells him right from wrong (cf. Moro. 7:12–19).'"

Keeping in mind that because of the light of Christ all people are accountable for their actions to a much higher degree than their actions might indicate, we will now proceed with this chapter. The prophecy against the Ammonites is given in verses 1-6. They lived east of Jerusalem, several miles east of the Jordan River. This area was originally given to the tribe of Gad when the children of Israel entered the Holy Land. However, the Ammonites (descendants of Lot) maintained a strong presence and at the time of Jeremiah's prophecy here, they were essentially their own nation.

1 CONCERNING the Ammonites, thus saith the LORD; Hath Israel no sons? hath he no heir? why *then* doth their king inherit Gad, and his people dwell in his cities?

2 Therefore, behold, the days come, saith the LORD, that **I will cause an alarm of war to be heard in Rabbah** [*the capital city*] **of the Ammonites**; and it shall be a desolate heap [*it will be destroyed*], and her daughters [*her people*] shall be burned with fire: then shall Israel be heir unto them that were his heirs, saith the LORD.

3 Howl, O Heshbon, for Ai is **spoiled**: cry, ye daughters of Rabbah, gird you [*dress yourselves*] with **sackcloth** [*a sign of mourning in their culture*]; **lament,** and run to and fro by the hedges; for **their king shall go into captivity,** *and* his **priests and his princes** together.

4 Wherefore gloriest thou in the valleys, thy flowing valley, O **backsliding daughter** [*apostate people*]? that trusted in her treasures [*materialism*], *saying,* Who shall come unto me [*who could possibly defeat us*]?

5 Behold, **I will bring a fear upon thee, saith the Lord** GOD of hosts, from all those that be about thee [*from surrounding nations*]; and ye shall be driven out every man right forth; and none shall gather up him that wandereth.

Verse 6, next, is the Lord's promise that the Ammonites would return again to their land. One probable fulfillment of this promise was when Cyrus the Persian, who defeated Babylon in about 538 BC, decreed that these people could return to their homeland. That decree also applied to the Jews who were allowed to return to Jerusalem.

6 And **afterward I will bring again the captivity of** [*I will overturn the captivity of*] **the children of Ammon**, saith the LORD.

7 ¶ **Concerning Edom** [*a mountainous country south of the Dead Sea where the descendants of Esau settled*], thus saith the LORD of hosts; *Is* **wisdom no more** in Teman [*doesn't anyone in Edom have common sense any more*]*? is* **counsel perished** from the prudent? is their **wisdom vanished?**

8 Flee ye, turn back, dwell deep, O inhabitants of Dedan; for I will bring the **calamity** of Esau upon him, the time *that* I will visit [*punish*] him.

Next, a comparison is made between harvesting, where there are always a few grapes left, and the complete destruction of Edom (Esau).

9 **If grapegatherers come to thee, would they not leave** *some* **gleaning grapes?** if thieves by night, they will destroy till they have enough [*they don't take everything*].

10 **But I have made Esau bare** [*I will completely destroy Edom as a nation*], I have uncovered his secret places [*his hiding places*], and he shall not be able to hide himself: his seed is spoiled, and his brethren, and his neighbours, and **he** *is* **not.**

11 Leave thy fatherless children, I will preserve *them* alive; and let thy widows trust in me [*the Lord will take care of the orphans and widows*].

12 For thus saith the LORD; Behold, **they whose judgment** *was* **not to drink of the cup** [*those who thought to avoid punishment*] **have assuredly drunken** [*have been punished*]; and *art* thou he *that* shall altogether go unpunished? **thou shalt not go unpunished**, but thou shalt surely drink *of it* [*the bitter cup of paying for their wickedness*].

13 For I have sworn by myself, saith the LORD, that **Bozrah** [*a city in Edom, about eighty miles south of modern-day Amman in Jordan*] **shall become a desolation**, a **reproach**, a **waste**, and a **curse**; and all the cities thereof shall be perpetual wastes;

14 I have heard a rumour from the LORD, and an ambassador is sent unto the heathen, *saying*, Gather ye together, and come against her, and rise up to the battle.

15 For, lo, **I will make thee small among the heathen, *and* despised among men.**

16 Thy terribleness [*your fierceness*] hath deceived thee [*has given you a false sense of security*], *and* **the pride of thine heart**, O thou that dwellest in the clefts of the rock, that holdest the height of the hill: **though thou shouldest make thy nest as high as the eagle, I will bring thee down** from thence, saith the LORD.

17 Also **Edom shall be a desolation** [*NIV: will become an object of horror*]: every one that goeth by it shall be astonished [*appalled, shocked*], and shall hiss at [*gossip, deride*] all the plagues thereof.

18 As in the overthrow of Sodom and Gomorrah and the neighbour *cities* thereof, saith the LORD, **no man shall abide there**, neither shall a son of man dwell in it.

19 Behold, he [*the Lord*] **shall come up like a lion** from the swelling [*the thickets of the floodplain*] of Jordan **against the habitation of the strong** [*against Edom*]: but I [*the Lord*] will suddenly make him run away from her [*the inhabitants of Edom will be driven out of their land in an instant*]: and who *is* a chosen *man, that* I may appoint over her? for who *is* like me? and who will appoint me the time? and who *is* that shepherd that will stand before me [*in other words, who would dare try to prevent the Lord from carrying out this prophecy*]?

20 Therefore hear the counsel of the LORD, that he hath taken **against Edom**; and his purposes, that he hath purposed against the inhabitants of Teman [*part of Edom*]: Surely the least of the flock shall draw them out: **surely he shall make their habitations desolate** with them.

21 The earth is moved at the noise of their fall, at the cry the noise thereof was heard in the Red sea [*in effect, the whole earth will be startled by what happens to once-proud Edom*].

22 Behold, he [*the Lord; could also refer to Nebuchadnezzar and his Babylonian armies*] **shall come up and fly as the eagle, and spread his wings over Bozrah** [*a large city in Edom*]: and at that day shall the heart of the mighty men of Edom be as the heart of a woman in her pangs [*in labor; in other words, desperate for relief from the pain*].

23 ¶ **Concerning Damascus** [*Syria*]. Hamath [*a city in Syria*] is **confounded**, and Arpad: for they have heard **evil tidings**: they are **fainthearted**; *there is* **sorrow** on the sea; it cannot be quiet.

24 Damascus is waxed **feeble** [*has grown weak*], *and* turneth herself to flee, and **fear** hath seized on *her*: **anguish** and **sorrows** have taken her, as a woman in travail [*in labor*].

25 How is **the city of praise not left**, the city of my joy!

26 Therefore **her young men shall fall** in her streets, and **all the men of war shall be cut off** in that day, saith the LORD of hosts.

27 And **I will kindle a fire in the wall of Damascus**, and it shall consume the palaces of Ben-hadad.

28 ¶ **Concerning Kedar** [*Arabia*], **and** concerning the kingdoms of **Hazor** [*in Arabia; this is not the city by the same name in Palestine*], which **Nebuchadrezzar king of Babylon shall smite**, thus saith the LORD; Arise ye, go up to Kedar, and **spoil** [*ruin*] the men of the east.

29 Their tents and their flocks shall they take away: they shall take to themselves their curtains, and all their vessels, and their camels; and they shall cry unto them, **Fear** *is* **on every side.**

30 ¶ Flee, get you far off, **dwell deep** [*hide in deep caves*], O ye inhabitants of Hazor, saith the LORD; **for Nebuchadrezzar king of Babylon hath taken counsel against you, and hath conceived a purpose against you.**

Verse 31, next, appears to be symbolic instruction to Nebuchadnezzar, king of Babylon, to attack the Arabians, who are wealthy and at ease, living in tents rather than in cities with walls and gates.

31 **Arise, get you** [*Nebuchadnezzar*] **up unto the wealthy nation** [*the inhabitants of Arabia*], that dwelleth without care, saith the LORD, which have neither gates nor bars, *which* dwell alone.

32 And **their camels shall be a booty** [*will provide wealth for the Babylonian conquerors*], and the multitude of their cattle a spoil [*more wealth for you*]: and I will scatter into all winds them *that are* in the utmost corners; and I will bring their **calamity from all sides** thereof, saith the LORD.

33 And Hazor shall be a dwelling for dragons [*jackals, wild dogs; symbolically representing lonely and desolate ruins inhabited by wild animals that avoid areas inhabited by humans*], *and* a desolation [*in ruins*] for ever: there shall no man abide there, nor *any* son of man dwell in it.

34 ¶ **The word of the LORD** that came to Jeremiah the prophet **against Elam** [*located east of Babylon, in what is southwest Iran today*] in the beginning of the reign of Zedekiah king of Judah [*about 598 B.C.*], saying,

35 Thus saith the LORD of hosts; Behold, **I will break the bow of Elam** [*I will disarm them*], the chief of their might.

36 And **upon Elam will I bring the four winds** [*destruction*] **from** the four quarters of heaven, **and will scatter them** toward all those winds; and **there shall be no nation whither the outcasts of Elam shall not come** [*they will be scattered into all the world*].

37 For I will cause Elam to be **dismayed** before their enemies, and before them that seek their life: and **I will bring evil** [*calamity, disaster—see footnote 37a in your Bible*] **upon them,** *even* **my fierce anger,** saith the LORD; and I will send **the sword** after them, till I have consumed them:

38 And **I will** set my throne in Elam, and will **destroy** from thence **the king and the princes,** saith the LORD.

39 ¶ But it shall come to pass **in the latter days,** *that* **I will bring again the captivity of Elam** [*I will restore them and they will have an opportunity to be converted and set free from the captivity of sin*], saith the LORD.

> We will quote from the *Old Testament Student Manual* regarding the phrase "I will bring again the captivity of Elam," in verse 39, above:
>
> "Verse 39 speaks of the Lord's bringing again the captivity of Elam in the latter days. Again, it is supposed that this passage means their conversion, as with the Moabites" (*Old testament Student Manual,* page 258).

JEREMIAH 50

Selection: all verses

FROM JEREMIAH 50:1 through 51:58, we have a prophecy against Babylon. Interspersed within this prophecy is a prophecy about the scattering and gathering of Israel.

Keep in mind that "Babylon" is often used in the scriptures as well as in the teachings of modern prophets and Apostles to mean both the literal ancient city of Babylon, and also extreme wickedness, the kingdom of the devil, and so forth.

Literally, Babylon was a huge city, whose walls were fifty-six miles in length, 335 feet high, and 85 feet wide (see Bible Dictionary under "Babylon"). It was a center of military power and wickedness and seemed invincible.

Symbolically, Babylon represents Satan's kingdom, with all its worldly wickedness. It, too, can seem invincible, but it is not. Just as ancient Babylon was defeated suddenly by Cyrus the Persian, in about 538 BC, so also will Satan's kingdom be defeated suddenly at the Second Coming. He will be let loose again at the end of the Millennium for "a little season" (D&C 88:111) and will ultimately be defeated completely and, with his evil followers, "be cast away into their own place" forever (D&C 88:112–15).

In this chapter you will see many examples of the kind of repetition used by Jeremiah, Isaiah, and others of the Old

Testament prophets to drive home a point. The prophet makes a statement and then says it again, then again, then again, and again, using a bit different wording or using different examples to illustrate the message. We will point out much of this "manner of prophesying among the Jews (2 Nephi 25:1) as we go along. Be aware that the terms "Babylonians" and "Chaldeans" are used interchangeably by Jeremiah. Technically, the Chaldeans lived in the southeast portion of Babylon.

1 THE word that the LORD spake against Babylon *and* **against the land of the Chaldeans [***Babylonians***] by Jeremiah the prophet.**

As you have no doubt noticed, one of Jeremiah's favorite techniques in prophesying is to speak of the future as if it has already taken place. Here, he uses this approach to prophesying as he foretells the future downfall and destruction of Babylon.

2 Declare ye [*spread the news***] among the nations, and publish, and set up a standard; publish,** *and* **conceal not: say, Babylon is taken, Bel [***the chief god of Babylon***] is confounded [***is powerless to stop it***], Merodach [***the name of a Babylonian god, perhaps another name for Bel***] is broken in pieces;** her idols are confounded, **her images are broken in pieces.**

3 For out of the north there cometh up a nation against her, which shall make her land desolate, and none shall dwell therein: they shall remove, they shall depart, both man and beast.

Verses 4–8, next, contain a prophecy about the gathering of Israel and Judah.

4 ¶ In those days, and in that time, saith the LORD, the children of **Israel** shall come, they **and** the children of **Judah** together, going and weeping: they **shall go, and seek the LORD their God.**

5 They shall ask the way to Zion with their faces thitherward [*with intense, internal desire to come to Zion*], **saying, Come, and let us join ourselves to the LORD in a perpetual covenant** *that* shall not be forgotten.

6 My people hath been lost sheep: their shepherds [*their false prophets and false priests, teachers, political leaders and so forth***] have caused them to go astray, they have turned them away on the mountains [***have used idol worship carried out in high places in the mountains to turn them away from Jehovah***]: they have gone** from mountain to hill [*from idol to idol, shrine to shrine*], they have forgotten their restingplace.

7 All that found them have devoured them [*they have been easy prey to their enemies***]: and their adversaries [***enemies***] said, We offend not [***we are not doing anything**

wrong in brutalizing Israel and Judah], because they have sinned against the LORD, the habitation of justice, even the LORD, the hope of their fathers.

> The message in verse 8, next, seems to be to get out of Babylon before it is conquered (verse 9). Symbolically, we must flee Babylon, Satan's kingdom, before we are destroyed with it.

8 Remove [flee] out of the midst of Babylon, and go forth out of the land of the Chaldeans [a repetition of the first phrase], and be as the he goats before the flocks [lead the way as they flee].

9 ¶ For, lo, I will raise and cause to come up against Babylon an assembly [alliance] of great nations from the north country: and they shall set themselves in array against her; from thence she shall be taken: their arrows shall be as of a mighty expert man; none shall return in vain.

> The alliance of nations, spoken of in verse 9, above, is described in the following quote:
>
> "The army of Cyrus was composed of Medes, Persians, Armenians, Caducians, Sacae, &c. Though all these did not come from the north; yet they were arranged under the Medes, who did come from the north, in reference to Babylon" (Clarke's Commentary, 4:383).

10 And Chaldea shall be a spoil

[Babylon will be left in ruins]: all that spoil her shall be satisfied, saith the LORD.

11 Because ye were glad, because ye rejoiced, O ye destroyers of mine heritage, because ye are grown fat as the heifer at grass, and bellow as bulls;

12 Your mother shall be sore confounded; she that bare you shall be ashamed: behold, the hindermost of the nations shall be a wilderness, a dry land, and a desert.

> In verse 13, next, Jeremiah prophesies that the ruins of Babylon will never be inhabited again nor built upon. Such is still the case today.

13 Because of the wrath of the LORD it shall not be inhabited, but it shall be wholly desolate: every one that goeth by Babylon shall be astonished, and hiss at all her plagues.

14 Put yourselves in array [lay siege] against Babylon round about: all ye that bend the bow, shoot at her, spare no arrows: for she hath sinned against the LORD.

15 Shout against her round about: she hath given her hand: her foundations are fallen, her walls are thrown down: for it is the vengeance of the LORD: take vengeance upon her; as she hath done, do unto her.

16 Cut off the sower [*farmer*] from Babylon, **and him that handleth the sickle in the time of harvest:** for fear of the oppressing sword they shall turn every one to his people, and **they shall flee every one to his own land** [*foreigners who have been living in Babylon because of the available protection and prosperity will flee away*].

Verses 17–20 contain another prophecy about the scattering and gathering of Israel.

Do you find it interesting that the prophecies about Babylon and those about Israel are going along simultaneously, interwoven with each other? Could it be that there is symbolism here, pointing out that the kingdom of Satan will exist at the same time as the kingdom of God, throughout the earth's history? "It must needs be that there is an opposition in all things" (2 Nephi 2:11) is a principle illustrated effectively here.

17 ¶ **Israel** [*referring here to both the lost ten tribes and the kingdom of Judah*] **is a scattered** sheep; the lions have driven him away: **first the king of Assyria hath devoured him** [*the northern ten tribes*]**; and last this Nebuchadrezzar king of Babylon hath broken his** [*Judah's*] **bones.**

18 Therefore thus saith the LORD of hosts, the God of Israel; Behold, I will punish the king of Babylon and his land, as I have punished the king of Assyria [*both kings can be symbolic of Satan*].

The gathering and restoration of Israel is prophesied in verse 19, next.

19 And **I will bring Israel again to his habitation,** and he shall feed on Carmel and Bashan, and his soul shall be satisfied upon mount Ephraim and Gilead.

The doctrine of repentance and forgiveness is taught in verse 20, next. Being gathered unto Christ is the ultimate meaning of the "gathering of Israel."

20 In those days, and in that time, saith the LORD, **the iniquity of Israel shall be sought for** [*looked for*]**, and** *there shall be* **none;** and the sins of Judah, and they shall not be found: **for I will pardon them whom I reserve** [*the Lord will forgive the righteous remnant of Israel whom He spares*].

This prophecy returns once again to the destruction of Babylon.

21 ¶ **Go up against the land of Merathaim** [*"double rebellion;" apparently a symbolical name for Babylon*]**,** *even* against it, **and against the inhabitants of Pekod** [*a place in Babylonia, perhaps meaning "punishment"*]**: waste and utterly destroy after them,** saith the LORD, and do according to all that I have commanded thee.

22 A sound of battle *is* in the land, and of great destruction.

23 How is the hammer [*Babylon*] of the whole earth cut asunder and broken [*how incredible it is that the "hammer" that pounded all other nations is now broken*]! how is Babylon become a desolation among the nations!

24 I have laid a snare for thee, and thou art also taken, O Babylon, and thou wast not aware [*it caught you by surprise*]: thou art found, and also caught, because thou hast striven against the LORD.

25 The LORD hath opened his armoury, and hath brought forth the weapons of his indignation: for this *is* the work of the Lord GOD of hosts in the land of the Chaldeans.

26 Come against her from the utmost border, open her storehouses: cast her up as heaps [*throw her in piles, like grain*], and destroy her utterly: let nothing of her be left.

27 Slay all her bullocks [*young bulls*]; let them go down to the slaughter: woe unto them! for their day is come, the time of their visitation [*punishment*].

28 The voice of them that flee and escape out of the land of Babylon, to declare in Zion the vengeance of the LORD our God, the vengeance of his temple.

In verse 29, next, we see at least two doctrines. One is that the unrepentant wicked will not escape the punishments of God. Another is that pride is the root cause of all sin.

29 Call together the archers against Babylon: all ye that bend the bow, camp against it round about; let none thereof escape: recompense her according to her work; according to all that she hath done, do unto her: for she hath been proud against the LORD, against the Holy One of Israel.

30 Therefore shall her young men fall in the streets, and all her men of war shall be cut off in that day, saith the LORD.

31 Behold, I *am* against thee, O *thou* most proud, saith the Lord GOD of hosts: for thy day is come, the time *that* I will visit [*punish*] thee.

32 And the most proud shall stumble and fall, and none shall raise him up: and I will kindle a fire in his cities, and it shall devour all round about him.

One of the major messages found in verses 33-34, next, is that the Savior has the power to redeem us from the bondage of sin. Satan does not want to let anyone escape from him, but he cannot prevent the Savior from setting us free if we repent.

33 ¶ Thus saith the LORD of hosts; The children of Israel [*the northern ten tribes who became the "lost ten tribes"*] and the children of Judah

[the Jews] *were* oppressed together: and all that took them captives held them fast; they refused to let them go.

34 Their Redeemer *is* strong; the LORD of hosts [*Jehovah, Jesus Christ*] *is* his name: he shall throughly plead their cause, that he may give rest to the land [*symbolic of the righteous*], and disquiet the inhabitants of Babylon [*while at the same time being a source of unrest for the wicked*].

> Now, back again to the punishment of the wicked in Babylon.

35 ¶ A sword *is* upon the Chaldeans, saith the LORD, and upon the inhabitants of Babylon, and upon her princes, and upon her wise *men.*

36 A sword *is* upon the liars [*NIV: "false prophets"*]; and they shall dote [*will become viewed as fools*]: a sword *is* upon her mighty men; and they shall be dismayed.

> In Old Testament symbolism, horses and chariots are used to symbolize military might.

37 A sword [*destruction*] *is* upon their horses, and upon their chariots, and upon all the mingled people [*foreigners*] that *are* in the midst of her [*outsiders who have chosen to live in Babylon*]; and they shall become as women [*a phrase meaning "weak" in the culture of the day*]: a

sword *is* upon her treasures; and they shall be robbed.

38 A drought *is* upon her waters; and they shall be dried up: for it *is* the land of graven images, and they are mad upon *their* idols.

> Whenever Jeremiah wants us to get the idea that a city will be destroyed completely and abandoned, he paints a picture with words depicting the ruins with lonely creatures and wild animals that live away from humans.

39 Therefore the wild beasts of the desert with the wild beasts of the islands shall dwell *there* [*in the ruins of Babylon*], and the owls shall dwell therein: and it shall be no more inhabited for ever; neither shall it be dwelt in from generation to generation.

40 As God overthrew Sodom and Gomorrah and the neighbour *cities* thereof, saith the LORD; *so* shall no man abide there, neither shall any son of man dwell therein.

> The prophecy again reminds us how the ancient wicked nation of Babylon was to be destroyed.

41 Behold, a people shall come from the north, and a great nation, and many kings [*a great alliance against Babylon*] shall be raised up from the coasts of the earth.

42 They shall hold the bow and the lance: they *are* cruel, and will not

shew mercy: their voice shall roar like the sea, and **they shall ride upon horses,** *every one* put in array, like a man **to the battle, against thee, O daughter** [*inhabitants*] **of Babylon.**

43 The king of Babylon hath heard the report of them, **and his hands waxed feeble: anguish took hold of him,** *and* pangs as of a woman in travail [*labor; in other words, he can't get out of it now*].

44 Behold, he [*the Lord, ultimately; can also refer to the alliance of nations who will conquer Babylon*] **shall come up like a lion** from the swelling of Jordan [*from the thickets on the Jordan River floodplain*] **unto the habitation of the strong** [*to Babylon*]: but I will make them suddenly run away from her: and who *is* a chosen *man, that* I may appoint over her? for who *is* like me? and who will appoint me the time? **and who** *is* **that shepherd that will stand before me** [*in other words, whom could Babylon call upon to successfully protect her from the wrath of the Lord*]?

45 Therefore hear ye the counsel [*the plan*] **of the LORD,** that he hath taken **against Babylon;** and his purposes, that he hath purposed against the land of the Chaldeans: Surely the least of the flock shall draw them out: **surely he shall**

make *their* habitation desolate with them.

46 At the noise of the taking of Babylon the earth is moved, and the cry is heard among the nations [*when Babylon falls, it will startle those who have enjoyed living in it*].

JEREMIAH 51

Selection: all verses

THIS CHAPTER IS a continuation of the prophecy about the downfall of Babylon, contained in chapter 50. The material in chapters 50–51 was written down in the days of Zedekiah, king of Judah, and sent to Babylon (see verses 59–64). You may wish to read Revelation, chapters 17–18, which prophesy the fall of Babylon, along with this chapter of Jeremiah.

As explained in the background notes for chapter 50, "Babylon" can have dual meaning: (1) the literal ancient city of Babylon, and (2) wickedness; Satan's kingdom. Also keep in mind that "Israel" can mean the literal descendants of Abraham, Isaac, and Jacob (whose name was changed to Israel—see Genesis 32:28), but can also mean any who choose to accept the gospel, be baptized, and keep the commandments. Those who desire to be part of the Lord's covenant people, Israel, are commanded to flee from Babylon (verse 6).

As in other prophecies of Jeremiah, this

one will make much use of symbolism and repetition. It will deal with events all the way from the literal fall of ancient Babylon (also referred to as Chaldea) to the fall of Satan's kingdom at the time of the Second Coming of the Savior.

Each time you see the word "Babylon" in this prophecy, you may wish to think of a major message as being that the Lord has power over Satan and thus will ultimately destroy his kingdom and cast him out into his "own place" (D&C 88:114). Another major message is that we must flee Babylon, in other words, wickedness, in order to be on the Lord's side when Babylon is a thing of the past.

Yet a third message to keep in mind comes from the fact that not all people who choose to live in "Babylon" know anything about the true gospel and thus have no chance at all to live it. One of the truths of the gospel is that the Lord is completely fair. Thus, before the day of final judgment, everyone, whether in this life, the postmortal spirit world mission field, or during the Millennium, will have a completely fair chance to hear, understand, accept, or reject the pure gospel of Jesus Christ.

Also, keep in mind that since everyone born into this world has the Light of Christ (John 1:9), everyone over age eight has a degree of accountability, and so those who choose to live the lifestyle found in "Babylon," despite the pricks of conscience that accompany such choices (especially initially), can rightly be taken down with the fall of Babylon. God will be the final judge as to gospel opportunities that still remain for them after their demise with the destruction of Satan's kingdom.

We will now proceed with the Lord's great prophecy through His humble prophet, Jeremiah, concerning the guaranteed fall of Babylon.

1 THUS saith the LORD; Behold, I will raise up against Babylon, and against them that dwell in the midst of them that rise up against me, **a destroying wind** [*the "east wind" which is symbolic of destruction*];

2 And will send unto Babylon fanners [*foreign enemies*], **that shall fan her** [*scatter her—see footnote 2a in your Bible*], and shall empty her land: for in the day of trouble they shall be against her round about.

3 Against *him that* **bendeth** [*strings his bow in preparation to defend Babylon*] **let the archer** [*in the foreign armies*] **bend his bow** [*prepare for battle*], and against *him that* lifteth himself up in his brigandine [*canvas or leather body armor, sometimes with metal strips in it*]: and **spare ye not her** [*Babylon's*] **young men; destroy ye utterly all her host.**

4 Thus the slain shall fall in the land of the Chaldeans [*Babylon*], and *they that are* thrust through in her streets.

Next, in verses 5–6, we see that the Lord will yet gather Israel and that they will be gathered to Him as they flee from the ways of Babylon.

5 For Israel *hath* **not** *been* **for-saken, nor Judah of his God,** of the LORD of hosts; though their land was filled with sin [*even though they were once involved in wickedness*] against the Holy One of Israel.

6 Flee out of the midst of Babylon, and deliver every man his soul [*and thus save your souls*]: **be not cut off in her iniquity;** for this *is* the time of the LORD's vengeance; **he will render unto her a recompence** [*those in Babylon will face God's punishments as they take the consequences of their sins*].

> The symbolism of the "golden cup" mentioned in verse 7, next, is likely the same as that found in the Book of Revelation, chapter 17. If so, it represents having one's "cup" or life full of gross wickedness. We will quote from Revelation and then go on to verse 7, here, in Jeremiah.
>
> <u>Revelation 17:4</u>
> 4 And the woman [*symbolic of Babylon; Satan's kingdom*] was arrayed in purple and scarlet colour, and decked with gold and precious stones and pearls, **having a golden cup in her hand full of abominations and filthiness** of her fornication [*wickedness; breaking of God's laws and commandments; counterfeits of the true gospel*]:

7 Babylon *hath been* **a golden cup** in the LORD's hand [*allowed by the Lord to exist during the mortal years of the earth's existence—compare with*

2 *Nephi 2:11, which says "for it must needs be, that there is an opposition in all things*], **that made all the earth drunken: the nations have drunken of her wine** [*have participated in her wickedness*]; **therefore the nations are mad** [*out of their mind with wickedness*].

8 Babylon is suddenly fallen and destroyed: howl for her; take balm for her pain, if so be she may be healed.

9 We would have healed Babylon [*if she had repented*], **but she is not healed:** forsake her, and let us go every one into his own country: for her judgment reacheth unto heaven, and is lifted up *even* to the skies.

> We will include a quote that verifies the interpretation of the first part of verse 9, above:
>
> "God would have healed them, as he would all his children, before their destruction, but sometimes, like Babylon, they resist turning to the Lord and therefore are not healed" (*Old Testament Student Manual*, page 258).
>
> Verse 10, next, depicts those who do repent, flee Babylon, and become part of righteous Israel.

10 The LORD hath brought forth our righteousness [*in effect, the Atonement of Christ has enabled us to become righteous*]: come, and let us declare in Zion the work of the LORD our God [*let's spread the word of God*].

Next, Jeremiah specifically prophesies that the Medes (an empire located east of Babylon, led by Cyrus the Persian) will defeat ancient Babylon. They did, in about 538 BC

As you will notice, one aspect of "the manner of prophesying among the Jews," spoken of by Nephi (2 Nephi 25:1), is nicely illustrated here. Rather than simply saying that the Medes will prepare for war against Babylon, as most in our modern culture prefer and do, the "manner of prophesying" used by ancient prophets consisted of elaborate and detailed descriptions, conjuring up pictures in the minds and imaginations of the readers of a variety of activities associated with preparing for war against Babylon. In effect, Jeremiah paints dramatic pictures in our minds and involves our emotions as he tells us what will happen.

11 Make bright the arrows; gather the shields [*prepare for battle*]: the LORD hath raised up the spirit of the kings of **the Medes**: for his device *is* **against Babylon, to destroy it;** because it *is* the vengeance of the LORD, the vengeance of his temple.

12 Set up the standard upon [*lift up a banner against*] the walls of Babylon, make the watch strong [*strengthen the guard*], set up the watchmen, **prepare the ambushes:** for the LORD hath both devised and done that which he spake **against the inhabitants of Babylon.**

13 O thou that dwellest upon many waters [*symbolic of Satan's kingdom— see 1 Nephi 14:11, Revelation 17:1, D&C 61 heading*], abundant in treasures, **thine end is come,** *and* the measure of thy covetousness.

14 The LORD of hosts **hath sworn by himself** [*has covenanted in His own name; the strongest oath or promise available in ancient Jewish culture*], **saying, Surely I will fill thee with men,** as with caterpillers [*enemy armies will break into your city; they will be everywhere, like an invasion of caterpillars*]; **and they shall lift up a shout against thee.**

Next, in verses 15–16, Jeremiah testifies that Jehovah, the Creator of earth and heaven, has the power to carry out this prophecy against Babylon.

15 He [*the Lord*] **hath made the earth by his power,** he hath established the world by his wisdom, and hath stretched out the heaven by his understanding.

16 When he uttereth *his* **voice** [*when He commands*], *there is* a multitude of waters in the heavens; and he causeth the vapours to ascend from the ends of the earth: he maketh lightnings with rain, and bringeth forth the wind out of his treasures [*in other words, all things obeyed His voice as He created the earth*].

Having reminded the people of

the power of Jehovah, Jeremiah now points out that idols and other false gods have absolutely no power, in verses 17–18, next.

17 Every man is brutish by *his* **knowledge** [*every idol worshiper is like a brute animal, completely without common sense and doesn't know what he is doing*]; **every founder** [*blacksmith who pours molten metal to form graven images*] **is confounded** by the graven image: for **his molten image** *is* **falsehood, and** *there is* **no breath in them.**

18 They *are* **vanity, the work of errors:** in the time of their visitation they shall perish [*when idol worshipers are destroyed, their powerless idols will perish with them*].

19 The portion of Jacob [*the benefit available to Israel from the true God*] *is* **not like them** [*is not like that from idols to their worshipers*]; **for he** [*the Lord*] *is* **the former** [*creator*] **of all things:** and *Israel is* **the rod** [*power*] **of his inheritance** [*Israel is the covenant people of the Lord through whom the power of salvation is taken to the whole earth—see Abraham 2:9–11*]: **the LORD of hosts** *is* **his name.**

In verses 20-23, next, we see that Israel, the Lord's covenant people, are the tool in the hand of the Lord through which the Church and kingdom of God will be taken to the whole earth (see Daniel 2:34, 44–45). The true gospel of Jesus Christ has the power to cut through falsehood

and error and defeat Satan's power and grasp upon the wicked, if they choose to repent.

20 Thou [*Israel*] **art my** [*the Lord's*] **battle axe** *and* **weapons of war: for with thee will I break in pieces the nations, and with thee will I destroy kingdoms;**

Remember that horses and chariots were used symbolically in Jeremiah's day to represent military might. You might think of verse 21, next, as referring to Satan's armies, the host of wicked mortals who follow his lead in their lives.

21 And with thee will I break in pieces the **horse** and his **rider;** and with thee will I break in pieces the **chariot** and his **rider** [*in other words, the enemy armies, or armies of the wicked*];

22 With thee also will I break in pieces man and woman; and with thee will I break in pieces **old and young;** and with thee will I break in pieces the young man and the maid [*in other words, all who oppose righteousness*];

23 I will also break in pieces with thee [*Israel*] **the shepherd** [*the false prophet and other misguided leaders*] **and his flock** [*followers*]; and with thee will I break in pieces the husbandman [*farmer*] and his yoke of oxen; and with thee will I break in pieces captains and rulers [*military and political leaders*].

One very important aspect of the message in verses 20–23, above, is the fact that goodness and righteousness will ultimately triumph over evil on earth.

24 And I will render [*pay back*] **unto Babylon and to all the inhabitants of Chaldea** [*another term for Babylon*] **all their evil** that they have done in Zion in your sight, saith the LORD.

The "destroying mountain" in verses 25–26, next, seems to be a reference to Babylon, both literally the ancient city and also, symbolically Satan's kingdom. See Revelation 8:8

25 Behold, I *am* **against thee, O destroying mountain** [*Babylon*], saith the LORD, **which destroyest all the earth: and I will stretch out mine hand upon thee, and roll thee down from the rocks, and will make thee a burnt mountain** [*compare with Revelation 8:8*].

26 And they shall not take of thee a stone for a corner, nor a stone for foundations; but **thou shalt be desolate for ever, saith the LORD** [*Babylon is still ruins today, and Satan and his evil followers will be cast into outer darkness, at the end of the Millennium—see Doctrine & Covenants 88:114*].

The next several verses continue to repeat much that has been said in the previous verses. As already pointed out, this type of repetition is typical in Jeremiah's culture. In some verses, he speaks prophetically

of the future as though it had already happened.

27 Set ye up a standard in the land, blow the trumpet among the nations, **prepare the nations against her** [*Babylon*], call together against her the kingdoms of Ararat, Minni, and Ashchenaz; appoint a captain against her; cause the horses to come up as the rough caterpillers.

28 Prepare against her the nations with the kings of the Medes, the captains thereof, and all the rulers thereof, and all the land of his dominion.

29 And the land shall tremble and sorrow: for **every purpose of the LORD shall be performed against Babylon, to make the land of Babylon a desolation without an inhabitant.**

30 The mighty men of Babylon have forborn to fight [*have stopped fighting*], **they have remained in** their **holds: their might hath failed**; they became as women: **they** [*Babylon's enemies*] **have burned her dwellingplaces; her bars are broken.**

31 One post [*messenger*] **shall run to meet another,** and one messenger to meet another, **to shew the king of Babylon that his city is taken at one end** [*captured completely—see footnote 31d in your Bible*],

32 And that **the passages** [*NIV: "river crossings"*] **are stopped, and the reeds** [*marshlands*] **they have burned with fire, and the men of war are affrighted** [*Babylon's soldiers are terrified*].

33 For **thus saith the LORD** of hosts, the God of Israel; **The daughter of Babylon** [*in other words, Babylon*] **is like a threshingfloor, it is time to thresh her:** yet a little while, and the time of her harvest shall come.

Symbolically, verses 34–35, next, have Israel saying that he has been beaten around badly by Satan's kingdom for thousands of years, and now (in the last days and at the Second Coming of Christ), all of Babylon's wickedness will catch up with her.

34 **Nebuchadrezzar** the king of **Babylon hath devoured me** [*Israel, Judah*], he hath **crushed me, he hath made me an empty vessel, he hath swallowed me up like a dragon,** he hath **filled his belly with my delicates,** he hath **cast me out.**

35 **The violence done to me and to my flesh** *be* **upon Babylon,** shall the inhabitant of Zion say; and my blood upon the inhabitants of Chaldea, shall Jerusalem say.

In verses 36–37, next, Jeremiah teaches us that it is the power of the Lord through which we are redeemed from Satan and the forces of evil.

36 **Therefore thus saith the LORD; Behold, I will plead thy cause** [*through the Atonement—see D&C 45:3–5*], **and take vengeance for thee; and I will dry up her sea, and make her springs dry** [*I will destroy Babylon*].

37 And **Babylon shall become heaps** [*ruins*], a dwellingplace for dragons [*jackals*], an astonishment [*an object of surprise and horror*], and an hissing [*scorn*], without an inhabitant.

Next, beginning with verse 38, Jeremiah prophetically depicts Babylon at its prime, when its inhabitants are feeling powerful and invincible in their wickedness.

38 **They shall roar together like lions: they shall yell as lions' whelps** [*cubs*].

39 In their heat I will make their feasts, and I will make them drunken, that they may rejoice [*they will keep right on partying and living riotously*], and sleep a perpetual sleep, and not wake, saith the LORD.

40 **I will bring them down like lambs to the slaughter, like rams** with he goats.

41 **How is Sheshach** [*another name for Babylon*] **taken** [*how quickly it falls*]! and **how** is the praise of the whole earth **surprised! how** is Babylon become **an astonishment among the nations!**

The imagery in verse 42, next, takes advantage of the fact that Babylon is built in a desert. Just as it would seem impossible to believe that a tidal wave would destroy Babylon, so also it seems impossible to many that such a large kingdom as that of the devil could be destroyed suddenly. It is not impossible for the Lord. Babylon was destroyed. Satan's kingdom will be destroyed.

42 The sea is come up upon Babylon: she is covered with the multitude of the waves thereof.

43 Her cities are a desolation, a dry land, and a wilderness, **a land wherein no man dwelleth,** neither doth *any* son of man pass thereby.

44 And I will punish Bel [*the main false god of Babylon*] **in Babylon,** and I will bring forth out of his mouth that which he hath swallowed up: and the nations shall not flow together any more unto him [*people will no longer gather to Babylon to participate in wickedness*]: yea, **the wall of Babylon shall fall.**

45 My people [*Those who wish to be part of righteous Israel*], **go ye out of the midst of her, and deliver ye every man his soul** [*save your souls*] from the fierce anger of the LORD.

After reading Revelation 18:9–10, quoted next, verses 46–49 of Jeremiah, which follow, appear to include the fall of spiritual Babylon in the last days.

Revelation 18:9–10

9 And the kings [*powerful, wicked leaders*] of the earth, who have committed fornication [*who have been extremely wicked*] and lived deliciously [*riotously*] with her [*the "whore," Satan's kingdom, Babylon*], shall bewail her [*mourn losing her*], and lament for her [*instead of repenting*], when they shall see the smoke of her burning [*the wicked will be devastated by the destruction of their lifestyle*],
10 Standing afar off for the fear of her torment, saying, Alas, alas, that great city Babylon, that mighty city! for in one hour is thy judgment come [*the Second Coming will change things quickly; they can't believe how fast she was destroyed!*].

46 And [*flee from Babylon—verse 45, above*] **lest your heart faint** [*lest you be sorry when Babylon falls*], **and ye fear for the rumour** [*the news that Babylon has fallen*] that shall be heard in the land; a rumour shall both come *one* year, and after that in *another* year *shall come* a rumour, and violence in the land, ruler against ruler.

47 Therefore, behold, the days come, that I will do judgment upon the graven images of Babylon: and her whole land shall be confounded [*in confusion; startled; perplexed*], and all her slain shall fall in the midst of her.

48 Then the heaven and the earth,

and all that *is* therein, shall sing for Babylon [*will rejoice because Babylon is gone*]: for the spoilers shall come unto her from the north, saith the LORD.

49 As Babylon *hath caused* the slain of Israel to fall, so at **Babylon shall fall** the slain of all the earth [*the wicked of the earth*].

50 Ye that have escaped the sword [*you who still have the opportunity to repent*], **go away, stand not still: remember the LORD afar off, and let Jerusalem come into your mind.**

51 We [*Israel*] **are confounded, because** we have heard reproach: shame hath covered our faces: for **strangers are come into the sanctuaries of the LORD's house** [*because of our wickedness, our temple has been defiled*].

> Now, back to the destruction of Babylon.

52 Wherefore, behold, **the days come, saith the LORD, that I will do judgment upon her graven images:** and through all her land the wounded shall groan.

> No matter how strong and powerful Satan's kingdom seems to get, the Lord can and will destroy it. Jeremiah continues using prophetic repetition to emphasize the details of this prophecy against Babylon.

53 Though [*even if*] **Babylon should mount up to heaven** [*as was attempted by the builders of the Tower of Babel*], **and though she should fortify the height of her strength, yet from me shall spoilers come unto her,** saith the LORD.

54 A sound of **a cry *cometh* from Babylon,** and great destruction from the land of the Chaldeans:

55 Because the LORD hath spoiled [*ruined, destroyed*] **Babylon,** and destroyed out of her the great voice; when her waves do roar like great waters, a noise of their voice is uttered:

56 Because the spoiler is come upon her, *even* upon Babylon, and **her mighty men are taken, every one of their bows is broken: for the LORD God of recompences shall surely requite** [*repay in full, in other words, the law of the harvest*].

> Since we know that the Lord does not make people wicked, we need to interpret verse 57, next, as saying that He will allow them their agency to choose wickedness. The idea is that Babylon is filled with people who are through and through wicked.

57 And I will make drunk her princes, and her wise *men*, her captains, and her rulers, and her mighty men: and **they shall sleep a perpetual sleep, and not wake** [*they will be destroyed*], saith the King, whose name *is* the LORD of hosts.

58 Thus saith the LORD of hosts; **The broad walls of Babylon shall be utterly broken, and her high gates shall be burned with fire** [*perhaps symbolic of the burning of the wicked at the time of the Second Coming*]; and the people shall labour in vain, and the folk in the fire, and they shall be weary.

> Verses 59–64, next, provide a historical note informing us that Jeremiah wrote down the prophecy contained in chapters 50–51 and sent them to Babylon with Seraiah, who accompanied King Zedekiah, king of Judah, when he traveled to Babylon on political business about 594 BC Seraiah was instructed to read the prophecy after he arrived in Babylon and then to tie a rock to the scroll and throw it into the Euphrates River. You will see the purpose behind this act as you read verse 64.

59 ¶ **The word which Jeremiah the** prophet **commanded Seraiah** the son of Neriah, the son of Maaseiah, **when he went with Zedekiah the** king of Judah **into Babylon** in the fourth year of his reign [*he reigned for eleven years—see Jeremiah 52:1*]. And *this* Seraiah *was* a quiet prince [*German Bible: Seraiah was the officer in charge of all details for the trip*].

60 So **Jeremiah wrote** in a book [*on a scroll*] **all the evil that should come upon Babylon,** *even* **all these words** [*chapters 50–51*] **that are written against Babylon.**

61 And **Jeremiah said to Seraiah, When thou comest to Babylon,** and shalt see, and shalt **read all these words;**

62 **Then shalt thou say, O LORD,** thou hast spoken against this place [*Babylon*], to cut it off, that none shall remain in it, neither man nor beast, but that it shall be desolate for ever.

63 **And** it shall be, **when thou hast made an end of reading this book** [*this scroll*], *that* thou shalt **bind a stone to it, and cast it into the midst of Euphrates** [*the Euphrates River*]:

64 **And** thou shalt **say, Thus shall Babylon sink, and shall not rise** from the evil that I [*the Lord*] will bring upon her: and they shall be weary. **Thus far** *are* **the words of Jeremiah** [*NIV* The words of Jeremiah end here].

> We see similar action by an angel in the vision of John as described in Revelation. It, too, depicts the final destruction of Babylon.
>
> **Revelation 18:21**
> 21 And a mighty angel took up a stone like a great millstone, and cast *it* into the sea, saying, **Thus with violence shall that great city Babylon be thrown down, and shall be found no more at all.**

JEREMIAH 52

Selection: all verses

BIBLE SCHOLARS DON'T really know who added this chapter on to the end of Jeremiah's writings, which end with the last verse of chapter 51 (see note at the end of 51:64 in this study guide). Jeremiah 52 is pretty much a repeat of the material in 2 Kings 24:18 through 25:21. It is also quite similar to parts of Jeremiah 39.

In this chapter, we are given a summary of events at the time Jerusalem fell to the Babylonian army of King Nebuchadnezzar. The prophecies given by Jeremiah concerning the fall of Jerusalem were fulfilled at this time. As stated previously, Jeremiah is one of the few prophets who have seen many of their prophecies fulfilled in their own lifetime. It begins with a brief history of King Zedekiah of Judah, who is mentioned by Nephi in 1 Nephi 1:4. As you will see, he was twenty-one years old when he became king.

1 ZEDEKIAH *was* one and twenty years old when he began to reign [*in about 598* B.C.]**, and he reigned eleven years in Jerusalem.** And his mother's name *was* Hamutal the daughter of Jeremiah of Libnah.

2 And he did *that which was* **evil in the eyes of the LORD,** according to all that Jehoiakim had done [*he was wicked just like the king who preceded him*].

3 For through the anger of the LORD it came to pass in Jerusalem and Judah, till he had cast them out from his presence, that **Zedekiah rebelled against the king of Babylon** [*not a wise political move*].

4 ¶ And it came to pass **in the ninth year of his** [*Zedekiah's*] **reign, in the tenth month, in the tenth** *day* **of the month,** *that* **Nebuchadrezzar king of Babylon came,** he and all his army, **against Jerusalem,** and pitched against it [*and laid siege to it*]**,** and built forts against it round about.

5 So the city was besieged unto the eleventh year of king Zedekiah.

> By the time we get to verse 6, the Babylonian armies have had Jerusalem under siege for about eighteen months. Consequently, the Jews there are suffering from severe lack of food

6 And in the fourth month, in the ninth *day* of the month, **the famine was sore** [*severe*] in the city, so that there was no bread for the people of the land.

7 **Then the city was broken up** [*the Babylonian soldiers broke into Jerusalem*]**,** and all **the men** of war **fled** [*including Zedekiah*]**,** and went forth out of the city **by night** by the way of the gate between the two walls, which *was* by the king's garden; (now the Chaldeans *were* by the city round about:) and they went by the way of the plain.

8 ¶ But the army of the Chaldeans pursued after the king, and overtook Zedekiah in the plains of Jericho; and all his army was scattered from him.

9 Then they took the king, and carried him up unto the king of Babylon to Riblah [*about two hundred miles north of Jerusalem*] in the land of Hamath [*in Syria*]; **where he gave judgment upon him** [*where he sentenced Zedekiah*].

10 And the king of Babylon slew the sons of Zedekiah before his eyes: he slew also all the princes of Judah in Riblah.

We know that one of the sons of Zedekiah was not killed. We know from the Book of Mormon that his son, Mulek, escaped, and was brought by the Lord to America. We will include two references from the Book of Mormon here:

Helaman 6:10

10 Now the land south was called Lehi and the land north was called Mulek, which was after the son of Zedekiah; for **the Lord did bring Mulek into the land north**, and Lehi into the land south.

Helaman 8:21

21 And now will you dispute that Jerusalem was destroyed? **Will ye say that the sons of Zedekiah were not slain, all except it were Mulek?** Yea, and do ye not behold that the seed of Zedekiah are with us, and they were driven out of the land of Jerusalem? But behold, this is not all—

11 Then he put out the eyes of Zedekiah; and the king of Babylon **bound him in chains, and carried him to Babylon, and put him in prison till the day of his death.**

12 ¶ Now in the fifth month, in the tenth *day* **of the month** [*about a month after the fall of Jerusalem*], which *was* the nineteenth year of Nebuchadrezzar king of Babylon, **came Nebuzar-adan, captain of the guard,** *which* **served the king of Babylon, into Jerusalem,**

13 And burned the house of the LORD [*the temple in Jerusalem*], **and the king's house** [*the palace*]; **and all the houses of Jerusalem, and all the houses of the great** *men***, burned he with fire:**

14 And all the army of the Chaldeans [*Babylonians*], that *were* with the captain of the guard, **brake down all the walls of Jerusalem** round about [*symbolizing that they had completely conquered the city*].

15 Then Nebuzar-adan the captain of the guard [*one of King Nebuchadnezzar's chief military officers*] **carried away captive** *certain* **of the poor of the people, and the**

residue of the people that remained in the city, and those that fell away, that fell to the king of Babylon, and the rest of the multitude.

16 But **Nebuzar-adan** the captain of the guard **left** *certain* **of the poor of the land for vinedressers and for husbandmen** [*to farm the area around Jerusalem*].

> Next, in verses 17–23, the Babylonians gather up the things of value from the temple in Jerusalem and take them to Babylon.

17 Also **the pillars of brass** that *were* in the house of the LORD, and the bases, and the **brasen sea** that *was* in the house of the LORD, the Chaldeans brake, **and carried all the brass of them to Babylon**.

18 The **caldrons** also, and the **shovels**, and the **snuffers**, and the **bowls**, and the **spoons**, and all the **vessels of brass** wherewith they ministered, took they away.

19 And the **basons**, and the **firepans**, and the **bowls**, and the **caldrons**, and the **candlesticks**, and the **spoons**, and the **cups**; *that* which *was* of **gold** *in* gold [NIV: *"made of pure gold"*], and *that* which *was* of **silver** *in* silver, took the captain of the guard away.

20 The **two pillars, one sea** [*large font*], and **twelve brasen bulls** that *were* under the bases, which king Solomon had made in the house of the LORD: the brass of all these vessels was without weight [*too much to weigh*].

21 And *concerning* the pillars, the height of one pillar *was* eighteen cubits [*about twenty-seven feet*]; and a fillet of twelve cubits did compass it; and the thickness thereof *was* four fingers: *it was* hollow.

22 And a chapiter of brass *was* upon it; and the height of one chapiter *was* five cubits, with network and pomegranates [*decorations made of brass*] upon the chapiters round about, all *of* brass. The second pillar also and the pomegranates *were* like unto these.

23 And there were ninety and six pomegranates [*made of brass*] on a side; *and* all the pomegranates upon the network *were* an hundred round about.

> Next, in verses 24–27, King Nebuchadnezzar's chief military officer in Judah rounds up several dignitaries of the Jews who had been close associates of King Zedekiah and takes them about two hundred miles north to Riblah, where Nebuchadnezzar executes them.

24 ¶ And **the captain of the guard took Seraiah** [*apparently not the same person as in Jeremiah 51:59*] the chief priest, and **Zephaniah** the second priest, and **the three keepers of the door**:

25 He took also out of the city **an eunuch** [*an officer—see footnote 25a in your Bible*], which had the charge of the men of war; and **seven men of them that were near the king's person** [*who had been close associates and advisors of King Zedekiah*], which were found in the city; and **the principal scribe** of the host, who mustered the people [*drafted people for military duty*] of the land; **and threescore** [*sixty*] men of the people of the land, **that were found in the midst of the city.**

26 So Nebuzar-adan the captain of the guard took them, and brought them to the king of Babylon to Riblah.

27 And the king of Babylon smote them, and put them to death in Riblah in the land of Hamath. **Thus Judah was carried away captive out of his own land** [*as prophesied*].

> Verses 28–30, next, inform us that Nebuchadnezzar (often spelled "Nebuchadrezzar," as seen in verse 28) carried a total of forty-six hundred Jews into captivity (see verse 30) over the next several years. He had already taken many others, including Daniel and Ezekiel, in earlier waves of conquest against the Jews in Jerusalem and Judah.

28 This *is* **the people whom Nebuchadrezzar carried away captive:** in the seventh year **three thousand Jews and three and twenty:**

29 In the eighteenth year of Nebuchadrezzar he carried away captive from Jerusalem **eight hundred thirty and two persons:**

30 In the three and twentieth year of Nebuchadrezzar Nebuzar-adan the captain of the guard carried away captive of the Jews **seven hundred forty and five** persons: **all the persons** *were* **four thousand and six hundred.**

> Verses 31–34, next, are a sort of appendix, containing a very brief history of Jehoiachin, who had been king of Judah for just a few months (about 598 BC) before he and his court were taken into exile to Babylon and imprisoned. King Zedekiah followed him as king. When Nebuchadnezzar died, his successor, Evil-merodach, freed Jehoiachin after thirty-seven years in prison and gave him good treatment in Babylon for the rest of his life.

31 ¶ And it came to pass **in the seven and thirtieth year of the captivity of Jehoiachin king of Judah,** in the twelfth month, in the five and twentieth *day* of the month, *that* **Evil-merodach king of Babylon** in the *first* year of his reign lifted up the head of Jehoiachin king of Judah [*released him from prison*], and **brought him forth out of prison,**

32 And spake kindly unto him, and set his throne [*gave him a status*] above the throne of the kings that *were* with him in Babylon [*other kings, probably from other nations that had also been conquered by Babylon*],

33 And changed his prison garments: and he did continually eat bread before him [*he ate at the king's table*] all the days of his life.

34 And *for* his diet, there was a continual diet given him of the king of Babylon, every day a portion until the day of his death, all the days of his life.

LAMENTATIONS

TO LAMENT IS to go into deep sorrow and morning because of a great loss. Thus, the Book of Lamentations is Jeremiah's expression of deep loss and mourning over what happened to his people, Israel (Judah especially), who were taken into captivity and scattered.

If you have studied Jeremiah in this study guide, you will be quite familiar with the language of Jeremiah and will likely do well in understanding Lamentations. For example, you will be familiar with the fact that Jeremiah uses vivid images and drama to express what he has seen in vision and received by direct revelation from the Lord.

LAMENTATIONS 1

Selection: all verses

BECAUSE OF SPACE limitations in this study guide, we will just do one chapter of Lamentations, chapter 1, in which Jeremiah laments and sorrows over what happened to Jerusalem. He has seen in vision the future destruction of Jerusalem by the Babylonians, the final scenes of which took place in about 587 BC Thus, he will speak of the future as if it had already taken place.

1 How doth the city [*Jerusalem*] sit solitary, *that was* full of people! *how* is she become as a widow! she

that was great among the nations, *and* princess among the provinces, how is she become tributary [*a servant to another nation*]!

2 She weepeth sore in the night, and her tears *are* on her cheeks: **among all her lovers** [*false gods, idols, priorities that take the place of God*] **she hath none to comfort her:** all her friends have dealt treacherously with her, they are become her enemies.

3 Judah is gone into captivity because of affliction, and because of great servitude: **she dwelleth among the heathen,** she findeth no rest: all her persecutors overtook her between the straits.

4 The ways of Zion [*the roads leading to Jerusalem*] **do mourn, because none come to the solemn feasts:** all her gates are desolate: her priests sigh, her virgins are afflicted, and she *is* in bitterness.

5 Her adversaries are the chief, her enemies prosper; for the LORD hath afflicted her for [*because of*] **the multitude of her transgressions:** her children are gone into captivity before the enemy.

6 And from the daughter of Zion [*another name for Jerusalem*] **all her beauty is departed:** her princes are become like harts [*deer*] *that* find no pasture, and they are gone without

strength before the pursuer.

7 Jerusalem remembered in the days of her affliction and of her miseries all her pleasant things that she had in the days of old, when her people fell into the hand of the enemy, and none did help her: the adversaries saw her, *and* did mock at her sabbaths.

8 Jerusalem hath grievously sinned; therefore she is removed: all that honoured her despise her, because they have seen her nakedness: yea, she sigheth, and turneth backward.

9 Her filthiness *is* in her skirts [*her filthiness clings to her like mud clings to clothing*]; **she remembereth not her last end** [*she did not think ahead and consider the final consequences of sin*]; **therefore she came down wonderfully** [*astonishingly*]: she had no comforter. O LORD, behold my affliction: for the enemy hath magnified *himself.*

10 The adversary hath spread out his hand upon all her pleasant things: for she hath seen *that* the heathen entered into her sanctuary, whom thou didst command *that* they should not enter into thy congregation.

11 All her people sigh, they seek bread [*they are hungry*]; they have given their pleasant things for meat [*food*] to relieve the soul [*to keep their bodies alive*]: see, O LORD, and consider; for **I am become vile** [*have become despised*].

In verses 12–22, Jeremiah depicts Judah (the Jews at this time in history) as a person, mourning what has become of her.

12 ¶ *Is it* **nothing to you, all ye that pass by** [*why don't you feel sorry for me*]? **Behold** [*look*], **and see if there be any sorrow like unto my sorrow,** which is done unto me, **wherewith the LORD hath afflicted** *me* **in the day of his fierce anger.**

13 **From above hath he sent fire into my bones,** and it prevaileth against them: **he hath spread a net for my feet** [*put me in captivity*], he hath turned me back: he hath made me desolate *and* faint all the day.

14 The yoke of my transgressions is bound by his hand: they **are wreathed** [*woven together*]**, and come up upon my neck:** he hath made my strength to fall, **the Lord hath delivered me into** *their* **hands** [*the Babylonians*]**,** *from whom* I am not able to rise up [*escape*].

15 **The Lord hath trodden under foot all my mighty** *men* in the midst of me: he hath called an assembly against me to crush my young men: the Lord hath trodden the virgin, the daughter of Judah, *as in a winepress* [*my people have been crushed like grapes*].

16 **For these** *things* I weep; mine eye, mine eye runneth down with water, because the comforter [*the Lord*] that should relieve my soul is far from me: my children are desolate, because the enemy prevailed.

17 **Zion spreadeth forth her hands** [*in a plea for help*]**, and there is none to comfort her:** the LORD hath commanded concerning Jacob [*wicked Israel*]*, that* his adversaries *should be* round about him: Jerusalem is as a menstruous woman [*rejected, shunned*] among them.

18 ¶ **The LORD is righteous** [*the Lord is in the right as He punishes me*]**; for I have rebelled against his commandment:** hear, I pray you, all people, and behold my sorrow: my virgins and my young men are gone into captivity.

19 I called for my lovers [*I called upon my false gods*]**, but they deceived me:** my priests and mine elders gave up the ghost [*died*] in the city, while they sought their meat to relieve their souls [*while they searched for food to save themselves from starving to death*].

20 **Behold, O LORD; for I** *am* **in distress:** my bowels are troubled [*I am deeply troubled*]; mine heart is turned within me [*my heart is tormented*]; for **I have grievously rebelled:** abroad the sword bereaveth, at home *there is* as death [*I'm

in trouble abroad and at home].

21 They have heard that I sigh: *there is* none to comfort me: all mine enemies have heard of my trouble; they are glad that thou hast done *it*: thou wilt bring the day *that* thou hast called, and they shall be like unto me *[the day will come that they too will be punished by Thee, and then they will be like me].*

22 Let all their wickedness come before thee; and do unto them, as thou hast done unto me for all my transgressions: for my sighs *are* many, and my heart *is* faint.

EZEKIEL

EZEKIEL WAS A prophet who served among the Jews who had been taken captive into Babylon during various waves of military action against Judah from about 606 BC until the fall of Jerusalem in about 587 BC. Bible scholars believe that Ezekiel was among the Jewish captives carried away by King Nebuchadnezzar, of Babylon, along with King Jehoiachin, king of Judah, somewhere around 598–597 BC. Five years after he arrived in Babylon, Ezekiel was called to be a prophet. He served the exiled Jews in captivity for about twenty-two years, until 570 BC. We will quote from the Bible Dictionary, which contains a brief outline of Ezekiel's writings.

Bible Dictionary: "Ezekiel"
"The book of Ezekiel has three main divisions: (1) 1–24, prophecies of judgment against Jerusalem and the nation; (2) 25–39, prophecies of restoration; (3) 40–48, visions of the reconstruction of the temple and its worship. Chs. 1–39 are similar in manner and contents to other prophetic writings; chs. 40–48 are unique in prophecy."

Probably the best-known scriptural passage in Ezekiel among the Latter-day Saints is Ezekiel 37:15–20, dealing with the stick of Judah and the stick of Joseph (the Bible and the Book of Mormon) and prophesying that in the last days, the two books would come together.

They have literally come together in many ways, including when the Saints carry their scriptures to church and elsewhere. Perhaps the best-known passage among Christians in general might be Ezekiel's vision of the valley of dry bones, in chapter 37:1–14, symbolizing both the resurrection and the restoration of Israel to the promised land.

Because of space limitations for this study guide, we will of necessity limit our treatment of Ezekiel to the prophecy concerning the "stick of Judah" and the "stick of Joseph." To do this, we will go to the relevant verses in chapter 37.

EZEKIEL 37

Selection: verses 15–28

TWO STICKS

The "stick of Judah" (the Bible) and the "stick of Joseph" (the Book of Mormon).

According to footnote 16a, for Ezekiel, chapter 37 in your Bible, the Hebrew word for "stick," in this context, is "wood," meaning a wooden writing tablet of the type commonly used in Babylon in the days of Ezekiel. We will quote from a fascinating article in the September 1977 *Ensign*, pages 24–26, which sheds additional light on the subject of such wooden writing tablets:

> "Recent exciting discoveries now confirm the correctness of Joseph Smith's interpretation in a way impossible in 1830. But before discussing these new discoveries,

let's take quick look at some linguistic points. Both stick, in the English King James Version, and rod, in the Greek Septuagint Version, are very unusual translations of the Hebrew word ets . . . whose basic meaning is wood. . . .

"The modern nation of Iraq includes almost all of Mesopotamia, the homeland of the ancient kingdoms of Assyria and Babylonia. In 593 BC, when Ezekiel was called to be a prophet, he was living in exile in Babylonia. . . . As he walked its streets, he would have seen the typical scribe pressing a wedge-shaped stylus into moist clay tablets to make the complex writings familiar to us as cuneiform (wedge-shaped). But scholars today know that other kinds of records were being made in Mesopotamia: papyrus, parchment, and wooden tablets. Though only the clay tablets have survived the millennia, writers referred to the other writing materials on their clay tablets. [One such writing style was called "wood tablets."]

"Modern archaeologists knew what papyrus and parchment were, but what were these wood tablets? How could cuneiform be written on wood? . . .

"
. . . Some years ago . . . San Nicolo [*an archaeologist*]

remembered that Romans and Greeks both made wooden wax tablets for record-keeping purposes out of boards whose surfaces had been cut below the edges in order to hold a thin coating of wax. Scribes wrote on the wax. The raised edges protected the inscribed surfaces when two tablets were put together.

"Could the Babylonians have done the same thing? . . . But five years later, . . . a discovery made in the territory that had been ancient Assyria confirmed his theory to the letter.

"The discovery, directed by archaeologist Max Mallowan, was made in a layer of sludge deep in a well in Nimrod, a city known as Calah in the Bible. . . . By the end of the day workmen had found . . . fragments of two complete sets of tablets, one of ivory and the other of walnut, each composed of sixteen boards. . . .

"All of the surfaces of the boards were cut down a tenth of an inch, leaving a half-inch-wide raised edge all around. The lowered surfaces provided a bed for wax filling, of which some thin biscuit-like fragments were found either still adhering to the boards or mixed in the sludge nearby. . . .

"The cover boards . . . had hinge marks on both sides, making it evident that all sixteen in each set had once been joined together like a Japanese folding screen. The whole work made such an extensive record that Mallowan could announce his discovery as the oldest known example of a book. . . .

"With these things in mind, we can see how we might translate Ezekiel 37:15–17 in this way:

"'These were the words of the Lord to me: Man, take one leaf of a wooden tablet and write on it, "Judah and his associates of Israel." Then take another leaf and write on it, "Joseph, the leaf [wooden tablet] of Ephraim and all his associates of Israel."

"'Now bring the two together to form one tablet; then they will be a folding tablet in your hand.'

"This translation is faithful to what we now know of Ezekiel's language and culture" (Keith H. Meservy, "Ezekiel's 'Sticks,'" Ensign, September 1977, pages 24–26, as quoted in the Old Testament Student Manual, page 283–284).

We will now go ahead and read the relevant verses in Ezekiel. You will see that this is a dual prophecy, meaning that it has two different meanings. First, it foretells the coming together of the Bible and the Book of Mormon in the last days. Second, it predicts the latter-day reuniting of the kingdoms of Judah (the Jews) and Joseph (Israel).

15 ¶ The word of the LORD came again unto me, saying,

16 Moreover, thou son of man, take thee one stick, and write upon it, For Judah [*the Bible*], **and for the children of Israel his companions: then take another stick, and write upon it, For Joseph** [*the Book of Mormon*], **the stick of Ephraim, and** *for* **all the house of Israel his companions** [*all of Israel will benefit from these two books*]:

17 And join them one to another into one stick; and they shall become one in thine hand.

Have you noticed that there are several ways in which this prophecy has been fulfilled in our day? One way is the literal fact that both the Bible and the Book of Mormon are part of our LDS "standard works." We literally hold them together as we pick up our scriptures. They are "one in [our] hand."

Another literal fulfillment is that the Bible and the Book of Mormon are cross-referenced in our Topical Guide, Bible Dictionary, and Index. Yet another fulfillment is that both books of scripture have come together in our hearts.

Another very important fulfillment is that the Book of Mormon bears witness of the truthfulness of the Bible. This is vital in our day, when so many Christians are discounting the Bible's importance and interpreting it to condone sin in our day.

You can no doubt think of other ways in which the Bible and the Book of Mormon have been "joined" together in our day.

18 ¶ And when the children of thy people shall speak unto thee, saying, Wilt thou not shew us what thou *meanest* **by these** [*would you please explain what you mean by this prophecy*]?

19 Say unto them, Thus saith the Lord GOD; Behold, I will take the stick of Joseph, which *is* **in the hand of Ephraim, and the tribes of Israel his fellows, and will put them with him,** *even* **with the stick of Judah, and make them one stick, and they shall be one in mine hand.**

20 ¶ And the sticks whereon thou writest shall be in thine hand before their eyes [*in other words, this is a literal prophecy; there will literally be two books, and they will come together such that you can see them together with your eyes*].

Next, we see the second meaning of this prophecy explained. The kingdoms of Judah and Israel will be reunited in the last days. Remember that the twelve tribes of Israel split into two nations after the death of King Solomon. They became the Northern Kingdom (the ten tribes), often referred to as Ephraim or Israel, with headquarters in Samaria; and the Southern Kingdom (Judah), consisting of the tribes of Judah and Benjamin, with headquarters in Jerusalem. These next verses are a major prophecy concerning the gathering of Israel. Remember that the most important aspect of the gathering of Israel is gathering them to Jesus Christ, who brings them to the Father to dwell in celestial glory.

21 And say unto them, **Thus saith the Lord GOD; Behold, I will take the children of Israel from among the heathen, whither they be gone, and will gather them on every side, and bring them into their own land:**

22 **And I will make them one nation** in the land upon the mountains of Israel; **and one king** [Christ] **shall be king to them all:** and they shall be no more two nations, neither shall they be divided into two kingdoms any more at all:

23 **Neither shall they defile themselves any more with their idols, nor with their detestable things, nor with any of their transgressions: but I will save them out of all their dwellingplaces, wherein they have sinned, and will cleanse them: so shall they be my people, and I will be their God.**

24 **And David** [symbolic of Christ in this context] **my servant shall be king over them;** and they all shall have one shepherd [Jesus Christ]: **they shall also walk in my judgments, and observe my statutes, and do them** [in other words, they will understand and keep the commandments].

25 And they shall dwell in the land that I have given unto Jacob my servant, wherein your fathers have dwelt; and they shall dwell therein, even they, and their children, and their children's children for ever [the righteous will inherit the earth, which will ultimately become the celestial kingdom—see Doctrine and Covenants 130:9–11]: and my servant David shall be their prince for ever.

26 Moreover **I will make** a covenant of peace with them; it shall be **an everlasting covenant with them:** and I will place them, and multiply them, and will set my sanctuary in the midst of them for evermore.

27 My tabernacle also shall be with them: yea, **I will be their God, and they shall be my people.**

28 And the heathen shall know that I the LORD do sanctify Israel, when my sanctuary shall be in the midst of them for evermore.

DANIEL

W E WILL DO a few things with Daniel within our space limitations for this study guide. He was taken captive to Babylon with other Jews by Nebuchadnezzar (perhaps the crown prince of Babylon at this time—according to some Bible scholars, his father was still alive), in about 606 BC, not quite twenty years before the fall of Jerusalem in 587 BC. It appears that he was among one of the first waves of captives, which included skilled craftsmen and likely candidates for being educated in Babylon. It was customary for the king of Babylon to take the cream of the crop among those he captured and treat them well, educating them and giving them responsibilities in his government. Daniel and three other Hebrew young men, Shadrach, Meshach, and Abednego, were among the promising young men chosen for privilege by Nebuchadnezzar.

The Book of Daniel can be divided into two general categories. Chapters 1–6 are accounts of Daniel and his three young friends in Babylon. Chapters 7–12 consist of prophetic visions that Daniel saw while in Babylon. As you know, some of our favorite Bible stories come from the Book of Daniel, including Daniel in the lions' den.

In a way, Daniel might be considered to be the "Joseph" in Babylonian captivity since his story and values closely parallel those of Joseph who was sold into Egypt.

There are several major messages in Daniel, including:

1. The value of living a healthy lifestyle and living according to the Lord's laws of health (1:5–15).

2. Being strictly loyal to God; having "no other gods" before Him (chapter 3).

3. The power of prayer (chapters 2, 6, and 9).

4. The value of a good reputation (4:8; 5:11–14; 6:14).

5. The value of showing gratitude (chapter 4).

6. The value of gifts of the Spirit (chapters 2, 4, 5, 7–12).

We will study selections from Daniel, using specific sets of verses as we go.

Major Message

Living according to the Lord's law of health provides both physical and spiritual blessings.

DANIEL 1

Selection: verses 1–20

I N THIS INTRODUCTORY chapter to the book of Daniel, we see that King Nebuchadnezzar of Babylon has laid siege to Jerusalem. Daniel and his young friends are among the Jews who are taken captive to Babylon, which is some 500 miles east of Jerusalem as the crow flies, but closer to 800–1000 miles of travel by the normal trade routes of the day.

1 IN the third year of the reign of

Jehoiakim king of Judah [*about 606 BC*] **came Nebuchadnezzar king of Babylon unto Jerusalem, and besieged it.**

> The gross wickedness of the Jews at this time made them weak and unable to defend themselves. Likewise, their lifestyles had separated them from the Lord and His help.

2 And **the Lord gave Jehoiakim king of Judah into his hand,** with part of the vessels of the house of God: which he carried into the land of Shinar to the house of his god; and he brought the vessels into the treasure house of his god.

3 ¶ And **the king** [*Nebuchadnezzar*] **spake** unto Ashpenaz the master of his eunuchs [*the chief of his palace officers*], that he should **bring certain of the children of Israel,** and of the king's seed, and of the princes;

4 Children **in whom** *was* **no blemish, but well favoured, and skilful in all wisdom, and cunning in knowledge, and understanding science,** and such as *had* ability in them to stand in the king's palace, and **whom they might teach the learning and the tongue of the Chaldeans** [*Babylonians*].

> According to verse 5, next, the plan was to feed them the same sumptuous food eaten by the king, and to educate them for three years, at which time they would be presented to the

king to enter into his service. Remember that the word "meat" in our Bible means "food." When Old Testament writers mean beef or lamb or whatever, they usually use the word "flesh."

It is almost certain that the "king's meat" included the meat of several different kinds of animals, many of which would have been against the Jews' "word of wisdom" (see Leviticus 11)—the Law of Moses regarding what a faithful Israelite could and could not eat. For example, the king's food could have included pork and meat that had not been bled before cooking. All of these would have violated the commitments of Daniel and his friends to the Lord, just as smoking and drinking would violate our covenants with the Lord.

5 And **the king appointed them a daily provision of the king's meat** [*had them eat the same food that the king ate*], **and** of the **wine** which he drank: so nourishing them three years, **that at the end thereof they might stand before the king** [*be given responsible positions in the king's service*].

6 Now among these were of the children of Judah [*from among the Jewish captives*], **Daniel, Hananiah** [*Shadrach*], **Mishael** [*Meshach*], and **Azariah** [*Abednego*]:

7 Unto **whom the prince of the eunuchs gave names:** for he gave unto **Daniel** *the name* of

Belteshazzar; and to Hananiah, of Shadrach; and to Mishael, of Meshach; and to Azariah, of Abed-nego.

8 ¶ But Daniel purposed in his heart that he **would not defile himself** [*break the covenants he had made with the Lord*] **with** the portion of **the king's meat, nor with the wine** which he drank: **therefore he requested of the prince of the eunuchs that he might not defile himself.**

> The "prince of the eunuchs"—in other words, the chief servant in charge of these young men—was put in a dangerous position by Daniel's request. If he granted Daniel's request, and it did not work out, he could be imprisoned or executed.

9 **Now God had brought Daniel into favour and tender love with the prince of the eunuchs.**

10 And **the prince of the eunuchs said unto Daniel, I fear my lord the king,** who hath appointed your meat [*food*] and your drink: **for why should he see** [*if he sees*] **your faces worse** liking than the children which *are* of your sort [*what if you look less healthy than others in your class*]? **then shall ye make** *me* **endanger my head to the king.**

11 **Then said Daniel to Melzar,** whom the prince of the eunuchs had set over Daniel, Hananiah, Mishael, and Azariah,

12 **Prove thy servants, I beseech thee, ten days;** and let them give us pulse [*seeds, grains—see footnote 12a in your Bible; NIV: "vegetables"*] to eat, and water to drink [*just try our Hebrew diet out on us for ten days*].

13 **Then let our countenances** [*faces*] **be looked upon before thee, and the countenance of the children that eat of the portion of the king's meat: and as thou seest, deal with thy servants** [*then see how healthy we look compared to others in our group of trainees, and then you make a decision*].

14 **So he consented** to them in this matter, and proved them ten days.

15 **And at the end of ten days their countenances appeared fairer and fatter** in flesh than all the children which did eat the portion of the king's meat.

16 **Thus Melzar took away** the portion of **their meat, and the wine** that they should drink; **and gave them pulse.**

17 ¶ **As for these four children, God gave them knowledge and skill in all learning and wisdom: and Daniel had understanding in all visions and dreams.**

> Let's see what happened when the three years ended.

18 Now at the end of the days that the king had said he should bring

them [*the group of trainees*] in, then the prince of the eunuchs brought them in before Nebuchadnezzar.

19 And the king communed with them; and among them all was found none like Daniel, Hananiah, Mishael, and Azariah: therefore stood they before the king [*they were chosen to take responsible positions in the government*].

20 And in all matters of wisdom *and* understanding, that the king enquired of them, he found them ten times better than all the magicians *and* astrologers that *were* in all his realm.

DANIEL 2

Selection: verses 1–45

THIS CHAPTER CONTAINS the great prophecy that, in the latter days, the kingdom of God will be restored and taken to the whole earth. The stone cut out of the mountain without hands will roll forth to fill the whole earth.

King Nebuchadnezzar had a troubling dream and demanded that his wise men, astrologers, magicians, and so forth interpret the dream for him but refused to tell them what the dream was.

1 And in the second year of the reign of Nebuchadnezzar **Nebuchadnezzar dreamed dreams**, wherewith **his spirit was troubled, and his sleep brake from him** [*he could not sleep*].

2 Then the king commanded to call the magicians, and the astrologers, and the sorcerers, and the Chaldeans [*NIV: "astrologers"*], for to shew [*interpret*] the king his dreams. So they came and stood before the king.

3 And the king said unto them, I have dreamed a dream, and my spirit was troubled to know the dream [*the interpretation of the dream*].

4 Then spake the Chaldeans to the king in Syriack [*Aramaic, a language related to Hebrew*], O king, live for ever: tell thy servants the dream, and we will shew the interpretation,

5 The king answered and said to the Chaldeans, The thing is gone from me [*he actually remembered the dream but was testing the astrologers—see footnote 5a in your Bible*]: if ye will not make known unto me the dream, with the interpretation thereof, ye shall be cut in pieces, and your houses shall be made a dunghill.

6 But if ye shew the dream [*tell me what the dream was*], and the interpretation thereof, ye shall receive of me gifts and rewards and great honour: therefore shew me the dream, and the interpretation thereof.

7 They answered again and said, Let the king tell his servants the dream, and we will shew the interpretation of it.

8 The king answered and said, I know of certainty that ye would gain the time [*you are stalling for time*], because ye see the thing is gone from me.

9 But if ye will not make known unto me the dream, *there is but* one decree for you [*as stated in verse 5*]: for ye have prepared lying and corrupt words to speak before me, till the time be changed [*hoping the situation will change*]: therefore tell me the dream, and I shall know that ye can shew me the interpretation thereof.

10 ¶ The Chaldeans answered before the king, and said, There is not a man upon the earth that can shew the king's matter: therefore *there is* no king, lord, nor ruler, *that* asked such things at any magician, or astrologer, or Chaldean.

11 And *it is* a rare thing that the king requireth, and there is none other that can shew it before the king, except the gods, whose dwelling is not with flesh.

12 For this cause the king was angry and very furious, and commanded to destroy all the wise *men* of Babylon.

13 And the decree went forth that the wise *men* should be slain; and they sought Daniel and his fellows to be slain.

14 ¶ Then Daniel answered [*responded*] with counsel and wisdom to Arioch the captain of the king's guard, which was gone forth to slay the wise *men* of Babylon:

15 He answered and said to Arioch the king's captain, Why *is* the decree so hasty from the king [*why is the king in such a hurry to kill us all*]? Then Arioch made the thing known [*explained the situation*] to Daniel.

16 Then Daniel went in, and desired of the king that he would give him time, and that he would shew the king the interpretation.

17 Then Daniel went to his house, and made the thing known to Hananiah, Mishael, and Azariah [*to Shadrach, Meshach, and Abednego*], his companions:

18 That they would desire mercies of the God of heaven concerning this secret [*so that they would join him in praying to God for help*]; that Daniel and his fellows should not perish with the rest of the wise *men* of Babylon.

19 ¶ Then was the secret revealed unto Daniel in a night vision. Then Daniel blessed [*praised and thanked*] the God of heaven.

20 Daniel answered and said, Blessed be the name of God for ever and ever: for wisdom and might are his:

21 And he changeth the times and the seasons: he removeth kings, and setteth up kings: he giveth wisdom unto the wise, and knowledge to them that know understanding:

22 He revealeth the deep and secret things: he knoweth what *is* in the darkness, and the light dwelleth with him.

23 I thank thee, and praise thee, O thou God of my fathers, who hast given me wisdom and might, and hast made known unto me now what we desired of thee: for thou hast *now* made known unto us the king's matter.

24 ¶ Therefore Daniel went in unto Arioch, whom the king had ordained [*assigned*] to destroy the wise *men* of Babylon: he went and said thus unto him; Destroy not the wise *men* of Babylon: bring me in before the king, and I will shew unto the king the interpretation.

25 Then Arioch brought in Daniel before the king in haste, and said thus unto him, I have found a man of the captives of Judah, that will make known unto the king the interpretation.

26 The king answered [*responded*]

and said to Daniel, whose name *was* Belteshazzar, Art thou able to make known unto me the dream which I have seen, and the interpretation thereof?

> This is a "missionary moment" for Daniel. Watch as he gives credit to the Lord.

27 Daniel answered in the presence of the king, and said, The secret which the king hath demanded cannot the wise *men*, the astrologers, the magicians, the soothsayers, shew unto the king;

28 But there is a God in heaven that revealeth secrets, and maketh known to the king Nebuchadnezzar what shall be in the latter days. Thy dream, and the visions of thy head upon thy bed, are these;

29 As for thee, O king, thy thoughts came *into thy mind* upon thy bed, what should come to pass hereafter [*you were shown the future*]: and he [*the Lord*] that revealeth secrets maketh known to thee what shall come to pass.

> Next, in verse 30, Daniel humbly tells the king that he, himself, is nothing special and that the Lord revealed the dream to him in order to save the advisers the king had ordered to be executed.

30 But as for me, this secret is not revealed to me for *any* wisdom that I have more than any living, but for *their* sakes that shall make known the interpretation to the king, and that thou mightest know the thoughts of thy heart.

Next, because of what the Lord had shown him, Daniel tells the king what he saw in his dream.

31 ¶ Thou, O king, sawest, and behold **a great image.** This great image, whose brightness *was* excellent [*dazzling*], stood before thee; and the form thereof *was* terrible [*awe inspiring*].

32 This image's head *was* **of fine gold, his breast and his arms of silver,** his **belly and his thighs of brass,**

33 His **legs of iron, his feet part of iron and part of clay.**

President Spencer W. Kimball gave the interpretation of the above images. He taught that:

a. The head of gold represented King Nebuchadnezzar and the kingdom of Babylon.

b. The breast and arms of silver symbolized Cyrus the Persian, whose armies would conquer Babylon.

c. The brass represented Philip and Alexander and the Greek or Macedonian kingdom.

d. The Roman Empire was represented by the legs of iron.

e. The feet of iron and clay symbolized a group of European nations.

("The Stone Cut Without Hands," *Ensign*, May 1976, page 8.)

Next, in verses 34–35, the stone, representing The Church of Jesus Christ of Latter-day Saints, goes forth into the whole earth, destroying all earthly kingdoms (D&C 65:2; D&C 87:6), until it fills the earth.

34 Thou sawest till that **a stone** was cut out without hands [*the stone is not man-made; in other words, it is the work of God, the true Church*], **which smote the image upon his feet** *that were* **of iron and clay, and brake them to pieces.**

One other consideration about the stone or rock, in verse 34, above, is that Jesus Christ is often referred to in scripture as the "Rock of our salvation," the sure Foundation. He and His gospel will ultimately overcome all obstacles and enemies and fill the earth with truth and light.

35 Then was the iron, the clay, the brass, the silver, and the gold, broken to pieces together, and became like the chaff of the summer threshingfloors; and the wind carried them away, that no place was found for them: **and the stone that smote the image became a great mountain, and filled the whole earth.**

36 ¶ This *is* **the dream; and we will tell the interpretation thereof** before the king.

37 Thou, O king, *art* **a king of kings:** for the God of heaven hath given thee a kingdom, power, and strength, and glory.

38 And **wheresoever the children of men dwell, the beasts of the field and the fowls of the heaven hath he given into thine hand, and hath made thee ruler over them all. Thou art this head of gold.**

39 And **after thee shall arise another kingdom inferior to thee,** and **another third kingdom of brass,** which shall bear rule over all the earth.

40 And **the fourth kingdom shall be strong as iron:** forasmuch as iron breaketh in pieces and subdueth all *things:* and as iron that breaketh all these, shall it break in pieces and bruise.

41 And whereas thou sawest **the feet and toes, part of potters' clay, and part of iron, the kingdom shall be divided;** but there shall be in it of the strength of the iron, forasmuch as thou sawest the iron mixed with miry clay.

42 And *as* **the toes of the feet** *were* **part of iron, and part of clay,** *so* the kingdom shall be **partly strong, and partly broken.**

43 And whereas thou sawest iron mixed with miry clay, **they shall mingle themselves with the seed of men: but they shall not cleave one to another,** even as iron is not mixed

with clay [*the nations of Europe will have a difficult time forming a solid union*].

44 And **in the days of these kings** [*in the last days, when the nations of Europe have been formed*] **shall the God of heaven set up a kingdom** [*The Church of Jesus Christ of Latter-day Saints*]**, which shall never be destroyed: and the kingdom shall not be left to other people** [*it will never go into apostasy and thus need to be saved by others*]**,** but it shall break in pieces and consume all these kingdoms, **and it shall stand for ever.**

Do you realize how important the phrase "shall not be left to other people" is? Over many years, especially while serving as a stake president, people occasionally approached me to say that the First Presidency of the Church had gone astray and that the apostles were not doing as they should. In several cases, I asked them if they still believed the Bible. They said they did. I then asked them to turn to Daniel 2:44 and tell me what it means when it says, "the kingdom shall not be left to other people." In one case in particular, the people said, "We have never noticed that verse before. It has to mean that the First Presidency will never lead us astray. The Church will never be turned over to someone else who will have to straighten it out and save it." With that realization, they returned to full activity and commitment in the Church.

45 Forasmuch as thou sawest that the stone was cut out of the mountain without hands, and that it brake in pieces the iron, the brass, the clay, the silver, and the gold; the great God hath made known to the king what shall come to pass hereafter [*what will happen in the future*]: and **the dream** *is* **certain, and the interpretation thereof sure.**

In other words, the Church will never go into apostasy again. It will continue strong and vibrant, ever increasing and expanding, until it fills the whole earth during the Millennium.

DANIEL 3

Selection: verses 1, 4–6, 21–26

IN DANIEL, CHAPTER 3, King Nebuchadnezzar has a huge, about 90 foot tall image made and commands all the people to fall down and worship it whenever a signal is given. Daniel's friends, Shadrach, Meshach, and Abednego put their lives on the line as they disobey Nebuchadnezzar in order to keep their covenants to God.

1 Nedbuchadnezzar the king made an image of gold, whose height *was* threescore cubits [*about ninety feet high—"score" means twenty, and a cubit was about eighteen inches*], and the breadth thereof six cubits [*about nine feet*]: he set it up in the plain of Dura, in the province of Babylon.

4 Then an herald cried aloud, **To you it is commanded**, O people, nations, and languages,

5 *That* **at what time ye hear the sound** of the cornet, flute, harp, sackbut, psaltery, dulcimer, and all kinds of musick, **ye fall down and worship the golden image** that Nebuchadnezzar the king hath set up:

6 And **whoso falleth not down and worshippeth shall the same hour be cast into the midst of a burning fiery furnace.**

As you know, Shadrach, Meshach, and Abednego refused to worship the statue and were cast into the fiery furnace. We will take a close look at the wording of verse 25. Understanding it will help you understand similar wording when you see it elsewhere in the scriptures. It has to do with the question, "Why didn't the writers just say 'the Lord' or 'the Savior' rather than using an oblique reference to Him?"

We will lead up to verse 25, starting with verse 21.

21 Then these men were bound in their coats, their hosen [*pants, trousers*], and their hats, and their *other* garments, **and were cast into the midst of the burning fiery furnace.**

22 Therefore because the king's commandment was urgent, and the furnace exceeding hot, **the flame**

of the fire slew those men that took up Shadrach, Meshach, and Abed-nego.

23 And these three men, Shadrach, Meshach, and Abed-nego, fell down bound into the midst of the burning fiery furnace.

24 Then Nebuchadnezzar the king was astonied, and rose up in haste, *and* spake, and said unto his counsellors, Did not we cast three men bound into the midst of the fire? They answered and said unto the king, True, O king.

25 He answered and said, Lo, I see four men loose, walking in the midst of the fire, and they have no hurt; and the form of the fourth is like the Son of God.

The point of our looking especially at verse 25 is the phrase "like the Son of God." This is a reference to Jesus Christ, or Jehovah, who is the God of the Old Testament and is the Son of God.

We see a similar phrase in Daniel 7:13 and another in Abraham 3:24, where it says "there stood one among them that was like unto God." Footnote 24a for Abraham 3 informs us that it is a reference to Jesus Christ. We see yet another such reference in 1 Nephi 1:8, where Lehi sees the Father, but as Nephi records it, he says concerning his father, "he thought he saw God sitting upon his throne."

The answer is simple. In Old Testament culture, people were careful not to take the name of the Lord in vain, as commanded in the Ten Commandments. They became so cautious that they avoided almost any chance of inappropriately using the sacred name and thus often used an indirect reference rather than directly stating it.

26 ¶ Then Nebuchadnezzar came near to the mouth of the burning fiery furnace, *and* spake, and said, Shadrach, Meshach, and Abed-nego, ye servants of the most high God, come forth, and come hither. Then Shadrach, Meshach, and Abed-nego, came forth of the midst of the fire.

DANIEL 6

Selection: verses 3–24, 28

AFTER NEBUCHAD-NEZZAR died (about 561 BC), his son, Belshazzar, succeeded him as king of Babylon. Belshazzar was later killed (Daniel 5:30), and Darius the Mede took over the kingdom (Daniel 5:31). Darius is the king who was tricked by jealous advisers to have Daniel thrown to the lions. Since Daniel, as a young man, was taken along with many other Jews of higher social status into Babylonian captivity about 606 BC (see chronology chart in the Bible Dictionary, where it says "Daniel carried captive," 606), he would now be getting along in years. He could easily be between seventy and eighty years old at the time he was cast into the lions' den. He is an example of one who is willing to place it all on the altar—in other words, he was willing to be loyal to his commitment to God at all costs.

As we look at this block of verses, we see that Daniel was highly thought of by King Darius, who was considering putting him in charge of all things in the kingdom, under himself (much the same as Joseph was when he became second in command in Egypt). This prompted jealousy among the king's top officers.

3 Then this Daniel was preferred above the presidents and princes, because an excellent spirit was in him; and the king thought to set him over the whole realm.

4 ¶ Then the presidents and princes sought to find occasion against Daniel concerning the kingdom; but they could find none occasion nor fault; forasmuch as he was faithful, neither was there any error or fault found in him.

5 Then said these men, We shall not find any occasion [any way to get him in trouble with the king] against this Daniel, **except we find it against him concerning the law of his God.**

The plot: If anyone prays to any god or person other than King Darius during the next thirty days (verses 6–9) . . .

6 Then these presidents and princes assembled together to the king, and said thus unto him, King Darius, live for ever.

7 All the presidents of the kingdom, the governors, and the princes, the counsellors, and the captains, have consulted together to establish a royal statute, and to **make a firm decree, that whosoever shall ask a petition of any God or man for thirty days, save of thee, O king, he shall be cast into the den of lions.**

8 Now, O king, establish the decree, and **sign the writing,** that it be not changed, according to the law of the Medes and Persians, which altereth not [*according to their laws, once the king puts it in writing, even he cannot change it*].

9 Wherefore king Darius signed the writing and the decree.

Despite the decree, Daniel continued his personal habit of praying formally, three times a day. He preferred to pray facing the direction of Jerusalem and the temple there.

10 ¶ Now when Daniel knew that the writing was signed, he went into his house; and his windows being open in his chamber toward Jerusalem, **he kneeled upon his knees three times a day, and prayed,** and gave thanks before his God, **as he did aforetime** [*just like he had been doing before the decree*].

11 Then these men assembled, and found Daniel praying and making supplication before his God.

Can you picture the faces of these men as they continue to pressure King Darius to carry out the law of the land?

12 Then they came near, and spake before the king concerning the king's decree; Hast thou not signed a decree, that every man that shall ask *a petition* of any God or man within thirty days, save of thee, O king, shall be cast into the den of lions? The king answered and said, The thing *is* true, according to the law of the Medes and Persians, which altereth not.

Next, they smoothly tattle on Daniel, as if they were just doing their duty and expressing their loyalty to the king and the laws of the kingdom.

13 Then answered [*responded*] they and said before the king, That Daniel, which *is* of the children of the captivity of Judah, regardeth not thee, O king, nor the decree that thou hast signed, but maketh his petition three times a day.

The king immediately realizes that he has been caught in a vicious trap by these jealous, self-serving advisers.

14 Then the king, when he heard *these* words, was sore displeased with himself, and set *his* heart on Daniel to deliver him [*and immediately began trying to figure out a way to save Daniel*]: and he laboured till the going down of the sun to deliver him.

15 Then these men assembled unto the king, and said unto the king, Know, O king, that the law of the Medes and Persians *is*, That no decree nor statute which the king establisheth may be changed.

Next, in verse 16, we feel the anxiety of Darius for Daniel, and we sense that he and Daniel must have had previous discussions about the Lord and the role of faith and prayer.

16 Then the king commanded, and they brought Daniel, and cast *him* into the den of lions. *Now* the king spake and said unto Daniel, Thy God whom thou servest continually, he will deliver thee.

17 And a stone was brought, and laid upon the mouth of the den; and the king sealed it with his own signet [*signet ring*], and with the signet of his lords; that the purpose might not be changed concerning Daniel.

18 ¶ Then the king went to his palace, and passed the night fasting: neither were instruments of musick brought before him: and his sleep went from him [*he couldn't sleep*].

19 Then the king arose very early in the morning, and went in haste unto the den of lions.

20 And when he came to the den, he cried with a lamentable [*worried*] voice unto Daniel: and the king spake and said to Daniel, **O Daniel, servant of the living God** [*in contrast to all the "dead" or inanimate idols and false gods*], **is thy God,** whom thou servest continually, **able to deliver thee from the lions?**

21 Then said Daniel unto the king, O king, live for ever.

22 **My God hath sent his angel, and hath shut the lions' mouths, that they have not hurt me:** forasmuch as before him innocency was found in me; and also before thee, O king, have I done no hurt [*I have done nothing wrong*].

23 **Then was the king exceeding glad for him** [*an understatement!*], **and commanded that they should take Daniel up out of the den.** So Daniel was taken up out of the den, and no manner of hurt was found upon him, because he believed in his God.

24 ¶ And the king commanded, and they brought those men which had accused Daniel, and they cast *them* into the den of lions, them, their children, and their wives; and the lions had the mastery of them, and brake all their bones in pieces or ever they came at the bottom of the den.

28 So this Daniel prospered in the reign of Darius, and in the reign of Cyrus the Persian.

DANIEL 7

Selection: verses 9–10, 13–14

IN CHAPTER 7, Daniel sees in vision the meeting at Adam-ondi-Ahman, to be held in the last days before the Second Coming of the Savior.

We will take a minute to discuss background to this vision that Daniel was given. About seventy miles, northeast of Independence, Missouri, is a sacred place called Adam-ondi-Ahman. "It is the place where Adam shall come to visit his people, or the Ancient of Days [*Adam*] shall sit, as spoken of by Daniel the prophet" (D&C 116:1).

In the Doctrine and Covenants we are taught that a great conference of Adam and Eve's righteous posterity was held at Adam-ondi-Ahman three years prior to Adam's death. We read:

Doctrine & Covenants 107:53–56

53 **Three years previous to the death of Adam, he** called Seth, Enos, Cainan, Mahalaleel, Jared, Enoch, and Methuselah, who were all high priests, **with the residue of his posterity who were righteous, into the valley of Adam-ondi-Ahman,** and there bestowed upon them his last blessing.

54 And **the Lord appeared**

unto them, and **they rose up and blessed Adam**, and called him Michael, the prince, the archangel.

55 And **the Lord administered comfort unto Adam**, and said unto him: I have set thee to be at the head; a multitude of nations shall come of thee, and thou art a prince over them forever.

56 **And Adam stood up** in the midst of the congregation; and, notwithstanding he was bowed down with age, **being full of the Holy Ghost, predicted whatsoever should befall his posterity unto the latest generation.**

Shortly before the Second Coming of Christ, another great council will be held at Adam-ondi-Ahman. We read of this in Daniel. He had a vision in which he saw that millions of righteous people will attend this great meeting.

9 I beheld till the thrones were cast down [*Daniel saw the future, including the downfall of governments in the last days, as spoken of in D&C 87:6*], and **the Ancient of days** [*Adam*] **did sit**, whose garment *was* **white as snow**, and the hair of his head like the **pure wool** [*see Isaiah 1:18, where "white as snow" and "pure wool" are associated with one's being completely cleansed by the Atonement of Christ*]: **his throne** [*Adam is in a position of great power and authority*] **was like the fiery flame**, *and* his wheels *as* burning fire.

10 A fiery stream issued and came forth from before him: **thousand thousands** [*millions*] **ministered unto him, and ten thousand times ten thousand** [*a hundred million*] **stood before him** [*this will be a large meeting*]: the judgment was set, and the books were opened.

13 I [*Daniel*] **saw in the night visions**, and, behold, **one like the Son of man** [*a biblically respectful way of saying Jehovah—in other words, Christ*] came with the clouds of heaven, and **came to the Ancient of days** [*Adam*], and they brought him [*Christ*] near before him [*Adam— see Teachings of the Prophet Joseph Smith, page 157*].

Next, we see in Daniel's vision that the keys of leadership are given back to Christ during this grand council in preparation for His ruling and reigning as "Lord of lords, and King of kings" (Revelation 17:14) during the Millennium.

14 And **there was given him** [*Christ*] **dominion, and glory, and a kingdom, that all people, nations, and languages, should serve him** [*during the Millennium*]: his dominion *is* an everlasting dominion, which shall not pass away, and his kingdom *that* which shall not be destroyed.

Joseph Fielding Smith taught about this meeting at Adam-ondi-Ahman before the Second Coming. He said that "all who have held keys will make their reports and deliver their stewardships, as they shall be required. Adam will . . . then . . . make his report, as the one holding the keys for this earth, to his Superior Officer, Jesus Christ. Our Lord will then assume the reins of government; directions will be given to the Priesthood; and He, whose right it is to rule, will be installed officially by the voice of the Priesthood there assembled. This grand council of Priesthood will be composed, not only of those who are faithful who now dwell on this earth, but also of the prophets and apostles of old, who have had directing authority. Others may also be there, but if so they will be there by appointment, for this is to be an official council called to attend to the most momentous matters concerning the destiny of this earth" (*Way to Perfection*, pages 290–91).

Among other things, Bruce R. McConkie taught the following about this council at Adam-ondi-Ahman (**bold** added for emphasis):

"But Daniel has yet more to say about the great events soon to transpire at Adam-ondi-Ahman. And we need not suppose that all these things shall happen in one single meeting or at one single hour in time. It is proper to hold numerous meetings at a general conference, some for the instruction of leaders, others for edification of all the Saints. In some, business is transacted; others are for worship and spiritual refreshment. And so Daniel says: 'I saw in the night visions, and, behold, one like the Son of man came with the clouds of heaven, and came to the Ancient of days, and they brought him near before him.' **Christ comes to Adam**, who is sitting in glory. He comes to conform to his own priestal order. He comes to hear the report of Adam for his stewardship. **He comes to take back the keys of the earthly kingdom**. He comes to be invested with glory and dominion so that he can reign personally upon the earth" (*The Millennial Messiah: The Second Coming of the Son of Man*, page 585).

You may wish to read more about this meeting at Adam-ondi-Ahman in *Millennial Messiah*, pages 578–88.

Elder McConkie also taught:

"At this council, all who have held keys of authority will give an accounting of their stewardship to Adam. Christ will then come, receive back the keys, and thus take one of the final steps preparatory to reigning personally upon the earth. (Dan. 7:9–14; *Teachings*, p. 157.)" (*Mormon Doctrine*, page 21).

Before we leave Daniel, we will consider one other insight. It is interesting to note that the Garden of Eden was located in what is now Jackson County, Missouri. Joseph Fielding Smith taught this:

"In accord with the revelations given to the Prophet Joseph Smith, we teach that the Garden of Eden was on the American continent located where the City Zion [in Jackson County, Missouri], or the New Jerusalem, will be built. . . . When Adam and Eve were driven out of the Garden, they eventually dwelt at a place called Adam-ondi-Ahman, situated in what is now Daviess County, Missouri" (*Doctrines of Salvation,* vol. 3, page 74).

Thus, when Adam and Eve were cast out of the Garden of Eden, they went to the area of Adam-ondi-Ahman to dwell. In other words, things got started in Missouri, in the Garden of Eden, as far as mortal life on this earth is concerned, and things will have gone full circle back to Missouri and the council at Adam-ondi-Ahman as the time for the Millennium nears.

HOSEA

HOSEA WAS A contemporary of Isaiah, Amos, and Micah. His ministry as a prophet went from about 755 BC to 725 BC If you read Hosea 1:1 and Isaiah 1:1, you will see that they both served as prophets during the reign of the same kings of Judah.

To understand Hosea's writings, you must be aware that he makes extensive use of metaphors and symbolism. A metaphor involves the use of one thing to represent another. For example, "sheep" are often used to represent Israel. The Savior is the "Shepherd." When Israel goes into apostasy and gets lost spiritually, we say "the sheep are lost," and the Shepherd goes into the wilderness to find them and bring them back to the "fold," which is symbolic of the Church and the celestial kingdom.

Hosea's writings and prophecies contain marvelous examples of the power of the Atonement of Jesus Christ to cleanse and heal.

For purposes of this study guide, we will study selections from Hosea 1–3 in order to give you a feel for this great but not well-known prophet.

HOSEA 1

Selection: verses 1–11

HOSEA USES THE marriage of a husband and wife to represent the covenant relationship between Israel and the Lord. The Lord (the husband) and Israel (the wife) have the potential to have a beautiful and tender relationship. But the wife commits adultery (symbolic of going into apostasy and worshiping false gods, materialism, and so forth). Despite the wickedness and infidelity of his wife, the husband invites her back and promises to forgive her and take good care of her and her children. It is the story of Israel (including Judah) and the Lord's willingness to take His covenant people back after they have continually broken their covenants ("marriage vows") with Him by choosing other "lovers" (false gods and wickedness).

1 The word of the LORD that came unto Hosea, the son of Beeri, **in the days of Uzziah, Jotham, Ahaz,** *and* **Hezekiah, kings of Judah** [*the same kings as ruled Judah during Isaiah's ministry—see Isaiah 1:1*], and in the days of Jeroboam the son of Joash, king of Israel.

2 The beginning of the word of the LORD by Hosea. And **the LORD said to Hosea, Go, take unto thee a wife of whoredoms** [*in other words, marry a harlot, a prostitute*] and children of whoredoms: **for the land** [*the people of Israel, including Judah*]

hath committed great whoredom [*spiritual adultery; breaking covenants made with the Lord*], **departing from the LORD.**

There has been much debate among Bible scholars as to whether verse 2, above, is literal or symbolic, or a combination of both. We will use a quote from LDS Bible scholar Sidney B. Sperry, as quoted in the *Old Testament Student Manual 1 Kings—Malachi*, page 104, to answer this question.

"Sperry said that Hosea never did actually contract such a marriage. He defends his viewpoint with an argument that seems authoritative to the Latter-day Saint: 'The Lord's call to Hosea to take a harlotrous woman to wife represents the prophet's call to the ministry—a ministry to an apostate and covenant-breaking people. The evil children of this apparent union represent the coming of the judgments of the Lord upon Israel, warning of which was to be carried to the people by the prophet. The figure of the harlotrous wife and children would, I believe, be readily understood at the time by the Hebrew people without reflecting on Hosea's own wife, or, if he was unmarried, on himself.' (*Voice of Israel's Prophets*, p. 281.)"

3 So he went and took Gomer the daughter of Diblaim; **which conceived, and bare him a son.**

4 And the LORD said unto him, **Call his name Jezreel** [*the name of a valley in Israel*]; for yet a little *while,*

449

and I will avenge the blood of Jezreel upon the house of Jehu, and will cause to cease the kingdom of the house of Israel.

5 And it shall come to pass at that day, that **I will break the bow** [*power; ability to defend*] **of Israel in the valley of Jezreel.**

6 ¶ **And she conceived again, and bare a daughter.** And *God* said unto him, **Call her name Lo-ruhamah** [*didn't obtain mercy—see footnote 6a in your Bible*]: **for I will no more have mercy upon the house of Israel** [*the northern ten tribes (in this context), with headquarters in Samaria—they will be conquered by Assyria in about 722 B.C. and taken away*]; **but I will utterly take them away** [*scatter them*].

7 **But I will have mercy upon the house of Judah** [*the Southern Kingdom, consisting of the tribes of Judah and Benjamin, with headquarters in Jerusalem*], **and will save them by the LORD their God, and will not save them by bow, nor by sword, nor by battle, by horses, nor by horsemen** [*they will be protected from the Assyrians by the power of the Lord, as recorded in 2 Kings 19:32–37, when 185,000 Assyrian soldiers died in one night*].

8 ¶ **Now when she had weaned Lo-ruhamah, she conceived, and bare a son.**

9 **Then said** *God,* **Call his name Lo-ammi** [*meaning they are not My people anymore*]: **for ye are not my people, and I will not be your God.**

Verses 10–11, next, are a prophecy of the gathering of Israel in the last days, when the righteous are gathered unto Christ by making and keeping covenants in His name. The implications of these verses continue into the Millennium and beyond that into celestial exaltation.

10 ¶ **Yet the number of the children of Israel shall be as the sand of the sea,** which cannot be measured nor numbered; **and it shall come to pass,** *that* **in the place where it was said unto them, Ye** *are* **not my people,** *there* **it shall be said unto them, Ye** *are* **the sons of the living God.**

11 **Then shall the children of Judah and the children of Israel be gathered together,** and appoint themselves one head [*perhaps meaning that they will come unto Christ and be loyal to Him as their King*], and they shall come up out of the land: for great *shall be* the day of Jezreel.

HOSEA 2

Selection: verses 1–19, 23

THIS CHAPTER PRO-PHESIES of the punishments that will come upon the people because of apostasy. It also foretells the restoration of the gospel in the last days and eventual millennial peace.

1 Say ye unto your brethren, Ammi; and to your sisters, Ruhamah.

2 Plead with your mother [*apostate Israel*], **plead: for she *is* not my wife, neither *am* I her husband** [*she has broken our marriage covenant*]: **let her therefore put away her whoredoms** out of her sight [*try to convince her to repent*], **and her adulteries from between her breasts;**

3 Lest I strip her naked [*leave her with no excuses, expose her sins—compare with 2 Nephi 9:14*], **and set her as in the day that she was born** [*without any cover up*], **and make her as a wilderness, and set her like a dry land, and slay her with thirst** [*famine*].

4 And I will not have mercy upon her children [*because they too have grown up and chosen wickedness*]; **for they *be* the children of whoredoms.**

5 For their mother hath played the harlot [*has broken her covenants with Me, the Lord*]: **she that conceived them hath done shamefully: for she said, I will go after my lovers** [*false gods, idols, all kinds of wickedness*], **that give *me* my bread and my water, my wool and my flax, mine oil and my drink** [*covenant Israel credits her false gods as being the power behind her prosperity; in other words, wicked*

people attribute their prosperity to their evil pursuits].

6 ¶ Therefore, behold, I will hedge up thy way with thorns, and make a wall, that she shall not find her paths [*she will not prosper*].

In verses 7–8, next, we are taught that troubles can sometimes bring wicked people back to the Lord.

7 And she shall follow after her lovers [*false gods and so forth*], **but she shall not overtake them; and she shall seek them, but shall not find *them*: then shall she say, I will go and return to my first husband** [*I will repent and return to the Lord*]; **for then *was it* better with me than now.**

8 For she did not know [*realize*] **that I gave her corn, and wine, and oil, and multiplied her silver and gold,** which **they prepared for Baal** [*a major false god adopted by the Israelites from neighboring nations*].

9 Therefore will I return, and take away my corn in the time thereof, and my wine in the season thereof, and will recover my wool and my flax *given* to cover her nakedness [*the Lord will take away the blessings of prosperity*].

10 And now will I discover [*uncover*] **her lewdness** [*symbolic of sins in this metaphor*] **in the sight of her lovers, and none shall deliver her out of**

451

mine hand [*no one, including her false gods, will be able to stop the punishments of God upon her*].

11 I will also cause all her mirth [*partying*] **to cease,** her feast days, her new moons, and her sabbaths, and all her solemn feasts [*elements of their religious worship*].

12 And I will destroy her vines and her fig trees, whereof she hath said, These *are* **my rewards that my lovers have given me**: and I will make them a forest [*no longer cultivated*], and the beasts of the field shall eat them.

13 And I will visit upon her the days of [*I will punish her for the days when she worshiped*] **Baalim** [*plural for Baal, a false god whose worship included sexual immorality and sometimes child sacrifice*], wherein she burned incense to them, and she decked herself with her earrings and her jewels, and she went after her lovers [*false gods*], and forgat me, saith the LORD.

> Next, beginning with verse 14, the Lord prophesies, through Hosea, that He will restore Israel, after her apostasy.

14 ¶ Therefore, behold, I will allure her [*attract her back to Me*], and bring her into the wilderness, **and speak comfortably unto her.**

15 And I will give her her vineyards [*she will once again prosper*] from thence, and the valley of Achor for a door of **hope:** and **she shall sing there, as in the days of her youth, and as in the day when she came up out of the land of Egypt.**

16 And it shall be at that day, saith the LORD, *that* **thou shalt call me Ishi** [*husband; a sweet, intimate relationship*]; and shalt call me **no more Baali** [*master, symbolizing a harsh servant-to-master relationship*].

17 For **I will take away the names of Baalim out of her mouth** [*the tribulation I send her through will purge the sins out of her*], and they shall no more be remembered by their name.

> Verse 18, next, can depict many things, including Millennial peace, eternal life, the peace in one's soul that comes from doing right and keeping covenants.

18 And in that day will I make a covenant for them with the beasts of the field, and with the fowls of heaven, and *with* **the creeping things of the ground** [*Millennial peace*]: and I will break the bow and the sword and the battle out of the earth [*there will be no fighting during the Millennium*], and will make them to lie down safely.

19 And I will betroth thee unto me for ever [*you will be My wife forever*]; yea, I will betroth thee unto me **in righteousness, and in judgment, and in lovingkindness, and in mercies.**

23 And I will sow her unto me in the earth; and **I will have mercy upon her that had not obtained mercy; and I will say to *them which were* not my people, Thou *art* my people; and they shall say, *Thou art* my God.**

Israel will go through a time of apostasy, during which time they will be far from God, but they will be brought back in the latter days.

HOSEA 3

Selection: verses 4–5

IN THIS CHAPTER, we see the gathering of Israel in the last days. We are a part of this. It is comforting to know that even though Israel will go through a time of apostasy, during which time they will be far from God, they will be brought back in the latter days.

4 For the children of Israel shall abide many days without a king [*without the Lord—in other words, in apostasy*], **and without a prince, and without a sacrifice, and without an image, and without an ephod, and *without* teraphim** [*in other words, without the ordinances of the priesthood*]:

5 Afterward shall the children of Israel return, and seek the LORD their God, and David [*Christ*] **their king; and shall fear** [*respect*] **the LORD and his goodness in the latter days.**

JOEL

BIBLE SCHOLARS HAVE not been able to determine with any degree of reliable accuracy when Joel lived. It could have been as early as 850 BC or as late as the return of the Jews from Babylon, in 537 BC. He was a prophet who ministered to Judah.

JOEL 2

Selection: verses 28–32

WE WILL JUST do one thing with Joel's writings. President Gordon B. Hinckley taught that one of Joel's best-known prophecies has been fulfilled. We will quote the prophecy and then quote President Hinckley's statement about it. It is a prophecy about the last days, and some signs of the times that will be fulfilled before the Second Coming of the Savior.

28 ¶ And it shall come to pass afterward [*in the last days*], *that* **I will pour out my spirit upon all flesh**; and your sons and your daughters shall prophesy, your old men shall dream dreams, your young men shall see visions:

29 And also upon the servants and upon the handmaids **in those days will I pour out my spirit.**

30 **And I will shew wonders** [*signs of the times*] **in the heavens and in the earth,** blood, and fire, and pillars of smoke [*wars and natural disasters will be everywhere*].

31 **The sun shall be turned into darkness, and the moon into blood,** before the great and the terrible day of the LORD [*the Second Coming*] come.

32 And it shall come to pass, *that* **whosoever shall call on the name of the LORD shall be delivered: for in mount Zion and in Jerusalem shall be deliverance** [*the gospel of Jesus Christ will once again be available on earth*], as the LORD hath said, and in the remnant whom the LORD shall call.

We will focus our attention on verse 31, above. One of the signs of the times spoken of several times in the scriptures is that the sun will be darkened and the moon will become as blood. As I lectured on the signs of the times over the course of many years at BYU Campus Education Week, Know Your Religion lectures, and in my classes in seminary and institute of religion, I told my students that we don't know what this means and we don't know whether it has been fulfilled.

However, in the October 2001 general conference of the Church, during the Saturday morning session, President Hinckley said something that changed my mind on this prophecy. He said (**bold** added for emphasis):

"The era in which we live is the fulness of times spoken of in the scriptures, when God has brought together all of the elements of previous dispensations. From the day that He and His Beloved Son manifested themselves to the boy Joseph, there has been a tremendous cascade of enlightenment poured out upon the world. The hearts of men have turned to their fathers in fulfillment of the words of Malachi. **The vision of Joel has been fulfilled wherein he declared:"** ("Living in the Fulness of Times," *Ensign*, November 2001, page 4).

He then quoted Joel 2:28–32. As soon as President Hinckley said that these words of Joel had been fulfilled, quoting them exactly as written, I accepted it on faith. We are now left to wonder exactly what "the sun shall be turned into darkness, and the moon into blood" means and how it has been fulfilled. We will not speculate but will wait for additional revelation from the Lord's living prophet, when the time is right.

AMOS

AMOS WAS A contemporary of Isaiah and Hosea. He was a shepherd from Tekoa, a small town in the Judean hills about six miles south of Bethlehem and twelve miles south of Jerusalem. He was assigned by the Lord to prophesy to the Northern Kingdom, the ten tribes, often referred to as Israel, with headquarters in Samaria. His major emphasis was on the perfect moral character of Jehovah, and the fact that the sacrifice He desires most from His covenant people is that of a righteous life.

AMOS 3

Selection: verse 7

PERHAPS THE BEST-KNOWN reference in Amos, among Latter-day Saints, is the one that emphasizes the role of prophets. It is used much in missionary work to help people realize that there are prophets today on earth who reveal the mind and will of the Lord to us today.

7 Surely the Lord **GOD will do nothing, but he revealeth his secret unto his servants the prophets.**

JONAH

JONAH LIVED SOME-WHERE around 800 BC and was called to preach in Nineveh, a terribly wicked city known for torturing and killing outsiders. The book of Jonah was not written by Jonah himself but by a later, unidentified writer.

A major message of Jonah is that the Lord wants to save the wicked. He loves them too and wants them to repent and come to live with Him eternally.

We will not do more with Jonah in this study guide other than to quote from Nahum to give you an idea as to why Jonah was reluctant to accept a mission call to preach to Nineveh. While we are not suggesting that it was at all proper for Jonah to run the other way when the call came, we may be a bit less critical when we realize the terrors of Nineveh to outsiders. A brief description of Nenevah, a prominent city in Assyria about five hundred miles northeast of Jerusalem, is given by the prophet Nahum as he prophesied against their wickedness.

Nahum 3:1–5

1 Woe to the bloody city [*Nineveh*]! it *is* all full of lies *and* robbery; the prey departeth not [*NIV: "never without victims"*];

2 The noise of a whip, and the noise of the rattling of the wheels, and of the pransing horses, and of the jumping chariots [*in other words, a mighty military power*].

3 The horseman lifteth up both the bright sword and the glittering spear: and *there is* a multitude of slain, and a great number of carcases; and *there is* none end of *their* corpses; they stumble upon their corpses [*there are so many dead bodies that the people in Nineveh are constantly tripping over them*]:

4 Because of the multitude of the whoredoms of the wellfavoured harlot, the mistress of witchcrafts, that selleth nations through her whoredoms, and families through her witchcrafts.

5 Behold, I *am* against thee, saith the LORD of hosts; and I will discover thy skirts upon thy face, and I will shew the nations thy nakedness, and the kingdoms thy shame [*your wickedness will be exposed by the Lord*].

MICAH

MICAH WAS ANO-THER prophet who served in Isaiah's day. He was a native of Moresheth Gath, in the lower plain country of Judah. Among other things, he prophesied the downfall of the nation of Judah. He also gave many prophecies about the mission of Israel in the last days.

We will take just a few moments and gather several of his prophecies about the gathering of Israel, the covenant people of the Lord, and their role and mission in the last days.

MICAH 2

Selection: verses 12–13

THIS SELECTION OF verses deals with the last days gathering of Israel, of which we are a part.

12 ¶ I will surely assemble [*gather*], O Jacob [*another name for Israel*], all of thee; I will surely gather the remnant of Israel; I will put [*gather*] them together [*bring them into the fold*] as the sheep of Bozrah [*a city southeast of the Dead Sea, famous for its large flocks of sheep*], as the flock in the midst of their fold: they shall make great noise by reason of *the multitude of*

men [*there will be large numbers of Israel gathered in the last days; the Church will grow rapidly and flourish*].

13 The breaker [*one who breaks open the way for others, leads them*] is come up before them: they have broken up, and have passed through the gate, and are gone out by it: and their king [*Christ*] shall pass before them [*will go in front of them*], and the LORD on the head of them [*they will follow the Lord*].

MICAH 4

Selection: verses 1–7, 11–13

THIS SELECTION IS a marvelous prophecy of the gathering of the Lord's covenant people to the top of the mountains in the last days. It is both symbolic and literal.

1 But in the last days it shall come to pass, *that* the mountain of the house of the LORD [*the restored Church, the temple*] shall be established in the top of the mountains [*one meaning of this is in the Rocky Mountains—compare with Isaiah 2:2*], and it shall be exalted above the hills; and people shall flow unto it.

2 And many nations shall come [*many converts from many nations will come into the Church*], and say, Come, and let us go up to the mountain of the LORD [*let us look to the living

prophets at Church headquarters], **and to the house of the God of Jacob** [*and let us learn in the temples of God*]; **and he will teach us of his ways, and we will walk in his paths** [*we will keep the commandments*]: for the **law shall go forth of Zion, and the word of the LORD from Jerusalem** ["*law*" *and* "*word of the Lord*" *are synonyms; in other words, there will be two headquartes of the Church during the Millennium; Zion, in Jackson County, Missouri, and Old Jerusalem—see Ether 13:3–5; compare with Isaiah 2:3—from which people will be taught the gospel*].

3 ¶ **And he** [*Christ*] **shall judge among many people, and rebuke strong nations afar off** [*the wicked will be destroyed at the Second Coming, thus paving the way for peace*]; **and they shall beat their swords into plowshares, and their spears into pruninghooks** [*there will be peace during the Millennium*]: **nation shall not lift up a sword against nation, neither shall they learn war any more.**

4 But they shall sit every man under his vine and under his fig tree; and **none shall make** *them* **afraid**: for the mouth of the LORD of hosts hath spoken *it* [*the Lord has prophesied this and it will happen*].

5 For all people will walk every one in the name of his god, and **we will walk in the name of the LORD our God** for ever and ever.

6 In that day, saith the LORD, will I assemble her that halteth, and I will gather her that is driven out, and her that I have afflicted [*Israel will be gathered again*];

7 **And I will make her that halted** [*was lame; perhaps symbolizing one who is spiritually lame, unable to move ahead on the strait and narrow path*] **a remnant** [*a part of covenant Israel*], **and her that was cast far off** [*Israel, who was rejected because of apostasy*] **a strong nation: and the LORD shall reign over them** in mount Zion from henceforth, even **for ever.**

11 ¶ Now also **many nations are gathered against thee** [*Israel*], that say, Let her be defiled, and let our eye look upon Zion.

12 But they know not the thoughts of the LORD, neither understand they his counsel [*plans*]: for he shall gather them as the sheaves into the floor.

13 **Arise and thresh** [*win the battle against your enemies, spiritually and physically*], **O daughter of Zion** [*people of the Lord*]: for I will make thine horn iron, and I will make thy hoofs brass: and **thou shalt beat in pieces many people** [*righteous Israel will finally triumph over all her enemies*]: and **I will consecrate their gain unto the LORD, and**

their substance unto the Lord of the whole earth.

MICAH 5

Selection: verses 2–4, 7–8

THIS SELECTION CONTAINS a prophecy that Christ will be born in Bethlehem. It also deals with the great spreading of the gospel in the last days and the fact that the Church, which was once severely persecuted, will become strong and a powerful influence for good throughout the earth.

2 But **thou, Beth-lehem** Ephratah, *though* thou be little among the thousands of Judah, *yet* **out of thee shall he** [*Jesus Christ*] **come forth unto me** *that is* to be ruler in Israel; whose goings forth *have been* from of old, from everlasting [*Jesus Christ will be born in Bethlehem*].

3 **Therefore will he give them up** [*the Lord will reject Israel for a time because of apostasy*], **until the time** *that* **she which travaileth hath brought forth** [*until the restoration of the gospel in the last days—see JST Revelation 12:7*]: **then the remnant of his brethren shall return unto the children of Israel.**

4 ¶ And he [*Israel*] **shall stand and feed in the strength of the LORD, in the majesty of the name of the LORD his God; and they shall**

abide: for now shall he be great unto the ends of the earth.

7 **And the remnant of Jacob** [*the members of the Church in the last days*] **shall be in the midst of many people as a dew from the LORD, as the showers upon the grass** [*will be as dew and refreshing rain among the spiritually parched inhabitants of the earth*], **that tarrieth not for man, nor waiteth for the sons of men.**

8 ¶ And **the remnant of Jacob shall be among the Gentiles in the midst of many people as a lion among the beasts of the forest** [*the members of the Church will become a strong influence throughout the earth*], as a young lion among the flocks of sheep: who, if he go through, both treadeth down, and teareth in pieces, and **none can deliver** [*none will stop the growth of the Church after it is restored in the last days*].

MICAH 6

Selection: verses 6–8

THESE THREE VERSES provide one of the clearest views of what kind of sacrifice the Lord desires from his people, the kind that will do them the most good.

6 ¶ **Wherewith shall** [*what kind of offering shall I bring when*] **I come before the LORD,** *and* **bow myself before the high God? shall I come**

before him with burnt offerings, with calves of a year old?

7 Will the LORD be pleased with thousands of rams, *or* with ten thousands of rivers of oil? shall I give **my firstborn** *for* my transgression, the fruit of my body *for* the sin of my soul?

8 He hath shewed thee, O man, what *is* good; and **what doth the LORD require of thee**, but to **do justly**, and to **love mercy**, and to walk humbly with thy God?

MICAH 7

Selection: verses 18–20

MICAH GIVES A beautiful description of the Atonement of Jesus Christ in action, couched in a setting where many believed in false gods who were often angry and vindictive, showing no mercy.

18 **Who** *is* **a God like unto thee** [*who can compare to Jehovah, Jesus Christ*], **that pardoneth iniquity,** and passeth by [*forgives*] **the trans-gression of the remnant of his heri-tage** [*in other words, Israel; those who wish to become His covenant people*]? **he retaineth not his anger for ever, because he delighteth** *in* **mercy.**

19 **He will turn again** [*He will turn toward us, with outstretched arms,*

welcoming us back*], **he will have com-passion upon us;** he will **subdue our iniquities** [*He will pay the price of our sins—compare with 2 Nephi 9:21*]; **and** thou **wilt cast all their sins into the depths of the sea.**

20 **Thou wilt perform the truth** [*keep the covenant made*] **to Jacob,** *and* **the mercy to Abraham, which thou hast sworn** [*promised, cov-enanted*] **unto our fathers** [*ances-tors*] **from the days of old** [*from the beginning*].

HABAKKUK

ABOUT ALL WE know about Habakkuk is that he was a prophet who was sent to preach to Judah, perhaps somewhere around 600 BC. It is possible that he was one of the "many prophets" (1 Nephi 1:4) sent by the Lord to warn the Jews in Jerusalem and Judah about the impending Babylonian captivity.

HABAKKUK 1

Selection: verses 2–17

HABAKKUK ASKS A question that many people would like to ask but don't dare. In effect, he asks the Lord why the wicked prosper and the righteous always have it rough. We will look at the question and how he poses it to the Lord in chapter 1, and then we'll look at the Lord's answer to him at the beginning of chapter 2. It is basically a question-and-answer session between Habakkuk and the Lord. We will have a bit of fun with it.

Question

2 O LORD, how long shall I cry [*pray*], **and thou wilt not hear** [*why don't you hear the prayers of the righteous*]! even **cry out unto thee of violence, and thou wilt not save** [*you are not doing a very good job of saving the righteous*]!

3 Why dost thou shew me iniquity, and cause *me* **to behold grievance** [*why don't you get rid of the wickedness I have to see all the time*]? for **spoiling and violence** *are* **before me** [*are all around me*]: and there are *that* raise up strife and contention [*everyone is always fighting and arguing*].

4 Therefore the law *is* **slacked** [*Your laws that say the wicked will be punished are never enforced*], **and judgment doth never go forth** [*I don't like the way You are running things*]: for **the wicked doth compass about the righteous** [*the righteous are surrounded with the wicked*]; **therefore wrong judgment proceedeth** [*You are making a mistake by ignoring it*].

Answer

5 ¶ Behold [*look*] **ye** [*Habakkuk*] **among the heathen, and regard**

[*pay close attention to what you see*], **and wonder marvelously** [*prepare to be surprised*]: for **I will work a work in your days,** *which* **ye will not believe,** though it be told *you* [*I will do something that you won't believe, even if I tell you in advance*].

> Next, the Lord tells Habakkuk that He is going to use the coming Babylonian army (the Chaldeans) to punish and hammer the wicked in heathen nations as well as in Judah and Jerusalem.

6 For, lo, I raise up the Chaldeans, *that* **bitter and hasty nation, which shall march through the breadth of the land,** to possess the dwelling-places *that are* not theirs [*they will occupy Judah*].

7 They *are* **terrible and dreadful:** their judgment and their dignity shall proceed of themselves.

8 Their horses also are swifter than the leopards, and are more fierce than the evening wolves: and their horsemen shall spread themselves, and their horsemen shall come from far; they shall fly as the eagle *that* hasteth to eat [*eager to gobble up the wicked among you, Habakkuk*].

9 They shall come all for violence: their faces shall sup up *as* the east wind [*devastating destruction*], and they shall gather the captivity as the sand.

10 And they shall scoff at the

kings, and the princes shall be a scorn unto them: **they shall deride every strong hold;** for they shall heap dust, and take it.

11 Then shall *his* mind change, and he shall pass over, and offend, *imputing* this his power unto his god [*the Babylonians will give credit to their false god, Bel, rather than realizing that the Lord has allowed them to do this*].

Next, Habakkuk is not satisfied with the Lord's answer and so he continues with his questions.

Question

12 ¶ *Art* thou not from everlasting [*don't You have power to smite them*], O LORD my God, mine Holy One? **we shall not die** [*nobody seems to get zapped anymore*]. O LORD, thou hast ordained them for judgment; and, O mighty God, thou hast established them for correction [*You say they are headed for punishment, but nothing seems to happen to them*].

Next, Habakkuk changes his approach and comes at the Lord from another direction.

13 *Thou art* of purer eyes than to behold evil [*You shouldn't have to be watching all this wickedness with Your pure eyes*], **and canst not look on iniquity** [*You are not supposed to be able to look upon iniquity "with the least degree of allowance"—D&C 1:31*]: **wherefore** [*so, why*] **lookest thou upon them that deal treacherously** [*the wicked*], **and holdest thy tongue** [*and never command them to be smitten*] **when the wicked devoureth** *the man that is* **more righteous than he** [*while the wicked are destroying the righteous; in other words, why do You just keep watching and never take any action*]?

14 And makest men as the fishes of the sea, as the creeping things, *that have* **no ruler over them?** [*It appears that we are no more important to You than fish or bugs, with no one to protect us. It is like we don't even have a God.*]

15 They [*the wicked*] take up all of them with the angle, they catch them in their net, and gather them in their drag: therefore they rejoice and are glad [*the wicked prosper in their business pursuits*].

16 Therefore [*because they are so successful*] **they sacrifice unto their net, and burn incense unto their drag** [*they worship their fishing equipment*]; **because by them their portion** *is* **fat, and their meat plenteous** [*because their false gods are blessing them bounteously*].

17 Shall they therefore empty their net, and not spare continually to slay the nations [*is there any good reason for them to stop plundering and pillaging*]?

HABAKKUK 2

Selection: verses 1–4

HABAKKUK IS NERVOUS about what he has just said to the Lord in chapter 1, so he stands by to see what the Lord will say when He scolds him. He begins to try to come up with an answer to defend himself.

1 I will stand upon my watch, and set me upon the tower, and will **watch to see what he** [*the Lord*] **will say unto me, and what I shall answer when I am reproved** [*chastised*].

Answer

2 And the LORD answered me, and said, Write the vision, and make *it* **plain upon tables** [*get this straight and write it down*], that he may run that readeth it [*so that the herald or messenger can take it throughout the city for others to read*].

3 For the vision [*the punishment of the wicked*] *is* yet for an appointed time [*will take place when I am ready—in other words, "in mine own due time"*], **but at the end it shall speak** [*but it will happen*], and not lie [*not be a false prophecy*]: **though it tarry** [*even if it takes longer than you think for the wicked to be punished*], **wait for it; because it will surely come, it will not tarry.**

4 Behold, his soul *which* **is lifted up is not upright in him** [*the person who

pridefully complains to the Lord is not righteous]: **but the just shall live by his faith** [*hint, hint, Habakkuk, you need to have more faith*].

One of the major messages we learn through the above dialogue between the Lord and Habakkuk is that the Lord is not eager to destroy the wicked. Indeed, He gives them chance after chance after chance to repent. He wants to save them, not destroy them.

ZECHARIAH

ZECHARIAH PROPHESIED AND taught from about 520 BC to 518 BC He was a contemporary of the prophet Haggai (see Ezra 5:1).

ZECHARIAH 9

Selection: verse 9

ONE OF THE significant things Zechariah prophesied was that the Savior would come triumphantly into Jerusalem, riding on a donkey.

9 ¶ Rejoice greatly, O daughter of Zion [*Jerusalem*]; shout, O daughter of Jerusalem: behold, **thy King cometh unto thee: he** *is* **just, and having salvation** [*He comes, bringing salvation to all who will follow the gospel*]; **lowly** [*humble*], **and riding upon an ass,** and upon a colt the foal of an ass.

We will mention two things in conjunction with verse 9, above. First, in the Jewish culture of the day, donkeys symbolized submission and humility. Horses symbolized military triumph and victory. The Savior rode into Jerusalem on a donkey, symbolizing His submission to the will of the Father, and to the Jewish leaders and Roman soldiers who would crucify Him.

Second, did you know that the donkey on which Jesus rode into Jerusalem had never been ridden? Mark tells us that the donkey that Jesus rode was "a colt . . . whereon never man sat" (Mark 11:2). This is a reminder of the Savior's power and mastery over all things, including the animal kingdom.

Among the many prophecies of Zechariah, some of the most fascinating deal with the last days. We will mention just two of them because of our space limitations in this study guide.

ZECHARIAH 12

Selection: verses 2–3

ZECHARIAH PRO-PHESIED THAT in the last days, before the Second Coming, the Jews would become a powerful and formidable military power among the nations of the earth. This is one of the signs of the times that we see being fulfilled in our day.

2 Behold, I will make Jerusalem [*the Jews*] **a cup of trembling unto all the people round about** [*the Jews*

will become a fearsome enemy to their adversaries]**, when they shall be in the siege both against Judah *and* against Jerusalem** [*when many nations are fighting against the Jews in the Holy Land*]**.**

3 ¶ And in that day will I make Jerusalem a burdensome stone for all people: all that burden themselves with it shall be cut in pieces, though all the people of the earth be gathered together against it [*even if every nation on earth joins together to fight against the Jews*]**.**

ZECHARIAH 14

Selection: verses 3–4

THIS PROPHECY OF Zechariah is one of the signs of the times, yet to be fulfilled. The Savior will appear on the Mount of Olives and it will split in two.

3 Then shall the LORD go forth, and fight against those nations, as when he fought in the day of battle.

4 ¶ And his feet shall stand in that day upon the mount of Olives, which *is* before Jerusalem [*just outside of Jerusalem*] on the east, **and the mount of Olives shall cleave** [*split*] in the midst thereof toward the east and toward the west, *and there shall be* a very great valley; and half of the mountain shall remove toward the north, and half of it toward the south.

We will turn to the Doctrine and Covenants for additional information about this marvelous event.

Doctrine & Covenants 45:48, 51–52

48 And then shall the Lord set his foot upon this mount, and it shall cleave in twain, and the earth shall tremble, and reel to and fro, and the heavens also shall shake.

51 And **then shall the Jews look upon me and say: What are these wounds in thine hands and in thy feet?**

52 **Then shall they know that I am the Lord** [*many of them will be converted*]; for I will say unto them: These wounds are the wounds with which I was wounded in the house of my friends. I am he who was lifted up. I am Jesus that was crucified. I am the Son of God.

MALACHI

THE BOOK OF Malachi was given about 430 BC (see Bible Dictionary, under "Malachi"). It is the last book of the Old Testament. After Malachi, there is about a 430 year gap in the Bible, until the New Testament.

The Savior quoted Malachi, chapters 3 and 4, to the Nephites (see 3 Nephi, chapters 24 and 25), and requested that they write them down.

MALACHI 3

Selection: verses 2, 8–12

IN THIS CHAPTER, a very important question is asked in two different ways. It deals with the Second Coming. The answer is vital to us.

2 But **who may abide the day of his coming** [*who will survive the Second Coming*]? and **who shall stand when he appeareth?** for he *is* like a refiner's fire, and like fullers' soap [*powerful soap; in other words, He will cleanse the earth when He comes again*]:

The answer to the question is those whose lifestyles would fit in with the standards of terrestrial glory (Doctrine & Covenants 76:71–79) or with the standards of celestial glory (Doctrine & Covenants 76:50–53). All others will be burned by the Savior's glory when He comes (see 2 Nephi 12:10).

Next, we see the importance of paying our tithing. First, in verses 8-9, the Lord's covenant people are severely chastised for not paying tithing. Then, in a marvelous teaching approach (verses 10-12), we are all reminded of the tender blessings that attend honest and willing payment of tithing.

8 ¶ Will a man rob God? Yet ye have robbed me. But ye say, Wherein have we robbed thee? In tithes and offerings.

9 Ye *are* cursed with a curse: for ye have robbed me, *even* this whole nation.

10 Bring ye all the tithes into the storehouse, that there may be meat [*food for the poor*] in mine house, and prove [*test*] me now herewith, saith the LORD of hosts, if I will not open you the windows of heaven, and pour you out a blessing, that *there shall* not *be room* enough *to receive it.*

11 And I will rebuke the devourer for your sakes, and he shall not destroy the fruits of your ground; neither shall your vine cast her fruit before the time in the field, saith the LORD of hosts.

12 And all nations shall call you blessed: for ye shall be a delightsome land, saith the LORD of hosts.

We will conclude our study of the Old Testament by going through Malachi, chapter 4, verse by verse.

MALACHI 4

Selection: all verses

ONE OF THE most significant events in the last days is the coming of Elijah, the prophet, to the Kirtland Temple, on April 3, 1836. He there restored the keys of sealing and work for the dead to Joseph Smith and Oliver Cowdery.

First, in verse 1, we find a direct and dire warning to the wicked who are on the earth at the time of the Second Coming.

1 For, behold, **the day cometh** [*the Second Coming*], **that shall burn as an oven; and all the proud,** yea, **and all that do wickedly, shall be stubble** [*dried grain stalks, which burn easily*]: and **the day that cometh shall burn them up,** saith the LORD of hosts, that **it shall leave them neither root nor branch** [*in effect, they will not have families, or "family trees," with roots and branches, in the next life; in other words, they will not inherit exaltation in the celestial kingdom, where the family unit will continue—see Doctrine & Covenants132:19–20*].

Next, the Lord tells us what will happen to the righteous at His coming.

2 ¶ But unto you that fear [*respect and honor*] my name shall the Sun of righteousness [*"Son of Righteousness"—see 3 Nephi 25:2*] arise with healing in his wings [*you will be blessed by the full powers of the Atonement*]; and ye shall go forth, and grow up as calves of the stall [*you will be protected from evil just as calves are protected from the elements by their stalls in the barn*].

3 And ye shall tread down the wicked [*you will triumph over all your former enemies, physical and spiritual*]; for they shall be ashes under the soles of your feet in the day that I shall do *this*, saith the LORD of hosts.

4 ¶ Remember ye [*keep, obey*] the law of Moses my servant, which I commanded unto him in Horeb [*another name for Sinai—see Bible Dictionary, under "Horeb"*] for all Israel, *with* the statutes and judgments.

Verses 5–6, next, are perhaps some of the most meaningful verses in the scriptures for Latter-day Saints because Elijah restored the keys of sealing families together when he came to Joseph Smith and Oliver Cowdery in the Kirtland Temple—see Doctrine & Covenants 110:13–16. These keys are the basis for the tremendous family history and temple work of the Church.

5 ¶ Behold, I will send you Elijah the prophet before the coming of the great and dreadful day of the LORD [*before the Second Coming*]:

6 And he shall turn the heart of the fathers to the children, and the heart of the children to their fathers [*families will desire to be sealed together for time and all eternity; also, people's hearts will yearn to seek out their ancestors in order to seal them to their families*], lest I come and smite the earth with a curse [*lest the main purpose of the earth, to bring exaltation to our Father's children, not be fulfilled*].

SOURCES

Book of Mormon Student Manual. Salt Lake City: The Church of Jesus Christ of Latter-day Saints, 1982.

Bryant, T. Alton. *The New Compact Bible Dictionary.* Grand Rapids, Mich.: Zondervan, 1981.

Clark, James R., comp. *Messages of the First Presidency of The Church of Jesus Christ of Latter-day Saints.* 6 vols. Salt Lake City: Bookcraft, 1965–75.

Conference Reports of The Church of Jesus Christ of Latter-day Saints. Salt Lake City: The Church of Jesus Christ of Latter-day Saints, 1898 to present.

Doctrines of the Gospel Student Manual. Salt Lake City: The Church of Jesus Christ of Latter-day Saints (Institutes of Religion), 2000.

Encyclopedia of Mormonism. Edited by Daniel H. Ludlow. 5 vols. New York: Macmillan, 1992.

Hymns of The Church of Jesus Christ of Latter-day Saints. Salt Lake City: The Church of Jesus Christ of Latter-day Saints, 1985.

International Bible Society. *The Holy Bible: New International Version (NIV).* Grand Rapids, Mich.: Zondervan, 1984.

Josephus. *Antiquities of the Jews.* Philadelphia: John C. Winston Co., n.d.

Journal of Discourses. 26 vols. London: Latter-day Saints' Book Depot, 1854–86.

Kiel, C. F., and F. Delitzsch. *Commentary on the Old Testament.* 10 vols. Grand Rapids, Mich.: William B. Eerdmans Publishing, 1991.

Kimball, Spencer W. *Faith Precedes the Miracle.* Salt Lake City: Deseret Book, 1972.

Ludlow, Victor L. *Isaiah: Prophet, Seer, and Poet.* Salt Lake City: Deseret Book, 1982.

Maxwell, Neal A. *Deposition of a Disciple.* Salt Lake City: Deseret Book, 1976.

McConkie, Bruce R. *A New Witness for the Articles of Faith.* Salt Lake City: Deseret Book, 1985.

—————. *Doctrinal New Testament Commentary.* 3 vols. Salt Lake City: Deseret Book, 1972.

—————. *Mormon Doctrine.* 2d ed. Salt Lake City: Bookcraft, 1966.

—————. *The Millennial Messiah.* Salt Lake City: Deseret Book, 1982.

—————. *The Promised Messiah—The First Coming of Christ.* Salt Lake City: Deseret Book, 1978.

Nyman, Monte S. *Great Are the Words of Isaiah.* Salt Lake City: Bookcraft, 1980.

Old Testament Gospel Doctrine Teacher's Manual. Salt Lake City: The Church of Jesus Christ of Latter-day Saints (Institutes of Religion), 2001.

Old Testament Student Manual: Genesis–2 Samuel. Salt Lake City: The Church of Jesus Christ of Latter-day Saints (Institutes of Religion), 1981.

Old Testament Student Manual, I Kings–Malachi (Religion 302). Salt Lake City: The Church of Jesus Christ of Latter-day Saints, 1981.

Petersen, Mark E. *Moses, Man of Miracles.* Salt Lake City: Deseret Book, 1977.

Rasmussen, Ellis. *An Introduction to the Old Testament and its Teachings.* 2d ed. 2 vols. Provo, Utah: BYU Press, 1972–74.

Richards, LeGrand. *Israel! Do You Know?* Salt Lake City: Deseret Book, 1954.

Smith, Joseph. *History of The Church of Jesus Christ of Latter-day Saints.* Edited by B. H. Roberts. 2d ed. rev., 7 vols. Salt Lake City: The Church of Jesus Christ of Latter-day Saints, 1932–1951.

—————. *Teachings of the Prophet Joseph Smith.* Selected by Joseph Fielding Smith. Salt Lake City: Deseret Book, 1977.

ABOUT THE AUTHOR

DAVID J. RIDGES taught for the Church Educational System for thirty-five years and taught for several years at BYU Campus Education Week. He taught adult religion classes and Know Your Religion classes for BYU Continuing Education for many years. He has also served as a curriculum writer for Sunday School, seminary, and institute of religion manuals.

He has served in many callings in the Church, including Gospel Doctrine teacher, bishop, stake president, and patriarch. He and Sister Ridges have served two full-time CES missions together. They are the parents of six children and grandparents of eleven grandchildren so far. They make their home in Springville, Utah.